3

CENTER STAGE

Express Yourself in English

Lynn Bonesteel

Samuela Eckstut-Didier

Teacher's Edition by Lynn Bonesteel

PEARSON
Longman

Center Stage 3: Express Yourself in English
Teacher's Edition

Pearson Education, 10 Bank Street, White Plains, NY 10606

Staff credits: The people who made up the **Center Stage 3 Teacher's Edition** team, representing
editorial, production, design, and manufacturing, are Elizabeth Carlson, Dave Dickey, Margot Gramer,
Gosia Jaros-White, Laura Le Dréan, Melissa Leyva, Wendy Long, Diana Nam, Julie Schmidt, and Jennifer Stem.

Text composition: ElectraGraphics, Inc.

Text font: 9.5/11 Minion Pro

Cover art: Gilbert Mayers/Superstock

Photo credits: **p. 5** Royalty Free/Corbis; **p. 7** Banana Stock/Alamy; **p. 8** Steve Cole/Getty Images; **p. 9** Royalty Free/Jupiter Images; **p. 10** Charles Gupton/Corbis; **p. 11** Titus Lacoste/Getty Images; **p. 12** Andersen-Ross/Corbis; **p. 18** Iconotec Royalty Free/Fotosearch; **p. 21** (top left) Robert W Ginn/photo edit, Inc, (top right) Han Blossey/Peter Arnold, Inc. (bottom left) Mark Leibowitz/Masterfile, (bottom right) PressNew/Topham/The Images Works; **p. 24** Chris Andrews/ Getty Images; **p. 25** Wolfgang Schmidt/Peter Arnold, Inc; **p. 26** Bruce Forster/Dorling Kindersley; **p. 27** Royalty Free/ Corbis; **p. 35** Mike Blake/ Reuters/Corbis; **p. 36** Vincent LaForet/Getty Images; **p. 37** Omar Torres/Getty Images; **p. 38** Monika Graff/The Image Works; **p. 40** Lisa Blumenfield/ Getty Images; **p. 41** Matthew Stockman/Getty Images; **p. 42** (left) Thomas Northcut/ Getty Images, (center) Royalty Free/Corbis; **p. 43** (left) JT photo/Brand X/Corbis; **p. 67** M Stock/ Alamy; **p. 69** The New Yorker Collection 1979 George Booth from Cartoonbank.com; **p. 74** Tanya Constantine/ Getty Images; **p. 76** Digital Vision/Getty Images; **p. 80** Royalty Free/ Corbis; **p. 90** (top) Royalty Free/Corbis, (bottom) Photodisc/Getty Images; **p. 92** (left) Royalty Free/ Corbis, (center) Royalty Free/Corbis, (right) Michael Goldman/Getty Images; **p. 94** Medioimages/Getty Images; **p. 95** Tom Grill/ Corbis; **p. 98** Laura DeSantis/ Getty Images; **p. 102** Viviane Moos/Corbis; **p. 103** Digital Vision/Getty Images; **p. 106** Royalty Free/Corbis; **p. 108** Stewart Cohen/Pam Ostrow/Getty Images; **p. 120** Royalty Free/Corbis; **p. 121** Images.com/Corbis; **p. 123** Bruce Ayres/Getty Images; **p. 124** Imagemore Co. Ltd/ Getty Images; **p. 130** (top) TouchLife Images/Getty Images, (bottom) Royalty Free/Corbis; **p. 131** Stockbyte/Getty Images; **p. 133** (top) Digital Vision/Getty Images, (bottom) Albane Naivzet/Corbis; **p. 135** Blend Stock Images/Fotosearch; **p. 137** (top) Monty Brinton/CBS photo Archive, (bottom) Matthias Clamer/ Getty Images; **p. 138** Keith Dannemiller/Corbis; **p. 139** Keith Dannemiller/Corbis; **p. 145** (top) Klaus Hackenberg/Zefa/Corbis, (bottom) Frank Krahmer/Zefa/Corbis; **p. 148** (left) Juniors Bildarchiv/Alamy, (right) GK Hart/Vikki Hart/Getty Images; **p. 150** (top left) Gallo Images/Corbis, (bottom left) Royalty Free/ Corbis, (top right) Juliet Coombe/Lonely Planet Images/Getty Images, (bottom right) Edmond Van Hoorick/ Getty Images; **p. 152** Tom Brakefield/Corbis; **p. 154** Dennis Scott/Corbis; **p. 157** Royalty Free/Corbis; **p. 161** McMillian Digital Art/Getty Images; **p. 162** Image Source/Corbis; **p. 165** Bettman/Corbis; **p. 166** (top) Imagebroker/Alamy, (bottom) The Slow Food Movement; **p. 168** photo Alto/Fotosearch; **p. 172** Andrew Wakeford/Getty Images; **p. 175** Peter Scholey/Getty Images; **p. 180** VeriChip Corporation; **p. 181** PhotoStock File/Alamy; **p. 185** Photodisc Green/Getty Images; **p. 188** Royalty Free/Corbis; **p. 189** Royalty Free/Corbis; **p. 191** Royalty Free/Corbis; **p. 195** Royalty Free/Corbis; **p. 204** (top left) Macduff Everton/Corbis, (top right) Royalty Free/Corbis, (bottom left) Royalty Free/Corbis, (bottom right) Dave & Les Jacobs/Corbis; **p. 209** Digital Vision/Getty Images, **p. 213** WP Simon/Getty Images; **p. 222** Janine Wiedel Photolibrary/Alamy; **p. 227** John Liend/Tiffany Schoepp/Getty Images; **p. 228** (top) Keith Brofsky/ Getty Images, (bottom) Bob Krist/Corbis; **p. 230** Howard Huang/Getty Images; **p. 235** Sarah-Maria Vischer-Masino/The Image Works; **p. 237** Photodisc Green/ Getty Images; **p. 245** (top) Royalty Free/Corbis, (bottom) LWA-Shane Kennedy/Corbis; **p. 250** Dave G Houser/Corbis; **p. 251** Les Waslker/NewSport/Corbis; **p. 256** Don Farrall/Getty Images; **p. 265** Glowimages/Getty Images; **p. 270** (left) Photographer's Choice/Getty Images, (right) Heritage The Image Works; **p. 273** Royalty Free/Corbis

Illustration credits: A Corazón Abierto (Marcela Gómez), Steve Attoe, Laurie Conley, Debby Fisher, Marty Harris, Christopher Hitz, Francisco Morales, Mari Rodríguez, Steve Schulman, Wendy Smith, Gary Torrisi, Meryl Treatner, Ralph Voltz

ISBN-13: 978-0-13-194781-8
ISBN-10: 0-13-194781-8

Printed in the United States of America
1 2 3 4 5 6 7 8 9 10—VHG—11 10 09 08 07

Contents

Scope and Sequence

Writing	Critical Thinking	CASAS	LAUSD Intermediate Low	FL. Adult ESOL Low Intermediate
Writing Tip: Use pronouns to avoid repeating nouns Prewriting: Answer questions Write a paragraph about making friends	Interpret a descriptive passage on an unfamiliar topic Utilize prior knowledge to analyze a text Infer word meaning from context Draw logical conclusions Support personal opinion with reasoning	0.1.2, 0.1.4, 0.2.1, 0.2.4	Competencies: 1, 3, 6, 48 Grammar: 1, 2a Language Skill Proficiencies: L: 1, 2, 5, 6; S: 1; R: 1; W: 5	4.05.01, 4.05.02, 4.14.02, 4.15.01, 4.15.03, 4.16.01, 4.16.04, 4.16.05, 4.16.06, 4.16.07, 4.16.08, 4.17.02, 4.17.03, 4.17.05
Writing Tip: Use correct subject-verb agreement Prewriting: Take notes Write a paragraph about a city you know	Make inferences from charts, maps, and illustrations Analyze and interpret population statistics Evaluate advantages and disadvantages Infer word meaning from context	0.1.2, 0.1.4, 0.2.1, 0.2.4, 2.6.1, 2.7.3, 5.6.1, 7.2.1	Competencies: 1, 3, 6 Grammar: 1, 24, 25e Language Skill Proficiencies: L: 1, 2, 5, 6; S: 1; R: 4; W: 5	4.05.01, 4.12.01, 4.13.01, 4.15.01, 4.15.02, 4.15.03, 4.15.06, 4.16.01, 4.16.02, 4.16.03, 4.16.04, 4.16.05, 4.16.06, 4.16.07, 4.16.08, 4.17.02, 4.17.03, 4.17.05
Writing Tip: Use commas with time clauses Prewriting: Use facts Write a paragraph about the history of a sport	Infer word meaning from context Support personal opinion with information from the text Hypothesize scenarios	0.1.2, 0.1.4, 0.1.6, 0.2.1, 0.2.4, 2.6.1	Competencies: 1, 3, 4, 6, 7 Grammar: 1, 5a, 22a, 22b Language Skill Proficiencies: L: 1, 2, 5, 6; S: 1, 2, 4, 7, 8; R: 1; W: 2, 5	4.05.01, 4.05.03, 4.15.01, 4.15.02, 4.15.03, 4.15.08, 4.16.01, 4.16.02, 4.16.03, 4.16.04, 4.16.05, 4.16.06, 4.16.07, 4.16.08, 4.17.02, 4.17.03, 4.17.04, 4.17.05
Writing Tip: Use different tenses to show when things happen Prewriting: Visualize Write a paragraph about an incredible or surprising event	Interpret and analyze diagrams Infer word meaning from context Compare and contrast different kinds of experiences	0.1.2, 0.1.4, 0.1.6, 0.2.1, 0.2.4, 8.2.3, 8.2.4	Competencies: 1, 2, 4, 7, 34, 35 Grammar: 5a, 6a, 6b, 22b Language Skill Proficiencies: L: 1, 2, 5, 6; S: 1, 2, 4, 7, 8; R: 1, 3; W: 2, 5	4.05.01, 4.05.03, 4.15.01, 4.15.02, 4.15.03, 4.15.08, 4.16.01, 4.16.02, 4.16.03, 4.16.04, 4.16.05, 4.16.06, 4.16.07, 4.16.08, 4.17.02, 4.17.03, 4.17.04, 4.17.05
List, prioritize, and organize ideas Writing Tip: Use and and or with verb clauses Prewriting: Use an outline Write a paragraph about the way something used to be and the way it is now	Compare and contrast different kinds of past experiences Compare and contrast customs in the present and the past Hypothesize past customs Evaluate changes in society Develop arguments Identify personal values and assumptions Interpret illustrations	0.1.2, 0.1.3, 0.1.4, 0.1.6, 0.2.1, 0.2.4, 1.7.4, 2.6.1, 3.5.7, 5.1.5, 5.1.6, 8.1.1, 8.1.4, 8.2.1, 8.2.2, 8.2.3, 8.2.4	Competencies: 1, 3, 6, 7, 50, 51 Grammar: 5a, 5b Language Skill Proficiencies: L: 1, 2, 5, 6; S: 1, 2, 4, 7, 8; R: 1, 2, 3, 4; W: 2, 5	4.05.01, 4.05.03, 4.07.02, 4.07.06, 4.14.04, 4.15.01, 4.15.02, 4.15.03, 4.15.08, 4.16.01, 4.16.02, 4.16.03, 4.16.04, 4.16.05, 4.16.06, 4.16.07, 4.16.08, 4.17.02, 4.17.03, 4.17.04, 4.17.05

Writing	Critical Thinking	CASAS	LAUSD Intermediate Low	FL. Adult ESOL Low Intermediate
Writing Tip: Use *and* with verb clauses Prewriting: Answer information questions Write a paragraph about future plans	Infer information not explicit in the text Hypothesize scenarios Evaluate and classify information Interpret charts and illustrations Compare and contrast schedules	0.1.2, 0.1.3, 0.1.4, 0.1.6, 0.2.1, 0.2.4, 2.1.8, 2.3.1, 2.6.1, 2.7.3, 3.5.7, 7.1.1, 7.1.2, 7.1.4, 7.2.3, 7.2.5, 7.2.6	Competencies: 1, 3, 4, 5, 6, 7, 51 Grammar: 2b, 3, 9, 25e Language Skill Proficiencies: **L:** 1, 2, 3, 5, 6; **S:** 1, 2, 3, 4, 7, 8; **R:** 1, 2, 3, 4, 6; **W:** 2, 5	4.01.02, 4.05.01, 4.05.03, 4.05.04, 4.06.02, 4.08.01, 4.14.04, 4.15.01, 4.15.02, 4.15.03, 4.15.08, 4.16.01, 4.16.02, 4.16.03, 4.16.04, 4.16.05, 4.16.06, 4.16.07, 4.16.08, 4.17.02, 4.17.03, 4.17.04, 4.17.05
Writing Tip: Use correct tenses with time clauses Prewriting: Take notes Write a paragraph about learning a new language	Interpret illustrations, lists, and forms Infer information not explicit in the text Classify information Draw conclusions Hypothesize scenarios Support personal opinion with reasoning	0.1.2, 0.1.3, 0.1.4, 0.1.5, 0.1.6, 0.2.1, 0.2.2, 0.2.4, 2.1.7, 2.1.8, 2.5.5, 4.1.8, 4.1.9, 4.4.1, 7.1.1, 7.1.2, 7.1.3, 7.4.1, 7.5.1	Competencies: 1, 3, 4, 5, 6, 7, 9, 10, 12a, 12b, 12c, 48, 54, 57, 59, 60, 64 Grammar: 3, 4, 17, 22a Language Skill Proficiencies: **L:** 1, 2, 3, 5, 6; **S:** 1, 2, 3, 4, 7, 8; **R:** 1, 2, 3, 4, 6; **W:** 2, 4, 5	4.01.03, 4.01.02, 4.03.02, 4.05.01, 4.05.02, 4.06.02, 4.14.01, 4.14.02, 4.14.04, 4.15.01, 4.15.02, 4.15.03, 4.15.08, 4.16.01, 4.16.02, 4.16.03, 4.16.04, 4.16.05, 4.16.06, 4.16.07, 4.16.08, 4.17.02, 4.17.03, 4.17.04, 4.17.05
Writing Tip: Use business letter format Prewriting: Answer questions Write a formal letter of complaint	Interpret illustrations, advertisements, and charts Classify and order information Compare and contrast past experiences and accomplishments Hypothesize scenarios	0.1.2, 0.1.3, 0.1.4, 0.1.6, 0.2.1, 0.2.4, 2.4.1, 4.1.2, 4.1.3, 4.1.4, 4.1.5, 4.1.6, 4.1.7, 4.1.8, 4.1.9, 4.4.1, 4.4.2, 4.4.5, 4.4.6, 4.4.7, 7.1.1, 7.1.2, 7.2.1, 7.2.2, 7.3.1	Competencies: 1, 3, 4, 5, 6, 7, 9, 42, 43, 44, 46, 47, 48, 51, 52 Grammar: 1, 5a, 7a, 7b, 7d Language Skill Proficiencies: **L:** 1, 2, 3, 4, 5, 6; **S:** 1, 2, 3, 4, 7, 8; **R:** 1, 2, 3, 4, 5; **W:** 2, 4, 5	4.01.01, 4.01.02, 4.01.03, 4.01.04, 4.01.06, 4.02.01, 4.02.02, 4.02.05, 4.03.01, 4.03.02, 4.03.03, 4.05.01, 4.05.02, 4.05.03, 4.15.01, 4.15.02, 4.15.03, 4.15.08, 4.15.12, 4.15.13, 4.16.01, 4.16.02, 4.16.03, 4.16.04, 4.16.05, 4.16.06, 4.16.07, 4.16.08, 4.17.02, 4.17.03, 4.17.04, 4.17.05
Writing Tip: Use linking words to connect ideas Prewriting: List reasons Write a paragraph about a recent change in people's lifestyle in your country	Infer information not explicit in the text Draw logical conclusions Interpret illustrations Compare and contrast personal experiences Hypothesize scenarios Support personal opinions with examples	0.1.2, 0.1.3, 0.1.4, 0.1.6, 0.2.1, 0.2.4, 3.5.7, 3.5.8, 3.5.9, 7.2.2, 7.2.3, 7.2.5, 7.2.7, 7.3.1, 7.3.2, 7.3.3, 7.5.1, 7.5.2, 7.5.5, 7.5.7	Competencies: 1, 3, 4, 5, 6, 7, 9, 50, 51, 52 Grammar: 1, 2, 7a, 7b, 7d, 8a, 29 Language Skill Proficiencies: **L:** 1, 2, 5, 6; **S:** 1, 2, 3, 6, 7, 8; **R:** 1, 2, 3; **W:** 2, 5	4.05.01, 4.05.02, 4.05.03, 4.05.04, 4.15.01, 4.15.02, 4.15.03, 4.15.08, 4.15.13, 4.16.01, 4.16.02, 4.16.03, 4.16.04, 4.16.05, 4.16.06, 4.16.07, 4.16.08, 4.17.02, 4.17.03, 4.17.04, 4.17.05
Write a scene from a TV show List, prioritize, and organize ideas Writing Tip: Use examples to explain main points Prewriting: Use examples Write a paragraph about an effect of TV	Support personal opinions with examples Compare and contrast television shows Hypothesize emotions of speakers Hypothesize scenarios Analyze and describe characters in a story	0.1.2, 0.1.3, 0.1.4, 0.1.6, 0.2.1, 0.2.4, 2.6.1, 2.7.2, 2.7.3, 2.7.6, 3.5.8, 7.2.1, 7.2.2, 7.2.3, 7.4.1, 7.4.2	Competencies: 1, 3, 6, 7, 48, 50, 52 Grammar: 1, 2, 5a, 26b, 26d, 29 Language Skill Proficiencies: **L:** 1, 2, 5; **S:** 1, 2, 4, 7, 8; **R:** 1, 2, 6, 7; **W:** 1, 2, 5	4.05.01, 4.05.03, 4.15.01, 4.15.02, 4.15.03, 4.15.08, 4.15.13, 4.16.01, 4.16.02, 4.16.03, 4.16.04, 4.16.05, 4.16.06, 4.16.07, 4.16.08, 4.17.02, 4.17.03, 4.17.04, 4.17.05

Unit	Grammar	Listening	Speaking	Reading
11 **The Animal Kingdom** Page 142	Comparative and Superlative of Adjectives and Adverbs Comparative and Superlative of Nouns Equatives	Listen to a conversation about pets Listen to an interview comparing wild animals Make inferences Understand requests for clarifications Listen for numbers	Compare animals Ask and answer questions about animals Understand common sayings / expressions Compare and contrast information in order to express opinions	Understand time order Read signs Read an article about wolves and dogs Reading skill: Recognize similarities and differences
12 **Let's Eat!** Page 156	Reflexive Pronouns *One / Ones* *Other*: Singular and Plural	Listen to people ordering food in a restaurant Listen to a report about fast-food restaurants Make inferences about speakers' emotions Understand how to make requests and offers Understand appropriate restaurant behavior Listen for main ideas Listen for details	Compare food customs Ask and answer questions about food-related habits Identify and describe places Make inferences about new vocabulary Work with peers to share information and solve problems Ask for and give oral directions to places	Read charts Read an article about Slow Food Reading skill: Recognize conclusions
13 **Technology** Page 170	*Can* and *Be able to* *Could* and *Be able to* *Will be able to*	Listen to a technician assisting a customer Listen to a speech about "concept car" technology Listen for details Understand how to make requests and offer help Use clarification strategies to check for understanding and ask for meaning Understand a sequence of instructions	Talk about technology-related abilities Compare past and present daily routines Make predictions about future events and capabilities Express opinions	Read advertisements Read an article about radio frequency technology Reading skill: Skim
14 **A Kid's Life** Page 184	*Have to / Have got to / Must*: Affirmative Statements and *Have to*: *Yes / No* Questions *Does not have to* and *Must not* *Had to*: Statements and Questions	Listen to a conversation about family obligations Listen to a report comparing American and Japanese children Understand child rearing practices and parenting skills Listen for details Listen for main ideas	Compare school customs Understand the American school system Talk about appropriate behavior for children Talk about appropriate classroom behavior Talk about safety and emergency procedures Express opinions	Skim Read notes Read a letter to the editor about academic performance Reading skill: Recognize point of view
15 **Manners** Page 198	*Should (not)* + Verb *Should (not)* + *Be* + Present Participle *Should* and *Have to*	Listen to a mother give instructions to her son Listen to a report about table manners around the world Understand child rearing practices and parenting skills Listen for details	Talk about appropriate behavior Compare polite and impolite behavior in different countries Give and respond to advice Express opinions Make offers	Preview / Scan Understand appropriate behavior for different jobs Read an article about business etiquette Reading skill: Recognize supporting details

Writing	Critical Thinking	CASAS	LAUSD Intermediate Low	FL. Adult ESOL Low Intermediate
Writing Tip: Use *like* and *both* to compare two things Prewriting: Use a Venn diagram Write a paragraph comparing and contrasting two animals	Interpret illustrations and forms Infer information not explicit in the text Compare and contrast common expressions in different cultures Infer word meaning from context	0.1.2, 0.1.3, 0.1.4, 0.1.6, 0.2.1, 0.2.4, 2.6.1, 2.6.3, 6.0.1, 6.9.2, 7.2.1, 7.2.2, 7.2.3, 7.2.4, 7.2.5, 7.4.2, 7.4.4	Competencies: 1, 3, 4, 5, 6, 7, 49, 50, 51, 52 Grammar: 1, 23a, 23b Language Skill Proficiencies: **L:** 1, 2, 5, 6, 7; **S:** 1, 2, 4, 6, 7, 8; **R:** 1, 2, 3, 4, 6, 7; **W:** 1, 2, 5	4.05.01, 4.05.03, 4.05.04, 4.15.01, 4.15.02, 4.15.03, 4.15.08, 4.15.12, 4.15.13, 4.16.01, 4.16.02, 4.16.03, 4.16.04, 4.16.05, 4.16.06, 4.16.07, 4.16.08, 4.17.02, 4.17.03, 4.17.04, 4.17.05
Writing Tip: Use *in conclusion* and *to sum up* for conclusions Prewriting: List reasons Write a paragraph about food preferences	Interpret illustrations Infer information not explicit in the text Classify information Compare and contrast eating customs Infer word meaning from context Support personal opinions with examples	0.1.2, 0.1.3, 0.1.4, 0.1.6, 0.2.1, 0.2.4, 2.6.4, 2.7.2, 2.7.3, 3.5.2, 3.5.8, 3.5.9, 7.2.1, 7.2.2, 7.2.3, 7.2.4, 7.2.5, 8.1.3, 8.2.1	Competencies: 1, 3, 4, 5, 6, 7, 49, 50, 51, 52 Grammar: 1, 9, 25c, 25d Language Skill Proficiencies: **L:** 1, 2, 5, 6, 7; **S:** 1, 2, 4, 6, 7, 8; **R:** 1, 2, 4, 6, 7; **W:** 2, 5	4.05.01, 4.05.03, 4.05.04, 4.07.06, 4.11.03, 4.15.01, 4.15.02, 4.15.03, 4.15.08, 4.15.12, 4.15.13, 4.16.01, 4.16.02, 4.16.03, 4.16.04, 4.16.05, 4.16.06, 4.16.07, 4.16.08, 4.17.02, 4.17.03, 4.17.04, 4.17.05
List, prioritize, and organize ideas Writing Tip: Use time expressions Prewriting: Use a timeline Write a paragraph about a technology and how it has changed over the years	Interpret illustrations Support personal opinions with examples Hypothesize past and future customs and technological changes Evaluate technology-based changes in society	0.1.2, 0.1.3, 0.1.4, 0.1.6, 0.2.1, 0.2.4, 1.2.5, 1.7.3, 4.5.1, 7.2.1, 7.2.2, 7.2.3, 7.2.4, 7.2.5	Competencies: 1, 2, 3, 5, 6, 7, 49, 50, 51, 52, 53 Grammar: 1, 5a, 15, 28 Language Skill Proficiencies: **L:** 1, 2, 5, 6, 7; **S:** 1, 2, 4, 6, 7, 8; **R:** 1, 2, 3, 4, 6, 7; **W:** 2, 5	4.04.01, 4.05.01, 4.06.01, 4.15.01, 4.15.02, 4.15.03, 4.15.08, 4.15.12, 4.15.13, 4.16.01, 4.16.02, 4.16.03, 4.16.04, 4.16.05, 4.16.06, 4.16.07, 4.16.08, 4.17.02, 4.17.03, 4.17.04, 4.17.05
List, prioritize, and organize ideas Writing Tip: Use *the point is*, *in my opinion*, and *as I see it* to express point of view Prewriting: Brainstorm Write a letter about a community problem	Interpret illustrations and charts Infer information not explicit in the text Classify information Support personal opinions with examples Hypothesize and identify point of view in a text Develop arguments for or against an issue	0.1.1, 0.1.2, 0.1.3, 0.1.4, 0.1.5, 0.1.6, 0.2.1, 0.2.3, 0.2.4, 2.7.2, 2.7.3, 3.4.2, 3.5.2, 3.5.7, 3.5.8, 3.5.9, 4.6.1, 5.6.1, 7.2.1, 7.2.2, 7.2.3, 7.2.4, 7.2.5, 7.3.1, 7.3.2, 7.3.3, 7.3.4, 8.2.1, 8.2.2, 8.2.3	Competencies: 1, 3, 4, 5, 6, 7, 9, 10, 12c, 49, 50, 51, 52, 59, 64 Grammar: 1, 5a, 10a, 10b, 10c, 11 Language Skill Proficiencies: **L:** 1, 2, 5, 6, 7; **S:** 1, 2, 4, 6, 7, 8; **R:** 1, 2, 3, 4, 6, 7; **W:** 1, 2, 4, 5	4.03.02, 4.03.04, 4.05.01, 4.05.02, 4.05.03, 4.05.04, 4.07.06, 4.09.06, 4.13.03, 4.14.04, 4.15.01, 4.15.02, 4.15.03, 4.15.08, 4.15.12, 4.15.13, 4.16.01, 4.16.02, 4.16.03, 4.16.04, 4.16.05, 4.16.06, 4.16.07, 4.16.08, 4.17.02, 4.17.03, 4.17.04, 4.17.05
Writing Tip: Use words like *in fact* and *for example* to identify supporting details Prewriting: Use an outline Write a paragraph about business etiquette in your country	Compare and contrast polite and impolite behavior Evaluate statements Infer information not explicit in the text Support personal opinion with information from the text Hypothesize scenarios	0.1.1, 0.1.2, 0.1.3, 0.1.4, 0.1.5, 0.1.6, 0.2.1, 0.2.4, 2.7.2, 2.7.3, 3.5.5, 3.5.7, 3.5.8, 3.5.9, 4.4.1, 4.6.1, 4.8.2, 4.8.6, 4.8.7, 7.1.1, 7.2.2, 7.2.3, 7.3.1, 7.5.1, 7.5.2, 7.5.6, 8.1.1, 8.1.2, 8.1.3, 8.1.4	Competencies: 1, 3, 4, 5, 6, 7, 16, 49, 50, 51, 52, 64 Grammar: 1, 9, 11, 12, 22a Language Skill Proficiencies: **L:** 1, 2, 5, 6, 7; **S:** 1, 2, 4, 6, 7, 8; **R:** 1, 2, 3, 4, 6, 7; **W:** 1, 2, 5	4.01.01, 4.01.02, 4.03.04, 4.05.01, 4.05.03, 4.05.04, 4.07.02, 4.14.04, 4.15.01, 4.15.02, 4.15.03, 4.15.08, 4.15.12, 4.15.13, 4.16.01, 4.16.02, 4.16.03, 4.16.04, 4.16.05, 4.16.06, 4.16.07, 4.16.08, 4.17.02, 4.17.03, 4.17.04, 4.17.05

Writing	Critical Thinking	CASAS	LAUSD Intermediate Low	FL. Adult ESOL Low Intermediate
Writing Tip: Use questions to get reader's attention Prewriting: Use questions Write a paragraph about a problem in your country and a possible solution	Draw logical conclusions Hypothesize scenarios Compare and contrast past experiences Infer word meaning from context Evaluate the quality of arguments Identify problems and propose solutions	0.1.1, 0.1.2, 0.1.3, 0.1.4, 0.1.5, 0.1.6, 0.2.1, 0.2.4, 2.7.3, 3.5.7, 3.5.8, 3.5.9, 4.1.8, 4.4.1, 4.6.1, 5.6.1, 7.2.2, 7.2.3, 7.2.4, 7.2.5, 7.2.6, 7.3.1, 7.3.2, 7.5.4, 7.5.5, 7.5.6, 8.2.5, 8.2.6	Competencies: 1, 2, 3, 4, 5, 6, 7, 49, 50, 51, 52 Grammar: 1, 2a, 8a, 18 Language Skill Proficiencies: **L**: 1, 2, 5, 6, 7; **S**: 1, 2, 4, 6, 7, 8; **R**: 1, 2, 3, 4, 6, 7; **W**: 1, 2, 5	4.01.01, 4.01.03, 4.02.04, 4.05.01, 4.05.03, 4.05.04, 4.11.08, 4.13.03, 4.14.04, 4.15.01, 4.15.02, 4.15.03, 4.15.08, 4.15.12, 4.15.13, 4.16.01, 4.16.02, 4.16.03, 4.16.04, 4.16.05, 4.16.06, 4.16.07, 4.16.08, 4.17.02, 4.17.03, 4.17.04, 4.17.05
Writing Tip: Use synonyms to make your writing more interesting Prewriting: Use a cluster Write a paragraph about a common health myth in your country	Interpret illustrations and posters Compare and contrast health advice Compare and contrast past experiences and personal habits Hypothesize appropriate health advice for different groups Infer information not explicit in the text Draw logical conclusions Infer word meaning from context	0.1.1, 0.1.2, 0.1.3, 0.1.4, 0.1.6, 0.2.1, 0.2.4, 1.2.1, 1.3.8, 1.6.1, 2.6.4, 2.7.2, 2.7.3, 3.1.1, 3.1.2, 3.1.3, 3.2.3, 3.5.11, 3.5.2, 3.5.4, 3.5.5, 3.5.7, 3.5.8, 3.5.9, 4.6.1, 4.8.7, 7.1.1, 7.1.2, 7.1.3, 7.2.1, 7.2.2, 7.2.3, 7.2.4, 7.2.5, 7.2.6, 7.3.1, 7.3.2, 7.4.2, 7.5.2, 7.5.4, 7.5.5, 8.1.1, 8.2.1, 8.3.1, 8.3.2	Competencies: 1, 3, 4, 5, 6, 7, 36, 37, 38, 39, 49, 50, 51, 52 Grammar: 1, 5a, 5b, 9, 10a, 12, 20a, 20d Language Skill Proficiencies: **L**: 1, 2, 5, 6, 7; **S**: 1, 2, 4, 6, 7, 8; **R**: 1, 2, 3, 4, 6, 7; **W**: 1, 2, 5	4.02.03, 4.02.04, 4.02.05, 4.05.01, 4.05.02, 4.05.03, 4.05.04, 4.07.01, 4.07.02, 4.07.03, 4.07.06, 4.11.12, 4.14.04, 4.15.01, 4.15.02, 4.15.03, 4.15.08, 4.15.12, 4.15.13, 4.16.01, 4.16.02, 4.16.03, 4.16.04, 4.16.05, 4.16.06, 4.16.07, 4.16.08, 4.17.02, 4.17.03, 4.17.04, 4.17.05
List, prioritize, and organize ideas Writing Tip: Use logical order Prewriting: Use an outline Write a paragraph about a free-time activity	Interpret illustrations and charts Draw logical conclusions Compare and contrast personal experiences and interests Infer word meaning from context Support personal opinions with examples	0.1.1, 0.1.2, 0.1.3, 0.1.4, 0.1.6, 0.2.1, 0.2.2, 0.2.4, 2.6.1, 2.6.3, 2.7.2, 2.7.3, 3.5.8, 3.5.9, 7.2.1, 7.2.2, 7.2.3, 7.2.4, 7.2.5, 7.5.1	Competencies: 1, 3, 4, 5, 6, 7, 49, 50, 51, 52 Grammar: 1, 2, 5a, 19a, 19b, 20b, 20c, 23a, 28 Language Skill Proficiencies: **L**: 1, 2, 5, 6, 7; **S**: 1, 2, 4, 6, 7, 8; **R**: 1, 2, 3, 4, 6, 7; **W**: 1, 2, 5	4.05.01, 4.05.02, 4.05.03, 4.05.04, 4.15.01, 4.15.02, 4.15.03, 4.15.08, 4.15.12, 4.15.13, 4.16.01, 4.16.02, 4.16.03, 4.16.04, 4.16.05, 4.16.06, 4.16.07, 4.16.08, 4.17.02, 4.17.03, 4.17.04, 4.17.05
Writing Tip: Use examples when giving advice Prewriting: Use examples Write a paragraph about advice that experts give	Interpret illustrations Infer information not explicit in the text Hypothesize scenarios Support personal opinion with examples Identify problems and propose solutions	0.1.1, 0.1.2, 0.1.3, 0.1.4, 0.1.5, 0.1.6, 0.2.1, 0.2.2, 0.2.3, 0.2.4, 1.9.7, 2.1.2, 2.5.1, 2.7.2, 2.7.3, 3.4.2, 5.3.5, 5.3.7, 5.3.8, 5.5.6, 5.6.1, 7.2.1, 7.2.2, 7.2.3, 7.2.4, 7.2.5, 7.2.6, 7.2.7, 7.3.1, 7.3.2, 7.3.3, 7.3.4, 8.3.2	Competencies: 1, 3, 4, 5, 6, 7, 34, 35, 49, 50, 51, 52, 53 Grammar: 1, 5a, 6a, 9, 12, 20e, 21a, 21b Language Skill Proficiencies: **L**: 1, 2, 5, 6, 7; **S**: 1, 2, 4, 6, 7, 8; **R**: 1, 2, 3, 4, 6, 7; **W**: 1, 2, 5	4.05.01, 4.05.02, 4.05.03, 4.05.04, 4.06.03, 4.09.05, 4.09.06, 4.10.01, 4.10.02, 4.15.01, 4.15.02, 4.15.03, 4.15.08, 4.15.12, 4.15.13, 4.16.01, 4.16.02, 4.16.03, 4.16.04, 4.16.05, 4.16.06, 4.16.07, 4.16.08, 4.17.02, 4.17.03, 4.17.04, 4.17.05
List, prioritize, and organize ideas Writing Tip: Use quoted and reported speech Prewriting: Use quoted and reported speech Write a paragraph about a funny or interesting travel story	Interpret illustrations and charts Infer information not explicit in the text Hypothesize scenarios Compare and contrast past travel experiences	0.1.1, 0.1.2, 0.1.3, 0.1.4, 0.1.5, 0.1.6, 0.2.1, 0.2.4, 1.2.5, 2.6.1, 2.6.3, 3.4.2, 3.5.8, 4.8.3, 7.4.4, 7.5.6, 8.3.2	Competencies: 1, 3, 4, 5, 6, 7, 22 Grammar: 1, 2a, 5a, 9 Language Skill Proficiencies: **L**: 1, 2, 5, 6, 7; **S**: 1, 2, 4, 6, 7, 8; **R**: 1, 2, 3, 4, 6, 7; **W**: 1, 2, 5	4.05.01, 4.05.03, 4.05.04, 4.09.03, 4.09.04, 4.09.05, 4.15.01, 4.15.02, 4.15.03, 4.15.08, 4.15.12, 4.15.13, 4.16.01, 4.16.02, 4.16.03, 4.16.04, 4.16.05, 4.16.06, 4.16.07, 4.16.08, 4.17.02, 4.17.03, 4,17.04, 4.17.05

To the Teacher

The Center Stage Program

Center Stage is a four-level, four-skills course that balances grammar instruction and successful communication. Practical language and timely topics motivate adult students to master speaking, listening, reading, and writing skills. The *Center Stage* program includes the following components:

- The **Student Book** features twenty units that explore relevant themes for the adult learner, integrating grammar practice with speaking, listening, reading, and writing activities.
- The **Teacher's Edition** includes step-by-step teaching notes as well as multilevel strategies, learner persistence tips, expansion activities, culture notes, and grammar notes.
- A **Teacher's Resource Disk** in the back of the Teacher's Edition offers worksheets for supplementary grammar exercises, supplementary vocabulary exercises, and learner persistence.
- The **ExamView® Assessment Suite** includes hundreds of test items, providing flexible, comprehensive assessment of the skills taught in *Center Stage*.
- **Color transparencies** and **worksheets** offer teachers a flexible way to introduce, practice, and review vocabulary.
- The **Audio Program** contains recordings for all listening activities in the Student Book.

The Student Book

Each unit in the Student Book is divided into seven lessons. Each lesson is presented on two facing pages and provides clear, self-contained instruction taking approximately 45 to 60 minutes of class time. The lessons include:

- **Vocabulary and Listening:** The unit opens with a vivid illustration that sets the context and presents high-frequency, leveled vocabulary that is recycled in the unit and throughout the course. After practicing the new words, students listen to a conversation related to the unit theme.
- **Grammar to Communicate:** The three *Grammar to Communicate* lessons present target structures in easy-to-read charts. Students practice each language point through a variety of exercises that progress from controlled to open-ended. Every *Grammar to Communicate* lesson ends with a speaking activity, *Time to Talk*. This communicative activity promotes fluency and self-expression by giving students additional practice with the language in speaking contexts.
- **Review and Challenge:** This section helps students review the unit material, consolidate their knowledge, and extend their learning with more challenging grammar, dictation, speaking, and listening activities.
- **Reading:** In the reading section, students practice essential reading skills such as understanding main ideas, reading for details, and recognizing topics. Students also encounter a wide variety of reading genres, including e-mails, formal letters, articles, and essays.
- **Writing:** In the writing section, students engage in prewriting activities such as listing, interviewing, and using graphic organizers to prepare for writing. Students then complete writing tasks such as e-mails, letters, and essays. For each assignment, students are given a model to guide their writing.

Standards

The Center Stage 3 Student Book is a comprehensive course, ensuring student success on key grammar and life skills standards. The scope and sequence on pages iv–xiii links the book with CASAS, LAUSD, and Florida Adult ESOL standards.

Assessment

Center Stage includes several assessment tools.

- *Time to Talk* activities and the *Review and Challenge* sections provide teachers with multiple opportunities to gauge students' performance in class.
- The printed unit tests found in the *Teacher's Edition* allow teachers to assess students' mastery at the end of each unit.
- The *ExamView® Assessment Suite,* sold separately, offers teachers additional ready-made unit tests and also allows them to create new tests by mixing and matching items from different units or skill areas. *ExamView®* tests can be administered as pre-tests before the print tests, or as achievement tests at any time during the course.

The Teacher's Edition

The *Teacher's Edition* includes:

- Step-by-step unit notes as well as learning goals, suggested teaching times, learner persistence tips, multilevel strategies, expansion activities, culture notes, and grammar notes.
- Unit tests with answer keys and audioscripts.
- A *Teacher's Resource Disk* with reproducible supplementary Grammar and Vocabulary Exercises worksheets and Learner Persistence tips worksheets.
- Audioscript, grammar summaries, grammar charts, and index from the *Student Book* for easy reference.

Classroom Management

Teachers of adult students face a number of specific challenges. *Center Stage* offers a wealth of specific strategies on how to address these challenges.

Multilevel Strategies

Many adult classes have students of widely differing English proficiencies. In these "multilevel" classes, teachers are asked to serve the needs of pre-level, at-level, and above-level students, all at the same time. Further, almost no student in any given class will be completely at any one level. Individual learners have different strengths—a student may be pre-level in one skill, at-level in another skill, and above level in another. Some students, for example, are quite proficient in reading but have more trouble when it comes to speaking activities.

Center Stage provides ample support for teachers of multilevel classes. Multilevel strategies are offered for many of the Student Book activities. These strategies are designed to help teachers tailor the activities to the needs of students at different levels of proficiency. In this way, students all work on a task that is appropriate for them while staying focused on the objectives of the lesson. In addition, the supplementary Grammar and Vocabulary Exercises worksheets on the *Teacher's Resource Disk* can serve as useful tools in multilevel classes. The teacher can assign these exercises as homework or independent study, giving individual students tasks that are appropriate to their level.

Learner Persistence

Learner persistence is often defined as *adults staying in programs for as long as they can, engaging in self-directed study when they must drop out of their programs, and returning to a program as soon as the demands of their lives allow.* This is something unique to adult learners because, unlike children, adults make a conscious decision to participate in educational programs. Also unlike children, most adult students have many "positive and negative forces" outside of their control that affect their ability to attend class, including caring for children or other relatives and working full-time. Should a "negative force" arise, students may have to "stop out" for a period of time. Teachers can address these concerns in a variety of ways:

- First, be sensitive to the positive and negative forces that help and hinder persistence.
- Second, help adult students build self-confidence about reaching their goals.
- Third, have students establish unique goals for themselves.
- Finally, provide services and systems for achieving these goals.

Every unit of the *Teacher's Edition* opens with a Learner Persistence tip—a concrete, easy-to-implement strategy for dealing with learner persistence issues. These tips can also help teachers foster a sense of classroom community and encourage good study practices which can be used during a "stop out" period. The Learner Persistence worksheets found on the *Teacher's Resource Disk* offer yet more practical strategies for keeping students engaged and motivated.

Creating a Dynamic Learning Environment

Research has shown that dynamic learning environments foster student engagement and learning. Here are some easy, tried and true "best practices" to help you create an active classroom.

1. Make sure that all students participate in lessons by teaching to the three learning styles (audio, visual, tactile/kinesthetic) and by providing a variety of expansion tasks to reinforce the learning.

2. Make sure that students personalize activities as much as possible so that they can easily make the connection between what they learn in class and what they experience in their lives outside the classroom.

3. Make sure that students have opportunities to work with a variety of partners for pair and group activities so that they get used to working with different people and to help build a sense of classroom community.

4. Always review the directions with the class before beginning any activity. Be sure that all students completely understand the task and what they must do to complete it.

5. Give students opportunities to guess the meanings of words from both pictures and text.

6. Before presenting a new point, remind students of what they already know and build upon it. This will increase students' understanding and confidence.

7. Always tell students how many times they will hear a recording. This will help reassure them and reduce their anxiety if they do not understand what they hear the first time. If students have difficulty, replay the corresponding track as many times as necessary.

8. Do not correct every error. Focus your feedback on the point(s) presented and practiced in that specific lesson.

9. Once you have corrected students' writing, have them revise their writing so that they can focus on correcting their errors.

10. Have students role-play conversations to give them useful practice in pronunciation and fluency.

11. Use graphic organizers (charts, mind maps, and Venn diagrams) to help students learn new words and ideas.

12. Show students how they can use classroom materials to study on their own outside of the classroom.

About the Authors

Lynn Bonesteel has been teaching ESL since 1988. She is currently a full-time senior lecturer at the Center for English Language and Orientation Programs at Boston University Center for English Language and Orientation Programs (CELOP). Ms. Bonesteel is also the author of *Password 3: A Reading and Vocabulary Text*.

Samuela Eckstut-Didier has taught ESL and EFL for over twenty-five years in the United States, Greece, Italy, and England. She currently teaches at Boston University, Center for English Language and Orientation Programs (CELOP). She has authored and co-authored numerous texts for the teaching of English, notably *Strategic Reading 1, 2, and 3; What's in a Word? Reading and Vocabulary Building; Focus on Grammar Workbook; In the Read World; First Impressions; Beneath the Surface; Widely Read;* and *Finishing Touches*.

About the Series Consultants

MaryAnn Florez is the lead ESL Specialist for the Arlington Education and Employment Program (REEP) in Arlington, Virginia, where she has program management, curriculum development, and teacher training responsibilities. She has worked with Fairfax County (VA) Adult ESOL and the National Center for ESL Literacy Education (NCLE), and has coordinated a volunteer adult ESL program in Northern Virginia. Ms. Florez has offered workshops throughout the U.S. in areas such as teaching beginning-level English language learners, incorporating technology in instruction, strategies for a multilevel classroom, and assessment. Her publications include a variety of research-to-practice briefs and articles on adult ESL education. Ms. Florez holds an M.Ed. in Adult Education from George Mason University.

Sharon Seymour is an ESL instructor at City College of San Francisco, where she has extensive experience teaching both noncredit adult ESL and credit ESL. She recently completed ten years as chair of the ESL Department at CCSF. She is also currently a co-researcher for the Center for Advancement of Adult Literacy Project on Exemplary Noncredit Community College ESL Programs. Ms. Seymour has been president of CATESOL and a member of the TESOL board of directors and has served both organizations in a variety of capacities. She has served on California Community College Chancellor's Office and California State Department of Education committees relating to ESL curriculum and assessment. Ms. Seymour holds an M.A. in TESOL from San Francisco State University.

Unit 1
Getting to Know You

Learning Goals

- Learn vocabulary that is used to describe people
- Learn about *have got* in affirmative and negative statements; the present progressive for extended time; and the difference between simple present and present progressive
- Listen to a conversation about people and a radio report
- Read an article about how people get to know each other and write about the best way to meet people and make friends
- Talk about personality traits and physical appearance

Learner Persistence

Encourage students to purchase the textbook for the class.

Warm-up

Teaching Time: 3–5 min.

- With books closed, ask students to call out words to describe hair on the head and face. Write their answers on the board. If possible, group the words. As needed, explain the meanings of the words or draw pictures to illustrate. Leave the words on the board and have students open their books to page 2.
- Have students circle the words in the box that are new to them.

Vocabulary

A Teaching Time: 10–15 min.

- Have students complete the first task.
- 🎧 Play Track 2 as students listen and check their answers.
- Call on students to say answers. Say each word and have students repeat chorally.

B Teaching Time: 10–15 min.

- Explain that the words in Exercise A describe the way someone looks, but the words in Exercise B describe other things about someone.

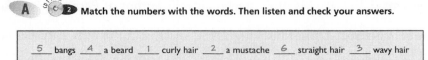

Unit 1
Getting to Know You

Vocabulary

A 🎧 **CD 1 TRACK 2** **Match the numbers with the words. Then listen and check your answers.**

> _5_ bangs   _4_ a beard   _1_ curly hair   _2_ a mustache   _6_ straight hair   _3_ wavy hair

B 🎧 **CD 1 TRACK 3** **Read about and listen to people at the party. What meaning do the boldface words have? Write + (good), – (bad), or O (not good or bad).**

_+_ 1. "Amy is really funny. I like her **sense of humor**."

_–_ 2. "Felicia has **a bad temper**. She's always angry about something."

_+_ 3. "Lupe has **a nice personality**. She's friendly and kind. Everybody likes her."

_O_ 4. "Ron has a new girlfriend. He **is going out with** Azalee."

_O_ 5. "Chris and Lupe moved here Friday. They **are getting to know** everybody."

_+_ 6. "I **get along with** all my neighbors. I like them very much."

2 Unit 1

- Explain the idea of positive, negative, and neutral words. Write the first sentence on the board as an example. Ask the students if *funny* is a positive or negative word. Put a + mark above it. Then ask them about *sense of humor*. Write a + mark above it also.
- 🎧 Play Track 3 as students complete the task. Tell them to circle the words in the context that helped them guess the meaning.
- Call on students to tell you which words they circled. Correct and explain as needed.

Culture Note

Vocabulary. Explain that in the United States, neighbors sometimes have a "getting to know you" party when someone new moves into the neighborhood. The party is at one person's house, but everyone brings some food or drinks to share. Everyone (not just the new neighbor) wears a name tag because neighbors sometimes forget one another's names.

Listening

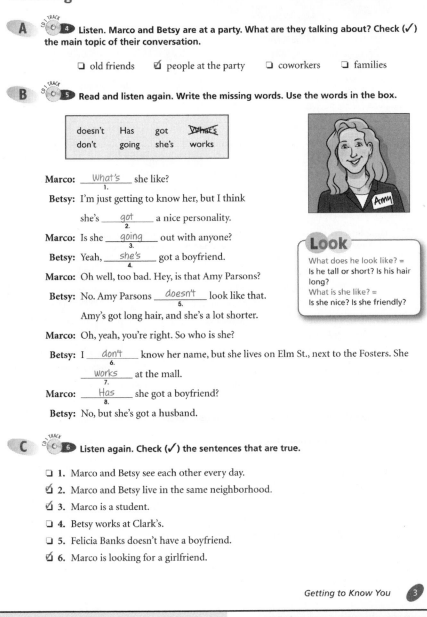

A 🎵 4 Listen. Marco and Betsy are at a party. What are they talking about? Check (✓) the main topic of their conversation.

❏ old friends ☑ people at the party ❏ coworkers ❏ families

B 🎵 5 Read and listen again. Write the missing words. Use the words in the box.

doesn't	Has	got	~~What's~~
don't	going	she's	works

Marco: _____What's_____ she like?
            1.

Betsy: I'm just getting to know her, but I think

she's _____got_____ a nice personality.
            2.

Marco: Is she _____going_____ out with anyone?
            3.

Betsy: Yeah, _____she's_____ got a boyfriend.
            4.

Marco: Oh well, too bad. Hey, is that Amy Parsons?

Betsy: No. Amy Parsons _____doesn't_____ look like that.
            5.

Amy's got long hair, and she's a lot shorter.

Marco: Oh, yeah, you're right. So who is she?

Betsy: I _____don't_____ know her name, but she lives on Elm St., next to the Fosters. She
            6.

_____works_____ at the mall.
            7.

Marco: _____Has_____ she got a boyfriend?
            8.

Betsy: No, but she's got a husband.

Look

What does he look like? =
Is he tall or short? Is his hair
long?

What is she like? =
Is she nice? Is she friendly?

C 🎵 6 Listen again. Check (✓) the sentences that are true.

❏ 1. Marco and Betsy see each other every day.

☑ 2. Marco and Betsy live in the same neighborhood.

☑ 3. Marco is a student.

❏ 4. Betsy works at Clark's.

❏ 5. Felicia Banks doesn't have a boyfriend.

☑ 6. Marco is looking for a girlfriend.

Getting to Know You ③

Watch Out!

Exercise B. Students are often confused by the use of *like* in the questions *What does he look like?* and *What is she like?* They might think that *like* is a verb, and that the question is about a person's *likes* and *dislikes*. Explain that *like* in these expressions means *similar to*. Give examples. Describe yourself and have students give you the question. For example, say: *I am tall and thin. What is the question? (What do you look like?)*

Option

Assign Unit 1 Supplementary Vocabulary Exercises on the Teacher's Resource Disk as homework or on the Student Persistence CD-ROM as self-access practice.

Multilevel Strategy

- **Pre-level:** Give students a handout with the words of the conversation already filled in and have them read along as they listen.
- **Above-level:** Have students try to fill in the words of the conversation before they listen.

Listening

A **Teaching Time: 10–15 min.**

- **Warm-up:** Tell students that they are going to listen to a conversation between a woman and a man at a party. Ask them what topics men and women talk about at parties in their countries. Write their answers on the board.

- Explain what a main topic is. Say: *The main topic of a conversation is what the conversation is about in general. One example of a main topic might be the weather.*

- Call on a student to read the topic choices aloud.

- 🎧 Play Track 4 while students listen and complete the task.

- After you have played the conversation once, read out each of the four topics. Pause after you've read each topic and have students raise their hands if they think that topic is the correct answer. Correct as needed.

B **Teaching Time: 10–15 min.**

- Tell students that they are going to listen to part of the conversation again, but this time they are going to focus on the specific language that the speakers use. Read the words in the box aloud and have students repeat chorally.

- Tell students to read the information in the Look Box. Explain that *What does he look like?* is a question about someone's physical appearance; *What is she like?* is a question about someone's personality.

- 🎧 Play Track 5 while students listen and complete the task.

- Call on students to say answers. Correct as needed.

Expansion Have pairs practice reading the conversation. After a few minutes, ask for volunteers to role-play the conversation in front of the class.

C **Teaching Time: 10–15 min.**

- PAIRS. Have students complete the task. If they are not sure whether a sentence is true, tell them to write a question mark (?).

- 🎧 Play Track 6 as students listen and check their answers.

- Call on students to say answers. If a statement is false, have them correct it to make it true.

Grammar to Communicate 1

Have Got: Statements

Teaching Time: 5–10 min.

- Have students study the chart.
- Use yourself as the example. Say: *I've got short / long hair.* Write the statement on the board. Point out the contraction and explain that we almost always contract *have* when we use *have got*. Ask several students: *How about you? (I've got short / long hair.)*
- Now ask about other students in the class: *How about [Juan]? (He's got long / short hair.)* Write the sentence on the board. Point out the contraction of *HE has got* to *HE's got*. Then ask: *How about [Juan and Stefan]? (They've got long / short hair.)*
- Do an oral drill with *have / has (not) got*, the new vocabulary, and the students in the class. For example, choose a student with a mustache and say: *mustache, Juan. (Juan's got a mustache.)* Then choose a student without a mustache and say: *mustache, Paolo. (Paolo hasn't got a mustache.)* Continue with other vocabulary items. Write students' sentences on the board. Correct as needed.
- Have students study the Look Box, then say: Have *and* have got *mean the same thing, but* have got *is less formal and is usually not written. We can use the contracted form of* have *with* have got—*for example,* I've got bangs—*but we can't use the contracted form of* have. *So it is incorrect to say:* I've bangs. Write this last example on the board and cross it out.

A **Teaching Time: 5–10 min.**

- Call on a student to read the example aloud. Then ask for the contracted form. (Chris's got a beard.)
- Have students complete the task.
- PAIRS. Have students compare answers.
- Call on students to read their answers. Correct as needed. For those items that have more than one correct answer, ask the class for other possibilities (e.g., for 5, students could answer *Lupe* or *Chris*.)

Grammar to Communicate 1

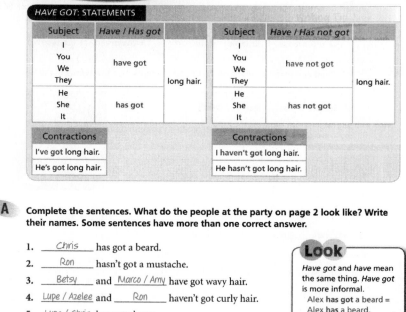

HAVE GOT: STATEMENTS

Subject	Have / Has got		Subject	Have / Has not got	
I You We They	have got	long hair.	I You We They	have not got	long hair.
He She It	has got		He She It	has not got	

Contractions		Contractions
I've got long hair.		I haven't got long hair.
He's got long hair.		He hasn't got long hair.

A Complete the sentences. What do the people at the party on page 2 look like? Write their names. Some sentences have more than one correct answer.

1. ___Chris___ has got a beard.
2. ___Ron___ hasn't got a mustache.
3. ___Betsy___ and ___Marco / Amy___ have got wavy hair.
4. ___Lupe / Azelee___ and ___Ron___ haven't got curly hair.
5. ___Lupe / Chris___ has got glasses.
6. ___Felicia___ and ___Chris / Ron___ haven't got bangs.

Look

Have got and *have* mean the same thing. *Have got* is more informal.

Alex **has got** a beard = Alex **has** a beard.
I **haven't got** long hair = I **don't have** long hair.

PAIRS. Compare sentences. How many of your sentences are the same?

B Rewrite the sentences. Use *have got, has got, haven't got,* or *hasn't got.*

1. My sister doesn't have bangs. — My sister hasn't got bangs.
2. My parents have brown eyes. — My parents have got brown eyes.
3. My brother has a mustache. — My brother has got a mustache.
4. My grandparents don't have grey hair. — My grandparents haven't got grey hair.
5. My mother and I don't have glasses. — My mother and I haven't got glasses.

Check (✓) the sentences that are true about your family.

4 Unit 1

B **Teaching Time: 5–10 min.**

- Write the example on the board, with one sentence immediately above the other. Draw an arrow from *doesn't* to *hasn't* and from *have* to *got*. Remind students that both sentences have the same meaning, even though the form is different.
- Have students complete the task.
- Call on students to say answers. Correct as needed.
- PAIRS. Have students tell their partners which sentences are true about their family.

Grammar Notes

1. *Have got* and *have* mean the same thing. We rarely use *have got* in writing, but we frequently use it in speaking.
2. Use *have got* with *I, you, we,* and *they.*
3. Use *has got* with the third person singular *(he, she, it).*
4. Contracted forms are more common, i.e., *'ve got / 's got.*
5. The negative forms are *have not (haven't) got* and *has not (hasn't got).*
6. For more information on this grammar topic, see page 282.

C Read the sentences about Carolina's family. Cross out the contraction(s) in each sentence. Then write the full form of the verb. Which two people does Carolina look like?

1. "My mother's~~'s~~ tall, and she's~~'s~~ got wavy,
   is   *has*
   red hair, and green eyes."

2. "My father's~~'s~~ a little heavy, but he's~~'s~~
   is   *is*
   good-looking. He's~~'s~~ got blue eyes."
   has

3. "My sister's~~'s~~ got blue eyes and a big
   has
   nose. Her hair's~~'s~~ long."
   is

4. "My older brother's~~'s~~ got big, brown
   has
   eyes and brown hair. He's~~'s~~ cute."
   is

5. "My younger brother's~~'s~~ very tall. He's~~'s~~
   is   *has*
   got a big nose and green eyes."

6. "My son's~~'s~~ got my eyes. He's~~'s~~ 8 years old."
   has   *is*

Carolina looks like her older brother and her son.

Look

The third-person singular of *be* and *have* are contracted the same way.

My **mother's** tall = My **mother is** tall
She's got wavy hair = **She has** got wavy hair

PAIRS. Describe your family. Who do you look like?

D Look at the picture on page 2. Complete the sentences. Use *have got, has got, haven't got,* or *hasn't got.*

1. Amy ___has got___ long hair.
2. Chris and Lupe ___have got___ glasses.
3. Chris ___has got___ a mustache.
4. Marco ___hasn't got___ a beard.
5. Ron and Lupe ___have got___ straight hair.
6. Betsy ___has got___ long, wavy hair.
7. Felicia and Ron ___haven't got___ bangs.
8. Lupe and Marco ___haven't got___ curly hair.

Change the underlined names above. Use the names of your classmates. Then compare sentences with another student. Did you write the same names?

Example: *José has got a beard.*

TIME to TALK

PAIRS. Write a description of one of your classmates.

WRAP UP. Read your description to the class. Can they guess the name of the classmate?

Example: *This person isn't very tall. He's got short, straight hair. He hasn't got a beard, but he's got a mustache. Who is this person?*

Getting to Know You   **5**

C Teaching Time: 10–15 min.

- Have students study the Look Box. Then read the examples.
- Have students complete the task.
- Call on students to say answers. Correct as needed.
- PAIRS. Model the activity by using yourself as an example. Talk about the person in your family whom you resemble most, for example, *My father is tall and thin. I look like him.* Then have students complete the task.
- Call on students to tell you who their partner looks like. Ask them to say what features their partner shares with his or her relative.

D Teaching Time: 5–10 min.

- Have a student read the first item. Tell students that *has got* is correct because *Amy* is a singular noun.
- Have students complete the first part of the task.
- Call on students to say answers. Correct as needed.
- Read the example for the second part of the task aloud. Tell students to write about their classmates.
- PAIRS. Have students compare their sentences.
- Call on a few students to read their sentences to the class. Ask the other students if they agree.

Watch Out!

Students might confuse the contraction for *has got* with the contraction for *is*. Write examples of both contractions on the board and ask students to change the contracted form to the full form. For example, write: *Mario's tall, and he's got red hair.* (Mario is tall, and he has got red hair.)

Option

Assign Unit 1 Supplementary Grammar to Communicate 1 Exercises on the Teacher's Resource Disk as homework or on the Student Persistence CD-ROM as self-access practice.

TIME to TALK

Teaching Time: 10–15 min.

- Read the example aloud.
- Model the activity by describing one of the students. Have the class guess which person you described.
- PAIRS. Have students complete the task.
- WRAP UP. Have students read their descriptions aloud while the class guesses who they are describing. Correct errors as needed.

Present Progressive: Extended Time

Teaching Time: 5–10 min.

- Have students study the chart and the Look Box.
- Talk about a student who has a job. Write on the board: *[Name of student] has got a job at [name of company].* Then write on the board: *Is [name of student] working right now? (No, he/she isn't.) What is he/she doing right now? (He/she is studying / is in class.) Is he/she looking for a job? (No, he/she isn't. He/she has a job.) Is he/she working these days? (Yes, he/she is.)*
- Write the time expressions *these days* and *right now* on the board.
- Say: These days *means* now, *but not* right now. *If you say that something is happening* these days, *it means it is true for the present time, but perhaps it isn't happening at exactly this moment. When something is true now, but is not happening at exactly this moment, we can use the present progressive. Of course, we can also use the present progressive for things that are happening right now, for example:* I am teaching right now.

A   **Teaching Time: 5–10 min.**

- Explain the example. Tell students that *RN* is the correct answer because Ana and Lou are talking about something that is happening at exactly this moment.
- Have students complete the task.
- Call on two students to read each conversation and tell you whether the time is *right now* or *these days.* Correct as needed.

Grammar to Communicate 2

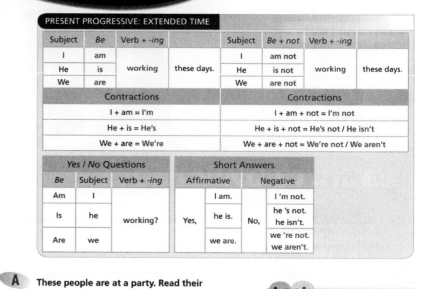

PRESENT PROGRESSIVE: EXTENDED TIME

Subject	Be	Verb + -ing		Subject	Be + not	Verb + -ing	
I	am			I	am not		
He	is	working	these days.	He	is not	working	these days.
We	are			We	are not		

Contractions	Contractions
I + am = I'm	I + am + not = I'm not
He + is = He's	He + is + not = He's not / He isn't
We + are = We're	We + are + not = We're not / We aren't

Yes / No Questions			Short Answers			
Be	Subject	Verb + -ing	Affirmative		Negative	
Am	I			I am.		I'm not.
Is	he	working?	Yes,	he is.	No,	he's not. / he isn't.
Are	we			we are.		we're not. / we aren't.

A   These people are at a party. Read their conversations. When is the underlined part happening? Write *RN* for right now and *TD* for these days.

Look

Use the present progressive for:
- activities right now.
  I can't talk right now. I'm working.
- activities these days (this week, this month, this year).
  Are you working these days?
  No, I'm looking for a job.

See page 295 for spelling rules with the present progressive.

     1.   **Ana:**   Are your kids here?
RN   **Lou:**   Yes. <u>They're playing</u> a computer game in their room.

     2.   **Amy:**   Hi, Bob. How are things?
TD   **Bob:**   Pretty good. <u>I'm getting ready</u> for a trip to Brazil.

     3.   **Rosa:**   Are you taking classes this semester?
TD   **Stan:**   No, I'm not. <u>I'm working</u> two jobs.

     4.   **Irina:**   Mmm . . . This cake is delicious.
TD   **Chris:**   Thanks. <u>I'm taking</u> a cooking class. We made it there.

     5.   **Lisa:**   Where's Tom?
RN   **Lucy:**   He<u>'s helping</u> Juan with something in the kitchen.

     6.   **Joe:**   Why do you want to work more hours?
TD   **Ray:**   Things <u>are getting</u> so expensive. I need the money.

Grammar Notes

1. Use the present progressive to talk about the extended present with these time expressions: *nowadays, this week, this month, this year.* These activities are likely to change in the future.

2. Activities in the extended present might or might not be happening right now, at the time of speaking.

3. For more information on this grammar topic, see page 282.

Teaching Tip

Grammar. Review the spelling of the *–ing* forms of verbs. Give students daily spelling quizzes. Short but frequent reinforcement is more effective than waiting until the end of the unit to test students.

B Complete the sentences. Make the first sentence negative and the second sentence affirmative. Use the words in the box and the present progressive.

cook	eat out	~~go~~	spend	~~take~~	visit
eat	get to know	look	stay	try	work

1. I ___am not going___ to school full time, but I ___am taking___ an English class this year.
2. My parents ___are not / aren't staying___ with me this month. They ___'re / are visiting___ my sister in Arizona.
3. My brother ___is not / isn't spending___ much time with his high school friends anymore. He ___'s / is getting to know___ a lot of new people at college.
4. My son ___is not / isn't working___ these days, but he ___'s / is looking___ for a job.
5. I ___'m / am not eating___ a lot of bread these days. I ___'m / am trying___ to lose weight.
6. My wife and I ___are not / aren't eating out___ a lot these days. We ___'re / are cooking___ more at home.

C Write *yes / no* questions about *these days*. Use the words in the boxes. Answers will vary.

you	do interesting things
you and your family	get to know new people
you and your friends	have a lot of fun
your boyfriend	make a lot of money
your children	sleep well
your girlfriend	spend a lot of money
your husband	spend time with family
your parents	take a class
your wife	work hard

1. ___Are you spending a lot of money these days?___
2. _____
3. _____
4. _____
5. _____
6. _____

TIME to TALK

PAIRS. Ask and answer the questions you wrote in Exercise C.

Example:
A: *Are you working hard these days?*   A: *Is your wife taking a class these days?*
B: *Yes, I am.*   B: *No, she isn't.*

Getting to Know You **7**

B Teaching Time: 5–10 min.

- Have a student read the example.
- Have students complete the task.
- Have students check their answers in pairs. Then call on students to say answers. Correct as needed.

C Teaching Time: 10–15 min.

- Have students work in pairs to complete the task.
- Call on students to read their questions. Correct as needed.

Watch Out!

Exercises A–C: Students often omit the auxiliary verb *be* when they form the present progressive. For example, they might say: *He cooking these days.* Write the verb *be* in large letters on the board and point to it as needed to prompt students to correct themselves.

Option

Assign Unit 1 Supplementary Grammar to Communicate 2 Exercises on the Teacher's Resource Disk as homework or on the Student Persistence CD-ROM as self-access practice.

TIME to TALK

Teaching Time: 10–15 min.

- Have a student ask you the first question: *Are you spending a lot of money these days?* Answer: *Yes, I am. I'm [verb + ing]* (e.g., *I'm buying a car, and I'm looking for a new house*).
- PAIRS. Have students complete the task.

Multilevel Strategy

- **Pre-level, At-level:** Pair pre-level students with at-level students to complete the task. Have pairs ask and answer three questions. Have them write their answers in their notebooks.
- **Above-level:** Pair above-level students for this exercise. Tell them to ask and answer all the questions. Then have them ask each other additional questions.

Simple Present and Present Progressive

Teaching Time: 5–10 min.

- Have students study the chart.
- Write on the board: *I drive to work most of the time, but this week my car is at the shop for repairs, so I'm not driving to work. I'm taking the bus.*
- Say: *We use the simple present for habits and routines. We use the present progressive when we are doing something that we do not usually do, or we are doing something for only a short period of time. In this example, my habit is to drive to work. However, because my car is at the shop for repairs, I can't drive to work this week. I'm doing something that I don't usually do—I'm taking the bus to work.*
- Read the examples in the chart and have students repeat chorally.

A **Teaching Time: 10–15 min.**

- Read the instructions to the class. Show them the explanations at the bottom of the page.
- 🎧 Play Track 7 while students listen and complete the task.
- Call on two students to read the first conversation. After they finish, ask the class: *What's Luke like?* (He's shy.) *Does he talk a lot?* (No, he doesn't.) *Is his personality probably going to change?* (No.) *Where does he live?* (In Dover.) *Is he probably going to move soon?* (No, he isn't.) *Do we use simple present or present progressive for things that are probably going to stay the same for a long time—in other words, things that are permanent?* (Simple present.)
- Call on two other students to read the second conversation aloud. Ask the class: *Where does Vera live?* (In L.A.) *Is she in L.A. now?* (No, she isn't.) *What is she doing?* (She's visiting.) *Where is she staying?* (At Dan and Meg's house.) *Is she going to stay there for a long time?* (No, she isn't. She's just visiting.) *What are Dan and Meg doing?* (They're driving from Texas to Guatemala.) *Do they drive from Texas to Guatemala every summer?* (No, they don't. They're just driving there this summer.) *Do we use*

simple present or present progressive for things that are probably going to change soon—in other words, things that are temporary? (Present progressive.)

- Call on students to say answers. Correct as needed.

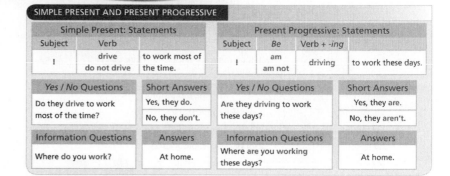

SIMPLE PRESENT AND PRESENT PROGRESSIVE

Simple Present: Statements		
Subject	Verb	
I	drive do not drive	to work most of the time.

Present Progressive: Statements			
Subject	*Be*	Verb + *-ing*	
I	am am not	driving	to work these days.

Yes / No Questions	Short Answers
Do they drive to work most of the time?	Yes, they do. No, they don't.

Information Questions	Answers
Where do you work?	At home.

Yes / No Questions	Short Answers
Are they driving to work these days?	Yes, they are. No, they aren't.

Information Questions	Answers
Where are you working these days?	At home.

A 🔊 CD 1 TRACK 7 **Read and listen to the conversations. Then read the explanations and circle** *simple present* **or** *present progressive.*

Conversation 1

Ann: Who's that guy in the corner?
Dia: His name's Luke Grava.
Ann: What's he like?
Dia: He's a little shy. He **doesn't talk** much, but he's got a nice personality.
Ann: **Does** he **live** here in the neighborhood?
Dia: He **lives** in Dover with his wife.

Conversation 2

Joe: She's got a good sense of humor. What's her name?
Ken: That's Vera. She**'s visiting** from L.A.
Joe: **Is** she **staying** with you?
Ken: No, she**'s staying** at Dan and Meg's. They're away for the summer. **They're driving** from Texas to Guatemala.
Joe: Wow. That's an adventure!
Ken: Yeah, they're very adventurous.

1. Conversation 1 uses the (simple present) / present progressive for something that is permanent (= probably going to stay the same for a long time).

2. Conversation 2 uses the simple present / (present progressive) for something that is temporary (= probably going to change soon).

Grammar Notes

- Use the present progressive to talk about activities that are temporary (= will probably change soon).
- Use the simple present to talk about activities that are permanent (= will probably stay the same for a long time).
- We do not use the present progressive with stative verbs, even if the activity is temporary. Turn to page 298 for a list of these verbs.
- For more information on this grammar topic, see the grammar summary on page 282.

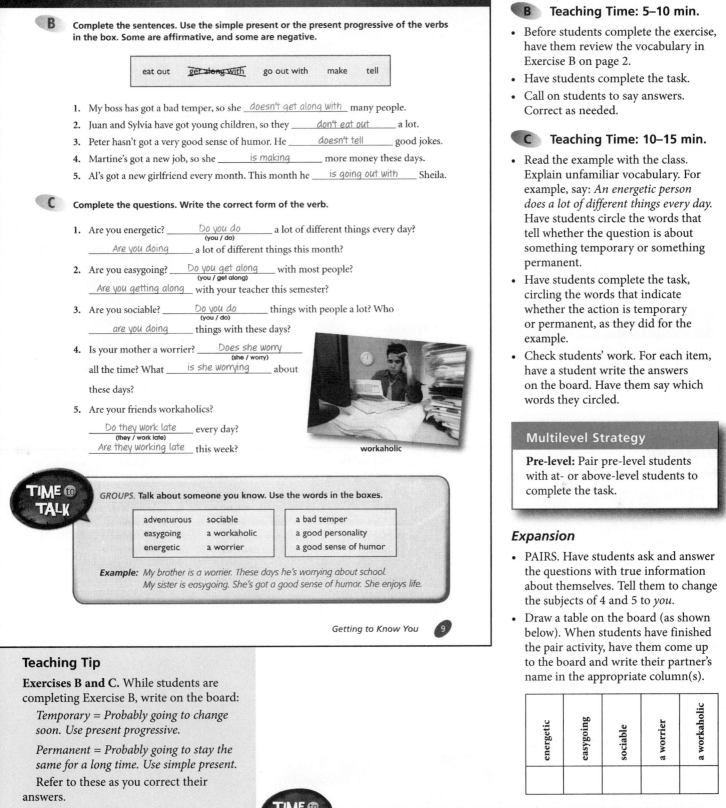

B Complete the sentences. Use the simple present or the present progressive of the verbs in the box. Some are affirmative, and some are negative.

> eat out   ~~get along with~~   go out with   make   tell

1. My boss has got a bad temper, so she _doesn't get along with_ many people.
2. Juan and Sylvia have got young children, so they _don't eat out_ a lot.
3. Peter hasn't got a very good sense of humor. He _doesn't tell_ good jokes.
4. Martine's got a new job, so she _is making_ more money these days.
5. Al's got a new girlfriend every month. This month he _is going out with_ Sheila.

C Complete the questions. Write the correct form of the verb.

1. Are you energetic? _Do you do_ a lot of different things every day?
   (you / do)
   Are you doing a lot of different things this month?

2. Are you easygoing? _Do you get along_ with most people?
   (you / get along)
   Are you getting along with your teacher this semester?

3. Are you sociable? _Do you do_ things with people a lot? Who
   (you / do)
   are you doing things with these days?

4. Is your mother a worrier? _Does she worry_
   (she / worry)
   all the time? What _is she worrying_ about
   these days?

5. Are your friends workaholics?
   Do they work late every day?
   (they / work late)
   Are they working late this week?

workaholic

TIME to TALK

GROUPS. Talk about someone you know. Use the words in the boxes.

adventurous	sociable		a bad temper
easygoing	a workaholic		a good personality
energetic	a worrier		a good sense of humor

Example: My brother is a worrier. These days he's worrying about school.
My sister is easygoing. She's got a good sense of humor. She enjoys life.

Getting to Know You   9

B Teaching Time: 5–10 min.

- Before students complete the exercise, have them review the vocabulary in Exercise B on page 2.
- Have students complete the task.
- Call on students to say answers. Correct as needed.

C Teaching Time: 10–15 min.

- Read the example with the class. Explain unfamiliar vocabulary. For example, say: *An energetic person does a lot of different things every day.* Have students circle the words that tell whether the question is about something temporary or something permanent.
- Have students complete the task, circling the words that indicate whether the action is temporary or permanent, as they did for the example.
- Check students' work. For each item, have a student write the answers on the board. Have them say which words they circled.

Multilevel Strategy

Pre-level: Pair pre-level students with at- or above-level students to complete the task.

Expansion

- PAIRS. Have students ask and answer the questions with true information about themselves. Tell them to change the subjects of 4 and 5 to *you*.
- Draw a table on the board (as shown below). When students have finished the pair activity, have them come up to the board and write their partner's name in the appropriate column(s).

energetic	easygoing	sociable	a worrier	a workaholic

Teaching Tip

Exercises B and C. While students are completing Exercise B, write on the board:

Temporary = Probably going to change soon. Use present progressive.

Permanent = Probably going to stay the same for a long time. Use simple present.

Refer to these as you correct their answers.

Option

Assign Unit 1 Supplementary Grammar to Communicate 3 Exercises on the Teacher's Resource Disk as homework or on the Student Persistence CD-ROM as self-access practice.

TIME to TALK

Teaching Time: 15–20 min.

- **Warm-up:** Read the words in the first box. Have students repeat chorally after you. Then ask about the words in the second box, for example, *What does a person with a bad temper do?* (scream a lot)
- Call on two students to read the example.
- GROUPS. Have students complete the task. Walk around and help as needed.

Review and Challenge

Grammar

Teaching Time: 5–10 min.

- Read the example with the class.
- Have students complete the task. Have them circle the words in the context that indicate whether the activity is temporary or permanent.
- 🎧 Play Track 8 while students check their answers.
- Call on students to read answers. For every verb, ask students to tell you whether it is temporary or permanent. Correct as needed.

Multilevel Strategy

Pre-level: Tell students what the mistakes are and have them rewrite the sentences and questions.

Dictation

Teaching Time: 5–10 min.

- 🎧 Play Track 9 while students listen and write what they hear.
- 🎧 Play Track 9 again while students check their answers.
- Call on students to write answers on the board.
- 🎧 Play Track 9 again and correct the sentences on the board.

Multilevel Strategy

Pre-level: Give students a worksheet with some of the words from the dictation already provided.

Speaking

Teaching Time: 10–15 min.

- Call on a student in the class to model the activity with you. Have the student ask you the questions. Write your answers on the board.
- Call on another student to read the example.

Review and Challenge

Grammar

🔘 **8** This conversation has seven mistakes. The first mistake is corrected for you. Find and correct the other six mistakes. Then listen and check your answers.

Stan: Hi, Jack. How ~~things going~~ *are things going*?

Jack: I'm pretty busy. I ~~take~~ *am taking* five classes this semester.

Stan: Really? That's a lot. I'm just taking three. Do you like your teachers?

Jack: Yes. I get along with all of them. I really like my math teacher. ~~He~~ *He's* got a good sense of humor, and ~~he's explaining~~ *he explains* things really well.

Stan: I like my teachers, too. So, where ~~you go~~ *are you going* now?

Jack: I'm going home. Peggy's ~~wait~~ *waiting* for me in the car.

Stan: Oh, are you two going out these days?

Jack: No, we're just friends. She ~~have~~ *has* got a boyfriend.

Dictation

🔘 **9** Listen. You will hear five sentences. Write them in your notebook. *See the audioscript on p. 307 for the sentences.*

Speaking

PAIRS. Talk about yourself. Use the words in the box and your own ideas. Answer these questions:

1. What's usually true about you?
2. What's true these days, but not always?
3. What's different these days?

cook a lot	exercise a lot	stay at home on weekends
eat a lot of fast food	play (your idea)	study hard
eat healthy food	sleep very well	watch sports on TV
eat out	spend time with family	work overtime

Example:
A: *I usually exercise a lot, but these days I'm not exercising much. I haven't got time. I'm working a lot of overtime.*

- PAIRS. Have students complete the task. Walk around and help as needed.
- Call on a few students to tell the class about their partners.

Multilevel Strategy

- **Pre-level:** Pair pre-level students together. Have them write out their answers before they speak.
- **Above-level:** Pair above-level students together. Tell them to discuss at least five of the activities in the box.

Listening

Listening

A 🔊 **1 TRACK 10** Listen to the radio report. What is the reporter trying to find out? Check (✓) the correct answer.

❏ **1.** Do people in the city have a lot of neighbors?

☑ **2.** Do people in the city get to know their neighbors?

❏ **3.** Do people in the city like their neighbors?

B 🔊 **1 TRACK 10** Listen again. Evangeline talks to three people: a young woman, a man, and an older woman. Read the sentences and write *T* (true) or *F* (false).

_F_ **1.** The young woman is living with her friend.

_T_ **2.** The man's neighbors have got pets.

_F_ **3.** The man knows one of his neighbors very well.

_F_ **4.** The old woman is not very sociable.

TIME to TALK

ON YOUR OWN. Read the sentences. Check (✓) the sentences that you agree with.

❏ **1.** I know most of the people in my neighborhood.

❏ **2.** My neighbors don't know very much about me, and that's a good thing.

❏ **3.** Most people haven't got time to get to know their neighbors.

❏ **4.** A lot of new people are moving into my neighborhood these days.

❏ **5.** The people in my neighborhood get along very well.

❏ **6.** It is important to have a close relationship with your neighbors.

❏ **7.** Most people in my country have close relationships with their neighbors.

❏ **8.** People in my country usually live in one place all their lives.

GROUPS. Talk about your answers. Do you agree?

Example: A: *I agree with Number 1. I know most of my neighbors.*
B: *I don't agree. I'm so busy. I haven't got time to meet my neighbors.*

Getting to Know You **11**

Listening

A Teaching Time: 5–10 min.

- **Warm-up:** Explain that in the United States, television and radio reporters often go out into the streets and interview ordinary people. This is sometimes called a "man (or woman)-on-the-street" interview. Ask students if reporters in their countries sometimes do these types of interviews.

- Have students read the questions before they listen. Tell them not to worry about understanding details. They should just listen for the main topic.

- 🎧 Play Track 10 while students listen and complete the task.

- Call on a student to say the answer. Correct as needed.

B Teaching Time: 5–10 min.

- To help students complete the task more easily, have them read through the statements before listening.

- Have students complete the task.

- 🎧 Play Track 10 while students listen and complete the task. If necessary, play the track again.

- Call on students to say answers. Correct as needed.

Multilevel Strategy

- **Pre-level:** Tell students that there are three false statements.

- **At-level, Above-level:** When checking answers, challenge students to correct the false statements.

Option

Assign Unit 1 Review and Challenge Supplementary Exercises on the Teacher's Resource Disk as homework or on the Student Persistence CD-ROM as self-access practice.

TIME to TALK

Teaching Time: 10–15 min.

- Ask for a show of hands in response to the question: *Are you close friends with any of your neighbors?*

- ON YOUR OWN. Have students complete the task individually. Walk around and help as needed.

- GROUPS. Have students read the example and complete the task.

- Read each sentence aloud and ask students to raise their hands if they agree with it. Write their responses on the board, like this:
  1: [number of students who agree], 2: [number of students who agree], and so on.

Reading

Getting Ready to Read

Teaching Time: 5–10 min.

- **Warm-up.** Ask for a show of hands in response to the question: *Do you have a best friend?* Call on a couple of the students who raised their hands and ask them when, where, and how they met their best friend.
- Ask a student to read the Reading Skill aloud.
- Have students complete the task and compare their answers with a partner.
- Have students look at the title of the article and the picture. Ask them to guess what new way of getting to know people they will probably read about. Write their responses on the board.

Reading

Teaching Time: 15–20 min.

- Tell students not to use a dictionary, but rather to try to understand the meaning of new words from the context. Tell them that the second exercise in the reading section is always a vocabulary exercise; it will help them with unfamiliar words. Assure them that they can understand the reading even if they don't understand the meaning of all the words.
- Have them read and complete the task. Call on students to say which of the things they wrote appeared in the article. Write their answers on the board.

Multilevel Strategy

- **Pre-level:** Give students extra time to complete the reading.
- **At-level, Above-level:** Faster readers should read the article again, this time circling unfamiliar words. When pre-level students have finished reading, pair them up with at- or above-level students. Have pre-level students ask their partner about anything they didn't understand.

Reading

Getting Ready to Read

How do people in your country meet and get to know new people? List four ways.
Answers will vary.

1. _____
2. _____
3. _____
4. _____

> **Reading Skill:**
> **Thinking about What You Know**
>
> Before you read, think about the topic of the text. What do you already know about the topic? That information will help you understand the text.

Reading

Read the article. Does the writer talk about any of the things you wrote about in Getting Ready to Read?

A NEW WAY OF GETTING TO KNOW PEOPLE

These days, people are getting to know other people in lots of different ways. Of course, many people make friends in traditional ways. They talk to **strangers** at parties. They join clubs, play team sports, or take classes. **Old friends** introduce people to new friends. But more and more people these days are making friends on the Internet.

How do people make friends on the Internet? They visit **chat rooms** and **blogs**. In chat rooms, people write messages to each other. Everyone in the chat room can read the messages. There are different chat rooms for people with different interests. For example, English students can go to special chat rooms to learn English.

On blogs, people write about many different topics. Other people read the blogs and write comments about them. You do not have to be important to write a blog, but the writers of some blogs become famous. For example, one woman wrote a blog about cooking dinner every night. She used a recipe from a famous French cookbook every night for a year. People loved it, so she made it into a book.

There are some problems with meeting people on the Internet. The Internet can be a dangerous place. Some Internet users are **criminals**. They want to steal your money or hurt you. For this reason, it's not a good idea to share your **private** information on the Internet.

On the other hand, some people say it is easier to make friends on the Internet? Some shy people are afraid to talk to new people **in person**, but they aren't afraid to write to people. Also on the Internet, it **doesn't matter** where you live. You can make friends with people all over the world.

Teaching Tip

Reading. If you have students complete the first few readings in class, you can monitor their dictionary use. After students get used to reading without a dictionary in class, you can save class time by assigning the readings for homework.

After You Read

A Look at the **boldface** words in the article. Guess their meaning. Then read the sentences, and circle the correct answer.

1. A **stranger**
   a. does not know you. ⟵ (circled)
   b. does bad things.

2. An **old friend** is
   a. not young.
   b. not new. (circled)

3. In a **chat room**, people
   a. can see each other.
   b. write to other people. (circled)

4. On a **blog**, people
   a. have conversations with other people.
   b. write things for other people to read. (circled)

5. A **criminal**
   a. does not know you.
   b. does bad things. (circled)

6. When something is **private**, you
   a. tell a lot of people about it.
   b. don't tell a lot of people about it. (circled)

7. When you talk to a friend **in person**, you
   a. can see, hear, and touch him or her. (circled)
   b. can hear him or her, but you can't touch or see him or her.

8. If something **doesn't matter** to you, it is
   a. not safe for you.
   b. not important to you. (circled)

B Read the article again. Write *T* (true) or *F* (false) for each statement. Then correct the false statements.

_F_ 1. People ~~aren't~~ *are* making friends in traditional ways these days.

_T_ 2. A lot of people make friends on the Internet.

_F_ 3. Writers of blogs are usually famous.

_T_ 4. In chat rooms, strangers read your messages.

_T_ 5. On the Internet, it doesn't matter if you are shy.

_T_ 6. It is easy to meet people on the Internet.

Option

Exercises A and B. After students have completed the reading exercises, have them underline two verbs in the article that are in the present progressive form and five verbs that are in the simple present. Call on students to explain why the different verb forms were used.

After You Read

A Teaching Time: 10–15 min.

- Read the example with the class.
- PAIRS. Have students complete the task with the same partner they had for the first activity.
- Call on students to say answers. Correct as needed. Refer to the text as necessary.

B Teaching Time: 10–15 min.

- Read the example with the class. Have students go back to the reading and find the paragraph that contains the answer (paragraph 1, sentence 2). Tell them to write the number 1 next to the place in the text where they found the answer.
- Tell students to complete the task without looking back at the text.
- Now let them check their answers in the text, writing the number of the item next to the place where they found the answer.
- Call on students to read their answers. Ask them to tell you where they found the answer in the text. Have them read aloud the relevant sentence, while their classmates read along silently. Correct as needed.

Expansion. Do an oral review of the information in the article. Write a series of questions on the board and have students work in groups of 3–5 to answer without looking back at the text. Assign a group secretary to write down the group's answers. Make the activity competitive. The group that gets the most correct answers is the winner. Suggested questions:

1. *What different ways of making friends does the writer mention? List them.*
2. *What are the differences between a blog and a chat room?*
3. *What are some of the problems with meeting people on the Internet?*
4. *What are some of the advantages of meeting people on the Internet?*

Getting Ready to Write

A **Teaching Time: 5–10 min.**

- **Warm-up.** Before students read the Writing Tip or the first example, write the example on the board (with *teenagers* appearing twice). Ask students to tell you how to improve the sentence. If they aren't able to answer, ask them to tell you which word is repeated (*teenagers*). Then ask them to replace it with a pronoun.
- Read the Writing Tip with students.
- Have students complete the task.
- Call on students to say answers. Correct as needed.

B **Teaching Time: 10–15 min.**

- Call on a student to read the model paragraph aloud.
- PAIRS. Have students complete the task.
- Call on students to answer the question about the model paragraph. Correct as needed.
- PAIRS. Have students complete the discussion task. Walk around and help as needed.

Expansion Ask students to explain what the writer of the model means in the last sentence: *We are real friends, not Internet friends.* Ask them what the writer's definition of a "real" friend probably is.

Writing

Getting Ready to Write

A Read the sentences. Change the repeated nouns to pronouns.

1. Many teenagers want to meet a lot of people, and ~~teenagers~~ *they* try to make friends on the Internet.

2. It isn't easy to get to know people well. You have to meet ~~people~~ *them* in person.

3. The Internet helps people make friends, but ~~the Internet~~ *it* is also dangerous.

4. Some people send messages to ~~people's~~ *their* friends every day.

5. You can send messages to strangers, but don't meet ~~strangers~~ *them* in person.

6. I like to take classes at night. ~~Classes~~ *They* are a good way to make friends.

B Read the model paragraph.

> More and more young people are making friends on the Internet these days. They are also sending messages to other people on their cell phones. They are not really talking. In my opinion, this is not the best way to meet people. You cannot really get to know a person on the Internet. People sometimes tell lies on the Internet. To make real friends, you have to meet people, look at them, and listen to them. For example, you can join a sports team. I met my best friend three years ago on a soccer team. We both love soccer. We play every weekend. After the games, we have dinner and talk about everything. We are real friends, not Internet friends.

PAIRS. Read the model again. According to the writer, what is the best way to make friends?

Do you agree? Discuss.

Teaching Tip

Exercise A. Review subject and object pronouns and possessive adjectives before having students complete Exercise A. Write the subject pronouns on the board and ask students to give you the object pronouns and the possessive adjectives.

Prewriting: Answering Questions

You are going to write a paragraph about making friends. Before you write, answer questions about the topic.

1. What do you think about the ways people are getting to know one another these days? Are they good or bad?

2. In your opinion, what is the best way to make new friends?

3. Describe how you met a new friend.

Writing

Now write a paragraph about making friends. The writing tip, the model paragraph, and your notes will help you. Write in your notebook.

Teaching Time: 10–15 min.

- Read the instructions aloud.
- Have students complete the task.
- Pair students and have them compare their answers.
- Walk around and help as needed.

Writing

Teaching Time: 15–20 min.

- Have students complete the task. Walk around and help as needed. Encourage students to refer to the model in the book as they write.
- If there is not enough time for students to complete the writing task during class time, tell them to finish it for homework.
- Before students hand in their paragraphs, tell them to review the grammar summary on page 282 and the Writing Tip on page 14. After they review the grammar, tell them to reread their paragraphs and underline the verbs. Then have them circle any nouns that are repeated. Have they used the correct verb forms? Have they used pronouns wherever possible?
- To correct students' paragraphs, focus your feedback on the grammar points presented and practiced in the unit.

Teaching Tip

Writing. Tell students to skip every other line when they write their paragraphs. That way you will have room to make comments and corrections.

Learning Goals

- Learn vocabulary used to describe places
- Learn about count and noncount nouns and quantifiers and how to use the correlative conjunctions *both, neither,* and *either*
- Listen to a conversation and a radio report
- Read an article about a city and write about a city with which you are familiar
- Talk about places around the world

Learner Persistence

Learn your students' names as quickly as possible.

Warm-up

Teaching Time: 3–5 min.

- Draw a graphic organizer on the board (as shown below).

This city	
I like	**I don't like**

- Ask the class: *What do you like about this city? What don't you like?*
- Write students' answers in note form in the graphic organizer.

Vocabulary

Teaching Time: 10–15 min.

- Have students complete the task.
- PAIRS. Have students compare answers.
- 🎧 Play Track 11 while students read and listen.
- Call on students to say answers. Read each word aloud and have students repeat chorally.

Expansion

- Draw the following graphic organizer on the board. Have students copy it into their notebooks.

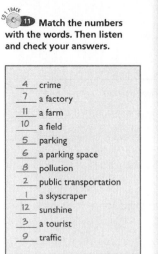

Unit 2
The World We Live In

Unit 2
The World We Live In

Grammar
- Count and Noncount Nouns: Quantifiers
- Count and Noncount Nouns: *Plenty of / Enough / Too much / Too many*
- *Both / Neither / Either*

Vocabulary

🎧 **CD 1 TRACK 11 Match the numbers with the words. Then listen and check your answers.**

4	crime
7	a factory
11	a farm
10	a field
5	parking
6	a parking space
8	pollution
2	public transportation
1	a skyscraper
12	sunshine
3	a tourist
9	traffic

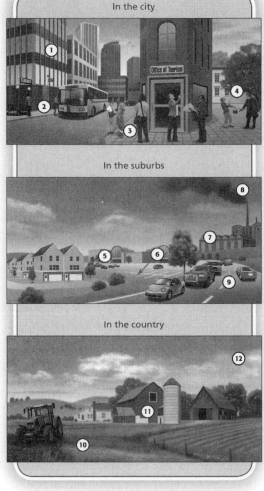

In the city

In the suburbs

In the country

16   Unit 2

- Write *skyscraper* in the city circle, *sunshine* in the overlapping space of the two circles, and *farm* in the country circle.
- Have students work in pairs to add the remaining words to the diagram. Tell them that answers may vary.
- Walk around the class and check their diagrams. Ask for clarification if necessary.

Culture Note

Vocabulary. Students might not understand the word *suburbs*. Write *the suburbs* on the board, along with the definition: *an area away from the center of the city, where a lot of people live.* Explain that in the United States, many people think that the suburbs are a good place to live. Ask: *Why do many Americans want to live in the suburbs?* (Possible answers = to leave problems of the city such as crime, traffic, etc; they want bigger houses; they want better schools for kids.) Have students name some local suburbs and write them on the board. Then ask: *Are the suburbs in your country similar to the suburbs in the United States? If not, how are they different?*

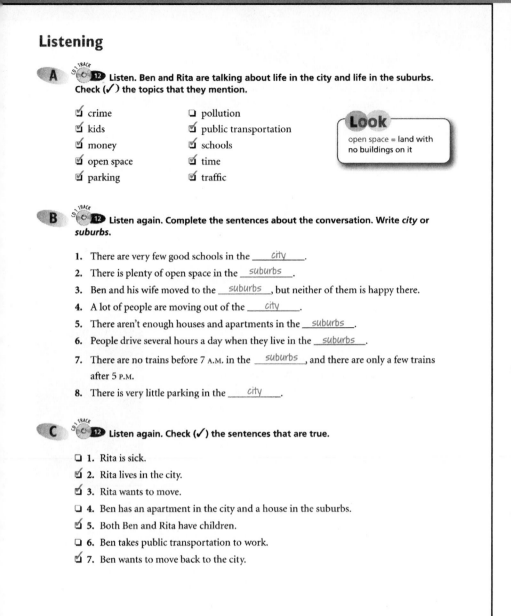

Listening

A 🎧 **12** Listen. Ben and Rita are talking about life in the city and life in the suburbs. Check (✓) the topics that they mention.

☑ crime
☑ kids
☑ money
☑ open space
☑ parking

❑ pollution
☑ public transportation
☑ schools
☑ time
☑ traffic

Look

open space = land with no buildings on it

B 🎧 **12** Listen again. Complete the sentences about the conversation. Write *city* or *suburbs*.

1. There are very few good schools in the ___city___.
2. There is plenty of open space in the ___suburbs___.
3. Ben and his wife moved to the ___suburbs___, but neither of them is happy there.
4. A lot of people are moving out of the ___city___.
5. There aren't enough houses and apartments in the ___suburbs___.
6. People drive several hours a day when they live in the ___suburbs___.
7. There are no trains before 7 A.M. in the ___suburbs___, and there are only a few trains after 5 P.M.
8. There is very little parking in the ___city___.

C 🎧 **12** Listen again. Check (✓) the sentences that are true.

❑ 1. Rita is sick.
☑ 2. Rita lives in the city.
☑ 3. Rita wants to move.
❑ 4. Ben has an apartment in the city and a house in the suburbs.
☑ 5. Both Ben and Rita have children.
❑ 6. Ben takes public transportation to work.
☑ 7. Ben wants to move back to the city.

The World We Live In **17**

Language Note

Exercise C. Write *I'm sick* and *I'm sick of the city* on the board. Ask: *Which sentence means that you aren't feeling well? Which sentence means that you are bored with something and want a change?* If someone is absent, ask: *Is [name of absent student] sick?* and *What is wrong with [name of absent student]?* Then call on students and ask: *Are you sick of the weather (your job, the traffic, etc.)?*

Option

Assign Unit 2 Supplementary Vocabulary Exercises on the Teacher's Resource Disk as homework or on the Student Persistence CD-ROM as self-access practice.

Listening

A **Teaching Time: 10–15 min.**

- **Warm-up:** Ask students where they would prefer to live: the city or the suburbs.
- Tell them that they are going to listen to a woman and a man talk about life in the city and life in the suburbs.
- Ask students to read the words in the list. Have them repeat the words chorally. Tell them that the people on the audio will talk about some of the topics, but not all of them.
- 🎧 Play Track 12 once while students just listen.
- 🎧 Play Track 12 again while students listen and complete the task.
- PAIRS. Have students compare answers.
- Call on students to say answers. Correct as needed.

B **Teaching Time: 10–15 min.**

- Tell students to complete the task. If they are not sure of an answer, tell them to guess.
- 🎧 Play Track 12 as students listen and check their answers.
- Call on students to say answers. Correct as needed.

C **Teaching Time: 10–15 min.**

- PAIRS. Have students complete the task together. If they are not sure whether a sentence is true, they should write a question mark (?).
- 🎧 Play Track 12 again as students listen and check their answers. Call on students to say answers. Correct as needed.

Multilevel Strategy

- **Pre-level:** Make photocopies of the audioscript and have students read along as they listen.
- **Above-level:** Write a part of the conversation on the board and erase some words. Have students close their books and attempt to recall the conversation while role-playing.

Unit 2 **T-17**

Grammar to Communicate 1

Count and Noncount Nouns: Quantifiers

Teaching Time: 5–10 min.

- Have students study the chart and the Look Boxes.
- Say: *We can count the count nouns. They have singular and plural forms. We can't count noncount nouns. They only have singular forms.*
- Write on the board: 1. *The traffic is terrible.* 2. *The school is good.* 3. *The schools are good.* Say: *Traffic is a noncount noun.* Ask: *Is school a count or a noncount noun?*
- Have students give examples of other noncount nouns and write them on the board. Correct as needed.
- Read the quantifiers in the chart aloud and have students repeat chorally. Say: *A quantifier tells the amount—how much or how many. Some quantifiers can only be used with count nouns, and others can only be used with noncount nouns. Some quantifiers can be used with both.* Have students underline the quantifiers that are used with both count and noncount nouns (*a lot of, some, any, no*).

A Teaching Time: 5–10 min.

- Call on a student to read the first two sentences aloud.
- Tell students there are two nouns in these sentences and ask what they are (*country, weather*). Then ask which noun is count (*country*) and which is noncount (*weather*). Ask them to explain how they know.
- Tell students to look at the picture of a village. Explain that a village is smaller than a town. Then ask if they think that the word *village* is count or noncount (*count*).
- 🎧 Play Track 13 as students listen and complete the task.
- Call on students to say answers. Correct as needed.

Multilevel Strategy

- **Pre-level, At-level:** Play the track twice. The first time the students should just read along for general comprehension.

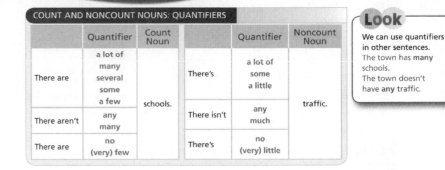

Grammar to Communicate 1

	Quantifier	Count Noun		Quantifier	Noncount Noun
There are	a lot of / many / several / some / a few	schools.	There's	a lot of / some / a little	traffic.
There aren't	any / many		There isn't	any / much	
There are	no / (very) few		There's	no / (very) little	

Look

We can use quantifiers in other sentences.
The town has **many** schools.
The town doesn't have **any** traffic.

A 🎧 13 Read and listen to a student's oral report about his country. Circle the count nouns and underline the noncount nouns.

I live in a beautiful (country). The <u>weather</u> is great. There's always a lot of <u>sunshine</u> and very little <u>rain.</u> There are a few big (cities), but most (people) live in small (towns) and (villages). I'm from the capital (city). It's an exciting (place). There are a lot of great (stores) and (restaurants), but there aren't any (skyscrapers). My (parents) and I live in an (apartment) near several (stores). The (apartment) is small and doesn't have much <u>space</u>, but we like it. Most (people) in my (country) haven't got a lot of <u>money</u>, but we've got many other good (things). I miss my (country) a lot.

Look

several = five or six
a little / a few = some
(very) little = not much
(very) few = not many

village

B Complete the sentences about your country. Write *is*, *isn't*, *are*, or *aren't*. Answers will vary.

1. The weather ___is/isn't___ good.
2. Our music ___is/isn't___ great.
3. The food ___is/isn't___ wonderful.
4. People ___are/aren't___ friendly.
5. There ___are/aren't___ a lot of skyscrapers.
6. People's homes ___are/aren't___ big.
7. There ___are/aren't___ a lot of villages.
8. There ___are/aren't___ many big cities.
9. There ___is/isn't___ a lot of open space.
10. There ___is/isn't___ a long river.

18   Unit 2

- **Above-level:** Have students cover the exercise in their books when they listen the first time.

B Teaching Time: 5–10 min.

- Have students circle the count nouns and underline the noncount nouns. Remind them that noncount nouns only have singular form.
- Have students complete the task. Walk around and help as needed.
- Call on a few students to read about their countries. Correct as needed.

Grammar Notes

1. Count nouns can be singular or plural.
2. Noncount nouns have no plural form. They are always used with a verb in the third person singular form.
3. You can use *a / an* in front of a singular count noun.
4. Never use *a / an* in front of a noncount noun. Use *some* in affirmative statements and *any* in questions and negative statements.
5. For more information on this grammar topic, see page 282.

C Complete the sentences with *a little*, *very little*, *a few*, or *very few*.

1. We never eat out because there are ___very few___ good restaurants around here.
2. There are ___a few___ restaurants near my home. Three of them are very good.
3. People need cars in my town because there's ___very little___ public transportation.
4. My street is almost always quiet. There's ___very little___ noise.
5. There are ___very few___ stores. We shop in another town.
6. You see ___very few___ people on the streets during the day. They're at work.
7. There are ___a few___ banks. Two are on my street, and one is around the corner.
8. There's ___a little___ crime, but we feel safe.

D What do people in your country eat? Write sentences with *a few*, *very few*, *a little*, *very little*, *a lot of*, or *no*. Use the words in the box and your own ideas. Answers will vary.

beans	bread	corn	fruit	hot peppers	pork	rice
beef	cheese	fish	hot dogs	ice cream	potatoes	spicy food

1. _In my country, we eat a lot of beef, but we eat very little cheese._
2. _____
3. _____
4. _____
5. _____
6. _____
7. _____

PAIRS. Talk to a student from a different country. Do people from your countries eat the same things?

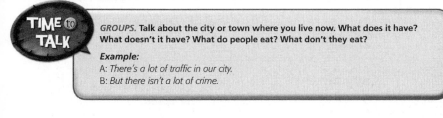

TIME to TALK

GROUPS. Talk about the city or town where you live now. What does it have? What doesn't it have? What do people eat? What don't they eat?

Example:
A: *There's a lot of traffic in our city.*
B: *But there isn't a lot of crime.*

The World We Live In 19

C Teaching Time: 5–10 min.

- Read the example with the class. Ask students to explain why the answer is *very few* and not *a few*. (*We never eat out* is the result, so we know that the number of good restaurants is VERY small.)
- Do number 2 with the class and compare it to the example. Point out that because the sentence says *three of them*, we know that there are more than three. So the answer is *a FEW*, not VERY few.
- Have students complete the task.
- Call on students to say answers. Correct as needed.

D Teaching Time: 10–15 min.

- Explain that students should write about the *customs* of people in their countries. Tell them to write about what is common in their country, even if their personal eating habits are different. If the food is different in different parts of the country, they should write, for example, *In the south, people eat* [type of food].
- Have students complete the task. Walk around and help as needed.
- PAIRS. Have students complete the task.
- Call on several students from different countries to read their sentences. Correct as needed.

Multilevel Strategy

- **Prelevel, At-level:** Have at-level students assist pre-level students with the task.
- **Above-level:** Have students report to the class what they learned about the customs of people in their partner's country.

Language Note

Exercise C. Students often have trouble understanding the difference between *a few* and *a little* and *few* and *little*. For many students, the difference in meaning is clearer when they add *very*. When they make a mistake and confuse *a few/a little* with *few/little*, ask them: *Do you mean a FEW (LITTLE) or VERY few (little)?*

Option

Assign Unit 2 Supplementary Grammar to Communicate 2 Exercises on the Teacher's Resource Disk as homework or on the Student Persistence CD-ROM as self-access practice.

Expansion Ask several students about what they eat. Talk about the food in the box and other common types of food. Get them to answer in full sentences to practice quantifiers.

TIME to TALK

Teaching Time: 10–15 min.

- Have students turn to page 16 and review the vocabulary. Tell them to think about which words describe the city where they live now.
- GROUPS. Have four students in one group read the example aloud. Ask the class if they all understand what to do. If not, explain.
- Have students complete the task. Walk around and help as needed.

Grammar to Communicate 2

Count and Noncount Nouns: *Plenty of / Enough / Too much / Too many*

Teaching Time: 5–10 min.

- Have students study the chart and the Look Box.
- To check students' understanding of the meaning of the various quantifiers, write them on the board. Draw three faces: a smiling face, a frowning face, and a neutral face. Ask students to tell you where to write each of the quantifiers. (Under the smiling face: *plenty of*; under the neutral face: *enough*; under the frowning face: *too much/too many/not enough*.)
- To check students' understanding of the difference between *too much* and *too many*, write sentences with blanks about the city where your school is located. Choose examples that most people would agree with. For example, if you are in a city with a traffic problem, you could write: *There _____ _____ _____ traffic here. There _____ _____ _____ cars.*
- Ask students a series of questions about the sentences on the board. Ask: *Is traffic a count or a noncount noun? (noncount) Which word goes with noncount nouns, too much or too many? (too much) Do we use a singular or a plural verb with a noncount noun? (singular) Are cars count or noncount? (count) Which word goes with count nouns—too much or too many? (too many) Is the word cars singular or plural? (plural)*
- Call on a student to complete the sentences. (*There is too much traffic here. There are too many cars.*)

A Teaching Time: 5–10 min.

- Read the first sentence with the class. Ask: *How many nouns are there in the sentence? (two: houses and money) Is money a count or a noncount noun? (noncount) House? (count)*
- Have students complete the task.
- Call on students to say answers. Correct as needed.

Grammar to Communicate 2

	Quantifier	Count Noun		Quantifier	Noncount Noun
There are	plenty of enough	houses.	There is	plenty of enough	space.
There aren't There are	enough too many	apartments. people.	There isn't There is	enough too much	sunshine. rain.

A Match the problems on the left and the information on the right.

_d_ **1.** Houses cost too much money.

_b_ **2.** There aren't enough police officers.

_e_ **3.** There are too many factories.

_a_ **4.** There aren't enough parking spaces.

_c_ **5.** There is too much rain.

a. There are too many cars.

b. There is too much crime.

c. There isn't enough sunshine.

d. There aren't enough inexpensive houses.

e. There aren't enough parks.

> **Look**
>
> enough = the correct amount
> not enough = less than the correct amount
> plenty of = a lot, more than enough
> too much / too many = more than the correct amount

B Complete the sentences. Be careful. Some are affirmative, and some are negative.

1. Tom and Linda's apartment has two bedrooms. They have seven children. They _____don't have enough_____ space.
(have / enough)

2. Ellen's home has two bedrooms. She has one child. She _____has enough_____ space.
(have / enough)

3. There are three bus stops, a train station, and a subway station near my home. There _____is plenty of_____ public transportation.
(be / plenty of)

4. There are 1 million people in my city and one hospital. There _____aren't enough_____ hospitals.
(be / enough)

5. Every night, I drive around for an hour looking for a place to park. There _____aren't enough_____ parking spaces.
(be / enough)

6. My wife and I have two phones in the house. We both have cell phones, too. We _____have enough_____ phones.
(have / enough)

7. There are four markets on my street. There _____are plenty of_____ markets.
(be / plenty of)

B Teaching Time: 5–10 min.

- Read the examples with the class and draw two pictures on the board. In one picture, show a two-bedroom house with seven stick figures crammed in one room—all are frowning. Draw two parents in the other room. In the other picture, show a two-bedroom house with two smiling stick figures, each in one of the bedrooms.
- Have students complete the task.
- Call on students to say answers. Correct as needed.

Grammar Notes

1. Use *plenty of* and *enough* with noncount nouns and plural nouns.
2. Use *too much* with noncount nouns. Use *too many* with plural nouns.
3. *Too much, too many,* and *not enough* have a negative meaning.
4. For more information on this grammar topic, see page 283.

Language Note

Exercise B. To illustrate the difference between *plenty of* and *too much / too many* draw a house with three bedrooms, and two smiling stick figures. Then draw another house with three bedrooms, but only one frowning stick figure in one of the rooms.

C Write a sentence about each picture. Use the words in the box and *too much* or *too many*.

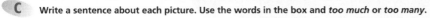

| buildings | people | rain | traffic |

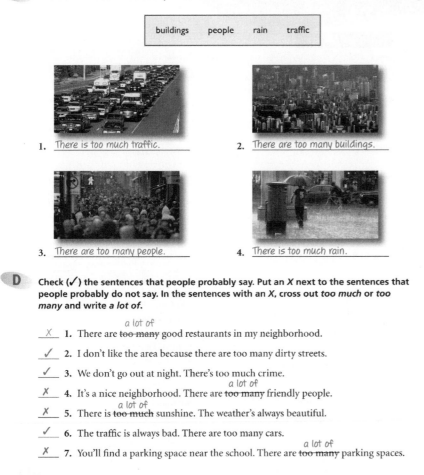

1. There is too much traffic.

2. There are too many buildings.

3. There are too many people.

4. There is too much rain.

D Check (✓) the sentences that people probably say. Put an X next to the sentences that people probably do not say. In the sentences with an X, cross out *too much* or *too many* and write *a lot of*.

    X   1. There are ~~too many~~ *a lot of* good restaurants in my neighborhood.

    ✓   2. I don't like the area because there are too many dirty streets.

    ✓   3. We don't go out at night. There's too much crime.

    X   4. It's a nice neighborhood. There are ~~too many~~ *a lot of* friendly people.

    X   5. There is ~~too much~~ *a lot of* sunshine. The weather's always beautiful.

    ✓   6. The traffic is always bad. There are too many cars.

    X   7. You'll find a parking space near the school. There are ~~too many~~ *a lot of* parking spaces.

TIME to TALK

GROUPS. Talk about the problems in big cities, small villages, the country, and the suburbs. Then discuss which place you prefer to live in, and why.

Example:
A: *In cities, there's too much crime.*
B: *There isn't much crime in villages, but there aren't enough activities for teenagers.*

The World We Live In   **21**

C Teaching Time: 5–10 min.

- Read the words in the box with the class.
- Have students complete the task.
- Call on students to say answers. Correct as needed.

Expansion Ask if any of the sentences are true about the city you are in.

D Teaching Time: 5–10 min.

- Write the first two (uncorrected) sentences on the board. Underline *too many* in both sentences and draw a frowning face next to each sentence.
- Ask whether good restaurants are a bad or a good thing. Cross out *too many* and write *a lot of*. Cross out the frowning face and draw a smiling face.
- Ask whether dirty streets are a bad thing or a good thing. Put a check mark next to the frowning face.
- Have students complete the task.
- Call on students to say answers. If a student gives an incorrect answer involving the meaning of the quantifiers, write the sentence on the board and draw a smiling (*a lot of*) or frowning (*too much / too many*) face next to it. If any students give incorrect answers involving the grammar of *too much* and *too many*, ask them if the noun is count or noncount. Then have them correct their answers.

Language Note

Exercise D. Students often have trouble understanding that *too* has a negative connotation in English. Use a visual image such as a frowning face to repeatedly reinforce this point. Draw a large frowning face and a large smiling face on the board. Have students point to one of the faces as they give their answers.

Option

Assign Unit 2 Supplementary Grammar to Communicate 2 Exercises on the Teacher's Resource Disk as homework or on the Student Persistence CD-ROM as self-access practice.

TIME to TALK

Teaching Time: 10–15 min.

- Draw a chart on the board with the following columns: *big cities, small villages, the country, the suburbs.* Have students copy it into their notebooks. Have a student read the instructions aloud. Then have two students read the example aloud. Ask the class to tell you where to write *too much crime* and where to write *not enough activities.*
- GROUPS. Have students complete the task. Walk around and encourage students to use *too much / too many / a lot of / plenty of* in their group discussions. Make sure they are taking notes in the chart.
- After a few minutes, ask one person from each group to report to the class about the problems in one of the places. Correct as needed. Add their ideas to the chart on the board.
- After problems in all of the places have been discussed, ask students to indicate which place they would prefer to live by a show of hands. Call on a few students to explain their choices.

Unit 2   **T-21**

Grammar to Communicate 3

Both / Neither / Either

Teaching Time: 5–10 min.

- Have students study the chart and the Look Box.
- Write the names of two big cities on the board, for example, Los Angeles and New York.
- Write on the board: *1. _____ cities are big. = _____ _____ the cities are big.*
  2. _____ city is small. = _____ _____ the cities is small.
  3. I don't live in _____ city. = I don't live in _____ _____ the cities.
- Have a student come up to the board and complete the sentences. Correct as needed.
- Have the class read the example sentences aloud.

Grammar to Communicate 3

A Teaching Time: 10–15 min.

- Put students into groups of three or four.
- Have them turn to the world map on pages 302–303 and find the cities. (Alternatively, bring in a world map and tape it to the board. Ask for a volunteer to come up to the front of the room and point to each of the countries in the exercise.) You might want to say that Mumbai, India, was formerly known as Bombay.
- Have students complete the task in their groups. Tell them to raise their hands when they think they have the correct answer. Go over to the group and check their answer. If it is correct, have them read it to the class. If it is incorrect, show them where they went wrong. For example, if they say that one of the cities in sentence 3 is New York, point to the sentence and say: *New York City is not the capital of the United States. Washington, D.C. is.*
- Students should continue to work until one of the groups gets the correct answer.
- PAIRS. Have students complete the task.
- Call on students to read the sentences with *of the*. Correct as needed.

BOTH / NEITHER / EITHER

Both / Neither / Either	Count Noun	Verb		Both / Neither / Either	of		Count Noun	Verb	
Both	places	are	fine.	Both	of	the / those / his	places	are	fine.
Neither Either	place	is		Neither Either	of	the / those / his	places	is	

The two places are good.	We	like	both	places.	We	like	both		the / those / his	places.
The two places are bad.	We	like	neither	place.	We	like	neither	of	the / those / his	places.
	We	don't like	either		We	don't like	either			

A Read the sentences. Which two cities are the sentences about? Write the names.

1. Both cities have more than 8,000,000 people.

2. Neither city is in South America.

3. Both cities are the capital of their country.

4. Most people don't speak Spanish in either city.

5. It snows in the winter in both cities.

6. There are no beaches because neither city is near the sea.

CITY	POPULATION
Seoul, South Korea	10,231,217
São Paulo, Brazil	10,009,231
Mumbai, India	9,925,891
Jakarta, Indonesia	9,373,900
Karachi, Pakistan	9,339,023
Moscow, Russia	8,297,056
Istanbul, Turkey	8,260,438
Mexico City, Mexico	8,235,744
Shanghai, China	8,214,384
Tokyo, Japan	8,130,408
New York City, United States	8,000,278
Bangkok, Thailand	7,506,700

The cities are _____Seoul_____ and _____Moscow_____.

PAIRS. **Take turns saying the sentences. Add *of the*.**

Look

We use *both*, *either*, and *neither*, to talk about two people, places, or things.
both = one and the other
either = one or the other
neither = not one and not the other

Expansion Ask students to name two cities in South America, two cities in Central America, two cities in Europe, two cities in Africa, two cities in the Middle East, two cities in the Far East, and two cities in North America. Have them make full sentences with *both* and *neither*, e.g., *Both Nairobi and Marrakech are in Africa. Neither of the cities is in Europe.*

Grammar Notes

1. *Both, neither,* and *either* can be subjects or objects.
2. *Not either* can be an object, but it can't be a subject.
3. Use a singular verb when *neither* or *either* is the subject of the sentence.
4. Use a plural verb when *both* is the subject of the sentence.
5. *Neither* can only be used in an affirmative sentence.
6. When *both* is the subject, the verb must be affirmative.

For information on this grammar topic, see page 283.

B Rewrite the sentences. Use *both, neither,* or *either* and *of the.* Write in your notebook.

1. São Paulo and Seoul have more than 10 million people.
   Both of the cities have more than 10 million people.

2. New York and Mexico City are not in South America.
   Neither of the cities is in South America.

3. It doesn't snow in Jakarta or Mumbai. *It doesn't snow in either of the cities.*

4. There are a lot of skyscrapers in Tokyo and Shanghai. *There are skyscrapers in both of the cities.*

5. People don't speak Chinese in Karachi or Istanbul. *People don't speak Chinese in either of the cities.*

6. Tokyo and Mumbai are not near the Atlantic Ocean. *Neither of the cities is near the Atlantic Ocean.*

PAIRS. Take turns saying the sentences without *of the.*

Example: *Both cities have more than 10 million people.*

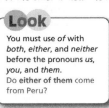

Look

You must use *of* with *both, either,* and *neither* before the pronouns *us, you,* and *them.*
Do **either of them** come from Peru?

C Complete the sentences with *both, neither,* or *either.* Add *of* where necessary.

1. **A:** Did you go to San Juan or Arecibo?
   B: We went to _____ both _____ places.

2. **A:** Who is from Mexico, Miguel or Pedro?
   B: _____ Neither of _____ them is from Mexico. They are from Peru.

3. **A:** Who comes from Bangkok, you or Aran?
   B: _____ Both of _____ us come from Bangkok. His home is a mile from mine.

4. **A:** Where do your son and daughter live?
   B: _____ Both _____ my children live in Toronto. They go to school there.

5. **A:** Who speaks Chinese, you or your wife?
   B: _____ Neither of _____ us. We don't know any Chinese.

6. **A:** Do you want to visit Mexico City or São Paulo?
   B: I can't visit _____ either _____ city. I haven't got enough money.

7. **A:** Do Jakarta and Mumbai have a lot of cold weather?
   B: No, it isn't cold in _____ either of _____ them.

TIME to TALK

GROUPS. Look at the world map on pages 302–303. Write sentences about two places.

WRAP UP. Read your sentences to the class. Can they guess the places?

Example:
Group A: *Both of the countries are in South America. Neither country is very large.*
  Class: *Are the countries Ecuador and Guyana?*
Group A: *No, they aren't. Here's more information. There are no beaches in either country.*

The World We Live In **23**

B **Teaching Time: 10–15 min.**

- Read examples 1 and 2 with students.
- Have students complete the task. Walk around and help as needed.
- Call on students to say answers. Correct as needed.
- PAIRS. Have students complete the task.
- Call on students to read sentences without *of the.* Correct as needed.

C **Teaching Time: 5–10 min.**

- Have the students study the Look Box.
- Read the example sentence with the class.
- Have students complete the task.
- Call on students to say answers. Correct as needed.

Watch Out!

Exercises A–C. Verb agreement with *both, neither,* and *either* is difficult for both native and nonnative speakers. Acknowledge this difficulty. Then reinforce it in practice exercises. Write answers on the board and explain why the singular or plural verb form is used.

Option

Assign Unit 2 Supplementary Grammar to Communicate 3 Exercises on the Teacher's Resource Disk as homework or on the Student Persistence CD-ROM as self-access practice.

TIME to TALK

Teaching Time: 10–15 min.

- Have students turn to the world map on pages 302–303. Tell them to listen to you and guess the places. Say: *Both countries are in western Europe. Neither country is on the coast.* (Switzerland and Lichtenstein [or Luxembourg])
- After students have guessed the countries, read the instructions aloud.
- GROUPS. Put students into groups of 3–5. Have students complete the task.
- WRAP UP. Have one student from each group read the group's sentences to the class. The class guesses the place.

Review and Challenge

Grammar

Teaching Time: 5–10 min.

- Read the example with the class.
- Have students complete the task.
- 🎧 Play Track 14 while students check their answers.
- Call on students to say answers. Correct as needed.

Dictation

Teaching Time: 5–10 min.

- 🎧 Play Track 15 while students listen and write what they hear.
- 🎧 Play Track 15 again while students check their answers.
- Call on students to write answers on the board.
- 🎧 Play Track 15 again and correct the sentences on the board.

Multilevel Strategy

- **Pre-level:** Give students a worksheet with some of the words from the dictation already provided.

Speaking

Teaching Time: 5–10 min.

- Read the instructions aloud. Ask students if crime is a serious problem in the place where you are.
- GROUPS. Have students complete the task. Walk around and help as needed.
- Ask one person from each group to talk about one of the problems the group discussed. Make notes on the board. Ask other groups if they agree.

Review and Challenge

Grammar

CD 1 TRACK 14 Complete the note with the words in the box. Then listen and check your answers. Some sentences have more than one correct answer. Be careful. There are extra words.

are	both	a few	isn't	much	no	too many	very few
aren't	enough	is	~~a little~~	neither	plenty of	too much	very little

I'm writing from my new home. The neighborhood is safe, and it's quiet most of the time. There's __a little__ noise in the morning, but I get up early anyway. The rent is very cheap, but there is __very little__ public transportation. Just one bus stops on my street. That's not great, but I'm lucky because there are __plenty of__ inexpensive stores and restaurants.

My apartment's fine, but there are __a few__ problems. First of all, the rooms are small, so there __isn't__ a lot of space. Second, there isn't __enough__ light. There isn't __much__ sunshine around here, and my bedroom has __no__ windows, zero! There are two windows in the living room, but __both__ of them are very small. I miss the sunshine back home!

Dictation

CD 1 TRACK 15 Listen. You will hear five sentences. Write them in your notebook. *See the audioscript on p. 308 for the sentences.*

Speaking

GROUPS. **What are some serious problems in the country where you are living? Use the words in the box and your own ideas.**

crime	natural disasters	poverty
health care	pollution	unemployment

Example:
A: *I think there is too much pollution in the big cities.*
B: *I agree. A lot of people have health problems because of the bad air.*

24 Unit 2

Option

Tell each student to bring in an article about a problem facing his or her community from a local newspaper. Put the students in pairs or small groups and have them summarize their articles.

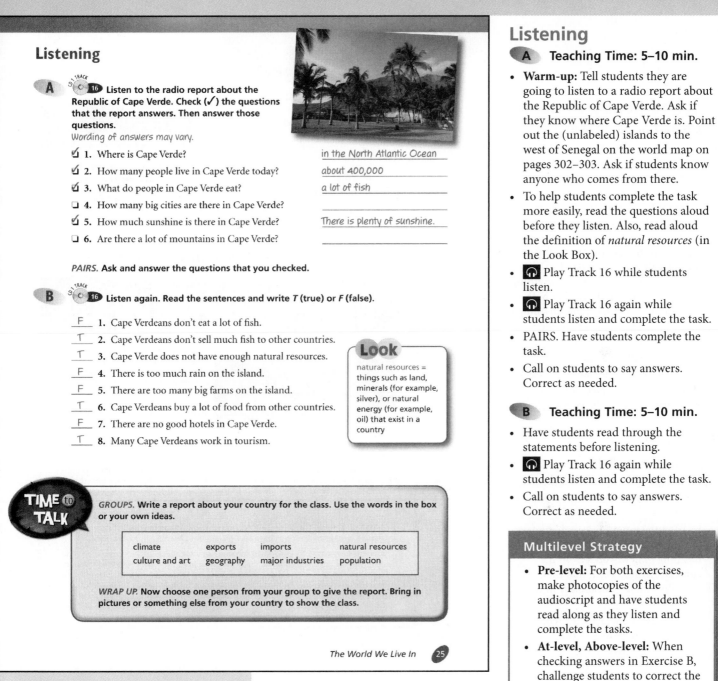

Listening

A 🎧 **16** Listen to the radio report about the Republic of Cape Verde. Check (✓) the questions that the report answers. Then answer those questions.
Wording of answers may vary.

✓ 1. Where is Cape Verde? — in the North Atlantic Ocean

✓ 2. How many people live in Cape Verde today? — about 400,000

✓ 3. What do people in Cape Verde eat? — a lot of fish

❑ 4. How many big cities are there in Cape Verde? _____

✓ 5. How much sunshine is there in Cape Verde? — There is plenty of sunshine.

❑ 6. Are there a lot of mountains in Cape Verde? _____

PAIRS. Ask and answer the questions that you checked.

B 🎧 **16** Listen again. Read the sentences and write *T* (true) or *F* (false).

F 1. Cape Verdeans don't eat a lot of fish.

T 2. Cape Verdeans don't sell much fish to other countries.

T 3. Cape Verde does not have enough natural resources.

F 4. There is too much rain on the island.

F 5. There are too many big farms on the island.

T 6. Cape Verdeans buy a lot of food from other countries.

F 7. There are no good hotels in Cape Verde.

T 8. Many Cape Verdeans work in tourism.

Look

natural resources = things such as land, minerals (for example, silver), or natural energy (for example, oil) that exist in a country

TIME to TALK

GROUPS. Write a report about your country for the class. Use the words in the box or your own ideas.

climate	exports	imports	natural resources
culture and art	geography	major industries	population

WRAP UP. Now choose one person from your group to give the report. Bring in pictures or something else from your country to show the class.

The World We Live In 25

Listening

A **Teaching Time: 5–10 min.**

- **Warm-up:** Tell students they are going to listen to a radio report about the Republic of Cape Verde. Ask if they know where Cape Verde is. Point out the (unlabeled) islands to the west of Senegal on the world map on pages 302–303. Ask if students know anyone who comes from there.

- To help students complete the task more easily, read the questions aloud before they listen. Also, read aloud the definition of *natural resources* (in the Look Box).

- 🎧 Play Track 16 while students listen.

- 🎧 Play Track 16 again while students listen and complete the task.

- PAIRS. Have students complete the task.

- Call on students to say answers. Correct as needed.

B **Teaching Time: 5–10 min.**

- Have students read through the statements before listening.

- 🎧 Play Track 16 again while students listen and complete the task.

- Call on students to say answers. Correct as needed.

Multilevel Strategy

- **Pre-level:** For both exercises, make photocopies of the audioscript and have students read along as they listen and complete the tasks.

- **At-level, Above-level:** When checking answers in Exercise B, challenge students to correct the false statements.

Option

Assign Unit 2 Review and Challenge Supplementary Exercises on the Teacher's Resource Disk as homework or on the Student Persistence CD-ROM as self-access practice.

TIME to TALK

Teaching Time: 15–20 min.

- BEFORE CLASS. Bring in some pictures of the Republic of Cape Verde. Prepare a model oral report for the class.

- Have a student read the instructions aloud.

- Model an oral report on the Republic of Cape Verde. Use the pictures that you brought in.

- GROUPS. A few days before you assign the task, tell students to bring pictures and interesting facts about their country. If there is more than one group of students from the same country, tell them to choose different topics. For example, one group could talk about the climate, geography, and natural resources of the country, while another could talk about the country's major industries, exports, and imports. Walk around and help as needed.

Getting Ready to Read

Teaching Time: 5–10 min.

- **Warm-up.** Tell students that they are going to read an article about Portland, Oregon. Have them turn to the world map on pages 302–303 and point to the northwestern part of the United States. Tell them that's where Portland is. Ask if anyone has visited Oregon; if so, have the student(s) tell the class about it. If no one has been there, ask them if they know anything about Portland, or Oregon, or both. For example, do they know anything about the weather there? Do they know anyone who lives there?
- Have a student read aloud the information in the Reading Skill box.
- Have students complete the task. Walk around and help as needed.

Reading

Teaching Time: 15–20 min.

- Assign the reading for homework or give students enough time to read it in class.
- Instruct them not to use a dictionary, but rather to try to understand the meaning of new words from the context. Remind them that they will get help with the vocabulary in the next exercise.
- Have students check their predictions. Call on a student to give the answer. Correct as needed.

Getting Ready to Read

Preview the article. Then check (✓) the topic of the article.

- ❑ housing in Portland
- ❑ retired people in Portland
- ☑ a problem in Portland

> **Reading Skill: Previewing**
>
> Before you read a text, you should **preview** it. This will help you to understand it. Look at the title and pictures, read the first paragraph, and read the first sentence of each paragraph.

Reading

Read the article. Was your answer to Getting Ready to Read correct?

WHERE ARE THE CHILDREN?

In many ways, Portland, Oregon is a **success story.** Well-educated people from all over the United States are moving there. In downtown Portland, there are a lot of new homes and businesses, and many new jobs. There are plenty of parks and open space, and there is not much crime. The public transportation system is excellent, so there is not a lot of air pollution or traffic. The weather is **mild**, with very few days of bad weather. But there is a problem in Portland: there are not enough children.

From 1990 to 2003, the population of Portland went up by about 90,000 people. However, very few of the new **residents** were children. In fact, Portland is closing many public schools because there aren't enough students to **fill** them. So who are these new residents? Many are **retired.** Others are single and are not planning to have any children.

Why aren't there more families in downtown Portland? The answer is simple: the high cost of housing. There are plenty of new houses and apartments, but they are very expensive. Young families don't have enough money to live in a city like Portland.

But is the low number of children in Portland really a problem for the retired and single residents of the city? According to Phillip Longman from the New America Foundation, it is a serious problem. ". . . Having fewer children really **diminishes** the quality of life in a city." Children ride their bikes on the streets and play in the parks. Their parents are **active** in the community. They care about **issues** such as public safety. And as children get older, they get jobs, open their own businesses, and begin their own families. All of these things are good for a city.

26   Unit 2

Culture Note

Reading. In many countries, the percentage of people who do not have children is very low compared to the United States. Students might have a hard time understanding why anyone would choose not to have children. You can explain that some of the reasons include the cost of raising a child in the United States today, the number of women choosing to have careers, the rising divorce rate, the fact that many people are choosing to get married at a later age, or just a lifestyle choice. Tell students that they shouldn't assume that everyone has children, and it is not polite to ask Americans *why* they don't have children.

After You Read

After You Read

A Look at the **boldface** words in the article. Guess their meaning. Match the words with the correct definitions.

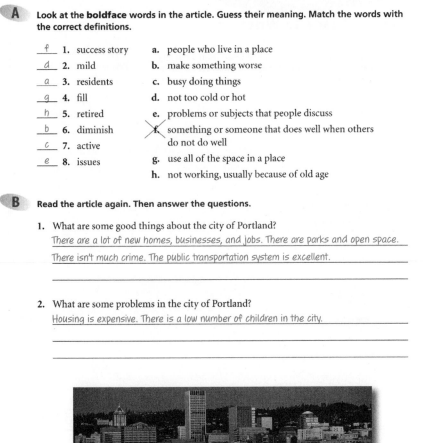

<u>f</u> 1. success story
<u>d</u> 2. mild
<u>a</u> 3. residents
<u>g</u> 4. fill
<u>h</u> 5. retired
<u>b</u> 6. diminish
<u>c</u> 7. active
<u>e</u> 8. issues

a. people who live in a place
b. make something worse
c. busy doing things
d. not too cold or hot
e. problems or subjects that people discuss
f. something or someone that does well when others do not do well
g. use all of the space in a place
h. not working, usually because of old age

B Read the article again. Then answer the questions.

1. What are some good things about the city of Portland?
   There are a lot of new homes, businesses, and jobs. There are parks and open space.
   There isn't much crime. The public transportation system is excellent.

2. What are some problems in the city of Portland?
   Housing is expensive. There is a low number of children in the city.

Downtown Portland

The World We Live In 27

Option

After students have completed the reading exercises, have them circle all of the quantifiers in the text. Then have them find five count and five noncount nouns in the reading. Write their answers on the board.

After You Read

A Teaching Time: 10–15 min.

- Read the example with students. Explain that sometimes students will need to read the sentences before and after a new word to figure out its meaning. Explain that *success story* is a good example of this; all of the context comes after the phrase. Have students find *success story* in the text and circle the other words in the context that can help them to understand the meaning of the phrase (*well-educated people; new homes and businesses; many new jobs; plenty of parks and open spaces; not much crime; excellent public transportation*—all very good things).

- Have students complete the task. Tell them to circle other words in the reading that help them understand the meanings of the new words.

- Call on students to say answers. Ask them which words they circled to find the answer. Correct as needed.

B Teaching Time: 10–15 min.

- Have students complete the task without looking back at the text. Tell them that it's okay if they make spelling or grammar mistakes or if they can't remember everything.

- Call on students to read their answers. Write their answers on the board. Correct as needed.

Expansion Start a discussion on the information in the reading. Ask students if they agree that not having enough children in a city "diminishes the quality of life in a city." Ask them if the neighborhood where they live now has a lot of children. In pairs, have them make a list of possible reasons why someone might choose not to have children. Write their reasons on the board.

Getting Ready to Write

- Write these sentences on the board: *Someone are / is calling. Something smell / smells good. Everyone love / loves him. Everything were / was fine. No one were / was there. There are / is nothing here.*
- Have students tell you which verb is correct in each sentence.
- Read the Writing Tip with students. Explain that while in some languages these pronouns are plural, in English they are always singular.
- Have students complete the task.
- Call on students to say answers. Correct as needed.

B Teaching Time: 10–15 min.

- Call on a student to read the model aloud. Explain any unfamiliar vocabulary.
- PAIRS. Have students complete the task.
- Call on students to answer the questions. Correct as needed.
- Call on a few students to list some good things and problems in other cities they know. Record their ideas on the board.

Writing

Getting Ready to Write

A Luis has just moved to a small town from a big city. Read his diary. Look at the underlined verbs. Circle the correct verb.

> **Writing Tip**
>
> These words are always singular.
>
> someone   something
> everyone   everything
> no one   nothing
>
> Example:
> Something **is** wrong.

> May 15
>
> I'm having a hard time here. Everything (is)/ are clean and beautiful, and the people is /(are) friendly, but something (is)/ are wrong. At first I wasn't sure what the problem was, but now I know. There isn't /(aren't) enough single people. Everyone (is)/ are married. Well, everyone except me. Everybody (works)/ work and (has)/ have children, so nobody (has)/ have any free time. There (is)/ are nothing to do, and nobody to do it with. There are only two restaurants in town, and both of them closes /(close) at 9:00. No one (goes)/ go out at night. It (is)/ are really strange. In my old city, there was /(were) plenty of single people, and there was /(were) fun things to do every night of the week. Where is /(are) all the single people? Am I really the only one?

B Read the model paragraph.

> Mexico City is in the south central part of Mexico. There are tall volcanoes and mountains near the city. More than 8.2 million people live in the city. With so many people, Mexico City is <u>a very exciting place</u>. Something is always happening. There are <u>famous museums, excellent nightclubs,</u> and <u>wonderful restaurants.</u> And <u>everything is open until very late.</u> Nobody goes to bed early in Mexico City! But there are also <u>too many cars, too much traffic,</u> and <u>too much air pollution.</u> Everyone in Mexico City complains about the pollution, but there are <u>no easy solutions.</u> People are trying to improve the air quality, but they haven't solved the problem yet.

PAIRS. Read the model again. According to the writer, what are the good things about Mexico City? What are the problems?

Now talk about another city. Discuss the good things and the problems.

Watch Out!

Exercise A. In many languages, collective pronouns are plural. Ask students if these pronouns are singular or plural in their languages. If they say that they are plural, tell them to pay extra attention to these words in English. Listen for and correct student errors such as *Everyone are here today.*

Prewriting: Taking Notes

You are going to write a paragraph about a city. Before you write, read the notes for the writing model. Then take notes about a city you know.

Writing Model
Mexico City

Location — south central part of Mexico

mountains and volcanoes around the city

Population — 8.2 million

Good things — large and exciting

museums, nightclubs, restaurants

everything is open late

no one goes to bed early

Problems — too many cars

too much traffic

air pollution

City:
Location
Population
Good things
Problems

Writing

Now write a paragraph about a city you know. The writing tip, the model paragraph, and your notes will help you. Write in your notebook.

Prewriting

Teaching Time: 10–15 min.

- Read the instructions aloud. Explain that it is very helpful to plan what you are going to write before you start writing. Point out that the notes for the model are not in full sentences.
- Have students complete the task. Tell them to write notes, not full sentences. Walk around and help as needed. If students are having trouble deciding which city to describe, make suggestions.
- PAIRS. Have students compare their notes.
- Have students show you their notes before moving on to the writing task. Make suggestions and corrections as needed.

Writing

Teaching Time: 20–25 min.

- Have students complete the task. Walk around and help as needed. Encourage students to refer to the model in the book as they write.
- If there is not enough time for students to complete the writing task during class time, tell them to finish it for homework.
- Before students hand in their paragraphs, tell them to review the grammar summaries on pages 282–283 and the Writing Tip on page 28. After they review the grammar, tell them to reread their paragraphs and pay attention to the nouns. Have they used the appropriate quantifiers? Do the subjects and verbs agree?

Learning Goals

- Learn vocabulary used to talk about sports
- Learn about the simple past: regular and irregular verbs and questions; and clauses with *because, before, after,* and *as soon as*
- Listen to a conversation about sports and a radio report about the origins of the first team sport
- Read an article about the life of a famous athlete and write about the origins of a sport
- Talk about sports and famous athletes

Learner Persistence

Help students identify the negative factors that can hinder persistence and teach them strategies to cope with these factors.

Warm-up

Teaching Time: 3–5 min.

- Have students cover the text and look at the illustrations. Tell them to work in pairs to think of as much vocabulary as they can to describe the three illustrations.
- Write *Nouns* and *Verbs* on the board. Have students call out the words they wrote. Ask them to tell you which column to put each word in.

Vocabulary

Teaching Time: 10–15 min.

- Have students complete the first part of the task (fill in words to complete the sentences).
- PAIRS. Have students compare answers.
- 🎧 Play Track 17 while students listen and check their answers.
- Have students complete the second part of the task (circle nouns, underline verbs).
- Call on students to read the paragraphs aloud. Ask them to tell you which words are nouns and which are verbs. Say each word and have students repeat chorally.

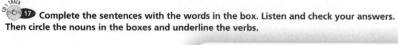

Unit 3
Sports

Grammar
- Simple Past: Regular and Irregular Verbs
- Simple Past: Questions
- Clauses with *Because, Before, After, As soon as*

Vocabulary

🔘 **17** Complete the sentences with the words in the box. Listen and check your answers. Then circle the nouns in the boxes and underline the verbs.

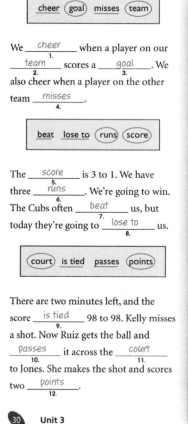

cheer (goal) misses (team)

We ___cheer___ when a player on our
1.
___team___ scores a ___goal___. We
2.   3.
also cheer when a player on the other
team ___misses___.
4.

beat lose to (runs) (score)

The ___score___ is 3 to 1. We have
5.
three ___runs___. We're going to win.
6.
The Cubs often ___beat___ us, but
7.
today they're going to ___lose to___ us.
8.

(court) is tied passes (points)

There are two minutes left, and the
score ___is tied___ 98 to 98. Kelly misses
9.
a shot. Now Ruiz gets the ball and
___passes___ it across the ___court___
10.   11.
to Jones. She makes the shot and scores
two ___points___.
12.

30   Unit 3

Soccer

YARDLEY STADIUM

Baseball

Basketball

Expansion Have students find the one word in each box that can only be used to describe that sport, and not the others (soccer: *goal*; baseball: *runs*; basketball: *court*).

Culture Note

Vocabulary. The United States is the only country in the world that does not use the word *football* to refer to *soccer*. Ask your students to describe some differences between the game of *American football* and the game that is called *football* in other countries.

Listening

A 🔘 **18** Listen. Why is Mina angry? Check (✓) the correct answer.

- ❏ 1. Tony didn't call her.
- ❏ 2. Tony went to the match last night with Barney.
- ☑ 3. Tony forgot about their date.
- ❏ 4. Tony didn't like the movie.

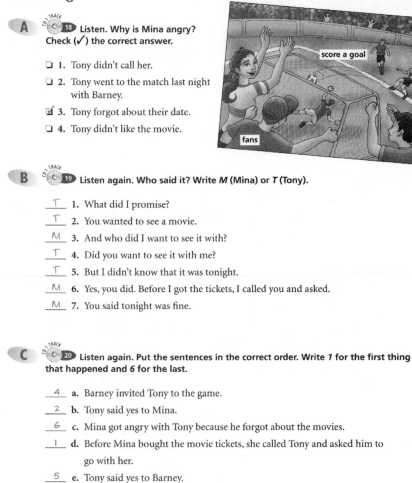

score a goal

fans

B 🔘 **19** Listen again. Who said it? Write *M* (Mina) or *T* (Tony).

- _T_ 1. What did I promise?
- _T_ 2. You wanted to see a movie.
- _M_ 3. And who did I want to see it with?
- _T_ 4. Did you want to see it with me?
- _T_ 5. But I didn't know that it was tonight.
- _M_ 6. Yes, you did. Before I got the tickets, I called you and asked.
- _M_ 7. You said tonight was fine.

C 🔘 **20** Listen again. Put the sentences in the correct order. Write *1* for the first thing that happened and *6* for the last.

- _4_ a. Barney invited Tony to the game.
- _2_ b. Tony said yes to Mina.
- _6_ c. Mina got angry with Tony because he forgot about the movies.
- _1_ d. Before Mina bought the movie tickets, she called Tony and asked him to go with her.
- _5_ e. Tony said yes to Barney.
- _3_ f. After Tony talked to Mina, Barney stopped by.

Sports **31**

Listening

A Teaching Time: 10–15 min.

- **Warm-up:** Have students read the directions and the answer choices. Ask: *What kind of a relationship do Tony and Mina probably have?* Write students' guesses on the board.
- 🎧 Play Track 18 while students listen.
- 🎧 Play Track 18 again while students listen and complete the task.
- Ask them if their predictions about Tony and Mina's relationship were correct.
- Read out each of the four answer choices. Pause after you've read each statement, and have students raise their hands if they think it is the correct answer. If more than a few students answer incorrectly, play the track again. Then call on a student to say the answer. Correct as needed.

B Teaching Time: 10–15 min.

- Tell students that if they are not sure of an answer, they can write a question mark (?) .
- 🎧 Play Track 19 as students listen and complete the task.
- Call on students to say answers. Correct as needed.

C Teaching Time: 10–15 min.

- 🎧 Play Track 20.
- PAIRS. Have students complete the task together.
- Call on a student to read the sentences in the correct order. Stop and correct as needed.
- PAIRS. Have students role-play the conversation.

Multilevel Strategy

- **Pre-level, At-level:** Make photocopies of the audioscript and have students role-play the conversation in pairs.
- **Above-level:** Have students role-play the conversation from memory. They can refer to Exercise C to help them remember the conversation.

Grammar to Communicate 1

Simple Past: Regular and Irregular Verbs

Teaching Time: 5–10 min.

- Have students study the chart.
- Copy the affirmative sentences with *missed* and *saw* from the chart onto the board.
- Ask which verb is regular in the past tense and which is irregular.
- Ask how to form the past tense of regular verbs (add *–ed* to the base form of the verb).
- Draw two columns on the board, one labeled *Regular* and the other *Irregular,* and have students tell you where to write the other verbs from the chart. Have students copy the columns and the verbs into their notebooks.
- Teach students the pronunciation rules for regular past tense verbs. Have them turn to page 300. Read each explanation aloud and have students follow along. Then read each verb in the chart and exaggerate the pronunciation of the final *–ed.* Have students repeat chorally.
- Write a few other regular verbs in the simple past on the board such as *washed, cleaned,* and *ended.* Call on students to read the words aloud. Pay attention to the pronunciation of the final *–ed* and correct as needed.
- Have students turn back to page 31 and find the past tense verbs. Have them write each verb in the appropriate column in their notebooks.
- Copy the negative sentences with *watch* and *lose* from the chart onto the board.
- Circle *didn't* in both sentences, and underline the base form of the verbs.
- Point out that the past tense form in both the affirmative and the negative is the same for all subjects (*I, you, he, she, it, we, they,* and *you* plural).

A Teaching Time: 5–10 min.

- Tell students to look at the pictures. Pantomime the actions and get students to call out the verb—first in the base form, and then in the past form. Correct their pronunciation as needed.

Grammar to Communicate 1

SIMPLE PAST : REGULAR AND IRREGULAR VERBS

Regular Verbs			Irregular Verbs		
Subject	Verb		Subject	Verb	
I	missed		I	saw	
You	didn't miss		You	didn't see	
He	watched	the game.	He	lost	the ball.
She	didn't watch		She	didn't lose	
We	played		We	got	
They	didn't play		They	didn't get	

Look
See pages 296 and 298 for spelling rules for regular and irregular verbs.

A Which sports are the sentences about? Write *S* (soccer), *BK* (basketball), or *BB* (baseball). In some sentences, more than one sport is correct.

S	**1.**	The player kicked the ball 100 feet.
S, BK	**2.**	The player shot the ball.
S, BB	**3.**	The player hit the ball.
BK, BB	**4.**	The player threw the ball.
BK, BB	**5.**	The player caught the ball.
S	**6.**	The player scored a goal.
S, BK, BB	**7.**	The player missed the ball.
S, BK	**8.**	The player passed the ball.
S, BK, BB	**9.**	The players jumped.
S, BK, BB	**10.**	My team beat your team.
S, BK, BB	**11.**	We won.
S, BK, BB	**12.**	We all cheered.

catch   hit   jump   kick   shoot   throw

B Write the verbs from Exercise A in the correct column. Then write the base form.

REGULAR VERBS		IRREGULAR VERBS	
Simple Past	Base Form	Simple Past	Base Form
kicked	kick	shot	shoot
scored	score	hit	hit
missed	miss	threw	throw
passed	pass	caught	catch
jumped	jump	beat	beat
cheered	cheer	won	win

32   Unit 3

- Call on a student to read the first two sentences aloud. Correct the pronunciation of the past tense as needed.
- Have students complete the task. Walk around and help as needed.
- Call on students to say answers. Correct pronunciation as needed.

B Teaching Time: 10–15 min.

- Copy the columns on the board.
- Call on students to come to the board and write the verbs in the appropriate columns. Correct as needed.

Grammar Notes

1. To form the simple past tense of regular verbs, add *–ed* to the verb.
2. Look at page 296 for information about spelling rules.
3. Many verbs are irregular. The simple past of these verbs does not have *–ed* at the end. See page 298 for a list of irregular verbs.
4. To form the negative of past tense verbs, use *did not* (or *didn't*) and the base form of the verb.
5. The past tense forms of *be* are *was / wasn't* and *were / weren't.* Do not use *didn't* with the past tense of *be.*
6. For more information on this grammar topic, see page 283.

C Complete the pairs of sentences. In each pair, the first sentence is affirmative and the second sentence is negative.

1. I won the first game. I __didn't win__ the second game.
2. They lost on Monday. They __didn't lose__ on Wednesday.
3. She __beat__ the older player. She didn't beat the younger player.
4. I bought two tickets for the game. I __didn't buy__ three tickets.
5. We __had__ good seats. We didn't have bad seats.
6. He relaxed at the end of the game. He __didn't relax__ at the beginning of the game.
7. We wanted to play in the morning. We __didn't want__ to play at night.
8. They __practiced__ yesterday. They didn't practice the week before the game.

D 🎧 **21** Complete the sports report. Use the past tense of the verbs. Be careful. Some are affirmative, and some are negative. Then listen and check your answers.

SPORTS NOW
Daryl Thompson: Broke his leg! Out for five games
No points for Sam Watson: What happened?
Peaks 113 ....Lions 110
Stars 121 .... Wings 78
Jags 96 ....Jets 88
Nets 112.......................Tigers 102
Greens 92 .... Sharks 86

Last night __was__ a big night for basketball fans.
         1. (be)
There __were__ five big games across the country.
       2. (be)
The most exciting game __took place__ in Detroit. It was
                        3. (take place)
close all night. In the final seconds, the Peaks and the

Lions __were tied__ 110 to 110. But then Mike Collins
        4. (be tied)
__passed__ the ball to Aaron Brown. Brown __shot__
  5. (pass)   6. (shoot)
the ball from the middle of the court and __won__
                                            7. (win)
the game for the Peaks. In New York, the Wings

__didn't play__ well at all. They __lost__ to the Stars, and it __wasn't__ pretty. The
  8. (play)   9. (lose)   10. (be)
Wings __didn't have__ their best player, Darryl Thompson, and their other top player, Sam
        11. (have)
Watson, __didn't score__ any points. He __missed__ every shot. The final score? The Stars
           12. (score)   13. (miss)
__beat__ the Wings 121 to 78. One thing's for sure: The Wings need help.
  14. (beat)

Look
take place = happen

TIME to TALK *PAIRS.* Imagine you are sports broadcasters. Discuss a game in your town or city. Then write a report. Use Exercise D as a model.

Sports **33**

C Teaching Time: 5–10 min.
- Read the example with the class.
- Have students complete the task.
- Call on students to say answers. Correct grammar and pronunciation as needed.

D Teaching Time: 5–10 min.
- Call on a student to read the example.
- Have students complete the task.
- 🎧 Play Track 21 while students check their answers. If necessary, play the recording twice.
- Call on students to read the sentences. Correct their grammar and pronunciation as needed. If they make a lot of mistakes, play the recording again, pausing after each verb is read.

Watch Out!

Students will often add an extra syllable when they pronounce the past tense, for example, they will say /mɪs-ɪd/ instead of /mɪst/. Conversely, they will neglect to add a syllable for verbs that end in /t/ or /d/ sounds, such as *want* and *need*. Listen for and correct these errors.

Option

Assign Unit 3 Supplementary Grammar to Communicate 1 Exercises on the Teacher's Resource Disk as homework or on the Student Persistence CD-ROM as self-access practice.

TIME to TALK

Teaching Time: 10–15 min.
- **Warm-up:** In pairs, have students take turns reading the report from Exercise D aloud. (If possible, pair the sports fans in the class with those who are less interested in sports.) Encourage students to read the report as they heard it on the recording—as a television sports reporter might read it.
- PAIRS. Have students complete the task.
- Call on one or two students to read their report aloud. Correct their grammar and pronunciation as needed.
- Collect students' reports. Correct them and give them back the next day. Focus your corrections on their use of the past tense.

Multilevel Strategy

Pre-level: Pair pre-level students together. Prepare a simple report similar to the one in Exercise D, but for a different sport. Instead of writing their own reports, students fill in the correct forms of the verbs, and then take turns reading the report aloud.

Unit 3 **T-33**

Grammar to Communicate 2

Simple Past: Questions

Teaching Time: 5–10 min.

- Have students study the chart.
- Say: *To form a yes / no question in the past tense, write* Did, *then the subject, then the base form of the verb.* Write the following on the board: *Did Carlo play on the team? Yes, he did.*
- Say: *When you answer yes, use the subject and* did. *When you answer no, use the subject and* did not *or* didn't.
- Say: *To make an information question in the past tense, write the question word, then* did, *then the subject, then the base form of the verb.* Under the first question and answer write: *When did the team play? They played on Saturday.*
- Under this, write the next question and answer: *Who did the team play against? They played against Milan.* Be careful to line up the *did* in both questions.
- Say: *But when the information question is about the subject, do not use* did. *Just write the question word, then the subject, then the simple past tense of the verb.* Add to the board: *Who played the best? Our team played the best.*
- Make sure students understand the difference between the third and the fourth questions. Say: *We used* did *with* who *in the third question because the question was about the object,* Milan, *and not about the subject,* The team. *In contrast, we didn't use* did *with* who *in the last question because the question was about the subject,* Our team.

A **Teaching Time: 5–10 min.**

- Call on two students to read the example. Have one student read the question, and the other the response.
- Have students complete the task.
- Ask for two volunteers, one to read David's questions, and one to read Mahtab's answers. Correct as needed.
- To make sure students have understood the conversation, ask: *Were the tickets easy to get?* (No) *How do you know?* (Because David was surprised that Mahtab got them.) *How does David feel when he hears*

that Mahtab left the game early to go to the movies? (He's surprised. He can't believe it.) *Why does he feel that way?* (Because it was probably an important game.)

B **Teaching Time: 5–10 min.**

- Have students complete the task.
- 🎧 Play Track 22 while students listen and check their answers.
- Ask for two volunteers to read the parts of David and Mahtab. Correct as needed.

Grammar to Communicate 2

SIMPLE PAST: QUESTIONS

Yes / No Questions				Short Answers	
Did	Subject	Verb			
Did	you	play	on the team?	Yes, I did.	No, I didn't.

Information Questions				Answer
Wh- word	*Did*	Subject	Verb	
Where	did	they	play	the game?	They played in Santiago.

Information Questions with *What / Who* as Subject			Answer
Wh- word	Verb		
Who	played	against Santiago?	Milan played against Santiago.

Information Questions with *How Many*			Answer
How many	Subject	Verb	
How many	people	watched	the game?	More than a million people watched it.

A David is asking Mahtab what she did last night. Match the questions and answers.

_d_ 1. What did you do last night?   **a.** I went with Paul.

_e_ 2. Wow! How did you get tickets?   **b.** I don't know. We left before the end.

_a_ 3. Who did you go with?   **c.** We didn't want to be late for the movies.

_b_ 4. So how was it? Who won?   **d.** I went to the Sparks/Tigers game.

_c_ 5. What? Why did you leave?   **e.** My boss gave them to me.

_f_ 6. Did you say the *movies*?   **f.** Yes, I did. We saw *Last Dream*. It was great!

B 🎧 **22** Complete Mahtab and David's conversation. Then listen and check your answers.

Mahtab: Why are you so upset? ___Did you want___ to go to the game?
1. (you / want)

David: Sure. The Sparks are great . . . wait a minute . . . you don't even like basketball! ___Did you tell___ your boss that?
2. (you / tell)

Mahtab: No, of course not! I told him I loved basketball.

David: ___Did he ask___ you about the game this morning?
3. (he / ask)

Mahtab: No, he didn't. Oh, no! Quick, tell me — who ___won___ ?
4. (win)

David: I don't know. ___Did you forget___ ? I didn't have any tickets.
5. (you / forget)

Grammar Notes

1. To make a *yes / no* question in the past tense, add *did* before the subject and use the base form of the verb. Use *did* or *didn't* in short answers.

2. In information questions, *did* comes after the question word (*what, where, why,* etc.).

3. When *who, what,* or *how many (much)* + *noun* is the subject of the question, do not use *did* in the question. Use the past tense form of the verb.

4. For questions with the verb *be,* do not use *did.* Use *was* or *were.*

5. For more information on this grammar topic, go to page 283.

T-34   Center Stage 3

C Write questions with *How many, Where, When,* and *Who.* Then answer the questions.

1. the first World Cup / take place
   When did the first World Cup take place?

   (a.) in 1902   **b.** in 1930   **c.** in 1950

2. the first World Cup / take place
   Where did the first World Cup take place?

   a. in China   **(b.)** in Uruguay   **c.** in the United States

3. people / watch / the World Cup on TV for the first time
   When did people watch the World Cup on TV for the first time?

   a. in 1926   **(b.)** in 1958   **c.** in 1974

4. England / win / the World Cup
   When did England win the World Cup?

   (a.) in 1966   **b.** in 1998   **c.** in 1966 and 1998

5. win / the 2002 World Cup
   Who won the 2002 World Cup?

   (a.) Brazil   **b.** Japan   **c.** the United States

6. people / see / the 2002 World Cup on TV
   How many people saw the 2002 World Cup on TV?

   a. 2 million   **b.** 10 million   **(c.)** 1.7 billion

PAIRS. **Compare your answers. Then check your answers on page 306.**

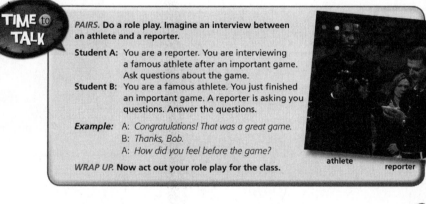

TIME to TALK

PAIRS. **Do a role play. Imagine an interview between an athlete and a reporter.**

Student A: You are a reporter. You are interviewing a famous athlete after an important game. Ask questions about the game.

Student B: You are a famous athlete. You just finished an important game. A reporter is asking you questions. Answer the questions.

Example: A: *Congratulations! That was a great game.*
B: *Thanks, Bob.*
A: *How did you feel before the game?*

WRAP UP. **Now act out your role play for the class.**

athlete   reporter

Sports   35

C Teaching Time: 10–15 min.

- Ask students who are soccer fans to raise their hands. Ask how many of them watched the last World Cup.
- Tell them that this exercise is about the first World Cup.
- Read the example. Tell students to guess if they are not sure of the answers.
- Have students complete the task.
- PAIRS. Have students take turns asking and answering the questions. Have them answer in full sentences. For example, for question 1, they would answer: *The first World Cup took place in 1902.*
- Call on students to read the questions. Correct as needed. Then ask for a show of hands for each answer choice.
- Say the correct answers, using full sentences.

Option

Exercise C. Pair soccer fans and nonsoccer fans and have them do the exercise together.

Option

Time to Talk. If you have a class with only a few sports fans, have the students work in groups of three with one sports fan in each group. The two nonsports fans can play the role of reporters.

Option

Assign Unit 3 Supplementary Grammar to Communicate 2 Exercises on the Teacher's Resource Disk as homework or on the Student Persistence CD-ROM as self-access practice.

TIME to TALK

Teaching Time: 10–15 min.

- **Warm-up:** Explain that an athlete is someone who is very good at a sport, and who usually plays the sport for money. Ask students for the names of their favorite athletes. Write the athletes' names and sports on the board.
- Pair sports fans and nonsports fans for this activity.
- Read the directions. The sports fan will choose the famous athlete and play that role. The nonsports fan will play the role of the interviewer.
- PAIRS. Have students complete the task.
- WRAP UP. Ask for volunteers to role-play their interview for the class.

Multilevel Strategy

Pre-level: Pair pre-level students. Give them a simple, generic script with several questions and responses. Have them practice reading the script. If they have a favorite athlete, encourage them to add a couple of questions specifically for that athlete.

Grammar to Communicate 3

Clauses with *Because, Before, After, As Soon As*

Teaching Time: 5–10 min.

- Have students study the chart and the Look Box.
- Write these sentences on the board, exactly as shown:

  After the first World Cup took place ,
  dependent clause
  → comma

  soccer became more popular.
  independent (main) clause

  Soccer became more popular
  independent (main) clause
  → no comma

  after the first World Cup took place.
  dependent clause

  Soccer became more popular. (a main clause: correct sentence)

  after the first World Cup took place (a dependent clause: not a sentence)

  The first World Cup took place. Soccer became more popular. (two sentences, each with one main clause: correct)

- As you point to the relevant examples on the board, say: *A clause always has a subject and a verb. An independent, or main, clause can be a sentence. A dependent clause begins with a connecting word, such as* after, before, *or* because, *and cannot be a sentence. It needs to be joined to a main clause. Sentences can have one or more clauses, but one of the clauses must be a main clause. If a sentence has a main clause and a dependent clause, either clause can come first. If the main clause comes first, there is no comma between the two clauses. If the dependent clause comes first, put a comma between the clauses.*

- Call on a student to read the sentences in the chart aloud. After the student has finished reading, ask the class what *as soon as* means. If they can't answer, say: As soon as *means immediately after.*

A Teaching Time: 5–10 min.

- Read the directions and the example with the class. Read the example as one sentence: *Because Pelé's father was a soccer player, Pelé learned to play soccer at a very young age.*

Grammar to Communicate 3

CLAUSES WITH *BECAUSE, BEFORE, AFTER, AS SOON AS*

Dependent Clause			Independent (Main) Clause		
	Subject	Verb		Subject	Verb	
Because		was	a good player,		won	a lot of games.
Before	he	joined	the Wings,	the team	was not	very good.
After		became	the number one player,		gave	him more money.
As soon as		left	the Wings,		started to lose	again.

A Make sentences about Brazilian soccer player Pelé. Match the information in the columns.

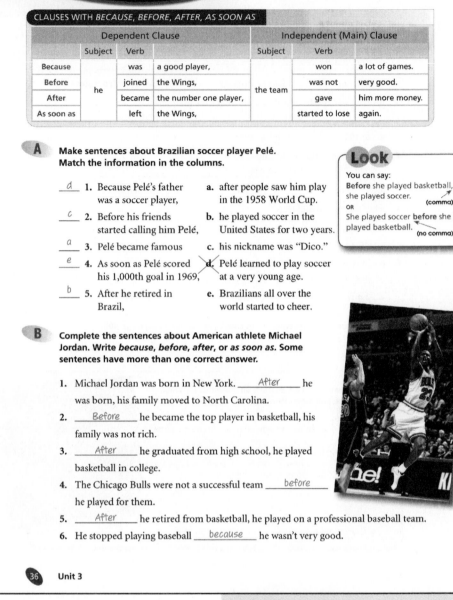

> **Look**
>
> You can say:
> **Before** she played basketball, she played soccer. (comma)
> OR
> She played soccer **before** she played basketball. (no comma)

_d_ 1. Because Pelé's father was a soccer player,

_c_ 2. Before his friends started calling him Pelé,

_a_ 3. Pelé became famous

_e_ 4. As soon as Pelé scored his 1,000th goal in 1969,

_b_ 5. After he retired in Brazil,

a. after people saw him play in the 1958 World Cup.

b. he played soccer in the United States for two years.

c. his nickname was "Dico."

d. Pelé learned to play soccer at a very young age.

e. Brazilians all over the world started to cheer.

B Complete the sentences about American athlete Michael Jordan. Write *because, before, after,* or *as soon as.* Some sentences have more than one correct answer.

1. Michael Jordan was born in New York. ___After___ he was born, his family moved to North Carolina.

2. ___Before___ he became the top player in basketball, his family was not rich.

3. ___After___ he graduated from high school, he played basketball in college.

4. The Chicago Bulls were not a successful team ___before___ he played for them.

5. ___After___ he retired from basketball, he played on a professional baseball team.

6. He stopped playing baseball ___because___ he wasn't very good.

- Have students complete the task.
- Call on students to read the complete sentences. Correct as needed.

B Teaching Time: 5–10 min.

- Ask how many students have watched Michael Jordan play basketball.
- Read the example with the class.
- Have students complete the task.
- Call on students to say answers. Correct as needed.

Grammar Notes

1. A clause is a group of words that has a subject and a verb. Some sentences have just one clause. That clause is the main, or independent, clause.

2. Some sentences have more than one clause. One clause is the main clause, and the other clause(s) is (are) the subordinate, or dependent, clause.

3. The subordinate clause begins with a connecting word like *because, before, after,* or *as soon as.* A subordinate clause is not a complete sentence. It needs a main clause.

4. For more information on this grammar topic, go to page 284.

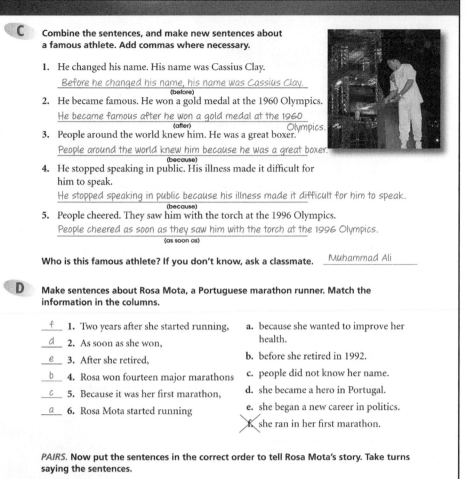

C Combine the sentences, and make new sentences about a famous athlete. Add commas where necessary.

1. He changed his name. His name was Cassius Clay.

   <u>Before he changed his name, his name was Cassius Clay.</u>
   (before)

2. He became famous. He won a gold medal at the 1960 Olympics.

   <u>He became famous after he won a gold medal at the 1960</u>
   (after)   Olympics.

3. People around the world knew him. He was a great boxer.

   <u>People around the world knew him because he was a great boxer.</u>
   (because)

4. He stopped speaking in public. His illness made it difficult for him to speak.

   <u>He stopped speaking in public because his illness made it difficult for him to speak.</u>
   (because)

5. People cheered. They saw him with the torch at the 1996 Olympics.

   <u>People cheered as soon as they saw him with the torch at the 1996 Olympics.</u>
   (as soon as)

Who is this famous athlete? If you don't know, ask a classmate. <u>Muhammad Ali</u>

D Make sentences about Rosa Mota, a Portuguese marathon runner. Match the information in the columns.

<u>f</u> **1.** Two years after she started running,

<u>d</u> **2.** As soon as she won,

<u>e</u> **3.** After she retired,

<u>b</u> **4.** Rosa won fourteen major marathons

<u>c</u> **5.** Because it was her first marathon,

<u>a</u> **6.** Rosa Mota started running

a. because she wanted to improve her health.

b. before she retired in 1992.

c. people did not know her name.

d. she became a hero in Portugal.

e. she began a new career in politics.

~~f.~~ she ran in her first marathon.

PAIRS. **Now put the sentences in the correct order to tell Rosa Mota's story. Take turns saying the sentences.**

Example: Rosa Mota started running . . .

GROUPS. **Write about a famous athlete. Do not write the athlete's name.**

Example: This tennis player became famous about ten years ago. After she started playing professionally, her sister began to play, too.

WRAP UP. **Read your sentences to the class. Ask the class to guess the name of the athlete.**

C Teaching Time: 5–10 min.

- Write the example on the board. Then switch the order of the clauses to remind students that when the main clause begins the sentence, there is no comma. Write: *His name was Cassius Clay before he changed it.* Point out that the order of the clauses also leads to the use of the pronoun *it* to replace *his name* in the subordinate clause.
- Have students complete the task.
- Call on students to say answers. Remind them to say *comma* if a comma is needed. Correct as needed.
- Have students identify the athlete (Mohammed Ali).

D Teaching Time: 5–10 min.

- Read the example with students.
- Have students complete the task.
- Call on students to read the complete sentences. Correct as needed.
- PAIRS. Have students complete the second part of the task. Tell them to write the reordered story in their notebooks.
- Call on a student to read the story. Correct as needed.

Multilevel Strategy

Pre-level, Above-level: If any of the pre-level students in the class are sports fans, pair them up with above-level students who are not sports fans. The pre-level sports fans can supply the content, and the above-level students can help them with the grammar.

Teaching Tip

Time to Talk. Bring in a variety of photographs of famous athletes from magazines or newspapers. If a group cannot think of an athlete to describe, give them one of the pictures.

Option

Assign Unit 3 Supplementary Grammar to Communicate 3 Exercises on the Teacher's Resource Disk as homework or on the Student Persistence CD-ROM as self-access practice.

TIME to TALK

Teaching Time: 10–15 min.

- Before class, find a magazine or newspaper photograph of Venus and Serena Williams, and bring it to class with you. Read the example aloud. Ask students who the athlete is (Venus Williams). If nobody knows the answer, give another hint: *Her younger sister won a major competition before she did.* If they still can't guess, hold up the picture of the sisters.
- Put the class into groups of 4–5 students. Make sure that each group has at least one sports fan.
- GROUPS. Have students complete the task. One of the nonsports fans in the group can be the secretary.
- WRAP UP: Have the secretary of each group read the group's sentences aloud. The class guesses who the sports figure is. Correct errors as needed.

Grammar

Teaching Time: 5–10 min.

- Read the example with the class.
- Have students complete the task.
- 🎧 Play Track 23 while students check their answers.
- Call on two students to read the conversation. Correct as needed.

Dictation

Teaching Time: 5–10 min.

- 🎧 Play Track 24 while students listen and write what they hear.
- 🎧 Play Track 24 again while students check their answers.
- Call on students to write answers on the board.
- 🎧 Play Track 24 again and have a student volunteer correct the sentences on the board. Provide help as needed.

Multilevel Strategy

- **Pre-level:** Give students a worksheet with some of the words from the dictation already provided.

Speaking

Teaching Time: 10–15 min.

- Read the directions aloud. Write *heroes, see a game in person,* and *autograph* on the board. Ask students to explain what the words mean.
- Call on two students to read the example.
- GROUPS. Have students complete the task. If necessary, help each group identify the person who is the biggest sports fan. If there is more than one sports fan in a group, the group can ask questions of more than one student. Walk around and help as needed.
- Ask for a sports fan to volunteer to come up in front of the class and answer his or her classmates' questions.

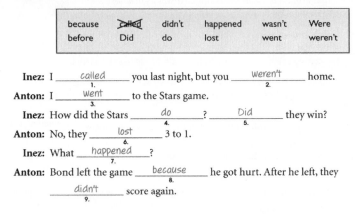

Review and Challenge

Grammar

🎧 **23** Complete the conversation with the words in the box. Then listen and check your answers. Be careful. There are extra words.

because	~~called~~	didn't	happened	wasn't	Were
before	Did	do	lost	went	weren't

Inez: I ___called___ you last night, but you ___weren't___ home.
1.   2.

Anton: I ___went___ to the Stars game.
3.

Inez: How did the Stars ___do___? ___Did___ they win?
4.   5.

Anton: No, they ___lost___ 3 to 1.
6.

Inez: What ___happened___?
7.

Anton: Bond left the game ___because___ he got hurt. After he left, they
8.

___didn't___ score again.
9.

Dictation

🎧 **24** **Listen. You will hear five sentences. Write them in your notebook.** *See the audioscript on p. 309 for the sentences.*

Speaking

GROUPS. Who in the group is the biggest sports fan? Ask him or her questions about sports. Use the questions below and your own ideas.

1. When did you first become interested in sports?
2. Why did you get interested in sports?
3. Who were your sports heroes when you were young and why?
4. Did you ever do any of these things when you were young?

- see a game in person
- get an autograph from a player
- talk to a player
- write to a player

Example:
A: *Did you ever get an autograph from a player?*
B: *Yes! I got an autograph from my favorite tennis player when I was 15 years old. It was so exciting!*

get an autograph

38 Unit 3

- Do not interrupt the interview, but write down any errors in question formation. After the class has finished interviewing the student, write the errors on board and have students correct them.

Language Note

Dictation. Students often do not use the past tense of regular verbs when they speak and write because they do not hear the endings. Explain that if the word after a regular past tense verb begins with a vowel sound, native speakers will often link the *–ed* ending /t/, /d/, or /ɪd/ to the beginning of the next word.

Teaching Tip

Dictation. It is often easier for students to hear the past tense endings of regular verbs in songs than in spoken English. Find a song with a lot of verbs in the past tense in it, and prepare a worksheet with the verbs blanked out. Play the song to the class and have them write in the verbs.

Listening

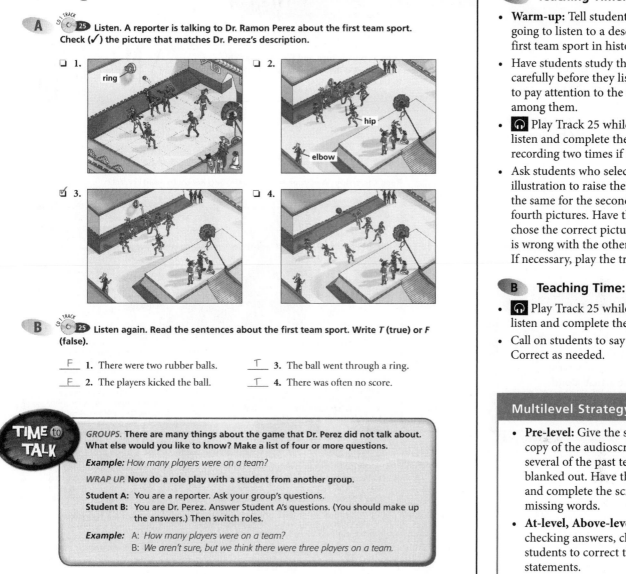

A 🎧 **25** Listen. A reporter is talking to Dr. Ramon Perez about the first team sport. Check (✓) the picture that matches Dr. Perez's description.

❏ 1. ring

❏ 2. hip elbow

☑ 3.

❏ 4.

B 🎧 **25** Listen again. Read the sentences about the first team sport. Write *T* (true) or *F* (false).

___F___ **1.** There were two rubber balls.

___F___ **2.** The players kicked the ball.

___T___ **3.** The ball went through a ring.

___T___ **4.** There was often no score.

TIME to TALK

GROUPS. There are many things about the game that Dr. Perez did not talk about. What else would you like to know? Make a list of four or more questions.

Example: How many players were on a team?

WRAP UP. Now do a role play with a student from another group.

Student A: You are a reporter. Ask your group's questions.
Student B: You are Dr. Perez. Answer Student A's questions. (You should make up the answers.) Then switch roles.

Example: A: How many players were on a team?
B: We aren't sure, but we think there were three players on a team.

Sports **39**

A **Teaching Time: 5–10 min.**

- **Warm-up:** Tell students that they are going to listen to a description of the first team sport in history.
- Have students study the pictures carefully before they listen. Tell them to pay attention to the differences among them.
- 🎧 Play Track 25 while students listen and complete the task. Play the recording two times if necessary.
- Ask students who selected the first illustration to raise their hands. Do the same for the second, third, and fourth pictures. Have those who chose the correct picture explain what is wrong with the other three pictures. If necessary, play the track again.

B **Teaching Time: 5–10 min.**

- 🎧 Play Track 25 while students listen and complete the task.
- Call on students to say answers. Correct as needed.

Multilevel Strategy

- **Pre-level:** Give the students a copy of the audioscript with several of the past tense verbs blanked out. Have them listen and complete the script with the missing words.
- **At-level, Above-level:** When checking answers, challenge students to correct the false statements.

Option

Time to Talk. After students complete the first part of the task, have a student from each group write one of their questions on the board. Correct as needed. Tell students they can use questions from other groups in their role-plays.

Option

Assign Unit 3 Review and Challenge Supplementary Exercises on the Teacher's Resource Disk as homework or on the Student Persistence CD-ROM as self-access practice.

TIME to TALK **Teaching Time: 10–15 min.**

- Read the example with the class.
- GROUPS. Have students complete the task. Make sure everyone in the group writes down the group's questions in his or her notebook. Walk around and help as needed.
- WRAP UP: Call on two students to read the example. Make sure they understand that they should make up the answers.
- Match up each student with a student from another group. Have students complete the task. Walk around and help as needed.

Getting Ready to Read

Teaching Time: 3–5 min.

- Have students study the picture and the photograph.
- Ask students if they recognize either of the two players in the photograph.
- Have students complete the task.

Reading

Teaching Time: 15–20 min.

- Have students read the article.
- Have students check their predictions.

Multilevel Strategy

- **Pre-level:** Assign the reading for homework. In class, put all pre-level students in a group and have them take turns reading the article aloud.
- **At-level, Above-level:** Have students read the text in class.

Reading

Getting Ready to Read

Look at the pictures and the photograph. What do you think the article is going to be about?

Answers will vary.

crooked straight

back brace

Reading

Read the article. Was your answer to Getting Ready to Read correct?

JAMES BLAKE'S STORY

Andre Agassi and James Blake at the 2005 U.S. Open

At the 2005 U.S. Open, James Blake and Andre Agassi played one of the best tennis matches in history. Blake's **performance** in the match was **impressive**, but his life story is even more impressive.

James Blake began to play tennis when he was very young. But when he was 13, he got a serious illness called scoliosis. Scoliosis makes a person's back crooked. Blake had to wear a back brace eighteen hours a day for the next four years. But that didn't stop him. In a few short years, Blake was the best college tennis player in the United States. Then he left college to become a professional player. Because Blake was handsome and polite, **the media** loved him. *People* magazine named him "the world's sexiest athlete."

Everything was perfect until May 6, 2004, when Blake had a terrible accident. He fell down during a tennis match and broke his neck. He wasn't **paralyzed**; however, he couldn't play tennis. But that was not the end of Blake's **troubles**. Two months after he had his accident, his father, Thomas, died. Then, a few days after his father's **death**, Blake woke up in terrible pain. He couldn't move his face. At the hospital, the doctors gave him some bad news. He had an illness called shingles. The doctors said that he got sick because he was **upset** about his father's death.

But Blake remembered his father's words: "If there's a problem, you're going to fix it." So as soon as he **recovered**, Blake started to play tennis again. A year after his father died, he played in the U.S. Open against one of the world's best players.

After You Read

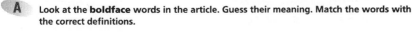

A Look at the **boldface** words in the article. Guess their meaning. Match the words with the correct definitions.

_f_ 1. performance   **a.** very special and excellent

_a_ 2. impressive   **b.** not able to move

_h_ 3. the media   **c.** got better after an illness

_b_ 4. paralyzed   **d.** very unhappy

_g_ 5. troubles   **e.** the end of a person's life

_e_ 6. death   **f.** the way he played

_d_ 7. upset   **g.** problems

_c_ 8. recovered   **h.** newspapers, television, and magazines

B Put the statements in order from 1 to 9. Write the numbers in the blanks.

> **Reading Skill:**
> **Understanding Time Order**
>
> When you read a story, it is important to understand when things happened. What happened first? Second? Third? Time phrases, such as *in a few years*, and dates tell you the order of events.

_6_ **a.** Blake broke his neck.

_3_ **b.** Blake was the best college player in the United States.

_4_ **c.** Blake left college.

_9_ **d.** Blake played against Agassi at the U.S. Open.

_7_ **e.** Blake's father died.

_8_ **f.** Blake got shingles.

_5_ **g.** *People* magazine named Blake the world's sexiest athlete.

_2_ **h.** Blake got scoliosis.

_1_ **i.** Blake learned how to play tennis.

James Blake during a match

Sports 41

Option

After students complete the reading exercises, have them underline the irregular past tense verbs in the article and circle the regular past tense verbs.

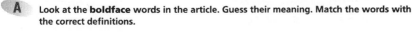

After You Read

A   Teaching Time: 10–15 min.

- Have students find the word *matches* in the reading. Tell them to circle other words in the context that help them to understand the meaning of the new word (*played, tennis*).
- Have students complete the task. Tell them to circle other words in the reading that help them understand the meanings of the new words.
- Call on students to say answers. Ask them which words they circled to find the answer. Correct as needed.

B   Teaching Time: 10–15 min.

- Call on a student to read the information in the Reading Skill box aloud.
- PAIRS. Have students complete the task without looking back at the text. When they have finished, they can go back to the text to check their answers.
- Call on a student to read the statements in order. If the student makes a mistake, stop him or her and call on another student to continue.

> **Multilevel Strategy**
>
> **Pre-level:** Allow students to look back at the article as they complete Exercise B. Have them write the letter of each sentence next to the place in the text where they find it.

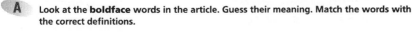

Unit 3   T-41

Writing

Getting Ready to Write

A   Teaching Time: 5–10 min.

- Call on a student to read the Writing Tip.
- Have students complete the task.
- Call on students to read the sentences where they added a comma. Correct as needed.

B   Teaching Time: 15–20 min.

- Ask for a volunteer to read the model aloud.
- PAIRS. Have students complete the task.
- Ask for a volunteer to talk about the history of his or her favorite sport.

Expansion Have students circle the commas in the model. Explain that in addition to putting a comma after a dependent clause, we also usually put a comma after time expressions such as *At first* or *By the . . .*, as well as other words that come before the subject of a sentence.

Writing

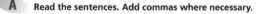

Getting Ready to Write

> **Writing Tip**
>
> Remember that when a time clause comes first, we use a comma.
>
> Examples:
> **As soon as he recovered,** he started to play tennis.
> Blake began to play tennis **when he was young.**

A   Read the sentences. Add commas where necessary.

Almost 1,000 years ago, Christian monks began to play a ball game called La Soule. Players hit the ball to each other with their hands or a stick. When ordinary people began to play the game, they played outside with gloves and a racket. Then in the 17th century, "real tennis" became the favorite game of the French royal family. However, after the French royal family was killed in the French Revolution, tennis became unpopular. It became popular again when rich English people started to play it on grass in the 19th century. The Wimbledon tennis championship started in 1877. It is still the world's most famous tennis championship.

B   Read the model paragraph.

> People first played golf in Scotland in the 1400s. At first, they played on the beach with sticks and rocks. Then golf moved from the beach to golf courses. When players began to use expensive clubs and balls instead of sticks and rocks, golf became a game for rich people. But after factories started to make cheap golf clubs, ordinary people began to play again. By the early 1900s, both men and women were professional golf players. Now professional golf players such as Tiger Woods are world famous. Some players make millions of dollars every year.

rocks

sticks

club

golf course

ball

PAIRS. Read the model again. Where and when did people first play golf?

What do you know about the history of your favorite sport? Do you know where it began? In what country? Discuss.

Prewriting: Using Facts

You are going to write a paragraph about the history of a sport. Before you write, read the list of facts for the writing model. Then read the list of facts for soccer and ice skating. Choose one of the sports to write about.

Writing Model: Golf

- First played in Scotland in the 1400s
- Played on beach with sticks and rocks
- Later, moved from beach to golf courses. Expensive clubs and balls, a game for rich people
- Factories made cheap golf clubs, ordinary people began to play
- Early 1900s, men and women professional golf players
- Players such as Tiger Woods make millions of dollars every year

Soccer

- First played by Chinese, more than 2,000 years ago
- Japanese, Greeks, and Romans also played
- British—modern soccer about 700 years ago
- 1880s, English Football League— teams of professional players
- Today, world's most popular sport for men and women all over the world

Ice Skating

- 5,000 years ago—ice skates for transportation on ice in winter
- 500 years ago—ice skates in Europe for fun
- 1908 Olympic Winter Games, first competitions in figure skating (dancing on ice) and speed skating (skating fast)
- Today, skating popular in cold countries
- Popular in all countries— professional figure skating on TV

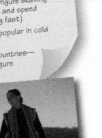

Writing

Now write a paragraph about the history of soccer or ice skating. The writing tip, the model paragraph, and the information above will help you. Write in your notebook.

Sports 43

- Point out that the notes for the writing model on page 42 are not in full sentences. Write the sentence from the model next to the notes for that sentence on the board:

  Notes: First played in Scotland in the 1400s.

  Sentence: People first played golf in Scotland in the 1400s.

  Ask students what is missing from the note (subject and object).

- Have students compare the rest of the notes to the writing model, and find what is missing (subject; verbs; connecting words; prepositions; *a/an, the*; periods). Write their answers on the board.

- Have students read the notes for soccer and ice skating, and choose one to write about.

Writing

Teaching Time: 15–20 min.

- Have students complete the task. Walk around and help as needed. Encourage students to refer to the model in the book as they write. Remind them that the notes are not in full sentences, and that they will have to add words and punctuation. Tell them to use time connecting words where appropriate.

- Before students hand in their paragraphs, tell them to review the grammar summaries on pages 283–284 and the Writing Tip on page 42. Tell them to reread their paragraphs, looking for errors with the past tense, clauses, and commas.

Multilevel Strategy

Pre-level: Prepare a worksheet that has the soccer or ice skating notes written in full sentences with the appropriate connecting words and commas. Put the sentences out of order. Have students match the notes to the sentences. Then have them write a paragraph by copying the sentences in the correct order.

Unit 4
Accidents

Learning Goals

- Learn vocabulary used to talk about common household accidents and automobile accidents
- Learn about the past progressive: statements and questions; and past time clauses with *when* and *while*
- Listen to a description of a fire and a conversation with an insurance agent about an automobile accident
- Read an article about a survivor of seven lightning strikes and write a narrative
- Describe an automobile accident
- Tell a story of an accident or other event

Learner Persistence

Help students identify positive factors in their learning experience that can help them to persist.

Warm-up

Teaching Time: 3–5 min.

- Have students cover the text for illustrations A and B and look at those illustrations. Ask: *What's happening?* Have students call out any words they can to describe the situations. Write their answers on the board.
- Then have students uncover and look at the vocabulary words for illustrations A and B. How many of the words did they guess?
- Repeat these steps for illustrations C and D and illustrations E and F.

Vocabulary

Teaching Time: 10–15 min.

- Have students complete the task.
- 🎧 Play Track 26 while students listen and check their answers.
- Say each word and have students repeat chorally.

Expansion Ask students if any of the accidents in the illustrations have happened to them. Ask for volunteers to describe what happened.

Grammar
- Past Progressive: Statements
- Past Progressive: Questions
- Past Progressive and Simple Past: *When* and *While*

Vocabulary

26 **Look at the pairs of pictures. Which action happened first, and which happened second? Write *1* and *2* under each pair of pictures. Then listen and check your answers.**

(A) __2__ fall off a ladder __1__ climb a ladder

(B) __1__ go down the stairs __2__ fall down the stairs

(C) __2__ break __1__ drop

(D) __2__ burn __1__ iron

(E) __1__ daydream __2__ slip

(F) __1__ chop __2__ cut

44 Unit 4

Listening

A 🔊 **27** Listen. What did Manny do this weekend? Check (✓) the correct answers.

- ❑ 1. He painted the house.
- ☑ 2. He dropped his paintbrush on his father-in-law.
- ❑ 3. He fell off a ladder.
- ❑ 4. He started a fire.

B 🔊 **27** Listen again. Put the pictures in the correct order. Write *1* for the first thing that happened and *6* for the last.

__2__ Suddenly, I heard a loud bang, and I dropped my paintbrush.

__1__ I was climbing up a ladder, and my father-in-law was standing below me.

__4__ Then my wife and mother-in-law ran out of the house. They were screaming.

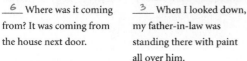

__6__ Where was it coming from? It was coming from the house next door.

__3__ When I looked down, my father-in-law was standing there with paint all over him.

__5__ While I was climbing down the ladder, I heard another bang. Then I smelled smoke.

C 🔊 **27** Listen again. Check (✓) the sentences that are true.

- ❑ 1. Manny dropped the paintbrush because he smelled smoke.
- ❑ 2. Manny's wife and mother-in-law ran out of the house because it was on fire.
- ❑ 3. The neighbors were at home when the fire started.
- ☑ 4. The fire was very serious.

Accidents **45**

Listening

A Teaching Time: 10–15 min.

- **Warm-up:** Have students read the directions and the sentences. Explain any unfamiliar vocabulary. Say, for example: *When you paint something, you cover it with a liquid to make it a certain color.* Pantomime painting a wall.
- 🎧 Play Track 27 while students listen.
- 🎧 Play Track 27 again while students listen and complete the task.
- Call on a student to say the answer. Correct as needed.

B Teaching Time: 10–15 min.

- Write the following vocabulary on the board: *bang, smoke, paint, scream, paintbrush.* Read each word aloud and have students point to each one in the pictures.
- Have students complete the task.
- 🎧 Play Track 27 while students listen and check their answers.
- Call on students to read the sentences in the correct order to retell the story. Stop and correct as needed. If necessary, play Track 27 again.

C Teaching Time: 10–15 min.

- 🎧 Play Track 27 while students listen and complete the task.
- PAIRS. Have students compare answers.
- Call on students to read the sentences that they checked. Correct as needed.

Multilevel Strategy

Pre-level: Make photocopies of the audioscript. Give it to students before they do Exercise C.

Expansion After students complete Exercise C, have them cover the sentences under the pictures and retell the story. Write their sentences on the board and correct as needed.

Option

Assign Unit 4 Supplementary Vocabulary Exercises on the Teacher's Resource Disk as homework or on the Student Persistence CD-ROM as self-access practice.

Grammar to Communicate 1

Past Progressive: Statements

Teaching Time: 5–10 min.

- Have students study the chart and the Look Box.
- Say: *We use the past progressive instead of the simple past when we want to show that an action was (or wasn't) happening at a particular time in the past. To describe these situations, we could NOT say: He ate at the time of the fire. or They watched TV at the time of the fire.* Write the incorrect sentences on the board, crossing them out to make the point that they are incorrect.
- Have students study the picture. Call their attention to the fire in the basement. Say: *There was a fire last night in an apartment building. What was the man in apartment 1A doing at the time of the fire? What were the people in apartment 2B doing?*
- Call on students to answer your questions. *(He was having dinner / eating. They were watching TV.)* Write their responses on the board, adding the time expression *at the time of the fire* to the end of the first sentence. Correct as needed. Underline the forms of *be* and the *–ing* on the ends of the *main* verbs. Label the sentences as follows:

	be – past	verb + ing	
He	was	eating	at the time of the fire.
They	were	watching	TV.

- Ask: *Why do we use* was *in the first sentence and* were *in the second?* (Because the subjects are different. Use *was* for I, he, she, it and *were* for you, we, they.)
- Ask: *Was the man in apartment 1A watching TV?* (No.) Write on the board: *The man in apartment 1A was not watching TV.*
- Say: *To make a sentence in the past progressive negative, add* not *after* was *or* were. *You can also use the contractions* wasn't *and* weren't.

Grammar to Communicate ①

PAST PROGRESSIVE: STATEMENTS

Subject	Be	Verb + -ing		Subject	Be + not	Verb + -ing	
I He She It	was			I He She It	was not wasn't		
		working	at 5:30.			working	at 5:30.
You We They	were			You We They	were not weren't		

A Look at the picture. There was a fire at 8:00 last night. What were the people doing? Write the correct apartment numbers.

Look

Use the past progressive to talk about activities in progress at a specific time in the past.

1. Mr. Gutierrez in apartment __1A__ wasn't watching TV. He was having dinner.
2. Mr. and Mrs. Liu in apartment __3B__ weren't sleeping. They were having dinner.
3. Cindy, Amos, and Al in apartment __2D__ weren't playing cards. They were watching TV.
4. Annie in apartment __3D__ wasn't playing computer games. She was sleeping.
5. Deb in apartment __1C__ wasn't doing the dishes. She was talking on the phone.
6. Johan in apartment __1B__ wasn't listening to music. He was watching TV.

46 Unit 4

A **Teaching Time: 5–10 min.**

- Have students complete the task. Tell them to underline the past progressive verb in each sentence.
- Call on students to read the sentences. As they answer, have them identify the past progressive verbs and their subjects. Correct as needed.

Grammar Notes

1. Use the past progressive to talk about activities in progress at a specific time in the past.

2. Do not use the simple past for activities in progress at a specific time, except if the verb is a nonaction (stative) verb. For a list of these verbs, go to page 298.

3. The time expressions *At the time of [an event such as a fire]* or *At [a specific time and date, such as 8:00 last night]* commonly appear with the past progressive.

4. For the spelling rules for the progressive form, go to page 295.

5. For more information on this grammar topic, go to page 284.

T-46 Center Stage 3

B Complete the sentences about the people in the apartments. Use the past progressive. Be careful. Some sentences are affirmative, and some are negative.

1. (Apt. 1A) Mr. Gutierrez (have) _____was having_____ dinner.
   He (watch) _____wasn't watching_____ TV.

2. (Apt. 2C) Charlie (sleep) _____wasn't sleeping_____.
   He (listen) _____was listening_____ to music.

3. (Apt. 2B) Lucy and her sisters (play) _____were playing_____ cards.
   They (read) _____weren't reading_____.

4. (Apt. 1D) Martha (read) _____was reading_____ the newspaper.
   She (do) _____wasn't doing_____ the dishes.

5. (Apt. 3A) Eric and Les (exercise) _____weren't exercising_____.
   They (play) _____were playing_____ computer games.

6. (Apt. 2A) Mr. Roberts (wash) _____was washing_____ the dishes.
   He (dry) _____wasn't drying_____ them.

C Other people in the apartment building were not at home last night at 8 P.M. Write what they probably said. Use the words in the box and quotation marks.

~~celebrate my wife's birthday~~	talk	walk my dog
go home	wait for the bus	work late

1. "I was at a restaurant with my family."   "We were celebrating my wife's birthday."
2. "I was with my girlfriend at a bus stop."   "We were waiting for the bus."
3. "I was in my car."   "I was going home."
4. "I was in the park."   "I was walking my dog."
5. "I was at my office."   "I was working late."
6. "I was on the phone with a friend."   "We were talking."

PAIRS. What about you? Where were you last night at 8 P.M.? What were you doing?

TIME to TALK

PAIRS. **Student A:** Study the picture in Exercise A. Then close your book and try to remember four things that people were doing at the time of the fire.
Student B: Keep your book open and give Student A the correct answers. Then switch roles.

Example: A: *A few people were sleeping.*
B: *No, you're wrong. Only one person was sleeping.*

Accidents **47**

B Teaching Time: 5–10 min.

- Read the example with the class.
- Have students complete the task.
- Call on students to say answers. Correct as needed.

C Teaching Time: 10–15 min.

- Call on a student to read the example and write it on the board.
- Point to the quotation marks and explain that we use them when we write the exact words that someone said.
- Draw students' attention to the dropped *e* in the spelling of *celebrating*. Tell them that the spelling rules for forming the past progressive are the same as those for the present progressive. Remind them that the spelling rules are on page 295 in their books.
- Have students complete the task.
- Call on students to say answers. Correct as needed.
- PAIRS. Have students tell the person sitting next to them what they were doing last night at 8:00.

Expansion

- Take an informal poll of what students were doing last night at 8:00. Write the results on the board like this:
  watching TV   sleeping   etc.
  3   1
- Call on students to make sentences for each activity, for example, *Three students were watching TV.*

Watch Out!

Exercises A–C. As with the present progressive, students have a tendency to drop the verb *be* when they are forming the past progressive. Conversely, some students will use the verb *be* correctly, but will drop the –*ing* on the main verb. Listen for and correct these errors.

Option

Assign Unit 4 Supplementary Grammar to Communicate 1 Exercises on the Teacher's Resource Disk as homework or on the Student Persistence CD-ROM as self-access practice.

TIME to TALK

Teaching Time: 10–15 min.

- Tell students that you are going to test their memories. Ask for a volunteer who thinks he or she has a good memory. Ask: *What were the students in this class doing at 8:00 last night?* See how many activities the student can remember. Correct as needed.
- Call on two students to read the example.
- PAIRS. Have students complete the task. Tell them to speak in full sentences. Have them record the number of activities their partner was able to remember correctly.
- Ask: *Whose partner has a good memory?* Find out who in the class remembered the most activities.

Grammar to Communicate 2

Past Progressive: Questions
Teaching Time: 5–10 min.

- Have students study the chart.
- Say: *To make a yes / no question in the past progressive write* Was *or* Were, *then the subject, then the main verb + ing. Write on the board:* Was he driving at the time of the accident? Yes, he was.
- Say: *When you answer yes, use the subject and* was *or* were. *When you answer no, use the subject and* was / were not *or* wasn't / weren't.
- Say: *To make an information question in the past progressive, write the question word, then* was *or* were, *then the subject, then the main verb + ing. Under the first question write:* Where was he looking? He was looking across the street. *Be careful to line up the* was *in both questions.*
- Write the next question under the last one: *Who was he looking at? He was looking at the child on the bike.*
- Say: *To make an information question about the subject, write the question word, then the subject, then the verb + ing. Under the last question, write:* Who was driving? Ben was driving.
- Ask students a few information questions and have them answer. For example, *Huang, were you watching TV last night?*

A   Teaching Time: 5–10 min.

- Read the example with the class.
- Have students complete the task.
- PAIRS. Have students take turns asking and answering the questions.
- Call on students to read the questions and say the answers. Correct as needed.

Grammar to Communicate 2

PAST PROGRESSIVE: QUESTIONS

Yes / No Questions

Be	Subject	Verb + -ing	
Was	he	driving	at the time of the accident?
Were	they		

Short Answers

Yes, he was.	No, he wasn't.
Yes, they were.	No, they weren't.

Information Questions

Wh- word	Be	Subject	Verb + -ing
Where	were	you	looking?
	was	he	
	were	they	

Answers

I was looking across the street.
He was looking across the street.
They were looking across the street.

Information Questions with *Who / What* as Subject

Wh- word	Be	Verb + -ing
Who	was	driving?
What		happening?

Answers

Ben was driving.
A lot of things were happening.

A   Look at the picture. Answer the questions about the accident.

At the time of the accident . . .

1. was the bus driver turning?
   <u>No, he wasn't.</u>
2. was the little girl standing on the corner?
   <u>No, she wasn't.</u>
3. were any people getting off the bus?
   <u>No, they weren't.</u>
4. where were the women standing?
   <u>They were standing on the corner.</u>
5. what was the little girl doing?
   <u>She was running after a ball.</u>
6. why was the man working?
   <u>He was working because there was a hole in the street.</u>

Multilevel Strategy

- **Pre-level:** Pair pre-level students together. Give them more time to do the exercise.
- **At-level, Above-level:** After students complete Exercise A, have them cover their responses and work with a partner to ask and answer questions about the picture.

Grammar Notes

1. To make a *yes / no* question, change the word order of the subject and the verb.
2. Use *was (not)* or *were (not)* in short answers.
3. In information questions, *was* or *were* comes after the question word (*what, where,* etc.).
4. When *who* or *what* is the subject of the question, there is no subject after *was*.
5. For more information on this grammar topic, see page 284.

B Write questions and answers about the accident.

1. Was the teenager watching his sister? — No, he wasn't.
   (the teenager / watch his sister)
2. Was the driver of the yellow car looking at the bus? — No, he wasn't.
   (the driver of the yellow car / look at the bus)
3. Was the little girl running after a ball? — Yes, she was.
   (the little girl / run after a ball)
4. Was the bus driver picking up passengers? — No, he wasn't.
   (the bus / pick up passengers)
5. Were the people on the bus talking to the driver? — No, they weren't.
   (the people on the bus / talk to the driver)
6. Were both cars going straight? — Yes, they were.
   (both cars / go straight)

C Read the statements. Then write questions to get more information.

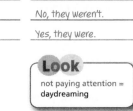
Look
not paying attention = daydreaming

1. The bus driver wasn't talking to the passengers. — Who was the bus driver talking to?
2. The women weren't standing at the bus stop. — Where were the women standing?
3. The girl's brother wasn't paying attention to her. — What was the girl's brother paying attention to?
4. The girl's brother wasn't driving the car. — Who was driving the car?
5. The girl wasn't running on the sidewalk. — Where was the girl running?
6. The bus driver wasn't looking at the women. — Who was the bus driver looking at?
7. The man was fixing the street. — Why was the man fixing the street?

PAIRS. Ask and answer the questions.

TIME to TALK

PAIRS. Talk about the last time the things in the box happened to you or someone you know. Ask and answer questions. Talk about what was happening at the time. If you can't remember, make up something.

be in a fire	break something valuable	lose something important
break a bone	get into a car accident	miss the bus

Example: A: Last month I got into a car accident.
B: Were you driving?
A: No, I wasn't.
B: Where were you sitting?
A: I was sitting in the back seat.

Accidents 49

B Teaching Time: 10–15 min.

- Read the example with the class. Make sure students understand that the questions are about the accident in the picture on page 48.
- Have students complete the task.
- Call on pairs of students to read the questions and answers. Correct as needed.

C Teaching Time: 10–15 min.

- Read the example with the class.
- Have students complete the task.
- PAIRS. Have students take turns asking and answering the questions.
- Call on pairs of students to read the questions and answers. Correct as needed.

Multilevel Strategy

- **Pre-level:** Sit in a group with the pre-level students. Guide them through the activity. First, find out who has really experienced one of the events. Then start asking that student questions about what happened. Encourage other students to ask questions as well. Create a relaxed atmosphere by focusing the activity on the story content.
- **At-level, Above-level:** While you are working with the pre-level students, have the other students complete the activity. When they finish, have them write a narrative describing one of the events in the box. Collect their descriptions and use them as the basis for an error analysis worksheet.

Watch Out!

Exercise C. Listen for errors such as *Who was the bus driver talking to the passengers?* Explain that the question does not make any sense because it contains both the question and the answer. If you already know the answer to a question, you have no need to ask it.

Option

Assign Unit 4 Supplementary Grammar to Communicate 2 Exercises on the Teacher's Resource Disk as homework or on the Student Persistence CD-ROM as self-access practice.

TIME to TALK

Teaching Time: 10–15 min.

- Have a student read the instructions aloud. Make sure everyone understands what *make up* means.
- Draw students' attention to the expressions in the box. Explain any unfamiliar vocabulary. Say, for example: *When you get into a car accident, you have an accident with your car.*
- Have two students read the example. Extend the example by asking more questions.
- PAIRS. Have students complete the task. Walk around and help as needed.
- Call on volunteers to present their stories to the class.

Past Progressive and Simple Past: *When* and *While*

Teaching Time: 5–10 min.

- Have students study the chart.
- Pantomime the following: *I was sleeping when the telephone rang.*
- Ask: *What just happened?* If students answer with the correct idea but incorrect grammar, for example, *You sleeping telephone ringing,* write their ideas on the board. Use them to build the correct sentence with *when*. If students do not get the idea of the two actions, write *sleep* and *ring* on the board, repeat the mime, and use the verbs to build a sentence with *when*.
- This sentence should now be on the board: *I was sleeping when the telephone rang.* Ask a series of questions, as follows: *Which action was in progress?* (was sleeping) *Which action interrupted, or stopped, the action in progress?* (rang) *Which verb form do we use to show that an action was in progress?* (past progressive) *Which verb form do we use to show that an action interrupted, or happened in the middle of, another action?* (simple past)
- Write *simple past* and *past progressive* under the verbs in the sentence. Circle the *when* and label it *time connector*.
- Repeat the same procedure with different actions.
- Read the sentences in the chart aloud, and have the class repeat chorally.

A Teaching Time: 5–10 min.

- Have students complete the task.
- Call on students to read the sentences and tell you which verbs they underlined or circled.

B Teaching Time: 10–15 min.

- Review the comma rule. Remind students that we only use a comma when the dependent clause comes before the main clause.
- Read the example with students. Ask them why there is no comma in this sentence.

- Have students complete the task. Tell them to pay attention to the capital letters as they form their sentences.
- Call on students to read their answers. Have them tell you where the commas go. Correct as needed.

Multilevel Strategy

Pre-level: Give students the first and last word of each sentence.

Grammar to Communicate 3

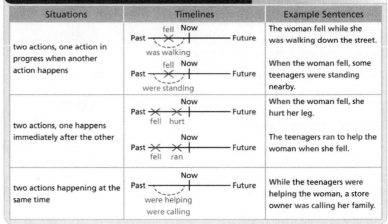

PAST PROGRESSIVE AND SIMPLE PAST: *WHEN* AND *WHILE*

Situations	Timelines	Example Sentences
two actions, one action in progress when another action happens	fell / Now / Past / Future / was walking	The woman fell while she was walking down the street.
	fell / Now / Past / Future / were standing	When the woman fell, some teenagers were standing nearby.
two actions, one happens immediately after the other	Now / Past / Future / fell hurt	When the woman fell, she hurt her leg.
	Now / Past / Future / fell ran	The teenagers ran to help the woman when she fell.
two actions happening at the same time	Now / Past / Future / were helping / were calling	While the teenagers were helping the woman, a store owner was calling her family.

A Read the sentences. Circle the action that happened first. If both actions happened at the same time, underline them.

1. I was daydreaming while I was chopping onions.
2. While I was chopping onions, I cut my finger.
3. When I cut my finger, I got a Band-Aid.
4. I was opening the box of Band-Aids when the phone rang.
5. While I was running to get the phone, I slipped and fell on the floor.

B Write sentences. Put the words in the correct order. Use commas where necessary.

1. I was playing with the dog when it bit me.
   (it / bit / with / when / I / playing / the dog / me / was)
2. While the old woman was walking, she slipped.
   (the old woman / walking / slipped / she / While / was)
3. I was standing on the chair when it broke.
   (on the chair / it / I / broke / when / standing / was)
4. When the boy touched the iron, he burned his hand.
   (the boy / When / burned / touched / he / the iron / his hand)
5. While the teenager was drying the knife, she cut her hand.
   (the teenager / cut her hand / she / drying / While / was / the knife)

50 Unit 4

Grammar Notes

1. Use the past progressive and the simple past with *when* and *while* to say that one activity was in progress when another activity interrupted it, or when another activity happened in the middle of it.

2. *While* must go with the progressive activity. *When* can go with either activity.

3. For more information on this grammar topic, go to page 284.

C How did the people have accidents? Write two sentences about each set of pictures. Use *when* or *while*. Answers will vary.

1. He was reading a recipe while he was cooking.
   (he / cook / read a recipe)

   He burned his hand while he was cooking.
   (he / cook / burn his arm)

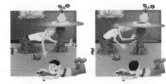

2. While he was riding his bike, he wasn't holding the handlebars.
   (he / ride his bike / not hold the handlebars)

   While he was riding his bike, he fell.
   (he / ride his bike / fall)

3. She was picking up her little boy's toy while she was looking at him.
   (she / look at him / pick up her little boy's toy)

   She was looking at her little boy when she hit her head.
   (she / hit her head / look at her little boy)

4. While she was walking down the stairs, she was talking on the phone.
   (she / walk down the stairs / talk on the phone)

   She fell down the stairs while she was talking on the phone.
   (she / fall down the stairs / talk on the phone)

PAIRS. **Now look at the pictures on page 44. Describe what happened in each picture. Use *when* and *while*. Then tell your sentences to the class.** Answers will vary.

> **TIME to TALK**
>
> *GROUPS.* **Write five sentences that describe five different kinds of accidents. Use *when*, *while*, the past progressive, and the simple past.**
>
> *WRAP UP.* **Now act out your sentences for the class. Can they guess what the sentences are?**
>
> **Example:**   Class: *Is the sentence, "I was driving while I was talking on the phone."?*
> Student A: *No, it isn't.*

Accidents 51

- Write the example on the board. Then switch the order of the clauses. Write: *While the man was cooking, he was reading a recipe.* Point out that the new order of the clauses requires a comma; it also leads to the use of the noun *the man* in the dependent clause and the pronoun *he* in the main clause.
- Have students complete the task.
- Call on students to read their sentences. Remind them to say *comma* if a comma is needed.
- PAIRS. Have students talk about the pictures on page 44.
- Call on students to write their sentences from the pairs activity on the board. Correct as needed.

Watch Out!

Exercise C. There are many correct ways to put the actions together into sentences, but there are also some incorrect ways. As students read their answers aloud, write them on the board so that others do not get confused. Repeat the correct sentences orally, but always write incorrect sentences on the board.

Option

Assign Unit 4 Supplementary Grammar to Communicate 3 Exercises on the Teacher's Resource Disk as homework or on the Student Persistence CD-ROM as self-access practice.

> **TIME to TALK**
> **Teaching Time: 10–15 min.**
>
> - WARM-UP: Write the sentence *I got into an accident while I was talking on my cell phone* on a piece of paper. Then ask an above-level student to pantomime it for the class. Have the class guess the action.
> - Read through both steps of the activity with students.
> - GROUPS. Have students complete the task.
> - WRAP UP. Have students complete the task. Write the students' guesses on the board. Correct as needed.

Multilevel Strategy

All levels: Balance the groups so that there is a mix of levels within each group. The pre-level students might not be able to come up with grammatical sentences on their own for the first stage of the activity, so they will benefit from the help of the more advanced students. However, they should be able to play just as active a role in the pantomimes and the guessing activity as their more advanced classmates.

Grammar

Teaching Time: 5–10 min.

- Read the example with the class. Ask two volunteers to pantomime the sentence for the class.
- Have students complete the task.
- Call on students to read their answers. Correct as needed. Use pantomime where appropriate to reinforce the correct answer.

Multilevel Strategy

- **Pre-level:** Tell students what the mistakes are and have them rewrite the sentences.

Dictation

Teaching Time: 5–10 min.

- 🎧 Play Track 28 while students listen and write what they hear.
- 🎧 Play Track 28 again while students check their answers.
- Call on students to write answers on the board.
- 🎧 Play Track 28 again and have a student volunteer correct the sentences on the board. Provide help as needed.

Multilevel Strategy

- **Pre-level:** Give students a worksheet with some of the words from the dictation already provided.

Speaking

Teaching Time: 10–15 min.

- ON YOUR OWN. Read the directions aloud. Ask a student: *What were you doing on Sunday at 3:00 P.M.?* Write your question and the student's answer on the board.
- Have students complete the task.
- CLASS. Call on three students to read the example conversation. After they've read the example, have them answer the question truthfully.

Grammar

Find the mistake in each sentence. Circle the letter and correct the mistake.

driving
1. I <u>was</u> <u>talking</u> <u>while</u> she <u>was</u> <del>drove</del>.
   A   B   C   D

fell
2. He <u>was</u> <u>running</u> when <u>he</u> <del>was falling</del>.
   A   B   C   D

started
3. <u>When</u> the fire <del>was starting</del>, I <u>left</u> the <u>building</u>.
   A   B   C   D

sleeping
4. <u>Were</u> you <u>and Bob</u> <del>sleep</del> <u>at the time</u> of the fire?
   A   B   C   D

was painting
5. <u>While</u> he <del>painted</del>, he <u>slipped</u> and <u>fell</u> off the ladder.
   A   B   C   D

Dictation

🎧 **28** **Listen. You will hear five sentences. Write them in your notebook.** *See the audioscript on p. 310 for the sentences.*

Speaking

ON YOUR OWN. **Think about what you were doing at the times in the box. Where were you? Who were you with? What were you doing? Write your answers in your notebook.**

Sunday at 3:00 P.M.	at 7:00 yesterday evening
at 9:00 yesterday morning	at midnight last night
between 12:00 and 2:00 yesterday afternoon	at 6:00 this morning

CLASS. **Then walk around the class and ask your classmates about their activities. Who was doing the same thing at the same time as you? Who was doing something different?**

Example:
A: *What were you doing at 9:00 yesterday morning?*
B: *I was driving to work.*
A: *I was too. Who were you driving with?*
B: *I wasn't with anybody. I was driving alone.*
A: *Me, too. How about you, Jean?*
C: *I was at home, feeding my baby.*

WRAP UP. **Now ask your classmates about the people that you didn't talk to.**

Example:
A: *David, what was Emily doing yesterday morning?*
D: *She was on the subway. She was coming home from work.*

52 Unit 4

- Have students stand up and walk around the class to complete the task. Tell them to try to find people who were doing the same thing they were for each of the times in the box. Tell them to take notes on their classmates' answers.
- WRAP UP. After they sit down, call on students to ask questions about classmates that they didn't have a chance to talk to. Correct errors as needed.

Expansion Survey the class on what they were doing at the different times in the box. Write their responses on the board. For example:

Sunday at 3:00 P.M.:   *working: 2*
                          watching a movie: 3
                          doing homework: 5

Listening

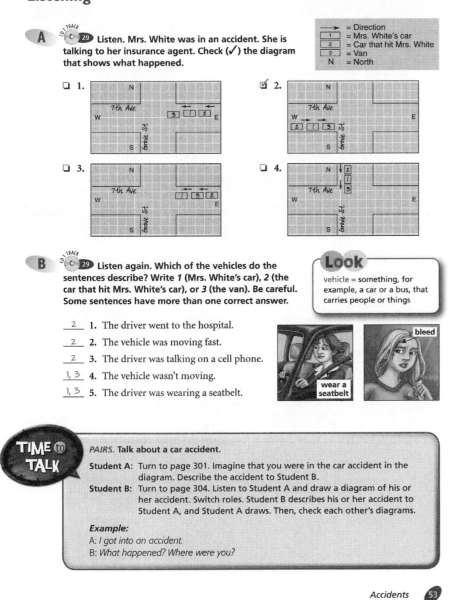

A 🎵 **29** Listen. Mrs. White was in an accident. She is talking to her insurance agent. Check (✓) the diagram that shows what happened.

	= Direction
1	= Mrs. White's car
2	= Car that hit Mrs. White
3	= Van
N	= North

❏ 1.

☑ 2.

❏ 3.

❏ 4.

B 🎵 **29** Listen again. Which of the vehicles do the sentences describe? Write *1* (Mrs. White's car), *2* (the car that hit Mrs. White's car), or *3* (the van). Be careful. Some sentences have more than one correct answer.

_2_ **1.** The driver went to the hospital.

_2_ **2.** The vehicle was moving fast.

_2_ **3.** The driver was talking on a cell phone.

_1, 3_ **4.** The vehicle wasn't moving.

_1, 3_ **5.** The driver was wearing a seatbelt.

Look

vehicle = something, for example, a car or a bus, that carries people or things

wear a seatbelt

bleed

TIME to TALK

PAIRS. Talk about a car accident.

Student A: Turn to page 301. Imagine that you were in the car accident in the diagram. Describe the accident to Student B.

Student B: Turn to page 304. Listen to Student A and draw a diagram of his or her accident. Switch roles. Student B describes his or her accident to Student A, and Student A draws. Then, check each other's diagrams.

Example:
A: *I got into an accident.*
B: *What happened? Where were you?*

Accidents **53**

Listening

A Teaching Time: 5–10 min.

- **Warm-up:** Have students look at the accident report diagrams. Explain that when you have an automobile accident in the United States, you have to call your insurance agent and fill out an accident report. Ask students what they have to do in their countries.
- Have students study the four diagrams carefully before they listen. Make sure they understand where north, south, east, and west are, and that the boxes with numbers on them represent the cars involved in the accident.
- 🎧 Play Track 29 while students listen.
- 🎧 Play Track 29 again while students listen and complete the task.
- Ask students who selected the first diagram to raise their hands. Do the same for the second, third, and fourth diagrams. Have those who chose the correct diagram explain what is wrong with the other three diagrams.

B Teaching Time: 5–10 min.

- Have students read the definition of *vehicle* in the Look Box. Say the word, and have them repeat chorally.
- Have students read the statements before listening.
- 🎧 Play Track 29 again while students listen and complete the task.
- Have students complete the task.
- Call on students to say answers. Correct as needed.

Multilevel Strategy

Pre-level: Give students a copy of the audioscript to follow while completing Exercises A and B.

Option

Time to Talk. Call on two volunteers to come up to the front of the class and do a role-play based on one of the accidents. One of the students is an insurance agent, and the other is a client who has just had an accident.

Option

Assign Unit 4 Review and Challenge Supplementary Exercises on the Teacher's Resource Disk as homework or on the Student Persistence CD-ROM as self-access practice.

TIME to TALK

Teaching Time: 10–15 min.

- Read the example with the class.
- PAIRS. Have students complete the task. Encourage them to use the simple past and past progressive as they describe their accidents.
- Ask a pair of students to come up to the board. One student describes the accident while the other asks questions and completes the diagram.
- Record any errors in simple past or past progressive, and write them on the board after the students have finished.

Reading

Getting Ready to Read

Teaching Time: 5–10 min.

- Read the information in the Reading Skill box aloud.
- Ask students to point to the picture of lightning on the page. Have them guess what *strike* means. If they have no idea, ask: *Does it mean* hit *or* fall?
- Read the directions aloud. Tell students they will have one minute to scan the text. Remind them to scan it, not read it. Ask them what they are scanning for. (numbers—years)
- Have students complete the task.

Reading

Teaching Time: 15–20 min.

- Have students read the article.
- Have students check their answers to the scanning exercise. Call on a student to read the answers.

Reading

Getting Ready to Read

Scan the article. In which years did lightning strike Roy Sullivan? Write the years.

<u>1942, 1969, 1970, 1972, 1973, 1974, 1977</u>

**Reading Skill:
Scanning**

When you **scan** a text, you are looking for specific information. You move your eyes very quickly over the text to find something, like a date or a name.

Reading

Read the article. Then check your answers to Getting Ready to Read.

LIGHTNING STRIKES
SEVEN TIMES!

Some people say that lightning never strikes twice. But sometimes, it does! Just ask Roy Sullivan. In his lifetime, Sullivan, a park ranger from Virginia, **survived** seven **incredible** lightning strikes.

Six of the strikes hit Sullivan at Shenandoah National Park. The first happened in 1942 when he was standing in a lookout tower. It **took off** one of his toenails. The second strike **occurred** in 1969 while he was driving. It burned off his eyebrows. The third strike came in 1970 as he was walking across his front yard. It burned his shoulders. The fourth, in 1972, hit him when he was standing in a ranger station. That strike burned off all of his hair. The fifth, sixth, and seventh strikes all occurred within just four years.

The fifth strike happened in 1973. Sullivan was at work when he saw that a storm cloud was forming. He got in his truck and tried to go faster than the cloud. As soon as he was sure that he was safe, he got out of his truck. But that was a mistake.

"I actually saw the lightning shoot out of the cloud this time," he said. "It was coming straight for me." The strike set his hair on fire and **traveled** down his leg. Then it took off his shoe. The sixth strike came in 1974 as he was checking a campground. Finally, the seventh found him in 1977 while he was fishing.

A park ranger in a lookout tower.

The lightning strikes **damaged** both Sullivan's health and his relationships. After people heard his story, they were afraid to be around him. "Naturally, people **avoid** me," Sullivan told a reporter. "I was walking with the chief ranger one day, and lightning struck way off, and he said, "I'll see you later, Roy.""

54   Unit 4

After You Read

A Look at the **boldface** words in the article. Guess their meaning. Match the words with the correct definitions.

_h_ 1. strikes   **a.** hurt

_g_ 2. survived   **b.** stay away from

_d_ 3. incredible   **c.** went

_e_ 4. took off   **d.** very strange and difficult to believe

_f_ 5. occurred   **e.** removed by a strong force

_c_ 6. traveled   **f.** happened

_a_ 7. damaged   **g.** continued to live after a serious accident

_b_ 8. avoid   ✗ **h.** hits someone or something

B What was Roy doing at the time of the lightning strikes? Write full sentences.

Strike 1:   He was standing in a lookout tower at a national park.

Strike 2:   He was driving.

Strike 3:   He was walking across his front yard.

Strike 4:   He was standing in a ranger station.

Strike 5:   He was working.
             (OR He was getting out of his truck.)

Strike 6:   He was checking a campground.

Strike 7:   He was fishing.

Accidents   **55**

Option

After students complete the reading exercises, have them underline the verbs in the article that are in the past progressive, and circle the ones that are in the simple past.

After You Read

A Teaching Time: 10–15 min.

- Do the example with the class. Tell them to go back to the article and circle any words that could help them to guess the meaning. (hit) Explain that sometimes students will need to use sentences or paragraphs before and after a new word to figure out its meaning. In this case, they need to read the second paragraph to learn that *strikes* means *hits*.

- Have students complete the task. Tell them to circle words in the reading that help them understand the meanings of the new words.

- Call on students to say answers. Ask them which words they circled to find the answer. Correct as needed.

B Teaching Time: 10–15 min.

- Read the example with the class. Make sure they understand that they should use the past progressive wherever possible.

- Have students complete the task without looking back at the text. When they have finished, they can go back to the text to check their answers.

Multilevel Strategy

Pre-level: Allow students to look back at the article as they complete Exercise B. Have them write the number of each sentence next to the place in the text where they find it.

Writing

Getting Ready to Write

A Teaching Time: 5–10 min.

- Call on a student to read the Writing Tip. Ask him/her to explain why the simple past and the past progressive were used in the example.
- Have students complete the task.
- Call on students to read their answers and say where commas are necessary.

B Teaching Time: 10–15 min.

- Read the model aloud.
- PAIRS. Have students complete the task.
- Ask for a volunteer to tell the class about something incredible that happened to him/her.

Expansion Have students underline the simple past and circle the past progressive in the model. Call on students to explain why each of the verb forms is appropriate in the story.

Writing

Getting Ready to Write

A Look at the pictures. Write sentences. Use the word in parentheses and the simple past or past progressive of the verbs. Add commas where necessary.

1. (while) I / swim / I / see a bolt of lightning
   <u>While I was swimming, I saw a bolt of lightning.</u> OR
   <u>I saw a bolt of lightning while I was swimming.</u>

2. (when) my mother / hear the storm / she / ran down to the beach
   <u>When my mother heard the storm, she ran down to the beach</u>
   <u>My mother ran down to the beach when she heard the storm</u>

3. (when) I / swim toward the beach / I / see my mother
   <u>I was swimming toward the beach when I saw my mother.</u>
   <u>When I saw my mother, I was swimming toward the beach.</u>

B Read the model paragraph.

> Last Saturday, a lot of people were enjoying the beautiful weather in the park. One woman was walking a big dog. Suddenly the dog saw a duck in the lake. The dog jumped into the lake and pulled the woman into the water! At first it was funny, but then the woman started to scream. I was getting ready to jump in the water when the dog grabbed a tree branch. He swam over to the woman with the branch, and she grabbed it. Then the dog swam back to the shore. When the dog pulled the woman out of the water, everybody started to cheer. It was incredible!

PAIRS. Read the model again. What was incredible about the day in the park? Answers will vary.

Then tell your partner about something incredible or surprising that happened to you.

56 Unit 4

Prewriting: Visualizing

You are going to write a story about the event you described to your partner on page 56. Before you write, draw a series of pictures to show the different things that happened. Visualizing will help you remember the details of your story.

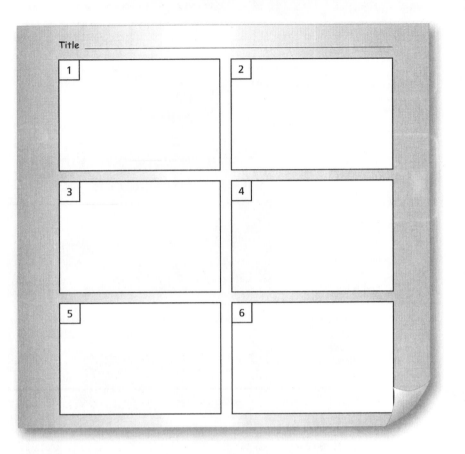

Title _____

| | |
|1| |2|
|3| |4|
|5| |6|

Writing

Now write a story about the incredible or surprising event. The writing tip, the model paragraph, and your pictures will help you. Write in your notebook.

Accidents 57

Teaching Time: 10–15 min.

- Explain that *visualizing* means *forming a picture in your mind.*
- Read the instructions aloud. Tell students that it is not necessary to be a good artist. Draw stick figures on the board to show them that they can keep the pictures very simple. Tell them that the important thing is for them to form a picture of the event in their minds when they draw.
- After students finish drawing, have them work with a new partner. Tell them to show their drawings to their partner, and see if their partner can guess what happened.

Writing

Teaching Time: 20–25 min.

- Have students complete the task. Walk around and help as needed. Encourage students to refer to the model in the book and their drawings as they write. Remind them to use the simple past and the past progressive to paint a picture with their words.
- Before students hand in their paragraphs, tell them to review the grammar summaries on page 284. Tell them to reread their paragraphs, looking for errors in simple past tense, past progressive, clauses, and commas.
- Have partners tell each other their stories. If a part of the story is not clear to their partner, they should rephrase it.

Multilevel Strategy

Pre-level: Allow students to write their stories at home and hand them in the next day.

Learning Goals

- Learn words to describe daily activities
- Learn about *used to:* statements and *yes / no* and information questions
- Listen to a conversation about dating customs in the past and to a radio interview about women's lives in the past
- Read an article about the evolution of transportation in the United States and write a paragraph comparing changes from the past to now
- Talk about changing family customs and gender roles

Learner Persistence

Make it as easy as possible for students to return to class after "stopping out." Students who feel welcomed back are more likely to persist.

Warm-up

Teaching Time: 3–5 min.

- Have students cover the text and look at the illustrations. Ask them questions about the pictures to see how much of the vocabulary they know. For example, ask: *What is the woman in the first picture doing? What is the woman in the second picture doing?*
- Write students' answers on the board. If they don't know the vocabulary, tell them they are going to learn it in this unit.

Vocabulary

Teaching Time: 10–15 min.

- Read the example with the class.
- Have students complete the task.
- 🎧 Play Track 30 while students listen and check their answers.
- Say each word or phrase and have students repeat chorally.

Expansion Ask students questions with the vocabulary. For example, ask: *How often do you get dressed up? Do you wear casual clothes to work? Do you wear casual clothes to school? Do you usually repair things, or do you throw them away?*

Unit 5
Then and Now

Vocabulary

🔘 CD 1 TRACK **30** Match the numbers with the words. Then listen and check your answers.

7	change a diaper
8	dress
10	feed
3	get dressed up
5	give a bath
1	give birth
2	make one's own clothes
4	repair
6	throw away
9	wear casual clothes

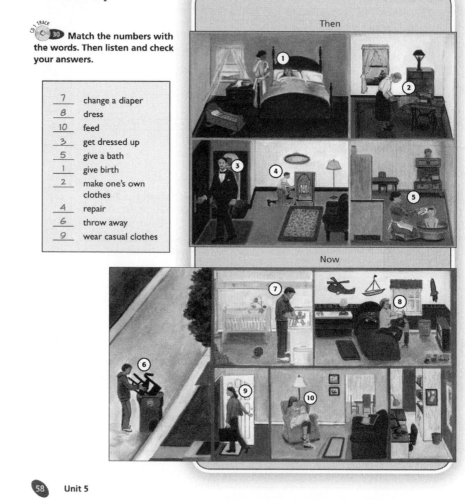

Then

Now

Culture Note

Listening. It is possible that some of your students will come from countries where dating is not a part of the culture. Be aware that those students might have a more difficult time understanding this listening exercise, and give them extra support.

Listening

A 🔊 **31** Listen. Tina is talking to her grandmother. What are they talking about? Check (✓) the main topic of their conversation.

❏ when Tina's grandmother was a little girl

❏ how Tina's grandmother and grandfather met

☑ dating in the past

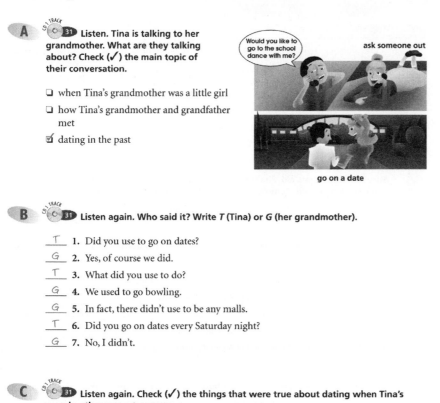

ask someone out

go on a date

B 🔊 **31** Listen again. Who said it? Write *T* (Tina) or *G* (her grandmother).

__T__ 1. Did you use to go on dates?

__G__ 2. Yes, of course we did.

__T__ 3. What did you use to do?

__G__ 4. We used to go bowling.

__G__ 5. In fact, there didn't use to be any malls.

__T__ 6. Did you go on dates every Saturday night?

__G__ 7. No, I didn't.

C 🔊 **31** Listen again. Check (✓) the things that were true about dating when Tina's grandmother was a teenager.

❏ 1. Young people didn't use to go to the movies on dates.

❏ 2. The girl used to pay.

☑ 3. The guys used to pick the girls up.

☑ 4. The guys used to meet the girls' parents.

❏ 5. The girls used to meet the guys' parents.

❏ 6. Boys and girls used to meet at the mall.

Then and Now 59

Teaching Tip

Exercises B and C. Students might ask you questions about the meaning of *used to*. Say: *It means something was true in the past, but isn't true now. We will study this grammar point in this unit, so don't worry if you don't understand it completely now.*

Option

Assign Unit 5 Supplementary Vocabulary Exercises on the Teacher's Resource Disk as homework or on the Student Persistence CD-ROM as self-access practice.

Listening

A Teaching Time: 10–15 min.

- **Warm-up:** Have students read the directions and look at the picture. Have them read the answer choices and guess which one will be correct.
- 🎧 Play Track 31 while students listen.
- 🎧 Play Track 31 again while students listen and complete the task.
- Call on a student to say the answer. Ask if his/her guess was correct. If more than a few students get the wrong answer, play the audio again.

B Teaching Time: 10–15 min.

- Read the directions and the example with the class.
- Have students complete the task.
- 🎧 Play Track 31 while students listen and complete the task.
- 🎧 Play Track 31 again while students listen and check their answers.
- Call on students to say answers. Correct as needed.

Multilevel Strategy

- **Pre-level:** Make photocopies of the tapescript. Give it to students before they do Exercise B.

C Teaching Time: 10–15 min.

- Read the directions and the sentences with the class.
- 🎧 Play Track 31 while students listen and complete the task.
- Call on students to read the sentences that they checked. Correct as needed.

Grammar to Communicate 1

Used to: Statements

Teaching Time: 5–10 min.

- Have students study the chart and the Look Box.
- Ask a series of questions about the sentences in the chart. Call on students to answer. Ask: *Do I live in Miami now?* (No, you don't.) *Did I live in Miami in the past?* (Yes, you did.) *Do I have a pet now?* (Yes, you do.) *Did I have a pet in the past?* (No, you didn't.)
- Read the sentences aloud and have students repeat chorally.
- Draw students' attention to the time expressions in the chart. Say: *You can use the time expressions* not anymore *and* now *to emphasize that things were different in the past from the way they are now. However, time expressions are not necessary with* used to. *They are only for extra emphasis.*
- Say: Now *can go at the end of the sentence or after* but.

A   Teaching Time: 5–10 min.

- Read the directions and the example with the class. Make sure they understand that they are completing the statements of Mrs. Stein, who is eighty-five years old. They are not completing the sentences with information about their own countries.
- Have students complete the task. Tell them to circle *used to* + verb in each sentence.
- Have students complete the task.
- Call on students to read the statements that Mrs. Stein made. For each one, ask the student if Mrs. Stein's statement is true about his/her country. If it isn't true, have the student explain what the situation really is. Do an example with the class. Say: *For example, for statement 1, you could say: This isn't true in my country. Women still wear skirts and dresses to work in my country.* (Write this last sentence on the board.)
- Explain that we use the word *still* to talk about a situation in the past that continues in the present.
- Correct students' answers as needed.

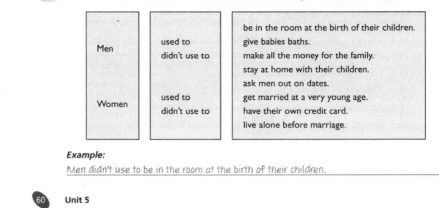

Grammar to Communicate 1

USED TO: STATEMENTS

Subject	Used to	Verb	Time Expression	Subject	Didn't use to	Verb	Time Expression
I	used to	live	in Miami,	but I don't anymore.	I	didn't use to	have	a pet,	but I do now.
You					You				
He	used to	live	in Miami.	He	didn't use to	have	a pet.
We					We			
They					They			

A   Mrs. Stein is 85 years old. She is giving her opinion about the lives of men and women when she was a child. Complete her sentences. Write *men* or *women*.

1. "___Women___ used to wear skirts and dresses to work, but now they don't."
2. "___Women___ used to make their own clothes, but they don't anymore."
3. "___Men___ didn't use to feed babies, but they often do now."
4. "___Women___ didn't use to keep their last name after marriage, but they do now."
5. "___Men___ didn't use to change diapers, but they do now."
6. "___Men___ used to be good at repairing things, but they aren't anymore."

Look

Used to + verb = happened in the past but doesn't happen often now.
People **used to** build their own houses.

Didn't use to + verb = didn't happen often in the past but happens often now.
Women **didn't use to** be police officers.

B   Write sentences with the words in the boxes. Write in your notebook. *Answers will vary.*

Men	used to	be in the room at the birth of their children.
	didn't use to	give babies baths.
		make all the money for the family.
		stay at home with their children.
Women	used to	ask men out on dates.
	didn't use to	get married at a very young age.
		have their own credit card.
		live alone before marriage.

Example:
Men didn't use to be in the room at the birth of their children.

60   Unit 5

B   Teaching Time: 10–15 min.

- Read the directions and the example with students. Tell them to write about the country they are in now.
- Have students complete the task.
- Call on students to read their sentences. Correct as needed. For each statement, take an informal poll. Ask the other students to raise their hands if they agree with the answer. Then give your opinion.

Grammar Notes

1. We use *used to* + base form of a verb to talk about things that happened often in the past. These things usually do not happen often or at all now.
2. For the negative of *used to*, use *didn't use to*.
3. We often use the time expressions *not anymore* and *now* with *used to* to emphasize that things were different in the past from the way they are now.
4. For more information on this grammar topic, go to page 285.

Watch Out!

Exercises A and B.

- Look for and correct errors such as: *I use to play soccer* instead of *I used to play soccer.*

C Write two sentences about each picture with *used to* and *didn't use to*. Use the words in the box.

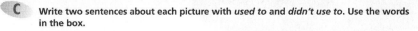

~~wash clothes by hand~~	make their own bread	make furniture by hand	grow their own vegetables
~~have washing machines~~	buy bread	make furniture in a factory	buy frozen vegetables

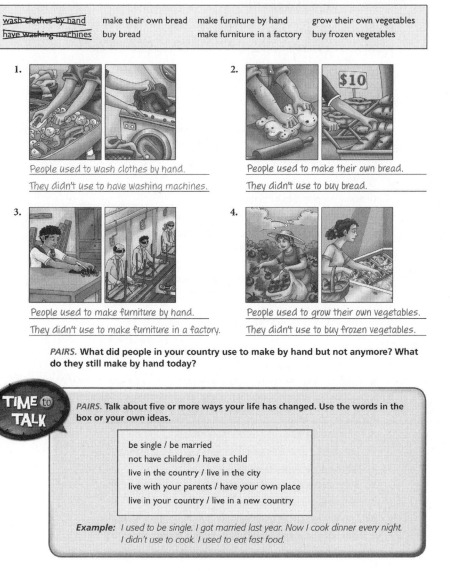

1. People used to wash clothes by hand.
They didn't use to have washing machines.

2. People used to make their own bread.
They didn't use to buy bread.

3. People used to make furniture by hand.
They didn't use to make furniture in a factory.

4. People used to grow their own vegetables.
They didn't use to buy frozen vegetables.

PAIRS. **What did people in your country use to make by hand but not anymore? What do they still make by hand today?**

TIME to TALK

PAIRS. **Talk about five or more ways your life has changed. Use the words in the box or your own ideas.**

be single / be married
not have children / have a child
live in the country / live in the city
live with your parents / have your own place
live in your country / live in a new country

Example: *I used to be single. I got married last year. Now I cook dinner every night. I didn't use to cook. I used to eat fast food.*

Then and Now 61

C Teaching Time: 10–15 min.

- Read the directions and the expressions in the word box.
- Have a student read the example. Ask the class to tell you what *by hand* means. (not by machine; with your own hands)
- Have students complete the task.
- Call on students to say answers. Correct as needed.
- PAIRS. Have students talk about their countries.
- Call on a few students to say something about their partners' countries. Correct as needed.

Expansion Have students talk about things that they know how to do by hand. Make sure they use the simple present *know* or the modal verb *can* in their sentences.

Teaching Tip

Time to Talk. While the students are talking, walk around and take notes on any mistakes with *used to* that you hear. Do not interrupt their conversations. After students have finished, write some of the errors that you noticed on the board. Have the class correct them together.

Option

Assign Unit 5 Supplementary Grammar to Communicate 1 Exercises on the Teacher's Resource Disk as homework or on the Student Persistence CD-ROM as self-access practice.

TIME to TALK

Teaching Time: 10–15 min.

- Read the directions with the class. Have a student read the example. Ask students to raise their hands if the example is true for them.
- PAIRS. Have students complete the task.
- Walk around and make sure students are using the grammar correctly in their conversations. Correct as needed.

Grammar to Communicate 2

Used to: Yes / No Questions

Teaching Time: 5–10 min.

- Have students study the chart.
- Point out that in a question *use to* is in the base form.
- Point out that the short answer for *used to* is the same as the short answer for the simple past: *Yes, I did. / No, I didn't.*
- Read the examples in the chart aloud and have students repeat chorally.

A Teaching Time: 10–15 min.

- Read the example with the class. Make sure students understand that they should answer with information about their countries.
- Have students complete the task.
- PAIRS. Have students take turns asking and answering the questions.
- Call on students to read the questions and say the answers for their countries. Correct as needed.

B Teaching Time: 10–15 min.

- Read the example with the class.
- Have students complete the task.
- Call on students to read their questions. Correct as needed.

Multilevel Strategy

- **Pre-level:** Group all the pre-level students for this exercise. Sit with them and break down the grammar as follows:
  - Have them circle the subject and underline the verb in each answer.
  - Have them write the base form of the verb that they have underlined.
  - Write out the pattern for them to follow: *Did + subject + use to + base form of the main verb + the rest of the sentence + ?*
  - Have them put their questions together by following the pattern.
- **At-level, Above-level:** After they have completed the task, have students get into pairs and take turns asking the questions and answering about their countries.

USED TO: YES / NO QUESTIONS				Affirmative			Negative		
Did	Subject	*Use to*	Verb						
Did	you he we they	use to	work?	Yes,	I he we they	did.	No,	I he we they	didn't.

A Imagine that someone is asking you questions about work life in your country fifty years ago. Complete the questions with the missing words. Then answer the questions.

1. Did women use __to__ work outside the home? ___Yes, they did. OR No, they didn't.___
2. __Did__ women use to go to college? _____
3. Did women __use__ to be in the military? _____
4. __Did__ parents use to put their children in daycare? _____
5. Did fathers use __to__ stay home with a sick child? _____
6. Did men __use__ to take time off for a child's birth? _____

PAIRS. Ask and answer the questions about your countries.

Example:
A: *Did women use to go to college in your country?*
B: *No, they didn't, but they do today.*

B Complete the questions with the correct form of *used to*.

1. **A:** Men are kindergarten teachers these days.
   B: ___Did they use to be kindergarten teachers___ years ago?
2. **A:** Women are directors of big companies.
   B: ___Did women use to be directors of big companies___ years ago?
3. **A:** Women drive buses and trucks these days.
   B: ___Did women use to drive buses and trucks___ years ago?
4. **A:** Women are college professors nowadays.
   B: ___Did women use to be college professors___ years ago?
5. **A:** Men work as nurses nowadays.
   B: ___Did men use to work as nurses___ years ago?
6. **A:** Men often wear jeans and T-shirts to work nowadays.
   B: ___Did men use to wear jeans and T-shirts to work___ years ago?

Grammar Notes

1. To make a *yes / no* question, use *did* before the subject and *use to* + verb after the subject.
2. Use *did* in short answers, even when the main verb is *be*.
3. For more information on this grammar topic, go to page 285.

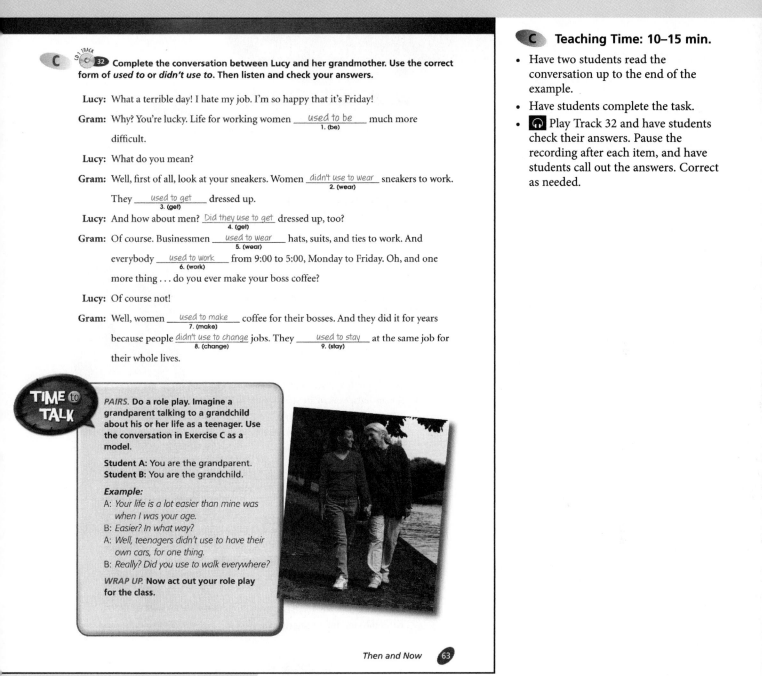

C 🔘 **32** Complete the conversation between Lucy and her grandmother. Use the correct form of *used to* or *didn't use to*. Then listen and check your answers.

Lucy: What a terrible day! I hate my job. I'm so happy that it's Friday!

Gram: Why? You're lucky. Life for working women ___used to be___ much more
                                                                 1. (be)
difficult.

Lucy: What do you mean?

Gram: Well, first of all, look at your sneakers. Women ___didn't use to wear___ sneakers to work.
                                                                 2. (wear)
They ___used to get___ dressed up.
          3. (get)

Lucy: And how about men? ___Did they use to get___ dressed up, too?
                                    4. (get)

Gram: Of course. Businessmen ___used to wear___ hats, suits, and ties to work. And
                                        5. (wear)
everybody ___used to work___ from 9:00 to 5:00, Monday to Friday. Oh, and one
                6. (work)
more thing . . . do you ever make your boss coffee?

Lucy: Of course not!

Gram: Well, women ___used to make___ coffee for their bosses. And they did it for years
                          7. (make)
because people ___didn't use to change___ jobs. They ___used to stay___ at the same job for
                      8. (change)   9. (stay)
their whole lives.

TIME to TALK

PAIRS. **Do a role play. Imagine a grandparent talking to a grandchild about his or her life as a teenager. Use the conversation in Exercise C as a model.**

Student A: You are the grandparent.
Student B: You are the grandchild.

Example:
A: *Your life is a lot easier than mine was when I was your age.*
B: *Easier? In what way?*
A: *Well, teenagers didn't use to have their own cars, for one thing.*
B: *Really? Did you use to walk everywhere?*

WRAP UP. **Now act out your role play for the class.**

Then and Now 63

C **Teaching Time: 10–15 min.**

- Have two students read the conversation up to the end of the example.
- Have students complete the task.
- 🎧 Play Track 32 and have students check their answers. Pause the recording after each item, and have students call out the answers. Correct as needed.

Culture Note

Exercise C. Explain that in English, people often use special words to refer to their grandparents. Ask students if they know any other words we use for grandmother or grandfather. (grandmother: grandma, ma, nana; grandfather: gramps, grandpa, pa, pops)

Option

Assign Unit 5 Supplementary Grammar to Communicate 2 Exercises on the Teacher's Resource Disk as homework or on the Student Persistence CD-ROM as self-access practice.

TIME to TALK

Teaching Time: 10–15 min.

- Call on two students to read the example aloud.
- PAIRS. For each pair, assign a Student A and a Student B. Have students complete the task.
- WRAP UP. Ask volunteers to perform their role-play for the class.
- Wait until the role-plays are finished to make corrections. Write errors on the board and have the class correct them.

Multilevel Strategy

Pre-level: Pair pre-level students together. Do not have them write their own role-play. Instead, have them role play the conversation in Exercise C. Encourage them to act it out, not merely read it. During the wrap up, have one pre-level pair do their role-play in front of the class.

Grammar to Communicate 3

Used to: Information Questions

Teaching Time: 5–10 min.

- Have students study the chart.
- Say: *To form most information questions with* used to, *we use the same pattern as for yes / no questions. The only difference is that we add a question word before* did.
- Write the following sentences on the board. Be careful to line up the *did* in both questions:

  <u>Did she use to go out?</u>

  Yes, she did.

  How often <u>did she use to go out?</u>

  She used to go out every weekend.

- Say: *But when the question is about the subject, the information question looks different from the yes / no question.*
- Under the *How often* question, write:
- *Who <u>used to go out</u> with her? <u>Her friends</u> used to go out with her.*
- Ask: *What is different about this question?* (There is no *did.*) *Why is there no* did? (Because the question is about the subject.)
- Call on two students to read the examples from the chart. One student reads the questions, and the other student reads the answers.

A   Teaching Time: 10–15 min.

- Explain that the questions are about how men and women used to behave toward each other, and how they behave today.
- Have students complete the task.
- Call on students to read their answers. Ask other students if they agree.

Expansion Start a discussion on differences between men's and women's behavior in different cultures, both today and in the past.

Grammar to Communicate 3

USED TO: INFORMATION QUESTIONS

Wh- word	Did	Subject	Use to	Verb	Answers
How often		she		go out?	She used to go out every weekend.
Where	did	you	use to	meet?	We used to meet at my home.
When		they		go?	They used to go on Sundays.
Who		he		date?	He used to date Mary.

Wh- word (Subject)	Used to	Verb		Answers
What	used to	happen	every Friday?	We used to go bowling.
Who		go?		Everyone on the team went.

A **Answer the questions about what men and women do these days and what they used to do in many parts of the world. If you are not sure, guess.**

Answers to the first question in each item will vary.

1. A man and a woman are standing near a door.

   Who opens the door these days?   *Who used to open the door?*

   a. The man opens the door.   (**a.**) The man used to open the door.

   b. The woman opens the door.   **b.** The woman used to open the door.

   c. It isn't important.   **c.** It wasn't important.

2. A woman comes into a room. Two men are sitting in the room.

   What do men do these days?   *What did men use to do?*

   a. They say hello.   **a.** They used to say hello.

   b. They stand up and say hello.   (**b.**) They used to stand up and say hello.

   c. They do nothing.   **c.** They used to do nothing.

3. A man and a woman are standing near a table.

   When does the man sit down these days?   *When did the man use to sit down?*

   a. before the woman   **a.** before the woman

   b. after the woman   (**b.**) after the woman

   c. at the same time as the woman   **c.** at the same time as the woman

---

Grammar Notes

1. In information questions, *did* comes after the question word (*what, how much,* etc.) and *use to* + verb comes after the subject.

2. When *who* or *what* is the subject of the question, do not use *did* in the question. Use *used to* + the base form of the verb.

3. For more information on this grammar topic, go to page 285.

Culture Note

Exercise A. If you have students who come from Asia, Africa, or the Middle East, you might want to change the directions to: *Answer the questions about the United States.*

B Write questions about dating fifty years ago. Put the words in the correct order.

1. What did girls use to wear on dates?
   (wear on dates / to / use / girls / did / what)
2. Who used to pay for the date?
   (used / pay for / who / the date / to)
3. Where did the man use to pick up the woman?
   (where / the man / pick up the woman / did / to / use)
4. What did young people use to do on dates?
   (young people / what / did / to / use / on dates / do)
5. At what age did girls use to start dating?
   (did / at what age / girls / start dating / to / use)

PAIRS. Ask and answer the questions about your country.

C Read the statements about family life in some parts of the world today. Write questions about life fifty years ago. Use the correct form of *used to.*

1. Today families rarely have dinner together.
   How often _____ did families use to have _____ dinner together?
   (have)
2. Today people eat fast food three or four times a week.
   How often _____ did people use to eat out _____?
   (eat out)
3. Today many women have their first child after age thirty.
   At what age _did women use to have their first child_?
   (have)
4. Many children's parents drive them to school.
   How _____ did children use to get _____ to school?
   (get)
5. Day care workers often take care of very young children today.
   Who _____ used to take care of _____ very young children?
   (take care of)

PAIRS. Ask and answer the questions. Do you and your partner agree on the answers?

TIME to TALK

GROUPS. Ask and answer questions about relationships between young people in your country today and in the past. Use the words in the box.

At what age . . . get engaged?	How . . . meet each other?
At what age . . . get married?	Where . . . live after marriage?
How many children . . . have?	Where . . . live before marriage?

Example:
A: *How do young people meet each other in your country today?*
B: *They usually meet at school, or their friends introduce them.*
A: *How did young people use to meet in the past?*

Then and Now **65**

B Teaching Time: 10–15 min.

- Read the example with the class.
- Have students complete the task.
- Call on students to read their questions. Correct as needed.
- PAIRS. Have students take turns asking and answering the questions.

Multilevel Strategy

Pre-level: Group all the pre-level students for this exercise. Give them extra support. See the multilevel strategy for Exercise B on page 62 for more information.

C Teaching Time: 10–15 min.

- Have a student read the example.
- Have students complete the task.
- Ask for volunteers to write the questions on the board. Correct as needed.
- PAIRS. Have students take turns asking and answering the questions.
- Take an informal poll of the class. For each item, ask students to raise their hands if the statement is true in their country today. If a student doesn't raise his/her hand, ask him/her what the custom is in his/her country today.

Multilevel Strategy

All levels: Balance the groups so that there is a mix of levels within each group. The pre-level students might not be able to come up with grammatical questions, so they will benefit from the help of the more advanced students. Choose the most advanced student in each group, and make him or her responsible for the grammar in the group. Have that student listen carefully and correct any errors in *used to* that he or she hears.

Teaching Tip

Exercise B. Because dating is not universal, some students may not be able to answer the questions in the PAIRS activity. Find out who those students are by asking: *Does anyone come from a culture where dating is not common?* Pair them with students who come from countries where dating is common. That way, the students who can't answer the questions can still participate in the activity by asking the questions.

Option

Assign Unit 5 Supplementary Grammar to Communicate 3 Exercises on the Teacher's Resource Disk as homework or on the Student Persistence CD-ROM as self-access practice.

TIME to TALK

Teaching Time: 10–15 min.

- Make sure everyone in the group knows the meaning of *get engaged.* To explain, say: *In many cultures, people get engaged before they get married. In the United States, for example, the man usually gives the woman an engagement ring, and they tell their family and friends about their wedding plans.*
- Have two students read the example. Call the class's attention to the use of the simple present in the first question, and the use of *used to* in the second question.
- GROUPS. Have students complete the task.
- Walk around and help as needed. Remind students to use *used to* when they are talking about the past.

Review and Challenge

Grammar

Teaching Time: 5–10 min.

- Read the directions with the class. Have two students read the conversation up to the example.
- Have students complete the task.
- 🎧 Play Track 33 and have students check their answers.
- 🎧 Play Track 33 again, this time pausing each time an answer is given. Call on a student to say the correct answer.

Dictation

Teaching Time: 5–10 min.

- 🎧 Play Track 34 while students listen and write what they hear.
- 🎧 Play Track 34 again while students check their answers.
- Call on students to write answers on the board.
- 🎧 Play Track 34 again and have a student volunteer correct the sentences on the board. Provide help as needed.

Speaking

Teaching Time: 10–15 min.

- Explain the meaning of any unfamiliar words in the box.
- Ask for three volunteers to read the example. You may want to point out that *there* is the subject of the

sentences with *used to*. Make sure everyone understands that this is a question-and-answer chain. Encourage students to listen carefully to each other. If necessary, have three advanced students do another example.
- GROUPS. Have students complete the task.
- Ask for a group to volunteer to do their question-and-answer chain for the class. Don't interrupt the chain, but keep track of any errors you hear. Write them on the board when the students finish. Correct them with the class.

Review and Challenge

Grammar

33 This conversation has seven mistakes. The first mistake is corrected for you. Find and correct the other six mistakes. Then listen and check your answers.

Rob: Do you always take your son to school?

Dan: Always.

Rob: ~~Your father use~~ *Did your father use* to take you to school?

Dan: No, never.

Rob: Did your father ~~use to did help~~ *use to help* around the house?

Dan: My father ~~usen't to do~~ *didn't use to do* a thing. He ~~used come~~ *used to come* home, have dinner, and watch TV.

Rob: Who ~~did use to~~ *used to* take care of the house?

Dan: My mother, of course.

Rob: ~~You used to~~ *Did you use to* help her?

Dan: No, I didn't. My brothers and sisters and I ~~were used to be~~ *used to be* the same as my father.

Dictation

34 Listen. You will hear five sentences. Write them in your notebook. *See the audioscript on p. 311 for the sentences.*

Speaking

GROUPS. Talk about how our lives are different today because of technology. Use the words in the box and your own ideas.

Student A: Make a statement and ask a question.
Student B: Answer Student A's question. Make another statement, and ask a question.
Student C: Answer Student B's question. Make another statement, and ask a question.

| airplanes | electricity | refrigerators | running water | televisions |

Example:
A: *There didn't use to be electricity. How did people use to read after dark?*
B: *People used to use candles. There didn't use to be televisions. What did people use to do for fun?*
C: *They used to sit around and talk. There didn't use to be . . .*

66 Unit 5

Language Note

Dictation. Explain that because the final *d* of *used* and the *t* of *to* sound like one sound, it is very difficult to hear the /d/ on the end of *used*. In an affirmative sentence or in an information question about the subject, tell students to write the *d* even if they don't hear it.

Listening

A 🎵 **35** Listen to the radio report. Check (✓) the topic of the report.

- ☑ changes in women's lives
- ❏ mothers and fathers in the past
- ❏ women's lives today

B 🎵 **35** Listen again. Complete the sentences with the correct information.

1. Lynn and Alice Thomas are twins. They are ___102___ years old.
2. Women used to do all of the _housework_.
3. There didn't use to be any _washing machines_, so women used to wash the family's clothes by _hand_.
4. Alice and Lynn used to do the laundry _on Mondays_.
5. They used to get up at ___4:00___ in the morning on Mondays, and they didn't finish until _8:00 or 9:00_ at night.
6. Men used to have _Sundays_ off.
7. The women used to work ___seven___ days a week.

TIME to TALK

GROUPS. Talk about changes in society in the past 100 years. Which changes are positive? Which changes are negative? Write five sentences for each category.

Examples:

Positive Changes
Housework today is easy. It used to be hard because there didn't use to be any machines.

Negative Changes
People eat a lot of fast food. They used to eat home cooking.

WRAP UP. Share your list with the class. Discuss any differences of opinion.

Then and Now **67**

Listening

A **Teaching Time: 5–10 min.**

- **Warm-up:** Have students look at the picture and tell you what the relationship between the women probably is. Give them a chance to answer, and then write *identical twins* on the board.
- Have students read the answer choices to Exercise A. Have them predict what the topic of the listening will be.
- 🎧 Play Track 35 while students listen.
- 🎧 Play Track 35 again while students listen and complete the task.
- Call on a student to say the answer. Ask students to raise their hands if they correctly predicted the answer before they listened.

B **Teaching Time: 5–10 min.**

- Have students complete the task without the audio. If they can't remember an answer, they should leave it blank.
- 🎧 Play Track 35 and have students check their answers.
- 🎧 Play Track 35 again, this time pausing each time an answer is given.
- Call on students to say answers. Correct as needed.

Multilevel Strategy

Pre-level: Give students a handout with the missing information on it, arranged out of order. Students listen and write the missing words in the appropriate blanks.

Option

Assign Unit 5 Review and Challenge Supplementary Exercises on the Teacher's Resource Disk as homework or on the Student Persistence CD-ROM as self-access practice.

TIME to TALK

Teaching Time: 10–15 min.

- Read the example with the class. Assign a secretary for each group. Explain that the secretary will write down the group's ideas and read them to the class.
- Remind students to use *used to* and *didn't use to* in their sentences.
- GROUPS. Have students complete the task.
- WRAP UP. Write two column headings on the board: *Positive Changes* and *Negative Changes*. Have the group secretaries take turns reading their groups' sentences. Write the sentences on the board in the correct column. Correct sentences as needed.

Expansion Start a discussion of the ideas on the board. Ask if everyone in the class agrees about which changes are positive and which changes are negative. Ask students who disagree to explain their opinions. Then have someone from the group who wrote the sentence defend the group's opinion.

Reading

Getting Ready to Read
Teaching Time: 3–5 min.

- Before students read the article, have them scan it to find which type of transportation came first, second, third, and fourth.
- Have students complete the task.

Reading
Teaching Time: 15–20 min.

- Have students read the article.
- Tell students to check their answers to the prereading exercise.
- Call on a student to give the answer. Ask for the paragraph and line number where the student found the answer. (paragraph 2, line 1)

Multilevel Strategy

- **Pre-level:** Give students more time to read the article.
- **At-level, Above-level:** Write the questions below on the board. When students finish reading, have them scan the article to find the answers. When the pre-level students have had enough time to read the article, have the other students read their answers to the questions on the board. Tell them to give the paragraph and line number where they found the answer.

  Before the 1800s, how did people use to get places? (They used to walk or ride horses.)

  When was the horsecar first used? (in the 1840s)

  Which type of transportation was invented in the 1880s? (the electric trolley)

  When did New York's subway open? (in 1904)

  When did public transportation in the United States start to get worse? (in 1908, with the invention of the Model T car)

  In 1908, what did the U.S. government start to spend a lot of money on? (highways)

Getting Ready to Read

Look at the pictures. Check (✓) which kind of transportation came first.

rails

❑ electric trolley   ❑ horsecar   ❑ Model T car   ☑ omnibus

Reading

Read the article. Was your answer to Getting Ready to Read correct?

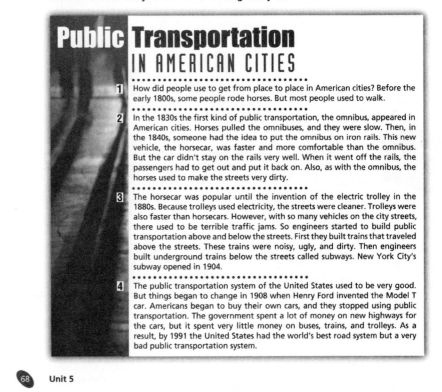

Public Transportation
IN AMERICAN CITIES

1 How did people use to get from place to place in American cities? Before the early 1800s, some people rode horses. But most people used to walk.

2 In the 1830s the first kind of public transportation, the omnibus, appeared in American cities. Horses pulled the omnibuses, and they were slow. Then, in the 1840s, someone had the idea to put the omnibus on iron rails. This new vehicle, the horsecar, was faster and more comfortable than the omnibus. But the car didn't stay on the rails very well. When it went off the rails, the passengers had to get out and put it back on. Also, as with the omnibus, the horses used to make the streets very dirty.

3 The horsecar was popular until the invention of the electric trolley in the 1880s. Because trolleys used electricity, the streets were cleaner. Trolleys were also faster than horsecars. However, with so many vehicles on the city streets, there used to be terrible traffic jams. So engineers started to build public transportation above and below the streets. First they built trains that traveled above the streets. These trains were noisy, ugly, and dirty. Then engineers built underground trains below the streets called subways. New York City's subway opened in 1904.

4 The public transportation system of the United States used to be very good. But things began to change in 1908 when Henry Ford invented the Model T car. Americans began to buy their own cars, and they stopped using public transportation. The government spent a lot of money on new highways for the cars, but it spent very little money on buses, trains, and trolleys. As a result, by 1991 the United States had the world's best road system but a very bad public transportation system.

68   Unit 5

Option

After students complete the reading exercises, have them skim the article and underline the verbs with *used to*.

After You Read

After You Read

A Check (✓) the features the article mentions for each type of transportation.

	OMNIBUS	HORSECAR	ELECTRIC TROLLEY
clean			✓
dirty	✓	✓	
comfortable		✓	
uncomfortable	✓		
fast		✓	✓
slow	✓		
with horses	✓	✓	
without horses			✓

B Read the article again. What is the main topic of the article?

<u>the history of public transportation in</u>

<u>American cities</u>

What is the topic of each paragraph? Write the paragraph number next to its topic.

__3__ electric transportation

__2__ the earliest public transportation

__1__ transportation before the 1800s

__4__ the car's effect on transportation

Reading Skill:
Identifying Topics

Identifying **topics** in a reading will help you to understand it. The main topic connects all of the paragraphs in the reading. Each paragraph also has its own topic. The topic of each paragraph develops part of the main topic.

Then and Now **69**

- Read the example with the class.
- Tell students to scan the text and find the information as quickly as they can, and circle the place in the text where they found it. When they have all of the answers, tell them to raise their hands.
- Have students complete the task.
- While the students are doing the exercise, copy the chart onto the board.
- Call on students to say answers, and complete the chart. Ask them where they found the answers (paragraph and line number). Correct as needed.

B Teaching Time: 10–15 min.

- Call on a student to read the information in the Reading Skill box. Make sure that students understand the difference between the topic of an article and the topic of each paragraph in the article. Explain that the topic of the whole article will always be more general than the topic of any one paragraph within it.
- Have students complete the tasks.
- Have students read their answers. Correct as needed.
- Draw the following diagram on the board.

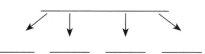

- Ask a volunteer to come up to the board and write the main topic on the top line of the diagram (the history of public transportation in American cities). Correct as needed.
- Have another student come up to the board and write the topics of the paragraphs, from left to right, in the order in which they appeared in the reading (transportation before the 1800s; the earliest public transportation; electric transportation; the car's effect on transportation). Correct as needed.

Writing

Getting Ready to Write

A **Teaching Time: 10–15 min.**

A **Teaching Time: 10–15 min.**

- Have students study the Writing Tip.
- Have a student read the example. Ask the class: *Why are the two sentences combined with* and? (because they are affirmative) *When should we use* or? (when we combine two negative sentences)
- Have students complete the task.
- Call on students to write their answers on the board. Write corrections on the board as needed.

B **Teaching Time: 10–15 min.**

- Have students read the writing model.
- PAIRS. Have students complete the task.

Expansion Have students underline the main verbs in the model that go with *used to*. Write them on the board (*have; drive; stay; do; have; walk; ride; be; ride*).

Writing

Getting Ready to Write

A Combine the two sentences. Use *and* or *or*.

1. My sister and I used to ride our bikes in nice weather. We used to walk in bad weather.

   My sister and I used to ride our bikes in nice
   weather and walk in bad weather.

2. We didn't use to take the bus. We didn't use to drive.

   We didn't use to take the bus or drive.

3. Parents didn't use to drop their kids off at school. Parents didn't use to pick them up after school.

   Parents didn't use to drop their kids off at school or pick them up after school.

4. Most families used to live close to their workplaces. Most families used to share one car.

   Most families used to live close to their workplaces and share one car.

5. People used to buy one car. People used to keep it for years.

   People used to buy one car and keep it for years.

B Read the model paragraph.

> In the United States, cars were much less common in the past than they are today. Fifty years ago, <u>families used to have only one car.</u> In most families, the father used to drive the car to work. The mother used to stay at home and do housework. Teenagers didn't use to have their own cars. They used to walk or ride their bikes everywhere. Things are different now. <u>Families often have several cars.</u> Often, all the people in the family have their own cars. It's more convenient now, but because so many people have cars, there's a lot more traffic and pollution than there used to be. Maybe things were better before when people used to ride bikes!

PAIRS. Read the model again. How many cars did Americans use to have, and how many do they have now? Is this true in your country?

Now talk about the way something used to be and the way it is now. You can talk about transportation, roles of men and women, free time activities, food, school life, work life, or your own idea.

Writing Tip

If you have one subject with two verbs with *used to*, write *used to* only one time. For affirmative sentences, join the two verbs with *and*. For negative sentences, use *or*.

Examples:

Americans used to walk or ride in carriages.

Poor people didn't use to own horses or ride in carriages.

Language Note

Writing Tip

- Make sure students understand that they can only combine sentences in this way if both sentences have the same subject. Write on the board: *My sister and I used to ride our bikes in nice weather. My brother used to walk.*
- Circle the different subjects.
- Say: *You can still join two sentences with* and *if the subjects are different, but you must repeat* used to.
- Write: *My sister and I used to ride our bikes in nice weather, <u>and</u> my brother <u>used to walk.</u>*

Prewriting: Using an Outline

You are going to write a paragraph about the way something used to be and the way it is now. Before you write, choose a main topic from the list, or choose your own main topic.

- Transportation
- Roles of men and women
- Free time activities
- Food
- School life
- Work life

Read the outline for the writing model. Then complete your outline with notes about your topic.

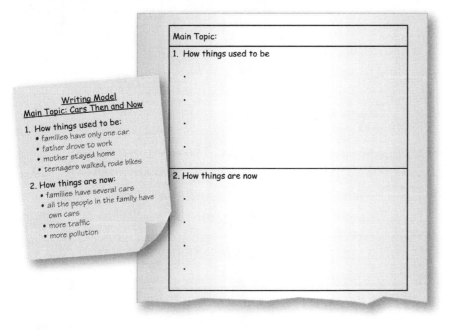

Writing Model
Main Topic: Cars Then and Now

1. How things used to be:
   - families have only one car
   - father drove to work
   - mother stayed home
   - teenagers walked, rode bikes

2. How things are now:
   - families have several cars
   - all the people in the family have own cars
   - more traffic
   - more pollution

Main Topic:

1. How things used to be
   -
   -
   -

2. How things are now
   -
   -
   -
   -

Writing

Now write a paragraph about the way something used to be and the way it is now. The writing tip, the model paragraph, and your notes will help you. Write in your notebook.

Then and Now 71

Prewriting

Teaching Time: 10–15 min.

- Give students a few minutes to choose a topic. Tell them that they can change their topics later if they want to.

- While students are choosing their topics, copy the outline for the writing model on the board.

- Explain what an outline is. Point to the outline on the board, and explain how it shows the relationship among the main topic, the subtopics, and the details. Explain that *sub-* means *under*. Explain that outlines show which ideas are most general and which ideas are most specific.

- Point to each part of the outline, and name it. Say and point: *Main topic (most general), subtopic 1 (more specific), details for subtopic 1 (most specific); subtopic 2, details for subtopic 2.*

- Have students complete the task. Allow them to change their topics if they want to. If they choose a topic that is not on the list, tell them to check with you before beginning the outline.

- Have students show you their outlines before the end of class. They shouldn't write their paragraphs until you have approved their outlines.

Multilevel Strategy

- **Pre-level:** Have pre-level students sit together in one group. Sit with them and help them get started on their outlines.

- **At-level, Above-level:** After the pre-level students have gotten started, walk around and assist other students. Encourage them to show their outlines to each other, and to give each other feedback. If possible, pair each at-level student with an above-level writer.

Writing

Teaching Time: 15–20 min.

- Assign the paragraph writing for homework. Encourage students to refer to the model in the book and their outlines as they write. Remind them to use *used to* when they write about things that were one way in the past, but are different now.

- Before students hand in their paragraphs, tell them to review the grammar summaries on page 285. Have them check for and correct errors in *used to* in their paragraphs.

Unit 6
Busy Lives

Learning Goals

- Learn vocabulary related to everyday life
- Learn about *will* and *be going to* and the present progressive for future arrangements
- Listen to a conversation between a mother and son about schedules and to short conversational exchanges containing set expressions used in shops, cabs, restaurants, etc.
- Read an article about personal assistants and write a paragraph about future plans
- Talk about future plans and arrangements
- Practice brief conversations with set expressions

Learner Persistence

Have students who are familiar with the class orient new students as they enter. Students who feel welcomed in your class are more likely to persist.

Warm-up

Teaching Time: 3–5 min.

- Take an informal poll. Have students raise their hands if they feel that their lives are too busy.
- Start a discussion about how students deal with all of the things that they have to do. Ask how many different things they do in a day. Ask how much free time they have every day and every week.

Vocabulary

Teaching Time: 10–15 min.

- Read the example with the class.
- Have students complete the task.
- 🎧 Play Track 36 while students listen and check their answers.
- Say each word or phrase and have students repeat chorally.

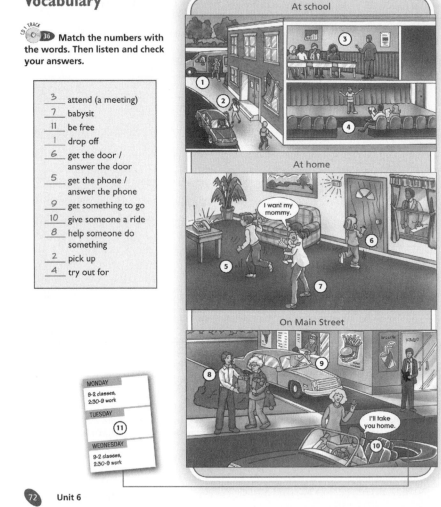

Expansion Write the following questions on the board, and have students ask and answer them in pairs.

Which of the activities in the picture do you do every day?
Which of the activities do you do every week?
Which of the activities do you never do?

Listening

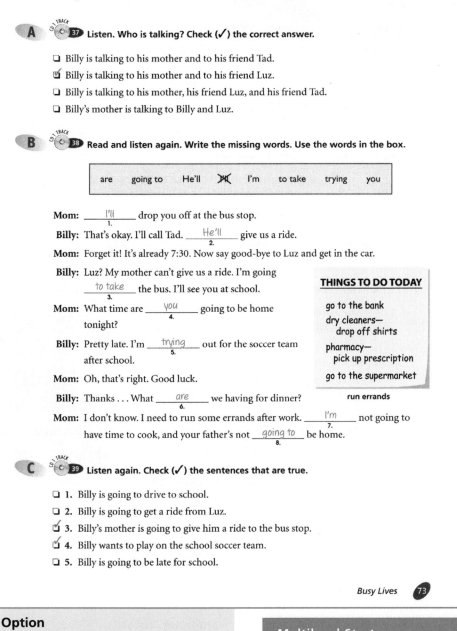

A 🎧 37 **Listen. Who is talking? Check (✓) the correct answer.**

❑ Billy is talking to his mother and to his friend Tad.

☑ Billy is talking to his mother and to his friend Luz.

❑ Billy is talking to his mother, his friend Luz, and his friend Tad.

❑ Billy's mother is talking to Billy and Luz.

B 🎧 38 **Read and listen again. Write the missing words. Use the words in the box.**

are	going to	He'll	~~I~~	I'm	to take	trying	you

Mom: _____I'll_____ drop you off at the bus stop.
1.

Billy: That's okay. I'll call Tad. _____He'll_____ give us a ride.
2.

Mom: Forget it! It's already 7:30. Now say good-bye to Luz and get in the car.

Billy: Luz? My mother can't give us a ride. I'm going _____to take_____ the bus. I'll see you at school.
3.

Mom: What time are _____you_____ going to be home tonight?
4.

Billy: Pretty late. I'm _____trying_____ out for the soccer team after school.
5.

Mom: Oh, that's right. Good luck.

Billy: Thanks . . . What _____are_____ we having for dinner?
6.

Mom: I don't know. I need to run some errands after work. _____I'm_____ not going to
7.
have time to cook, and your father's not _____going to_____ be home.
8.

> **THINGS TO DO TODAY**
>
> go to the bank
> dry cleaners—
>   drop off shirts
> pharmacy—
>   pick up prescription
> go to the supermarket
>
> **run errands**

C 🎧 39 **Listen again. Check (✓) the sentences that are true.**

❑ 1. Billy is going to drive to school.

❑ 2. Billy is going to get a ride from Luz.

☑ 3. Billy's mother is going to give him a ride to the bus stop.

☑ 4. Billy wants to play on the school soccer team.

❑ 5. Billy is going to be late for school.

Busy Lives **73**

Option

Assign Unit 6 Supplementary Vocabulary Exercises on the Teacher's Resource Disk as homework or on the Student Persistence CD-ROM as self-access practice.

Multilevel Strategy

Pre-level: Make photocopies of the audioscript. Give it to students before they do exercise C.

Listening

A **Teaching Time: 10–15 min.**

- **Warm-up:** Have students read the directions and the answer choices. Ask if the names Tad and Luz are men's or women's names. (Tad = man; Luz = woman)

- 🎧 Play Track 37 while students listen and complete the task.

- 🎧 Play Track 37 again, pausing it at the point where the answer becomes clear.

- Call on a student to say the answer.

Expansion Have students look at the list of vocabulary on page 72 as they listen. Tell them to circle the words that they hear in the listening exercise.

B **Teaching Time: 10–15 min.**

- Tell students to look at the Things to Do Today list. Make sure they understand the word *errands* by asking them to give examples of other common errands that are not on the list.

- Have students read the directions and the words in the box. Pronounce *He'll* and *I'll* and have students repeat chorally.

- 🎧 Play Track 38 while students listen and complete the task.

- 🎧 Play Track 38 again, pausing after each of the answers is given.

- Call on students to say answers. Correct as needed.

- PAIRS. Have students role-play the conversation. Ask for volunteers to perform their role-play for the class.

C **Teaching Time: 10–15 min.**

- Have students complete the task without the audio. If they are not sure of an answer, tell them to write a question mark (?).

- 🎧 Play Track 39 as students check their answers.

- 🎧 Play Track 39 again, pausing after each of the answers is given.

- Call on students to read the sentences that they checked. Correct as needed.

Expansion Have students correct the sentences that they did not check to make them true.

Grammar to Communicate 1

Future: *Will* for Decisions and Promises

Teaching Time: 5–10 min.

- Have students study the chart and the Look Box.
- Say: *We use will + the base form of the verb when we decide to do something without planning it first. For example, if you hear the phone ring, you say, "I'll get it." You didn't know that the phone would ring. You decide at that moment to answer it. You didn't plan to answer it.*
- Say: *We use will with all subjects.* Write on the board:
  I'll do it.
  You'll do it.
  She'll do it.
  He'll do it.
  They'll do it.
  We'll do it.
- Say: *When we speak, we almost always make a contraction with* will. *It can be difficult to hear the contracted* will, *so let's practice listening and saying it.*
- Read the sentences on the board aloud, and have students repeat chorally.
- Write the negatives on the board: *I won't do it; You won't do it,* etc.
- Say: *The contraction of* will not *is* won't. *The pronunciation of* won't *can be difficult. Let's practice it.*
- Read the negative sentences aloud, and have students repeat chorally. Correct pronunciation as needed.

 A Teaching Time: 5–10 min.

- Call on two students to read the example.
- Have students complete the task.
- Ask for two volunteers. Have one student read the statements and the other student the responses. Correct as needed.

B Teaching Time: 10–15 min.

- 🎧 Play Track 40 while students listen and complete the task.
- 🎧 Play Track 40 again, pausing as each answer is read.
- Call on students to read the answers. Correct as needed.

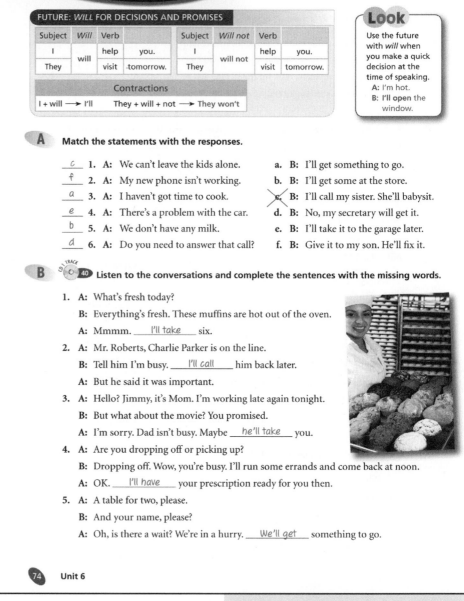

- PAIRS. Have students read the conversations in pairs. Tell them to guess where the people are and who they are talking to.

Multilevel Strategy

- **Pre-level:** Before students listen to the recording, give them a handout with a list of the verbs arranged in alphabetical order. Have them fill in the blanks with the verbs (*call, get, have, take*) and *I'll, we'll,* or *he'll.*

Grammar Notes

1. Use *will* for an action that you decide to do at the time you are talking.
2. Use *will* or *won't* when you make a promise.
3. Use *will* or *won't* with all subjects.
4. For more information on this grammar topic, see page 285.

C What promises do these people make? Use *won't* or *will* and the words in the box.

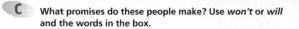

Look

Use the future with *will* or *won't* when you make a promise.
I'll do it tomorrow. I promise.

answer babysit be forget give open ~~wash~~

1. The dishes are in the sink. Paul is busy right now. What does he promise his wife?
   "I ___will wash___ them later."

2. Sara has to work on Saturday, but she doesn't want to leave her kids alone. What do her parents promise?
   "We ___will babysit___."

3. Lori's boss wants her to work late on Mondays, but she is worried about taking the bus late at night. What does her boss promise?
   "I ___will give___ you a ride home."

4. It's Carl's lunch hour, and he's getting something to go. What does the server promise?
   "Your food ___will be___ ready in ten minutes."

5. Dan forgot to pick his brother up after class last week. What does Dan promise?
   "I ___won't forget___ this time."

6. Vera's working late. Her kids are alone at home. What do they promise?
   "Don't worry. We ___won't open___ the door for anyone."

7. Ed's boss always call him during dinner. His wife is angry. What does Ed promise?
   "I ___won't answer___ the phone during dinner anymore."

TIME to TALK

PAIRS. Write three short conversations. Use a different sentence in the box in each conversation. Use the conversations in Exercise B as models.

"Don't worry. I'll help you do it."	"Thanks! I'll remember this!"
"We'll help you find an apartment."	"He'll pick them up for you."
"My husband will give you a ride."	"I'll get something to go."

Example:
A: *I don't want to paint my apartment. It's so much work.*
B: *Don't worry. I'll help you do it.*
A: *Really? That's great!*

WRAP UP. Now act out one of your conversations for the class.

Busy Lives 75

- Have students study the Look Box. Say: *We use* will *when we make a quick decision without planning. We also use* will *when we make a promise to someone. Some promises are negative; they mean that you are promising NOT to do something. For example, dentists often say, "I won't hurt you."* Write *I won't hurt you* on the board.
- Call on a student to read the example.
- Have students complete the task.
- Call on students to read their answers. Correct as needed.

Expansion PAIRS. Have students role-play the situations. One student says something, and the other student responds with the promises from the exercise. Encourage students to use contractions in their role-plays. For example:

A: *Just look at all these dirty dishes.*
B: *I'll wash them later.*

Multilevel Strategy

Pre-level: Pair pre-level students for the expansion activity. Give them a worksheet with the first line for each role play, arranged out of order. Tell them to match each line to the appropriate response and then role-play the conversations. (2: "The babysitter's sick, and I have to work on Saturday night." 3: "I don't have a car, and it's not safe for me to take the bus at night." 4: "I'm in a hurry. How long do you think it will take?" 5. "Please remember to pick me up this time." 6: "Remember: If someone comes to the door, don't open it." 7: "Why does your boss always call at dinnertime?")

Option

Assign Unit 6 Supplementary Grammar to Communicate 1 Exercises on the Teacher's Resource Disk as homework or on the Student Persistence CD-ROM as self-access practice.

TIME to TALK

Teaching Time: 10–15 min.

- Read the directions with the class. Have two students read the example.
- PAIRS. Have students complete the task.
- WRAP UP. Ask volunteers to role-play their conversations in front of the class.

Grammar to Communicate 2

Future: *Be going to* and *Will*

Teaching Time: 5–10 min.

- Have students study the chart.
- Draw the following chart on the board, and have students complete it with the correct forms of *be*.

Subject	verb be— am/is/ are	*going to*	base form of verb
I		going to	make a cake.
You			
He			
She			
They			
We			

- Write the following examples on the board:
  1. *A: Was that the doorbell?*
     B: Yes. I'll get it.
  2. *A: What are you going to buy Ed for his birthday?*
     B: I'm going to buy him a watch. How about you?
  3. *A: Don't forget to pick me up.*
     B: Don't worry. I won't be late this time.

  Ask students: *Which example shows a plan?* (2) *Which example shows a promise?* (3) *Which example shows a quick decision?* (1)

A Teaching Time: 5–10 min.

- Copy the example onto the board. Then write next to it:
  A: Honey, I'm going to get some gas.
  B: Okay.
- Ask students to compare the two conversations. Say: *In the example from the book, A just told B that there wasn't any gas. B didn't know that they needed gas, so we know he didn't make a plan to get gas. However, in the example on the board, A has already decided to get some gas. He's telling B about his plan.*
- Have students complete the task.
- Call on students to say answers. Correct as needed.

Grammar to
Communicate 2

FUTURE: *BE GOING TO* AND *WILL*	
Rule	**Example**
Use *be going to* for future actions that you plan before the time of speaking.	**A:** Why are the eggs, sugar, and flour on the kitchen table? **B:** I'm going to make a cake. It's Ed's birthday tomorrow.
Use *will* for future actions that you decide at the time of speaking.	**A:** It's Ed's birthday tomorrow. **B:** Really? I'll make him a cake. He likes chocolate, right?
Use *will* for promises about the future.	**A:** Can we go to Ed's birthday party? **B:** I'm sorry, but I have to work this weekend. We'll visit him next weekend. I promise.

A What is the meaning of the **boldface** words? What is the speaker talking about? Write **PL** (a plan before the time of speaking), **D** (a decision at the time of speaking), or **P** (a promise).

D 1. **A:** We need to get some gas.
   B: Okay. I**'ll stop** at the next station.

PL 2. **A:** Who's picking up the kids tomorrow?
   B: Betty. She**'s going to be** here at 3:00.

D 3. **A:** I need a ride home.
   B: Amy's got a car. She**'ll take** you.

PL 4. **A:** **Are you going to try out** for the play?
   B: No, I haven't got time this year.

P 5. **A:** But you said we could go to the zoo.
   B: I**'ll take** you next week. I promise.

PL 6. **A:** Do you need help with the kids?
   B: No, my Mom**'s going to babysit**.

B CD 1 TRACK 41 Complete the conversations. Circle the correct answer. Then listen and check your answers.

1. **Joe:** Why are you putting on your sneakers?
   Tim: (I'm going to)/ I'll play soccer.

2. **Amy:** Are you free this evening?
   Ann: No, (I'm going to)/ I'll babysit for the Miller kids.

3. **Paul:** I'm tired.
   Tina: Then give me the keys. I'm going to / (I'll) drive.

4. **Lisa:** Mom's busy tonight and can't take me to the party.
   Dad: I told you yesterday. (I'm going to)/ I'll take you to the party.

5. **Fran:** You have a new schedule at work, right?
   Adam: Yes. (I'm not going to)/ I won't work on weekends anymore.

76 Unit 6

B Teaching Time: 10–15 min.

- Read the first item with the class. Ask: *Is it a plan?* (yes) *How do you know?* (Joe is putting on his soccer clothes, so we know that he's already decided to play soccer.)
- Have students complete the task.
- 🎧 Play Track 41 as students listen and correct their answers. Pause the recording as each answer is given.
- Call on students to say answers. For sentences with *be going to* (2, 4, and 5), ask how they know it's a plan, and not a promise or a quick decision. (2: Ann isn't free because she already decided to babysit; 4: Dad told her yesterday; 5: Adam already knows his new schedule.)

Grammar Notes

1. Use *be going to* to tell someone about your plans: actions that you have already decided to do.

2. Use *will* for an action that you decide to do at the time you are talking. You don't have a plan. You just decide at that moment. Do <u>not</u> use a form of *be going to* when you decide to do something at the time you are talking.

3. Use *will* or *won't* when you make a promise. Do <u>not</u> use a form of *be going to* when you make a promise.

4. For more information on this grammar topic, see page 285.

T-76 Center Stage 3

C Complete the conversations. Use *will* or the correct form of *be going to*. Then listen and check your answers.

1. **Rao:** Could you get sandwiches for the party?

   Ada: I talked to Charlie yesterday. He_'s going to get_ the sandwiches. (get) But I _'ll get_ the drinks. (get)

2. **Clara:** Why is the soap and water outside?

   Felix: I _'m going to wash_ the car. (wash)

3. **Solana:** Is this your plane ticket?

   Renée: No, it's Javier's. He _'s going to visit_ his parents next month. (visit)

4. **Sarita:** Please hurry. My train leaves at 6:00.

   Cab driver: Don't worry. I _'ll get_ you there on time. (get)

5. **Sergei:** Why do you need the car?

   Barbara: We _'re going to run_ some errands. (run)

6. **Matt:** Did you make an appointment for Tammy?

   Juan: Yes, the doctor _is going to see_ her tomorrow at 2:00. (see)

7. **Rita:** Mr. Miller called.

   Ming: Oh, good, thanks. I _'ll call_ him back right away. (call)

8. **Max:** Are you going to pick up Andy after school?

   Sheila: No, he _'s going to get_ a ride from Sue. She drives on Mondays. (get)

9. **Robert:** I'm late for work.

   Irene: I've got the car today. I _'ll give_ you a ride. (give)

TIME to TALK

PAIRS. **Do a role play. Sam and Stella are 17 years old. Sam is picking Stella up for their first date. Stella's father has a lot of questions for Sam. Write a conversation between Stella's father and Sam.**

Student A: You are Stella's father. This is Stella's first date. You want to know exactly what she and Sam are going to do. Ask Sam questions.
Student B: You are Sam. Answer Stella's father's questions politely. Use *be going to* to talk about your plans. Try to get him to trust you. Make promises.

Example:
A: *Is that the doorbell? I'll get it.*
B: *Good evening, Mr. Davis. I'm Sam. It's very nice to meet you.*
A: *It's nice to meet you, too. Please come in. . . . So, Sam, where are you going to take my daughter tonight?*

WRAP UP. **Now act out your role play for the class.**

Busy Lives **77**

C Teaching Time: 10–15 min.

- Have two students read the example. Ask the class to explain why Ada uses *be going to* in her first sentence, but *will* in the second. (Charlie has already decided to get the sandwiches. We know that's his plan because he told Ada yesterday. In the second sentence, Ada is responding to a request at that moment, and she's also promising to do something, so she uses *will*.)
- Have students complete the task.
- Play Track 42 and have students check their answers. Pause the recording after each item, and have students call out the answers. Ask them whether the action is a plan, a promise, or a decision. Correct as needed.

Expansion Have students work in pairs to identify each of the actions as a plan, a promise, or a decision before they write their answers. Tell them to circle the words in the context that helped them decide.

Option

Assign Unit 6 Supplementary Grammar to Communicate 2 Exercises on the Teacher's Resource Disk as homework or on the Student Persistence CD-ROM as self-access practice.

TIME to TALK

Teaching Time: 10–15 min.

- Call on two students to read the example aloud.
- PAIRS. For each pair, assign a Student A and a Student B. Have students complete the task.
- WRAP UP. Ask for volunteers to perform their role play for the class.
- Wait until the role plays are finished to make corrections. Then write errors on the board and have the class correct them.

Multilevel Strategy

Pre-level: Pair pre-level students for this activity. Give them a worksheet with a conversation between Sam and Stella's father already written, but with the verbs in the base form. Tell students to complete the conversation with *be going to* or *will*, and then practice reading it. Call on at least one pair of pre-level students to perform their role play for the class.

Future: Present Progressive for Future Arrangements

Teaching Time: 5–10 min.

- Have students study the chart.
- Read the first sentence in the chart aloud and ask: *What is the time?* (future—tomorrow) *What is the verb tense?* (present progressive)
- Say: *Sometimes we use the present progressive instead of* be going to *when we are talking about our future plans. We usually do this when the plans are very certain because we have already made specific arrangements. For example, we have already bought tickets. We can also use* be going to *in these situations.*
- Write this example on the board:
  I'm flying to New York tomorrow.
  I have a ticket for the 9:00 flight.
  OR
  I'm going to fly to New York tomorrow.
- Read the sentences in the chart and have students repeat chorally.

A   Teaching Time: 5–10 min.

- Read the example with the class. Explain that when we write things on our calendars, they are usually things that we are sure we are going to do. We have already arranged to do them. For example, we have made an appointment or bought tickets. That is why we can use the present progressive to describe those activities.
- Have students complete the task.
- Call on students to read their answers. Correct as needed.

B   Teaching Time: 5–10 min.

- Have a student read the example.
- Have students complete the task.
- Call on students to read their answers. Correct as needed.

Expansion Ask students who have personal calendars with them to raise their hands. Pair them with students who don't have calendars. (If more than half the class has calendars, it's fine to pair up students who each have calendars.) Have them look at their calendars and talk about their plans for

the next week and/or month. Tell them to use the present progressive. Have their partners ask them questions.

Grammar to Communicate 3

FUTURE: PRESENT PROGRESSIVE FOR FUTURE ARRANGEMENTS

Statements	
Lynn is babysitting tomorrow night.	She isn't babysitting tomorrow morning.

Yes / No Question	Short Answers	
Are you babysitting tomorrow night?	Yes, I am.	No, I'm not.

Information Questions	Answers
What is Lynn doing tomorrow night?	She's babysitting.
Where are you babysitting tomorrow night?	At the Petrov's.

A Look at the October calendar of Jimena and Mike Romero and their children, Annie and Paul. Circle the correct answers.

SUNDAY	MONDAY	TUESDAY	WEDNESDAY	THURSDAY	FRIDAY	SATURDAY
1 M-help Oscar move	2	3 J & M- neighborhood meeting 8 P.M.	4	5 J & M look at new apartment 5:30 P.M.	6 A-babysit 7 P.M.	7 P-baseball game J & M-salsa night
8 P's birthday party	9 A-try out for school play	10 A-dentist appointment 2 P.M.	11	12 J & M-parent/teacher night 6:15	13	14 P-try out for soccer team

1. Annie **is** / **isn't** trying out for the school play on October 9th.
2. Jimena and Mike **are** / **aren't** meeting their children's teachers on October 5th.
3. Jimena **is** / **isn't** taking Annie to the dentist on October 10th.
4. Jimena and Mike **are** / **aren't** looking at a new apartment on October 3rd.
5. Jimena and Mike **are** / **aren't** going dancing on October 7th.

B Complete the sentences about the Romero family's busy schedule. Use the correct forms of the verbs from the box. (Today is Saturday, September 30th.)

attend	take
have	try out for
~~help~~	

1. Mike ___is helping___ Oscar move tomorrow.
2. Paul ___is trying out for___ the soccer team in two weeks.
3. Jimena says, "I ___'m taking___ Paul to his baseball game next Saturday."
4. Mike says, "We ___aren't having___ a birthday party for Paul next week."
5. Jimena and Mike ___are attending___ a neighborhood meeting in a few days.

78 Unit 6

Grammar Notes

1. Use the present progressive for the future when the future activity was planned or arranged in advance (before the moment of speaking).

2. When we use the present progressive for the future, we usually use a time expression. Without a time expression, people understand the present progressive is for *now*.

3. You can always use *be going to* + verb instead of the present progressive for future activities that are planned or arranged in advance.

4. For more information on this grammar topic, see pages 285–286.

C Complete the questions about next week.

1. Jim usually works on Tuesday night. _____Is he working_____ next Tuesday night?

2. Cindy usually visits relatives on Sunday. _____Is she visiting relatives_____ next Sunday?

3. Chris usually cleans on Saturday. _____Is she cleaning_____ next Saturday?

4. Javier and Luisa usually go dancing on Saturday night. _____Are they going dancing_____ next Saturday?

5. Mia and Luis usually go food shopping on Monday night. _____Are they going food shopping_____ next Monday?

6. Jenny usually gets a ride to work on Fridays. _____Is she getting a ride to work_____ this Friday?

PAIRS. **Find out about your partner's schedule next week. Ask and answer the questions above.**

Example: A: *Are you working next Tuesday night?*
B: *Yes, I am.* OR *No, I'm not.*

D 🎧 **43** **Complete the conversation. Use the present progressive. Then listen and check your answers.**

Alba: _____Are you doing_____ anything after class?
_{1. (you / do)}

Lili: I _'m picking up_ my daughter from day care.
_{2. (pick up)}
Why? What _____are you doing_____?
_{3. (you / do)}

Alba: I _'m having_ lunch with Jenny and Elena. We wanted to invite you.
_{4. (have)}

Lili: Oh, that's nice! I'm sorry I can't go. Where _____are you going_____?
_{5. (you / go)}

Alba: To Jenny's house. She _'s cooking_.
_{6. (cook)}

Lili: Now I'm really sorry I can't go! How _____are you getting_____ there?
_{7. (you / get)}

Alba: We _'re taking_ the subway. Why?
_{8. (take)}

Lili: I _'m driving_ that way. I'll give you a ride.
_{9. (drive)}

TIME to TALK

GROUPS. **Plan a time to get together for a party. When is everyone in the group free? Ask and answer questions about your schedules.**

Example:
A: *I'm free on Tuesday evening. What are you doing on Tuesday?*
B: *Tuesday's not good for me. I'm working late. How about Thursday night? I'm not working on Thursday.*

Busy Lives **79**

C Teaching Time: 10–15 min.

- Read the example with the class.
- Have students complete the task.
- Call on students to read their questions. Correct as needed.
- PAIRS. Have students ask and answer the questions about their own schedules.

D Teaching Time: 5–10 min.

- Call on a student to read the example.
- Have students complete the task.
- 🎧 Play Track 43 while students listen and check their answers. Pause the recording as each answer is given.
- Ask for two volunteers to read the conversation. Correct as needed.

Option

Assign Unit 6 Supplementary Grammar to Communicate 3 Exercises on the Teacher's Resource Disk as homework or on the Student Persistence CD-ROM as self-access practice.

TIME to TALK

Teaching Time: 10–15 min.

- Call on two students to read the example.
- GROUPS. Have students complete the task. Walk around and help as needed.

Expansion Have students plan a class party. Have them decide on the place, food, music, and any other details. Then have the party!

Grammar

Teaching Time: 5–10 min.

- Have two students read the example.
- Remind students that the present progressive and *be going to* are both for future arrangements.
- Have students complete the task.
- 🎧 Play Track 44 and have students check their answers.
- 🎧 Play Track 44 again, this time pausing each time an answer is given.
- Call on students to read the answers. Have them identify whether the action is a plan, a decision made at the time of speaking, or a promise. Point out that the present progressive and *be going to* are correct for numbers 3, 4, and 6.

Dictation

Teaching Time: 5–10 min.

- 🎧 Play Track 45 while students listen and write what they hear.
- 🎧 Play Track 45 again while students check their answers.
- Call on students to write answers on the board.
- 🎧 Play Track 45 again and have a student volunteer correct the sentences on the board. Provide help as needed.

Multilevel Strategy

- **Pre-level:** Give students a worksheet with some of the words from the dictation already provided.

Speaking

Teaching Time: 10–15 min.

- PAIRS. Have students complete the first part of the task.
- Have students say their sentences to the class as their classmates guess who is talking. Correct as needed.

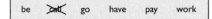

Review and Challenge

Grammar

🔊 **44** Complete the conversations. Write the correct future form of the verbs in the box. Some are affirmative, and some are negative. Then listen and check your answers.

be	~~call~~	go	have	pay	work

1. **A:** Bye, darling. Have a good day.
    B: Bye-bye. I _'ll call_____ you later.

2. **A:** Oh, no! I haven't got my wallet with me!
    B: That's OK. I _'ll pay_____. You can pay next time.

3. **A:** Is Linda pregnant?
    B: Yes, she _'s going to have_ a baby in three months.

4. **A:** So, what did you decide? _____ _Are_____ you
    _____ _going_____ to New York this weekend?
    B: No, we haven't got the money.

5. **A:** Don't forget about tonight.
    B: Don't worry. We _____ _won't be_____ late.

6. **A:** Which days _____ _are_____ you _going to work_ this week?
    B: Monday to Saturday. I'm off on Sunday.

Dictation

🔊 **45** Listen. You will hear five sentences. Write them in your notebook. *See the audioscript on p. 313 for the sentences.*

Speaking

PAIRS. **Look at the pictures on page 72. What are the people in the pictures saying? Use** *will*, *be going to*, **or the present progressive.**

Example:
A: *Oh, honey. Please don't cry. Your mommy will be home very soon. I promise.*

Say your sentences to the class. Can they guess who is talking?

Example:
B: *The babysitter is talking to the little girl.*
A: *You're right.*

80 Unit 6

Multilevel Strategy

Pre-level: Pair pre-level students for this activity. Give them a worksheet with sentences for the people in the pictures on page 72 already written out, but with the verbs written in the base form. Tell students to complete the sentences with *be going to, will,* or the present progressive.

Listening

A 🎧 **46** Listen. Who is talking in each conversation? Check (✓) the correct column.

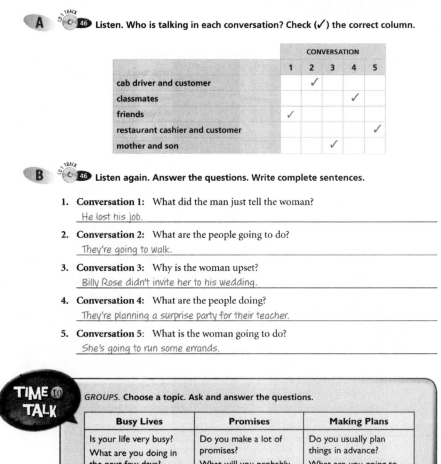

	CONVERSATION 1	2	3	4	5
cab driver and customer		✓			
classmates				✓	
friends	✓				
restaurant cashier and customer					✓
mother and son			✓		

B 🎧 **46** Listen again. Answer the questions. Write complete sentences.

1. **Conversation 1:** What did the man just tell the woman?
   He lost his job.

2. **Conversation 2:** What are the people going to do?
   They're going to walk.

3. **Conversation 3:** Why is the woman upset?
   Billy Rose didn't invite her to his wedding.

4. **Conversation 4:** What are the people doing?
   They're planning a surprise party for their teacher.

5. **Conversation 5:** What is the woman going to do?
   She's going to run some errands.

TIME to TALK

GROUPS. **Choose a topic. Ask and answer the questions.**

Busy Lives	Promises	Making Plans
Is your life very busy? What are you doing in the next few days?	Do you make a lot of promises? What will you probably do for someone this week?	Do you usually plan things in advance? What are you going to do this month? This year?

Example:
A: I choose Busy Lives.
B: Is your life very busy?
A: Yes, it is. Today, I'm working until 9:00. I'm going to get home late, so I'll study Monday.

Busy Lives **81**

Listening

A Teaching Time: 5–10 min.

- **Warm-up:** Tell students they will hear a series of short conversations.
- Have students read the answer choices.
- 🎧 Play Track 46 while students listen and complete the task.
- 🎧 Play Track 46 again, pausing the recording at the end of each conversation. Call on a student to give the answer before moving on to the next conversation.

B Teaching Time: 5–10 min.

- Have students read the questions before listening.
- 🎧 Play Track 46. Have students complete the task.
- 🎧 Play Track 46 again, pausing at the end of each conversation. Call on students to read their answers. Correct as needed. If necessary, play the recording again.

Multilevel Strategy

- **Pre-level:** Give students a copy of the audioscript before they complete Exercise B. After you have gone over the answers to Exercise B, have them role-play the conversations.
- **At-level, Above-level:** Have students role-play the conversations from memory.

Option

Assign Unit 6 Review and Challenge Supplementary Exercises on the Teacher's Resource Disk as homework or on the Student Persistence CD-ROM as self-access practice.

TIME to TALK

Teaching Time: 10–15 min.

- Have two students read the example.
- GROUPS. Have students complete the task.
- Walk around the class and listen to students' grammar. Make a note of errors in future forms. At the end of the discussion, write the errors on the board and have the class correct them.

Unit 6 **T-81**

Reading

Getting Ready to Read

Teaching Time: 5–10 min.

- Read the instructions aloud. Ask for a volunteer to explain the word *personal*. Ask for another volunteer to explain the word *assistant*. Write their definitions on the board.
- Tell students to look at the title of the reading and the picture, and complete the task.
- Call on several students to say their guesses. Write them on the board. Leave the guesses up on the board while students read the article.

Reading

Teaching Time: 15–20 min.

- Have students read the article.
- Have students check their guesses from the prereading exercise. Read the guesses on the board, and check those that the writer talked about.
- Ask students to explain the title of the article.

Multilevel Strategy

- **Pre-level:** Put the pre-level students in a group and read the article aloud as they follow along in their books. Pause frequently and ask them questions to check their general comprehension.
- **At-level, Above-level:** After students have finished reading, tell them to work with a partner, and underline two verbs with *will*, two verbs with *be going to*, and two verbs with the present progressive as future. Have them discuss why each form was used. Have them refer to the explanations that you have written on the board:
  1. *Future plan (be going to)*
  2. *Future arrangement (present progressive or be going to)*
  3. *Promise (will)*
  4. *Decision at the time of speaking (will)*

Reading

Getting Ready to Read

The article talks about the job of a personal assistant. What kind of things do you think personal assistants do? List three things. *Answers will vary.*

1. _____
2. _____
3. _____

Reading

Read the article. Does the writer talk about any of the things you wrote about in Getting Ready to Read?

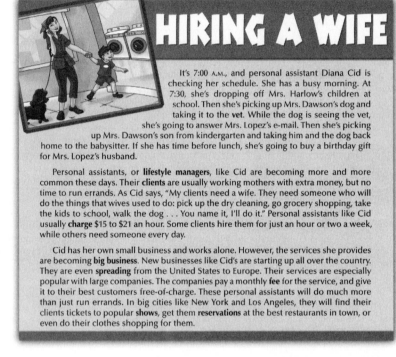

HIRING A WIFE

It's 7:00 A.M., and personal assistant Diana Cid is checking her schedule. She has a busy morning. At 7:30, she's dropping off Mrs. Harlow's children at school. Then she's picking up Mrs. Dawson's dog and taking it to the **vet**. While the dog is seeing the vet, she's going to answer Mrs. Lopez's e-mail. Then she's picking up Mrs. Dawson's son from kindergarten and taking him and the dog back home to the babysitter. If she has time before lunch, she's going to buy a birthday gift for Mrs. Lopez's husband.

Personal assistants, or **lifestyle managers**, like Cid are becoming more and more common these days. Their **clients** are usually working mothers with extra money, but no time to run errands. As Cid says, "My clients need a wife. They need someone who will do the things that wives used to do: pick up the dry cleaning, go grocery shopping, take the kids to school, walk the dog . . . You name it, I'll do it." Personal assistants like Cid usually **charge** $15 to $21 an hour. Some clients hire them for just an hour or two a week, while others need someone every day.

Cid has her own small business and works alone. However, the services she provides are becoming **big business**. New businesses like Cid's are starting up all over the country. They are even **spreading** from the United States to Europe. Their services are especially popular with large companies. The companies pay a monthly **fee** for the service, and give it to their best customers free-of-charge. These personal assistants will do much more than just run errands. In big cities like New York and Los Angeles, they will find their clients tickets to popular **shows**, get them **reservations** at the best restaurants in town, or even do their clothes shopping for them.

After You Read

A **Teaching Time: 10–15 min.**

A Look at the **boldface** words in the article. Guess their meaning. Then read the sentences and circle the correct answer.

1. A **vet** is a
   a. doctor for animals. *(circled)*   **b.** hairdresser for dogs.

2. A **lifestyle manager** is another name for a
   a. large company.   **b.** personal assistant. *(circled)*

3. When you have **clients,**
   a. they pay you. *(circled)*   **b.** you pay them.

4. If someone **charges** you $16 an hour,
   a. you pay him or her. *(circled)*   **b.** you pay the credit card company.

5. If something is **big business**, it is
   a. successful. *(circled)*   **b.** unsuccessful.

6. When something **spreads**, it
   a. costs more money.   **b.** becomes more common. *(circled)*

7. A **fee** is money that you
   a. pay for a service. *(circled)*   **b.** put in the bank.

8. A **show** has
   a. waiters and waitresses.   **b.** actors and actresses. *(circled)*

9. When you make a **reservation** at a restaurant, you want to
   a. eat at a particular time. *(circled)*   **b.** get your food to go.

B Read the article again. Then find the pronouns. What do they refer to? Write the noun.

1. it (line 5)   Mrs. Dawson's dog
2. him (line 7)   Mrs. Dawson's son
3. They (line 12)   Cid's clients
4. them (line 15)   personal assistants
5. she (line 17)   Cid
6. them (line 23)   their clients

> **Reading Skill:**
> **Understanding Pronouns**
>
> **Pronouns** replace nouns. To understand a text, you need to know which nouns the pronouns refer to.

After You Read

A **Teaching Time: 10–15 min.**

- Remind students that sometimes the words that will help them are not in the same sentence as the unfamiliar word. Sometimes they will need to look at the sentences or paragraphs before or after the sentence that contains the unfamiliar word.
- Read the example with students. Point out that the word that will help them to understand the word *vet* is in the following sentence, "While the dog is seeing the doctor. . . ."
- Have students complete the task. Tell them to circle the words in the text that helped them understand the meaning.
- Call on students to say the answers. Have them tell you which words they circled to help them. Correct as needed.

B **Teaching Time: 10–15 min.**

- Call on a student to read the information in the Reading Skill box. Ask students to give you some examples of pronouns.
- Read the example with the class. Have them circle *dog* in line 4 and *it* in line 5.
- Have students complete the task. Tell them to circle the pronoun and the word it replaces in the text.
- Call on students to read their answers. Correct as needed.

Writing

Getting Ready to Write

A Teaching Time: 10–15 min.

- Have students study the Writing Tip.
- Write the sentences in number 1 on the board. (I am going to go to college. I am going to study business.) Ask: *What is the subject of the first sentence?* (I) *What is the subject of the second sentence?* (I) Then ask: *What is the verb in the first sentence?* (am going to go) *What is the verb in the second sentence?* (am going to study) Ask: *Are the verbs the same tense?* (yes) Tell students that when two sentences have the same subject and verb tense, they can make them into one sentence with *and*. Show students how they can combine the two sentences into one.

  I am going to go to college. ^ I am going to study business.

   and

- Have students complete the task.
- Call on students to write answers on the board. Write corrections on the board as needed.

B Teaching Time: 10–15 min.

- Have students read the writing model.
- PAIRS. Have students complete the task.

Expansion Call on students to explain the different future forms that are used in the model. Write the same explanations that you gave for the Multilevel Strategy on page 82 on the board. Have students refer to the explanations when they answer. Explain the first sentence as an example. Say: *In the first sentence, the writer uses the present progressive as future because he already made arrangements. He probably told his boss that he's leaving his job, and he probably rented a place for the restaurant. These are all future arrangements so we can use the present progressive.*

Writing

Getting Ready to Write

A Combine the sentences with *and*.

1. I am going to go to college. I am going to study business.

   I am going to go to college and study business.

2. I am retiring in two years. I am moving to Florida.

   I am retiring in two years and moving to Florida.

   _____

3. I am selling my apartment. I am buying a house.

   I am selling my apartment and buying a house.

4. I will borrow some money. I will start my own business.

   I will borrow some money and start my own business.

5. I am going to quit this job. I am going to open a restaurant.

   I am going to quit this job and open a restaurant.

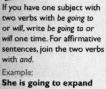

Writing Tip

If you have one subject with two verbs with *be going to* or *will*, write *be going to* or *will* one time. For affirmative sentences, join the two verbs with *and*.

Example:
She is going to expand her business **and hire** more employees.

B Read the model paragraph.

> Next month, I am quitting my job and opening a restaurant in Chelsea. I am getting a loan from the bank and a lot of help from my family. It is going to be a family restaurant, and it will serve traditional Haitian food. My mother will cook, my father will take care of the bills, my sisters will wait on tables, and my little brother will wash dishes. I will be responsible for everything else. <u>I owned a successful restaurant in my country, and that experience will help me</u>. Things are a little different here, but <u>my mother is a fantastic cook, and people everywhere like good food</u>. I think that my restaurant will be a success.

PAIRS. **Read the model again. Why does the writer think his restaurant will be a success?** Answers will vary.

Do you have any interesting future plans? Discuss.

Prewriting: Answering Information Questions

You are going to write a paragraph about your future plans. Before you write, read the notes for the writing model. Then answer the information questions about your future plans.

Writing Model
Plans to open a restaurant

What?	restaurant traditional Haitian food
Where?	Chelsea
When?	next month
How?	bank loan family help
Who?	Mom: cook Dad: bills Rose: waitress Mark: dishes me: manager, owner
Why will the plans succeed?	past experience mother good cook good food

My plans:

What?

Where?

When?

How?

Who?

Why will the plans succeed?

Writing

Now write a paragraph about your future plans. The writing tip, the model paragraph, and your notes will help you. Write in your notebook.

Busy Lives 85

Prewriting

Teaching Time: 10–15 min.

- Have students complete the task.
- PAIRS. Have students show a partner their notes. If the partner doesn't understand something in the notes, tell him or her to ask for clarification.
- Before students begin writing their paragraphs, tell them to show you their notes. Help them clarify their ideas as needed.

Multilevel Strategy

Pre-level: While the other students are reading each other's notes in pairs, work with the pre-level students in a group. Have them read their answers to the questions aloud. Help them make their meaning clearer.

Writing

Teaching Time: 20–25 min.

- Have students complete the task.
- Before students hand in their paragraphs, tell them to review the grammar summaries on pages 285–286. Tell them to reread their paragraphs. Have them check for and correct errors in the use of *be going to, will,* or the present progressive as future.

Learning Goals

- Learn vocabulary related to education
- Learn about *if* clauses for possibility; future time clauses; and *may / might* for possibility
- Listen to a conversation between a teacher and a parent, and to a radio interview about education
- Read an article about bilingualism and write about how to raise a bilingual child
- Talk about educational expectations, plans, and goals and different education systems around the world

Learner Persistence

Make sure that your students get a student ID card.

Warm-up

Teaching Time: 3–5 min.

- Have students look at the words in the box and circle those that they don't know.
- GROUPS. Have students who know the vocabulary explain it to those who don't. Tell them to try to point to the pictures as they explain.

Vocabulary

Teaching Time: 10–15 min.

- Read the example with the class.
- Have students complete the task in small groups.
- 🎧 Play Track 47 while students listen and check their answers.
- Say each word or phrase and have students repeat chorally.

Expansion

- Write three columns on the board: *Positive +*, *Negative –*, and *Not positive or negative*. Ask students to tell you which of the new words are positive, which are negative, and which are neutral. Add words to the correct columns. (Positive + : get good grades, get a scholarship, improve, pass a class / course; Negative – : cheat, fail a class / course; Not positive or negative: apply for, major

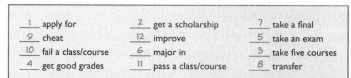

Grammar
- Future: *If* Clauses for Possibility
- Future: Time Clauses
- Future: *May* and *Might* for Possibility

Vocabulary

🎧 TRACK **47** **Match the numbers with the words. Then listen and check your answers.**

1	apply for	2	get a scholarship	7	take a final
9	cheat	12	improve	5	take an exam
10	fail a class/course	6	major in	3	take five courses
4	get good grades	11	pass a class/course	8	transfer

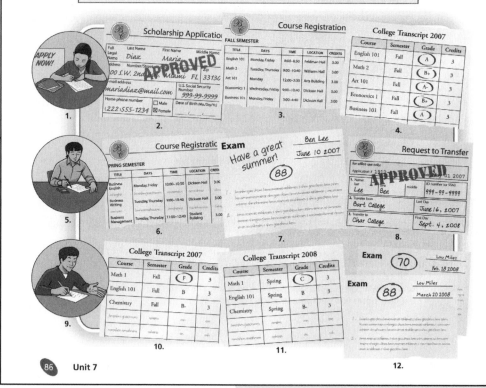

in, take a final, take an exam, take five courses, transfer)
- Ask students questions about the pictures. For example, say: *Look at picture 6. What is the student majoring in?* (business) *Look at picture 8. Where is the student studying now?* (Bart College) *Which college is the student transferring to?* (Char College)

Listening

A 🔊 **48** Listen. Why did Mrs. Parker call Mrs. Martin? Check (✓) the correct answer.

❏ **1.** Mrs. Parker is going to be Tommy Martin's teacher next year.

❏ **2.** Mrs. Martin sent Mrs. Parker an e-mail.

❏ **3.** Mrs. Martin is worried about her son, Tommy.

☑ **4.** Tommy Martin is not doing well in school.

❏ **5.** The principal tried to contact Mrs. Martin.

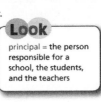

Look

principal = the person responsible for a school, the students, and the teachers

B 🔊 **49** Listen again. For each pair of sentences, check (✓) the sentence that you hear.

1. ☑ **a.** He might not be ready for high school next year.

❏ **b.** He might be ready for high school next year.

2. ❏ **a.** As soon as I get home tonight, I'll take Tommy out of the house.

☑ **b.** As soon as I get home tonight, I'll take care of this.

3. ☑ **a.** If he tries harder, he'll be fine.

❏ **b.** If he doesn't try harder, he'll fail.

4. ❏ **a.** We want to know exactly, so we'll test him.

☑ **b.** We won't know exactly until we test him.

5. ☑ **a.** I'll call you when we finish.

❏ **b.** I'll call you when it finishes.

C 🔊 **50** Listen again. Answer the questions. Write complete sentences.

1. Where is Mrs. Martin when Mrs. Parker calls?

She is at work.

2. What will Tommy have to do this summer?

He will have to attend summer school.

3. Why didn't Mrs. Martin answer Mrs. Parker's calls or e-mails?

She has been very busy.

4. What does Mrs. Parker think Tommy's problem is?

She thinks he might have a learning problem.

5. What is going to happen in an hour?

Mrs. Martin is going to call Mrs. Parker back.

Education **87**

Listening

A Teaching Time: 10–15 min.

- **Warm-up:** Have students read the information in the Look Box. Make sure they understand the word *principal*. Say: *I am the teacher of this class. I am responsible for the students in this class. I am not responsible for the students in other classes. The principal of a school is responsible for the students and the teachers of all the classes.*

- Have students read the answer choices.

- 🎧 Play Track 48 while students listen and complete the task. If necessary, play the track again.

- Call on a student to say the answer.

B Teaching Time: 10–15 min.

- PAIRS. Have students take turns reading the sentences aloud to the person sitting next to them.

- 🎧 Play Track 49 while students listen and complete the task. Pause the recording as each answer is given. Have students call out the answers when you pause the recording.

C Teaching Time: 10–15 min.

- Have students read the questions.

- 🎧 Play Track 50 while students listen and complete the task.

- 🎧 Play Track 50 again, pausing after each answer is given.

- Ask volunteers to write their answers on the board. Correct as needed.

Multilevel Strategy

Pre-level: Make photocopies of the audioscript. Give it to students before they complete Exercise C.

Expansion If a lot of students in the class have school-age children, start a discussion about relationships between teachers and parents. Ask questions such as: *Do teachers ever call you about your children? How often do you visit your child's school? What should you do if your child has a problem with one of his/her teachers?*

Culture Note

Listening. If necessary, explain the following words to students:

- *Summer school:* During the summer, many schools in the United States have special classes for students who have failed a class or who are in danger of failing.

- *Learning disabilities:* Ask students if they know what learning disabilities are. In U.S. schools, it is common for students who are having trouble in school to be tested for learning disabilities.

Option

Assign Unit 7 Supplementary Vocabulary Exercises on the Teacher's Resource Disk as homework or on the Student Persistence CD-ROM as self-access practice.

Grammar to Communicate 1

Future: *If* Clauses for Possibility

Teaching Time: 5–10 min.

- Have students study the chart and the Look Box.
- Write these sentences on the board, labeled as shown:

MEANING

If you study, = *(It is possible that you will study.)*

you will pass. = *(This will be the result of studying.)*

FORM

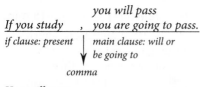

If you study , you are going to pass.
if clause: present | main clause: will or be going to
↓
comma

You will pass
You are going to pass if you study.
main clause: | if clause: present
will or be going to
↓
no comma

- As you point to MEANING on the board, say: *We use an if clause and a main clause when we want to say that something is possible in the future. The if clause introduces a possible situation in the future. The main clause introduces the result of the possible situation.*
- As you point to FORM and the corresponding sentences on the board, say: *The if clause is about the future, but we do not use will or be going to in the if clause. We use the present.*
- Point to the two different positions of the *if* clauses in the sentences under FORM and say: *In sentences with an if clause, either the if clause or the main clause can come first. When the main clause comes first, there is no comma between the two clauses. When the if clause comes first, put a comma between the clauses.*

A Teaching Time: 5–10 min.

- Read the example with the class. Pronounce *kindergarten* and have students repeat chorally. Make sure they understand the meaning.
- Have students complete the task. Tell them to circle the words in the

sentences that helped them decide whether the speaker was a kindergarten or a high school teacher.

- Call on students to say answers. Correct as needed.

B Teaching Time: 10–15 min.

- Read the example with the class.
- Have students complete the task.
- Call on students to say answers. If a comma is necessary, tell the students to say *comma.*

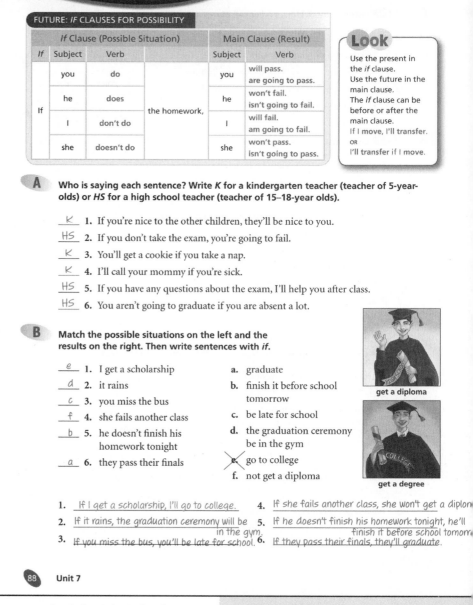

Grammar to Communicate 1

FUTURE: *IF* CLAUSES FOR POSSIBILITY					
If Clause (Possible Situation)			Main Clause (Result)		
If	Subject	Verb		Subject	Verb
If	you	do	the homework,	you	will pass. / are going to pass.
	he	does		he	won't fail. / isn't going to fail.
	I	don't do		I	will fail. / am going to fail.
	she	doesn't do		she	won't pass. / isn't going to pass.

Look

Use the present in the *if* clause. Use the future in the main clause. The *if* clause can be before or after the main clause.
If I move, I'll transfer.
OR
I'll transfer if I move.

A Who is saying each sentence? Write *K* for a kindergarten teacher (teacher of 5-year-olds) or *HS* for a high school teacher (teacher of 15–18-year olds).

_K_ 1. If you're nice to the other children, they'll be nice to you.

_HS_ 2. If you don't take the exam, you're going to fail.

_K_ 3. You'll get a cookie if you take a nap.

_K_ 4. I'll call your mommy if you're sick.

_HS_ 5. If you have any questions about the exam, I'll help you after class.

_HS_ 6. You aren't going to graduate if you are absent a lot.

B Match the possible situations on the left and the results on the right. Then write sentences with *if.*

_e_ 1. I get a scholarship
_d_ 2. it rains
_c_ 3. you miss the bus
_f_ 4. she fails another class
_b_ 5. he doesn't finish his homework tonight
_a_ 6. they pass their finals

a. graduate
b. finish it before school tomorrow
c. be late for school
d. the graduation ceremony be in the gym
e. go to college
f. not get a diploma

get a diploma

get a degree

1. _If I get a scholarship, I'll go to college._
2. _If it rains, the graduation ceremony will be in the gym._
3. _If you miss the bus, you'll be late for school._
4. _If she fails another class, she won't get a diploma._
5. _If he doesn't finish his homework tonight, he'll finish it before school tomorrow._
6. _If they pass their finals, they'll graduate._

88 Unit 7

Grammar Notes

1. Sentences with *if* have a dependent clause and a main clause. The *if* clause introduces a possible situation in the future. The main clause introduces the result of the possible situation.

2. The *if* clause is about the future, but we do <u>not</u> use *will* or *be going to* in the *if* clause. We usually use the simple present.

3. When the *if* clause comes at the *beginning* of the sentence, put a comma between the *if* clause and the main clause. When the *if* clause comes after the main clause, do <u>not</u> put a comma.

4. For more information on this grammar topic, see page 286.

 Center Stage 3

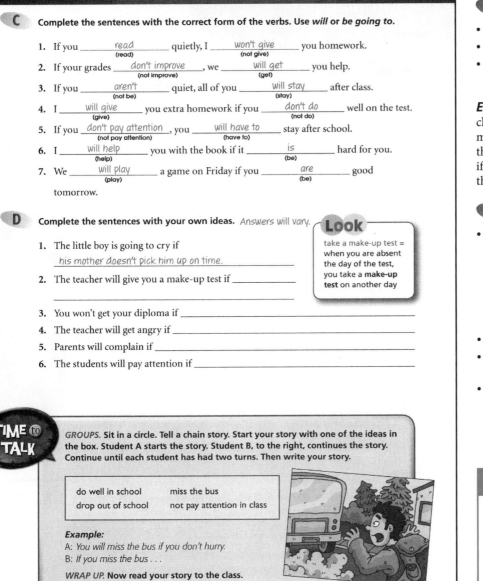

C Complete the sentences with the correct form of the verbs. Use *will* or *be going to.*

1. If you ___read___ (read) quietly, I ___won't give___ (not give) you homework.

2. If your grades ___don't improve___ (not improve), we ___will get___ (get) you help.

3. If you ___aren't___ (not be) quiet, all of you ___will stay___ (stay) after class.

4. I ___will give___ (give) you extra homework if you ___don't do___ (not do) well on the test.

5. If you ___don't pay attention___ (not pay attention), you ___will have to___ (have to) stay after school.

6. I ___will help___ (help) you with the book if it ___is___ (be) hard for you.

7. We ___will play___ (play) a game on Friday if you ___are___ (be) good tomorrow.

D Complete the sentences with your own ideas. Answers will vary.

1. The little boy is going to cry if
   ___his mother doesn't pick him up on time.___

2. The teacher will give you a make-up test if _____
   _____

3. You won't get your diploma if _____

4. The teacher will get angry if _____

5. Parents will complain if _____

6. The students will pay attention if _____

Look

take a make-up test =
when you are absent
the day of the test,
you take a **make-up
test** on another day

TIME to TALK

GROUPS. Sit in a circle. Tell a chain story. Start your story with one of the ideas in the box. Student A starts the story. Student B, to the right, continues the story. Continue until each student has had two turns. Then write your story.

| do well in school | miss the bus |
| drop out of school | not pay attention in class |

Example:
A: *You will miss the bus if you don't hurry.*
B: *If you miss the bus . . .*

WRAP UP. Now read your story to the class.

Education 89

C Teaching Time: 5–10 min.

- Call on a student to read the example.
- Have students complete the task.
- Call on students to read their answers. Correct as needed.

Expansion PAIRS. Have students check the sentences that a good teacher might say. Then have them compare their answers with other students to see if they agree. Call on students to read the sentences that they checked.

D Teaching Time: 5–10 min.

- Have students read the Look Box. Make sure they all understand the meaning of *make-up test.* Tell them that in some classes, teachers do not give make-up tests. If you are absent, you get a zero. Ask them if there are make-up tests in their countries.
- Read the example with the class.
- PAIRS. Have students complete the task together.
- Ask for volunteers to write their answers on the board. Have each volunteer complete a different sentence. Correct as needed.

Multilevel Strategy

All levels: Pair pre-level students with at- or above-level students for this activity. That way, if the pre-level students can't come up with the vocabulary or grammar they need, their partner can help them.

Option

Exercise D. Have students write their sentences on a piece of paper. Collect their papers. That way you can check all of their sentences, not just those of the volunteers.

Option

Assign Unit 7 Supplementary Grammar to Communicate 1 Exercises on the Teacher's Resource Disk as homework or on the Student Persistence CD-ROM as self-access practice.

TIME to TALK

Teaching Time: 10–15 min.

- Read the directions with the class. Have two students read the example.
- GROUPS. Tell each group to assign a secretary to write down the group's story.
- Have students complete the task.
- WRAP UP. Have the group secretaries read the stories to the class. Correct as needed.

Expansion At the end of the activity, have students write down as much of their group's story as they can remember and hand it in. Do not allow the students to look at the secretary's notes.

Grammar to Communicate 2

Future: Time Clauses

Teaching Time: 5–10 min.

- Have students study the chart and the Look Box.
- Write these examples on the board, labeled as shown:

  She is going to get her own apartment
      main clause: future

  after she gets a job.
      time clause: present

  She will get her own apartment
  main clause: future

  after she gets a job.
      time clause: present

- As you point to the relevant parts of the example sentences, say: *We use a time clause and a main clause when we want to show the order of future events. In this example, what will happen first? (She will get a job.) What will happen after that? (She will get her own apartment.)*
- Explain: *The time clause is about the future, but we do <u>not</u> use* will *or be going to in the time clause. We use the present. In the main clause, we use the future with* be going to *or* will. *There is no difference in meaning between* be going to *and* will.
- Write on the board: *After she gets a job, she is going to get her own apartment.* Point to the two different positions of the time clause in the examples and say: *In sentences with a time clause, either the time clause or the main clause can come first. When the main clause comes first, there is no comma between the two clauses. When the time clause comes first, put a comma between the clauses.*

A   **Teaching Time: 5–10 min.**

- Have students complete the task. As they complete the task, tell them to think about the order of the events, and write the number 1 or 2 above each one.
- Call on students to say answers. Correct as needed.

B   **Teaching Time: 10–15 min.**

- Read the example with the class. Make sure students understand that they can use *be going to* or *will* in the main clause, with no change in meaning.

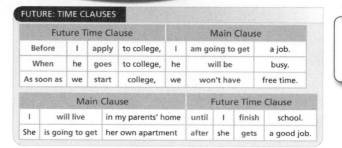

Grammar to Communicate 2

FUTURE: TIME CLAUSES

Future Time Clause				Main Clause		
Before	I	apply	to college,	I	am going to get	a job.
When	he	goes	to college,	he	will be	busy.
As soon as	we	start	college,	we	won't have	free time.

Main Clause			Future Time Clause			
I	will live	in my parents' home	until	I	finish	school.
She	is going to get	her own apartment	after	she	gets	a good job.

Look

Remember: We can use *will* or *be going to* for the future.

A   **Complete the paragraphs.**

1. (as soon as / until / before)

   <u>As soon as</u> I graduate, I'm going to get a full-time job. I'll work <u>until</u> I get married. Then I'm going to stop working and have a baby. <u>Before</u> I have a baby, I'm going to buy a house.

2. (after / before / when)

   <u>After</u> I graduate, I'm going to start college. I'm going to visit my family in Guatemala <u>before</u> classes start in September. I'll take a lot of different courses <u>when</u> I'm in college, but I think I will major in biology.

B   Two other students are writing about their plans after high school. Complete the sentences with the correct form of the verbs. Use *be going to* or *will*.

1. (graduate / help / work / save / go / major in)

   When I <u>graduate</u>, I <u>'m going to help OR I will help</u> my parents in their store. I <u>'m going to work</u> there until I <u>save</u> enough money for college. When I <u>go</u> to college, I <u>'ll major in</u> business.

2. (end / find / take / start / get / transfer)

   Before high school <u>ends</u>, I <u>'m going to find</u> a part-time job. I <u>'m going to take</u> some evening classes at a community college as soon as the new semester <u>starts</u>. After I <u>get</u> my associate's degree, I <u>'ll transfer</u> to a four-year college.

90   Unit 7

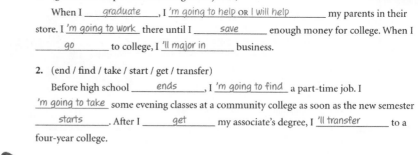

- Have students complete the task.
- Call on students to say answers. Correct as needed.

Multilevel Strategy

- **Pre-level:** Give students more time to complete Exercises A and B. Walk around and help as needed.
- **At-level, Above-level:** Have students complete Unit 7 Supplementary Grammar Exercise B, on the Teacher's Resource Disk. Provide them with the answer key so that they can correct themselves.

Grammar Notes

1. Future time clauses begin with a time word: *after, as soon as, before, until,* or *when.*

2. The time clause is about the future, but we do <u>not</u> use *will* or *be going to.* We usually use the simple present.

3. Use *be going to* or *will* in the main clause of the sentence.

4. When the future time clause comes at the *beginning* of the sentence, put a comma between the time clause and the main clause. When the time clause comes after the main clause, do *not* put a comma.

5. For more information on this grammar topic, go to page 286.

C Complete the sentences about the people's dreams for the future. Use *when*, *as soon as*, *before*, or *after*. Some sentences have more than one correct answer.

1. (I / finish / become) _____After I finish_____ high school, _____I am going to become_____ a model.

2. (I / be / graduate) _____I am going to be_____ a professional basketball player, _____after I graduate._____.

3. (he / go / ask) _____Before he goes_____ away to college, _____he is going to ask_____ her to marry him.

4. (she / retire / be) _____She is going to retire_____ _____when she is_____ 40.

5. (she / graduate / apply) _____After she graduates_____, _____she is going to apply_____ to beauty school.

6. (they / get / celebrate) _____As soon as they get_____ their diplomas, _____they will celebrate._____.

> **TIME to TALK**
>
> *PAIRS.* Look at page 301. It is Tommy's junior year of high school, and he is thinking about college. Read the checklist. Talk about the things that he is going to do and when he is going to do them.
>
> *Example:*
> *In the spring, Tommy is going to make an appointment with the school guidance counselor. When she meets with him, she'll discuss several different colleges with him. After he chooses colleges. . . .*

Education **91**

C **Teaching Time: 10–15 min.**

- Have students read the directions and look at the picture. Call on a student to read the example. Tell students to point to the person that the sentence is about.
- Have students complete the task.
- Call on students to say answers. Correct as needed.

Multilevel Strategy

- **Pre-level:** Give students more time to complete the exercise.
- **At-level, Above-level:** After students finish writing their answers in the books, have them work in pairs. Tell them to cover the sentences and say what each person in the picture is thinking. Then have them uncover the sentences and check their answers.

Expansion If some of the students in your class have attended college in their countries, start a discussion about the similarities and differences between the application process in their countries and in the United States.

Culture Note

Time to Talk. In the United States, there are guidance counselors in most high schools. The guidance counselor's job is to help students set goals and plan for their future. Guidance counselors help students with the college application process, but they also help students who don't want to go to college. Guidance counselors also meet with parents to discuss their children's future.

Option

Assign Unit 7 Supplementary Grammar to Communicate 2 Exercises on the Teacher's Resource Disk as homework or on the Student Persistence CD-ROM as self-access practice.

> **TIME to TALK**
>
> **Teaching Time: 10–15 min.**
>
> - Put the students into pairs. Have one student open his or her book to page 301. Have the other student read the example on this page.
> - Explain new vocabulary as needed.
> - Have students complete the task.
> - Call on students to say their answers. Write them on the board. Point out places where more than one answer is correct.

Multilevel Strategy

- **Pre-level:** Group pre-level students. Sit with them and give them extra help with the activity.

Unit 7   **T-91**

Grammar to Communicate 3

Future: *May* and *Might* for Possibility

Teaching Time: 5–10 min.

- Have students study the chart.
- Say: *We use* may *or* might *when something is possible in the future, but we are not sure.* Write on the board: *It might rain tomorrow.* Point to the sentence and say: *It's possible that it will rain, but it is also possible that it will not rain.*
- Say: *The meaning of* may *and* might *is the same. It means something is possible in the future. Use the base form of the verb after* may *or* might.
- Say: *The negatives of* may *and* might *are* may not *and* might not. Write on the board: *It may not rain tomorrow. = It might not rain tomorrow.*
- Say: *Do not make contractions with* may *or* might.
- Read the sentences in the chart and have students repeat chorally.

A Teaching Time: 3–5 min.

- Explain that we use *be going to* for future plans that we are pretty sure about. We can also use *may* or *might* for future plans, but when we use *may* or *might*, it means we are not sure about our plans.
- Have students complete the task.
- Call on a student to say the answer. Correct as needed.

B Teaching Time: 10–15 min.

- Have students study the Look Box.
- Write the example on the board, as follows:

Maybe   I'll
Maybe
or Perhaps   *subject + will*

learn   to use a computer. =
base form
of the verb

I   may
subject   *may or might*

learn   to use a computer.
base form
of the verb

- Explain that *may* and *might* are verbs, so they come after the subject, but *maybe* and *perhaps* are not verbs.

They come before the subject. When we use *maybe* or *perhaps*, we need to use *will* in front of the main verb to show that the time is future.

- Have students complete the task.
- Call on students to say answers. Correct as needed.

Grammar to Communicate 3

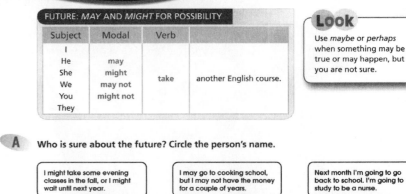

Subject	Modal	Verb	
I			
He	may		
She	might	take	another English course.
We	may not		
You	might not		
They			

FUTURE: *MAY* AND *MIGHT* FOR POSSIBILITY

Look
Use *maybe* or *perhaps* when something may be true or may happen, but you are not sure.

A Who is sure about the future? Circle the person's name.

I might take some evening classes in the fall, or I might wait until next year.

Tom

I may go to cooking school, but I may not have the money for a couple of years.

Joe

Next month I'm going to go back to school. I'm going to study to be a nurse.

Yolanda

B Rewrite the sentences with *may*. Do not change the meaning.

1. Maybe I'll learn to use a computer.   I may learn to use a computer.
2. Perhaps he'll take a class in car mechanics.   He may take a class in car mechanics.
3. Maybe she won't have money to take a class.   She may not have money to take a class.
4. Perhaps they're going to apply to college.   They may apply to college.

Rewrite these sentences with *might*. Do not change the meaning.

5. Perhaps I'll go to the community college.   I might go to the community college.
6. Maybe she's not going to study full time.   She might not study full time.
7. Maybe he's going to become a plumber.   He might become a plumber.
8. Perhaps I won't transfer to a new school.   I might not transfer to a new school.

Grammar Notes

1. Use *may* and *might* to talk about future possibility. Use the base form of the verb after *may* or *might*.
2. Use *may not* or *might not* for negative statements. Do not contract them.
3. The affirmative and negative forms are the same for all persons (*I, you, he, she, it, we, they*).
4. Be careful. *May be* is a modal + a verb. *Maybe* is an adverb that comes at the beginning of the sentence. It means *possible*. *Perhaps* means the same thing as *maybe*, and is used in the same way. Use *maybe* and *perhaps* with *will*.
5. For more information on this grammar topic, see page 286.

C Read about what the students are doing now. Then complete the sentences about their future. Use *might* or a form of *be going to* and the words in the box.

get	graduate	improve	major in	pass	~~take~~

1. Lyn is looking at brochures for an art class, but she is not sure about the class.
   She might take an art class.

2. Henry is writing a check for a car mechanics class.
   He is going to take a car mechanics class.

3. Ricky is applying for a scholarship, but a lot of other people are also applying.
   Ricky might get a scholarship.

4. Rosa knows that she wants be a math teacher. She loves math and teaching.
   Rosa is going to major in math.

5. Fatima's English isn't very good, but she's studying a lot in her English class.
   Fatima is going to improve her English.

6. Marsha and Jane are in their last year at college. They have very good grades.
   Marsha and Jane are going to graduate.

7. Joe and Ann's grades aren't good, but it's the end of the semester, and they're trying.
   Joe and Ann might pass.

PAIRS. Compare your answers.

TIME to TALK

CLASS. **Play this game.**

STEP 1: Write four sentences about the future. Write about one thing that you are definitely going to do, two things that you might do, and one thing that you might not do. Use *be going to, may, might*, and *might not*.

STEP 2: Your teacher will collect the papers and put them in a box.

STEP 3: Each student will take a paper from the box and read the sentences out loud.

STEP 4: The other students will guess who wrote the sentences.

Example:
I am going to go to nursing school. I may go home to visit my family first. . . .

Education 93

C Teaching Time: 10–15 min.

- Read the examples with the class.
- Have students complete the task.
- PAIRS. Have students compare their answers. If their answers are different, tell them to decide whose answer is better.
- Call on students to say answers. Correct as needed.

Teaching Tip

Time to Talk. When you record students' errors and use them to teach from, only focus on the grammar point that you are working on at that time. If there are other errors in the students' sentences, correct them before you write the sentences on the board. That way, students will not be distracted by errors that are not related to the grammar point they are practicing.

Option

Assign Unit 7 Supplementary Grammar to Communicate 3 Exercises on the Teacher's Resource Disk as homework or on the Student Persistence CD-ROM as self-access practice.

TIME to TALK

Teaching Time: 15–20 min.

- Read the directions and the example with the class.
- CLASS. Have students play the game.
- After students have guessed who wrote the sentences, write errors from their sentences on the board. Have the class correct the errors.

Multilevel Strategy

Pre-level: Have students write only two sentences—one with *be going to*, and another with *might* or *may*. Give them extra assistance.

Review and Challenge

Grammar

Teaching Time: 5–10 min.

- Have a student read the corrected sentence in the example aloud.
- Have students complete the task.
- Call on students to read the answers. Correct as needed.

Multilevel Strategy

- **Pre-level:** Tell students what the mistakes are and have them rewrite the sentences.

Dictation

Teaching Time: 5–10 min.

- 🎧 Play Track 51 while students listen and write what they hear.
- 🎧 Play Track 51 again while students check their answers.
- Call on students to write answers on the board.
- 🎧 Play Track 51 again and correct the sentences on the board.

Multilevel Strategy

- **Pre-level:** Give students a worksheet with some of the words from the dictation already provided.

Speaking

Teaching Time: 10–15 min.

- Make sure students understand both situations. Explain any unfamiliar vocabulary.
- Have two students read the example.
- PAIRS. Have students write the conversations and practice role-playing them.
- Ask volunteers to role-play their conversations in front of the class.
- Wait until the role plays are finished to make corrections. Write errors on the board and have the class correct them.

Review and Challenge

Grammar

Find the mistake in each sentence. Circle the letter and correct the mistake.

 as soon as

1. I'm going to transfer to Center College as soon the semester ends.
     A   B   Ⓒ   D

2. I might to major in music, or I may study Spanish.
     A Ⓑ   C D

3. If you will study for the next test, you will get a good grade.
     Ⓐ   B   C D

4. Until she is going to go to college, she is going to work full time.
     Ⓐ   Ⓑ   C   D
   goes

5. I take a makeup exam next month if I don't take the final exam Friday.
    Ⓐ   B   C   D
   will take

Dictation

🎧 **51** **Listen. You will hear five sentences. Write them in your notebook.** *See the audioscript on p. 314 for the sentences.*

Speaking

PAIRS. **Choose a situation and write a conversation. Then act it out for the class.**

> **Situation 1**
>
> *Student A:* You are a new student in an evening course that started last week. Ask the teacher about information you missed. Ask about things such as absences and tests.
>
> *Student B:* You teach an evening course that started last week. Answer the questions of a student who missed the first week of class.

> **Situation 2**
>
> *Student A:* You are a parent of a 12-year-old. Your son didn't get good grades on his report card. You go to parent-teacher's night to talk to the teacher about your son.
>
> *Student B:* You are a teacher. Your students are 12 years old. It is parent-teacher's night, and you are talking to the parent of one of your students.

Example: (Situation 1)
A: *Excuse me. I have some questions about the course. I might need to stay home with my son sometimes. Will there be a problem if I miss class?*
B: *Well, if you are absent too much, you will not get a certificate at the end of the course.*

94 Unit 7

Multilevel Strategy

All levels: Pair pre-level and at-/above-level students for this role play. Allow the pre-level students to read from their papers when performing the role play. Have at- and above-level students perform their roles from memory.

Culture Note

Speaking. Explain that public schools in the United States have several parent-teacher nights a year. On parent-teacher nights, parents go in to the school to meet with their children's teacher(s). Ask students if they have anything similar to parent-teacher nights in their countries. If your students have children in public school, ask if any of them have attended a parent-teacher night. If they have, ask them to describe their experience to the class. If they haven't, encourage them to attend parent-teacher nights.

Listening

A 🎧 **52** Listen to the radio show. A reporter is talking to two people who want to become the mayor. They are talking about the problems with the city's schools. Check (✓) the problems that they mention.

Look
mayor = the leader of a city or town
candidate = someone who is competing in an election or trying to get a job

☑ Student test scores are very low.

☑ There are not enough teachers.

☑ Teachers don't make enough money.

❑ There aren't any good principals.

B 🎧 **52** Listen again. If Ms. West becomes mayor, what will she do? If Mr. Lee becomes mayor, what will he do? Check (✓) the correct column.

	MS. WEST	MR. LEE
1. Who will listen to a lot of people before he/she does anything?	✓	
2. Who wants to pay teachers more?		✓
3. Who will visit every school in the city?	✓	
4. Who will act quickly?		✓
5. Who will talk with students?	✓	
6. Who will meet with public school principals?	✓	

TIME to TALK

GROUPS. Talk about the public schools in your city or town. Answer the questions and take notes as you listen to the discussion.

1. Talk about the good and bad things about the public schools in your area. Which schools are the best? Which are the worst? What are the problems?

2. Should there be changes in the public schools in your area? Why or why not? Which changes might happen? Which changes might not happen? Which changes won't happen?

3. Do you think that the public schools in your area will stay the same, improve, or get worse in the future?

Example:
A: *Our principal is going to meet with the mayor to ask for money to buy new computers.*
B: *That's great. Our principal may do the same thing.*

WRAP UP. Now compare notes with other groups.

Education 95

Teaching Tip

Time to Talk. Make sure at least one person in each group knows something about the public schools in the area. If there are students in the class who do not know anything about the topic, assign them to be the notetakers for their group. During the WRAP UP, call on them to highlight the most important or interesting points that came up during the discussion.

Option

Assign Unit 7 Review and Challenge Supplementary Exercises on the Teacher's Resource Disk as homework or on the Student Persistence CD-ROM as self-access practice.

Listening

A **Teaching Time: 5–10 min.**

- **Warm-up:** Tell students that they are going to listen to a radio interview with two candidates for mayor. Write the definitions from the Look Box on the board, and make sure everyone understands the meaning of *mayor* and *candidate*. Ask if anyone knows the name of the mayor of the city you are in. Write his or her name on the board. If there is an election happening soon, ask if anyone knows who the candidates are. Write their names on the board.

- Have students read the answer choices. Ask students to predict what the main topic of the interview will be. (education)

- 🎧 Play Track 52 while students listen and complete the task.

- 🎧 Play Track 52 again, this time pausing as each problem is discussed.

- Call on a student to say the answers. Correct as needed.

B **Teaching Time: 5–10 min.**

- Have students read the questions before listening.

- 🎧 Play Track 52 while students listen and complete the task.

- 🎧 Play Track 52 again, pausing as each answer is given. Call on students to give the answer before starting the tape again.

Multilevel Strategy

Pre-level: Give students a copy of the audioscript before they complete Exercise B. Tell them to read along as they listen and complete the task.

TIME to TALK

Teaching Time: 10–15 min.

- Call on students to read the directions and the questions aloud.
- Call on two students to read the example.
- GROUPS. Have students complete the task.
- Spend a few minutes with each group. Encourage them to use the grammar from the unit in their discussion.
- WRAP UP. Have one person from each group tell the class the most interesting point that came up in the discussion.

Getting Ready to Read

Teaching Time: 3–5 min.

- Read the statements aloud.
- PAIRS. Have students complete the task in pairs.

Reading

Teaching Time: 15–20 min.

- Have students read the article.
- Have students check their guesses to Getting Ready to Read. Tell them to mark the place in the text where they found the answers.
- Call on students to read the statements from Getting Reading to Read aloud and say which ones are true. Have them tell you where they found the answers.

Multilevel Strategy

- **Pre-level:** Put the pre-level students in a group, and read the article aloud as they follow along in their books. Pause frequently and ask them questions to check their general comprehension.
- **At-level, Above-level:** After students have finished reading, tell them to underline all of the *if* clauses and future time clauses in the article, and circle *may* and *might*.

Getting Ready to Read

Check (✓) the statements that are true. If you are not sure, guess.

- ❏ 1. A bilingual person can speak, read, and write in three languages.
- ☑ 2. When they are born, all children can hear the sounds of all languages.
- ❏ 3. Children start to learn a language when they are about six months old.
- ☑ 4. Children with two first languages sometimes confuse the two languages.
- ❏ 5. Children with two first languages do not do well in school.

Reading

Read the article. Then check your answers to Getting Ready to Read.

HOW MANY LANGUAGES?

If you live in an English-speaking country but your first language is not English, what language will you speak to your children at home? What if you and your **spouse** speak different languages? Which language will you use with your children? If your children hear both languages at home, will they have problems when they get to school? Here is some information that might help to answer these questions.

First, which language should you use with your children at home? At birth, all children can hear the sounds of all languages. However, if you speak to children in just one language, after about six to nine months, they will hear only the sounds of that language. If you want children to have two first languages, they will need to hear each of them at least 30 percent of the time when they are babies. If you and your spouse speak two different languages, you may each decide to talk to your baby in your first language, or you might choose the language that the child will not hear in school. In either case, your child will **benefit**.

Second, how well do bilingual children do in school? When children grow up with two first languages, they will sometimes confuse them. If they can't think of a word in one language, they might use a word from the other language. However, this will stop as soon as the child learns enough vocabulary. It is also true that bilingual children might learn to read later than **monolingual** children. However, they will soon **catch up**. Then they will be able to read, write, and speak two languages for the rest of their lives. And that is a wonderful gift to give any child.

After You Read

A Look at the **boldface** words in the article. Try to guess the meaning from the context. Write a definition or description.

1. spouse: _a husband or wife_
2. benefit: _help_
3. monolingual: _speaking only one language_
4. catch up: _reach the same level as others_

Now look up the words in the dictionary. Were your definitions close to the dictionary definitions?

Reading Skill:
Guessing Meaning From Context

Often, you do not need to use a dictionary to understand the meaning of a new word in a text. You can guess the meaning from the **context** (the words and sentences before and after the new word).

B Read the article again. Then answer the questions. Answers will vary, but should include the following.

1. At what age do babies lose their ability to hear the sounds of all languages?
   at six to nine months

2. How much time should a baby listen to a language every day?
   about 30% of the time

3. If you and your spouse speak two different languages and you want your child to speak both, what can you do?
   each speak to your child in your first language, or speak to your child in the language that the child will not hear in school

4. In what ways might school be more difficult at first for a bilingual child than for a monolingual child?
   A bilingual child might confuse the two languages. He or she might learn to read later than a monolingual child.

Education 97

After You Read

A Teaching Time: 10–15 min.

- Call on a student to read the information in the Reading Skill box.
- Have students complete the task. Tell them to circle the words in the text that helped them guess the meaning.
- Call on students to say the answers. Have them tell you which words they circled to help them.
- Have them check their answers in their dictionaries.

Multilevel Strategy

- **Pre-level:** Students will probably not be able to write their own definitions. Copy a page from a dictionary for each of the four vocabulary items. Have students find the definition that matches the way the word is used in the reading.

B Teaching Time: 10–15 min.

- Have students read the questions before they read the article again.
- Have students complete the task. Tell them to mark the place in the text where they found the answers. Encourage them to put their answers in their own words, rather than copying.
- PAIRS. Have students compare their answers. Tell them to refer to the places they marked in their books if they have different answers.
- Call on students to read their answers. Correct as needed by referring to the places in the text where the answers can be found.

Watch Out!

Exercise A. Students need to be taught how to use an English monolingual dictionary effectively. Copy the page from a learner's dictionary (or the assigned dictionary for the class, if applicable) that contains the word *spouse*. Point to various parts of the definition, and ask students what they mean. For example, ask students what *n.* means (noun), and what the symbols between the brackets are for (pronunciation). Be careful, however. Don't try to teach everything about the dictionary in one class. Rather, give students frequent but brief practice using a dictionary. Each time, show them only one or two important things that are contained in a dictionary entry.

Writing

Getting Ready to Write

A Teaching Time: 5–10 min.

- Have students study the Writing Tip.
- Read the example with the class.
- Have students complete the task.
- Call on students to say answers. Correct as needed.
- Ask students if they or anyone they know has had an experience similar to the writer's experience.

B Teaching Time: 10–15 min.

- Have students read the writing model.
- PAIRS. Have students complete the task.

Expansion Have students tell their stories about raising bilingual children to the class. Then start a discussion about bilingual education. Ask students whether they would like their children to study in a bilingual class or in a monolingual one. Have them explain their opinions.

Writing

> ### Writing Tip
> Remember: When you use a time clause to talk about the future, you use the present tense in the time clause.
> Example:
> I will send my son to a bilingual school **when he is five.**

Getting Ready to Write

A Complete the sentences with the correct form of the verbs.

I just moved to Boston from Brazil. My daughter is five. She __will start__
   1. (start)
school as soon as she ___is___ six. Of course, when her teachers __speak__ to her
   2. (be)   3. (speak)
in English, she __will answer__ in English. My husband and I will continue to speak to her
   4. (answer)
in Portugese. My son is four, and he speaks Portugese. After he __starts__ school, he
   5. (start)
__is going to speak__ English too. I want all of us to know both languages. I __will take__ an English
   6. (speak)   7. (take)
class as soon as I __finish__ unpacking!
   8. (finish)

B Read the model paragraph.

> My husband and I are Russian. We live in the United States, but we speak Russian at home. Our four-year-old son, Sergei, understands Russian very well, but he almost never speaks it. I am worried that after he starts school, he will not understand Russian anymore, and he will never learn to speak it. My mother might come to live with us next year. She does not speak any English. If Sergei wants to speak to her, he will need to use Russian. If she does not come, we are going to send Sergei to a private bilingual school. It is expensive, but we want our son to understand our language and culture.

PAIRS. **Read the model again. How is the writer going to help her child to be bilingual?**
Answers will vary.

Talk about things you are doing to learn English. What are you doing now? What will you do in the future?

Prewriting: Taking Notes

You are going to write a paragraph about learning a new language. Before you write, read the notes for the writing model. Then complete the chart with notes about your ideas.

Writing Model
Helping our son learn a new language

Now
Living in U.S.
Russian at home
Sergei: Understands Russian/Eng
    Speaks only Eng
Problem—future?

Future
Grandmother?
Bilingual school?

Goal: Sergei will be bilingual.

Learning a new language

Now

Future

Writing

Now write a paragraph about learning a new language. The writing tip, the model paragraph, and your notes will help you. Write in your notebook.

Prewriting
Teaching Time: 15–20 min.

- Have students complete the task. If students do not know anyone who is raising a bilingual child, tell them to imagine that they have a child and want to raise him or her to be bilingual. What will they do?
- PAIRS. Have students show a partner their notes. If the partner doesn't understand something in the notes, tell him or her to ask for clarification.
- Before students begin writing their paragraphs, tell them to show you their notes. Help them clarify their ideas.

Writing
Teaching Time: 20–25 min.

- Have students reread the model paragraph if necessary.
- Have students complete the task. Walk around and help as needed.
- Collect students' work and offer individual feedback.

Multilevel Strategy

Pre-level: This assignment might be beyond the ability of your pre-level students. If so, have them work together on the Unit 7 Review and Challenge Supplementary Exercises on the Teacher's Resource Disk. Have them hand in their answers.

Unit 8
Getting a Job

Learning Goals

- Learn vocabulary related to work, job searching, and job training
- Learn about the present perfect: regular and irregular verbs and *yes / no* questions
- Listen to a conversation about a job search and to an interview for a management training program
- Read an article about a job and write a letter of complaint
- Talk about work experience and how to search for a job

Learner Persistence

Encourage students to get a library card.

Warm-up

Teaching Time: 3–5 min.

- PAIRS. Have students look at the pictures without looking at the paragraph. Have them guess what the story is going to be about. Write their guesses on the board.

Vocabulary

Teaching Time: 10–15 min.

- Read the example with the class.
- PAIRS. Have students complete the task.
- Play Track 2 while students listen and check their answers.
- Say each word or phrase and have students repeat chorally.
- Check students' comprehension of the meaning of each word or phrase. Have them explain the meanings in their own words. Correct as needed.

Expansion

- Have students circle the verbs and verb phrases in the story. Ask them which are regular and which are irregular. Write two columns on the board: *Regular verbs* and *Irregular verbs.* Write each verb in the correct column. (Regular verbs: search, contact, own, need, use, like, hire, learn, train, work, handle, fire; Irregular verbs: hear from, go, tell, know, make, be, quit)

Unit 8
Getting a Job

> **Grammar**
> - Present Perfect: Regular Verbs
> - Present Perfect: Irregular Verbs
> - Present Perfect: *Yes / No* Questions

Vocabulary

 2 Read the story, and look at the pictures. The pictures are not in the correct order. Write the number of each picture in the correct place in the story. Then listen and check your answers.

___4___ Adam **searched** for a job in the newspaper and online. ___5___ He **contacted** Sam Alvarez on Monday. Mr. Alvarez **owned** a 24-hour convenience store. He needed a cashier.

___1___ Adam **heard from** Mr. Alvarez on Tuesday. ___6___ Adam went to see Mr. Alvarez. Adam told him he didn't know how to use a **cash register**. But Mr. Alvarez liked Adam and **hired** him as the new cashier. ___8___ Adam learned how to use the cash register. Mr. Alvarez **trained** him.

___7___ The first month, Adam worked **the day shift**. But the second month, he worked **the night shift**. ___2___ All the cashiers **handled** a lot of money. One cashier made many mistakes, so Mr. Alvarez **fired** her. ___3___ After that, Adam worked **overtime**. He often worked sixty hours a week. He was very tired. After six months, Adam **quit** his job. Now he's searching for a new job.

100   Unit 8

- Ask students questions about the pictures. Tell them to answer with the verbs on the board. For example, ask: *Picture 4: Where did Adam search for a job?* (He searched for a job online and in the newspaper.) *Picture 5: When did he contact Mr. Alvarez?* (He contacted Mr. Alvarez on Monday.) *Why did he contact Mr. Alvarez?* (Because Mr. Alvarez owned a store and he needed a cashier.)

Listening

A 🔘 **3** Listen. What is the relationship between the two speakers? Check (✓) the correct answer.

❑ boss and employee ☑ classmates ❑ father and daughter ❑ husband and wife

B 🔘 **4** Read and listen again. Write the missing words. Use the words in the box.

already	~~ever~~	gotten	has	Have	haven't	I've	started

Ignacio: Have you ___ever___ handled money?
   1.
Natalia: Just when I sold vegetables at a farm last summer. But ___I've___ never used
   2.
a cash register.
Ignacio: Oh, it's easy.
Natalia: Really? ___Have___ you ever used one?
   3.
Ignacio: Uh, no, I ___haven't___. But a lot of my friends have. Just go in and apply.
   4.
Natalia: Hmmm . . . maybe I will. Thanks for the information. So, how about Tracy?
Has she ___started___ her new job?
   5.
Ignacio: Yes, she ___has___.
   6.
Natalia: And how does she like it?
Ignacio: She loves it.
Natalia: Has she ___gotten___ her first paycheck yet?
   7.
Ignacio: No, she hasn't, but I think she's ___already___ spent more than she's made!
   8.

C 🔘 **5** Listen again. Check (✓) the sentences that are true.

❑ 1. Ignacio has a job as a cashier.
☑ 2. Natalia might apply for a job at Danny's.
❑ 3. Ignacio's friends are going to teach Natalia how to use a cash register.
☑ 4. Tracy is working.
❑ 5. Tracy has two jobs.
☑ 6. Natalia is nervous about looking for a job.

Getting a Job 101

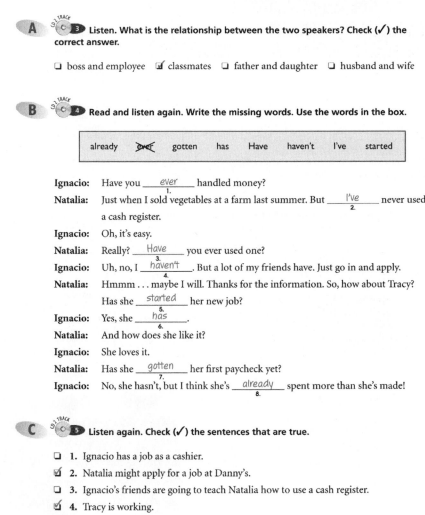

Listening

A **Teaching Time: 10–15 min.**

- **Warm-up.** Take an informal poll. Ask students to raise their hands if they have ever used a cash register. Then ask students to raise their hands if they've ever had to handle money at a job.
- 🎧 Play Track 3 while students listen and complete the task. If necessary, play the track again.
- Call on a student to say the answer. Correct as needed.

B **Teaching Time: 10–15 min.**

- Have students read the words in the box.
- Read the example with the class.
- 🎧 Play Track 4 while students listen and complete the task. Pause the recording as each answer is given. Have students say the answers when you pause the recording.
- 🎧 Play Track 4 again as students read along.

C **Teaching Time: 10–15 min.**

- 🎧 Play Track 5 while students listen and complete the task.
- 🎧 Play Track 5 again, pausing after each answer is given.

Expansion Have students correct the statements to make them true. Call on students to read the corrected sentences.

Multilevel Strategy

Pre-level: Make photocopies of the audioscript. Give it to students before they complete Exercise C.

Option

Assign Unit 8 Supplementary Vocabulary Exercises on the Teacher's Resource Disk as homework or on the Student Persistence CD-ROM as self-access practice.

Grammar to Communicate 1

Present Perfect: Regular Verbs

Teaching Time: 5–10 min.

- Have students study the chart and the Look Box.
- Write these sentences on the board, labeled as shown:

  We have called the manager. (Present Perfect: Indefinite, or unspecified, time in the past)

  We called him yesterday. (Simple Past: Definite, or specified, time in the past)

- As you point to the first sentence on the board, say: *We use the present perfect when we talk about things that happened sometime before now, but we don't say exactly when they happened. In this example, we say that we called the manager, but we don't say exactly when—the time is not specified. The time is indefinite, so we can use the present perfect.*

- As you point to the second sentence on the board, say: *We use the simple past, not the present perfect, if we are talking about when something happened in the past. The time is definite and specified. In this example, you see the word* yesterday, *which is a definite, specific time. We cannot use the present perfect because the time is given.*

- Say: *We form the present perfect with* have *or* has + *the past participle of the main verb. For regular verbs, the past participle is the same as the simple past form:* verb + -ed. *Use* have *for the subjects* I, you, we, *and* they. *Use* has *for he, she, and it. The contracted form of* has *in the present perfect is* 's: *he's, she's, it's. The contracted from of* have *in the present perfect is* 've: *I've, you've, we've, they've. The negative contractions are* haven't *and* hasn't.

A Teaching Time: 5–10 min.

- Call on a student to read the definitions in the Look Box aloud.
- Take an informal poll. Ask students to raise their hands if they've ever contacted an employment agency, talked to a job counselor, searched for a job online, or attended a job fair.
- Read the examples with the class.

Grammar to Communicate 1

PRESENT PERFECT: REGULAR VERBS

Subject	Have / Has	Past Participle	Subject	Have not / Has not	Past Participle
I We You They	have	called.	I We You They	have not	called.
He She	has		He She	has not	

Contractions	
I + have = I've	I + have not = I haven't
He + has = He's	He + has not = He hasn't

Look

Use the present perfect to talk about indefinite times in the past.
I **have started** a new job.

Use the simple past to talk about definite times in the past.
I **started** a new job yesterday.

A The people in the chart are looking for jobs. Complete the sentences. Use *has, hasn't, have,* or *haven't*.

	CARLOS	JENNIFER	MIKE	SANDRA
apply for a job	yes	yes	no	no
look in the newspaper	yes	no	yes	yes
attend a job fair	no	no	yes	yes
contact an employment agency	no	no	no	yes
talk to a job counselor	no	yes	yes	yes
search for jobs online	yes	no	no	no

1. Jennifer _____has_____ applied for a job.
2. Mike and Sandra ___haven't___ applied for a job.
3. Sandra, Mike, and Carlos ___have___ looked in the newspaper.
4. Jennifer ___hasn't___ looked in the newspaper.
5. Carlos and Jennifer ___haven't___ attended a job fair.
6. Sandra ___has___ attended a job fair.

Look

employment agency = a company that helps people find jobs
job counselor = a person who gives people advice about jobs to apply for
online = on the Internet
job fair = a place where companies look for workers, and workers look for jobs

attend a job fair

- Have students complete the task.
- Call on students to say answers. Correct as needed.

Grammar Notes

1. Use the present perfect to talk about actions at an *indefinite* time in the past, or when the time is not specified in the sentence.

2. Use the simple past to talk about actions at a *definite* time in the past.

3. To form the present perfect, use *has* or *have* and the past participle of the verb. To make the past participle of regular verbs, add *–ed* to the verb.

4. Look at page 296 for information about the spelling rules for past participles. Look at page 300 for information about pronunciation.

5. For more information on this grammar topic, see pages 286–287.

B Write new sentences about the people in Exercise A. Write an affirmative sentence and a negative sentence. Use the present perfect.

1. apply for a job
   Mike hasn't applied for a job.
   Jennifer and Carlos have applied for a job.

2. contact an employment agency
   Sandra has contacted an employment agency.
   Carlos, Jennifer, and Mike haven't contacted an employment agency.

3. talk to a job counselor
   Jennifer, Mike, and Sandra have talked to a job counselor.
   Carlos hasn't talked to a job counselor.

4. search for jobs online
   Carlos has searched for jobs online.
   Jennifer, Mike, and Sandra haven't searched for jobs online.

PAIRS. Talk about yourself. Use the verbs in the chart in Exercise A.

C Write sentences with *ever* and *never*. Some are affirmative, and some are negative.

1. *I haven't ever applied for a job.*
   (I / ever / apply / for a job)
2. *My mother has never worked full-time.*
   (My mother / never / work / full-time)
3. *My father hasn't ever owned a business.*
   (My father / ever / own / a business)
4. *I have never handled a lot of money.*
   (I / never / handle / a lot of money)
5. *My friends haven't ever helped me find a job.*
   (My friends / ever / help / me find a job)
6. *I haven't ever trained people.*
   (I / ever / train / people)

> **Look**
>
> Use *ever* with a negative verb.
> I haven't ever worked.
> Use *never* with an affirmative verb.
> I have never worked.

TIME to TALK

GROUPS. Talk about the things that you have never done in your work life. Would you like to do those things someday? Use the ideas in the box.

fire a worker	work for a relative
hire a worker	work outdoors
manage a department	work overtime
start your own business	work the day shift
work for a large corporation	work the night shift

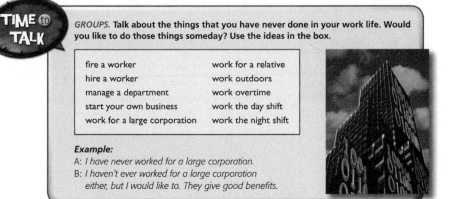

Example:
A: *I have never worked for a large corporation.*
B: *I haven't ever worked for a large corporation either, but I would like to. They give good benefits.*

Getting a Job 103

B Teaching Time: 10–15 min.

- Read the example with the class.
- Have students complete the task.
- Call on students to say answers.
- PAIRS. Have students take turns talking about themselves.

Expansion Start a discussion about how people look for jobs in the students' countries. Ask students which of the various ways of looking for a job in the chart in Exercise A are common in their countries. Ask if there are other ways of looking for a job that are not listed in the chart.

C Teaching Time: 10–15 min.

- Have students study the Look Box. Make sure they understand that *never* means the same thing as *not ever*.
- Call on a student to read the example.
- Have students complete the task.
- Call on students to say answers. Correct as needed.

Watch Out!

Exercise C. English does not permit double negatives. However, double negatives are used in many languages. This can lead students to produce errors such as: *My mother hasn't never worked full-time.* Listen for and correct these errors.

Option

Assign Unit 8 Supplementary Grammar to Communicate 1 Exercises on the Teacher's Resource Disk as homework or on the Student Persistence CD-ROM as self-access practice.

TIME to TALK

Teaching Time: 10–15 min.

- Read the directions with the class. Make sure students understand that they should talk about things that they have *never* done.
- Read the ideas in the box with the class. Explain new words as needed. Say, for example: *a relative is a person in your family.*
- Have two students read the example.
- GROUPS. Have students complete the task. As students are working, sit with each group for a few minutes and correct any errors that you hear in the use of the present perfect. Encourage students to explain why they would or wouldn't like to do that thing someday.
- Write a few of the errors that you heard on the board. Ask for a volunteer to come up to the board and correct them.

Grammar to Communicate 2

Present Perfect: Irregular Verbs

Teaching Time: 5–10 min.

- Have students study the chart.
- Ask: *What is the past participle of the verb* be? (been) *Is it regular or irregular?* (irregular)
- Say: *Many of the most common verbs in English have irregular past participle forms. Sometimes the past participle of irregular verbs is the same as the irregular simple past form, but often it is not. The only way to learn the irregular past participle forms is to memorize them.*
- Tell students they will find a list of irregular verbs on page 298.

A Teaching Time: 5–10 min.

- Have a student read the example.
- Have students complete the task.
- Call on students to say answers. Correct as needed.

B Teaching Time: 5–10 min.

- Read the example with the class.
- Have students complete the task.
- Call on students to say the answers. Correct as needed.

Multilevel Strategy

- **Pre-level:** Give students more time to complete Exercises A and B. Walk around and help as needed.
- **At-level, Above-level:** Have students quiz each other on the three forms of the irregular verbs.

Grammar to Communicate 2

PRESENT PERFECT: IRREGULAR VERBS

Subject	Has / Have	Past Participle		Subject	Has not / Have not	Past Participle	
I You We They	have	been	there.	I You We They	have not	been	there.
He She	has			He She	has		

A Match the parts of sentences.

_g_ 1. She's <u>quit</u> her job, but

_c_ 2. They've <u>made</u> many phone calls, but

_d_ 3. She's <u>taken</u> the test, but

_e_ 4. I've <u>done</u> the report, but

_b_ 5. They've <u>met</u> two people from the company, but

_a_ 6. I've <u>sent</u> two e-mails, but

_f_ 7. I've <u>gone</u> to several job fairs, but

a. I haven't <u>heard</u> from anyone.

b. they haven't <u>seen</u> the boss.

c. they haven't <u>spoken</u> to anyone.

d. she hasn't <u>gotten</u> her score.

e. I haven't <u>given</u> it to my boss.

f. I haven't <u>had</u> any interviews.

g. she hasn't <u>found</u> a new job.

B Complete the table. Look at the chart and the underlined words in Exercise A for help.

BASE FORM OF VERB	SIMPLE PAST	PAST PARTICIPLE	BASE FORM OF VERB	SIMPLE PAST	PAST PARTICIPLE
1. be	was / were	been	9. make	made	made
2. do	did	done	10. meet	met	met
3. find	found	found	11. quit	quit	quit
4. get	got	gotten	12. see	saw	seen
5. give	gave	given	13. send	sent	sent
6. go	went	gone	14. speak	spoke	spoken
7. have	had	had	15. take	took	taken
8. hear	heard	heard			

Grammar Notes

1. Many verbs have irregular past participles. The past participles of these verbs do not have *–ed* at the end. See page 298 for a list of irregular past participles.

2. We often use *already* between *has* or *have* and the past participle. *Already* means *by* or *before now*. It is an indefinite time.

3. We often use *yet* at the end of negative sentences with the present perfect. *Yet* means *until now*. It is an indefinite time, and it is never used with affirmative statements.

4. For more information on this grammar topic, see page 287.

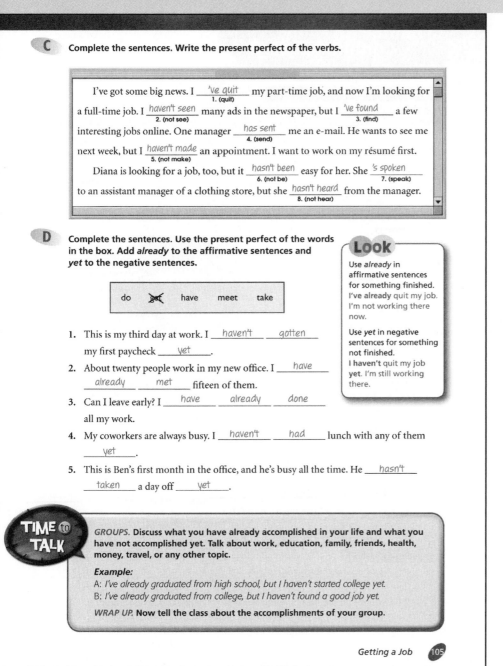

C Complete the sentences. Write the present perfect of the verbs.

> I've got some big news. I __'ve quit__ my part-time job, and now I'm looking for
> _1. (quit)_
> a full-time job. I __haven't seen__ many ads in the newspaper, but I __'ve found__ a few
> _2. (not see)_ _3. (find)_
> interesting jobs online. One manager __has sent__ me an e-mail. He wants to see me
> _4. (send)_
> next week, but I __haven't made__ an appointment. I want to work on my résumé first.
> _5. (not make)_
> Diana is looking for a job, too, but it __hasn't been__ easy for her. She __'s spoken__
> _6. (not be)_ _7. (speak)_
> to an assistant manager of a clothing store, but she __hasn't heard__ from the manager.
> _8. (not hear)_

D Complete the sentences. Use the present perfect of the words in the box. Add *already* to the affirmative sentences and *yet* to the negative sentences.

do	~~get~~	have	meet	take

Look

Use *already* in affirmative sentences for something finished.
I've **already** quit my job. I'm not working there now.

Use *yet* in negative sentences for something not finished.
I haven't quit my job **yet**. I'm still working there.

1. This is my third day at work. I __haven't__ __gotten__ my first paycheck __yet__.

2. About twenty people work in my new office. I __have__ __already__ __met__ fifteen of them.

3. Can I leave early? I __have__ __already__ __done__ all my work.

4. My coworkers are always busy. I __haven't__ __had__ lunch with any of them __yet__.

5. This is Ben's first month in the office, and he's busy all the time. He __hasn't__ __taken__ a day off __yet__.

TIME to TALK

GROUPS. Discuss what you have already accomplished in your life and what you have not accomplished yet. Talk about work, education, family, friends, health, money, travel, or any other topic.

Example:
A: *I've already graduated from high school, but I haven't started college yet.*
B: *I've already graduated from college, but I haven't found a good job yet.*

WRAP UP. Now tell the class about the accomplishments of your group.

Getting a Job **105**

C Teaching Time: 5–10 min.

- Have a student read the example aloud. Ask students when the writer quit his job. *(Sometime before now, but we don't know exactly when.)* Then remind students that we can use the present perfect here because the exact time is not given.
- Have students complete the task.
- Call on students to say answers. Correct as needed.

D Teaching Time: 5–10 min.

- Have students study the Look Box.
- Explain that *already* and *yet* are often used with the present perfect because they both mean *sometime before now*, but the exact time is not specified. *Already* means *by* or *before now*. *Yet* means *until now*. *Yet* is used with negative statements.
- Point out the different positions of *already* and *yet* in sentences. Explain that *already* comes between *has* or *have* and the past participle. *Yet* comes at the end of negative sentences.
- Have students complete the task.
- Call on students to say answers. Correct as needed.

Teaching Tip

Have students learn a few irregular past participle forms every night. Give them daily quizzes that are cumulative, for example: five verbs the first day, those five plus five new verbs the next, those ten plus five new verbs the next, etc. Students are more likely to remember the forms if they study them frequently for short periods of time, rather than all at once.

Option

Assign Unit 8 Supplementary Grammar to Communicate 2 Exercises on the Teacher's Resource Disk as homework or on the Student Persistence CD-ROM as self-access practice.

TIME to TALK

Teaching Time: 10–15 min.

- Read the instructions with the class. Call on two students to read the example.
- Make sure that students understand the word *accomplish*. Write this definition on the board: *accomplish = succeed in doing something, especially after trying very hard.*
- Explain that accomplishments do not have to be related to work or school. They can be personal accomplishments, such as having a baby, losing weight, or quitting smoking.
- GROUPS. Have students complete the task.
- WRAP UP. Have each group choose the most interesting accomplishment of someone in their group. Call on that student to tell the class what he or she has accomplished. Correct grammar as needed.

Grammar to Communicate 3

Present Perfect: *Yes / No* Questions

Teaching Time: 5–10 min.

- Have students study the chart.
- Read the first question in the chart aloud: *Has he ever had a job?* Ask: *What is the main verb?* (had) *What is the auxiliary verb?* (has) *What is the time?* (ever = sometime before now, but not a definite, specified time) *What is the short answer to the question?* (Yes, he has or No, he hasn't.) *In the short answer, is* has *the main verb or the auxiliary verb?* (It's the auxiliary verb.)
- Now read the second question in the chart aloud and ask the same series of questions: *What is the main verb? What is the auxiliary verb? What is the time? What is the short answer to the question? In the short answer, is* have *the main verb or the auxiliary verb?*

A Teaching Time: 10–15 min.

- Have students read the ad and the speech bubble. Ask students where they might see an ad like this (in the Help Wanted section of the newspaper, online, etc.). If necessary, explain *long-distance* and *no tickets*.
- Have students complete the task.
- Call on students to say answers. Correct as needed.

Expansion Take an informal poll. Ask students to raise their hands if they have ever driven 1,500 miles or more (the number of miles from New York to Texas). Have those who raised their hands tell the class about their trip. Then ask students who have driver's licenses to raise their hands if they have ever gotten a ticket. Finally, ask students to raise their hands if they have ever worked as a truck driver. Have those who raised their hands tell the class about their experience.

B Teaching Time: 10–15 min.

- Have students complete the task.
- PAIRS. Have students ask and answer the questions.
- Call on students to ask and answer the questions. Correct as needed.

Grammar to Communicate 3

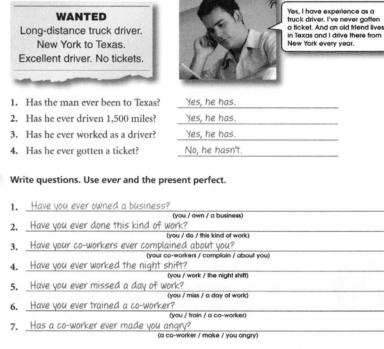

Have/ Has	Subject		Past Participle		Affirmative			Negative		
Has	he she	ever	had	a job?	Yes,	he she	has.	No,	he she	hasn't.
Have	you they		driven	a truck?		I we they	have.		I we they	haven't.

A Answer the questions. Use short answers.

WANTED
Long-distance truck driver.
New York to Texas.
Excellent driver. No tickets.

Yes, I have experience as a truck driver. I've never gotten a ticket. And an old friend lives in Texas and I drive there from New York every year.

1. Has the man ever been to Texas? <u>Yes, he has.</u>
2. Has he ever driven 1,500 miles? <u>Yes, he has.</u>
3. Has he ever worked as a driver? <u>Yes, he has.</u>
4. Has he ever gotten a ticket? <u>No, he hasn't.</u>

B Write questions. Use *ever* and the present perfect.

1. <u>Have you ever owned a business?</u>
   (you / own / a business)
2. <u>Have you ever done this kind of work?</u>
   (you / do / this kind of work)
3. <u>Have your co-workers ever complained about you?</u>
   (your co-workers / complain / about you)
4. <u>Have you ever worked the night shift?</u>
   (you / work / the night shift)
5. <u>Have you ever missed a day of work?</u>
   (you / miss / a day of work)
6. <u>Have you ever trained a co-worker?</u>
   (you / train / a co-worker)
7. <u>Has a co-worker ever made you angry?</u>
   (a co-worker / make / you angry)

Which questions would an interviewer probably <u>not</u> ask at an interview?

Expansion Start a discussion about the types of questions that are usually asked at a job interview in the students' countries and in the United States. Make a note of any differences.

Multilevel Strategy

- **Pre-level:** Give students more time to complete Exercises A and B. Walk around and help as needed.
- **At-level, Above-level:** While you are working with the pre-level students, have the other students complete Unit 8 Supplementary Grammar Exercise B on the Teacher's Resource Disk. Provide them with the answer key so that they can correct themselves.

Grammar Notes

1. To make a *yes / no* question in the present perfect, use *has* or *have* before the subject and the past participle of the verb. Use *has* or *have* in short answers.
2. When we ask someone a question with *Have you ever . . . ,* we are asking about the time period from any time in the past until now. The time is indefinite.
3. We cannot use *ever* in affirmative statements or short answers.
4. We can also ask a question with *yet*. Put *yet* at the end of the question.
5. We can also use *yet* in negative statements and short answers.
6. For more information on this grammar topic, see page 287.

C Three people have applied for a job as manager of a supermarket. Look at the information about them. Write questions with *ever*. Then answer the questions.

	BE A MANAGER	TRAIN WORKERS	HAVE A PROBLEM WITH A CO-WORKER	FIRE PEOPLE	HANDLE A LOT OF CASH	HIRE PEOPLE
Lenore Johnson	yes	no	yes	yes	yes	yes
Christine Huggins	no	no	yes	no	no	yes
Roger Mendoza	no	yes	no	yes	yes	yes

1. Has Ms. Johnson ever been a manager?   Yes, she has.
   (Ms. Johnson / be a manager)
2. Have Ms. Huggins and Mr. Mendoza ever been managers?   No, they haven't.
   (Ms. Huggins and Mr. Mendoza / be managers)
3. Has Ms. Huggins ever trained workers?   No, she hasn't.
   (Ms. Huggins / train workers)
4. Have Ms. Johnson and Ms. Huggins ever had problems with a co-worker?   Yes, they have.
   (Ms. Johnson and Ms. Huggins / have problems with a coworker)
5. Have Ms. Johnson and Mr. Mendoza ever fired people?   Yes, they have.
   (Ms. Johnson and Mr. Mendoza / fire people)
6. Has Ms. Huggins ever handled a lot of cash?   No, she hasn't.
   (Ms. Huggins / handle a lot of cash)
7. Has Mr. Mendoza ever hired people?   Yes, he has.
   (Mr. Mendoza / hire people)

PAIRS. Ask and answer other questions about the job candidates. Who do you think should get the job?

TIME to TALK

GROUPS. What kinds of jobs do the people in your group want in the future? What questions might an interviewer ask for each job? Write two or more questions for each person in your group.

STUDENT	JOB	QUESTIONS
Marcella	hairdresser	Have you ever been to beauty school? Have you ever worked in a hair salon?

WRAP UP. Now tell the class about the jobs the people in your group want. Does a student in another group want the same job? If so, compare the questions.

Getting a Job 107

- Read the examples with the class.
- Have students complete the task.
- Call on students to ask and answer the questions. Correct as needed.
- PAIRS. Have students complete the second part of the task.
- Ask volunteers to write their additional questions on the board.
- Call on several students to say who they think should get the job. Have them explain their answers.

Culture Note

Exercise A. Students may not understand exactly how far 1,500 miles is. You might want to give students the equivalent in kilometers (2,414 km). Even if students have learned the system of weights and measures used in the United States, it might be difficult for them to do the conversions in their heads. Provide students with a list of common weights and measures and their equivalents.

Option

Assign Unit 8 Supplementary Grammar to Communicate 3 Exercises on the Teacher's Resource Disk as homework or on the Student Persistence CD-ROM as self-access practice.

TIME to TALK

Teaching Time: 10–15 min.

- Read the directions and the example with the class.
- GROUPS. Have students complete the task. As they are working, walk around and help with vocabulary and grammar.
- WRAP UP. Ask volunteers to write their groups' questions on the board. Then have the class guess the jobs that the students in the group want. Finally, have the class match each person in the group to a job. The group tells them if their guesses are correct.
- Point out any questions on the board are not common or are inappropriate in job interviews in the United States.

Review and
Challenge

Grammar

Teaching Time: 5–10 min.

- Have a student read the corrected example.
- Have students complete the task.
- 🎧 Play Track 6 as students listen and check their answers.
- 🎧 Play Track 6 again, this time pausing after each answer is given.
- Call on students to read the answers. Correct as needed.

Multilevel Strategy

- **Pre-level:** Give students the audioscript. Tell them to compare it to the conversation in the book, and find the errors.
- **At-level, Above-level:** When students give each answer, have them also identify the type of error, and explain why it is wrong. For example, in the first error, *Have* is incorrect because the subject is Annie—she. In the present perfect, the subject *she* takes *has*, not *have*.

Dictation

Teaching Time: 5–10 min.

- 🎧 Play Track 7 while students listen and write what they hear.
- 🎧 Play Track 7 again while students check their answers.
- Call on students to write sentences on the board.
- 🎧 Play Track 7 again and correct the sentences on the board.

Multilevel Strategy

- **Pre-level:** Give students a worksheet with some of the words from the dictation already provided.

Speaking

Teaching Time: 10–15 min.

- Read the directions with the class.
- Call on two students to read the example.

Review and Challenge

Grammar

🎧 **6** This conversation has seven mistakes. The first mistake is corrected for you. Find and correct the other six mistakes. Then listen and check your answers.

Raj: Hi, Liz. How are you and the family? ~~Have~~ *Has* Annie found a job?

Liz: No, she ~~doesn't~~ *hasn't*. It's ~~ever~~ *never* been easy for her to find a job.

Raj: ~~Is~~ *Has* she ever searched for a job online? I've found lots of jobs that way.

Liz: I'm not sure. But she's ~~go~~ *gone* to several employment agencies. How about your new job? ~~You have~~ *Have you* started yet?

Raj: Yes, ~~I've~~ *I have*. It's a little hard because I have to work the night shift.

Liz: Oh, that is hard. I guess I'm lucky. I've always had the day shift.

work the night shift

Dictation

🎧 **7** Listen. You will hear five sentences. Write them in your notebook. *See the audioscript on p. 315 for the sentences.*

Speaking

ON YOUR OWN. Look at the experiences in the chart. Make questions with *ever*. Then walk around the classroom and ask the questions. Write your classmates' names in the chart.

Example:
You: *Raul, have you ever had a job?*
Raul: *No, I haven't had a job yet.*

EXPERIENCES	CLASSMATES
never had a job	Raul
never spoken English at work	
never worn a uniform at work	
never had a bad boss	
never disliked a co-worker	
never been late to work	
never quit a job	
never worked overtime	
never worked the night shift	

108   Unit 8

- Have students complete the task.
- While students are working, copy the chart from the book onto the board.
- Call on students to give you the names of their classmates who have had each experience. Have them use full sentences, for example: *Raul and Sonam have never had a job.* Correct as needed. Write the names in the chart.

Multilevel Strategy

Pre-level: Help students form the first couple of questions from the prompts. Continue to provide support as needed.

Listening

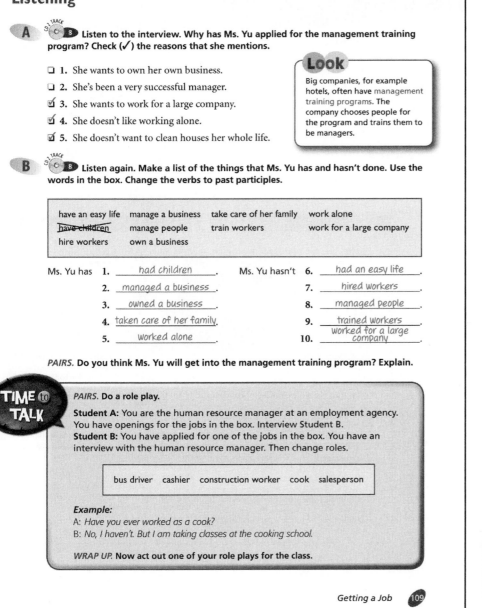

A 🎧 TRACK 8 Listen to the interview. Why has Ms. Yu applied for the management training program? Check (✓) the reasons that she mentions.

❑ 1. She wants to own her own business.

❑ 2. She's been a very successful manager.

☑ 3. She wants to work for a large company.

☑ 4. She doesn't like working alone.

☑ 5. She doesn't want to clean houses her whole life.

Look

Big companies, for example hotels, often have management training programs. The company chooses people for the program and trains them to be managers.

B 🎧 TRACK 8 Listen again. Make a list of the things that Ms. Yu has and hasn't done. Use the words in the box. Change the verbs to past participles.

have an easy life	manage a business	take care of her family	work alone
~~have children~~	manage people	train workers	work for a large company
hire workers	own a business		

Ms. Yu has 1. _____had children_____.

2. _____managed a business_____.

3. _____owned a business_____.

4. _____taken care of her family_____.

5. _____worked alone_____.

Ms. Yu hasn't 6. _____had an easy life_____.

7. _____hired workers_____.

8. _____managed people_____.

9. _____trained workers_____.

10. _____worked for a large company_____.

PAIRS. Do you think Ms. Yu will get into the management training program? Explain.

TIME to TALK

PAIRS. **Do a role play.**

Student A: You are the human resource manager at an employment agency. You have openings for the jobs in the box. Interview Student B.
Student B: You have applied for one of the jobs in the box. You have an interview with the human resource manager. Then change roles.

bus driver	cashier	construction worker	cook	salesperson

Example:
A: *Have you ever worked as a cook?*
B: *No, I haven't. But I am taking classes at the cooking school.*

WRAP UP. **Now act out one of your role plays for the class.**

Option

Assign Unit 8 Review and Challenge Supplementary Exercises on the Teacher's Resource Disk as homework or on the Student Persistence CD-ROM as self-access practice.

Listening

A Teaching Time: 5–10 min.

- **Warm-up:** Write *management training program* on the board. Ask students what they think it means. Then tell them to read the explanation in the Look Box. Ask if anyone has ever been in a management training program. Have them tell the class about their experience. Ask if students know of any companies in the area that have management-level training programs. Write the names of the companies on the board.
- 🎧 Play Track 8 while students listen and complete the task.
- 🎧 Play Track 8 again, this time pausing as each reason is mentioned.
- Call on a student to say answers. Correct as needed.

B Teaching Time: 5–10 min.

- Have students read the words in the box before listening.
- 🎧 Play Track 8 while students listen and complete the task.
- 🎧 Play Track 8 again, pausing as each answer is given. Call on students to give the answer before starting the tape again.
- PAIRS. Have students complete the task. Ask for volunteers to explain their opinions.

Multi-level Strategy

Pre-level: Give students a copy of the audioscript before they complete Exercise B. Tell them to read along as they listen and complete the task. Have them circle the places in the audioscript where they find the answers.

TIME to TALK

Teaching Time: 10–15 min.

- Explain that *human resources* refers to the department in a company that deals with hiring, training, and firing employees.
- Have two students read the example.
- PAIRS. Have students complete the task. Walk around and help as needed.
- WRAP UP. Call on volunteers to perform their role plays for the class.

Multilevel Strategy

Pre-level: Pair pre-level students together for this activity. Rather than asking them to write their own role play, have them practice reading the audioscript.

Reading

Getting Ready to Read

Teaching Time: 5–10 min.

- Call on a student to read the information in the Reading Skill box aloud.
- Have students complete the task.
- Call on several students to tell you what they think the main topic is. Write their answers on the board, and leave them up as they read the article.

Reading

Teaching Time: 15–20 min.

- Have students read the article.
- Discuss what the main topic is. Have students check their answers from the previous exercise.
- Ask students to explain what a mystery shopper does. Tell them to point to the mystery shopper in the illustration. Ask: *What is she holding in her hand?* (a stop watch) *What is she probably doing?* (timing the salesperson; keeping track of how long he spends with each customer, or how long the customers have to wait)

Multilevel Strategy

- **Pre-level:** Give students more time to complete the reading. Explain unfamiliar vocabulary. However, if the vocabulary is not necessary to their understanding of the text, encourage them to ignore it and continue reading.
- **At-level, Above-level:** After students have finished reading, tell them to underline all of the verbs in the text that are in the present perfect.

Reading

Getting Ready to Read

Read the first paragraph of the article. What is the main topic of the article?

_____what a mystery shopper does_____

Reading

Read the article. Was your answer to Getting Ready to Read correct?

MYSTERY SHOPPERS

Mary Beth has been at the mall all day. She has bought some shoes, gotten a haircut, and had a nice lunch, but she has not spent one penny of her own money. In fact, she's made $40. How? Mary Beth is a mystery shopper.

Mystery shoppers have been around for years, but most people have never heard of them. That is because mystery shoppers look like regular customers. Businesses hire mystery shoppers because they want information that is difficult to get. For example, imagine that a restaurant owner has received several complaints about poor service. However, when he is at the restaurant, there are no problems. That is not surprising, since most employees work harder when the boss is around. To find out the truth about the complaints, he might decide to use a mystery shopper. If he does, he will contact an agency. That agency will e-mail the mystery shopper and ask him or her to go to the restaurant. The shopper will look and act like a regular customer. Afterwards, he or she will answer detailed questions about the experience. In some cases, the shopper will also be paid, usually from $10 to $20.

To become a mystery shopper, you need to take a training course. Sometimes the course is free, but sometimes you have to pay. You also need to have a computer and an e-mail address. You might not make any money at first, but you will get a free meal or a store discount. Mystery shoppers who have had a lot of experience get paid, but even they rarely do it full time. For most mystery shoppers, it is not really a job. It is a good way to get free meals and store discounts by doing what they love to do: Eat out and shop.

110   Unit 8

After You Read

After You Read

A Read the article again. Put the following statements in order from 1 to 8. Write the numbers on the blanks.

_6_ a. The mystery shopper answers the list of questions about the service at the store.

_2_ b. The store owner visits the store, but he doesn't see any service problems.

_8_ c. The mystery shopper gets paid.

_4_ d. The mystery shopper gets an e-mail from the agency about the job, along with a list of questions.

_5_ e. The mystery shopper visits the store and acts like a regular customer.

_1_ f. The store owner gets several complaints about the service at his store.

_7_ g. The mystery shopper e-mails the answers back to the mystery shopping agency.

_3_ h. The store owner contacts an agency.

B Read the article again. Answer the questions. *Wording of answers will vary.*

1. What kinds of businesses use mystery shoppers?
   stores, restaurants, hair salons

2. Do most people notice mystery shoppers? Why or why not?
   No, they don't, because mystery shoppers look and act like regular customers.

3. Why do business owners need to hire mystery shoppers?
   Because they want to find out information that is difficult to get, for example, they
   want to find out if a customer complaint is true.

4. How do mystery shoppers find out about available jobs?
   An agency will e-mail the mystery shopper.

5. What do mystery shoppers get for their services?
   free meals, store discounts, and sometimes money

Getting a Job 111

A Teaching Time: 10–15 min.

- Explain that many texts are not organized in time order. It is often necessary for the reader to put things in the correct order to understand an article, especially if the text explains a process.
- Read the example with the class.
- Have students complete the task. Tell them to mark the places in the text where each step is explained.
- Call on a student to read the statements in order. Stop the student if he or she makes a mistake. Call on another student to correct the mistake and continue.

Multilevel Strategy

All levels: Pair each pre-level student with an at- or above-level student for Exercise A. Make sure the higher-level student in each pair shows the pre-level student the places in the text where each step is explained.

B Teaching Time: 10–15 min.

- Have students read the questions before they read the article again.
- Have students complete the task. Tell them to mark the place in the text where they found the answers. Encourage them to put their answers in their own words wherever possible.
- PAIRS. Have students compare their answers. Tell them to refer to the places they marked in their books if they have different answers.
- Call on students to read their answers. Correct as needed by referring to the places in the text where the answers can be found.

Multilevel Strategy

Above-level: Have students complete the exercise without reading the article again or looking back at the text. Then have them check their answers against the text.

Writing

Getting Ready to Write

A Teaching Time: 5–10 min.

- Have students study the Writing Tip.
- Take an informal poll. Ask students to raise their hands if they have ever written a business letter in English.
- Have students complete the task.
- Call on a student to give the answer. Correct as needed.

B Teaching Time: 10–15 min.

- Have students read the writing model.
- PAIRS. Have students complete the task.

Expansion Start a discussion about service in the students' countries.

- Draw the following table and key on the board:

1 = poor 3 = good			
2 = not bad 4 = very good			
	[country name 1]	[country name 2]	[country name 3]
Post Office			
Taxicabs			
Clothing stores			
Supermarkets			
Fast-food restaurants			
Sit-down restaurants			
Department stores			

- Ask: *How is the service in these places in your country?* Complete the table with the names of the students' countries and the appropriate numbers.

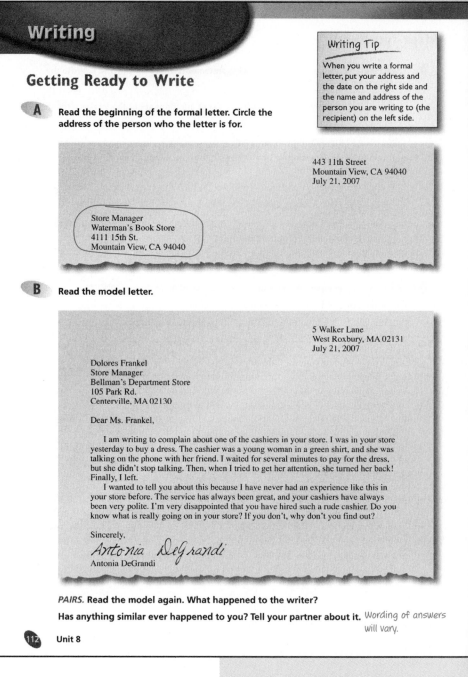

Writing

Writing Tip

When you write a formal letter, put your address and the date on the right side and the name and address of the person you are writing to (the recipient) on the left side.

Getting Ready to Write

A Read the beginning of the formal letter. Circle the address of the person who the letter is for.

> 443 11th Street
> Mountain View, CA 94040
> July 21, 2007
>
> Store Manager
> Waterman's Book Store
> 4111 15th St.
> Mountain View, CA 94040

B Read the model letter.

> 5 Walker Lane
> West Roxbury, MA 02131
> July 21, 2007
>
> Dolores Frankel
> Store Manager
> Bellman's Department Store
> 105 Park Rd.
> Centerville, MA 02130
>
> Dear Ms. Frankel,
>
> I am writing to complain about one of the cashiers in your store. I was in your store yesterday to buy a dress. The cashier was a young woman in a green shirt, and she was talking on the phone with her friend. I waited for several minutes to pay for the dress, but she didn't stop talking. Then, when I tried to get her attention, she turned her back! Finally, I left.
>
> I wanted to tell you about this because I have never had an experience like this in your store before. The service has always been great, and your cashiers have always been very polite. I'm very disappointed that you have hired such a rude cashier. Do you know what is really going on in your store? If you don't, why don't you find out?
>
> Sincerely,
>
> *Antonia DeGrandi*
> Antonia DeGrandi

PAIRS. Read the model again. What happened to the writer?

Has anything similar ever happened to you? Tell your partner about it. Wording of answers will vary.

112 Unit 8

Prewriting: Answering Questions

You are going to write a formal letter to complain about something bad that happened to you. Before you write, answer the questions.

1. What is your address?

2. What is today's date?

3. What is the address of the person you are writing to?

4. What happened to you?

5. Has anything like this ever happened to you before?

6. What do you want the recipient to do?

Writing

Now write a formal letter to complain about something bad that happened to you. The writing tip, the model letter, and your notes will help you. Write in your notebook.

Prewriting

Teaching Time: 15–20 min.

- Have students complete the task.
- PAIRS. Have students show a partner their notes. If the partner doesn't understand something in the notes, tell him or her to ask for clarification.
- Before students begin writing their paragraphs, tell them to show you their notes. Help them to clarify their ideas.

Writing

Teaching Time: 15–20 min.

- Have students complete the task and hand in their letters.

Expansion Have students send their letters. Tell them to bring in any responses that they receive. Pass the responses around the class, along with copies of the students' letters.

Unit 9
Relationships

Learning Goals

- Learn vocabulary to describe relationships
- Learn about the present perfect and present perfect progressive with *for* and *since* and the present perfect progressive: questions
- Listen to a conversation between two sisters and a radio talk show
- Read an article about changing family relationships in China and write a paragraph about recent changes in lifestyles
- Talk about relationships and lifestyles

Learner Persistence

Have students continually identify short-term goals and monitor their success in achieving those goals.

Warm-up

Teaching Time: 5–10 min.

- Have students cover the word boxes and paragraphs and look at the pictures. Have them say what the relationships are among the people in the pictures.
- Write their answers on the board.

Vocabulary

Teaching Time: 10–15 min.

- Have students complete the first task.
- PAIRS. Have students compare their answers.
- 🎧 Play Track 9 while students listen and check their answers.
- Have students look again at the relationships on the board. Which relationships did they guess correctly?
- Have students complete the second task.
- Say each word or phrase and have students repeat chorally.
- Have students say whether the word is a noun or a verb. Correct as needed.

Expansion

- PAIRS. Tell students to look at the pictures and the word boxes. Have them take turns retelling the stories.

Center Stage 3

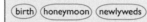

Unit 9
Relationships

Grammar
- Present Perfect: *For* and *Since*
- Present Perfect Progressive: *For* and *Since*
- Present Perfect Progressive: Questions

Vocabulary

🎧 CD 2 TRACK 9 **Complete the sentences with the words in the box. Listen and check your answers. Then circle the nouns in the boxes and underline the verbs.**

(birth) (honeymoon) (newlyweds)

Mira and Andy got married in May. Like many ___newlyweds___, they went to Hawaii on
1.
their ___honeymoon___. Now they are waiting for
2.
the ___birth___ of their first child.
3.

(marriage) remarried (widow) (widower)

Liz and her husband, Joe, had a happy
___marriage___. Joe died last year, and Liz
4.
became a ___widow___. Last week, Liz was
5.
___remarried___. Her new husband, Al, was a
6.
___widower___. It's his second marriage too.
7.

argued broke up (fight)

Ana and Ed went out for a year, but they did not get along very well. They ___argued___
8.
a lot. They had a ___fight___ almost every
9.
day, so they ___broke up___. Now, Ana has a
10.
new boyfriend.

Mira and Andy

Liz and Al

Ana and Ed

114   Unit 9

Multilevel Strategy

- **Pre-level:** Have students take turns reading the stories with a partner.
- **At-level, Above-level:** Have students take turns retelling the stories from memory. Call on students to retell the stories with the new vocabulary.

Listening

A 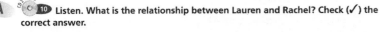 **10** Listen. What is the relationship between Lauren and Rachel? Check (✓) the correct answer.

❏ an aunt and a niece ❏ best friends ❏ neighbors ☑ sisters ❏ sisters-in-law

B **11** Listen again. For each pair of sentences, check (✓) the sentence that you hear.

1. ☑ **a.** We've been getting along great.
   ❏ **b.** We're getting along great.

2. ☑ **a.** We've been busy with the new house, and I've been making friends in the neighborhood.
   ❏ **b.** We're very busy with the new house, and I'm making friends in the neighborhood.

Look

make friends = start to know and like people you meet

3. ❏ **a.** And have you be running much?
   ☑ **b.** And have you been running much?

4. ❏ **a.** It's going to rain for weeks.
   ☑ **b.** It's been raining for weeks.

5. ☑ **a.** We've been wearing summer clothes since the beginning of June.
   ❏ **b.** We've worn summer clothes since the beginning of June.

6. ❏ **a.** But you're only getting married in February.
   ☑ **b.** But you've only been married since February.

C **12** Listen again. Check (✓) the sentences that are true.

❏ **1.** Rachel and Lauren talked on the phone yesterday.
☑ **2.** Rachel didn't use to cook a lot.
❏ **3.** Rachel and Lauren live near each other.
❏ **4.** Rachel's husband doesn't like children.
☑ **5.** Rachel doesn't see her nephews often.
❏ **6.** Rachel has children.

Relationships **115**

Option

Assign Unit 9 Supplementary Vocabulary Exercises on the Teacher's Resource Disk as homework or on the Student Persistence CD-ROM as self-access practice.

Listening

A **Teaching Time: 10–15 min.**

- **Warm-up.** Write the words from Exercise A on the board. Take an informal poll. Ask students to raise their hands if they have a niece, a best friend, a neighbor, a sister, or a sister-in-law. Ask them if they are close to any of them.
- Play Track 10 while students listen and complete the task. If necessary, play the track again.
- Call on a student to say the answer.

B **Teaching Time: 10–15 min.**

- Read the definition in the Look Box. Ask students if it is easy or difficult for them to make friends.
- Call on students to read the sentences.
- Play Track 11 while students listen and complete the task.
- Play Track 11 again, pausing as each answer is given. Have students call out the answers. Correct as needed.

Multilevel Strategy

Pre-level: Make photocopies of the audioscript. Give it to students before they do exercise B.

C **Teaching Time: 10–15 min.**

- Have students read the sentences.
- Play Track 12 while students listen and complete the task.
- Play Track 12 again, pausing as each answer is given. Have students say the answers. Correct as needed.

Multilevel Strategy

- **At-level, Above-level:** When checking answers, challenge students to correct the sentences that are not true.

Grammar to Communicate 1

Present Perfect: *For* and *Since*

Teaching Time: 5–10 min.

- Have students study the chart and the Look Box.
- Draw these graphic organizers on the board, with the sentences from the chart under them.

I have known Jim for 10 years.

since 2002

today

She has known Jim since 2002.

- Say: *We use the present perfect with* for *to show that something has happened over a period of time, such as* ten years. *We use the present perfect with* since *to show that something started at one point in time in the past, such as* 2002.

A   Teaching Time: 5–10 min.

- Read the example with the class.
- Have students complete the task.
- Call on students to say answers. Correct as needed.

B   Teaching Time: 10–15 min.

- Read the example with the class.
- Have students complete the task.
- Call on students to say answers. Correct as needed.

Expansion

- Write the headings *FOR* and *SINCE* on the board.

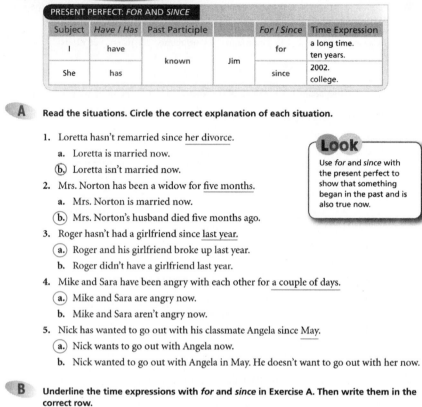

A   Read the situations. Circle the correct explanation of each situation.

1. Loretta hasn't remarried since <u>her divorce</u>.
   a. Loretta is married now.
   (b.) Loretta isn't married now.
2. Mrs. Norton has been a widow for <u>five months</u>.
   a. Mrs. Norton is married now.
   (b.) Mrs. Norton's husband died five months ago.
3. Roger hasn't had a girlfriend since <u>last year</u>.
   (a.) Roger and his girlfriend broke up last year.
   b. Roger didn't have a girlfriend last year.
4. Mike and Sara have been angry with each other for <u>a couple of days</u>.
   (a.) Mike and Sara are angry now.
   b. Mike and Sara aren't angry now.
5. Nick has wanted to go out with his classmate Angela since <u>May</u>.
   (a.) Nick wants to go out with Angela now.
   b. Nick wanted to go out with Angela in May. He doesn't want to go out with her now.

Look

Use *for* and *since* with the present perfect to show that something began in the past and is also true now.

B   Underline the time expressions with *for* and *since* in Exercise A. Then write them in the correct row.

FOR	five months, a couple of days
SINCE	her divorce, last year, May

Complete the statements. Circle the correct answer.

1. Use *for* before
   a. a specific time (for example, *yesterday*)
   (b.) a period of time (for example, *five minutes*)

2. Use *since* before
   (a.) a specific time (for example, *yesterday*)
   b. a period of time (for example, *five minutes*)

116   Unit 9

- Write these time expressions on the board: *their wedding day, years, two days, last month, yesterday, a few minutes*
- Have students tell you where to put each time expression and write it under the correct column. (*FOR*: years, two days, a few minutes; *SINCE*: their wedding day, last month, yesterday)

Grammar Notes

1. Use *for* and *since* with the present perfect to show that something began in the past and is continuing now.
2. Use *for* with a period of time. The period of time must include now.
3. Use *since* with a specific time in the past. The activity began at that specific time, is continuing now, and might continue into the future.
4. For more information on this grammar topic, see page 287.

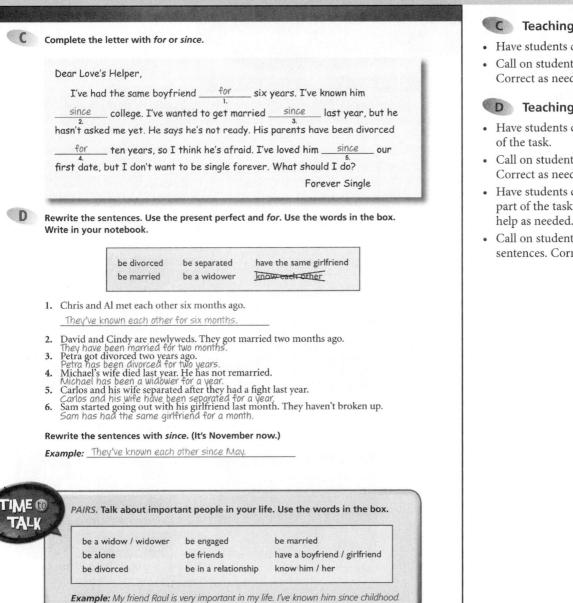

C Complete the letter with *for* or *since*.

Dear Love's Helper,

I've had the same boyfriend __for__ six years. I've known him
__since__ college. I've wanted to get married __since__ last year, but he
hasn't asked me yet. He says he's not ready. His parents have been divorced

__for__ ten years, so I think he's afraid. I've loved him __since__ our
first date, but I don't want to be single forever. What should I do?

Forever Single

D Rewrite the sentences. Use the present perfect and *for*. Use the words in the box.
Write in your notebook.

be divorced	be separated	have the same girlfriend
be married	be a widower	~~know each other~~

1. Chris and Al met each other six months ago.
   They've known each other for six months.

2. David and Cindy are newlyweds. They got married two months ago.
   They have been married for two months.
3. Petra got divorced two years ago.
   Petra has been divorced for two years.
4. Michael's wife died last year. He has not remarried.
   Michael has been a widower for a year.
5. Carlos and his wife separated after they had a fight last year.
   Carlos and his wife have been separated for a year.
6. Sam started going out with his girlfriend last month. They haven't broken up.
   Sam has had the same girlfriend for a month.

Rewrite the sentences with *since*. (It's November now.)

Example: *They've known each other since May.*

TIME to TALK

PAIRS. Talk about important people in your life. Use the words in the box.

be a widow / widower	be engaged	be married
be alone	be friends	have a boyfriend / girlfriend
be divorced	be in a relationship	know him / her

Example: My friend Raul is very important in my life. I've known him since childhood.
He used to be married to my best friend, but they have been divorced for several years.

Relationships 117

C Teaching Time: 5–10 min.

- Have students complete the task.
- Call on students to say answers.
  Correct as needed.

D Teaching Time: 5–10 min.

- Have students complete the first part
  of the task.
- Call on students to say answers.
  Correct as needed.
- Have students complete the second
  part of the task. Walk around and
  help as needed.
- Call on students to read their
  sentences. Correct as needed.

Option

Assign Unit 9 Supplementary Grammar to
Communicate 1 Exercises on the Teacher's
Resource Disk as homework or on the
Student Persistence CD-ROM as self-
access practice.

TIME to TALK

Teaching Time: 10–15 min.

- Read the words in the box with the class. Write *be engaged, be in a relationship,*
  and *be alone* on the board.
- Ask the class: *Which do couples do first, get married or get engaged?* (get
  engaged) *If you are in a relationship, is it a friendship or a romantic relationship?*
  (a romantic relationship) *When someone is alone, are they married or single?*
  (single)
- Call on a student to read the example.
- PAIRS. Have students complete the task.
- Ask volunteers to tell you about their relationships. Correct as needed.

Unit 9 T-117

Grammar to Communicate 2

Present Perfect Progressive: *For* and *Since*

Teaching Time: 5–10 min.

- Have students study the chart and the Look Box.
- Write on the board:
  We have been talking for ten minutes.
- Say: *We use the present perfect progressive with action verbs when we want to stress that something started in the past and is still happening now. In the example, we started talking ten minutes ago, and we are still talking right now.*
- Point to the sentence on the board, and say: *We form the present perfect progressive with* have *or* has + *the past participle of* be (been) *and the present participle, or verb* + *ing.*
- Ask: *What time is it now? When did class start? So how long have we been studying today?* (We've been studying for [amount of time]; since [time].)

 A **Teaching Time: 10–15 min.**

- Have a student read the example. Make sure students notice the two times in each picture.
- Have students complete the task.
- PAIRS. Have students compare their answers.
- Call on students to say answers. Correct as needed.

Multilevel Strategy

- **Pre-level:** Give students more time to complete the exercise. Assist them as needed.
- **At-level, Above-level:** In pairs, have students take turns covering the sentences and saying them from memory.

Expansion Ask students why the people in the pictures are upset. Then ask them if they have ever gotten angry at someone for doing any of the things in the pictures.

PRESENT PERFECT PROGRESSIVE: *FOR* AND *SINCE*

Subject	Have / Has	Been + Present Participle	For / Since	Time Expression	Subject	Have not / Has not	Been + Present Participle	For / Since	Time Expression
I We You They	have	been talking	for	10 minutes.	I We You They	have not	been talking	for	25 minutes.
He She	has		since	11:00.	He She	has not		since	11:00.

A Complete the sentences with the missing time expressions.

Look

Use the present perfect progressive to show that something began in the past and is also true now.

1.

She's been waiting for 15 minutes .
It's been raining since 6:00 .

2.

She's been talking since 11:00 .
He's been waiting for 30 minutes .

3.

They've been watching TV since
  2:00 .
They've been making a mess for
an hour and a half .

4.

They've been driving around for
  45 minutes .
She's been reading the map since
  2:00 .

118 Unit 9

Grammar Notes

1. We often use the present perfect progressive with these time expressions: *recently, lately, for* (+ period of time), *since* (+ specific time).

2. We use the present perfect progressive and *for* and *since* with <u>action</u> verbs (for example, *go*) to show that something began in the past and continues now.

3. We use the present perfect with <u>nonaction</u> verbs (for example, *know*) to show that something began in the past and continues now. See page 298 for a list of nonaction (stative) verbs.

4. For more information on this grammar topic, see pages 287–288.

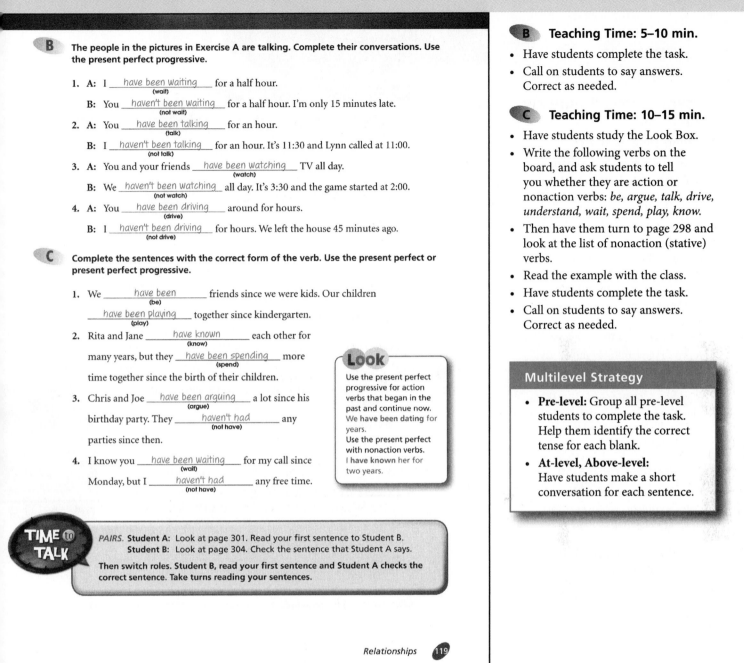

B The people in the pictures in Exercise A are talking. Complete their conversations. Use the present perfect progressive.

1. **A:** I ___have been waiting___ for a half hour.
       (wait)
   B: You ___haven't been waiting___ for a half hour. I'm only 15 minutes late.
       (not wait)

2. **A:** You ___have been talking___ for an hour.
       (talk)
   B: I ___haven't been talking___ for an hour. It's 11:30 and Lynn called at 11:00.
       (not talk)

3. **A:** You and your friends ___have been watching___ TV all day.
       (watch)
   B: We ___haven't been watching___ all day. It's 3:30 and the game started at 2:00.
       (not watch)

4. **A:** You ___have been driving___ around for hours.
       (drive)
   B: I ___haven't been driving___ for hours. We left the house 45 minutes ago.
       (not drive)

C Complete the sentences with the correct form of the verb. Use the present perfect or present perfect progressive.

1. We ___have been___ friends since we were kids. Our children
       (be)
   ___have been playing___ together since kindergarten.
       (play)

2. Rita and Jane ___have known___ each other for
       (know)
   many years, but they ___have been spending___ more
       (spend)
   time together since the birth of their children.

3. Chris and Joe ___have been arguing___ a lot since his
       (argue)
   birthday party. They ___haven't had___ any
       (not have)
   parties since then.

4. I know you ___have been waiting___ for my call since
       (wait)
   Monday, but I ___haven't had___ any free time.
       (not have)

Look

Use the present perfect progressive for action verbs that began in the past and continue now. We have been dating for years.
Use the present perfect with nonaction verbs. I have known her for two years.

TIME to TALK

PAIRS. **Student A:** Look at page 301. Read your first sentence to Student B.
Student B: Look at page 304. Check the sentence that Student A says.

Then switch roles. Student B, read your first sentence and Student A checks the correct sentence. Take turns reading your sentences.

Relationships 119

B Teaching Time: 5–10 min.

- Have students complete the task.
- Call on students to say answers. Correct as needed.

C Teaching Time: 10–15 min.

- Have students study the Look Box.
- Write the following verbs on the board, and ask students to tell you whether they are action or nonaction verbs: *be, argue, talk, drive, understand, wait, spend, play, know.*
- Then have them turn to page 298 and look at the list of nonaction (stative) verbs.
- Read the example with the class.
- Have students complete the task.
- Call on students to say answers. Correct as needed.

Multilevel Strategy

- **Pre-level:** Group all pre-level students to complete the task. Help them identify the correct tense for each blank.
- **At-level, Above-level:** Have students make a short conversation for each sentence.

Option

Assign Unit 9 Supplementary Grammar to Communicate 2 Exercises on the Teacher's Resource Disk as homework or on the Student Persistence CD-ROM as self-access practice.

TIME to TALK

Teaching Time: 10–15 min.

- Read the example with the class.
- PAIRS. Have students complete the task.
- Have students look at their partner's page to check their work.

Present Perfect Progressive: Questions

Teaching Time: 5–10 min.

- Have students study the chart.
- Call on two students to read the *yes / no* questions and answers from the chart aloud.
- Point out that in a *yes / no* question with the present perfect progressive, the subject comes after *has / have*.
- Write the example with *How long* from the chart on the board:

  Q: *How long has he been going out with her?*

  A: *For a month.* OR *Since June.*
- As you point to the example, say: *We often use the question phrase* How long *with the present perfect progressive.* How long *means* for how much time *or* for what period of time. *We usually answer* How long *questions with* for *or* since.

- Have students complete the task.
- Call on students to say answers. Correct as needed.

Expansion Ask questions about Deb and Jim's relationship, for example: *What is their relationship? Do you think they are married? Why or why not? Do you think they have a good relationship? Why or why not? What advice can Carla give Deb?* Have students answer in full sentences. Correct their grammar as needed.

- Have students complete the task.
- Call on students to say answers. Correct as needed.
- PAIRS. Have students complete the second part of the task.

Multilevel Strategy

All levels: Pair pre-level students with at- or above-level students for the pairs activity. The more advanced students can help the lower-level students.

PRESENT PERFECT PROGRESSIVE: QUESTIONS

Have / Has	Subject	Been + Present Participle		Affirmative			Negative	
Has	he she	been dating?	Yes,	he she	has.	No,	he she	hasn't.
Have	you they			I they	have.		I they	haven't.

Information Questions with *How long*				Answers
How long	has	he	been going out with her?	For a month. Since June.
	have	you		

 A   Deb is talking to Carla about her relationship with Jim. Answer the questions.

1. **Carla:** Have you and Jim been arguing a lot?   **Deb:** Yes, ___we have___.
2. **Carla:** Have you been going out with other guys?   **Deb:** No, ___I haven't___.
3. **Carla:** Has Jim been talking to other girls?   **Deb:** Yes, ___he has___.
4. **Carla:** Has Jim been spending all his free time with you?   **Deb:** No, ___he hasn't___.
5. **Carla:** Has Jim been going to your house on weekends?   **Deb:** No, ___he hasn't___.

B   Tony is unhappy because he doesn't know many people. Ask questions with *how long* and the present perfect progressive of the underlined words.

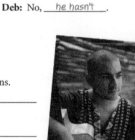

1. I'm living in the United States, but I don't know any Americans.
   How long have you been living in the United States?

2. I'm staying at my relatives' house. They work all the time.
   How long have you been staying at your relatives' house?

3. I'm trying to find a nice person to date, but it isn't easy.
   How long have you been trying to find a nice person to date?

4. I'm working here. I have a lot of co-workers, but I'm not friends with any of them.
   How long have you been working here?

5. I'm taking an English class, but my classmates are always busy after class.
   How long have you been taking an English class?

PAIRS. Check (✓) the sentences that are true for you. Then ask and answer the questions.

Expansion Start a discussion about whether it is easy or difficult to make friends in the city where you are. If you are teaching in the United States or another English-speaking country, ask students if they think it is easier to make friends in their countries than where they are living now. Have them explain their answers.

Grammar Notes

1. To make a *yes / no* question in the present perfect progressive, add *has* or *have* before the subject + *been* + the present participle of the verb. Use *has* or *have* in short answers.

2. To make information questions, *has* or *have* comes after the question word (*how long, what,* etc.).

3. For more information on this grammar topic, see page 288.

C What has been happening? Write questions with the
present perfect progressive and *lately* or *recently*.

1. <u>Have you been feeling homesick lately?</u>
   (feel homesick / lately)
2. <u>Have you been spending a lot of time alone recently?</u>
   (spend a lot of time alone / recently)
3. <u>Have you been working a lot lately?</u>
   (work a lot / lately)
4. <u>Have you been going to a lot of parties recently?</u>
   (go to a lot of parties / recently)
5. <u>Have you been going out a lot with your friends lately?</u>
   (go out a lot with your friends / lately)
6. <u>Have you been speaking a lot of English recently?</u>
   (speak a lot of English / recently)
7. <u>Have you been dating anyone lately?</u>
   (date anyone / lately)

Look

Use *recently* and *lately*
to talk about something
that began a short time
ago and is continuing
now.
Last year, my wife and
I had a lot of fights,
but **lately** we've been
getting along very well.

PAIRS. Ask and answer the questions.

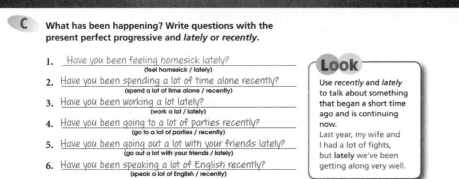

TIME to TALK

CLASS. Walk around the class and talk to your
classmates. For each question, find one person
who answers "yes." Then ask a question with *How
long* and write the person's name and answer. If
someone answers "no," ask another classmate.

Example: You: *Are you married?*
      Homero: *Yes, I am.*
         You: *How long have you been married?*
   Homero: *I've been married since 1999. How about you?*

If you don't want to answer a
personal question, you can say,
"I'd rather not say."

QUESTION	NAME	HOW LONG . . .
Are you married?	Homero	**(be)** *since 1999*
Are you a parent?		(be)
Do you live alone?		(live)
Do you have a roommate?		(have)
Do you have a best friend?		(have)
Do you have a pet?		(have)
Do you play a musical instrument?		(play)
Do you play on a sports team?		(play)

WRAP UP. Now tell the class about a few of your classmates.

Relationships 121

C Teaching Time: 10–15 min.

- Call on a student to read the
  information in the Look Box aloud.
- Read the example with the class.
- Have students complete the task.
- Call on students to say answers.
  Correct as needed.
- PAIRS. Have students take turns
  asking and answering the questions.
- Ask for volunteers to ask and answer
  the questions.

Culture Note

Time to Talk. Explain that in the United
States, some people might think that it is
impolite to ask some of these questions
the first time you meet them. For example,
an American would probably wait until
he had gotten to know you better before
asking the first six questions on the list.
Ask students which questions are polite
to ask the first time they meet someone in
their countries.

Option

Assign Unit 9 Supplementary Grammar to
Communicate 3 Exercises on the Teacher's
Resource Disk as homework or on the
Student Persistence CD-ROM as self-
access practice.

TIME to TALK

Teaching Time: 15–20 min.

- Read the instructions with the class.
- Call on two students to read the example.
- Point out the information in the cartoon. Make sure students understand that
  they don't have to answer a question if they don't want to.
- CLASS. Have students stand up and complete the task. As they are working,
  walk around and help with vocabulary and grammar.
- WRAP UP. Ask volunteers to tell the class about their classmates. Correct their
  sentences as needed.

Grammar

Teaching Time: 5–10 min.

- Have a student read the corrected example.
- Have students complete the task.
- 🎧 Play Track 13 as students listen and check their answers.
- 🎧 Play Track 13 again, this time pausing after each answer is given.
- Call on students to read the answers. Correct as needed.

Multilevel Strategy

- **Pre-level:** Give students the audioscript. Pair them and have them practice reading the corrected conversation.
- **At-level, Above-level:** Have students practice the conversation a couple of times, and then have them role-play it from memory.

Dictation

Teaching Time: 5–10 min.

- 🎧 Play Track 14 while students listen and write what they hear.
- 🎧 Play Track 14 again while students check their answers.
- PAIRS. Have students compare their answers and decide who has the correct answer, based on the grammar.
- Ask volunteers to write their sentences on the board.
- 🎧 Play Track 14 again and correct the sentences on the board.

Multilevel Strategy

Pre-level: Group all pre-level students. Work with them while their classmates are checking each other's dictations. Read the sentences in the dictation as many times as the students need.

Speaking

Teaching Time: 10–15 min.

- Have students look at number 1 on page 118.
- Call on two students to read the example on page 122.

Grammar

🎧 CD 2 TRACK 13 **This conversation has seven mistakes. The first mistake is corrected for you. Find and correct the other six mistakes. Then listen and check your answers.**

Kate: John, how long ~~we have~~ *have we* been going out?

John: Let's see. It's December. I moved back here in June. So we've been going out ~~since~~ *for* six months.

Kate: And how long have we ~~been knowing~~ *known* each other?

John: For a year.

Kate: And have ~~we any~~ *we had any* conversations since last year?

John: Sure. Every day. We're having a conversation right now.

Kate: No. I mean a real conversation, a conversation about our relationship.

John: About our relationship?

Kate: Yeah. This is probably a surprise to you, but ~~I'm not~~ *I haven't been* happy for about a month.

John: Really? Why not?

Kate: You've been ~~work~~ *working* a lot and you have ~~been not~~ *not been* paying attention to me.

John: Oh, come on, Katie. You know I love you.

Dictation

🎧 CD 2 TRACK 14 **Listen. You will hear five sentences. Write them in your notebook.** *See the audioscript on p. 316 for the sentences.*

Speaking

PAIRS. **Look at the sentences and illustrations on page 118. Choose one of the situations and do a role play. Then act out your role play for the class.**

Example:

A: *I can't believe it! I've been waiting for 15 minutes! We're going to be late for the party. You've known about this party for two weeks!*

B: *I'm sorry, but you know I've been working late every night. I've told you how busy I am at work, but you haven't been listening.*

A: *I've been listening. I think* you *haven't been trying!*

122   Unit 9

- Have students complete the task. Walk around and help as needed.
- Call on volunteers to do their role play for the class.

Multilevel Strategy

All levels: Pair pre-level students with at- or above-level students for this activity. The pre-level student should read the sentence that is given in the book while the other student comes up with a response. If the role play is more than two exchanges long, have the more advanced student write down his/her partner's lines. Allow pre-level students to read their lines while their partners perform their roles from memory.

Option

Assign Unit 9 Review and Challenge Supplementary Exercises on the Teacher's Resource Disk as homework or on the Student Persistence CD-ROM as self-access practice.

Listening

A 🔘 **15** Listen to the radio show. What is the major problem in Mary's relationship? Check (✓) the correct answer.

❑ her children   ❑ her house   ❑ her husband's job   ☑ money   ❑ music

B 🔘 **15** Listen again. Check (✓) the correct answers.

1. What is true about Mary and her husband?
   ❑ **a.** She has never worked.
   ❑ **b.** They've been married a long time.
   ☑ **c.** He has been working since he was a teenager.
   ❑ **d.** They've bought a new house.
   ☑ **e.** They haven't had any children yet.

2. What is Mary worried about?
   ☑ **a.** She and her husband have been arguing a lot recently.
   ☑ **b.** Her husband has been spending a lot of money lately.
   ☑ **c.** Her husband has never saved any money.
   ❑ **d.** Her husband hasn't found a job.
   ☑ **e.** They won't have the money to buy a house.

TIME to TALK

GROUPS. **Discuss the questions.**

1. Have you ever had a fight with someone over money?

2. In your opinion, what are the most common things that couples argue about?

3. Divorce has become more and more common in the U.S. in the past fifty years. Why do you think it has become so common? In your opinion, is that a good thing or a bad thing?

4. What has been happening with the number of divorces in your country recently? Has it been going up or down, or has it stayed the same?

WRAP UP. **Share your answers with the class.**

Example: The number of divorces has been going down in my country. I think it is because fewer people are getting married.

Relationships 123

Listening

A **Teaching Time: 5–10 min.**

- **Warm-up:** Explain that students are going to listen to a radio call-in show. Ask if radio call-in shows are popular in their countries. Then ask if they ever listen to talk radio. Ask them to tell you which topics are popular on talk radio, either in their countries or in the United States. Make a list on the board.

- Have students read the directions and the answer choices.

- 🎧 Play Track 15 while students listen and complete the task.

- 🎧 Play Track 15 again, and have students check their answers.

- Call on a student to say answers. Correct as needed.

Multilevel Strategy

Pre-level: Give students a copy of the audioscript before they complete Exercise A. Tell them to read along as they listen and complete the task. Have them circle the place in the audioscript where they find the answer. If you think they can handle the challenge, collect the audioscripts before they complete Exercise B.

B **Teaching Time: 5–10 min.**

- Have students read the questions and possible answers before listening.

- Have them check any answers that they are already sure are true.

- 🎧 Play Track 15 while students listen and complete the task.

- 🎧 Play Track 15 again, pausing as each answer is given. Call on students to give the answer before starting the recording again.

Teaching Tip

Time to Talk. Before the discussion, look on the Internet for some recent statistics on divorce in the United States and/or in the countries your students come from. Try these search terms: *divorce statistics (country name) 20___ (current or previous year)*. At the end of the discussion, give the information to the students. Alternatively, you can have students look up the statistics for homework and present them to the class the next day.

TIME to TALK

Teaching Time: 10–15 min.

- Call on students to read the questions. Explain any unfamiliar vocabulary.

- GROUPS. Have students complete the task.

- WRAP UP. Ask each group to tell the class one interesting thing that they learned in the discussion. Write what they say on the board. Correct any mistakes in forming the present perfect or present perfect progressive.

Multilevel Strategy

Pre-level: Group all pre-level students. Join the group and lead the discussion.

Reading

Getting Ready to Read

Teaching Time: 5–10 min.

- **Warm-up.** Have students read the title of the article and look at the picture. Have them guess what the article will be about. Write their guesses on the board.
- Call on a student to read the information in the Reading Skill box aloud.
- Have students complete the task. Tell them to raise their hands as soon as they have found all three answers; then they can start reading the article.
- Make a note of the order in which students raised their hands. Walk around the class and check their answers to the scanning exercise as they are reading. Make a note of any students with incorrect answers, but do not interrupt them.

Reading

Teaching Time: 15–20 min.

- Have students read the article.
- Have students look again at the guesses on the board. Were any of them correct?
- Call on students to give the answers to Getting Ready to Read. Correct as needed.

Multilevel Strategy

- **Pre-level:** Group all pre-level students. Read the article aloud as students follow along in their books. Encourage them to stop and ask questions about anything they don't understand.
- **At-level, Above-level:** After students have finished reading, tell them to underline the verbs in the text that are in the present perfect or present perfect progressive, and to circle the verbs that are in the simple past tense. Have them work in pairs, and discuss why the different tenses were used.

Reading

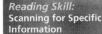

Getting Ready to Read

Reading Skill:
Scanning for Specific Information

When you need to find information quickly in a reading, look for specific information like numbers or dates. You will find them more quickly than words.

Read the questions. Then scan the article to find the answers.

1. When did the One-Child Policy begin?

   in 1979

2. How many only children have been born in China since the One-Child Policy began?

   eighty million

3. What is "4-2-1"?

   four grandparents and two parents
   focus on one child

Reading

Read the article. Were your answers in Getting Ready to Read correct?

THE ONE-CHILD POLICY

In 1979, the Chinese government introduced the One-Child Policy to slow down **population growth**. Families in the city could have only one child. Families in the countryside could have two, but only if the first child was a girl. The policy has been very successful. It has slowed population growth to about 10 million people a year. Now the first **generation** of children born under the policy are becoming adults. It is clear that the policy has changed Chinese family life.

Eighty million children with no brothers or sisters ("only children") have been born in China since 1979. This has resulted in what the Chinese call "4-2-1": four grandparents and two parents **focus** all of their attention **on** one child. But some young Chinese are not happy. Many say that they have always felt lonely because they have no brothers or sisters. They also feel a lot of **pressure** from their parents to be successful. Some people, on the other hand, complain that parents and grandparents have been **spoiling** their children. They believe that the new generation has become too **dependent** on their parents.

In the future, China could have a serious problem. Many Chinese do not have **pensions**, so they depend on their children to take care of them when they retire. In the past, brothers and sisters shared the responsibility for their parents. But only children do not have anyone to share the responsibility with. As Wan Bo, a young Chinese woman says, "My boyfriend and I often talk about how, after marriage, we will need to take care of four old people. Both of us are so busy trying to make money."

The Chinese government has been studying the situation for some time and has decided to allow only children to have two children. That is probably good news to Wan Bo and the 80 million other only children like her.

124 Unit 9

After You Read

A Look at the **boldface** words in the article. Guess their meaning. Then read the sentences, and circle the correct answer.

1. When there is **population growth**, the number of people gets _____.
   (a.) larger   **b.** smaller

2. When a child, her parents, and her grandparents all live in one house, _____ **generations** are living together.
   a. two   **(b.)** three

3. When you **focus on** something, you _____.
   a. forget about it   **(b.)** think about it a lot

4. When someone puts **pressure** on you, you feel _____.
   a. comfortable   **(b.)** uncomfortable

5. When you **spoil** a child, you _____.
   (a.) give the child too many things   **b.** don't give the child enough things

6. **Dependent** children can _____ take care of themselves.
   a. usually   **(b.)** rarely

7. A **pension** is _____.
   a. money that you give to your children   **(b.)** money that you get after you retire

B Read the article again. Answer the questions. *Wording of answers will vary.*

1. Why did the Chinese government introduce the One-Child Policy?
   to slow down population growth

2. Has the One-Child Policy been successful?
   Yes, it has.

3. What do Chinese parents want their children to do?
   be successful

4. What do some Chinese people think about the new generation of young Chinese?
   They're spoiled and too dependent on their parents.

5. What will Chinese children have to do for their parents after they retire?
   take care of them

6. What has the Chinese government decided to allow only children to do?
   have two children

Relationships **125**

After You Read

A Teaching Time: 10–15 min.

- Read each of the boldface vocabulary items aloud. For each one, ask students to raise their hands if they think they know the meaning of the word. If they do, tell them to choose the correct answer without looking back at the reading.
- Have students complete the task. Tell them to circle the words in the reading that help them understand the meanings of the new words. Those who have already chosen an answer should change their answers if necessary.
- Call on students to say answers. Ask them which words they circled to find the answer. Correct as needed. For students who indicated that they already knew the words, ask them if they changed any of their answers after looking back at the context.

B Teaching Time: 10–15 min.

- Write the questions on the board. Ask if anyone can answer any of the questions without reading again. Write their answers on the board.
- Have students complete the task. Tell them to mark the places in the text where they found the answers. Encourage them to put their answers in their own words wherever possible.
- PAIRS. Have students compare their answers. Tell them to refer to the places they marked in the text if they have different answers.
- Call on students to read their answers. Correct as needed by referring to the places in the text where the answers can be found. Compare the answers to the ones that are on the board. Were they correct? Write the correct answers.

Multilevel Strategy

Pre-level: Group all pre-level students, and do the exercise with them. Read the article aloud as the students follow along in their books. Tell them to stop you when they find an answer to one of the questions on the board. Make sure they mark that place in the text.

Writing

Getting Ready to Write

A **Teaching Time: 10–15 min.**

- Have students study the Writing Tip.
- Write the first sentence from the Writing Tip on the board.
- Ask: *What is the reason in the sentence? What is the result?* Label the clauses.

Because the cost of raising a child has been going up,
dependent clause: reason = cost of children ↑

the birth rate has been going down.
main clause: result = birth rate ↓

- Ask: *What is another way to write this sentence?* Write on the board, and label as follows:

The birth rate has been going down
main clause: result

because the cost of raising a child has been going up.
dependent clause: reason

- Remind students that if the main clause comes first, there is no comma. Point out that the *because* clause always contains the reason, while the main clause contains the result.
- Write the second sentence from the Writing Tip on the board.
- Ask: *What is the reason in the sentence? What is the result?* Label the clauses.

The cost of raising a child has been going up,
reason

so the birth rate has been going down.
result

- Ask: *Can we change the order of the clauses?* (No)
- Point out that the *so* clause always contains the result, and the other clause contains the reason.
- Explain that in sentences with *so,* we need a comma between the clauses, before *so.* Point to the second sentence on the board (with *because* in the middle and no comma) to contrast the comma use.
- Have students complete the task.
- Ask volunteers to write their answers on the board. Correct as needed.

Writing

Getting Ready to Write

A Rewrite each sentence. Use *because* or *so.*

1. Families have been getting smaller, so children are getting a lot of attention.
   Because families have been getting smaller,
   children are getting a lot of attention.

2. Both parents have to work, so they don't have time to take care of more than one child.
   Because both parents have to work, they don't have time to take care of more than
   one child.

3. Because some people get married when they are older, they save money before marriage.
   Some people get married when they are older, so they save money before marriage.

4. Travel has been getting easier, so a lot of families take trips together.
   Because travel has been getting easier, a lot of families take trips together.

5. Many older people are active these days, so they can do more with their grandchildren.
   Because many older people are active these days, they can do more with their
   grandchildren.

B Read the model paragraph.

> In many parts of the world, families have been getting smaller recently. There are many reasons for this change. The cost of raising a child has gone up in many parts of the world, so people cannot afford to have large families. Also, in many families both parents work, so they do not have enough time to take care of more than one child. The divorce rate has also been going up. Some couples get divorced before they have children. Finally, in many parts of the world women have careers, so they have been waiting longer to have children. If a woman has her first child when she is 35, she may not have many more children.

PAIRS. Read the model again. Is the information true about your country?

Now talk about another recent change in lifestyles in your country. Discuss the reasons why this change is happening. You can talk about relationships, money, health, education, or your own idea.

126   Unit 9

Writing Tip

Use linking words to connect one idea to another. Both *because* and *so* show a cause and effect relationship.

Examples:
Because the cost of raising a child has been going up, the birth rate has been going down.

The cost of raising a child has been going up, **so** the birth rate has been going down.

B **Teaching Time: 10–15 min.**

- Have students read the writing model.
- PAIRS. Have students complete the task.
- Call on a few students to tell you about recent changes in their countries.

Multilevel Strategy

All levels: Adjust the level of your questions to the student's level.

- **Pre-level:** Has the divorce rate in your country been going up or down?
- **At-level, Above-level:** How have people's lifestyles been changing in your country recently?

Language Note

Getting Ready to Write. Students often have trouble with the punctuation of sentences containing *because* and *so.* Common errors are *People have been living longer. Because health care has been getting better;* or *Health care has been getting better. So, people have been living longer.* To help students correct these errors, explain that when we use *so* and *because,* the reason and the result must be in the same sentence, not in two different sentences.

Prewriting: Listing Reasons

You are going to write a paragraph about a recent change in people's lifestyles in your country. Before you write, choose a main topic from the list or use your own idea.

- education
- health
- money
- relationships

Read the notes for the writing model. Then complete the chart with notes about your topic.

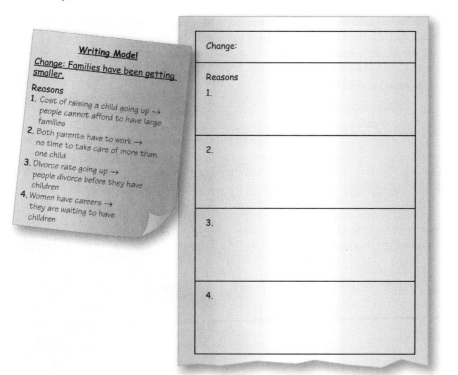

Writing Model

Change: Families have been getting smaller.

Reasons
1. Cost of raising a child going up → people cannot afford to have large families
2. Both parents have to work → no time to take care of more than one child
3. Divorce rate going up → people divorce before they have children
4. Women have careers → they are waiting to have children

Change:

Reasons
1.

2.

3.

4.

Writing

Now write a paragraph about a recent change in people's lifestyles in your country. The writing tip, the model paragraph, and your notes will help you. Write in your notebook.

Relationships 127

Prewriting

Teaching Time: 10–15 min.

- Have students read the writing model.
- Have students complete the task. Walk around and help as needed.

Writing

Teaching Time: 15–20 min.

- Have students complete the task.
- Have students exchange papers with a partner.
- Have them read their partner's paragraph and write down the change and the reasons for the change that they find in the paragraph.
- Have them look at their partner's list.
- Give students time to make changes to their paragraphs based on their partner's feedback.

Multilevel Strategy

Pre-level: While the other students are writing their paragraphs and giving each other feedback, work with the pre-level students in a group. Take one of the student's notes, and construct a paragraph on the board with the group. Have the students copy the final paragraph into their notebooks.

Unit 10
Television

Unit 10
Television

Learning Goals

- Learn common adjectives and adverbs and how to use adverbs of manner and degree
- Listen to scenes from different types of television shows
- Listen for intonation that characterizes strong emotions
- Read an article about soap operas and telenovelas and write a paragraph expressing an opinion about television
- Talk about popular television shows and actors and give opinions about the positive and negative effects of television

Learner Persistence

Set up individual conferences with students to check on their progress.

Warm-up

Teaching Time: 5–10 min.

- Have students look at the pictures of the three types of TV shows.
- Take an informal poll. Ask students to raise their hands if they watch these types of programs. Write on the board how many students watch each type of show, for example:

Talk Shows	The News
4	10

Cooking Shows	
2	

Vocabulary

Teaching Time: 10–15 min.

- Read the words in the boxes aloud as students listen, repeat, and circle the words that they already know.
- Have students complete the task.
- PAIRS. Have students compare their answers.
- 🎧 Play Track 16 while students listen and check their answers.
- Ask volunteers to read the paragraphs aloud. Correct as needed.
- Say each word in the word boxes and have students repeat chorally.

Vocabulary

🔘 16 **Complete the sentences with the words in the box. Then listen and check your answers.**

fashionable romantic secret stars

The young man and woman are movie ___stars___. Their clothes are very
1.
___fashionable___. They just got married
2.
in a ___secret___ ceremony. It was a
3.
___romantic___ way to get married.
4.

attractive calm clear nervous

Both the man and woman are
___attractive___. The woman is
5.
___calm___. The man is ___nervous___.
6.   7.
His speech is not very ___clear___.
8.

awful strange successful terrific

Many people watch *Cook with the Chefs*.
It is a ___successful___ show. Today, Chef
9.
Chick is wearing a ___strange___ hat.
10.
His food tastes ___awful___. Chef Bob's
11.
food tastes ___terrific___.
12.

128 Unit 10

Expansion PAIRS. Tell students to look at the pictures and the word boxes, but not the paragraphs. Have them take turns describing each scene with the new vocabulary.

Multilevel Strategy

Pre-level: PAIRS. Pair pre-level students together. While the other students are describing the pictures to each other, have them take turns reading the paragraphs aloud.

Listening

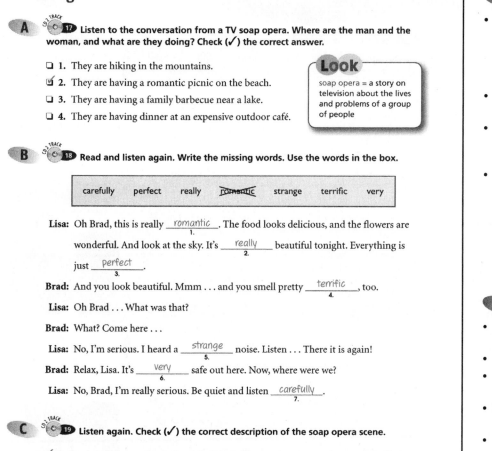

A 🎧 **17** Listen to the conversation from a TV soap opera. Where are the man and the woman, and what are they doing? Check (✓) the correct answer.

❑ 1. They are hiking in the mountains.

☑ 2. They are having a romantic picnic on the beach.

❑ 3. They are having a family barbecue near a lake.

❑ 4. They are having dinner at an expensive outdoor café.

Look

soap opera = a story on television about the lives and problems of a group of people

B 🎧 **18** Read and listen again. Write the missing words. Use the words in the box.

carefully	perfect	really	~~romantic~~	strange	terrific	very

Lisa: Oh Brad, this is really _romantic_. The food looks delicious, and the flowers are
wonderful. And look at the sky. It's _really_ beautiful tonight. Everything is
just _perfect_.

Brad: And you look beautiful. Mmm . . . and you smell pretty _terrific_, too.

Lisa: Oh Brad . . . What was that?

Brad: What? Come here . . .

Lisa: No, I'm serious. I heard a _strange_ noise. Listen . . . There it is again!

Brad: Relax, Lisa. It's _very_ safe out here. Now, where were we?

Lisa: No, Brad, I'm really serious. Be quiet and listen _carefully_.

C 🎧 **19** Listen again. Check (✓) the correct description of the soap opera scene.

☑ 1. Brad and Lisa meet secretly at the beach. The evening starts quite romantically, but then something terrible happens.

❑ 2. Brad and Lisa are walking on the beach. Lisa decides that it is time to tell Brad her secret, but is Brad ready to hear it?

❑ 3. Brad and Lisa are having a romantic evening on the beach. Everything is going perfectly, but then Brad says something really strange.

Television 129

Option

Exercise B. Have students try to complete the conversation with the words from the box *before* they listen.

Option

Assign Unit 10 Supplementary Vocabulary Exercises on the Teacher's Resource Disk as homework or on the Student Persistence CD-ROM as self-access practice.

Multilevel Strategy

- **Pre-level:** PAIRS. Have students role-play the conversation in Exercise B. Allow them to look at the conversation as they role-play.
- **At-level, Above-level:** PAIRS. Write the adjectives from the conversation on the board, and have students role-play the conversation from memory: *beautiful, delicious, perfect, quiet, romantic, safe, serious, strange, terrific, wonderful.*

Listening

A **Teaching Time: 10–15 min.**

- **Warm-up.** Call on a student to read the definition from the Look Box aloud. Ask students to name some popular soap operas. Write their answers on the board.
- Call on students to read the answer choices aloud.
- 🎧 Play Track 17 as students listen and complete the task. If necessary, play the track again.
- Call on a student to say the answer. Ask the student to explain why the other choices are not correct. (1. You can hear the sound of the ocean waves, and they don't sound like they're hiking or exercising; 3. They are alone; 4. You cannot hear any other people, as you would at a café.)

B **Teaching Time: 10–15 min.**

- Read the words in the word box and have students repeat chorally.
- Have students read the conversation.
- 🎧 Play Track 18 as students listen and complete the task.
- 🎧 Play Track 18 again, pausing the recording as each answer is given.
- Ask for volunteers, one male and one female, to read the conversation. Correct as needed.

C **Teaching Time: 10–15 min.**

- Call on students to read the answer choices aloud.
- 🎧 Play Track 19 as students listen and complete the task.
- Call on a student to give the answer. Ask students to explain why the other choices are not correct. (2. Lisa doesn't say anything about a secret, and they aren't walking; 3. Brad doesn't say anything strange. They *hear* something strange.)

Multilevel Strategy

Pre-level: Make photocopies of the audioscript, but delete the excerpted part of the conversation that students must complete in Exercise B. Give them to students before they do Exercise A. Let them look at the audioscript as they complete Exercises A and C.

Unit 10 T-129

Grammar to Communicate 1

Adverbs and Adjectives

Teaching Time: 5–10 min.

- Have students study the chart and the Look Box.
- Write the first two sentences on the board: *I am a slow eater. I eat slowly.*
- Underline the adjective *slow* in the first sentence. Ask: *In this sentence, what word does* slow *describe?* (eater) *What part of speech is the word* eater—*noun, verb, adjective, or adverb?* (Eater is a person, so it is a noun.) *What part of speech is the word* slow? (adjective—It describes the noun *eater.*) *Nouns name people, places, or things. What do adjectives do?* (They describe nouns.) *Do we put an adjective before or after the noun it describes?* (before)
- Circle the adverb *slowly* in the second sentence. Ask: *In this sentence, what word does* slowly *describe?* (eat) *What part of speech is the word* eat—*noun, verb, adjective, or adverb?* (verb) *What part of speech is the word* slowly? (adverb—It describes the verb *eat.*) *What do adverbs do?* (They describe verbs.) *Do we put an adverb before or after the verb it describes?* (after)
- Call on students to read the other sentences in the chart. Explain that many adverbs are formed by adding *–ly* to the adjective form. Ask them to tell you which words the adjectives and adverbs in the chart describe. (careful/driver; carefully/drives; bad/dresser; badly/dress)
- Call on students to read the words in the Look Box. Explain that some adverbs are irregular and do not end in *–ly.*

A Teaching Time: 10–15 min.

- Read the example with the class.
- Have students complete the task.
- Call on students to say answers. Correct as needed.

B Teaching Time: 10–15 min.

- Explain that this question-and-answer is from a magazine. The question is from a reader about a star on a show.
- Have students complete the task.
- Call on students to say answers. Correct as needed.

ADVERBS AND ADJECTIVES

Regular Adjectives					Regular Adverbs		
Subject	Verb	Article	Adjective	Noun	Subject	Verb	Adverb
I	am	a	slow	eater.	I	eat	slowly.
She	is		careful	driver.	She	drives	carefully.
They	are		bad	dressers.	They	dress	badly.

Look

Some adverbs are irregular and do not take *-ly.*

ADJECTIVE	ADVERB
fast	fast
good	well
hard	hard

A   Underline the adjectives. Circle the adverbs.

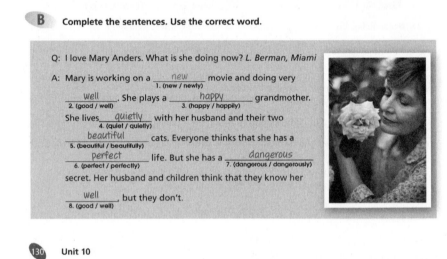

WHERE IS DARREN McDOUGAL NOW?

McDougal, the star of the <u>popular</u> soap opera *You and Me* lives (quietly) with his <u>beautiful</u> family in Los Angeles.

Last year he was <u>busy</u> all the time. He worked (hard) on *You and Me*, and the show did (well). But now he's doing things (differently). This year he is <u>happy</u> at home with his <u>young</u> children, Tara, 5, and Ben, 4. His wife, the actress Sara Miller, has a <u>successful</u> show. She is the <u>smart</u>, <u>attractive</u> police officer in *Life on the Street.* She lives (dangerously) in the show, but her life with Darren and the children is <u>quiet</u>.

B   Complete the sentences. Use the correct word.

Q: I love Mary Anders. What is she doing now? *L. Berman, Miami*

A: Mary is working on a ___new___ movie and doing very
       1. (new / newly)

___well___. She plays a ___happy___ grandmother.
2. (good / well)   3. (happy / happily)

She lives ___quietly___ with her husband and their two
    4. (quiet / quietly)

___beautiful___ cats. Everyone thinks that she has a
5. (beautiful / beautifully)

___perfect___ life. But she has a ___dangerous___
6. (perfect / perfectly)   7. (dangerous / dangerously)

secret. Her husband and children think that they know her

___well___, but they don't.
8. (good / well)

130   Unit 10

Expansion   Bring in some copies of soap opera digests. Ask students if they know what a soap opera digest is. If they don't, give them this definition: *A soap opera digest is a weekly magazine for soap opera fans. It contains information about the real lives of soap opera stars, as well as information about what happened in the shows the previous week.* Pass the digests around the room, and have students look through them before doing the exercises. Find out if students are familiar with the soap operas covered in the digests.

Grammar Notes

1. Adjectives describe nouns. They come before the nouns they modify.
2. Adverbs can describe verbs, adjectives, or other adverbs.
3. We use adjectives, not adverbs, after the main verb *be.*
4. Some verbs describe our senses. We use adjectives, not adverbs, after these verbs: *feel, look, smell, sound, taste.*

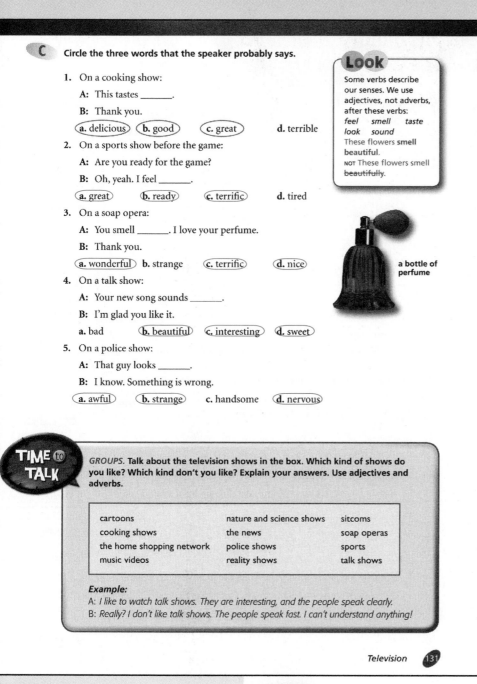

C Circle the three words that the speaker probably says.

1. On a cooking show:

   A: This tastes _____.

   B: Thank you.

   (a. delicious) (b. good) (c. great) d. terrible

2. On a sports show before the game:

   A: Are you ready for the game?

   B: Oh, yeah. I feel _____.

   (a. great) (b. ready) (c. terrific) d. tired

3. On a soap opera:

   A: You smell _____. I love your perfume.

   B: Thank you.

   (a. wonderful) b. strange (c. terrific) (d. nice)

4. On a talk show:

   A: Your new song sounds _____.

   B: I'm glad you like it.

   a. bad (b. beautiful) (c. interesting) (d. sweet)

5. On a police show:

   A: That guy looks _____.

   B: I know. Something is wrong.

   (a. awful) (b. strange) c. handsome (d. nervous)

Look

Some verbs describe our senses. We use adjectives, not adverbs, after these verbs:

feel   smell   taste
look   sound

These flowers **smell** beautiful.

NOT These flowers smell ~~beautifully~~.

a bottle of perfume

TIME to TALK

GROUPS. Talk about the television shows in the box. Which kind of shows do you like? Which kind don't you like? Explain your answers. Use adjectives and adverbs.

cartoons	nature and science shows	sitcoms
cooking shows	the news	soap operas
the home shopping network	police shows	sports
music videos	reality shows	talk shows

Example:
A: *I like to watch talk shows. They are interesting, and the people speak clearly.*
B: *Really? I don't like talk shows. The people speak fast. I can't understand anything!*

Television 131

C Teaching Time: 10–15 min.

- Have students study the Look Box.
- Read the example with the class.
- Have students complete the task.
- Call on students to read answers. Correct as needed.

Option

Time to Talk. If possible, show students a short (one minute or less) clip of each type of show in the box, and ask them to identify the type of show.

Option

Assign Unit 10 Supplementary Grammar to Communicate 1 Exercises on the Teacher's Resource Disk as homework or on the Student Persistence CD-ROM as self-access practice.

TIME to TALK

Teaching Time: 10–15 min.

- Read the words and phrases in the box with the class. Make sure everyone is familiar with the various types of shows. Ask students to give one example of each type of show.
- Call on two students to read the example.
- GROUPS. Have students complete the task.
- Ask volunteers to tell the class what kinds of shows they like and why. Correct their use of adverbs and adjectives as needed.

Unit 10   T-131

Grammar to Communicate 2

Adverbs of Manner

Teaching Time: 5–10 min.

- Have students study the chart and the Look Box.
- Write the following adjectives on the board, and ask volunteers to come up to the board and write the adverb form of each: *serious, responsible, artistic* (seriously, responsibly, artistically)
- Correct as needed. Refer students to the spelling rules in the chart.

A Teaching Time: 10–15 min.

- Play Track 20 while students listen and complete the task.
- Call on students to say answers. Correct as needed. Play the recording again if necessary.

B Teaching Time: 10–15 min.

- Read the example with the class.
- Have students complete the task.
- Call on students to say answers. Correct as needed.

Grammar to Communicate 2

ADVERBS OF MANNER

Subject	Verb	Adverb	Forming adverbs from adjectives
The children	sat	silently.	Most adjectives → + *ly* (silent / silently)
They	won	easily.	Adjectives with two or more syllables ending in consonants and *y* → change *y* to *i* and add *ly* (easy / easily)
The actors	dressed	fashionably.	Adjectives ending in –*le* → change *e* to *y* (fashionable / fashionably)
The couple	spoke	romantically.	Adjectives ending in –*ic* → + *ally* (romantic / romantically)

Look

Adverbs of manner answer the question *how*. How do they speak? They speak clearly.

A CD 2 TRACK 20 **Listen. How are the people speaking?**

angrily	nervously	romantically	slowly	softly

Look

softly = quietly

The person is speaking . . .

1. __slowly__. 2. __romantically__. 3. __nervously__. 4. __angrily__. 5. __softly__.

B Underline the adverbs. Then write the adverb and its adjective form.

	ADVERB	ADJECTIVE
The Happy Kitchen Learn how to make dinner successfully. With Chef Peter's help, you won't work hard in the kitchen. And all your dinner guests will think you cook terrifically.	successfully / hard / terrifically	successful / hard / terrific
Doctors' Hospital Dr. Black meets secretly with Charlotte. The student nurses do badly on their exam. Ten patients complain angrily about Dr. Lee.	secretly / badly / angrily	secret / bad / angry
The Apartment Last week Ruth and Ed were getting along well and living together happily. But things change this week. Do they change temporarily? Or do they change permanently?	well / happily / temporarily / permanently	good / happy / temporary / permanent

Grammar Notes

1. Adverbs of manner answer the question *how*. We usually put adverbs of manner after the verb, but we can also put some adverbs of manner before the main verb. For example: *He ran quickly to her side.* OR *He quickly ran to her side.*
2. Some adverbs are the same form as adjectives, for example, *fast* and *hard*.
3. The adverb form of *good* is *well*.
4. Some adjectives do not have adverb forms. For example, adjectives that end in –*ly* (*friendly, lovely, ugly, elderly*) do not have adverb forms.
5. For more information on this grammar topic, see page 288.

C A director of a soap opera is telling the actors and actresses how to act. Complete the directions with adverbs.

1. "You need to be careful. You don't want the police to stop you. Drive ___carefully___."

2. "You're angry. You saw your boyfriend with another woman. Look at him ___angrily___."

3. "You need to be romantic. You're in love. Talk to her ___romantically___."

4. "You're sad. Your friend is very sick. Look at her ___sadly___."

5. "Everyone in the room is very quiet. Don't make a lot of noise. Come in ___quietly___."

6. "You haven't seen your friend in a long time, and you're very happy to see her. Enter the room ___happily___."

7. "You're nervous when you make the call. Speak ___nervously___."

TIME to TALK

PAIRS. Talk about famous television shows or movies and the people in them. Make sentences with the words in the boxes. Use one word from each box for every sentence.

cartoon	the news	sitcom
cooking show	police show	soap opera
music	reality show	talk show

Verbs	Adverbs
act	badly
behave	beautifully
dance	fashionably
dress	fast
laugh	realistically
sing	strangely
speak	terribly
walk	terrifically

Dennis Franz in *NYPD Blue*

Example:
In my favorite police show, the star of the show dresses badly.

- Have a student read the example aloud. Point out the adjective *careful* in the first sentence.
- Have students complete the task. Tell them to underline the adjective in the first sentence of each item.
- Call on students to say answers. Have them say the adjective and the adverb, and then have them spell the adverb as you write it on the board. Correct as needed.

Option

Assign Unit 10 Supplementary Grammar to Communicate 2 Exercises on the Teacher's Resource Disk as homework or on the Student Persistence CD-ROM as self-access practice.

TIME to TALK

Teaching Time: 10–15 min.

- Read the example with the class.
- PAIRS. Have students complete the task.
- Ask volunteers to write their sentences on the board. Correct as needed.

Grammar to Communicate 3

Adverbs of Degree

Teaching Time: 5–10 min.

- Have students study the chart and the Look Box.
- Draw three faces on the board: a frowning face with many tears; a frowning face and one tear; a frowning face and no tears.
- Write the following sentences on the board.

  He's really sad. / He's speaking really sadly.

  He's very sad. / He's speaking very sadly.

  He's extremely sad. / He's speaking extremely sadly.

  He's pretty sad. / He's speaking pretty sadly.

- Ask volunteers to come up to the board and write the sentences under the appropriate faces.

  (Under the frowning face with many tears: *He's extremely sad. / He's speaking extremely sadly.*)

  (Under the frowning face and one tear: *He's really sad. / He's speaking really sadly; He's very sad. / He's speaking very sadly.*)

  (Under the frowning face and no tears: *He's pretty sad. / He's speaking pretty sadly.*)

- Say: *The adverbs very, extremely, really, and pretty are used with both adjectives and adverbs to make their meaning stronger.*

A   Teaching Time: 10–15 min.

- Call on a student to read the example. Ask the class which words in the context helped them choose the answer. (You liked it a lot.)
- Have students complete the task. Tell them to circle words in the context that help them choose the answer.
- Call on students to say answers. Have them say which words they circled. Correct as needed. (2: like her looks; don't think she's beautiful; 3: don't think she dances badly; don't think she's ready for music videos; 4: started at 8:00 P.M., finished after midnight; very boring; 5: can't understand; 6: starts at 11:00 P.M., be at work at 6:00 A.M.)

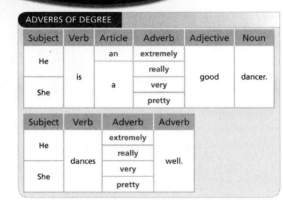

Grammar to Communicate 3

ADVERBS OF DEGREE					
Subject	Verb	Article	Adverb	Adjective	Noun
He		an	extremely		
	is		really	good	dancer.
She		a	very		
			pretty		

Subject	Verb	Adverb	Adverb
He		extremely	
	dances	really	well.
She		very	
		pretty	

Look

Very, extremely, pretty, and *really* make an adjective or adverb stronger.

↑ MORE

extremely

very, really

pretty

↓ LESS

A   Read the situations, and complete the sentences. Write the correct word.

1. There was a new show on TV last night. You liked it a lot. What do you say?

   "The show was _____really_____ good."
   (pretty / really)

2. You are talking about an actress on TV. You like her looks, but you don't think she's beautiful. What do you say?

   "She is _____pretty_____ attractive."
   (extremely / pretty)

3. Your neighbor's daughter wants to be a dancer and lives in Hollywood. You don't think she dances badly, but you don't think she's ready for music videos. What do you say?

   "She dances _____pretty_____ well."
   (pretty / very)

4. The baseball game started at 8:00 P.M. last night and finished after midnight, and it was very boring. What do you say?

   "The game was _____extremely_____ long."
   (extremely / pretty)

5. You like the newscaster on Channel 2. She speaks clearly. But you can't understand the newscaster on Channel 10. What do you say?

   "He talks _____really_____ fast."
   (pretty / really)

6. Your friend wants you to watch a show on TV with her, but it starts at 11:00 P.M. and you have to be in work at 6:00 A.M. What do you say?

   "It's _____very_____ late. I can't watch the show with you."
   (pretty / very)

Grammar Notes

1. Adverbs of degree change how strong an adjective or adverb is. Put adverbs of degree in front of the adjective or adverb that they describe.

2. Do not use *very* or *extremely* with adjectives or adverbs that are already very strong. Some examples of words that you should not use with *very* or *extremely* are: *gorgeous / gorgeously; hideous / hideously; perfect / perfectly; terrible / terribly; wonderful / wonderfully.*

3. *Pretty* can be an adjective or an adverb, but the meaning is different. Compare:

   She is pretty. (pretty = adjective)

   She is pretty smart. (pretty = adverb)

4. For more information on this grammar topic, see page 288.

B Write *very* where possible. If *very* is not possible, write *really*.

1. Talk shows are ____very____ interesting.
2. Some TV shows are ____really____ excellent.
3. Some newscasters talk ____very____ quickly.
4. Some actors on TV are ____really____ terrible.
5. A lot of actors in soap operas act ____very____ well.
6. TV actors get jobs ____very____ easily.
7. Singers in music videos sing ____really____ perfectly.
8. Most actresses and actors are ____really____ gorgeous.

Look

These words have a strong meaning.
great, wonderful, excellent, perfect = very good
terrible, awful = very bad
gorgeous = very beautiful or very handsome

Do not use *very* or *extremely* with these words. Use *really* or *pretty*.

He is really great.
NOT He is ~~very~~ great.

C Look at the pictures on page 128. Write five new sentences about the people in the pictures. Use *extremely*, *pretty*, *really*, or *very*. Then read your sentences to a partner.
Answers will vary.

1. _The woman in the first picture is really gorgeous._
2. _____
3. _____
4. _____
5. _____
6. _____

TIME to TALK

ON YOUR OWN. Complete the statements with *pretty*, *very*, *really*, or *extremely*. If you don't agree with the statement, make the verb negative.

1. Television is _____ bad for children.
2. Television is _____ educational.
3. Sitcoms are _____ funny.
4. Police shows are _____ violent.
5. Television commercials are _____ annoying.
6. People in reality shows behave _____ stupidly.
7. Actors and actresses have to work _____ hard.

Example:
A: *I think that television is really bad for children.*
B: *I don't agree. Television isn't always bad for children. Some shows are very good.*

GROUPS. Talk about your opinions.

Television **135**

B Teaching Time: 10–15 min.

- Have students study the Look Box.
- Write the following words on the board, and ask students whether they can be used with *very* or *extremely*: *perfect* (no), *nice* (yes), *terrific* (no), *good* (yes), *awful* (no), *bad* (yes).
- Read the examples with the class.
- Have students complete the task.
- Call on students to say answers. Correct as needed.

C Teaching Time: 10–15 min.

- Read the example with the class.
- Have students complete the task. Walk around and help as needed.
- Ask volunteers to write their sentences on the board. Correct as needed.

Multilevel Strategy

- **Pre-level:** Give students a handout with five sentences using *extremely*, *pretty*, *really*, and *very*. Have them guess which person in the pictures each sentence is about. Have them copy the sentences onto the lines in Exercise C.

Option

Assign Unit 10 Supplementary Grammar to Communicate 3 Exercises on the Teacher's Resource Disk as homework or on the Student Persistence CD-ROM as self-access practice.

TIME to TALK

Teaching Time: 10–15 min.

- Read the directions with the class.
- ON YOUR OWN. Have students complete the task.
- Read the example with the class.
- GROUPS. Have students complete the task.
- Have one student from each group report on some of the opinions in the group. For example, *In our group, three students think that television is really bad for children. Only one person thinks that television is very educational.*

Grammar

Teaching Time: 5–10 min.

- Have students complete the task.
- Ask volunteers to write the corrected sentences on the board. Have them underline the adjectives and circle the adverbs in each sentence, and draw a line from the adjective or adverb to the word it modifies.
- Correct as needed.

Multilevel Strategy

Pre-level: Tell students what the mistakes are and have them rewrite the statements.

Dictation

Teaching Time: 5–10 min.

- 🎧 Play Track 21 while students listen and write what they hear.
- 🎧 Play Track 21 again while students check their answers.
- Ask for volunteers to write their sentences on the board. Have them underline the adjectives and circle the adverbs in each sentence, and draw a line from the adjective or adverb to the word it modifies.
- 🎧 Play Track 21 again and correct the sentences on the board.

Multilevel Strategy

Pre-level: Give students a worksheet with some of the words from the dictation already provided.

Speaking

Teaching Time: 5–10 min.

- Read the directions with the class.
- Choose an above-level student to help you model the example. Say the following sentence very quickly: *Hurry up! We're going to be late!* The above-level student reads Student B's part in the example. You read Student A's part.

Review and Challenge

Grammar

Find the mistake in each sentence. Circle the letter and correct the mistake.

1. TV actresses <u>always</u> <u>look</u> <u>really</u> <u>perfectly</u>.   *perfect*
   A   B   C   D

2. It <u>doesn't sound</u> <u>very</u> <u>good</u>, but it isn't <u>very awful</u>.   *really*
     A   B   C   D

3. Some <u>very</u> <u>famously</u> people behave <u>pretty stupidly</u>.   *famous*
        A   B   C   D

4. Chef Bob's food <u>looks great</u>, but does it <u>taste well</u>?   *good*
                   A   B   C   D

5. He's <u>pretty</u> <u>attractive</u>, but he dresses <u>very bad</u>.   *badly*
        A   B   C   D

Dictation

🎧 **CD 2 TRACK 21** **Listen. You will hear five sentences. Write them in your notebook.** *See the audioscript on p. 317 for the sentences.*

Speaking

PAIRS. **Student A:** Choose one word from each box and think of a sentence. Then act it out. Do not tell your partner your sentence.

Student B: Guess what Student A's sentence is. Then switch roles. Each student should act out five sentences.

Example: B: *Are you speaking nervously?*
A: *No, I'm not.*
B: *Are you speaking fast?*
A: *Yes, I am.*

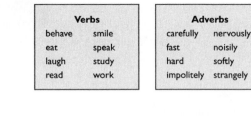

Verbs		Adverbs	
behave	smile	carefully	nervously
eat	speak	fast	noisily
laugh	study	hard	softly
read	work	impolitely	strangely

- PAIRS. Have students complete the task.
- Ask volunteers to come up in front of the class and say a sentence. The class guesses what the sentence is.

Option

Speaking. Make a sentence, and have two volunteers act it out for the class. Ask the class to vote on which student is a better actor. Here are some possible sentences:

You are speaking carefully.
You are smiling strangely.
You are laughing nervously.

Listening

Listening

A 🎵 **22** Listen to scenes from television shows. Write the correct scene number next to the show. Be careful. There is one extra show.

1. cooking show ___3___
2. police show ___1___
3. nature show ___5___
4. soap opera ___2___
5. newscast ___4___
6. talk show _____

B 🎵 **22** Listen again. Complete the sentences. Use the words in the box.

badly	calmly	hard	nervous	serious
calm	excited	impatient	romantic	softly

Scene 1: The man is trying to sound ___calm___, but he is really ___nervous___.

Scene 2: They are both speaking ___softly___. This is a ___romantic___ scene.

Scene 3: The man cooks ___badly___. The woman sounds ___impatient___.

Scene 4: The situation is very ___serious___, but they are speaking pretty ___calmly___.

Scene 5: They are extremely ___excited___, but they are trying ___hard___ to be quiet.

TIME to TALK

PAIRS. **Choose one of the situations below, and write a short scene for a television show. Read it like an actor.**

A Game Show:
Student A: You are the host. Speak enthusiastically.
Student B: You are a contestant. You are really excited.

A Police Show:
Student A: You are a police officer. You stop a car because it is going very fast. The driver is behaving strangely. You are suspicious.
Student B: You are the driver, but the car is not yours. You stole it. You are nervous, but try to look and sound relaxed.

WRAP UP. **Now, act out your scene for the class.**

Television (137)

Listening

A **Teaching Time: 5–10 min.**

- Tell students they are going to listen to scenes from different types of television shows. Read the types of shows with the class.
- 🎧 Play Track 22 as students listen and complete the task.
- 🎧 Play Track 22 again, this time pausing at the end of each scene. Have students say answers. Ask them to explain how they came up with their answers.

B **Teaching Time: 10–15 min.**

- Read the words in the box aloud, and have students repeat chorally.
- Have students read the sentences.
- 🎧 Play Track 22 as students listen and complete the task.
- 🎧 Play Track 22 again, pausing at the end of each scene. Call on a student to read the completed sentence before starting the recording again.

Expansion Before students complete Exercise B, have them underline the adjectives in the box and circle the adverbs. Then have them decide whether each blank requires an adjective or an adverb. Tell them to write *adj* or *adv* in the margin next to each sentence.

Option

Assign Unit 10 Review and Challenge Supplementary Exercises on the Teacher's Resource Disk as homework or on the Student Persistence CD-ROM as self-access practice.

TIME to TALK

Teaching Time: 10–15 min.

- Ask students if they know what a game show is. If not, explain that it is a show where people compete to win a prize, usually money, a trip, a car, or something else that is valuable. Ask them if game shows are popular in their countries.
- Read the directions and each of the situations aloud. Make sure that students understand what *enthusiastically* and *suspicious* mean. If necessary, write the following definitions on the board: *enthusiastically = in a very excited, interested way; suspicious = thinking that someone might be responsible for a crime.*
- Ask students to raise their hands if they like to watch police shows. Then ask those who like game shows to raise their hands. If possible, pair students according to their interests.
- PAIRS. Have students complete the task.
- WRAP UP. Ask volunteers to perform their scenes for the class.

Getting Ready to Read

Teaching Time: 5–10 min.

- **Warm-up.** Have students read the title of the article and look at the picture. Point out that the word *telenovela* is not English. Ask them to tell you what they think the translation is in English. If no one answers, give them the following hint: *It is a type of television show.* If they still can't answer, ask a series of *yes / no* questions to elicit the answer, for example: *Is it a talk show? Is it a police show? Is it a soap opera?*
- Call on students to read the answer choices aloud.
- Have students complete the task.

Reading

Teaching Time: 15–20 min.

- Have students read the article.
- Have students check their predictions.
- Call on students to give the answers to the questions in Getting Ready to Read. Correct as needed.

Multilevel Strategy

- **Pre-level:** Give students more time to complete the reading. Walk around and help as needed.
- **At-level, Above-level:** After students have finished reading, tell them to underline the adjectives in the text and circle the adverbs. Have them draw a line from each adjective and adverb to the word in the sentence that it modifies. Have them compare their answers in pairs.

Getting Ready to Read

Look at the picture and the title of the article, and read the first and last sentence of each paragraph. Check (✓) the questions that you think the article will answer.

- ❏ 1. Which countries make the best soap operas?
- ☑ 2. What are the differences between soap operas and telenovelas?
- ❏ 3. How much money do the directors of telenovelas make?
- ☑ 4. Are telenovelas from different countries the same?
- ☑ 5. Which topics do telenovelas focus on?
- ☑ 6. How are actors in telenovelas different from actors in soap operas?

Reading

Read the article. Were your predictions in Getting Ready to Read correct? Answer as many of the questions as you can in your notebook.

TELENOVELAS

Today almost every country has television soap operas. In Latin America, soap operas are called *telenovelas*. Telenovelas and English-language soap operas are similar in many ways. However, there are some important differences. For example, soap operas are on during the daytime. Telenovelas, on the other hand, are usually on in the evening, during prime time (the most popular time for television viewing). Men and women of all ages and social classes, from the very poor to the very rich, watch telenovelas. In contrast, women between the ages of 18 and 49 usually watch English-language soap operas. Popular soap operas commonly continue for years, but telenovelas usually end **dramatically**, with an exciting surprise, after about six months.

There are also differences between the actors. The actors in telenovelas often become extremely famous in Latin America. They sometimes act in both telenovelas and movies at the same time. The stars of English-language soap operas, in contrast, are popular with their viewers, but they are not as famous as movie stars. The few soap opera actors who **go on to** become movie stars **rarely** continue to appear in soap operas.

Finally, soap operas and telenovelas **deal with** very different topics. Like English-language soap operas today, most telenovelas used to be about romantic relationships. However, telenovelas **increasingly** focus on serious social topics. The topics differ from country to country. For example, telenovelas in Brazil have dealt with single motherhood, government **dishonesty**, and **environmental** problems such as water and air pollution. Mexican telenovelas, on the other hand, are often about differences in social class. In Colombia telenovelas have dealt with crime and **violence**. Telenovelas, therefore, give people an opportunity to **talk** about the serious problems their countries **face** today.

138 Unit 10

Option

Getting Ready to Read. PAIRS. Before they read, have students answer as many of the questions as they can. Ask volunteers to write their answers on the board. After students have completed the reading, have them check to see if any of their answers were correct.

After You Read

A Look at the **boldface** words in the article. Guess the meaning. Then match the words with their definitions.

c 1. dramatically   a. relating to the air, land, or water on earth
f 2. go on to   b. more and more
i 3. rarely   ~~c.~~ in an exciting way
h 4. deal with   d. lying
b 5. increasingly   e. accept that a difficult situation or problem exists
d 6. dishonesty   f. do something new when you have finished something else
a 7. environmental   g. the act of hurting people on purpose
g 8. violence   h. discuss or be about a particular subject
e 9. face   i. not often

B Read the article again. Match each main point with the example that goes with it.

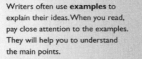

Reading Skill:
Understanding Examples

Writers often use **examples** to explain their ideas. When you read, pay close attention to the examples. They will help you to understand the main points.

MAIN POINT

d 1. Today almost every country has television soap operas.

c 2. Telenovelas and English-language soap operas are similar in many ways. However, there are some important differences.

b 3. There are also differences between the actors.

a 4. The topics differ from country to country.

EXAMPLE

a. Telenovelas in Brazil have dealt with single motherhood.

b. The actors in telenovelas often become extremely famous.

c. Soap operas are on during the daytime. Telenovelas are usually on in the evening.

d. In Latin America, soap operas are called *telenovelas*.

Actors and television crew working on a telenovela

After You Read

A Teaching Time: 10–15 min.

- Read the example with the class.
- Have students complete the task. Tell them to circle words in the reading that help them to understand the meanings of the new words.
- Call on students to say answers. Ask them which words they circled to find the answers. For each adjective and adverb in the exercise (1, 3, 5, 7), have students say which word it describes in the sentence. Correct as needed. (1. end; 2. continue; 5. focus on; 7. problems)

Multilevel Strategy

- **All level:** Pair pre-level students with at- or above-level students for Exercise A. Make sure the higher-level student in each pair shows the pre-level student words in the text that help them understand the new words.

B Teaching Time: 10–15 min.

- Have students study the Reading Skill box.
- Explain that sometimes examples are easy to find because the writer uses the words *for example*, or *such as*. However, sometimes the writer does not tell the reader directly which sentences are examples. The reader needs to understand from the context.
- Read the example with the class.
- Have students complete the task.
- Call on students to say answers. Correct as needed.

Getting Ready to Write

A   **Teaching Time: 10–15 min.**

- Have students study the Writing Tip.
- Read the example with the class.
- Have students complete the task.
- Call on students to read answers. Correct as needed.

B   **Teaching Time: 10–15 min.**

- Have students read the writing model.
- PAIRS. Have students complete the task.
- Call on students to say answers. Correct as needed.
- Start a discussion about how to use television as a language-learning tool. Call on students to tell you about their personal experience with television and language learning. Write their ideas on the board.
- Encourage students to try the suggestions in the writing model, as well as others that came up during the discussion.

Writing

Getting Ready to Write

A   **Rewrite the sentences using *for example*.**

> **Writing Tip**
>
> Include examples to explain your main points. Use the expression *for example* to introduce an example.
>
> Example:
> The topics differ from country to country. **For example,** telenovelas in Brazil have dealt with single motherhood.

1. Television has some positive effects. It entertains people.

   Television has some positive effects. For example, it entertains people.

2. There are some serious negative effects of TV. Children watch too much TV and don't exercise enough.

   There are some serious negative effects of TV. For example, children watch too much TV and don't exercise enough.

3. I think television is a good thing. It teaches people a lot about the world.

   I think television is a good thing. For example, it teaches people a lot about the world.

4. TV has negative effects on people. People become more violent when they watch violent TV shows.

   TV has negative effects on people. For example, people become more violent when they watch violent TV shows.

B   **Read the model paragraph.**

> Television can improve your language skills. For example, it can teach you vocabulary. To learn vocabulary from your TV, simply turn on the captions. When you see a new word on the screen, copy it quickly and guess the meaning. Then check it later in your dictionary. Another example of something television can help you with is improving your listening comprehension. To work on your listening comprehension, watch TV with the captions off. Choose one show, and watch it regularly. Listen carefully, but don't worry if you don't always understand. After a few shows, you will become more familiar with the actors' voices. You will also understand the words and expressions that they usually use.

Read the model again. According to the writer, how can you improve your vocabulary by watching TV? How can you improve your listening? *Wording of answers will vary.*

Now talk about your personal experience. Has television helped you to improve your English? Explain.

Prewriting: Using Examples

You are going to write a paragraph about a positive or negative effect of television. Before you write, read the notes for the writing model. Then write examples that explain your ideas.

Writing Model

Positive Effect of TV:
TV can improve language skills

Example 1
improve vocabulary when captions on

Example 2
improve listening comprehension when captions off

_____ Effect of TV:
_____

Example 1

Example 2

Writing

Now write a paragraph about a positive or negative effect of television. The writing tip, the model paragraph, and your notes will help you. Write in your notebook.

Prewriting

Teaching Time: 15–20 min.

- Have students complete the task.

Writing

Teaching Time: 15–20 min.

- Have students complete the task.
- Have students exchange paragraphs with a partner.
- Have them read their partner's paragraph and make a simple outline of it.
- Have them look at the outline their partner made of their paragraph.
- If the outline does not match their original outline, have them decide whether they want to hand their paragraph in, or work on it at home and hand it in the next day.

Multilevel Strategy

Pre-level: While other students are writing their paragraphs and then giving each other feedback, work with pre-level students in a group. Take one of the student's notes, and construct a paragraph on the board with the group. Have students copy the final paragraph into their notebooks.

Unit 11
The Animal Kingdom

Learning Goals

- Learn the names of animals
- Learn how to use comparatives, superlatives, and equatives of adjectives, adverbs, and nouns
- Listen to a conversation about pets in different countries and to an interview about animal behavior
- Read an article about dogs and wolves and write a paragraph comparing two kinds of animals
- Talk about animals, pets, and animal behavior and compare animals and animal behavior

Learner Persistence

Try to ground English instruction in everyday experiences by identifying practical, real world tasks related to the topics covered in each unit.

Warm-up

Teaching Time: 3–5 min.

PAIRS. Have students cover the word box and say and spell the names of as many of the animals in the pictures as they can. Write their answers on the board, even those that are misspelled or misidentified. Ask if everyone in the class agrees with the answers and the spelling. If not, have students come up to the board and correct those that they think are wrong. Even if they are not able to correct all of the mistakes, do not correct them. Just leave them on the board.

Vocabulary

Teaching Time: 10–15 min.

- Read the words in the box aloud as students listen and repeat chorally. Correct any misspellings on the board, and cross out any animal names that are not listed in the box.
- Have students complete the task.
- 🎧 Play Track 23 while students listen and check their answers.

Expansion PAIRS. Tell students to discuss the animals in the pictures. Write these questions on the board:

Unit 11
The Animal Kingdom

Grammar
- Comparative and Superlative of Adjectives and Adverbs
- Comparative and Superlative of Nouns
- Equatives

Vocabulary

🎧 CD 2 TRACK 23 **Match the numbers with the words. Then listen and check your answers.**

_8_ bear	_4_ chimpanzee	_6_ donkey	_10_ lion	_7_ rabbit	_2_ bat				
_9_ camel	_3_ dolphin	_11_ elephant	_5_ penguin	_1_ rat	_12_ whale				

Which animals have you seen? Where did you see them? (Write on the board and explain the following phrases to help students in their discussions: *at the zoo, at the circus, in the wild, on a farm, at an aquarium, in the ocean*) *Which animals are native to your country? Which of the animals do you like, and why? Which don't you like, and why? Have you ever had any of the animals as pets? Which one(s)?*

Listening

A **24** Listen. Ahmed and May mention one of the animals in the pictures. Check (✓) the animal that they mention.

❑ **1. a mouse / mice**

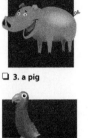

❑ **2. a snake**

❑ **3. a pig**

❑ **4. a cheetah**

☑ **5. a falcon**

❑ **6. a parrot**

B **24** Listen again. Who said it? Write *M* (May) or *A* (Ahmed).

_M_ **1.** A lot more people own cats than dogs.

_A_ **2.** There are as many dogs as children.

_A_ **3.** Pets aren't as popular as they are in the United States.

_A_ **4.** In fact, dogs are the least popular pets.

_M_ **5.** We don't have as much space as Americans do.

_M_ **6.** What is the most common pet?

_A_ **7.** It's one of the oldest sports in Asia.

C **24** Listen again. Who probably agrees with each statement? Check (✓) Ahmed, May, or both Ahmed and May.

	Ahmed	May
1. "Dogs make good pets."	❑	☑
2. "Birds are cleaner than dogs."	☑	❑
3. "Small dogs or cats are the best pets for people in my country."	❑	☑
4. "Big dogs are not common pets in my country."	☑	☑
5. "Falcons are popular in my country today."	☑	❑

The Animal Kingdom **143**

Listening

A **Teaching Time: 10–15 min.**

- **Warm-up.** Read the names of the animals in the pictures aloud. Have students repeat chorally. Ask students if any of the animals are native to their countries.
- 🎧 Play Track 24 as students complete the task.
- Call on a student to say the answer. Correct as needed.

B **Teaching Time: 10–15 min.**

- Read the example with the class.
- 🎧 Play Track 24 as students listen and complete the task.
- 🎧 Play Track 24 again, pausing the recording as each sentence is read. Have students check their answers.

C **Teaching Time: 10–15 min.**

- Have students read the sentences and answer if they can. If they are not sure of an answer, tell them to write a question mark (*?*) next to it.
- 🎧 Play Track 24 as students listen and complete the task.
- Call on students to say answers.
- 🎧 Play Track 24 again, pausing the recording as each answer is given.

Expansion GROUPS. Have students discuss the statements in Exercise C, and answer the following questions: *Which statements do you agree with? Why do you agree or disagree? Which statements are true about your country? What kinds of pets are popular in your country? Do you have any pets? If so, what kind of pet do you have? If not, would you like to have a pet? Why or why not?*

Option

Assign Unit 11 Supplementary Vocabulary Exercises on the Teacher's Resource Disk as homework or on the Student Persistence CD-ROM as self-access practice.

Multilevel Strategy

Pre-level: Make photocopies of the audioscript with the animal names (cat, dog, falcon) deleted. Have students read along and fill in the missing words as they listen.

Grammar to Communicate 1

Comparative and Superlative of Adjectives and Adverbs

Teaching Time: 5–10 min.

- Have students study the chart.
- Draw the following chart on the board. Ask the questions below the chart to guide students to complete it.

Adjective	Comparative form
slow	
easy	
comfortable	
Adverb	**Comparative form**
slowly	
easily	
comfortably	

- Ask: *What are the rules for forming comparative adjectives?* (one syllable = add *–er*; two syllables ending in *–y* = change *–y* to *–i* and add *–er*; two or more syllables not ending in *–y: more* + adjective)
- Ask: *What are the rules for forming comparative adverbs?* (one syllable = add *–er*; two or more syllables = *more* + adverb)
- Write *quicklier* and *prettier* on the board, and ask: *Which is incorrect?* (quicklier) *Why?* (It ends in *–y*, but it's an adverb, not an adjective, so we don't use *–er*. In contrast, *pretty* is an adjective. It ends in *–y*, so we change the *–y* to *–i* and add *–er*.)
- Point out the irregular comparative forms of *good, bad,* and *far*.

A   Teaching Time: 5–10 min.

- Have students look at the pictures. Write the following definitions on the board: *able to take care of yourself; following the rules; refusing to do something that others want you to do or refusing to change your mind; making you feel afraid or nervous.*
- Have students match the words under the pictures with the definitions on the board.
- Read the example with the class.
- Have students complete the task.
- PAIRS. Have students compare their answers.

- Call on students to say answers. Correct as needed. If their answers are unusual, ask them to explain. For example, if a student says: *Pigs are prettier than parrots,* ask the student to explain why he or she thinks so.

B   Teaching Time: 5–10 min.

- Read the example with the class.
- Have students complete the task.
- PAIRS. Have students read their answers to each other. If they disagree, have them defend their answers.
- Call on students to say answers. Correct as needed. (Note: Numbers 3 and 4 are opinion questions.)

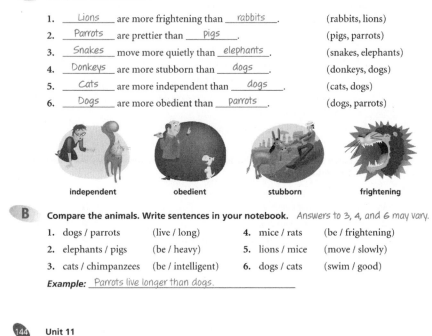

COMPARATIVE OF ADJECTIVES AND ADVERBS

Regular Adjectives	Comparative	Regular Adverbs	Comparative
One syllable		One syllable	
old	older (than)	fast	faster (than)
nice	nicer (than)	late	later (than)
Two syllables		Two syllables	
easy	easier (than)	quickly	more quickly than
Three or more syllables		Three or more syllables	
beautiful	more beautiful (than)	beautifully	more beautiful than
Irregular Adjectives		Irregular Adverbs	
good	better (than)	well	better
bad	worse (than)	badly	worse
far	farther (than)	far	farther

A   **Complete the sentences.**

1. ___Lions___ are more frightening than ___rabbits___.   (rabbits, lions)
2. ___Parrots___ are prettier than ___pigs___.   (pigs, parrots)
3. ___Snakes___ move more quietly than ___elephants___.   (snakes, elephants)
4. ___Donkeys___ are more stubborn than ___dogs___.   (donkeys, dogs)
5. ___Cats___ are more independent than ___dogs___.   (cats, dogs)
6. ___Dogs___ are more obedient than ___parrots___.   (dogs, parrots)

independent   obedient   stubborn   frightening

B   **Compare the animals. Write sentences in your notebook.**   *Answers to 3, 4, and 6 may vary.*

1. dogs / parrots   (live / long)   4. mice / rats   (be / frightening)
2. elephants / pigs   (be / heavy)   5. lions / mice   (move / slowly)
3. cats / chimpanzees (be / intelligent)   6. dogs / cats   (swim / good)

Example: ___Parrots live longer than dogs.___

144   Unit 11

Grammar Notes

1. Use the comparative to compare *two* people, places, or things.

2. In formal English, use the subject pronoun (*I, you, he, she, we, they*) after *than*. In informal English, use the object pronoun (*me, you, him, her, us, them*).

3. We sometimes put *a little, a lot,* or *much* before the comparative of adjectives and adverbs. *Much* and *a lot* have the same meaning.

4. The opposite of *more* is *less*. Use *less* with most adjectives and adverbs that have two or three syllables. Use *not as . . . as* with adjectives and adverbs that have one syllable.

5. For more information about this grammar topic, see pages 288–289.

SUPERLATIVE OF ADJECTIVES AND ADVERBS

Regular Adjectives	Superlative	Regular Adverbs	Superlative
One syllable		One syllable	
old	the oldest	fast	the fastest
nice	the nicest	late	the latest
Two syllables		Two syllables	
easy	the easiest	quickly	the most quickly
Three or more syllables		Three or more syllables	
beautiful	the most beautiful	beautifully	the most beautifully
Irregular Adjectives		Irregular Adverbs	
good	the best	well	the best
bad	the worst	badly	the worst
far	the farthest	far	the farthest

C Write sentences about four animals: elephants, penguins, bears, and whales. Use the superlative. Add *not* where necessary. Write in your notebook.

1. elephants / heavy / animal
2. penguins / cute / animal
3. bears / sleep / long
4. whales / swim / far

Example: Elephants are not the heaviest animals. (Whales are.)

D Complete the sentences with the comparative or superlative of the words. Then write *T* (true) or *F* (false). Check your answers on page 306.

_T_ 1. Whales are ___the largest___ animals in the animal kingdom. (large)

_T_ 2. Dolphins hear ___the best___ of all animals. (good)

_T_ 3. ___The heaviest___ snake weighs 500 pounds (227 kilos). (heavy)

_T_ 4. Camels can live ___the longest___ without water. (long)

_T_ 5. Snails move ___the most slowly___ of all animals. (slowly)

_F_ 6. Gorillas live ___longer___ than chimpanzees. (long)

_T_ 7. Lions run ___more quickly___ than rabbits. (quickly)

_F_ 8. Bats see ___better___ at night than humans do. (well)

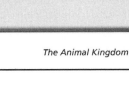

TIME to TALK

GROUPS. Write sentences about animals. Then ask other groups if your statements are true or false. Use Exercise D as a model.

Example: Cats live longer than dogs.

The Animal Kingdom (145)

Option

Assign Unit 11 Supplementary Grammar to Communicate 1 Exercises on the Teacher's Resource Disk as homework or on the Student Persistence CD-ROM as self-access practice.

Superlative of Adjectives and Adverbs

Teaching Time: 5–10 min.

- Have students study the chart.
- Draw the following chart on the board. Ask the questions below the chart to guide students to complete it.

Adjective	Superlative form
slow	
easy	
comfortable	

Adverb	Superlative form
slowly	
easily	
comfortably	

- Ask: *What are the rules for forming superlative adjectives?* (one syllable = add –est; two syllables ending in –y = change –y to –i and add –est; two or more syllables not ending in –y: *the most* + adjective)
- Ask: *What are the rules for forming superlative adverbs?* (one syllable = add –est; two or more syllables = *the most* + adverb)
- Point out the irregular superlative forms of *good, bad,* and *far.*

C **Teaching Time: 5–10 min.**

- Read the example with the class.
- Have students complete the task.
- Call on students to say answers. Correct as needed.
- Note that number 2 is an opinion. Call on a few students to read their sentences. Ask other students if they agree.

D **Teaching Time: 5–10 min.**

- Read the example with the class.
- Have students complete the task.
- Call on students to say answers. Correct as needed.

TIME to TALK

Teaching Time: 5–10 min.

- GROUPS. Have students complete the task.
- Have each group read their statements aloud. Other groups say whether the statement is true or false. If there is disagreement about the content of an answer, assign a student to research the answer and report back to the class the next day.

Grammar to Communicate 2

Comparative and Superlative of Nouns

Teaching Time: 5–10 min.

- Have students study the chart.
- Have students identify all of the count nouns in the chart (*lions, birds, visitors, bears, chimpanzees, snakes, mice*).
- Then have them identify the noncount nouns (*noise, money, space*).

A Teaching Time: 10–15 min.

- Read the example with the class. Have students identify the price information on each poster. Say: *Zoo B has the lowest price. It costs the least money.*
- Have students complete the task.
- Call on students to say answers. Correct as needed.

B Teaching Time: 10–15 min.

- Have students complete the task.
- Call on students to say answers. Correct as needed.

Multilevel Strategy

Pre-level: Before students do Exercises A and B, have them underline the count nouns and circle the noncount nouns.

Grammar to Communicate 2

COMPARATIVE AND SUPERLATIVE OF NOUNS

	Comparative	Count Nouns		Comparative	Noncount Nouns
Lions have	more visitors than	birds.	Birds make	more noise than	bears.
Birds have	fewer visitors than	lions.	Bears make	less noise than	birds.

	Superlative	Count Nouns		Superlative	Noncount Nouns
Chimpanzees have	the most	visitors.	Lions cost	the most	money.
Snakes have	the fewest	visitors.	Mice need	the least	space.

A Complete the sentences. Write *Zoo A, Zoo B,* or *Zoo C.*

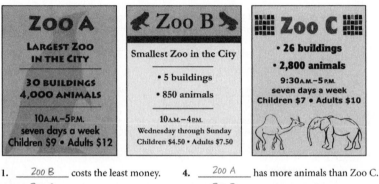

ZOO A

LARGEST ZOO IN THE CITY

30 BUILDINGS
4,000 ANIMALS

10 A.M.–5 P.M.
seven days a week
Children $9 • Adults $12

Zoo B

Smallest Zoo in the City

- 5 buildings
- 850 animals

10 A.M.–4 P.M.
Wednesday through Sunday
Children $4.50 • Adults $7.50

Zoo C

- 26 buildings
- 2,800 animals

9:30 A.M.–5 P.M.
seven days a week
Children $7 • Adults $10

1. __Zoo B__ costs the least money.
2. __Zoo C__ is open the most hours.
3. __Zoo B__ has the fewest animals.
4. __Zoo A__ has more animals than Zoo C.
5. __Zoo B__ has fewer buildings than Zoo C.
6. __Zoo A__ has more space than Zoo C.

B Write comparative or superlative sentences about the zoos.

1. (Zoo C / has / buildings / Zoo B) — *Zoo C has more buildings than Zoo B.*
2. (Zoo B / has / animals / Zoo A) — *Zoo B has fewer animals than Zoo A.*
3. (Zoo C / costs / money / Zoo A) — *Zoo C costs less money than Zoo A.*
4. (Zoo A / has / space / Zoo C) — *Zoo A has more space than Zoo C.*
5. (Zoo B / has / space / of the three) — *Zoo B has the least space of the three.*
6. (Zoo A / costs / money / of the three) — *Zoo A costs the most money of the three.*
7. (Zoo B / is open / hours / of the three) — *Zoo B is open the fewest hours of the three.*
8. (Zoo A / has / buildings / of the three) — *Zoo A has the most buildings of the three.*

146 Unit 11

Grammar Notes

1. Use *less* or *more* to compare two noncount nouns.
2. Use *fewer* or *more* to compare two count nouns.
3. Use *the least* or *the most* to compare three or more noncount nouns.
4. Use *the fewest* or *the most* to compare three or more count nouns.
5. For more information on this grammar topic, see page 289.

C **C** CD 2 TRACK **25** Ten-year-old Stephanie is writing a report about animals. Complete her conversation with a zookeeper. Then listen and check your answers.

Stephanie: Which animals make _____*more*_____ noise, elephants or lions?
　　　　　　　1. (more / the most)

Zookeeper: Hmm. That's a good question. Here at the zoo, probably the lions.

Stephanie: And which animals make _____*the least*_____ noise?
　　　　　　　2. (the fewest / the least)

Zookeeper: Oh, that's easy—the snakes.

Stephanie: Which animals cause _____*the fewest*_____ problems?
　　　　　　　3. (the fewest / the least)

Zookeeper: The snakes again!

Stephanie: And which animals cause _____*the most*_____ problems? The
　　　　　　　4. (more / the most)
chimpanzees?

Zookeeper: Yes, probably. But they also make _____*the most*_____ money for the
　　　　　　　　　　　　　　　　　　　5. (more / the most)
zoo because they get _____*more*_____ visitors than all of the other
　　　　　　　　　　　6. (more / the most)
animals.

Stephanie: Really? Even more than the lions?

Zookeeper: Oh yes. The lions definitely get _____*fewer*_____ visitors. And the
　　　　　　　　　　　　　　　　　　7. (less / fewer)
poor snakes get _____*the fewest*_____ visitors of all.
　　　　　　　　　8. (fewer / the fewest)

TIME to TALK

GROUPS. Ask and answer the questions about animals. Use the information in the box and **more, less, fewer, the most, the least,** and **the fewest.**

> eat / fruit (a bat, a chimpanzee, a parrot)
> eat / meat (a shark, a lion, a chimpanzee)
> have / babies in a lifetime (a rat, a chimpanzee, a whale)
> have / mates in a lifetime (a lion, a dolphin)
> have / teeth (a shark, a dolphin)
> make / noise (a whale, an elephant)
> sleep / hours a day (a lion, a horse, a bat)
> travel / miles in a day (an eagle, a rabbit)

Examples: *Which animal has fewer teeth: a shark or a dolphin?*
Which animal has the most babies in a lifetime: a rat, a chimpanzee, or a whale?

WRAP UP. Now ask your questions to the class. [The answers are on page 304.]

The Animal Kingdom (147)

C Teaching Time: 10–15 min.

C **Teaching Time: 10–15 min.**

- Read the example with the class.
- Have students complete the task.
- Tell students to underline the count nouns and circle the noncount nouns as they complete the exercise.
- Remind students that we use the words *more, less,* and *fewer* when we compare two things and we use the words *the most, the least,* and *the fewest* when we compare three or more things.
- 🎧 Play Track 25 as students listen and check their answers.
- Ask two volunteers to read the conversation. Correct as needed.

Option

Time to Talk.

- Make the activity a team competition. Do not allow students to check their answers.
- Write the groups' answers on the board, as follows:

most	Group 1	Group 2	Group 3	Group 4
fruit?	bat	bat	chimpanzee	parrot

- Give the correct answers. The group with the most correct answers wins.

Option

Assign Unit 11 Supplementary Grammar to Communicate 2 Exercises on the Teacher's Resource Disk as homework or on the Student Persistence CD-ROM as self-access practice.

TIME to TALK

Teaching Time: 10–15 min.

- Have a student read the first question in the example. Call on volunteers to guess the answer. Repeat with the second question in the example.
- GROUPS. Have students complete the task. Tell them that they should decide as a group on the correct answers.
- WRAP UP. Have groups take turns asking questions to the class. For each question, take an informal poll. Have groups raise their hands to indicate what they think the correct answer is. Tell them to check their answers on page 304. How many did they get correct? Which group knows the most about animals?

Equatives

Teaching Time: 5–10 min.

- Have students study the chart.
- Write on the board:

  Adjective:

  A horse is bigger than a dog. =

  A dog is/isn't _____ big _____ a horse is.

  Adverb:

  You can train both a dog and a horse easily. =

  You can/can't train a dog _____ easily _____ a horse.

  Count nouns:

  There are more dog owners than horse owners. =

  There are/aren't _____ horse owners _____ dog owners.

  Noncount nouns:

  A horse needs more food than a dog. =

  A dog doesn't need/needs _____ food _____ a horse does.

- Call on students to come up to the board. Have them circle the correct verb form and fill in the missing words for each sentence. Make sure they understand that the sentence with *as . . . as* must have the same meaning as the first sentence in each set.

A   Teaching Time: 10–15 min.

- Have students read the information about the two dogs. Read the example with the class.
- Have students complete the task.
- Call on students to read the answers. Correct as needed.

B   Teaching Time: 10–15 min.

- Have students study the Look Box. Write on the board:

  Cats aren't as obedient as dogs are.

  Cats aren't as obedient as dogs. —

  Dogs don't need as much food as horses do.

  Dogs don't need as much food as horses. —

- Point to the verbs *aren't / are* and *don't / do* in the examples, and explain that we can include the auxiliary or

delete it from the second part of the sentence.

- Have students complete the task.
- Call on students to give answers. Tell them to read you the sentence two ways—first with the auxiliary verb, and then without it. For example: *Cats aren't as obedient as dogs are; Cats aren't as obedient as dogs.*

Multilevel Strategy

- **Pre-level:** Help students form the first couple of sentences from the prompts. Continue to provide support as needed.

EQUATIVES

	as . . . as (= the same)	*not as . . . as* (not the same)
ADJECTIVES	A dog is as cute as a cat is.	A rat isn't as cute as a dog is.
ADVERBS	Fish swim as well as whales do.	Dogs don't swim as well as whales do.
COUNT NOUNS	There are as many cat toys as dog toys.	There aren't as many rabbit toys as cat toys.
NONCOUNT NOUNS	Horses need as much exercise as big dogs do.	Small dogs don't need as much exercise as big dogs do.

A   Complete the sentences. Write *Max* or *Gypsy*.

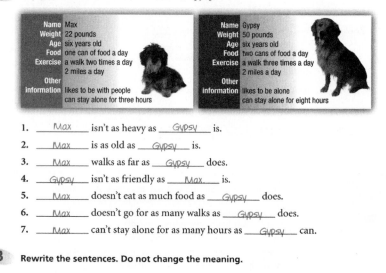

Name	Max
Weight	22 pounds
Age	six years old
Food	one can of food a day
Exercise	a walk two times a day 2 miles a day
Other information	likes to be with people can stay alone for three hours

Name	Gypsy
Weight	50 pounds
Age	six years old
Food	two cans of food a day
Exercise	a walk three times a day 2 miles a day
Other information	likes to be alone can stay alone for eight hours

1. ___Max___ isn't as heavy as ___Gypsy___ is.
2. ___Max___ is as old as ___Gypsy___ is.
3. ___Max___ walks as far as ___Gypsy___ does.
4. ___Gypsy___ isn't as friendly as ___Max___ is.
5. ___Max___ doesn't eat as much food as ___Gypsy___ does.
6. ___Max___ doesn't go for as many walks as ___Gypsy___ does.
7. ___Max___ can't stay alone for as many hours as ___Gypsy___ can.

B   Rewrite the sentences. Do not change the meaning.

1. Dogs are more obedient than cats.   *Cats aren't as obedient as dogs.*
2. Dogs understand people better than cats.   *Cats don't understand people as well as dogs (do).*
3. Dogs are friendlier than cats.   *Cats aren't as friendly as dogs (are).*
4. Cats are more independent than dogs.   *Dogs aren't as independent as cats (are).*
5. Dogs learn more easily than cats.   *Cats don't learn as easily as dog (do).*
6. Cats live longer than dogs.   *Dogs don't live as long as cats (do).*

Grammar Notes

1. Use *as . . . as* to say two people, places, or things are the same.

2. We use *not as . . . as* for the opposite of *more than.*

3. For more information on this grammar topic, see page 289.

Culture Note

Exercise A. In the United States, most cities and towns have animal shelters. Animal shelters are places where people can go to adopt dogs and cats that have no owners. The animals are vaccinated and given medical attention if needed. When someone comes to the shelter to adopt an animal, the staff asks about his or her lifestyle to help him or her choose an appropriate animal.

C A woman is talking about her pets. Complete the sentences with *as . . .* or *as . . . as*.

1. Pets can be ___as helpful as___ people.
   (helpful)

2. My pets are ___as important___ to me as my friends are.
   (important)

3. A pet can make you smile ___as often as___ people.
   (often)

4. Animals are ___as smart as___ people are.
   (smart)

5. My pets know me ___as well as___ my friends do.
   (well)

6. I can communicate ___as easily___ with animals as I can with my friends.
   (easily)

Look

Cats aren't as obedient as dogs are.

OR

Cats aren't as obedient as dogs.

Do you have a pet? If so, do you agree with the statements?

D Write sentences. How are the pets similar? How are they different? Use *(not) as . . . as* and the words in the boxes. Then compare sentences with other students. Answers will vary.

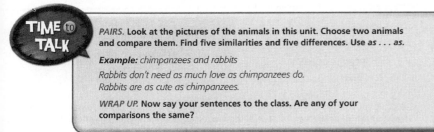

Popular pets	Verbs		Count Nouns	Noncount Nouns
cats	be	make	hours	food
dogs	cause	need	mice	fun
fish	eat	sleep	problems	mess
parrots	live	understand	words	noise
rabbits			years	space

1. _Cats are as much fun as dogs. Cats don't cause as many problems as dogs._
2. _____
3. _____
4. _____
5. _____

TIME to TALK

PAIRS. Look at the pictures of the animals in this unit. Choose two animals and compare them. Find five similarities and five differences. Use *as . . . as.*

Example: chimpanzees and rabbits

Rabbits don't need as much love as chimpanzees do.
Rabbits are as cute as chimpanzees.

WRAP UP. Now say your sentences to the class. Are any of your comparisons the same?

The Animal Kingdom 149

C Teaching Time: 10–15 min.

- Read the example with the class.
- Have students complete the task.
- Call on students to say answers. Correct as needed.

Expansion Start a discussion about people and their pets. Ask students to say whether they agree with any of the statements in Exercise C. Have them explain their answers by giving specific examples. For example, if a student agrees with statement 1, ask: *How are pets helpful to people? Give me some examples.*

D Teaching Time: 10–15 min.

- Read the directions with the class, and write the first sentence from the example on the board. Explain that students need to choose words from the boxes to build their sentences. Point to the example and show them that it uses two words from the first box (*cats / dogs*); one word from the second box (*are*) and one word from the fourth box (*fun*).
- Have students complete the task.
- Ask volunteers to write their sentences on the board. Correct as needed.

Option

Assign Unit 11 Supplementary Grammar to Communicate 3 Exercises on the Teacher's Resource Disk as homework or on the Student Persistence CD-ROM as self-access practice.

TIME to TALK

Teaching Time: 10–15 min.

- Call on a student to read the example.
- PAIRS. Have students complete the task.
- WRAP UP. Have each student say one of their sentences. Write their sentences on the board and have the class correct any errors.

Unit 11 T-149

Review and Challenge

Grammar

Teaching Time: 5–10 min.

- Read the example with the class.
- Have students complete the task.
- 🎧 Play Track 26 while students listen and check their answers.
- Call on students to read the corrected sentences. Correct as needed.

Dictation

Teaching Time: 5–10 min.

- 🎧 Play Track 27 while students listen and write what they hear.
- 🎧 Play Track 27 again while students check their answers.
- Ask volunteers to write their sentences on the board.
- 🎧 Play Track 27 again and correct the sentences on the board.

Speaking

Teaching Time: 5–10 min.

- Have students read the words in the box and look at the labeled pictures.
- PAIRS. Have students complete the task.
- Call on students to read their answers. Correct as needed.
- CLASS. Start a discussion based on the questions in the text. Write the expressions students tell you on the board.

Review and Challenge

Grammar

🔘 **26** This paragraph has seven mistakes. The first mistake is corrected for you. Find and correct the other six mistakes. Then listen and check your answers.

I have two parrots, Gertie and Peter. Gertie is ~~the oldest~~ *older*. She's 25 years old. Peter's only 10. He is gray. Gertie is more colorful ~~as~~ *than* Peter. She's green, blue, and yellow. Both parrots talk a lot. Gertie ~~is talkative~~ *is as talkative* as Peter. Gertie knows ~~less~~ *fewer* words than Peter, but Peter doesn't know as many big words as Gertie does. And they both say the ~~most funny~~ *funniest* things. Parrots are always messy, but Gertie isn't as ~~messier~~ *messy* as Peter. He always makes a big mess. I love both my parrots. They cause the ~~least~~ *fewest* problems of any pet, and they are the most fun.

Dictation

🔘 **27** Listen. You will hear five sentences. Write them in your notebook. *See the audioscript on p. 318 for the sentences.*

Speaking

PAIRS. Complete the sentences to make common expressions. Use the words in the box.

a bee	a fox	a mule
a bird	a mouse	an ox

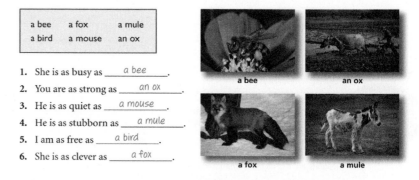

a bee

an ox

a fox

a mule

1. She is as busy as _____ *a bee* .
2. You are as strong as _____ *an ox* .
3. He is as quiet as _____ *a mouse* .
4. He is as stubborn as _____ *a mule* .
5. I am as free as _____ *a bird* .
6. She is as clever as _____ *a fox* .

CLASS. Check your answers with your teacher. Do you have similar expressions in your language? Which animals do you use in the expressions? What other expressions do you have with animals? Tell the class.

150 Unit 11

Expansion Have students explain the characteristics that are associated with particular animals in their cultures. Write some characteristics on the board, such as: *intelligent / stupid; honest / dishonest; strong / weak; greedy / generous; lazy / hardworking; serious / playful; lucky / unlucky.* Ask students which animals are associated with these characteristics in their culture or language. Write animal names next to each characteristic on the board.

Listening

A 🔘 **28** Listen. Check (✓) the animals that Dr. Downey talks about.

- ☐ bears
- ☑ cats
- ☑ dogs
- ☑ giraffes
- ☑ mosquitoes
- ☐ rats
- ☑ brown bats
- ☑ chimps
- ☑ elephants
- ☐ lions
- ☑ pigs
- ☑ whales

B 🔘 **28** Listen again. What does Dr. Downey say about the animals in Exercise A? Complete the sentences with the correct animals.

1. _____Pigs_____ aren't the dirtiest animals.
2. Pigs are almost as intelligent as _____chimps_____.
3. Some of the smartest animals are _____whales_____, _____elephants_____, and _____pigs_____.
4. _____Cats_____ sleep more hours than _____dogs_____.
5. _____Brown bats_____ sleep the most hours.
6. _____Giraffes_____ sleep the fewest hours.
7. _____Mosquitoes_____ kill the most people every year.

TIME to TALK

GROUPS. Discuss your opinions about animals.

Which animals are:

the best pets?	the most important in your culture?
the cutest?	the most intelligent?
the friendliest?	the most interesting?
the most disgusting?	the most useful to humans?
the most frightening?	the strangest?

Example: I think dogs are the best pets. They are smart and fun.

WRAP UP. Share your opinions with the class.

The Animal Kingdom 151

Listening

A **Teaching Time: 10–15 min.**

- **Warm-up:** Have students look at the pictures and read the directions and answer choices. Have them guess what the listening is going to be about. Write their guesses on the board.
- 🎧 Play Track 28 as students listen and complete the task.
- 🎧 Play Track 28 again, this time pausing as each animal is mentioned.

B **Teaching Time: 10–15 min.**

- PAIRS. Have students complete the task in pairs before you play the audio.
- 🎧 Play Track 28 while students check their answers.
- 🎧 Play Track 28 again, pausing as each answer is given. Call on a student to read the completed sentence before starting the recording again.

Multilevel Strategy

- **Pre-level:** Give students more time to complete the task. Have them circle the comparative, superlative, and equative forms in the sentences.
- **At-level, Above-level:** Have students complete Unit 11 Review and Challenge Supplementary Exercises on the Teacher's Resource Disk. Give them the answer key so that they can correct their answers.

Option

Assign Unit 11 Review and Challenge Supplementary Exercises on the Teacher's Resource Disk as homework or on the Student Persistence CD-ROM as self-access practice.

TIME to TALK

Teaching Time: 5–10 min.

- Read the example with the class.
- GROUPS. Have students complete the task.
- WRAP UP. Draw the following table on the board, and write the animals the groups mention in each column. Then take an informal poll for each animal, and write the number of students who agree in the chart.

the best pets	the cutest	the friendliest	the most disgusting	the most frightening
Ex.: *dogs* (8)				

Getting Ready to Read

Teaching Time: 5–10 min.

- Call on a student to read the information in the Reading Skill box.
- Make sure students know what a wolf is. Point to the picture in the reading.
- Have students complete the task. Remind them that it's okay to guess.
- Write the headings *Similarities* and *Differences* on the board.
- Call on students to give their answers.
- Write their answers on the board. Leave them there while they read the article.

Reading

Teaching Time: 15–20 min.

- Have students read the article.
- Have students look at the chart on the board. Ask them which of the similarities and differences were mentioned in the article. Check (✓) those that were mentioned. Cross out the others.

Multilevel Strategy

- **Pre-level:** Put pre-level students in a group. Read the article aloud as students follow along in their books. Pause frequently to ask them questions to check their general comprehension. In addition, encourage them to stop and ask questions about anything they don't understand.
- **At-level, Above-level:** After students have finished reading, tell them to underline the comparative, superlative, and equative forms in the article, and circle the words *like, both, unlike,* and *in contrast to.* Then have them compare what they have underlined and circled with a partner.

Reading

Getting Ready to Read

How are dogs and wolves similar? How are they different? If you are not sure, guess. *Answers will vary.*

Similarities

1. _____ .
2. _____ .

Differences

1. _____ .
2. _____ .

Reading

Read the article. Can you find the similarities and differences you wrote in Getting Ready to Read?

a wolf and her cub

FROM Wolves TO Dogs

Most people know that dogs **evolved from** wolves. But how? Scientists believe that between 20,000 and 100,000 years ago, wolves and humans came into contact for the first time. Some wolves lived near the camps of humans. As they became more **familiar with** people, they moved closer to human camps to find food. That is how the two **species** began to **interact** with each other.

Humans also hunted wolves for meat, so sometimes they killed adult wolves with cubs. Humans **took in** the cubs, probably because young wolves are cute, sociable, and playful. In other words, they are very similar to modern dogs. And like dogs, they are easy to train because they will **obey** the strongest member of the group — in this case, humans.

As young wolves become adults, however, they become more **aggressive** and much more difficult to control than wolf cubs. Humans probably killed most of the wolves as soon as they grew up and became aggressive and dangerous. However, the calmest, least aggressive wolves lived **side by side** with humans. These wolves had cubs, and often their cubs were also calm and lived easily with humans. Finally, after many generations, the wolves that lived with humans were a new species — the dog.

Dogs were as cute and as easy to train as wolf cubs, but their personalities and behavior did not change as they got older. In contrast to the wolf cubs, they continued to see humans as their leaders. For this reason, adult dogs did not become as aggressive or as dangerous as adult wolves. That is how wolves became dogs, and dogs became "man's best friend."

After You Read

After You Read

A Look at the **boldface** words in the article. Guess their meaning. Then read the sentences and circle the correct answer.

1. When one animal **evolves from** another animal, it ____.
   a. stays the same as that animal   (b.) becomes a new kind of animal

2. When you become **familiar with** someone, you ____.
   (a.) get to know the person   b. feel uncomfortable with the person

3. A new **species** is a new ____.
   (a.) type of plant or animal   b. type of idea

4. When you **interact with** someone, you ____.
   a. have no contact with each other   (b.) have contact with each other

5. When you **take in** an animal, ____.
   a. you kill it   (b.) the animal lives with you

6. When you **obey** someone, you ____.
   (a.) do what the person says   b. don't do what the person says

7. When an animal is **aggressive**, it might ____.
   (a.) bite you   b. play with you

8. An example of an animal that lives **side by side** with humans is a ____.
   a. shark   (b.) horse

B Put the statements in order from 1 to 9. Write the numbers in the blanks.

_4_ a. Humans took the wolf cubs in and took care of them.
_7_ b. The least aggressive young wolves continued to live with humans.
_9_ c. After many generations, a new species, the dog, evolved.
_1_ d. Wolves started to live near human camps.
_5_ e. The wolf cubs became adults and most became aggressive and dangerous.
_2_ f. Wolves got familiar with humans.
_6_ g. Humans killed most of the adult wolves.
_8_ h. The least aggressive young wolves had cubs.
_3_ i. Humans sometimes killed the parents of wolf cubs.

The Animal Kingdom **153**

After You Read

A Teaching Time: 10–15 min.

- Read the directions, and do the example with the class. Show students how to check their answers by replacing the word(s) in the article with the answer they have chosen. Write the first sentence from the article on the board, along with the two answer choices from Exercise A:

  Most people know that dogs evolved from wolves.
      a. *stayed the same as wolves.*
              OR
      b. *became a new kind of animal.*

- Ask which answer is logically correct, a or b? (b)

- Have students complete the task. Tell them to check their answers by replacing the word(s) in the article with the answer they have chosen.

- Call on students to say answers. Have them reread the sentences from the article with their answer choices. Write the original sentences and the replacements on the board. For example:

  2. they became more familiar with people = they got to know people
  3. the two species = the two types of animals

B Teaching Time: 10–15 min.

- Read the example with the class.
- Have students complete the task.
- Call on students to say answers. Correct as needed.

Multilevel Strategy

All levels: PAIRS. Pair pre-level students with at- and above-level students. Tell students to find the place in the article that corresponds to each sentence in Exercise B. For example, have them write *1* next to line 4 in paragraph 1. Continue until they have written the numbers of all 9 of the sentences in Exercise B next to the corresponding places in the article. Then have them complete Exercise B. Walk around and help as needed.
(*2*: paragraph 1, line 5; *3*: paragraph 2, line 2; *4*: paragraph 2, line 2; *5*: paragraph 3, line 2; *6*: paragraph 3, line 3; *7*: paragraph 3, lines 5–6; *8*: paragraph 3, line 6; *9*: paragraph 3, lines 8–9)

Getting Ready to Write

- Have students study the Writing Tip.
- Write the first sentence from the exercise on the board: *Like dogs, cows live side by side with humans.* Call on a student to come up to the board and rewrite it with *both*. (*Both dogs and cows live side by side with humans.*)
- Read the example with the class, and add the sentence *Unlike dogs, cows are not pets* to the board.
- Have students complete the task.
- Call on students to say answers. Correct as needed.

Expansion Have students rewrite the sentences in the exercise with *like, both,* or *unlike* (for example, 2: *Unlike dogs, fish live under water.*)

B Teaching Time: 10–15 min.

- Have students read the writing model.
- PAIRS. Have students complete the task. Write some examples of animals they could compare on the board: *dogs / cats; cats / lions; dogs / wolves; horses / donkeys; chimps / gorillas; mice / rats.*

Writing

Getting Ready to Write

A Write new sentences. Use the words in parentheses.

1. Like dogs, cows live side by side with humans.
   <u>Unlike dogs, cows are not pets.</u>
   (unlike / are not pets)
2. In contrast to dogs, fish live under water.
   <u>Both dogs and fish can swim.</u>
   (both / can swim)
3. Both wolves and lions have fur.
   <u>Like wolves, lions eat meat.</u>
   (like / eat meat)
4. Like wolves, bears live in forests.
   <u>In contrast to wolves, bears can weigh 500 pounds.</u>
   (in contrast to / can weigh 500 pounds)
5. Both cats and dogs are trainable.
   <u>Unlike cats, dogs are easy to train.</u>
   (unlike / easy to train)

B Read the model paragraph.

> Sharks and dolphins are similar in many ways. <u>Both animals have fins on their back and sides</u>, and their bodies have a similar shape. <u>Like sharks, dolphins are some of the fastest swimmers in the ocean.</u> However, in contrast to sharks, dolphins are warm-blooded, and they breathe air. Dolphins have much better eyesight and hearing than sharks do. But unlike dolphins, sharks have a very good sense of smell. Some people think that <u>sharks are as intelligent as dolphins</u>, but dolphins are easier to train. They are also much friendlier toward humans.

PAIRS. Read the model again. According to the writer, what are the similarities and differences between sharks and dolphins? Wording of answers will vary.

Now talk about two other animals. Discuss the similarities and differences between them.

Writing Tip

Use *like* and *both* to compare two things:

Example:

Like wolves, dogs are good at hunting.

Both wolves and dogs are good at hunting.

Use *unlike* and *in contrast to* to contrast two things:

Example:

Unlike wolves, dogs are trainable.

In contrast to wolves, dogs are easy to train.

Prewriting: Using a Venn Diagram

You are going to write a paragraph comparing and contrasting two animals. Before you write, look at the Venn diagram for the writing model.

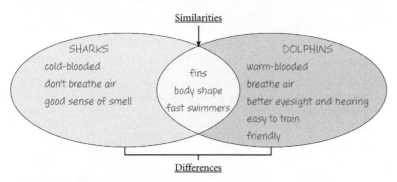

Similarities

SHARKS
cold-blooded
don't breathe air
good sense of smell

fins
body shape
fast swimmers

DOLPHINS
warm-blooded
breathe air
better eyesight and hearing
easy to train
friendly

Differences

Choose two animals and complete the Venn diagram. Choose one of the animal pairs in the box or use your own ideas.

| dogs / cats | lions / tigers | cows / horses | monkeys / gorillas |

If you need more information, look in the library or on the Internet. To search the Internet:

- Go to an Internet search engine such as www.google.com.
- Choose two animals that you want to write about. For example, type in "sharks and dolphins."
- Choose a site and click on its Web address.
- Read some of the information on the site. Write notes in your Venn diagram.

Writing

Now write a paragraph comparing and contrasting two animals. The writing tip, the model paragraph, and your notes will help you. Write in your notebook.

The Animal Kingdom 155

Prewriting

Teaching Time: 5–10 min.

- Have students look at the example Venn diagram. Explain the information in each part of the diagram.
- Assign the task for homework.
- In class the next day, have students exchange their Venn diagrams. Tell them to ask and answer questions about anything in their diagrams that is not clear.

Writing

Teaching Time: 20–25 min.

- Have students use their Venn diagrams to complete the task.
- Encourage students to use comparatives and the words *like, both, unlike,* and *in contrast to* in their paragraphs.
- Before students hand their paragraphs in, tell them to review the unit grammar summary on pages 288–289, and revise their paragraphs as necessary.

Multilevel Strategy

Pre-level: While the other students are exchanging their Venn diagrams and writing their paragraphs, work with the pre-level students in a group. Take one of the student's diagrams, and use it to construct a paragraph on the board with the group. Have students copy the final paragraph into their notebooks.

Unit 12
Let's Eat!

Learning Goals

- Learn vocabulary related to eating and hospitality
- Learn how to use reflexive pronouns, *one / ones,* and the singular and plural forms of *other*
- Listen to a conversation in a restaurant and a report about the history of fast food restaurants
- Read an article about the Slow Food Movement and write a paragraph about diet
- Talk about restaurants, dining etiquette and hospitality in different countries, and cultural food preferences

Learner Persistence

Ask students what they want to learn. Make sure to include that information in the unit lessons.

Warm-up

Teaching Time: 5–10 min.

Have students look at the picture. Ask: *Where are the people? How often do you eat out? How often do you eat at a restaurant like the one in the picture? When you eat out, do you usually go alone or with someone? If you go with someone, who do you usually go with?*

Vocabulary

Teaching Time: 10–15 min.

- Read the words in the box aloud as students listen and repeat chorally. Tell them to check (✓) the words that they already know.
- Read the example with the class.
- Have students complete the first part of the task (matching).
- 🎧 Play Track 29 while students listen and check their answers.
- Have students complete the second part of the task (identifying nouns and verbs).
- Call on students to say answers. Correct as needed.

Unit 12
Let's Eat!

Grammar
- Reflexive Pronouns
- *One / Ones*
- *Other*: Singular and Plural

Vocabulary

🎧 **29** Match the numbers with the words. Circle the nouns and underline the verbs. Then listen and check your answers.

8	appetizer
10	dessert
1	enjoy herself
12	help herself
9	main dish
2	napkin
7	order
13	salad bar
5	seat
4	serve
11	specials
3	stuff herself
6	treat

156   Unit 12

Expansion

- PAIRS. Have students make sentences about the people in the picture with the words in the box. For example: *The hostess is seating a man and a woman. A woman is helping herself to the salad bar. A man is ordering. The waitress is taking his order.*
- Ask volunteers to write their sentences on the board. Correct as needed.

Listening

A 🎵 **30** Listen. A man goes out to lunch with his wife. Write *W* for the words that describe the woman. Write *M* for the words that describe the man. Be careful. There are two extra answers.

____ **1.** bored   _M_ **3.** impatient   _M_ **5.** rude

_W_ **2.** friendly   _W_ **4.** polite   ____ **6.** smart

B 🎵 **31** Listen again. Put the sentences in each group in order from 1 to 4.

Group 1

_3_ By the window?

_4_ One of them is, but the others are free.

_1_ The one in the corner? It's reserved.

_2_ How about the ones over there? Are they reserved, too?

Group 2

_3_ This one is dirty.

_4_ Oh, I'm sorry. I'll get you another one.

_1_ You can serve yourselves whenever you're ready.

_2_ I need another fork.

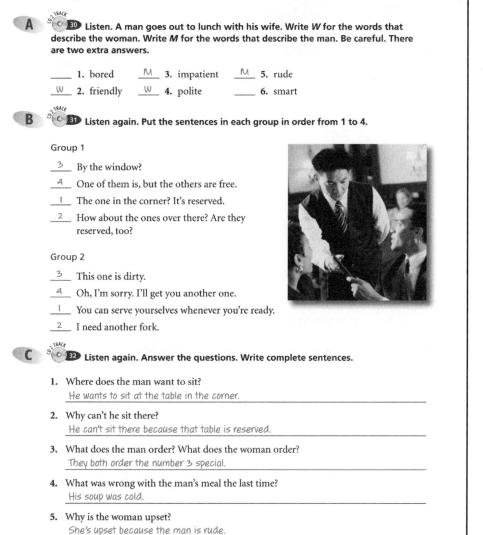

C 🎵 **32** Listen again. Answer the questions. Write complete sentences.

1. Where does the man want to sit?
He wants to sit at the table in the corner.

2. Why can't he sit there?
He can't sit there because that table is reserved.

3. What does the man order? What does the woman order?
They both order the number 3 special.

4. What was wrong with the man's meal the last time?
His soup was cold.

5. Why is the woman upset?
She's upset because the man is rude.

Let's Eat! **157**

Culture Note

- **Tipping:** At most restaurants in the United States, waiters expect a tip of at least 15 percent. In fact, they depend on their tips to support themselves and their families.

- **Getting the waiter's attention:** It is not polite to whistle, snap your fingers, or clap your hands to get a waiter's attention at an American restaurant. Instead, try to make eye contact with the waiter.

Option

Assign Unit 12 Supplementary Vocabulary Exercises on the Teacher's Resource Disk as homework or on the Student Persistence CD-ROM as self-access practice.

Listening

A **Teaching Time: 10–15 min.**

- **Warm-up.** Have a student read the answer choices aloud. Ask which words are positive and which are negative. (positive: *friendly, polite, smart*; negative: *bored, impatient, rude*)

- 🎧 Play Track 30 as students complete the task.

- 🎧 Play Track 30 again as students check their answers. Pause the recording as each answer is given. Ask: *Which word describes what the [woman or man] just said?*

B **Teaching Time: 10–15 min.**

- Read the example with the class.

- 🎧 Play Track 31 as students listen and complete the task.

- 🎧 Play Track 31 again, pausing the recording at the end of each conversation. Call on two students to read each conversation in order.

Multilevel Strategy

- **Pre-level:** Make photocopies of the audioscript to give to students after they have completed Exercise B. Have them work in pairs and practice reading the conversation aloud. Encourage them to imitate the attitudes of the man and the woman on the recording (e.g., impatient, rude, polite).

- **At-level, Above-level:** Have students work in pairs to recall the part of the conversation that is not on the page. Ask volunteers to role-play the conversation for the class.

C **Teaching Time: 10–15 min.**

- PAIRS. Have students try to complete the task before they hear the recording again.

- 🎧 Play Track 32 as students listen and check their answers.

- Ask volunteers to write their answers on the board.

- 🎧 Play Track 32 again, pausing as each answer is given. Correct the sentences on the board as needed.

Grammar to Communicate 1

Reflexive Pronouns

Teaching Time: 5–10 min.

- Have students study the chart.
- Write on the board:

  She serves me / myself.
  I don't serve me / myself.
  She serves you / yourself.
  You don't serve you / yourself.
  She serves us / ourselves.
  We don't serve us / ourselves.

- Have students tell you which pronoun to circle in each sentence, the object pronoun or the reflexive pronoun (me, myself, you, yourself, us, ourselves).
- Say: *We use the object pronoun after the verb when the subject and the object are different. We use the reflexive pronoun after the verb when the subject and the object are the same.*
- Write on the board:

  Please serve you / yourself.
  Please serve you / yourselves.
  Please serve him / himself.

- Have students tell you which pronoun to circle in each sentence, the object pronoun or the reflexive pronoun.
- Ask: *Why do we use the reflexive pronouns in the first two sentences, but the object pronoun in the third sentence?* (In the first two, we use the reflexive pronouns because they are imperative sentences, or commands. In imperative sentences, the understood subject is always *you*—either *you* singular, as in the first sentence, or *you* plural, as in the second. In the third sentence, we use the object pronoun because the subject and object are different. It's an imperative sentence, so the understood subject is *you*. The object is *him,* so we can't use a reflexive pronoun.)

A **Teaching Time: 10–15 min.**

- Read the example with the class.
- Have students complete the task.
- Call on students to give answers. Have students identify the subject of the sentences containing reflexive pronouns. Correct as needed.

Grammar to Communicate 1

REFLEXIVE PRONOUNS

Singular				Plural			
Subject Pronoun		Verb	Reflexive Pronoun	Subject Pronoun		Verb	Reflexive Pronoun
I	always	serve	myself.	We			ourselves.
You			yourself.	You	always	serve	yourselves.
He			himself.	They			themselves.
She	always	serves	herself.				
It			itself.				

A Circle the reflexive pronouns.

1. I've really stuffed (myself.) No dessert for me!
2. We can't seat (ourselves.) We have to wait for the hostess.
3. Look at the guy near the window. He's talking to (himself.)
4. Put that knife down. You could hurt (yourself.)
5. If your children don't behave (themselves,) they're going to have to leave.
6. The salad bar is over there. Please help (yourselves.)
7. It's her birthday, so she's treating (herself) to lunch in a nice restaurant.

B Complete the sentences. Use the correct reflexive pronoun.

1. I don't go to restaurants by ___myself___ .
2. My friend Anna feels uncomfortable if she sits by ___herself___ in a restaurant.
3. My father never eats out by ___himself___ .
4. When I go to a restaurant, I like to pay for ___myself___ .
5. My friends and I always enjoy ___ourselves___ when we eat out together.
6. I never go to restaurants with children that don't behave ___themselves___ .
7. On their anniversary, my parents treat ___themselves___ to a meal in a nice restaurant.

Look

By + reflexive pronoun = alone
I live **by myself.** = I live **alone.**

PAIRS. **Make the sentences true about yourself or people you know.**

Examples: *I don't go to restaurants by myself.* OR *I like to go to restaurants by myself.* OR *My children don't go to restaurants by themselves.*

158 Unit 12

B **Teaching Time: 10–15 min.**

- Have students study the Look Box.
- Read the example with the class.
- Have students complete the task.
- Call on students to give answers. Correct as needed.
- PAIRS. Have students make sentences about themselves and people they know.
- Call on students to tell the class something about their partners. Correct as needed.

Grammar Notes

1. We use reflexive pronouns when the subject and the object are the same.
2. We often use reflexive pronouns after these verbs: *burn, cut, enjoy, hurt.*
3. For more information about this grammar topic, see page 289.

Watch Out!

Common errors include using *hisself* instead of *himself,* and *theirself* or *theirselves* instead of *themselves.* Listen carefully for these errors and correct them.

C Complete the sentences. Circle the correct answer.

1. The children stuffed _____ with candy. Now they won't eat dinner.
   a. each other　　b. them　　(c.) themselves

2. Our children started throwing food at _____ in the restaurant last night. It was very embarrassing.
   (a.) each other　　b. them　　c. themselves

3. Make _____ at home. Our home is your home. If you're hungry, there's food in the refrigerator.
   a. each other　　b. you　　(c.) yourselves

4. My husband hurt his hand, so he can't feed _____.
   a. each other　　b. him　　(c.) himself

5. That man ordered three desserts. Do you think that they're all for _____?
   a. each other　　(b.) him　　c. himself

6. We haven't seen _____ in months! Let's meet for dinner.
   (a.) each other　　b. us　　c. ourselves

7. Come on. You've had a bad day. I'll treat _____ to dinner.
   a. each other　　(b.) you　　c. yourself

8. If you stuff _____ like that all the time, you're going to get fat.
   a. each other　　b. you　　(c.) yourself

Look

They're looking at **them.**

They're looking at **themselves.**

They're looking at **each other.**

TIME to TALK

ON YOUR OWN. Check (✓) the statements that describe your culture.

☐ 1. People usually seat themselves at restaurants. They don't wait for a waiter.
☐ 2. Children order for themselves. Their parents don't order for them.
☐ 3. When people visit their friends' homes, they help themselves to food.
☐ 4. Children must excuse themselves before they leave the table.
☐ 5. When a couple eats out, the man always treats. The woman never pays.
☐ 6. People often sit by themselves at restaurants.

GROUPS. **Compare eating customs in your cultures.**

Let's Eat! 159

- Have students study the Look Box. Have them point to the object of each sentence in each picture.
- Read the example with the class.
- Have students complete the task.
- Call on students to say answers. Correct as needed.

Teaching Tip

Exercise C. Simple illustrations can be very helpful in getting students to understand the difference between *each other* and *themselves, yourselves,* and *ourselves.* For example, for sentence 1, draw two faces side by side, each with an arrow pointing up at the mouth. For sentence 2, draw two faces side by side, each with an arrow pointing towards the other.

Option

Assign Unit 12 Supplementary Grammar to Communicate 1 Exercises on the Teacher's Resource Disk as homework or on the Student Persistence CD-ROM as self-access practice.

TIME to TALK

Teaching Time: 10–15 min.

- ON YOUR OWN. Have students complete the task. If necessary, explain *help oneself to something* (= It's okay to take something without asking); and *excuse oneself* (= Say, "Excuse me.").
- GROUPS. Have students complete the task.
- Ask each group to tell you something interesting that they learned about another culture.

Grammar to Communicate 2

One / Ones

Teaching Time: 10–15 min.

- Have students study the chart and the Look Box.
- To illustrate the use of the pronoun *one,* hold up three pencils, each one a different color (or three other small objects, such as pieces of candy or erasers, identical except in color).
- Look at one student and say: *I have some extra pencils. Would you like one?* If the student says no, keep asking until someone says yes.
- Now ask: *Which one would you like? The red one, the blue one, or the yellow one?* Give the student the pencil he asks for.
- Hold up the remaining two pencils and point at each one in turn, asking: *Who would like this pencil? And this one?* Give the pencils to the students who answer first.
- Write the sentences you have just used on the board, along with the explanations in brackets.

  I have some extra pencils. Would you like one? [= one of the three—but not any particular one]

  Which pencil would you like? The red one, the blue one, or the yellow one? [= one of the three—specific]

  Who would like this pencil? And this one? [= this particular thing that I'm pointing at—specific]

 A **Teaching Time: 5–10 min.**

- Read the example with the class.
- Have students complete the task.
- 🎧 Play Track 33 while students listen and correct their answers.
- Call on students to say answers. Correct as needed.
- Have two volunteers read each conversation aloud.

B **Teaching Time: 5–10 min.**

- Read the example with the class. Then ask: *What is the noun in the first sentence?* (dish) *Is it singular or plural?* (singular) Explain: *We use the singular form* one *because it refers to a singular noun,* dish.

- Have students identify the noun in each sentence and complete the task.
- Call on students to say answers. Correct as needed.

Grammar to Communicate 2

ONE / ONES

	Singular Count Nouns	Plural Count Nouns
THINGS OR PEOPLE IN GENERAL	This glass isn't clean. Can you give us a clean one?	These glasses aren't clean. Can you give us clean ones?
SPECIFIC THINGS OR PEOPLE	That's not our waiter. Ours is the one with the beard.	I don't want these cookies. I want the big ones.
WITH *THIS* OR *THAT*	I don't want to sit at this table. I want to sit at that one.	

A 🎧 33 **Complete the conversations. Circle the correct words. Then listen and check your answers.**

> **Look**
> Use *one* or *ones* to replace singular or plural count nouns.

1. A: Do you want your (sandwich) / sandwiches with mayonnaise or mustard?
   B: I want one with both, please.
2. A: Do you like hot **sandwich** / (**sandwiches**) or cold ones?
   B: Hmm . . . That's a good question.
3. A: We need more **napkin** / (**napkins.**)
   B: I'll get some extra ones.
4. A: I can't find my (**napkin**) / **napkins.**
   B: Is this one yours?
5. A: Which **main dish** / (**main dishes**) should we have?
   B: The ones at the next table look good.
6. A: Which (**main dish**) / **main dishes** did you order?
   B: The one with the potatoes.

B **Complete the conversations. Use *one* or *ones.***

1. I don't want the chicken dish with peppers. I'll have the _____one_____ with mushrooms.
2. Put the small forks here, and put the big _____ones_____ there.
3. You're drinking my glass of water. That _____one_____ is yours.
4. We need two tables. Can we sit at the _____ones_____ over there?
5. These knives are dirty. Can you give us two clean _____ones_____?
6. This appetizer is good, and that _____one_____ is, too.
7. Are we going to get a large pizza or a small _____one_____?

160 Unit 12

Grammar Notes

1. We use *one* or *ones* when we do not want to repeat a noun. Compare:

   This glass is dirty.   Can I have a clean *one*?

   INCORRECT: Can I have ~~a clean it~~?

2. Use *one* for singular count nouns. Use *ones* for plural count nouns. Do not use *one* or *ones* for noncount nouns.

3. For more information on this grammar topic, see page 289.

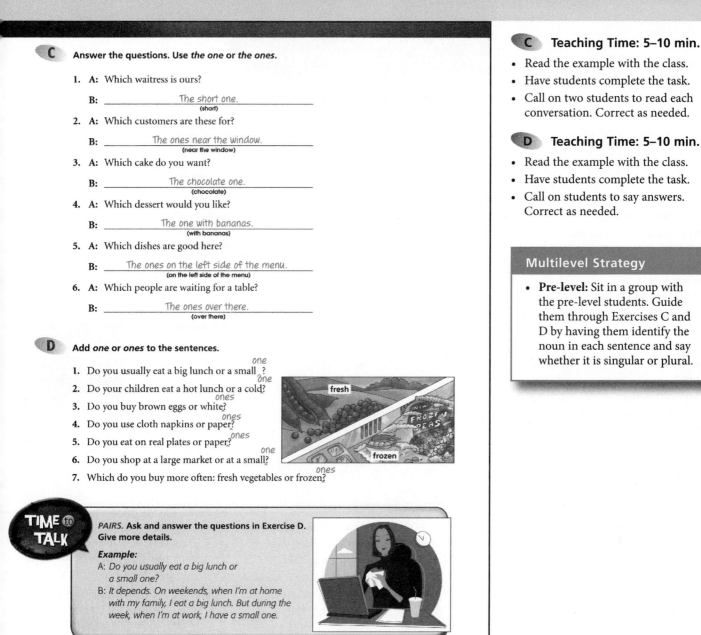

C Answer the questions. Use *the one* or *the ones*.

1. **A:** Which waitress is ours?

   B: _____ The short one. _____
   (short)

2. **A:** Which customers are these for?

   B: ___ The ones near the window. ___
   (near the window)

3. **A:** Which cake do you want?

   B: _____ The chocolate one. _____
   (chocolate)

4. **A:** Which dessert would you like?

   B: _____ The one with bananas. _____
   (with bananas)

5. **A:** Which dishes are good here?

   B: __ The ones on the left side of the menu. __
   (on the left side of the menu)

6. **A:** Which people are waiting for a table?

   B: _____ The ones over there. _____
   (over there)

D Add *one* or *ones* to the sentences.

1. Do you usually eat a big lunch or a small ⟨one⟩?
2. Do your children eat a hot lunch or a cold ⟨one⟩?
3. Do you buy brown eggs or white ⟨ones⟩?
4. Do you use cloth napkins or paper ⟨ones⟩?
5. Do you eat on real plates or paper ⟨ones⟩?
6. Do you shop at a large market or at a small ⟨one⟩?
7. Which do you buy more often: fresh vegetables or frozen ⟨ones⟩?

TIME to TALK

PAIRS. **Ask and answer the questions in Exercise D. Give more details.**

Example:
A: *Do you usually eat a big lunch or a small one?*
B: *It depends. On weekends, when I'm at home with my family, I eat a big lunch. But during the week, when I'm at work, I have a small one.*

Let's Eat! 161

C Teaching Time: 5–10 min.

- Read the example with the class.
- Have students complete the task.
- Call on two students to read each conversation. Correct as needed.

D Teaching Time: 5–10 min.

- Read the example with the class.
- Have students complete the task.
- Call on students to say answers. Correct as needed.

Multilevel Strategy

- **Pre-level:** Sit in a group with the pre-level students. Guide them through Exercises C and D by having them identify the noun in each sentence and say whether it is singular or plural.

Option

Assign Unit 12 Supplementary Grammar to Communicate 2 Exercises on the Teacher's Resource Disk as homework or on the Student Persistence CD-ROM as self-access practice.

TIME to TALK

Teaching Time: 10–15 min.

- Have two students read the example.
- PAIRS. Have students complete the task. Walk around and make a note of errors in the use of *one / ones*.
- Write the errors on the board. Have students correct them.

Unit 12 T-161

Grammar to Communicate 3

Other: Singular and Plural

Teaching Time: 5–10 min.

- Have students study the charts.
- Hold up three different-colored pencils. Say: *I have three pencils. One pencil is yellow. Another pencil is blue. The other pencil is red.*
- Write the sentences on the board, as follows:

  Adjective: *One pencil is yellow.*

  Singular pronoun: *One is yellow.*

  Adjective: *Another pencil is blue.*

  Singular pronoun: *Another is blue.*

  Adjective: *The other pencil is red.*

  Singular pronoun: *The other is red.*

- As you point to the appropriate parts of the sentences on the board, say: *We can use* one, another, *and* the other *as adjectives or pronouns.*
- Hold up the pencils again. Say: *I have three pencils. One is yellow. The others are blue and red.*
- Write the sentences on the board:

  Adjective: *The other pencils are blue and red.*

  Plural pronoun: *The others are blue and red.*

A Teaching Time: 10–15 min.

- Draw the following on the board:

  Read the example with the class as you point to the corresponding "cookies."
- Have students complete the task.
- Call on students to read the sentences and the answers. As students answer, draw the appropriate picture on the board (see below). Read the sentences again, this time pointing to the different circles in the pictures as you read the sentences aloud.

- Sentence 2:

- Sentence 3:

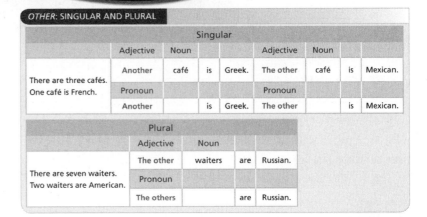

OTHER: SINGULAR AND PLURAL								
		Singular						
		Adjective	Noun			Adjective	Noun	
There are three cafés. One café is French.		Another	café	is	Greek.	The other	café	is	Mexican.
		Pronoun				Pronoun		
		Another		is	Greek.	The other		is	Mexican.

		Plural			
		Adjective	Noun		
There are seven waiters. Two waiters are American.		The other	waiters	are	Russian.
		Pronoun			
		The others		are	Russian.

A How many cookies are there? Circle the correct answers.

1. One cookie is small. The others are big.
   a. 1   b. 2   **c.** 3
2. One cookie is small. The other is big.
   a. 1   **b.** 2   c. 3
3. One cookie is small. Another is big. The other is medium-size.
   a. 1   b. 2   **c.** 3   d. more than 3
4. One cookie is small. Another is big. The others are medium-size.
   a. 1   b. 2   c. 3   **d.** more than 3

B **34** Rewrite the answers. Use pronouns. Then listen and check your answers.

1. A: Would you like another cookie?
   B: Sure, I'll have another cookie.
      Sure, I'll have ___another___.

2. A: Are these the forks that you want?
   B: No, I meant the other forks.
      No, I meant ___the others___.

3. A: Have you got enough spoons?
   B: No, I need another spoon.
      No, I need ___another___.

4. A: Is one napkin enough?
   B: No, please give me another napkin.
      No, please give me ___another___.

- Sentence 4:

B Teaching Time: 10–15 min.

- Have students complete the task.
- Play Track 34 while students listen and check their answers.
- Call on two students to read each conversation. Correct as needed.

Grammar Notes

1. *One* can be a pronoun. We use it when we do not want to repeat a singular count noun.

2. *Another* means *an additional . . .* or *a different . . .* It can be an adjective or a pronoun.

3. *The other* means *the last one in a group.* We use *the other* as an adjective before singular and plural nouns, or as a pronoun to refer to one person or thing.

4. *The others* is a pronoun. We use *the others* to refer to more than one person or thing.

5. For more information on this grammar topic, see pages 289–290.

C Look at the information about different restaurants. Complete the sentences with *another*, *the other*, or *the others*.

	Type of food	Meals served	Open	Location	Price*
China Palace	Chinese	lunch, dinner	7 days a week	341 Main St.	$
Dynasty Inn	Chinese	lunch, dinner	7 days a week	56 Elm St.	$
Jack's Family Diner	American	breakfast, lunch, dinner	7 days a week	658 Main St.	$
La Provence	French	breakfast, lunch	Closed Sunday	10 Park St.	$
Mexico Lindo	Mexican	lunch, dinner	7 days a week	466 Pine St.	$
Napolitana	Italian	lunch, dinner	Closed Sunday and Monday	539 Pine St.	$$$

*$ = inexpensive; $$$ = expensive

1. One is closed on Sundays. _Another_ is closed Sunday and Monday. _The others_ are open seven days a week.
2. Two serve breakfast. _The other_ four serve lunch and dinner only.
3. One serves Italian food. _Another_ serves American food. _Another_ serves French food. _Another_ serves Mexican food. _The others_ serve Chinese food.
4. Two of the restaurants are on Main Street. _Another_ restaurant is on Elm Street. _Another_ restaurant is on Park Street. _The other_ restaurants are on Pine Street.
5. Five of the restaurants are inexpensive. _The other_ is expensive.

TIME to TALK

PAIRS. Talk about places near where you work, go to school, and live.

How many restaurants are there? What kind of food do they serve? Which one is your favorite?	How many coffee shops are there? Which one is the most popular? Which one has the best coffee?
How many supermarkets are there? At which one or ones do you shop?	How many places are there to buy fresh fruit and vegetables? Which one has the best prices?

Example:
A: *How many restaurants are there near where you work?*
B: *There are three. There's one next to my office, and the others are across the street.*
A: *What kind of food do they serve?*
B: *The one next to my building is a Greek restaurant. The others are fast-food restaurants.*

Let's Eat! **163**

C Teaching Time: 10–15 min.

- Have students look at the information in the chart. Then read the example with the class.
- Have students complete the task.
- Call on students to read their completed sentences. Correct as needed. After they read the answer, have them read the sentences again, but this time with the names of the restaurants. For example, for sentence 1, first the student reads: *One is closed on Sundays. Another is closed on Sunday and Monday. The others are open seven days a week.* Then the same student reads: *La Provence is closed on Sundays. Napolitana is closed on Sunday and Monday. China Palace, Dynasty Inn, Jack's Family Diner, and Mexico Lindo are open seven days a week.*

Watch Out!

Students who speak languages in which adjectives have singular and plural forms might make the following mistake with *the others*. Listen for and correct errors such as: *The others cookies are big.*

Option

Assign Unit 12 Supplementary Grammar to Communicate 3 Exercises on the Teacher's Resource Disk as homework or on the Student Persistence CD-ROM as self-access practice.

TIME to TALK

Teaching Time: 10–15 min.

- Call on two students to read the example conversation.
- PAIRS. Have students complete the task. Encourage them to use the questions in the boxes.
- Ask a volunteer to come up to the front of the room and answer the class's questions. Correct as needed.

Expansion Write the names of local restaurants, coffee shops, and stores on the board. Start a discussion about which one has the best food, the best coffee, the best prices, the best service, etc.

Unit 12 **T-163**

Review and Challenge

Grammar

Teaching Time: 5–10 min.

- Read the example with the class.
- Have students complete the task.
- 🎧 Play Track 35 while students listen and check their answers.
- Call on three students to read the conversation. Correct as needed. If necessary, play the recording again.

Dictation

Teaching Time: 5–10 min.

- 🎧 Play Track 36 while students listen and write what they hear.
- 🎧 Play Track 36 again while students check their answers.
- Ask volunteers to write their sentences on the board.
- 🎧 Play Track 36 again and correct the sentences on the board.

Multilevel Strategy

Pre-level: Give students a worksheet with the words from the dictation already provided, except for the pronouns.

Speaking

Teaching Time: 5–10 min.

- PAIRS. Have students complete the task. Encourage students to use the following format when writing their definitions:

  Self-employed people work for themselves.

- WRAP UP. Call on students to say answers. Correct as necessary. Have the class vote on the most creative definition.

Review and Challenge

Grammar

🎧 **35** Complete the conversation with the words in the box. Then listen and check your answers. Be careful. There are extra words.

another	herself	me	one	ourselves	the others	~~yourself~~
each other	himself	myself	ones	the other	you	yourselves

Amy: Come in. Make ___yourself___ at home. Here, give ___me___ your jacket.
        1.   2.

Jan: Sorry I'm late. I missed the bus and waited an hour for the next ___one___.
                                                                          3.

Amy: Don't worry. Two couples, the ___ones___ from Chester, still aren't here.
                                    4.

Jan: Yeah, Chester is far away. Bill, is that you? How are you?

Bill: Oh, Jan, nice to see ___you___. I'm great.
                            5.

Amy: How do you two know ___each other___? Did you meet at ___another___ party?
                          6.   7.

Jan: Yeah. We met at Lin's. It was great. We really enjoyed ___ourselves___.
                                                            8.

Amy: So Jan, do you know ___the other___ people here?
                          9.

Jan: Well, I know your boyfriend, of course, but I don't think I know ___the others___.
                                                                      10.

Dictation

🎧 **36** Listen. You will hear five sentences. Write them in your notebook. *See the audioscript on p. 319 for the sentences.*

Speaking

PAIRS. Most restaurant owners are *self-employed*. They work for themselves. What do the phrases with *self* in the box mean? Write your ideas.

self-addressed envelope	self-cleaning oven	self-made man (or woman)
self-centered person	self-defrosting refrigerator	self-serve restaurant

WRAP UP. Now share your ideas with the class. Who has the best definitions? Finally, check your definitions in a dictionary or ask your teacher.

Listening

A 🎵 **37** Listen to the report. Check (✓) the best title for the report.

- ❑ 1. A History of American Restaurants
- ❑ 2. Eating in Your Car: An American Tradition
- ❑ 3. The McDonald Brothers
- ✓ 4. The Birth of Fast Food

B 🎵 **38** Listen again. Check (✓) the features of the Speedy Service System.

- ✓ 1. There are only a few choices on the menu.
- ❑ 2. The food is made to order.
- ❑ 3. The waiters are very fast.
- ✓ 4. People serve themselves.
- ✓ 5. The food is ready very quickly.
- ❑ 6. There are no tables. People eat in their cars.
- ✓ 7. People seat themselves.
- ✓ 8. People clean up after themselves.
- ❑ 9. Customers wash their own dishes.

Model-T Ford

assembly line

TIME to TALK

GROUPS. **Talk about fast-food restaurants in your country. Discuss the answers to the questions.**

1. What are the most popular fast-food restaurants where you live? What kinds of food do they serve? Why are they so popular?

2. How often do you eat fast food? What is your favorite kind of fast food? Where do you like to go to eat fast food?

3. Are there American fast-food restaurants in your country? Which ones are there? Which ones are the most popular?

Let's Eat! 165

Listening

A Teaching Time: 10–15 min.

- Have students read the answer choices.
- 🎧 Play Track 37 as students listen and complete the task.
- Call on a student to say the answer.

B Teaching Time: 10–15 min.

- Have a student explain what the Speedy Service System is.
- 🎧 Play Track 38 while students listen and complete the task.
- 🎧 Play Track 38 again, pausing the recording as each answer is given.

Multilevel Strategy

Pre-level: After students have completed Exercise A, give them a copy of the audioscript and tell them to read along as they do Exercise B.

Option

Assign Unit 12 Review and Challenge Supplementary Exercises on the Teacher's Resource Disk as homework or on the Student Persistence CD-ROM as self-access practice.

TIME to TALK

Teaching Time: 10–15 min.

- GROUPS. Have students complete the task.
- Put a list of popular fast-food chains in your area on the board. Find out which one is most popular among the students in your class by taking an informal poll.

Reading

Getting Ready to Read

Teaching Time: 5–10 min.

- Call on a student to read the information in the Reading Skill box.
- Have students complete the task.
- Ask a volunteer to read his/her main idea sentence. Write it on the board and leave it up as the students read the article.

Reading

Teaching Time: 15–20 min.

- Have students read the article.
- Have students read the main idea sentence on the board. Ask: *Is it close to the main idea? If not, how should it be changed?*

Multilevel Strategy

- **All levels:** Have students complete the reading section over two days. On the first day, have all students do the Getting Ready to Read and the initial reading in class. On the following day, discuss the answers to After You Read with the whole class.

- **Pre-level:** Day 1: Tell the pre-level students to reread the article and complete the After You Read exercises for homework. Day 2: While the at- and above-level students are completing the exercises, put the pre-level students in a group. Read the article aloud as students follow along in their books. Encourage them to stop and ask questions about anything they don't understand.

- **At-level, Above-level:** Day 1: Students do Getting Ready to Read and read the article in class. Do not assign them the exercises for homework. Day 2: Have students complete the After You Read exercises in class while you work with the pre-level students.

Reading

Getting Ready to Read

Read the introduction and the conclusion of the article. What do you think the main idea of the article is? *Wording of answers will vary.*

_____

Reading Skill:
Recognizing Conclusions

Sometimes, the writer repeats the main idea of the text in the last sentence (the **concluding sentence**) or the last paragraph (the **conclusion**). When you read, look for words like *to sum up*. These words are often used at the beginning of the conclusion.

Reading

Read the article. Then check your answer to Getting Ready to Read.

SLOW FOOD, SLOW CITIES ... BETTER LIFE?

Life in today's world has been getting faster and faster. Fast food has become very popular because people don't have enough time to cook. The situation has gotten so bad that a group of people in Europe decided to start the Slow Food Movement. The goal of this movement is to live an unhurried life, beginning at the dinner table.

a truffle

The Movement's **headquarters** are in Bra, Italy, in an area famous for its wine, white truffles, cheese, and beef. There are other Slow Food offices all over the world, including one in Switzerland, another in Germany, and others in the United States, France, and Japan. Slow Food has 80,000 members in more than 100 countries, organized into more than 800 local groups. The leaders of the groups organize special events and they **promote local** products and food growers. In short, they educate the public about good food.

The Slow Food Movement has also **led to** another movement called *Città Slow* (Slow Cities). The Città Slow are a group of towns and cities that try to improve the quality of life for their citizens. According to the Città Slow Web site, the movement is looking for "...towns with **untouched landscapes**...where people are still able to recognize the slow course of the seasons and their...products."

Slow Food®

Members of Città Slow have found many ways to make their cities and towns better places to live. One way is to close the center of town to traffic one day a week. Another brings members of the community to markets and town squares—places where local food growers offer their fruits and vegetables.

To sum up, members of the Slow Food Movement and Città Slow try to live like snails. The snail is the **symbol** of the Slow Food Movement because "... it moves slowly and calmly eats its way through life."

After You Read

A Look at the **boldface** words in the article. Guess their meaning. Match the words with the correct definitions.

_h_	**1.** movement	**a.**	main office
_g_	**2.** unhurried	**b.**	made something happen as the result of something else
_a_	**3.** headquarters	**c.**	help something develop and be successful
_c_	**4.** promote	**d.**	relating to a particular place or area
_d_	**5.** local	**e.**	an area of land
_b_	**6.** led to	**f.**	a picture, person, or object that means or shows something else
_i_	**7.** untouched		
_e_	**8.** landscape	**g.**	slow, not in a hurry
_f_	**9.** symbol	~~**h.**~~	a group of people who share the same ideas and work together
		i.	in a natural state or condition

B Read the article again. Then answer the questions. Wording of answers will vary.

1. Why did a group of people start the Slow Food Movement?

   They started the Slow Food Movement because they thought that the fast pace of modern life, including fast food, was not good for people.

2. Where did the Slow Food Movement start?

   It started in Europe. It's headquarters are in Italy.

3. What do the offices and local groups of the Slow Food Movement do?

   They organize events to promote local products and food growers. They educate the public about good food.

4. What is the Città Slow Movement?

   The Città Slow are a group of towns and cities that have committed themselves to improving the quality of life for their citizens by slowing down the pace of life.

5. How does the Città Slow Movement make towns and cities better places to live?

   They close the center of town to traffic one day a week. They make it possible for local food growers to sell their fruits and vegetables in the markets and town squares.

6. Why is the snail the symbol of the Slow Food Movement?

   The snail is the symbol of the Slow Food Movement because it "moves slowly and calmly eats its way through life."

Let's Eat!   167

After You Read

A **Teaching Time: 10–15 min.**

- Read the example with the class.
- Have students complete the task. Tell them to check their answers by replacing the word in the article with the answer they have chosen. (See page 153 for an explanation of the procedure.)
- Call on students to say answers. Have them reread the sentences from the article with their answer choices. Write the original sentences and the replacements on the board. For example: *1. The situation. . . . Movement (= group of people who share the same ideas and work together).*

B **Teaching Time: 10–15 min.**

- Have students complete the task. Encourage them to write the answers in their own words wherever possible.
- Call on students to say answers. Correct as needed.

Multilevel Strategy

- **Pre-level:** Tell students in which paragraph they can find the answer to each question in Exercise B. (1. paragraph 1; 2. paragraph 1; 3. paragraph 2; 4. paragraph 3; 5. paragraph 4; 6. paragraph 5)
- **At-level, Above-level:** Challenge students to answer the questions without looking back at the article.

Teaching Tip

Exercise B. One way to encourage students to answer reading comprehension questions in their own words is to have them answer without looking back at the text. Follow this procedure:

- Have students read the list of questions first.
- Have them reread the entire article. Tell them not to stop to answer the questions. Instead, they should make a mental note of the answers as they are reading.
- Have them answer the questions without looking back at the text.

Writing

Getting Ready to Write

Writing

A   Teaching Time: 5–10 min.

- Read the example with the class. Ask which words show it is a concluding sentence (In conclusion).
- Have students study the Writing Tip.
- Have students complete the task.
- Call on students to read answers. Correct as needed.

B   Teaching Time: 10–15 min.

- Have students read the writing model.
- PAIRS. Have students complete the task.
- Call on students to say answers. Correct as needed.

Expansion Draw a graphic organizer similar to the one on page 169 on the board, with some of the information from the writing model filled in. Have students copy it into their notebooks and complete it.

What kind of food do you like to eat? fast food
Reason 1: no time to cook
Reason 2: very tired after work
Reason 3:
Reason 4:
Concluding Sentence:

Getting Ready to Write

A   Read the sentences from different articles. Write **C** next to the concluding sentences.

  _C_ **1.** In conclusion, many people are too heavy because they eat too much fast food.

  ____ **2.** There is a problem with the way we eat today.

  ____ **3.** One healthy food people can eat is fruit, and another is vegetables.

  _C_ **4.** To sum up, I enjoy cooking dinner at home, but I usually don't have time.

  _C_ **5.** In conclusion, people who eat healthy foods usually feel better about themselves.

B Read the model paragraph.

> I agree with some of the ideas of the Slow Food Movement. Of course good, healthy food is better than fast food. But sometimes it is easier to eat fast food. One reason is that many people don't have time to buy and cook good food. When my wife and I both work late, we sometimes fight with each other about who should make dinner. We're too tired to cook for ourselves. Another reason is that our children love fast food. If I cook dinner with good food, they won't eat it. And yet another reason is that good food is often more expensive than fast food. I don't have enough money to buy from local food growers! To sum up, the Slow Food Movement has some good ideas, but I can't live like a snail!

PAIRS. According to the writer, does the Slow Food Movement have good ideas about food? Does the writer use the ideas? Why or why not? Wording of answers may vary.

Now discuss your ideas about food. What kind of food do you eat? What are the reasons why you eat certain foods?

> ### Writing Tip
> Use words like *in conclusion* and *to sum up* to show readers that you are ending your paragraph.
> Examples:
> **In conclusion**, members of the Slow Food Movement try to live like snails.
>
> **To sum up**, members of the Slow Food Movement try to live like snails.

Prewriting: Listing Reasons

You are going to write a paragraph about the kind of food you like to eat. Before you write, complete the chart with notes about the topic.

What kind of food do you like to eat?
Reasons:
1.
2.
3.
Concluding Sentence:

Writing

Now write a paragraph about the food you eat. The writing tip, the model paragraph, and your notes will help you. Write in your notebook.

Teaching Time: 20–25 min.

- Students might need help naming the different types of food they eat. Write on the board, and explain as needed:

  home cooking; TV dinners; cold food (for example, sandwiches); take out (what kind?); organic products; free-range chicken and beef; canned food; frozen food; fresh produce; junk food; seafood

- Have students complete the task.
- PAIRS. Have students ask and answer the questions.

Multilevel Strategy

- **Pre-level:** Have pre-level students sit together in a group. Sit with them and help them get started on their notes.
- **At-level, Above-level:** After the pre-level students have gotten started, walk around and assist the other students. Encourage them to show their notes to each other and to give each other feedback. If possible, pair each at-level student with an above-level writer.

Writing

Teaching Time: 5–10 min.

- Assign the task for homework.
- Remind students to include a concluding sentence for their paragraphs.

Learning Goals

- Learn vocabulary related to technology
- Learn how to use *can* for present ability and *be able to* for ability in the present, past, future, and present perfect forms
- Listen to a conversation about a computer problem and to a report about automobiles in the future
- Read an article about a new type of technology and write a paragraph about technological changes over time
- Talk about individual uses of technology, the effects of technology, and the development of technology

Learner Persistence

Use your sense of humor in the classroom.

Warm-up

Teaching Time: 3–5 min.

- Have students look at the pictures. Start a discussion on students' feelings about technology. Write the following questions on the board, and take notes on students' responses: *What is technology? What are some positive (good) effects of technology? What are some negative (bad) effects of technology? How has technology such as computers changed our lives?*

Vocabulary

Teaching Time: 10–15 min.

- Read the words in the boxes aloud as students listen and repeat chorally. Tell them to circle the words that they already know.
- Have students complete the task. Remind them to look at the pictures for help.
- 🎧 Play Track 39 while students listen and check their answers.
- Read the words again and have students repeat chorally.

Expansion PAIRS. Have students identify the things in the picture that they know how to operate.

Grammar
- *Can* and *Be able to*
- *Could* and *Be able to*
- *Will be able to*

Vocabulary

🎧 **39** Complete the sentences with the words in the box. Then listen and check your answers.

burn CDs	camcorder	download	record

I love my new _camcorder_ . I _record_
1.   2.
my son Sam all the time. Then I _download_
3.
everything onto my computer. Sometimes
I _burn CDs_ and give them to friends or
4.
family.

battery	charge	install	software

First, put in the _battery_ . Then
5.
charge it for twenty-four hours. Finally,
6.
install the _software_ on your
7.   8.
computer.

online	operate	remote control	Web

Use the _remote control_ for your TV and DVD
9.
player. It's easy to _operate_ . Just press
10.
the "On" button, and the TV goes on. If you
need help, go _online_ . There's a lot of
11.
information on the _Web_ .
12.

170   Unit 13

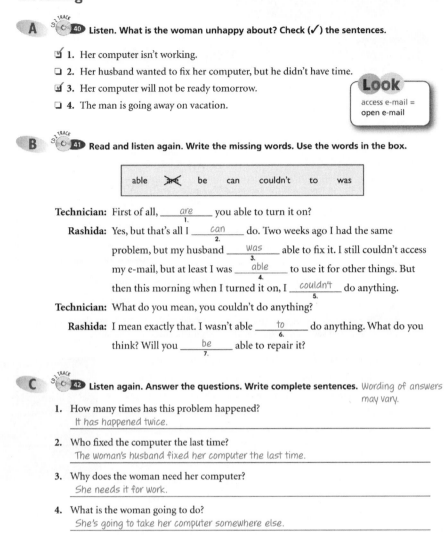

Listening

A 🔊 CD2 TRACK 40 **Listen. What is the woman unhappy about? Check (✓) the sentences.**

☑ 1. Her computer isn't working.

❏ 2. Her husband wanted to fix her computer, but he didn't have time.

☑ 3. Her computer will not be ready tomorrow.

❏ 4. The man is going away on vacation.

> **Look**
> access e-mail =
> open e-mail

B 🔊 CD2 TRACK 41 **Read and listen again. Write the missing words. Use the words in the box.**

| able | ~~are~~ | be | can | couldn't | to | was |

Technician: First of all, ___are___ you able to turn it on?
                              1.

Rashida: Yes, but that's all I ___can___ do. Two weeks ago I had the same
                              2.

    problem, but my husband ___was___ able to fix it. I still couldn't access
                              3.

    my e-mail, but at least I was ___able___ to use it for other things. But
                             4.

    then this morning when I turned it on, I ___couldn't___ do anything.
                              5.

Technician: What do you mean, you couldn't do anything?

Rashida: I mean exactly that. I wasn't able ___to___ do anything. What do you
                              6.

    think? Will you ___be___ able to repair it?
                     7.

C 🔊 CD2 TRACK 42 **Listen again. Answer the questions. Write complete sentences.** *Wording of answers may vary.*

1. How many times has this problem happened?
   It has happened twice.

2. Who fixed the computer the last time?
   The woman's husband fixed her computer the last time.

3. Why does the woman need her computer?
   She needs it for work.

4. What is the woman going to do?
   She's going to take her computer somewhere else.

Technology (171)

Listening

A **Teaching Time: 10–15 min.**

- **Warm-up.** Tell the students that they are going to listen to a conversation between a man and a woman. Have them read the answer choices and guess what the relationship is between the man and the woman. Write their guesses on the board.
- 🎧 Play Track 40 as students listen and complete the task.
- Ask: *What is the relationship between the man and the woman?* (technician and customer) *Did anyone guess correctly?*
- 🎧 Play Track 40 again, pausing the recording as each answer is given.

B **Teaching Time: 10–15 min.**

- Have students read the words in the box before they listen.
- 🎧 Play Track 41 as students listen and complete the task.
- 🎧 Play Track 41 again, this time pausing the recording as each answer is given.
- Call on two students to read the completed conversation. Correct as needed.

C **Teaching Time: 10–15 min.**

- Have students complete the task.
- 🎧 Play Track 42 as students listen and complete the task.
- Ask volunteers to write their answers on the board.
- 🎧 Play Track 42 again, pausing as each answer is given. Correct the sentences on the board as needed.

> **Multilevel Strategy**
>
> **Pre-level:** Make photocopies of the audioscript to give to students after they have completed Exercise B. Allow them to use the audioscript as they complete Exercise C.

Expansion Pair at-level and above-level students with pre-level students. Have pre-level students read one of the roles from the audioscript, while their partner role-plays without looking at the audioscript. Then ask two volunteers to perform their role play for the class.

Option

Assign Unit 13 Supplementary Vocabulary Exercises on the Teacher's Resource Disk as homework or on the Student Persistence CD-ROM as self-access practice.

Grammar to Communicate 1

Can and *Be Able To*

Teaching Time: 5–10 min.

- Have students study the chart and the Look Box.
- Say: Can *and* be able to *have the same meaning: present ability. Be able to is a little more formal than* can. *You will often see* be able to *in writing or in formal situations, such as when someone is giving a speech.*
- Read the sentences below with *can;* after each sentence, call on a student to repeat, replacing *can* with *be able to.* Write what the student says on the board, and call on other students to correct as needed.

  I can take pictures with my cell phone.

  He cannot take pictures with his cell phone.

  We can download pictures from our cell phones.

  You cannot take pictures with this cell phone.

A Teaching Time: 10–15 min.

- Have students complete the task. Tell them to answer truthfully about their individual abilities.
- Call on students to read their answers. Ask for a show of hands for each sentence. Is there anyone in the class who can do all five things?

B Teaching Time: 10–15 min.

- Read the example with the class.
- Have students complete the task.
- Play Track 43 as students listen and check their answers.
- Call on a student to read the paragraph. Correct as needed.
- PAIRS. Have students complete the task.
- Call on students to share their answers with the class.

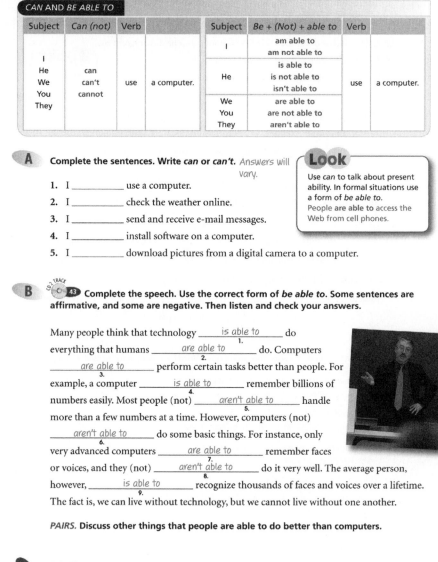

Grammar to Communicate 1

CAN AND *BE ABLE TO*							
Subject	Can (not)	Verb		Subject	Be + (Not) + able to	Verb	
I				I	am able to / am not able to		
He	can			He	is able to / is not able to / isn't able to		
We	can't	use	a computer.	We	are able to	use	a computer.
You	cannot			You	are not able to		
They				They	aren't able to		

A   **Complete the sentences. Write *can* or *can't*.** Answers will vary.

1. I _____ use a computer.
2. I _____ check the weather online.
3. I _____ send and receive e-mail messages.
4. I _____ install software on a computer.
5. I _____ download pictures from a digital camera to a computer.

> **Look**
>
> Use *can* to talk about present ability. In formal situations use a form of *be able to*.
> People **are able to** access the Web from cell phones.

B   CD 2 TRACK **43**   **Complete the speech. Use the correct form of *be able to*. Some sentences are affirmative, and some are negative. Then listen and check your answers.**

Many people think that technology ___is able to___ do
                                         1.
everything that humans ___are able to___ do. Computers
                                      2.
___are able to___ perform certain tasks better than people. For
                               3.
example, a computer ___is able to___ remember billions of
                                     4.
numbers easily. Most people (not) ___aren't able to___ handle
                                      5.
more than a few numbers at a time. However, computers (not)
___aren't able to___ do some basic things. For instance, only
                             6.
very advanced computers ___are able to___ remember faces
                                    7.
or voices, and they (not) ___aren't able to___ do it very well. The average person,
                               8.
however, ___is able to___ recognize thousands of faces and voices over a lifetime.
                            9.
The fact is, we can live without technology, but we cannot live without one another.

PAIRS. **Discuss other things that people are able to do better than computers.**

172   **Unit 13**

Grammar Notes

1. Use *can* or *can't* to talk about present ability. *Can* and *can't* are the same for all subjects (*I, you,* etc.).
2. We also use *be able to* and *not be able to* to talk about ability. The verb *be* changes for different subjects. (*I am able to, he is able to, they are able to,* etc.).
3. *Can* and *can't* are more common when we are talking about present ability. *Be able to* in the present sounds more formal than *can* and *can't.*
4. We use *be able to* with other forms—for example, the present perfect (*has been able to*) and modals (*might be able to*).
5. For more information about this grammar topic, see page 290.

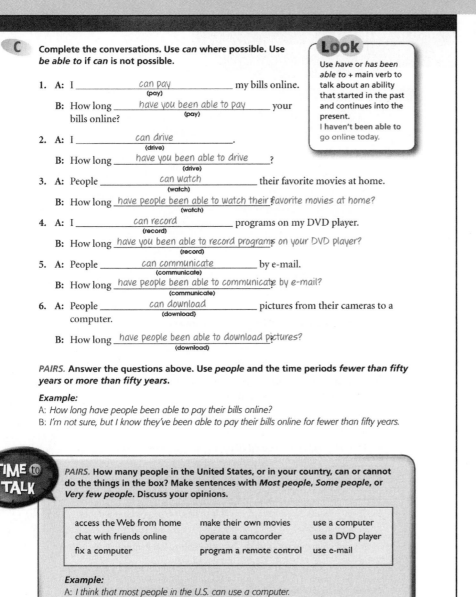

C Complete the conversations. Use *can* where possible. Use *be able to* if *can* is not possible.

1. A: I _____ can pay _____ my bills online.
   (pay)
   B: How long _____ have you been able to pay _____ your bills online?
   (pay)

2. A: I _____ can drive _____ .
   (drive)
   B: How long _____ have you been able to drive _____ ?
   (drive)

3. A: People _____ can watch _____ their favorite movies at home.
   (watch)
   B: How long _____ have people been able to watch their favorite movies at home?
   (watch)

4. A: I _____ can record _____ programs on my DVD player.
   (record)
   B: How long _____ have you been able to record programs on your DVD player?
   (record)

5. A: People _____ can communicate _____ by e-mail.
   (communicate)
   B: How long _____ have people been able to communicate by e-mail?
   (communicate)

6. A: People _____ can download _____ pictures from their cameras to a computer.
   (download)
   B: How long _____ have people been able to download pictures?
   (download)

> **Look**
>
> Use *have* or *has been able to* + main verb to talk about an ability that started in the past and continues into the present.
> I haven't been able to go online today.

PAIRS. Answer the questions above. Use *people* and the time periods *fewer than fifty years* or *more than fifty years*.

Example:
A: *How long have people been able to pay their bills online?*
B: *I'm not sure, but I know they've been able to pay their bills online for fewer than fifty years.*

TIME to TALK

PAIRS. How many people in the United States, or in your country, can or cannot do the things in the box? Make sentences with *Most people*, *Some people*, or *Very few people*. Discuss your opinions.

access the Web from home	make their own movies	use a computer
chat with friends online	operate a camcorder	use a DVD player
fix a computer	program a remote control	use e-mail

Example:
A: *I think that most people in the U.S. can use a computer.*
B: *Really? I don't agree. Some people are able to use a computer, but many people can't because they don't have access to one.*

Technology 173

C Teaching Time: 10–15 min.

- Have students study the Look Box. Say: *Can is only for present ability. If we want to talk about an ability that started in the past and continues up until now, we must use the present perfect of* be + able to + *the main verb.*
- Write on the board: *I can swim. My father taught me when I was 5 years old. I ___ since I was five years old.*
- Call on a student to complete the sentence to show ability from the past up to now. (*have been able to swim*)
- Read the example with the class.
- Have students complete the task.
- Call on students to say answers. Correct as needed.
- PAIRS. Have students complete the task.
- Call on students to answer the questions. Correct as needed.

Language Note

Students often have difficulty distinguishing between the affirmative *can* and the negative *can't* in natural speech. Teach students to listen for the sentence stress. If both *can't* and the main verb are stressed equally, then the sentence is usually negative. If only the main verb is stressed, then the sentence is usually affirmative.

Option

Assign Unit 13 Supplementary Grammar to Communicate 1 Exercises on the Teacher's Resource Disk as homework or on the Student Persistence CD-ROM as self-access practice.

TIME to TALK

Teaching Time: 10–15 min.

- Call on two students to read the example. Make sure students understand that they are just giving their opinions. They do not need to be sure of their answers. If students seem reluctant to make generalizations about their countries, tell them to think about the people they know and answer for them, for example: *Most/Some/Very few people I know are able to . . . .*
- PAIRS. Have students complete the task.
- Call on students to tell the class something about their partners' country. Correct as needed.

Expansion Have some of the more advanced students in the class look up information about cell phone and Internet use in the countries of the students in the class. Then have them report to the class. Many statistical databases include this type of information. They usually present the information as number of users for every 1,000 people.

Grammar to Communicate 2

Could and Be Able To

Teaching Time: 5–10 min.

- Have students study the chart and the Look Boxes.
- Write on the board:

  1. The guys at that shop were great. They could fix / were able to fix any kind of computer. Unfortunately, the shop isn't in business anymore.

  General or specific?

  2. My computer wasn't working. I wasn't able to fix / couldn't fix the problem.

  General or specific?

  3. I called my friend, and he could fix / was able to fix the problem over the phone.

  General or specific?

- Ask: *Which sentence is about general ability in the past?* (1) *Which sentences are about ability at one specific time in the past?* (2 and 3) Circle *General* for 1 and *specific* for 2 and 3.
- Ask: *For number 1, which answer is correct: could fix, were able to fix, or both?* (both) *Why?* (Because for general ability in the past, we can use either *could* or *be able to.*) Circle both verb forms.
- Ask: *For number 2, which answer is correct: wasn't able to fix, couldn't fix, or both?* (both) *Why?* (Because in negative sentences about past ability, we can use either *couldn't* or *was / were not able to.*) Circle both verb forms.
- Ask: *In sentence 3, can we use could fix, was able to fix, or both?* (just *was able to fix*) *Why?* (Because in affirmative sentences about specific past events, we do not use *couldn't.* We must use *was / were able to.*) Circle *was able to fix.* Cross out *could fix.*

A   Teaching Time: 10–15 min.

- Have students complete the task.
- Call on students to say answers. Correct as needed.
- PAIRS. Have students complete the second task.

Grammar to Communicate 2

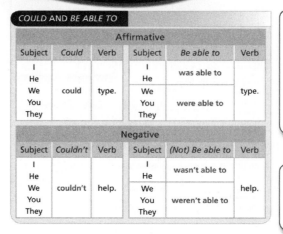

COULD AND BE ABLE TO

Affirmative

Subject	Could	Verb	Subject	Be able to	Verb
I He We You They	could	type.	I He	was able to	type.
			We You They	were able to	

Negative

Subject	Couldn't	Verb	Subject	(Not) Be able to	Verb
I He We You They	couldn't	help.	I He	wasn't able to	help.
			We You They	weren't able to	

Look

Use *could* or *be able to* to talk about general ability in the past.
I **could** type well years ago, but now I can't.
I **was able to** type well years ago, but now I can't.

Use *be able to* to talk about a specific event.
I **was able to** finish on time.

Look

Couldn't and *(not) be able to* mean the same thing.
I tried, but I **couldn't** help.
I tried, but I **wasn't able to** help.

A   Complete the sentences. Circle the correct answers.

1. Four hundred years ago, people <u>were able to</u> make clothes _____.
   - **(a.)** by hand
   - **b.** with machines

2. My aunt's sewing machine was broken, but she <u>was able to</u> make the dress _____.
   - **(a.)** by hand
   - **b.** with the machine

3. There was a lot of traffic, so we <u>were able to</u> drive only ten miles in _____.
   - **a.** ten minutes
   - **(b.)** an hour

4. Fifty years ago, people <u>could</u> communicate with each other by _____.
   - **(a.)** mail
   - **b.** e-mail

5. His computer wasn't working yesterday, so I <u>couldn't</u> send him _____.
   - **a.** a letter
   - **(b.)** an e-mail message

6. Twenty years ago, people <u>weren't able to</u> talk on the phone when they _____.
   - **a.** were at home
   - **(b.)** were walking down a street

7. My cell phone wasn't working, but I <u>was able to</u> use it after I _____.
   - **a.** left
   - **(b.)** charged the battery

Change the underlined words where possible.

Example: *Four hundred years ago, people **could** make clothes _____.*

174   Unit 13

- Call on students to say answers. For affirmative sentences, ask students if the sentence is about a general ability or a specific event. If it is about a specific event, remind them not to use *could*. Refer to the examples on the board as necessary.

Grammar Notes

1. *Could* and *couldn't* are the past forms of *can't*. Use *could* and *couldn't* to talk about general ability in the past.

2. We also use *was / were able to* and *was not / were not able to* to talk about general ability in the past.

3. Use *was / were able to* (<u>not</u> *could*) to talk about a specific event in the past.

4. *Couldn't* and *wasn't / weren't able to* have the same meaning. We can use either *couldn't* or *wasn't / weren't able to* for both general and specific ability in the past.

5. For more information on this grammar topic, see page 290.

B Write six sentences about people's abilities in the past. Use the words in the boxes and *could*, *couldn't*, *were able to*, or *weren't able to*. Write in your notebook.

500 years ago	communicate by cell phone	listen to music in their cars
100 years ago	communicate by phone	take photographs
50 years ago	cook food	take showers in their homes
30 years ago	grow food	travel by train
	listen to music	use batteries in radios

C CD 2 TRACK **44** Complete the conversations. Write *could* where possible. If *could* is not possible, write *was able to* or *were able to*. Then listen and check your answers.

1. **A:** You're good with computers. When did you learn to use one?
   B: I don't even remember. I ___could___ use a computer before
   I ___could___ read.
2. **A:** Did you repair my printer?
   B: Yes, I ___was able to___ repair it, but you really need a new one.
3. **A:** Did your grandfather have a computer for his farm business?
   B: No. It was strange. He ___could___ learn to operate almost any
   machine, but he was never able to use a computer.
4. **A:** Kids today are amazing. They understand technology so much better than we do.
   B: I know. My son ___could___ use a cell phone before he ___could___ read!
5. **A:** Did you put the information on the company's Web site?
   B: Yes. I ___was able to___ do it last night.
6. **A:** Did you take a lot of pictures at the wedding?
   B: I ___was able to___ take a few before the battery died.

TIME to TALK

PAIRS. Talk about five things that you were able to do yesterday because of technology. How many of those things could your grandparents do when they were your age?

Example:
A: *I took the subway. I was able to get to work in 15 minutes.*
B: *My grandfather couldn't take the subway because there was no subway in his town.*

WRAP UP. Now think of something that we can't do today because of technology, but most people in the past could do. Then tell the class.

Example:
Most people could ride horses. Now, they can drive, but they can't ride a horse.

Technology 175

B Teaching Time: 10–15 min.

- Have students complete the task.
- Ask volunteers to write their sentences on the board. Correct both grammar and content as needed.

Multilevel Strategy

- **Pre-level:** Group pre-level students and help them make sentences.
- **At-level, Above-level:** PAIRS. After students finish making sentences, have them work in pairs to complete Unit 13 Supplementary Grammar to Communicate 2 Exercise B on the Teacher's Resource Disk. Give them the answer key so that they can correct themselves.

C Teaching Time: 10–15 min.

- Have students complete the task. Remind them to think about whether the affirmative sentences are general or specific. Remind them not to use *could* for specific events.
- 🎧 Play Track 44 while students listen and check their answers.
- Call on students to say answers. Correct as needed.
- Have students read each short conversation with a partner.

Option

Assign Unit 13 Supplementary Grammar to Communicate 2 Exercises on the Teacher's Resource Disk as homework or on the Student Persistence CD-ROM as self-access practice.

TIME to TALK

Teaching Time: 10–15 min.

- Have two students read the example.
- PAIRS. Have students complete the task. Walk around and make a note of errors in the use of *could* and *be able to*.
- Write the errors you noted on the board. Have students correct them.
- WRAP UP. Give students five minutes to think of as many things as they can. Call on volunteers to say their sentences to the class. Who thought of the most?

Unit 13 T-175

Grammar to Communicate 3

Will Be Able To

Teaching Time: 5–10 min.

- Have students study the chart and the Look Box.
- Say: *We use* will be able to *to talk about future ability. We do not use* can *for future ability.*
- Write the following sentences on the board, and have students fill in the blanks with *will (not) be able to* and *can (not).*

  We ___ [can't] travel to the Moon now, but in the future we ___ [will be able to] live on the Moon.

  Today doctors ___ [can] help people with cancer, but they ___ [can't] cure them. In the future they ___ [will be able to] cure people of cancer.

  In the future, people ___ [will be able to] live longer, but they ___ [won't be able to] live forever.

  What other diseases (doctors) ___ [will doctors be able to] cure in the future?

A **Teaching Time: 10–15 min.**

- Read the example with the class.
- Have students complete the task.
- Call on students to say answers. Correct as needed.

Expansion Bring in advertisements from magazines that contain direct or implied promises. Have students look at the ads and make sentences with *will be able to.* For example, for an ad for a health club, students might write: *Join Body Works and you will be able to fit into a bikini this summer!*

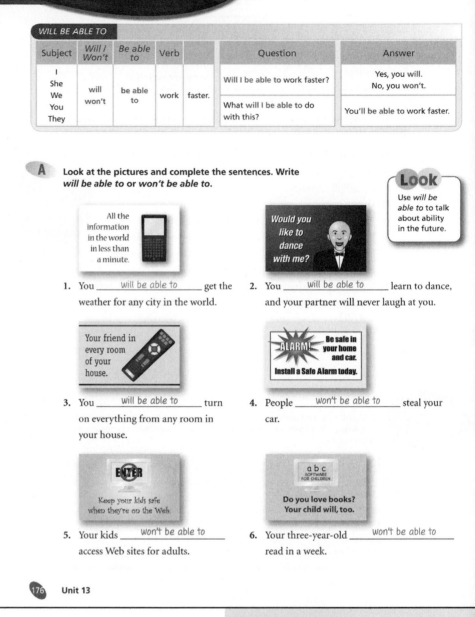

Grammar to Communicate 3

WILL BE ABLE TO

Subject	Will I / Won't	Be able to	Verb		Question	Answer
I She We You They	will won't	be able to	work	faster.	Will I be able to work faster?	Yes, you will. No, you won't.
					What will I be able to do with this?	You'll be able to work faster.

A Look at the pictures and complete the sentences. Write *will be able to* or *won't be able to.*

Look
Use *will be able to* to talk about ability in the future.

All the information in the world in less than a minute.

1. You ____will be able to____ get the weather for any city in the world.

Would you like to dance with me?

2. You ____will be able to____ learn to dance, and your partner will never laugh at you.

Your friend in every room of your house.

3. You ____will be able to____ turn on everything from any room in your house.

ALARM! Be safe in your home and car. Install a Safe Alarm today.

4. People ____won't be able to____ steal your car.

ENTER
Keep your kids safe when they're on the Web.

5. Your kids ____won't be able to____ access Web sites for adults.

a b c SOFTWARE FOR CHILDREN
Do you love books? Your child will, too.

6. Your three-year-old ____won't be able to____ read in a week.

Grammar Notes

1. Use *will be able to* and *won't be able to* to talk about ability in the future. Do not use *can* or *cannot* to talk about future ability.

2. To make a *yes / no* question, put *will* before the subject. Use *will* or *won't* in short answers.

3. For more information on this grammar topic, see page 290.

B Write questions customers have about the products in the pictures.

1. Will I be able to get the weather for my hometown?
   (the weather / I / will / for my hometown / be able to / get)
2. Will the robot be able to teach me every dance?
   (teach me / the robot / will / be able to / every dance)
3. Will I be able to use the remote for everything?
   (I / will / use the remote / for everything / be able to)
4. Will the police be able to hear the car alarm?
   (be able to / will / hear the car alarm / the police)
5. Which Web sites will my kids be able to access?
   (access / which Web sites / my kids / will / be able to)
6. What kinds of things will my child be able to read?
   (be able to / my child / what kinds of things / read / will)

PAIRS. **Ask and answer the questions. The person who asks the questions is a customer. The person who answers is a salesperson.**

Example:
A: *Will the police be able to hear the car alarm?*
B: *Yes. The alarm has special software. The software will send a message to a computer at the police station.*

C Complete the sentences with *are able to, will be able to,* or *won't be able to.* Answers will vary.

1. People _____are able to_____ call their friends with their computers now.
2. People _____are able to_____ get a college degree and never leave their home now.
3. People _will / won't be able to_ eat only one meal a month and stay healthy in 2100.
4. People _will / won't be able to_ look young when they are very old in 2100.
5. People _will / won't be able to_ live forever in 2100.
6. People _will / won't be able to_ travel around the world in one hour in 2100.
7. People _will / won't be able to_ take vacations on Mars in 2100.

PAIRS. **Compare your opinions. Which of these things would you like to do?**

TIME to TALK

GROUPS. **Discuss how the items in the box will be different in the future. What will people be able to do with them that they can't do now? Then compare ideas with other groups.**

| books   cell phones   clothing   pens   sunglasses   umbrellas   watches |

Example: *Books will be able to talk, so people will be able to listen and read at the same time.*

Technology **177**

B **Teaching Time: 10–15 min.**

- Read the example with the class.
- Have students complete the task.
- Call on students to read their questions. Correct as needed.
- PAIRS. Have students complete the task.
- Ask volunteers to role-play the conversations in front of the class.

Multilevel Strategy

- **Pre-level:** Give students the first and last word or phrase of each question.

C **Teaching Time: 10–15 min.**

- Have students complete the task. Remind them that they are making predictions for numbers 3–7. They're giving their opinions for these items.
- PAIRS. Have students complete the task.
- Call on students to give their opinions. Correct grammar as needed.

Option

Assign Unit 13 Supplementary Grammar to Communicate 3 Exercises on the Teacher's Resource Disk as homework or on the Student Persistence CD-ROM as self-access practice.

TIME to TALK

Teaching Time: 10–15 min.

- Call on a student to read the example.
- GROUPS. Have students complete the task.
- Have each group tell one of their ideas to the class. Write the ideas on the board. Correct as needed.

Expansion Have the class vote on the most original idea.

Review and Challenge

Grammar

Teaching Time: 5–10 min.

- Read the example with the class.
- Have students complete the task.
- 🎧 Play Track 45 while students listen and check their answers.
- Call on a student to read the corrected note aloud. Correct as needed.

Multilevel Strategy

- **Pre-level:** Give students a copy of the audioscript. Have them compare it to the note in their books to find and correct the mistakes.

Dictation

Teaching Time: 5–10 min.

- 🎧 Play Track 46 while students listen and write what they hear.
- 🎧 Play Track 46 again while students check their answers.
- Call on students to read the dictated sentences aloud. Write exactly what you hear. Ask them to spell the new vocabulary.
- Have students correct the sentences on the board, as needed.
- 🎧 Play Track 46 again and correct the sentences on the board.

Multilevel Strategy

Pre-level: Give students a worksheet with the words from the dictation provided, except for *can, can't, could, couldn't,* forms of *be able to,* and the new vocabulary.

Speaking

Teaching Time: 10–15 min.

- Call on two students to read the example. Explain that their goal is to make a list of the different types of machines or equipment their

Review and Challenge

Grammar

🎧 **45** Correct the note. There are seven mistakes. The first mistake is corrected for you. Then listen and check your answers.

> Hi,
>
>   I have good news and bad news. First, the bad news. I haven't been
> ~~to~~ able ~~fix~~ the TV yet. When I turn it on, I ~~can to see to~~ a picture; but
> [can see]
> I can't hear a thing. That's strange because yesterday I ~~can~~ hear
> [was able to]
> things, but I ~~not~~ able to see anything. I'm going to look at the TV
> [was not]
> again tomorrow. Maybe I ~~could~~ fix it then.
> [will be able to]
>   Now, the good news. I ~~could~~ fix the radio yesterday. At first, ~~I'm~~
> [was able to]
> ~~not able~~ to find the problem, but actually there wasn't really a
> [I wasn't able]
> problem. It only needed new batteries.
>
>   Sam

Dictation

🎧 **46** Listen. You will hear five sentences. Write them in your notebook. *See the audioscript on p. 320 for the sentences.*

Speaking

GROUPS. Make a list of all the things that people in your group can do with technology. Describe what things they can (and can't) do with technology. How long has each person been able to do these things? Think of as many things as possible.

Example:
A: *Sasha, what can you do? Can you use any technology?*
B: *I can do a lot of things. I can use a microwave oven, I can cook very well, I can sew . . .*
C: *Really? Can you use a sewing machine?*
B: *Yes, I can.*

Now tell the class about your group. Which group can operate the most machines or equipment?

group members can operate, along with what they can do with the machines or equipment.

- GROUPS. Encourage groups to compete against each other. Give them a time limit, for example five minutes. Have students complete the task.
- Ask each group to name the machines and equipment the group members can operate. Write them on the board. The winner is the group that has the longest list.

Listening

A 🔘 **47** Listen to the report. Check (✓) the picture that best matches the reporter's description.

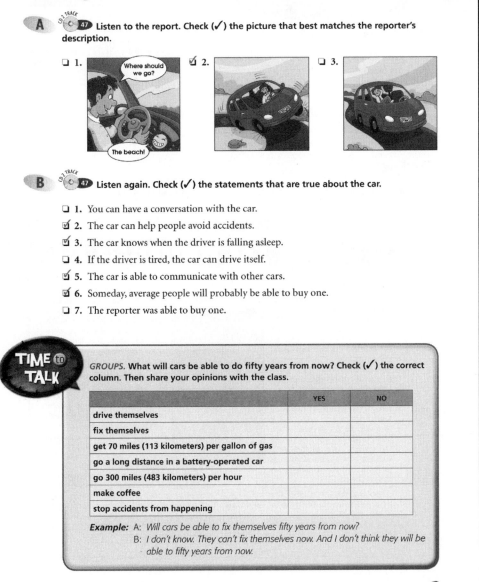

❑ 1.   ☑ 2.   ❑ 3.

B 🔘 **47** Listen again. Check (✓) the statements that are true about the car.

❑ 1. You can have a conversation with the car.

☑ 2. The car can help people avoid accidents.

☑ 3. The car knows when the driver is falling asleep.

❑ 4. If the driver is tired, the car can drive itself.

☑ 5. The car is able to communicate with other cars.

☑ 6. Someday, average people will probably be able to buy one.

❑ 7. The reporter was able to buy one.

TIME to TALK

GROUPS. What will cars be able to do fifty years from now? Check (✓) the correct column. Then share your opinions with the class.

	YES	NO
drive themselves		
fix themselves		
get 70 miles (113 kilometers) per gallon of gas		
go a long distance in a battery-operated car		
go 300 miles (483 kilometers) per hour		
make coffee		
stop accidents from happening		

Example: A: *Will cars be able to fix themselves fifty years from now?*
   B: *I don't know. They can't fix themselves now. And I don't think they will be able to fifty years from now.*

Technology **179**

Listening

A **Teaching Time: 5–10 min.**

- **Warm-up.** Have students look at the pictures and guess the topic of the report. Write their guesses on the board.
- 🎧 Play Track 47 as students listen and complete the task. Play the recording again if necessary.
- Call on a student to say the answer. Correct as needed.

B **Teaching Time: 10–15 min.**

- PAIRS. Have students read the answer choices and check the answers that they think are true before they listen. If they are not sure about an answer, tell them to write a question mark (?).
- 🎧 Play Track 47 while students listen and complete the task.
- 🎧 Play Track 47 again, pausing the recording as each answer is given.
- Ask students if they think the information in the report is true or not. (The answer is yes. The features mentioned in the report are in the development or testing stages in the research departments of automobile companies. Whether or not these features will become commercially available, however, is unknown at this time.)

Multilevel Strategy

Pre-level: After students have completed Exercise A, give them a copy of the audioscript and tell them to read along as they do Exercise B.

Option

Assign Unit 13 Review and Challenge Supplementary Exercises on the Teacher's Resource Disk as homework or on the Student Persistence CD-ROM as self-access practice.

TIME to TALK

Teaching Time: 5–10 min.

- Call on two students to read the example.
- GROUPS. Have students complete the task. Walk around the class and make sure students are asking questions and responding in full sentences.
- Copy the chart from the student book onto the board. Call on students to make questions. Take an informal poll. Have students raise their hands if they think the answer is *yes*. Record the numbers on the board.

Getting Ready to Read

Teaching Time: 5–10 min.

- Call on a student to read the information in the Reading Skill box.

- Give students thirty seconds to skim the text. Explain that they should not read. Instead, they should quickly run their eyes over the text, reading just a few words every few lines. Tell them that their goal is for their eyes to reach the end of the text in thirty seconds.

- After thirty seconds, have students close their books and tell you anything they remember about the text, even if they don't understand it; it could be a word, a phrase, or a main idea. Write everything they tell you on the board.

- Have students choose the main idea by looking at the information on the board.

Reading

Teaching Time: 15–20 min.

- Have students read the article and check their answer to Getting Ready to Read.

- Call on a student to read the answer. Correct as needed.

Multilevel Strategy

- **Pre-level:** Group pre-level students. Read the article aloud as students follow along in their books. Encourage them to stop and ask questions about anything they don't understand.

- **At-level, Above-level:** In their notebooks, have students copy the sentences from the text where the writer uses a form of *can* or *be able to*. Tell them to rewrite *be able to* sentences with *can* or *could* wherever possible, and to replace *can* or *could* with the correct form of *be able to*. Collect their papers. In class the next day, write the original sentences and the rewrites on the board, and have

---

Reading Skill:
Skimming

When you **skim** a text, you do not read every word. Instead, you read very quickly to find the main idea. Read the first and last paragraphs and the first sentences of the body paragraphs.

Getting Ready to Read

Skim the article. Check (✓) the main idea of the reading.

- ❑ **1.** how RFID technology helps pet owners find their lost pets
- ☑ **2.** how RFID technology is getting more and more useful
- ❑ **3.** how RFID technology prevents kidnapping

Reading

Read the article. Then check your answer to Getting Ready to Read.

The WONDERS of
RFID TECHNOLOGY

For years, pet owners have been able to find their lost pets with the help of radio frequency technology, or RFID. An RFID tag is a very small computer chip. The tag is a little larger than a grain of rice. Veterinarians (doctors for animals) put the tags under the animal's skin. Then someone types the number of the tag into a computer database. Most vets' offices and animal hospitals in the United States have machines to **scan** lost animals. If someone finds a lost animal and takes it to a vet, the vet can scan it and get the contact information of the owner. As a result of RFID technology, many more lost pets go back to their owners today than in the past.

Recently, the use of RFID tags has begun to spread from vets' offices to local hospitals. About 900 hospitals across North America now use RFID tags on the **ankle** bracelets of **newborns**. If someone takes a baby with an

an RFID chip next to a grain of rice

RFID bracelet out of the hospital, an alarm rings. A few months ago, the technology stopped the **kidnapping** of a baby from a hospital in North Carolina. Hospital officials were able to catch the kidnapper when the RFID tag on the baby's bracelet **set off** an alarm.

Now some hospitals are putting the chip in their patients. The chips contain information about the patients' medical conditions and medications. If a patient with a chip comes into the hospital, doctors are able to read his or her medical information very quickly. This is especially useful for seriously ill patients who cannot remember the different medications that they are taking. It is also useful for elderly patients with **diseases** that affect their memory, such as Alzheimers disease. These patients often get lost and forget where they are. With the help of RFID technology, their relatives can **locate** them more quickly.

---

the class correct any mistakes. (Paragraph 1, line 1: have been able to—no change possible; Paragraph 1, line 15: can scan it and get = is able to scan it and get; Paragraph 2, lines 10–11: were able to catch—no change possible; Paragraph 3, line 7: are able to read = can read; Paragraph 3, lines 10–11: cannot remember = are not able to remember; Paragraph 3, lines 16–17: can locate = are able to locate)

After You Read

A Find the **boldface** words in the article that have similar meanings to the words below.

1. find — locate
2. very young babies — newborns
3. illnesses — diseases
4. make something start operating — set off
5. read or look for information with a special machine — scan
6. "stealing" a person — kidnapping
7. the joint between the foot and leg — ankle

B Read the article again. Which uses of RFID technology did you read about in the article? Check (✓) them.

With the help of RFID technology, . . .

☑ 1. pet owners are able to find their lost animals.

☐ 2. sick pets receive faster and better care from the veterinarian.

☑ 3. hospitals are able to protect newborn babies.

☐ 4. parents can check where their children are at all times.

☑ 5. doctors can give patients better care.

☑ 6. relatives can protect their elderly, sick family members.

Veterinarian scans a cat to look for an RFID tag.

Technology ·181·

After You Read

A Teaching Time: 10–15 min.

- Read the example with the class.
- Have students complete the task. Tell them to circle words in the text that helped them find the answer and then check their answers by replacing the word in the text with the answer they have chosen. (See page 153 of this book for an explanation of the procedure.)
- Call on students to say answers. Have them tell you which words they circled, and then have them reread the sentences from the text with their answer choices. For example, a student might answer:

(*1. find = locate   I circled the words get lost in the previous sentence.
With the help of RFID technology, their relatives can* find *them more quickly.*)

B Teaching Time: 10–15 min.

- Have students complete the task. Tell them to underline the sentences in the article where they find the answers.
- Call on students to say answers. Have them tell you the paragraph and the line number where the answer can be found in the article. Then have them read those sentences from the article aloud as the other students follow along in their books.

(1. Paragraph 1, lines 1–3;
3. Paragraph 2, lines 5–10;
5. Paragraph 3, lines 5–14;
6. Paragraph 3, lines 9–14)

Multilevel Strategy

All Levels: PAIRS. Pair pre-level students with at- and above-level students for Exercises A and B. Walk around the class and encourage the more advanced students to help the less advanced ones by explaining how and where they found the answers.

Teaching Tip

It is important that students not only hear the correct answers to reading comprehension exercises, but also understand how and where they can find the correct answers. When you go over comprehension exercises in class, always have the student who is answering give the paragraph and line number of the sentence he or she is referring to *before* reading a sentence from the text. This will ensure that everyone is looking at the same place in the text.

Writing

Getting Ready to Write

A Teaching Time: 10–15 min.

- Read the example with the class.
- Have students study the Writing Tip.
- Have students complete the task.
- Call on students to read answers. Correct as needed.

B Teaching Time: 10–15 min.

- Have students read the writing model. As they read, have them circle the time expressions.
- PAIRS. Have students complete the task.

Writing

Getting Ready to Write

A Read the sentences. Which happened first, second, and third? Write the time order (*1*, *2*, and *3*) next to the sentences.

> **Writing Tip**
>
> Use time expressions to indicate that you are changing the time you are writing about.
>
> Examples:
>
> **For years**, pets had RFID tags.
>
> **Recently**, hospitals have started giving babies tags.
>
> **Nowadays**, many patients have RFID chips.

1. _2_ At first, most Americans couldn't buy a car because it was too expensive.

   _1_ Almost 100 years ago, Henry Ford invented the Model T car.

   _3_ Nowadays, most Americans are able to afford a car.

2. _3_ Nowadays, some people are able to use their cell phones as computers.

   _1_ For many years, computers were very big and expensive.

   _2_ Not long ago, most people were not able to operate a computer.

3. _1_ For years, people could only watch television in black and white.

   _3_ Today, more and more people are buying huge flat-screen TVs.

   _2_ Then, stores stopped selling black and white TVs.

B Read the model paragraph.

> In the 1950's, people used transistor radios to listen to music. Transistor radios were small, so people could carry them around easily. In 1980, the Sony Walkman was invented. About five years later, portable CD players became popular. They were light, so people could wear them when they exercised. Now many young people have iPods. With an iPod, you can download hundreds of songs and you don't have to carry any CDs. People can also listen to music on their cell phones these days. How will people be able to listen to music in the future? Maybe they will be able to implant tiny music players in their ears!

PAIRS. **Read the model again. How has the way people listen to music changed over the years?** Wording of answers will vary.

Now choose another type of technology. Talk about how the technology has changed over the years. You can talk about television, telephones, computers, or your own ideas.

Prewriting: Using a Timeline

You are going to write a paragraph about how a type of technology has changed over the years. Read the timelines on cars and computers. Then choose one or make a timeline on another technology you know.

Cars

- **1876**: first car engine invented
- **1876-1908**: cars are very expensive
- **1908**: Henry Ford produced Model T—first cheap car
- **1910**: cars become popular in USA
- **1990s**: cars got bigger and bigger—SUVs popular
- Today: hybrid cars (run on gas and electricity) getting more popular

Computers

- **1930s**: computer invented—very big and expensive
- **1970s**: personal computers invented
- **1980s**: Apple computers and Microsoft Windows
- **1990s**: most people in U.S. use computers
- Today: computers everywhere, even on phones

Writing

Now write a paragraph about a technology and how it has changed over the years. The writing tip, the model paragraph, and your notes will help you. Write in your notebook.

Technology 183

Prewriting

Teaching Time: 10–15 min.

- Have students read through the notes and ask you questions about anything they don't understand.

Writing

Teaching Time: 5–10 min.

- Assign the task for homework. Remind students to use time expressions in their paragraphs.

Multilevel Strategy

- **Pre-level, At-level:** Have students use the given notes and write a paragraph about computers or cars.
- **Above-level:** Encourage students to research a different kind of technology to write about. If your students have access to computers, have them use a search engine such as Google® to find information on the technology they have chosen. The following search string should work well: "history of the [name of technology, for example refrigerator or television]." Alternatively, students can go to the library and look up information about the history of the technology in an encyclopedia such as the *World Book Encyclopedia* or the *Encyclopedia Britannica*.

Learning Goals

- Learn vocabulary related to parenting and family responsibilities
- Learn how to use *have to / have got to / must* for necessity; *not have to* and *must not* for lack of necessity and prohibition; and *had to* for past necessity
- Listen to a conversation about family responsibilities and to a report comparing children's lives in the United States and Japan
- Read and write a letter to the editor of a newspaper
- Talk about the relationship between parents and children in different cultures, the lives of children in different cultures, and personal childhood responsibilities and experiences

Learner Persistence

Have students keep a journal.

Warm-up

Teaching Time: 5–10 min.

Have students cover the word boxes and look at the pictures. Have them tell you what is happening in the pictures. Encourage them to use full sentences. Write their sentences on the board.

Vocabulary

Teaching Time: 10–15 min.

- Have students complete the task.
- 🎧 Play Track 48 while students listen and check their answers.
- Read the words in the word boxes and have students repeat chorally.

Expansion Lead a discussion about your students' relationships with their parents. Ask: *Were your parents strict?* Ask students who say yes to explain their answers with specific examples.

Unit 14
A Kid's Life

Grammar

- *Have to / Have got to / Must:* Affirmative Statements and *Have to:* Yes / No Questions
- *Does not have to* and *Must not*
- *Had to:* Statements and Questions

Vocabulary

CD 2 TRACK **48** Complete the sentences with the words in the box. Then listen and check your answers.

> apologize   do chores   take out the trash

The Morgans have four children. The two older children __do chores__ around the house. Henry needs to __take out the trash__, and Claire usually washes the dishes. When they forget, they feel bad and __apologize__ to their mother.

> bothers   crosses   holds

Billy Morgan is six years old. When he __crosses__ the street, his mother __holds__ his hand. This __bothers__ Billy. He's six, not three!

> behave   obey   punishes   strict

Mrs. Morgan is very __strict__ with her children, and they usually __obey__ her. When the children do not __behave__ well, she __punishes__ them. For example, if they fight or make too much noise, they can't watch TV.

> Mom, sorry I didn't do the dishes yesterday.

184   Unit 14

Listening

A 🔘 **49** Listen. What is bothering Nick the most? Check (✓) the correct answer.

☐ 1. His sister never comes home early.

☐ 2. His mother and father work a lot.

☑ 3. He helps more around the house than his sister.

☐ 4. His father always works late.

B 🔘 **49** Listen again. Then check (✓) the things that Nick is unhappy about.

☐ 1. He's got to go to school.

☐ 2. He must not walk home alone.

☐ 3. His father has to work late.

☑ 4. He's got to cook.

☑ 5. His sister doesn't have to cook.

☑ 6. His sister didn't have to do any chores last month.

☑ 7. He doesn't get any money for doing chores.

☑ 8. His mother had to go back to work.

C 🔘 **49** Listen again. Answer the questions. Write complete sentences.

1. Why does Nick have to cook tonight?
   He has to cook tonight because his father has to work late and his sister is babysitting.

2. Why does the dinner have to be ready by 6:00?
   Dinner has to be ready by 6:00 because Suzy has to get to basketball practice.

3. What did Nick have to do last week?
   He had to cook dinner.

4. Why did Nick's mother have to go back to work?
   She had to go back to work because they needed to pay the bills.

A Kid's Life **185**

Listening

A **Teaching Time: 10–15 min.**

- **Warm-up.** Have students read the instructions and the answer choices. Ask: *How old do you think Nick is? Why?*

- 🎧 Play Track 49 as students listen and complete the task. Make sure students understand that they should check the one thing that bothers Nick the most.

- Call on a student to say the answer. If necessary, play the recording again.

B **Teaching Time: 10–15 min.**

- Have students read the answer choices, and answer if they can. Tell them to write a question mark (?) if they are not sure of an answer.

- 🎧 Play Track 49 as students listen and complete the task.

- 🎧 Play Track 49 again, this time pausing the recording as each answer is read.

Multilevel Strategy

Pre-level: Make photocopies of the audioscript to give it to students after they have completed Exercise A. Allow them to use the audioscript as they complete Exercises B and C.

C **Teaching Time: 10–15 min.**

- 🎧 Play Track 49 as students listen and complete the task.

- Ask volunteers to write their answers on the board.

- 🎧 Play Track 49 again, pausing as each answer is given. Correct the sentences on the board as needed.

Have to / Have got to / Must: Affirmative Statements

Have to: Yes / No Questions

Teaching Time: 5–10 min.

- Have students study the chart and the Look Box.
- Write on the board:

  He needs to visit his grandmother. It's her birthday.

- Point to *need to* and say: *We use* need to *to say that something is necessary. What are three other ways of saying that something is necessary?* (have got to, must, have to)
- Have a student come up to the board and rewrite the sentence with *have got to, have to,* and *must.*
- Say: Have got to, have to, *and* must *all mean the same thing. However,* have to *and* have got to *are more common in speaking.* Have got to *is a little more informal than* have to. *The contraction of* have / has got to *is* 've got to *or* 's got to. *Write on the board: We often pronounce* got to *as one word—*gotta*—/ɡɑtə/ but we never write it that way. There is no contraction for* have / has to *or* must, *but we often pronounce* have to *as one word: hafta /hæftə/.*
- Read the sentences from the chart aloud, pronouncing *got to* as /ɡɑtə/ and *have to* as /hæftə/. Have students repeat chorally.
- Write on the board: *What does he need to do?* Ask: *We use* need to *to ask about necessity. What is another way of asking if something is necessary? How can we rewrite this question?* Write on board: *What does he have to do?*
- *Do we use* have got to *or* must *in questions?* (*No, we don't. We use* do / does have to.)

A Teaching Time: 10–15 min.

- Have students read the definition in the Look Box.
- Have students complete the task.
- Call on students to give their opinions. Write the following pattern on the board, and then model an example:

HAVE TO / HAVE GOT TO / MUST: AFFIRMATIVE STATEMENTS
HAVE TO: YES / NO QUESTIONS

Affirmative Statements

I You We They	have to have got to must	be	on time.	He She	has to has got to must	be	on time.

Yes / No Questions

Do	you we they	have to	buy	books?
Does	she			

Short Answers

Yes,	I you they	do.	No,	I you they	don't.
	she	does.		she	doesn't.

Look

Use *have to, have got to,* and *must* to talk about necessity.

Use *have to* to ask questions about necessity.

A What do you think? Check (✓) the column you agree with. *Answers will vary.*

Look

respect = be polite to someone because the person is important

	ALL OF THE TIME	SOME OF THE TIME
1. Children have got to respect adults.		
2. Children have to obey their parents.		
3. Children have to behave well.		
4. Parents have got to be strict with children.		
5. Parents must play with their children.		

B These teenagers have responsibilities at home. Write sentences about them.

1. *Jessica has got to make her bed every day.*
   (Jessica / have got to / make her bed every day)
2. *Frank has got to take out the trash every Tuesday night.*
   (Frank / have got to / take out the trash every Tuesday night)
3. *John and his sister have got to help with the family's bills.*
   (John and his sister / have got to / help with the family's bills)
4. *Nora has to make dinner for the family.*
   (Nora / have to / make dinner for the family)
5. *Anna and her brother have to feed the dog.*
   (Anna and her brother / have to / feed the dog)

I think that ___ some of the time / all of the time. For example, I think that children have got to behave some of the time, but they've got to respect their elders all of the time. What do you think?

B Teaching Time: 10–15 min.

- Read the example with the class.
- Have students complete the task.
- Call on students to read answers. Correct as needed.

Expansion Ask students if they have any of the same responsibilities as the people in the exercise. If they answer yes, have them make sentences about themselves, for example: *I've got to make my bed every day, too.*

Grammar Notes

1. Use *have to, have got to,* and *must* to talk about necessity. *Have to* and *have got to* are more common in conversation than *must. Have got to* is the least formal of the three.

2. Use *have to* or *have got to* with *I, you, we,* and *they.* Use *has to* or *has got to* with the third person singular (*he, she, it*). Use *must* with all subjects.

3. Use *do* or *does* + subject + *have to* + base form of the verb to ask questions about necessity. Use *do / does* or *don't / doesn't* in short answers.

4. For more information about this grammar topic, see pages 290–291.

C ⬤ 50 **Read the note Eleanor left the babysitter, Kate. Complete the conversations. Then listen and check your answers.**

1. **Kate:** Esme, it's time for bed.

   Esme: _Do I have to go to bed_ now?
   1. (I / have to / go to bed)

   Kate: Yup. Your mother's note says

   you have to go to bed
   2. (you / have got to / go to bed)

   at 8, and it's 8 now.

2. **Kate:** Laura, finish your vegetables.

   Laura: _Does Alex have to finish_ his?
   3. (Alex / have to / finish)

   Kate: Yes, but he's already finished.

   You have to finish yours.
   4. (you / have to / finish)

3. **Kate:** Alex, have you finished your homework?

   Alex: Not yet. _I've got to watch_
   5. (I / have got to / watch)

   the rest of this movie. It's really cool.

   Kate: No, _you've got to do your homework_ .
   6. (you / have got to / do your homework)

   Do I have to help you?
   7. (I / have to / help)

   Alex: No, you don't. It's really easy.

Look

In casual speech, *have to* is often pronounced "hafta," and *got to* is often pronounced "gotta."

Kate,

Please remember:

Esme must go to bed at 8:00.
Laura must eat her vegetables.
Alex must do his homework.

If there are any problems, call me on my cell phone at 600-555-8760.

Eleanor

TIME to TALK

PAIRS. Talk about the things that schoolchildren have to do in your country. Use the words in the box and your own ideas. Ask and answer questions.

erase the board for the teacher	stand up when the teacher enters the room
go home for lunch	study English
go to school for _____ years	wear school uniforms

Example:
A: *Kids in my country have got to go to school for ten years. Do kids in your country have to go to school for ten years, too?*
B: *No, they don't. They have to go to school for twelve years.*

WRAP UP. Now talk about children in another country you know about. Do they have to do the same things? If not, what do they do differently?

A Kid's Life 187

- Read the example with the class.
- Have students complete the task.
- 🎧 Play Track 50 as students listen and check their answers.
- Call on two students to read each conversation. Correct as needed.

Culture Note

In the United States, most of the funding for public schools comes from the property taxes of the people who live in the community where the school is located. Therefore, schools in poorer communities have less money than schools in richer communities.

Option

Assign Unit 14 Supplementary Grammar to Communicate 1 Exercises on the Teacher's Resource Disk as homework or on the Student Persistence CD-ROM as self-access practice.

TIME to TALK

Teaching Time: 10–15 min.

- Call on two students to read the example.
- PAIRS. Have students complete the task. Walk around and make sure they are asking questions as well as answering them.
- Call on students to tell the class something about their partners' country. Correct as needed.
- WRAP UP. If you are in the United States, start a discussion about differences between schools in the students' countries and schools in the United States. (See Culture Note.)

Grammar to Communicate 2

Does not have to and Must not

Teaching Time: 5–10 min.

- Have students study the chart and the Look Box.
- Write on the board:

  A. *It is not permitted, so it is <u>not</u> okay to do it.*

  B. *It is not necessary, but it is okay to do it.*

  Situation 1

  Mother: Remember, you ___ walk home alone after the party.

  Daughter: But the party is only a few blocks away.

  Mother: I don't care. It's dangerous to walk alone late at night.

  Situation 2

  Classmate 1: You ___ walk home. Here's the bus.

  Classmate 2: But I want to walk. It's a beautiful day.

  Classmate 1: Okay. I'll see you later.

- Ask: *Which situation matches meaning A? Which situation matches meaning B? (A–1; B–2)*

  Which verb do we use for meaning A— not have to or must not? For meaning B? (A: must not; B: not have to)

- Call on a student to tell you what to write in the blanks for situations 1 and 2.

A Teaching Time: 10–15 min.

- Have students complete the task.
- Call on students to say answers.

B Teaching Time: 10–15 min.

- Read the example with the class.
- Have students complete the task.
- Call on students to say answers. Correct as needed.
- Have partners read the completed conversations.

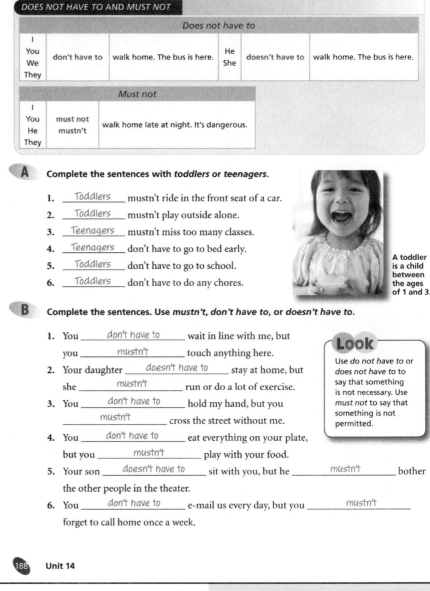

Grammar Notes

1. *Do not / Does not have to* means that something is *not necessary.*
2. *Must not* means that something is *not permitted.*
3. We also use *can't* to say that something is not permitted.
4. For more information on this grammar topic, see page 291.

Watch Out!

Students often confuse *must not* and *don't / doesn't have to.* For example, *In my country, children don't have to be late to class.* You can help students avoid these kinds of errors by teaching them to think "but it is okay" whenever they use *not have to.*

C Complete the sentences with *don't have to* or *mustn't*. Use the words in the box.

bother	get up early	miss	stay home	~~touch~~
cook	give	obey	tell	walk home

1. The stove is hot. You _____ mustn't touch _____ it.
2. There's no school tomorrow. I don't have to get up early.
3. The birthday party is a surprise for your mother. You _____ mustn't tell _____ her.
4. I'll pick you up after school if you want. You don't have to walk home.
5. This medicine isn't for children. You _____ must not give _____ any to your child.
6. My mother makes every meal. I _____ don't have to cook _____ .
7. The meeting is very important. Your children _____ must not miss _____ it.
8. I'm 14 years old! You don't have to stay home with me. I'll be fine alone.
9. Your father is working. You _____ mustn't bother _____ him.
10. You're not my mother! You're just the babysitter. I _____ don't have to obey _____ you.

TIME to TALK

PAIRS. Talk about the things that children at different ages *don't have to do* and the things that they *mustn't do.* Complete the chart.

	DON'T HAVE TO . . .	MUST NOT . . .
infants (0–11 months)	do any chores.	
toddlers (1–3 years)		cross the street alone.
young children (4–8 years)		
pre-teens (9–12 years)		

Example:
A: *Infants don't have to do any chores.*
B: *Toddlers mustn't cross the street alone.*

A Kid's Life 189

C Teaching Time: 10–15 min.
- Read the example with the class.
- Have students complete the task.
- Call on students to say answers. For each item, ask who is speaking. For example, in sentence 1, an adult is talking to a small child. In sentence 2, a schoolchild is speaking.

Option

Assign Unit 14 Supplementary Grammar to Communicate 2 Exercises on the Teacher's Resource Disk as homework or on the Student Persistence CD-ROM as self-access practice.

TIME to TALK

Teaching Time: 10–15 min.
- Have two students read the example. Tell students to try to think of as many sentences as they can for each age group.
- PAIRS. Have students complete the task. Walk around and make sure that students are speaking in full sentences.
- Call on students to say their sentences. Correct as needed.

Had to: Statements and Questions

Teaching Time: 5–10 min.

- Have students study the chart and the Look Box.
- Say: *Had to is just like* have to, *but it's about the past. The negative of* had to *is* didn't have to. *Like* don't have to, didn't have to *means not necessary.*
- Write the following sentences on the board, and call on students to fill in the blanks with a form of *had to.*

   A: When I was a child, I ___ walk to school, but my kids don't have to walk. I drive them to school.

   B: How far (you) ___ walk?

   A: About a mile.

   B: (you) ___ walk when it snowed?

   A: Yes, I ___. But when the weather was really bad, we ___ go to school. We stayed at home.

A   Teaching Time: 10–15 min.

- Have students complete the task.
- Call on students to read their answers.
- For each item, take an informal poll. Say, for example: *Carla had to take a nap every day. Raise your hand if you had to take a nap every day, too.*

B   Teaching Time: 10–15 min.

- Read the example with the class.
- Have students complete the task.
- Call on students to say answers.

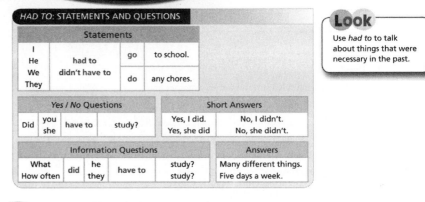

HAD TO: STATEMENTS AND QUESTIONS			
Statements			
I He We They	had to didn't have to	go	to school.
		do	any chores.

Yes / No Questions			
Did	you she	have to	study?

Short Answers	
Yes, I did. Yes, she did	No, I didn't. No, she didn't.

Information Questions			
What How often	did	he they	have to	study? study?

Answers
Many different things. Five days a week.

Look

Use *had to* to talk about things that were necessary in the past.

A Complete the sentences about yourself. Write *had to* or *didn't have to*.   Answers will vary.

1. When I was three, I _____ take a nap every day.
2. When I was six, I _____ drink milk every day.
3. When I was ten years old, I _____ do a lot of chores.
4. When I was twelve, I _____ eat all the food on my plate.
5. When I was fifteen, I _____ work.

B Rewrite the sentences. Use *had to* or *didn't have to*.

1. It was necessary for Bob to go to school six days a week.
   Bob had to go to school six days a week.

2. It was necessary for Sylvia to help her mother clean every Saturday.
   Sylvia had to help her mother clean every Saturday.

3. It was necessary for my older sister to take care of the younger kids.
   My older sister had to take care of the younger kids.

4. It wasn't necessary for my friends to walk to school.
   My friends didn't have to walk to school.

5. It wasn't necessary for me to do homework on the weekend.
   I didn't have to do homework on the weekend.

6. It wasn't necessary for Vera to behave well all the time.
   Vera didn't have to behave well all the time.

Multilevel Strategy

- **Pre-level:** Give students more time to complete the exercise.
- **At-level, Above-level:** PAIRS. Have students work in pairs. Tell them to say true sentences about themselves when they were young. For example: *When I was young, I didn't have to go to school six days a week. I only had to go to school five days a week.*

Grammar Notes

1. Use *had to* to talk about things that were necessary in the past. *Had to* is the past of *have to, have got to,* and *must.*

2. The past of *must not* (not permitted) is *could not.*

3. The past of *do not / does not have to* is *did not* (or *didn't*) + *have to* + the base form of the verb.

4. To make a *yes / no* question with *had to,* add *did* before the subject and use the base form of the verb.

5. When *who* is the subject of the question, do not use *did* in the question. Use *had to.*

6. For more information on this grammar topic, see page 291.

C Write questions.

1. **A:** I had to work after school.

   B: <u>Did you have to work after school</u> every day?

2. **A:** We had to wear uniforms in elementary school.

   B: <u>Did you have to wear uniforms</u> in high school?

3. **A:** We had to go to bed early on school nights.

   B: <u>Did you have to go to bed early</u> on weekends?

4. **A:** I had to get up very early for school.

   B: What time <u>did you have to get up?</u>

5. **A:** I had to take a lot of different subjects in school.

   B: Which subjects <u>did you have to take?</u>

6. **A:** I had to walk to school.

   B: How far <u>did you have to walk?</u>

7. **A:** I had to take care of my younger brothers and sisters.

   B: Why <u>did you have to take care of your younger</u> brothers and sisters?

Schoolchildren wearing uniforms

PAIRS. Read the sentences that are true for you. Your partner will ask you the follow-up questions. Then switch roles.

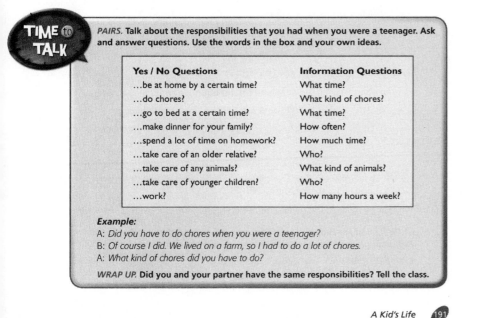

TIME to TALK

PAIRS. Talk about the responsibilities that you had when you were a teenager. Ask and answer questions. Use the words in the box and your own ideas.

Yes / No Questions	Information Questions
…be at home by a certain time?	What time?
…do chores?	What kind of chores?
…go to bed at a certain time?	What time?
…make dinner for your family?	How often?
…spend a lot of time on homework?	How much time?
…take care of an older relative?	Who?
…take care of any animals?	What kind of animals?
…take care of younger children?	Who?
…work?	How many hours a week?

Example:
A: *Did you have to do chores when you were a teenager?*
B: *Of course I did. We lived on a farm, so I had to do a lot of chores.*
A: *What kind of chores did you have to do?*

WRAP UP. Did you and your partner have the same responsibilities? Tell the class.

A Kid's Life **191**

C Teaching Time: 10–15 min.

- Read the example with the class.
- Have students complete the task.
- Call on students to read their questions. Correct as needed.
- PAIRS. Have students complete the task. Walk around and make sure that they are answering their partners' follow-up questions.
- Call on students to tell the class something about their partners.

Option

Assign Unit 14 Supplementary Grammar to Communicate 3 Exercises on the Teacher's Resource Disk as homework or on the Student Persistence CD-ROM as self-access practice.

TIME to TALK

Teaching Time: 10–15 min.

- Call on two students to read the example. Make sure they understand that they must ask full questions, and not just read what is in the box.
- PAIRS. Have students complete the task. Walk around and make sure students are asking and answering questions.
- WRAP UP. Have students tell the class something that both they and their partners had to do when you were teenagers. Correct as needed. Encourage the class to ask follow-up questions. For example, one student says: *Both Luz and I had to make dinner for our families.* The class asks: *Did you have to make dinner every night?* or *How many people did you have to cook for?*

Review and
Challenge

Grammar

Teaching Time: 5–10 min.

- Have students read the words in the box.
- Read the example with the class.
- Have students complete the task.
- 🎧 Play Track 51 while students listen and check their answers.
- Call on two students to read the completed conversation aloud. Correct as needed.

Multilevel Strategy

At-level, Above-level: Have students complete the conversation before they listen.

Dictation

Teaching Time: 5–10 min.

- 🎧 Play Track 52 while students listen and write what they hear.
- 🎧 Play Track 52 again while students check their answers.
- Call on students to read the dictated sentences aloud. Write exactly what you hear. Ask them to spell the new vocabulary.
- Have students correct the sentences on the board, as needed.
- 🎧 Play Track 52 again and correct the sentences on the board.

Multilevel Strategy

Pre-level: Give students a worksheet with the words from the dictation provided, except for forms of *have to*, *have got to*, and *must* and the vocabulary.

Speaking

Teaching Time: 5–10 min.

- Call on a student to read the example.
- GROUPS. Have students complete the task.

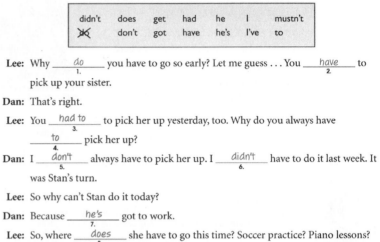

Review and Challenge

Grammar

🔊 **51** Complete the conversation with the words in the box. Then listen and check your answers. Be careful. There are extra words.

didn't	does	get	had	he	I	mustn't
~~he~~	don't	got	have	he's	I've	to

Lee: Why __do__ (1.) you have to go so early? Let me guess . . . You __have__ (2.) to pick up your sister.

Dan: That's right.

Lee: You __had to__ (3.) to pick her up yesterday, too. Why do you always have __to__ (4.) pick her up?

Dan: I __don't__ (5.) always have to pick her up. I __didn't__ (6.) have to do it last week. It was Stan's turn.

Lee: So why can't Stan do it today?

Dan: Because __he's__ (7.) got to work.

Lee: So, where __does__ (8.) she have to go this time? Soccer practice? Piano lessons?

Dan: She's __got__ (9.) to go to the dentist. I'm sorry, but __I__ (10.) really have to go. She __mustn't__ (11.) be late for her appointment.

Lee: And I've got to __get__ (12.) a new boyfriend — one with no little sister!

Dictation

🔊 **52** Listen. You will hear five sentences. Write them in your notebook. *See the audioscript on p. 321 for the sentences.*

Speaking

GROUPS. Compare your responsibilities when you were a teenager and your parents' and grandparents' responsibilities when they were teenagers.

Example: When I was a teenager, I didn't have to take care of my younger brothers and sisters. My grandmother had to take care of her younger sister and her grandmother.

Listening

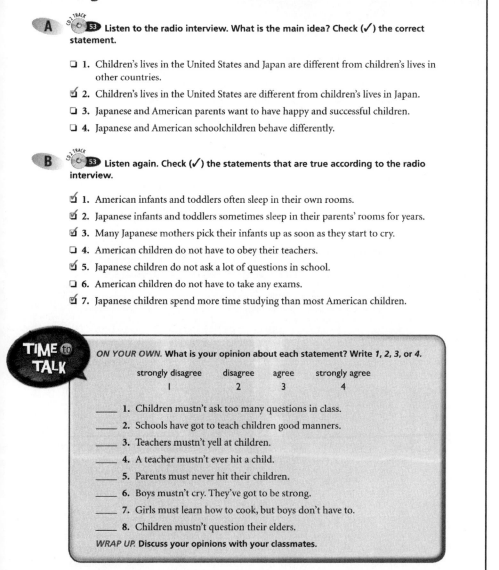

A 🎵 **53** Listen to the radio interview. What is the main idea? Check (✓) the correct statement.

❑ **1.** Children's lives in the United States and Japan are different from children's lives in other countries.

☑ **2.** Children's lives in the United States are different from children's lives in Japan.

❑ **3.** Japanese and American parents want to have happy and successful children.

❑ **4.** Japanese and American schoolchildren behave differently.

B 🎵 **53** Listen again. Check (✓) the statements that are true according to the radio interview.

☑ **1.** American infants and toddlers often sleep in their own rooms.

☑ **2.** Japanese infants and toddlers sometimes sleep in their parents' rooms for years.

☑ **3.** Many Japanese mothers pick their infants up as soon as they start to cry.

❑ **4.** American children do not have to obey their teachers.

☑ **5.** Japanese children do not ask a lot of questions in school.

❑ **6.** American children do not have to take any exams.

☑ **7.** Japanese children spend more time studying than most American children.

TIME to TALK

ON YOUR OWN. **What is your opinion about each statement? Write** *1, 2, 3,* **or** *4.*

strongly disagree	disagree	agree	strongly agree
I	2	3	4

_____ **1.** Children mustn't ask too many questions in class.

_____ **2.** Schools have got to teach children good manners.

_____ **3.** Teachers mustn't yell at children.

_____ **4.** A teacher mustn't ever hit a child.

_____ **5.** Parents must never hit their children.

_____ **6.** Boys mustn't cry. They've got to be strong.

_____ **7.** Girls must learn how to cook, but boys don't have to.

_____ **8.** Children mustn't question their elders.

WRAP UP. **Discuss your opinions with your classmates.**

A Kid's Life 193

Listening

A **Teaching Time: 5–10 min.**

- **Warm-up.** Start a discussion. Ask: *Do you think children's lives today are easier or more difficult than your life was when you were a child?* Have students explain their answers with specific examples.
- Have students read the answer choices.
- 🎧 Play Track 53 as students listen and complete the task.
- Call on a student to say the answer. Play the recording again if necessary.

B **Teaching Time: 10–15 min.**

- PAIRS. Have students read the answer choices and check the answers that they think are true before they listen. If they are not sure about an answer, tell them to write a question mark (?).
- 🎧 Play Track 53 while students listen and complete the task.
- 🎧 Play Track 53 again, pausing as each answer is given.
- Call on students to say answers.

Multilevel Strategy

Pre-level: After students have completed Exercise A, give them a copy of the audioscript and tell them to read along as they do Exercise B.

Option

Assign Unit 14 Review and Challenge Supplementary Exercises on the Teacher's Resource Disk as homework or on the Student Persistence CD-ROM as self-access practice.

TIME to TALK

Teaching Time: 10–15 min.

- ON YOUR OWN. Have students complete the task. Walk around the class and help with vocabulary as needed.
- WRAP UP. Read the statements aloud one by one. Ask students who strongly agree with the statement to raise their hands. Then ask students who strongly disagree with the statement to raise their hands. Have a student from each side explain his/her reasons. Then repeat the procedure with the next statement.

Reading

Getting Ready to Read

Teaching Time: 5–10 min.

- Give students thirty seconds to skim the letter. Remind them that when they skim, they should not read every word. Instead, they should quickly run their eyes over the letter, reading just a few words every few lines.
- After thirty seconds, have students close their books and tell you anything they remember about the letter, even if they don't understand it; it could be a word, a phrase, or a main idea. Write everything they tell you on the board.
- Have students choose the main topic of the letter by looking at the information on the board.

Reading

Teaching Time: 15–20 min.

- Have students read the article and check their answer to Getting Ready to Read.
- Call on a student to read the answer. Correct as needed.

Expansion PAIRS. Have students find and circle places in the text where the writer uses *have got to, (not) have to, had to,* and *must.*

Reading

Getting Ready to Read

Skim the letter. Check (✓) the main topic.

- ☑ the way to improve the academic performance of American kids
- ❑ the differences between the United States and other countries
- ❑ the reasons American kids do better in school than kids in other countries

Reading

Read the letter. Then check your answer to Getting Ready to Read.

> To the Editors,
>
> I am a parent of two children in the Lakeville School District. After I read yesterday's **editorial** on the latest "solution" to the **poor** academic **performance** of American children today, I felt that I had to **respond.** Your editorial uses the same arguments that we have been hearing for years. You say the government must provide more money for public schools, and schools have to spend more on teacher training. I am so tired of these arguments! It is time for new ideas. We have got to **come up with** solutions that work.
>
> In the United States, we **ignore** what is going on in countries where children perform better than American kids, such as India and China. In these countries, children are taught that they must respect their teachers as much as they respect their parents. A parent's highest goal in these countries is the education of their children. Unlike in the United States, children do not have to do chores or work part-time. All they have to do is study! This is a **sacrifice** the children make for the family. And in turn, the adult members of the family make sacrifices for the children. Perhaps the parents work two jobs to pay school fees, while the grandparents take care of everything at home. I think that education is not just the responsibility of teachers and schools, or even of the student. It is the whole family's responsibility.
>
> **As I see it,** if we really want to improve our children's school performance, we should be looking at the differences between our society and those countries where children perform better. I am sure that we will find that the biggest difference is in the families' attitudes toward education.
>
> *Emma Vanderbrook*
> Emma Vanderbrook
> Los Angeles

Culture Note

Warm-up: Bring in several copies of the editorial pages from a newspaper and pass them around the room. Explain that most newspapers have one section for opinions, called the editorial pages. In the editorial pages, there are usually two sections: one where the editors of the newspaper express their opinions on the news, and another where readers express their opinions in letters to the newspapers' editors. Every week, the editors choose the most interesting letters and put them in the paper. Ask: *Do newspapers in your country have editorial pages? Have you ever written a letter to the editor? If so, what was the topic of the letter?*

After You Read

A Look at the **boldface** words in the letter. Guess their meaning. Match the words with the correct definitions. Be careful. There are two extra definitions.

_h_ 1. editorial
_d_ 2. poor
_b_ 3. performance
_j_ 4. respond
_e_ 5. come up with
_c_ 6. ignore
_i_ 7. sacrifice
_a_ 8. as I see it

a. in my opinion
b. how well or badly someone does something
c. not pay attention to
d. very bad
e. think of
f. not having any money
g. opportunity
h. an article in a newspaper that expresses the opinion of the editors
i. something valuable that you decide not to have, in order to get something that is more important
j. say or write something as a reply

B Read the letter again. Check (✓) the statement that best expresses the writer's point of view.

❏ 1. Schools and teachers are not very important to children's academic success.

☑ 2. Parents' attitudes toward education are more important to their children's academic success than the schools or teachers.

❏ 3. If the government does not spend more money on education, children will not be successful in the future.

> **Reading Skill:**
> **Recognizing Point of View**
>
> A writer's **point of view** is his or her opinion about or attitude toward the topic. Look for words like *I think* or *as I see it* in the text. They often come at the beginning of sentences that give the writer's point of view.

A Kid's Life ⟨195⟩

After You Read

A Teaching Time: 10–15 min.

- Read the example with the class.
- Have students complete the task. Tell them to circle the words in the letter that helped them find the answer, and then check their answers by replacing the word in the letter with the answer they have chosen. (See page 153 in this book for an explanation of the procedure.)
- Call on students to say answers. Have them tell you which words they circled.

B Teaching Time: 10–15 min.

- Call on a student to read the information in the Reading Skill box.
- Have students reread the letter. Tell them to underline phrases or sentences where the writer makes it clear that she is expressing a personal opinion. (paragraph 1, line 3: *I felt*; paragraph 1, line 6: *I am so tired of*; paragraph 2, line 9: *I think*; paragraph 3, line 1: *As I see it*; paragraph 3, lines 1–2: *we should*; paragraph 3, line 3: *I am sure*)
- Call on a student to read the opinion words in the text aloud. Then have the student say the answer.

> **Multilevel Strategy**
>
> **All Levels:** Pair pre-level students with at-level and above-level students for Exercises A and B. Walk around the class and encourage the more advanced students to help the less advanced ones by explaining how and where they found the answers.

Writing

Getting Ready to Write

 A   **Teaching Time: 10–15 min.**

- Have students study the Writing Tip.
- Read the example with the class.
- Have students complete the task.
- Call on students to read answers. Correct as needed.

B   **Teaching Time: 10–15 min.**

- Have students read the model letter. As they read, have them circle the words that the writer uses to express point of view.
- PAIRS. Have students complete the task.

Writing

Getting Ready to Write

A   **Rewrite each sentence two ways. Use phrases that express a point of view.**

1. As I see it, children need more places to play.

   In my opinion, children need more places to play.

   The point is, children need more places to play.

   _____

2. In my opinion, the schools in our city are terrible.

   The point is, the schools in our city are terrible.

   As I see it, the schools in our city are terrible.

3. The point is, parents must teach their children good manners.

   In my opinion, parents must teach their children good manners.

   As I see it, parents must teach their children good manners.

4. The point is, children had to do too many chores fifty years ago.

   In my opinion, children had to do too many chores fifty years ago.

   As I see it, children had to do too many chores fifty years ago.

B   **Read the model letter.**

> To the Editors,
>
> I am writing because there is a serious problem in our community. As I see it, this city doesn't have enough parks. Parks are important because most people in our city don't have yards. <u>Parks are the only places we can sit and enjoy nature.</u> Also, <u>parks are great for kids.</u> Kids love to run and play on the grass. Because there <u>aren't enough parks, our kids have to play in the streets.</u> That can be really dangerous! If parents want to keep their children safe, <u>they have to keep them inside the house.</u> That's not fair to the children. In my opinion, our city has got to start building parks for our children as soon as possible!
>
> Ned Bates
> Centerville

PAIRS. **Read the model again. Why is it important to a community to have parks?** Wording of answers may vary.

Now choose a problem in your community. Talk about why it is important to solve the problem. You can talk about housing, traffic, schools, crime, or your own ideas.

196   **Unit 14**

Writing Tip

Use *the point is*, *in my opinion*, and *as I see it* to express your point of view:

Examples:

The point is, children should respect their teachers.

In my opinion, children should respect their teachers.

As I see it, children should respect their teachers.

Option

Exercise B. Bring in copies of letters to the editor from a local newspaper. Have students read them and identify each writer's point of view.

Prewriting: Brainstorming

You are going to write a letter to the editor about a community problem. Before you write, look at the brainstorming ideas for the writing model. Then brainstorm, or write down very quickly, as many ideas as you can think of. Check (✓) the ideas you would like to include in your letter.

Writing Model

Problem: the city needs more parks

Ideas:
our city parks are boring and small
our city parks are dirty
not enough parks ✓
people don't have yards ✓
parks only place to enjoy nature ✓
people use parks for exercise
children need to be outside ✓
children play on the street: dangerous ✓
children have to stay inside ✓
children need sunshine

Problem:

Ideas:

Writing

Now write a letter to the editor about a community problem. The writing tip, the model letter, and your notes will help you. Write in your notebook.

A Kid's Life 197

Prewriting
Teaching Time: 10–15 min.

- Have students read through the notes.
- Have students complete the task.

Writing
Teaching Time: 20–25 min.

- Have students complete the task. Remind them to use expressions such as *as I see it* to express their point of view.

Multilevel Strategy

- **Pre-level:** Have pre-level students work in a group to brainstorm ideas about one topic. Students can include any of these ideas in their letters.
- **At-level, Above-level:** After students have written their letters, have them exchange the letters with a partner. Tell them to read each other's letters and identify their partner's point of view. Give students the option of revising their letters (based on their partner's feedback) and handing them in the next day.

Option

If your students are having trouble thinking of issues to write about, do a class brainstorming session on local problems. Start by having students read some editorials from a local newspaper. Then ask them to call out problems in their communities. Write their ideas on the board.

Unit 15
Manners

Learning Goals

- Learn vocabulary related to good manners
- Learn how to use *should (not) + verb*; *should (not) + be + present participle*; and the difference between *should* and *have to*
- Listen to a conversation about manners and to a report about dining etiquette around the world
- Read and write about appropriate business etiquette around the world
- Talk about manners, etiquette, and polite and impolite behavior around the world

Learner Persistence

Keep a teaching journal.

Warm-up

Teaching Time: 3–5 min.

- Have students look at the pictures. Ask: *Are the people in the pictures doing anything wrong? If so, what?*

Vocabulary

Teaching Time: 10–15 min.

- Read the example with the class.
- Have students complete the task.
- 🎧 Play Track 2 while students listen and check their answers.
- Read the sentences aloud and have students repeat chorally as they point to the appropriate pictures.

Expansion PAIRS. Have one student cover the sentences and try to remember them while the other student checks his or her answers. After a few minutes, have them switch roles.

Unit 15
Manners

Grammar
- *Should (not)* + Verb
- *Should (not)* + Be + Present Participle
- *Should* and *Have to*

Vocabulary

🔊 **2** Read the sentences and look at the pictures. What do adults say to children? Match the sentences with the pictures. Then listen and check your answers.

1.   2.   3.   4.

5.   6.   7.   8.

    3   **a.** "Don't **lick** your fingers."

    5   **b.** "Don't **whisper.**"

    7   **c.** "Don't **talk with your mouth full.**"

    2   **d.** "**Knock on the door** before you enter a room."

    6   **e.** "Don't **interrupt.**"

    1   **f.** "**Cover your mouth** when you sneeze."

    8   **g.** "Don't **put your elbows** on the table."

    4   **h.** "Don't **talk about her behind her back.**"

198   Unit 15

Listening

A CD 3 TRACK **3** **Listen. What is Allen doing wrong? Check (✓) the pictures.**

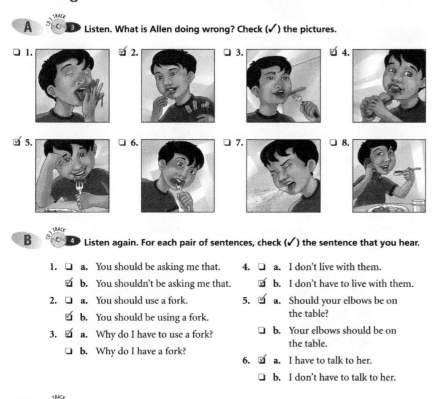

☐ 1.   ☑ 2.   ☐ 3.   ☑ 4.

☑ 5.   ☐ 6.   ☐ 7.   ☐ 8.

B CD 3 TRACK **4** **Listen again. For each pair of sentences, check (✓) the sentence that you hear.**

1.   ☐ **a.** You should be asking me that.
      ☑ **b.** You shouldn't be asking me that.

2.   ☐ **a.** You should use a fork.
      ☑ **b.** You should be using a fork.

3.   ☑ **a.** Why do I have to use a fork?
      ☐ **b.** Why do I have a fork?

4.   ☐ **a.** I don't live with them.
      ☑ **b.** I don't have to live with them.

5.   ☑ **a.** Should your elbows be on the table?
      ☐ **b.** Your elbows should be on the table.

6.   ☑ **a.** I have to talk to her.
      ☐ **b.** I don't have to talk to her.

C CD 3 TRACK **5** **Listen again. Answer the questions. Write complete sentences.** Wording of answers may vary.

1.   What is Allen's excuse for eating with his hands?
   He is eating French fries, and all of his friends eat French fries with their hands.

2.   Why doesn't Allen's mother care about his friends' manners?
   She doesn't have to live with them.

3.   What is Allen's excuse for putting his elbows on the table?
   He forgot.

4.   What is Allen's excuse for answering the telephone at dinnertime?
   The phone call is important.

Manners   199

Listening

A   **Teaching Time: 10–15 min.**

- **Warm-up.** Have students look at the pictures and describe what is happening in each one.
- 🎧 Play Track 3 as students complete the task.
- 🎧 Play Track 3 again, this time pausing as each answer is given.
- Call on a student to say answers.

B   **Teaching Time: 10–15 min.**

- Have students read the answer choices.
- 🎧 Play Track 4 as students listen and complete the task.
- 🎧 Play Track 4 again, this time pausing the recording after each answer is given.

C   **Teaching Time: 10–15 min.**

- Have students complete the task before they hear the recording again.
- 🎧 Play Track 5 as students listen and check their answers.
- Ask volunteers to write their answers on the board.
- 🎧 Play Track 5 again, pausing the recording as each answer is given. Correct the sentences on the board as needed.

Multilevel Strategy

Pre-level: Make photocopies of the audioscript and give it to students after they have completed Exercise C. Tell them to read along as you play the recording the final time.

Should (not) + Verb

Teaching Time: 5–10 min.

- Have students study the chart and the Look Box.
- Say: *We use* should *and* should not *when we want to give someone our advice or our opinion.*
- Read the sentences from the chart aloud. Point out that *should* is the same for all subjects, that the main verb is in the base form, and that in questions *should* comes before the subject.

A **Teaching Time: 5–10 min.**

- Have students look at the pictures and complete the task.
- Call on students to give their opinions. Correct grammar and content as needed.
- PAIRS. Have students complete the task.
- Call on students to tell the class about manners in their countries.

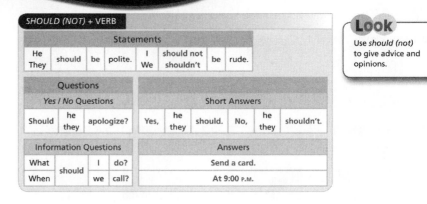

Grammar to Communicate 1

Look

Use *should (not)* to give advice and opinions.

SHOULD (NOT) + VERB						
Statements						
He They	should	be	polite.	I We	should not shouldn't	be rude.

Questions			**Short Answers**				
Yes / No Questions							
Should	he they	apologize?	Yes,	he they	should.	No,	he they	shouldn't.

Information Questions			**Answers**	
What	should	I	do?	Send a card.
When		we	call?	At 9:00 P.M.

A What do you know about manners in the United States? Complete the sentences. Write *should* or *shouldn't*.

1.

You ___should___ hold the door open for other people.

2.

You ___should___ wait for people to get off a bus before you get on.

3.

You ___should___ look people in the eyes when you talk to them.

4.

You ___shouldn't___ stare at people.

PAIRS. Are these manners the same in your country? Discuss.

Grammar Notes

1. Use *should* and *should not* to give advice and express opinions.
2. Use the base form of the verb after *should* or *should not*. Use *shouldn't* for negative statements when speaking.
3. To make a *yes / no* question, put *should* before the subject and use the base form of the verb. Use *should* or *shouldn't* in short answers.
4. In information questions, *should* comes after the question word (*when, what,* etc.).
5. For more information about this grammar topic, see page 291.

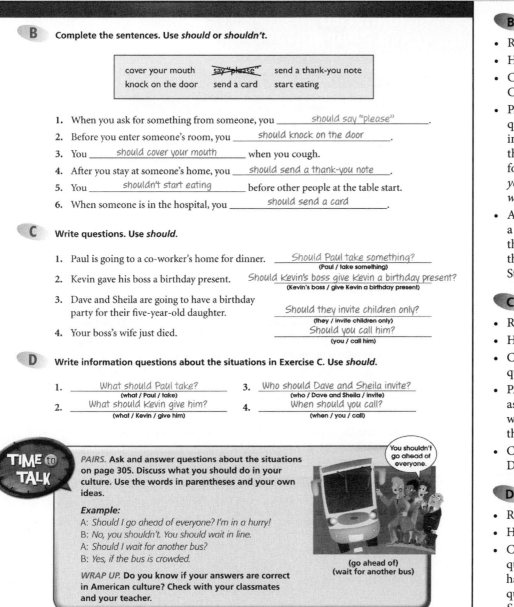

B Complete the sentences. Use *should* or *shouldn't*.

cover your mouth ~~say "please"~~ send a thank-you note
knock on the door send a card start eating

1. When you ask for something from someone, you ___should say "please"___.
2. Before you enter someone's room, you ___should knock on the door___.
3. You ___should cover your mouth___ when you cough.
4. After you stay at someone's home, you ___should send a thank-you note___.
5. You ___shouldn't start eating___ before other people at the table start.
6. When someone is in the hospital, you ___should send a card___.

C Write questions. Use *should*.

1. Paul is going to a co-worker's home for dinner. ___Should Paul take something?___
   (Paul / take something)
2. Kevin gave his boss a birthday present. ___Should Kevin's boss give Kevin a birthday present?___
   (Kevin's boss / give Kevin a birthday present)
3. Dave and Sheila are going to have a birthday party for their five-year-old daughter. ___Should they invite children only?___
   (they / invite children only)
4. Your boss's wife just died. ___Should you call him?___
   (you / call him)

D Write information questions about the situations in Exercise C. Use *should*.

1. ___What should Paul take?___   3. ___Who should Dave and Sheila invite?___
   (what / Paul / take)   (who / Dave and Sheila / invite)
2. ___What should Kevin give him?___   4. ___When should you call?___
   (what / Kevin / give him)   (when / you / call)

TIME to TALK

PAIRS. Ask and answer questions about the situations on page 305. Discuss what you should do in your culture. Use the words in parentheses and your own ideas.

Example:
A: *Should I go ahead of everyone? I'm in a hurry!*
B: *No, you shouldn't. You should wait in line.*
A: *Should I wait for another bus?*
B: *Yes, if the bus is crowded.*

WRAP UP. Do you know if your answers are correct in American culture? Check with your classmates and your teacher.

You shouldn't go ahead of everyone.

(go ahead of)
(wait for another bus)

Manners 201

B Teaching Time: 10–15 min.

- Read the example with the class.
- Have students complete the task.
- Call on students to say answers. Correct as needed.
- PAIRS. Have students ask and answer questions to find out whether the information in the exercise applies to their partner's culture. For example, for sentence 1, students should ask: *In your culture, should you say "please" when you ask someone for something?*
- Ask volunteers to give an example of a difference between their culture and their partner's culture, or between their culture and that of the United States.

C Teaching Time: 10–15 min.

- Read the example with the class.
- Have students complete the task.
- Call on students to read their questions. Correct as needed.
- PAIRS. Have students take turns asking the questions and answering with what would be appropriate in their culture.
- Call on students to give their answers. Discuss cultural differences.

D Teaching Time: 5–10 min.

- Read the example with the class.
- Have students complete the task.
- Call on students to read their questions. Correct as needed. Then have the student who asked the question answer it. For example, say: *So, what do you think? What should Paul take?*
- Discuss any differences of opinion.

Option

Assign Unit 15 Supplementary Grammar to Communicate 1 Exercises on the Teacher's Resource Disk as homework or on the Student Persistence CD-ROM as self-access practice.

TIME to TALK

Teaching Time: 5–10 min.

- Call on two students to read the example.
- PAIRS. Have students complete the task.
- WRAP UP. Have two volunteers ask and answer questions about each picture. Ask other students in the class if they agree with the answer. Ask students if the answer is correct in American culture.

Grammar to Communicate 2

Should (not) + Be + Present Participle

Teaching Time: 5–10 min.

- Have students study the chart and the Look Box.
- Say: *Imagine you are on a bus. You are standing. There are no empty seats. A very old woman gets on the bus. She is having trouble standing. A teenage boy is sitting. You say to him:* (write the following on board)

  You should not (sit). You should (give) your seat to her.

- Ask: *What is the boy doing wrong right now? (He is sitting.) So what verb form should I use with* sit? *(should not be sitting) What is your opinion about what he should do to correct his mistake? What verb form should I use with* give? *(should give)*

- Say: *We use the progressive form—* should (not) + be + verb + ing—*when someone is doing something wrong right now, and we want to say that it is wrong.* (Write: *doing something wrong now* on the board under *You should not be sitting.*)

- Say: *We use the simple form—* should + base form—*when we give someone general advice, or when we state our opinion about what he or she should do in the future.* (Write: *opinion / advice for future / in general* on the board under *You should give your seat to her.*)

A Teaching Time: 10–15 min.

- Have students complete the task.
- Call on students to say answers. Correct as needed

Expansion Have students circle the verbs that are in the progressive form in the exercise. Then have them rewrite the sentences in their notebooks, changing the negative to affirmative and the affirmative to negative. For example: sentence 1: *The child should be eating rice with his fork;* sentence 2: *He shouldn't be standing in front of the other people.*

Grammar to Communicate 2

SHOULD (NOT) + BE + PRESENT PARTICIPLE						
	Should	Be	Present Participle	Should + Not	Be	Present Participle
I You He We They	should	be	standing.	I You He We They	should not shouldn't	be	sitting.

Look

Use *should (not) + be + present participle* when someone is doing something wrong.

A Complete the sentences. Circle the correct answers.

1. The child shouldn't be eating rice with his ____.   a. fork   **b.** fingers
2. Jim arrived after the other people in the line. He should be standing in ____ of the other people.   **a.** back   b. front
3. Ann and Ed are studying. Ann uses Ed's phone without asking him. Ann shouldn't be using Ed's ____.   **a.** phone   b. books
4. There's one bottle of juice for John and his family. John shouldn't be drinking juice from the ____.   **a.** bottle   b. glass
5. Marta is going into a building. A man in a wheelchair is going in at the same time. Marta should be going in ____.   a. first   **b.** second

B What are these people doing wrong? Write sentences with *should* or *shouldn't*.

1. Susan is at dinner with friends. She is eating with her mouth open.
   Susan shouldn't be eating with her mouth open.

2. Tom is eating dinner with his family. He is reading the newspaper.
   He shouldn't be reading the newspaper.

3. Mark is eating chocolate ice cream. He is licking his fingers.
   He shouldn't be licking his fingers.

4. Lucy is with some friends at a movie. She is talking on her cell phone.
   She shouldn't be talking on her cell phone.

5. David is at a wedding. He's wearing jeans.
   He shouldn't be wearing jeans.

202   Unit 15

B Teaching Time: 10–15 min.

- Read the example with the class.
- Have students complete the task.
- Call on students to say answers. Correct as needed.

Grammar Notes

1. Use *should (not) + be +* present participle to give advice and opinions about something happening now. We use the progressive form of *should* when someone is doing something wrong <u>right now</u>.

2. Use *should (not) +* base form of the verb to talk about something that is true all the time. We use this form of *should* to make <u>a general statement</u> expressing our opinion or giving someone advice.

3. Use *should (not) +* base form of the verb to give someone specific advice about <u>the future</u>. Do *not* use the progressive form of *should* for the future.

4. For more information on this grammar topic, see page 291.

C Look at the picture. People are doing things wrong. Write sentences with *should* or *shouldn't*. *Answers will vary.*

1. The man should be waiting. He shouldn't be getting on the bus before the other passengers get off.
2. The man on the sidewalk should be helping the woman with her packages.
3. The children should not be staring at the man in the wheelchair.
4. The people who are running to catch the bus shouldn't be pushing.
5. The man shouldn't be throwing trash out of his car window.
6. The boy should be holding the door for the old man.

TIME to TALK

PAIRS. **Student A:** Act out something that is impolite in your culture.

Student B: Watch your partner. First guess what he or she is doing. Then make a sentence with *should (not) be doing*.

Talk about whether the action is impolite in Student B's culture, too. Then switch roles. Continue until each of you has done three impolite things.

You shouldn't be licking your fingers. It's impolite.

Manners 203

C Teaching Time: 10–15 min.

- Read the example with the class.
- Have students complete the task.
- Call on students to read their sentences. Have them identify which character they are talking about. For example: The man <u>in the car</u> shouldn't be throwing his trash in the street.

Multilevel Strategy

- **Pre-level:** Give students more time to complete Exercise C.
- **At-level, Above-level:** After students finish writing their sentences, have them work in pairs. Tell them to cover the sentences and say what things the people are doing wrong. Then have them uncover the sentences and check their answers.

Expansion Make a transparency of the illustration and project it so that the whole class can see it. Ask a volunteer to come up to the front of the room. Call on students to read their sentences as the volunteer points to the people in the illustration.

Watch Out!

Time to Talk. During the class discussion, students will probably continue to use the progressive form with *should*, for example: *You should never ~~be licking~~ (lick) your fingers in Brazil.*

Remind students that we only use the progressive form with *should* when someone is doing something wrong at the moment.

Option

Assign Unit 15 Supplementary Grammar to Communicate 2 Exercises on the Teacher's Resource Disk as homework or on the Student Persistence CD-ROM as self-access practice.

TIME to TALK

Teaching Time: 10–15 min.

- Read the directions with the class.
- Write the following three questions on the board: *What am I doing wrong? What shouldn't I be doing? What should I be doing?*
- PAIRS. Have students complete the task. Tell them to ask the questions on the board after they act out each impolite thing.
- Ask volunteers to act out something impolite in their culture while the class guesses what it is. Make sure students use the progressive form with *should*.
- Discuss whether or not that action is impolite in other cultures. Make sure students use the simple form of *should*. (See Watch Out!)

Grammar to Communicate 3

Should and Have to

Teaching Time: 5–10 min.

- Have students study the chart.
- Write on the board:

  1. A doctor has to ask patients questions.

  2. A doctor should speak politely.

  3. A doctor doesn't have to go to sick people's homes.

  4. A doctor shouldn't be rude to patients.

  a. But he doesn't have to.

  b. But sometimes he might.

  c. That's his job.

- Ask: *Which sentence can I add a to?* (2)

  Which sentences can I add b to? (3 and 4)

  Which sentence can I add c to? (1)

- Add a, b, and c to the sentences on the board.
- Ask: *Which of the sentences express opinions, but there is a choice?* (2, 3, 4)

  Which sentence is about a situation without a choice? (1)

- Write *no choice* next to 1, and *choice* next to 2, 3, and 4.
- Say: *We use* should / shouldn't *and* don't /doesn't have to *when there is a choice. We use* has / have to *when there is no choice.*

A **Teaching Time: 10–15 min.**

- Have students look at the pictures and read the captions.
- Have students complete the task.
- Call on students to say answers. Correct as needed.
- Call on students to read the sentences one by one. For every sentence, ask: *Does he have a choice?*

B **Teaching Time: 5–10 min.**

- Call on a student to read the examples. Ask: *Is it necessary or just a good idea?* (1 = a good idea; 2 = necessary)
- Say: *If something is necessary, use* has / have to. *If something is a good idea, but not necessary, use* should.

SHOULD AND HAVE TO

Rule	Example
Use *have to / has to* when something is necessary. There isn't any choice.	A doctor has to ask a patient questions.
Use *should* for advice and opinions.	A doctor should speak politely to a patient.
Use *don't have to / doesn't have to* when something is <u>not</u> necessary, but there is a choice.	A doctor doesn't have to go to patients' homes.
Use *shouldn't* for advice and opinions.	A doctor shouldn't be rude to a patient.

A Read the descriptions. What are the jobs? Write *bellhop, cab driver, chauffeur,* or *doorman*.

1. He has to open the door for his boss, and he has to be polite all the time. He doesn't have to do favors for his boss, but he usually does. He shouldn't use the car phone to call his friends. This person is a ____chauffeur____.

2. He doesn't have to open the door for his passengers. He usually opens the door only for elderly passengers. He shouldn't be rude to the passengers, and they shouldn't be rude to him. He has to talk to his passengers at the beginning and end of the ride, but he doesn't have to talk all the time. This person is a ____cab driver____.

doorman

cab driver

bellhop

chauffeur

B Complete the sentences with *has to, have to,* or *should*.

1. Police officers ___should___ have good manners.
2. People who work in expensive hotels ___have to___ have good manners.
3. Young people ___should___ open the door for older people.
4. Ed is a doorman. He ___has to___ open the door for people.
5. Alfred is a bellhop in a hotel. He ___has to___ help people with their bags.
6. You ___should___ carry your mother's bag. It looks heavy.

204 **Unit 15**

- Have students complete the task.
- Call on students to say answers. If they give the wrong answer, ask: *Is it necessary, or is it just a good idea?*
- Have students self-correct.

Grammar Notes

1. Use *should* to say that it is a good idea for someone to do something.

2. Use *has to* or *have to* to say that it is necessary for someone to do something.

3. Use *shouldn't* to say that it is not a good idea for someone to do something.

4. Use *doesn't have to* or *don't have to* to say that it is <u>not</u> necessary for someone to do something.

5. For more information on this grammar topic, see pages 291–292.

C Write sentences. Use *have to*, *don't have to*, *should*, *shouldn't*, and the words in the boxes.
Answers will vary.

Classmates	be polite with each other	have dinner together
Co-workers	buy each other presents	invite each other to their homes
Friends	celebrate holidays together	take care of each other
Relatives	eat lunch together	talk behind each other's backs
	get along with each other	talk to each other every day

1. _Classmates should be polite with each other._
2. _____
3. _____
4. _____
5. _____
6. _____

PAIRS. **Compare sentences.**

Example: A: *Classmates should be polite with each other.*
B: *I agree, but classmates don't have to invite each other to their homes.*

TIME to TALK

GROUPS. **Discuss the statements below. Write *A* if you agree with the statement and *D* if you disagree.**

____ 1. If you call your friend's house and his mother answers, you should talk to her for a few minutes before you ask to speak to your friend.

____ 2. If you see an elderly woman who is trying to cross the street, you have to help her.

____ 3. Children have to be quiet at the dinner table.

____ 4. Children have to ask for permission to leave the table.

____ 5. If you are invited to someone's house, you shouldn't arrive early.

____ 6. If you are eating at someone's house and you do not want any more food, you should say "No, thank you. I'm full."

____ 7. When you invite people to dinner, you should ask the guests if there is anything that they don't like to eat.

____ 8. When you are invited to someone's house for dinner, you don't have to bring anything.

WRAP UP. **Now discuss your opinions with the class.**

Manners 205

C Teaching Time: 10–15 min.

- Read the example with the class.
- Have students complete the task.
- PAIRS. Have students compare sentences.
- Call on students to read their sentences. Discuss differences of opinion. If students disagree about a sentence, have them explain their answers.

Teaching Tip

Time to Talk. Make sure that students rephrase the statements in a way that truly expresses their meaning. You can ask a series of questions to check comprehension of the slight but important differences in meaning between *should (not)* and *(not) have to*. Ask questions such as: *Is that your personal opinion, or is it the rule in your country? Do you have a choice about it in your culture?*

Option

Assign Unit 15 Supplementary Grammar to Communicate 3 Exercises on the Teacher's Resource Disk as homework or on the Student Persistence CD-ROM as self-access practice.

TIME to TALK

Teaching Time: 10–15 min.

- Read the directions. Explain that if students disagree with the statement, they should change it so that it expresses their cultural or personal beliefs. Say: *For example, for statement 1, an American might say:*
(write the following on the board) *In my culture, you don't have to talk to your friend's mother for a few minutes. Nobody does. You just say your name and ask if your friend is at home.*
Someone from Ecuador, on the other hand, might say:
(write the following on the board) *In my culture, you have to talk to your friend's mother for a few minutes. If you don't, she won't let you be friends anymore.*
- GROUPS. Have students take turns reading the sentences aloud. If they disagree, have them change the statement to reflect their opinion. Walk around and help as needed.
- WRAP UP. Call on students to give their opinions. Correct grammar as needed.

Grammar

Teaching Time: 5–10 min.

- Read the example with the class.
- Have students complete the task.
- 🎧 Play Track 6 while students listen and check their answers.
- Call on three students to read the conversation aloud. Correct as needed.

Expansion Start a discussion about cell phone use in public. Ask: *Have you ever asked someone to stop talking on his or her cell phone? If so, what was the situation? Has anyone ever asked you to stop talking on your cell phone? What was the situation? In your opinion, where is it appropriate to use a cell phone? Where isn't it appropriate?*

Dictation

Teaching Time: 5–10 min.

- 🎧 Play Track 7 while students listen and write what they hear.
- 🎧 Play Track 7 again while students check their answers.
- PAIRS. Have students compare dictations. If there are any differences, they should decide who has the correct answer.
- Call on students to read the dictated sentences aloud. Write exactly what you hear. Ask them to spell the new vocabulary.
- 🎧 Play Track 7 again and correct the sentences on the board.

Multilevel Strategy

Pre-level: Have pre-level students work together. While the other students are comparing dictations, give them a copy of the audioscript. Have them correct their mistakes.

Speaking

Teaching Time: 10–15 min.

- Call on two students to read the example.
- PAIRS. Have students complete

Review and Challenge

Grammar

🎧 **6** **Correct the conversation. There are seven mistakes. The first mistake is corrected for you. Then listen and check your answers.**

Lori: Listen to that woman with the cell phone. She shouldn't be ~~talk~~ *talking* on her cell phone here. You should be ~~telling~~ *tell* her.

Kirk: What ~~I should~~ *should I* say?

Lori: You should say, "Stop talking on your cell phone."

Kirk: That's not very polite. I don't think I should ~~to be~~ *be* rude because she's rude.

Lori: Sometimes you have ~~be~~ *to* be rude to people. They don't listen if you're polite.

Kirk: I don't agree. Watch. Excuse me?

Stranger: What?

Kirk: I'm sorry, but you really ~~don't have to~~ *shouldn't* be using your cell phone here.

Stranger: And you ~~should not interrupting~~ *shouldn't interrupt* other people's conversations.

Dictation

🎧 **7** **Listen. You will hear five sentences. Write them in your notebook.** *See the audioscript on p. 323 for the sentences.*

Speaking

PAIRS. **Choose one set of sentences. Make two short conversations, one for each sentence in the set. Then act out one of your conversations for the class.**

1. You don't have to stand up.
   You shouldn't be standing up.

2. You don't have to talk to her.
   You shouldn't talk behind her back.

Example:
A: *Thank you, but you don't have to stand up. I can stand.*
B: *Are you sure?*
A: *Yes, of course.*

3. You don't have to tell the teacher.
   You shouldn't tell the teacher.

4. You don't have to do her a favor.
   You shouldn't do her a favor.

A: *Here's a seat, Mom.*
B: *That's okay. I'll stand.*
A: *Come on, you shouldn't be standing up. You just had an operation.*

---

the task. Make sure they understand that they need to make two different conversations.

- Call on students to role-play their conversations for the class.

Multilevel Strategy

All levels: Pair pre-level students with at-level and above-level students for this task. The more advanced students can help the others.

Listening

 A **Listen to the report. Put the topics in the order in which you hear them in the report. Be careful. There are two extra topics.**

body language	conversation	how to eat	what to wear
children's behavior	food	~~seating~~	

Topic 1: _seating_   Topic 4: _conversation_

Topic 2: _how to eat_   Topic 5: _food_

Topic 3: _body language_

B **Listen again. Write the number of the correct topic from Exercise A next to each question.**

1. Which utensils should you use?   Topic _2_
2. Do men and women eat together, or do they have to sit in separate rooms?   Topic _1_
3. Do you have to eat everything on your plate?   Topic _5_
4. Which topics should you discuss? Which topics shouldn't you discuss?   Topic _4_
5. Where should guests sit at the table?   Topic _1_
6. What should you do if you don't like something?   Topic _5_
7. What should you do with your legs?   Topic _3_

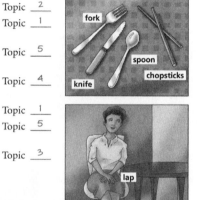

TIME to TALK

GROUPS. Ask and answer questions about table manners in your countries. Talk about differences between manners at home and manners at a restaurant or at someone else's house.

Example:
A: In your country, do you have to eat everything on your plate?
B: No, you don't. In fact, if you are invited to someone's house, you should leave a little food on your plate. Then the host will know that you are full.

WRAP UP. Now tell the class about the most interesting thing that you learned.

Manners   207

Listening

A   **Teaching Time: 5–10 min.**

- **Warm-up.** Have students look at the word box and the pictures in Exercise B. Then ask them to guess what the topic of the listening will be. Write their guesses on the board.
- Play Track 8 as students listen and complete the task.
- Play Track 8 again as students check their answers. Pause the recording after each topic, and have students call out the topic.
- Point to students' guesses on the board. Did they guess correctly?

B   **Teaching Time: 5–10 min.**

- Have students complete the task.
- Play Track 8 while students listen and check their answers.
- Call on students to say answers.

Multilevel Strategy

Pre-level: After students have completed Exercise A, give them a copy of the audioscript to read as they complete Exercise B.

Option

Assign Unit 15 Review and Challenge Supplementary Exercises on the Teacher's Resource Disk as homework or on the Student Persistence CD-ROM as self-access practice.

TIME to TALK

Teaching Time: 10–15 min.

- Call on two students to read the example.
- GROUPS. Have students complete the task.
- WRAP UP. Have someone from each group tell you the most interesting thing that they learned.

Expansion Write the names of the students' countries on the board in a simple table. Fill in the table with the rules the students tell you about. Ask students from each country if the rule is the same in their countries. Check the columns.

Reading

Getting Ready to Read

Teaching Time: 5–10 min.

- **Warm-up:** Have students look at the picture. Ask: *What is happening? How does the man feel? Why does he feel that way?*
- Have students complete the task.
- Ask a volunteer to tell you the definition of *etiquette*. Write it on the board. Leave it on the board as the students read the article.

Reading

Teaching Time: 15–20 min.

- Have students read the article.
- Read the definition on the board aloud. Ask students if it is correct. If not, have them correct it.

Getting Ready to Read

Preview the article. Look at the title and the picture and read the first paragraph. What do you think *etiquette* means? Write a definition.

etiquette = ___polite behavior, good manners___

Reading

Read the article. Then check your answer to Getting Ready to Read.

INTERNATIONAL BUSINESS ETIQUETTE

Like social manners, business **etiquette** differs from country to country. Sometimes the rules change only a little, but even small differences can result in a serious **misunderstanding**. Fortunately, there are a lot of books and information on the Internet to help businesspeople **avoid** cultural misunderstandings. If you do business with people from another culture, you should not expect them to understand your culture; instead, you have to learn about their culture and be ready to **adapt** to it.

In American culture, for example, business **colleagues** usually shake hands to **greet** each other. However, they do not always shake hands to say goodbye. In contrast, in many other countries, such as Colombia and Turkey, you must shake hands to both greet and say goodbye to colleagues. If you do not, people will think you are rude.

Let's look at another example. In the United States, if a business colleague invites you out for a meal, you should never try to pay. Everyone understands that the person who invited the other person, male or female, must pay. In the Philippines, however, a businesswoman should never pay the bill for a male colleague. If she does, it might **destroy** their business relationship.

Of course, if your foreign business colleagues are familiar with your culture, they might understand and **excuse** your behavior. However, you should never **assume** that others have such cultural knowledge, because you might be wrong. And you do not want your business colleagues to think that you are rude, or even worse, to imagine that you are trying to **insult** them. In conclusion, you should always learn the cultural rules of your foreign colleagues. It's just good business sense.

After You Read

A Find the **boldface** words in the article that have similar meanings to the words below.

1. say bad things about someone _insult_
2. keep away from _avoid_
3. think that something is true _assume_
4. change your behavior to fit a new situation _adapt_
5. forgive _excuse_
6. co-workers _colleagues_
7. when you can't understand something or someone _misunderstanding_
8. say hello to and welcome someone _greet_
9. manners _etiquette_
10. damage something so badly that it does not exist anymore _destroy_

B Read the article again. Write three supporting details from the article. Look for the words ***example*** and ***such as***. Wording of answers may vary.

1. In American culture, for example, business colleagues usually shake hands to greet each other.
2. In other countries, such as Colombia and Turkey, you must shake hands to both greet and say goodbye.
3. Let's look at another example. In the United States, if a business colleague invites you out, you should never try to pay.

Reading Skill: Recognizing Supporting Details

Writers use **supporting details** to give more information about the main idea. When you read, look for words like *example* and *such as*. These words are used to give examples that support the main idea.

After You Read

A Teaching Time: 10–15 min.

- Read the example with the class.
- Have students complete the task. Tell them to check their answers by replacing the word in the article with the answer they have chosen. (See page 153 in this book for an explanation of the procedure.)
- Call on students to say answers. As they give the answers, have them read the sentences from the article, replacing the words in boldface with the words from Exercise A.

B Teaching Time: 10–15 min.

- Call on a student to read the information in the Reading Skill box.
- Have students reread the article. Tell them to underline phrases or sentences that contain examples. Then have them complete the task.
- Call on students to read their answers.

Multilevel Strategy

- **Pre-level, At-level:** Give students more time to read the article and complete the exercises.
- **Above-level:** After students have completed the reading and After You Read exercises, put them in pairs. Have them practice orally summarizing the article without looking back at the text. Then have them discuss the examples in the article, comparing the cultures mentioned to their own. Walk around and provide help and feedback. After you have gone over the answers to Exercises A and B with the class, call on a student to orally summarize the article from memory.

Writing

Getting Ready to Write

A   Teaching Time: 10–15 min.

- Have students study the Writing Tip.
- Have students complete the task.
- Call on students to read answers. Correct as needed.

B   Teaching Time: 10–15 min.

- Have students read the model paragraph. As they read, have them underline the supporting details.
- PAIRS. Have students complete the task.

Writing

Getting Ready to Write

A 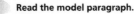 Read the sentences from a paragraph. Check (✓) the supporting details.

✓ 1. For example, Germans will be insulted if you do not use their titles.

☐ 2. In the U.S., you do not always have to use titles.

☐ 3. To sum up, you have to learn the appropriate language to use with businesspeople from other countries.

☐ 4. American businesspeople are generally less formal than businesspeople from most other countries.

✓ 5. In fact, in Japan, you must never call your colleagues by their first names.

☐ 6. The language of business can be formal or informal, depending on the country.

B Read the model paragraph.

> Both Chinese and American businesspeople like to have business dinners. However, polite behavior at a Chinese business dinner is not the same as polite behavior at an American business dinner. For example, <u>in China, business dinners usually have 20 or 30 courses. You should always taste a little bit of each dish</u>. But at the end of the meal, <u>you have to leave a little food on your plate</u>. In fact, <u>if you don't, the host will think that he did not order enough food</u>. In the United States, in contrast, <u>business dinners usually have only two or three courses</u>. You should <u>finish all the food on your plate</u> because this shows that you liked the food. To sum up, if someone invites you to a business dinner in China or the United States, you should remember these important rules of etiquette.

PAIRS. **Read the model again. According to the writer, what are the differences in business etiquette in China and the United States? Why are they important?**

Wording of answers may vary.

Now think about your country. Talk about business etiquette in your country. You can talk about appointments, clothes, giving gifts, or your own ideas.

Prewriting: Using an Outline

You are going to write a paragraph about some aspect of business etiquette in your country. Before you write, complete the outline with notes about your topic.

Writing Model

Main Idea: Polite behavior at a Chinese business dinner is not the same as polite behavior at an American business dinner.

Supporting Details:

1. China—business dinners usually have 20 or 30 courses

2. If you don't leave food, host will think he didn't order enough

3. U.S.—business dinners usually have only one or two courses. Should finish all the food—shows you liked it

Concluding Sentence: To sum up, if someone invites you to a business dinner in China or the U.S., remember etiquette rules.

Main Idea:

Supporting Details:

1.

2.

3.

Concluding Sentence:

Writing

Now write a paragraph about an aspect of business etiquette in your country. The writing tip, the model paragraph, and your notes will help you. Write in your notebook.

Manners 211

Prewriting

Teaching Time: 15–20 min.

- Have students read through the notes.
- Have students complete the task.
- PAIRS. Have students show a partner their notes. If the partner doesn't understand something in the notes, tell him or her to ask for clarification.

Writing

Teaching Time: 15–20 min.

Have students complete the task. Remind them to include examples to support their main idea.

Option

If your students do not have any experience in business, give them the option of writing about general rules of etiquette in their culture. For example, they could write about appropriate gifts for different occasions, or appropriate greetings.

Unit 16
Neighbors

Learning Goals

- Learn vocabulary to describe neighbors
- Learn how to use *must + verb*; *must + be + present participle*; and *must not* and *can't* for logical conclusions
- Listen to a conversation between neighbors and to a radio talk show about problems between neighbors
- Read an article about homelessness and write a paragraph about a problem in a community or country
- Talk about the causes of homelessness and some possible solutions
- Talk about relationships between neighbors

Learner Persistence

Encourage students to get tutoring.

Warm-up

Teaching Time: 3–5 min.

- Have students look at the picture.
- Ask: *Would you like to live in this neighborhood? Why or why not?*

Vocabulary

Teaching Time: 10–15 min.

- Read the example with the class.
- Have students complete the task.
- 🎧 Play Track 9 while students listen and check their answers.
- Read the words in the box aloud and have students repeat chorally as they point to the numbers in the picture.

Expansion

- Write on the board:
  Actions   People   Places   Things
- PAIRS. Have students copy the headings in their notebooks. Tell them to write the words from the box in the correct columns.
- Call on students to tell you under which heading to write each word. (Actions: *bark, chat, slam the door, shout*; People: *gardener, musician*; Places: *driveway, garden, yard*; Things: *junk*)

Vocabulary

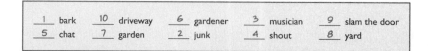

🎧 CD3 TRACK 9 **Match the numbers with the words. Then listen and check your answers.**

_1_ bark	_10_ driveway	_6_ gardener	_3_ musician	_9_ slam the door
_5_ chat	_7_ garden	_2_ junk	_4_ shout	_8_ yard

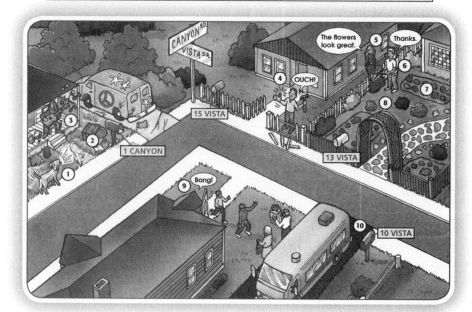

212   Unit 16

Listening

Listening

A **10** Listen. Ann and Bob live in a large apartment building. Check (✓) the correct statement.

- ☑ **1.** The man has been away for a month and wants to know about his neighbors.
- ❑ **2.** The woman is not very interested in her neighbors' lives, but the man is.
- ❑ **3.** The man and the woman don't like their neighbors very much.
- ❑ **4.** The man and the woman are not very interested in their neighbors' lives.

B **10** Listen again. Who said it? Write *B* (Bob) or *A* (Ann).

- _A_ **1.** You must be tired.
- _A_ **2.** She must be doing well at work.
- _A_ **3.** She must not be very happy about that.
- _B_ **4.** But they can't be getting along.
- _A_ **5.** He must be at his mother's.
- _B_ **6.** She can't be staying with Mrs. O'Hara.
- _A_ **7.** She can't be alone!

C **10** Listen again. Write *T* (true) or *F* (false). If the statement is false, correct it to make it true.

- _F_ **1.** Bob's grandchildren were visiting him.   Bob was visiting his grandchildren.
- _F_ **2.** Emily Rose is doing well at her job.   Emily Rose lost her job last week.
- _F_ **3.** Roberta was wearing a new suit.   Emily Rose was wearing a new suit.
- _T_ **4.** Roberta and Andy are fighting.
- _F_ **5.** Andy is staying at his mother's house.   Andy is staying with his brother.
- _F_ **6.** Mr. and Mrs. Russel are on vacation with Mrs. O'Hara.   Mrs. O'Hara is visiting her son.
- _F_ **7.** The Russels' daughter is alone in the apartment.   The Russels' daughter isn't alone.
- _T_ **8.** Sarah's grandmother has a car.

Neighbors **213**

Language Note

Exercise C.

- The final time you play the conversation, pause it after "And speaking of unhappy . . ."
- Say: *We use the expression* and speaking of *in a conversation when we want to introduce a new topic by connecting it to a previous topic. Bob introduced a new topic—a different neighbor, Roberta. The connection to the previous topic is the word* unhappy.

Option

Assign Unit 16 Supplementary Vocabulary Exercises on the Teacher's Resource Disk as homework or on the Student Persistence CD-ROM as self-access practice.

Listening

A **Teaching Time: 10–15 min.**

- **Warm-up.** Tell students that they are going to listen to a conversation between two neighbors. Start a discussion about neighbors. Ask: *Do you know your neighbors? How well do you know them? Do you know their names? How often do you talk to them? Are you friends with any of them?*
- Have students read the answer choices.
- 🎧 Play Track 10 as students listen and complete the task.
- Call on a student to say the answer. Play the conversation again if necessary.

B **Teaching Time: 10–15 min.**

- Have students read the sentences.
- 🎧 Play Track 10 as students listen and complete the task.
- Call on students to say answers.
- 🎧 Play Track 10 again, this time pausing the recording after each answer is given. Confirm the answers students gave previously.

Multilevel Strategy

Pre-level: Make photocopies of the audioscript, but blank out the names of the speakers (*Bob* and *Ann*). Give the audioscript to students after they have completed Exercise A. Tell them to read along as they listen. Allow them to use the audioscript to complete Exercises B and C.

C **Teaching Time: 10–15 min.**

- Read the example with the class.
- Have students complete the task before listening again. If they are not sure of an answer, tell them to write a question mark (?).
- 🎧 Play Track 10 as students listen and check their answers.
- Call on students to say answers.
- 🎧 Play Track 10 again, pausing the recording as each answer is given. Confirm the answers students gave previously.

Grammar to Communicate 1

Must + Verb

Teaching Time: 10–15 min.

- Have students study the chart and the Look Box.
- Say: *We use* must *+ verb for logical conclusions. A logical conclusion is something that we decide after we consider all the information we have. For example, imagine a new student comes into the class right now. The student has never met me before, so he doesn't know who I am. However, he will probably make a logical conclusion that I am the teacher. Why? Because of the information he has: I'm standing in front of the class; the students are listening and taking notes; I'm speaking English; I'm dressed like a teacher. He doesn't <u>know</u> that I'm the teacher because we have not been introduced yet, but he's 95 percent sure. He thinks to himself:* (write on board) *She must be the teacher.* (Write *logical conclusion* under the sentence.)
- Explain the difference between *must* of logical conclusion and *must* of necessity: *Don't confuse this meaning of* must *with* must *of necessity. For example:* (write on board) *Students must respect their teachers. In this sentence,* must respect *is not a logical conclusion. It means necessity. The students do not have a choice.* (Write *necessity / no choice* under the sentence.)
- Write the examples from the chart on the board:
  The house has a big garden. You must like flowers.
  People are wearing heavy coats. It must be cold out.
- Point to the first example on the board and ask: *Have I told you that I like flowers?* (No, you haven't.) *Why do you think that I like flowers?* (Because your house has a big garden.)
- Point to the second example on the board and ask: *Have I been out?* (No.) *Why do I think that it's cold out?* (Because you can see that people are wearing heavy coats. People usually wear heavy coats when it is cold out.)

Grammar to Communicate 1

MUST + VERB			
Fact	**Logical Conclusion**		
	Subject	*Must*	Verb
The house has a big garden.	You She They	must	like	flowers.
People are wearing heavy coats.	It	must	be	cold out.

Look

Use *must* when you are 95 percent sure that something is true. Do not use *must* if you <u>know</u> that something is true.
My neighbor is a teacher. He told me.
NOT My neighbor ~~must be~~ a teacher. He told me.

A   Match the sentences.

   _d_   1. The woman next door has a beautiful garden.
   _b_   2. The old people on the other side never have visitors.
   _e_   3. The man on the corner is always fixing things.
   _c_   4. The neighbors around the corner have four cats.
   _a_   5. The man across the street has a lot of parties.

   a. He must have a lot of friends.
   b. Their family must live far away.
   c. They must like animals.
   d. She must be a good gardener.
   e. He must be good with his hands.

Look

good with his hands = to be good at fixing or building things

B   🎵 TRACK 11   Complete the answers with *must*. Then listen and check your answers.

1. **A:** Do the people across the street have a lot of visitors?
   B: ___They must have___ a lot of visitors. There are always cars in front of their house.

2. **A:** Does Mrs. Cho like children?
   B: ___She must like them___ them. She babysits all the time.

3. **A:** Is that house empty?
   B: ___It must be___ empty. There's never anyone there.

4. **A:** Does John know his neighbors' names?
   B: ___He must know___ their names. He talks to them all the time.

5. **A:** Does that woman live near here?
   B: ___She must live___ around here. I see her on the bus all the time.

6. **A:** Are Vic and Cindy at home?
   B: ___They must be___ there. Their car is in the driveway.

A   Teaching Time: 5–10 min.

- Read the example with the class. Point out that the sentences on the left are facts, and the sentences on the right are logical conclusions based on those facts.
- Have students complete the task.
- Call on students to say answers. Correct as needed.

B   Teaching Time: 10–15 min.

- Read the example with the class. Ask: *What are the facts?* (There are always cars in front of their house.)
- Have students complete the task.
- 🎧 Play Track 11 while students listen and check their answers.

Grammar Notes

1. Use *must* when you are 95 percent sure that something is true, but you are not 100 percent sure.
2. Do not use *must* when you are 100 percent sure.
3. Use *may* or *might* when you are less than 50 percent sure that something is true. You don't really know. You are just guessing.
4. *Must* also means *necessary*.
5. For more information about this grammar topic, see page 292.

Barbara and Don are going to buy a home. They're looking in different neighborhoods. Write sentences about the people who live in the homes. *Answers may vary.*

1. (be) _They must be_ _doctors._

2. (have) _They must_ _have children._

3. (be) _They must_ _be rich._

4. (have) _They must_ _have a dog._

5. (like) _They must_ _like the color yellow._

6. (love) _They must_ _love gardening._

PAIRS. **Which neighbors would you like to have? Why?**

TIME to TALK

PAIRS. **Read the logical conclusions. Then think of a fact each conclusion could be based on.**

Fact	Logical Conclusion
1. _She is always carrying a guitar._	Your neighbor must be a musician.
2. _____	The man next door must love dogs.
3. _____	Your landlord must be single.
4. _____	The woman next door must be a good cook.

Now, read the facts and think of a logical conclusion you could make based on each fact.

5. Her phone rings all the time. _____

6. His TV is always very loud. _____

7. They have a party every weekend. _____

8. She never has any visitors. _____

Neighbors **215**

C **Teaching Time: 10–15 min.**

- Read the directions and the example with the class. Ask: *Why do you think they are doctors? What are the facts?* (The cars in the driveway have license plates with MD. MD = doctor)
- Have students complete the task.
- Call on students to say answers. Have them tell you why they made that logical conclusion. Ask: *What are the facts?* Correct as needed.
- PAIRS. Have students complete the task.
- Call on a few students to say which neighbors they would like to have and why. Then ask the class: *Is there anyone you wouldn't want to have as a neighbor? Why not?*

Expansion Have one student in each pair give facts about his or her real neighbors. The other student makes logical conclusions based on the facts. The first student says whether the logical conclusions are correct or not. Then they switch roles. For example:

A: *My neighbor sleeps all day. She goes out at night.*

B: *She must work the night shift.*

A: *Yes, that's right. She works the night shift at the hospital. She's a nurse.*

Option

Assign Unit 16 Supplementary Grammar to Communicate 1 Exercises on the Teacher's Resource Disk as homework or on the Student Persistence CD-ROM as self-access practice.

TIME to TALK

Teaching Time: 10–15 min.

- Read the directions and the example with the class.
- PAIRS. Have students complete the task.
- Call on students to read their answers. Correct as needed.

Multilevel Strategy

- **All-levels:** Pair pre-level students with at-level and above-level students for this task. The more advanced students can help the others.

Unit 16 **T-215**

Grammar to Communicate 2

Must + *Be* + Present Participle

Teaching Time: 5–10 min.

- Have students study the chart and the Look Box.
- Write on the board: *He is standing at the bus stop. He must be waiting for the bus.*
- Point to the sentence on the board and say: *We use* must + be + verb + ing *when we make a logical conclusion about something that is happening right now.*
- Ask: *Why do we think that he is waiting for the bus? What are the facts?* (He is standing at the bus stop.) *Do we* know *that he is waiting for the bus?* (No, we don't, but we are 95 percent sure.)

A   Teaching Time: 10–15 min.

- Read the example. Point out that the facts are in the speech bubbles.
- Have students complete the task.
- Call on students to say answers. Correct as needed.

B   Teaching Time: 10–15 min.

- Call on two students to read the example. Ask: *What is the logical conclusion?* (Billy Johnson must be crying.) *What are the facts that the logical conclusion is based on?* (Your neighbors have kids; one of them cries a lot.)
- Have students complete the task. Remind them to use *must* + *be* + verb + *ing* because the actions are happening now.
- 🎧 Play Track 12 as students listen and check their answers.
- Call on students to say answers. For each item, ask them to identify the logical conclusion and the facts that it is based on. Correct as needed.
- PAIRS. Have students practice reading the conversations.

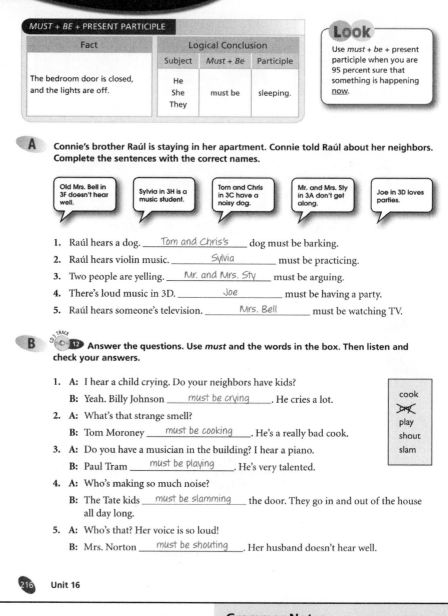

Grammar Notes

1. Use *must* + *be* + present participle when you are 95 percent sure that something is happening, but you are not 100 percent sure.
2. Do not use *must* + *be* + present participle when you are 100 percent sure that something is happening.
3. Do not use *must* + *be* + present participle with stative verbs. Use the simple form: *must* + base form.
4. For more information on this grammar topic, see page 292.

C 🎧 **TRACK 13** Lois and Ed are talking about Ed's neighbors. Complete the conversation. Use *must* and the correct form of the verbs in the box. Then listen and check your answers.

be sick	go to work	~~look for her keys~~	visit her mother
fight	~~have a new boyfriend~~	sell	

Lois: A woman across the street is taking everything out of her bag.

Ed: Oh, Linda ___must be looking for her keys___.
1.
She always loses them.

Lois: And the college student is holding hands with a good-looking young man.

Ed: Katie ___must have a new boyfriend___. Her
2.
last boyfriend wasn't good-looking at all.

Lois: A police officer is coming out of the house next door.

Ed: Oh, that's Officer Timmons. He lives there. He ___must be going to work___.
3.

Lois: Your next-door neighbors aren't home.

Ed: Mia and Tom ___must be visiting her mother___. They see her every Monday.
4.

Lois: Some little girls in green uniforms are going from house to house.

Ed: They ___must be selling___ Girl Scout cookies. They always come
5.
in the spring.

Lois: A nurse is going into the small yellow house.

Ed: Mr. Romero ___must be sick___.
6.

Lois: Two people are going into the green house. They look very angry.

Ed: Tim and Ann ___must be fighting___. They are not a happy couple
7.
these days.

Look

Stative verbs do not take *-ing*.
He must have a dog.
NOT He must be having a dog.
She must be tired.
NOT She must be being tired.
See page 298 for a list of stative verbs.

TIME to TALK

PAIRS. Look at the picture of the neighborhood on page 212. Make logical conclusions about the people you see in the picture.

Example:
The people at 10 Vista Drive must be visiting their grandchildren.

WRAP UP. Now share some of your sentences with the class. Did other students make the same conclusions?

Neighbors **217**

C **Teaching Time: 10–15 min.**

- Have students study the Look Box.
- Ask students for other examples of stative verbs (verbs that cannot take *–ing*). Write them on the board. Have students look at page 298 in their books for a list of common stative verbs.
- Call on two students to read the example. Then write the word *nosy* on the board. Say: *Ed and Lois are nosy. Who can tell me what nosy means?* If no one answers, ask: *How does Ed know so much about his neighbors? Do you think he watches his neighbors a lot or a little?* (*a lot*) Say: *A nosy person is someone who puts his or her "nose" in other people's business.* Ask: *Do any of you have nosy neighbors?*
- Have students complete the task.
- 🎧 Play Track 13 as students listen and correct their answers.
- Ask two volunteers to act out the parts of Ed and Lois.

Option

Assign Unit 16 Supplementary Grammar to Communicate 2 Exercises on the Teacher's Resource Disk as homework or on the Student Persistence CD-ROM as self-access practice.

TIME to TALK

Teaching Time: 10–15 min.

- Have a student read the example while the other students look at the picture.
- PAIRS. Have students complete the task.
- WRAP UP. Ask volunteers to write their conclusions on the board. Have them state the facts that they based their conclusions on. Correct as needed.

Expansion Make a transparency of the illustration and project it so that the whole class can see it as they complete the exercise. When students write their sentences on the board for the Wrap Up, instruct them NOT to write the address of the people they are making logical conclusions about. After they've written their sentences on the board, ask a volunteer to come up to the front of the room. Tell the volunteer to read the sentences and point to the people in the pictures.

Grammar to Communicate 3

Must not and *Can't*

Teaching Time: 10–15 min.

- Have students study the chart and the Look Box.
- Write on the board:

  Fact

  1. Rita and Bert don't live together.

  Logical Conclusion

  They must not be married.

- Ask: *Are you sure that they aren't married?* (No.) Say: *They might be married, but they probably aren't, because most married couples live together.*
- Write on the board:

  A: Rita and Bert must be married. They are together all the time, and she wears a wedding ring.

  B: But Rita and Bert can't be married! Bert told me that his wife's name is Lou.

- Say: *We often use* can't *when we are correcting someone else. For example, in this example, A makes a logical conclusion. B corrects A, saying that A's logical conclusion is incorrect. Then B gives another fact to show that A's logical conclusion is impossible.*
- To explain the difference between *can't be* and *aren't,* use the following example. Write on the board:

  A: Rita and Bert <u>can't be</u> married. Bert is married to a woman named Lou.

  B: Rita and Bert <u>aren't</u> married. Bert is married to Lou.

- Say: *Now let's look at the difference between* can't *and* aren't. *In the first example, A is sure that Rita and Lou are two different people, so A concludes that it is impossible for Bert to be married to Rita. However, A hasn't actually met Lou. There is a very small chance that Rita and Lou are the same person.* (Write *logical conclusion* under *can't be.* Write *fact* under *is married to a woman named Lou.*)
- Say: *In the second example, B has met both Rita and Lou, and knows that they are two different people. That is a fact. It is also a fact that Bert isn't married to Rita.* (Write *fact* under *aren't married* and *is married to Lou.*)

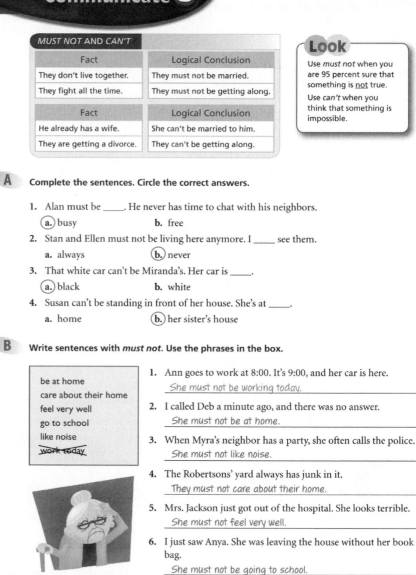

Grammar to Communicate 3

MUST NOT AND CAN'T	
Fact	**Logical Conclusion**
They don't live together.	They must not be married.
They fight all the time.	They must not be getting along.

Fact	**Logical Conclusion**
He already has a wife.	She can't be married to him.
They are getting a divorce.	They can't be getting along.

Look

Use *must not* when you are 95 percent sure that something is <u>not</u> true.

Use *can't* when you think that something is impossible.

A Complete the sentences. Circle the correct answers.

1. Alan must be _____. He never has time to chat with his neighbors.
   - (a.) busy
   - b. free
2. Stan and Ellen must not be living here anymore. I _____ see them.
   - a. always
   - (b.) never
3. That white car can't be Miranda's. Her car is _____.
   - (a.) black
   - b. white
4. Susan can't be standing in front of her house. She's at _____.
   - a. home
   - (b.) her sister's house

B Write sentences with *must not*. Use the phrases in the box.

be at home
care about their home
feel very well
go to school
like noise
~~work today~~

1. Ann goes to work at 8:00. It's 9:00, and her car is here.
   She must not be working today.
2. I called Deb a minute ago, and there was no answer.
   She must not be at home.
3. When Myra's neighbor has a party, she often calls the police.
   She must not like noise.
4. The Robertsons' yard always has junk in it.
   They must not care about their home.
5. Mrs. Jackson just got out of the hospital. She looks terrible.
   She must not feel very well.
6. I just saw Anya. She was leaving the house without her book bag.
   She must not be going to school.

218 Unit 16

A Teaching Time: 5–10 min.

- Have students complete the task.
- Call on students to say answers. Correct as needed.

B Teaching Time: 5–10 min.

- Read the example with the class.
- Have students complete the task.
- Call on students to say answers. Correct as needed.

Grammar Notes

1. Use *must not* when you are 95 percent sure that something is not true, but you are *not* 100 percent sure.
2. Use *can't* when you <u>think</u> that something is impossible. In fact, it might be possible, but you think that it is impossible.
3. We also say *couldn't* when we think that something is impossible.
4. Use *be* + present participle with *must not, can't,* or *couldn't* when you are making a logical conclusion about something that is <u>not</u> happening right now.
5. For more information on this grammar topic, see page 292.

C Joe and Ann are talking about their neighbors. Ann thinks that Joe's conclusions are wrong. Match Ann's statements and Joe's conclusions.

Ann says . . .

<u>d</u> 1. Your neighbors must be angry with you.

<u>f</u> 2. Mrs. Lee next door must be moving.

<u>a</u> 3. Mrs. Jones must be pregnant.

<u>c</u> 4. Their grandchildren must be visiting.

<u>b</u> 5. Sue in 1A must be having a party.

<u>e</u> 6. That must be his girlfriend.

Joe's conclusions . . .

a. She can't be. She's 50 years old!

b. She can't be. She's on vacation.

c. They can't be. It's not school vacation.

d. They can't be. I'm an excellent neighbor.

e. She can't be. He's married.

f. She can't be. She loves it here.

D 🎵 **14** Complete the conversations. Use *can't*, *must not*, or *must*. Then listen and check your answers.

1. **A:** Sue and Dave have the same last name. They ___*must*___ be married.

   B: They ___*can't*___ be married. Sue's husband's name is Brad. Dave ___*must*___ be her brother.

2. **A:** Oh look, there's Lena's dog.

   B: That ___*can't*___ be Lena's dog. Her dog died. That ___*must*___ be her son's dog.

3. **A:** Adam's not here. He ___*must*___ be out running.

   B: He ___*can't*___ be running. His running shoes are right here.

4. **A:** The new neighbors ___*must*___ love pink. Even their house is pink.

   B: Annie Sullivan across the street ___*must not*___ be very happy! She hates pink.

TIME to TALK

PAIRS. **You live in the same building. Make conversations about your neighbors from the situations below. Make as many conclusions as you can with** *must*, *mustn't*, **and** *can't*.

Jill isn't paying rent on time.	Pete has a lot of boxes in his apartment.
Luz is going to lose her job.	Sam is working a lot of late nights.
Ms. Yu has stayed home for 3 days.	The Bradys are fighting a lot.

Example:
A: *The Bradys are fighting a lot. They must be getting a divorce.*
B: *They can't be getting a divorce. They've been married for 20 years. They must be going through hard times.*

Neighbors 219

C Teaching Time: 5–10 min.

- Call on two students to read the example.
- Have students complete the task.
- Call on two students to read the matching sentences. Correct as needed.

D Teaching Time: 5–10 min.

- Call on two students to read the example.
- Have students complete the task.
- 🎧 Play Track 14 as students listen and check their answers.
- Call on two students to read each conversation. Correct as needed.

Multilevel Strategy

- **Pre-level:** Pair pre-level students. Allow them to write down the conversation.
- **At-level:** Pair at-level students. Have students complete the conversations orally first. Then have them write their conversations.
- **Above-level:** Pair above-level students. Have students complete the conversations orally. Do not allow them to write anything down.

Language Note

Exercise D. The difference between *must not* and *can't* is often difficult for students to understand. Explain that we usually use *can't* when we are disagreeing with someone else's logical conclusion. When we are just making a logical conclusion on our own, and not disagreeing with anyone, we use *must not*, not *can't*.

Option

Assign Unit 16 Supplementary Grammar to Communicate 3 Exercises on the Teacher's Resource Disk as homework or on the Student Persistence CD-ROM as self-access practice.

TIME to TALK

Teaching Time: 10–15 min.

- Read the directions with the class.
- Call on two students to read the example. Explain that B uses *can't* because he is disagreeing with A's logical conclusion. Remind students to use *can't* only when they are disagreeing with their partner's logical conclusion. If they are just making a negative logical conclusion, but not disagreeing, they should use *must not*. (See Language Note.)
- PAIRS. Have students complete the task.
- Call on students to role-play their conversations for the class and take notes on errors in logical conclusions.
- Write the errors on the board after the role plays are complete. Have the class correct the mistakes.

Review and Challenge

Grammar

Teaching Time: 5–10 min.

- Read the example with the class.
- Have students complete the task.
- 🎧 Play Track 15 while students listen and check their answers.
- Call on two students to read each conversation. Correct as needed.

Multilevel Strategy

- **Pre-level:** Tell students what the mistakes are and have them rewrite the conversations correctly.

Dictation

Teaching Time: 5–10 min.

- 🎧 Play Track 16 while students listen and write what they hear.
- 🎧 Play Track 16 again while students check their answers.
- PAIRS. Have students compare dictations. If there are any differences, they should decide who has the correct answer.
- Call on students to read the dictated sentences aloud. Write exactly what you hear. Ask them to spell the new vocabulary.
- 🎧 Play Track 16 again and correct the sentences on the board.

Speaking

Teaching Time: 5–10 min.

- Read the first situation to the class. Call on a student to read the example story.
- Make sure students understand what to do. Explain: *You have to imagine the story behind the sentences. That is, what is the story that would lead someone to say those sentences? Use your imagination. There are many possible stories for each sentence.*
- PAIRS. Have students complete the task.
- Call on students to tell their stories to the class. Tell them not to read the sentences at the end of the story. The class will guess the conclusion.

Review and Challenge

Grammar

🎧 **CD 3 TRACK 15** **Correct the mistake in each conversation. Then listen and check your answers.**

1. **A:** It ~~can't~~ *must* be difficult to find a good apartment around here.

   B: You're right. It is. I've been looking for a place for three months.

2. **A:** Laura's walking to the bus stop. That's strange.

   B: Her husband ~~must use~~ *must be using* her car today.

3. **A:** Mrs. Olsen must ~~not~~ be feeling lonely since her husband's death.

   B: I know. We should visit her next weekend.

4. **A:** Look, there's Tommy. He must be going to school.

   B: But it's Saturday. He can't ~~go~~ *be going* to school.

5. **A:** Hello? Could I please speak to Donna?

   B: Donna? There's no Donna here. You must ~~be having~~ *have* the wrong number.

Dictation

🎧 **CD 3 TRACK 16** **Listen. You will hear five sentences. Write them in your notebook.** *See the audioscript on p. 324 for the sentences.*

Speaking

PAIRS. **Choose one of the situations. Make up a story.**

- She can't be paying for that. Her son must be helping her.
- They must be joking. They can't be serious.
- It can't be all her fault. He must be responsible, too.
- He can't be the murderer! The police must have the wrong man.
- That can't be true. She must be wrong.

Now tell your story to the class. Who has the best story?

Example: *Mrs. Ephran is a retired school teacher. She's a widow. One day you see two men carrying a plasma TV into her house. You know that her son makes a lot of money. You say, "She can't be paying for that. Her son must be helping her."*

220 Unit 16

Multilevel Strategy

Pre-level: This speaking exercise might be beyond the ability of pre-level students. If you believe that is the case in your class, put the pre-level students in a group. While the other students are completing the Speaking task, help them complete Unit 16 Grammar to Communicate 3, Exercise B, on the Teacher's Resource Disk.

Option

Assign Unit 16 Review and Challenge Supplementary Exercises on the Teacher's Resource Disk as homework or on the Student Persistence CD-ROM as self-access practice.

Listening

Listening

A Teaching Time: 10–15 min.

- **Warm-up.** Tell students that they are going to listen to a radio talk show. Have students look at the pictures. Then ask them to guess what the topic of the talk show is. Write their guesses on the board.
- 🎧 Play Track 17 as students listen and complete the task.
- 🎧 Play Track 17 again as students check their answers.
- Call on students to say answers. Were the guesses they made during the warm-up correct?

B Teaching Time: 10–15 min.

- Have students read through the facts and logical conclusions before listening.
- 🎧 Play Track 17 while students listen and complete the task.
- 🎧 Play Track 17 again, this time pausing as each logical conclusion is given.
- Call on students to say answers.

A 🔘 **17** Listen to the radio talk show. Check (✓) the pictures that match the stories.

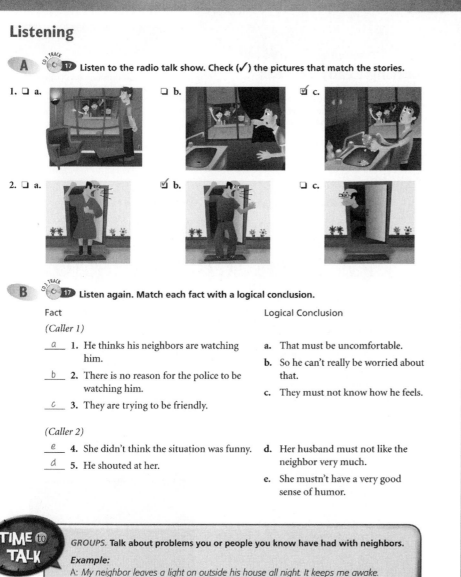

1. ☐ a.   ☐ b.   ☑ c.

2. ☐ a.   ☑ b.   ☐ c.

B 🔘 **17** Listen again. Match each fact with a logical conclusion.

Fact		Logical Conclusion
(Caller 1)		
_a_ **1.** He thinks his neighbors are watching him.		**a.** That must be uncomfortable.
_b_ **2.** There is no reason for the police to be watching him.		**b.** So he can't really be worried about that.
_c_ **3.** They are trying to be friendly.		**c.** They must not know how he feels.
(Caller 2)		
_e_ **4.** She didn't think the situation was funny.		**d.** Her husband must not like the neighbor very much.
_d_ **5.** He shouted at her.		**e.** She mustn't have a very good sense of humor.

TIME to TALK

GROUPS. **Talk about problems you or people you know have had with neighbors.**

Example:
A: *My neighbor leaves a light on outside his house all night. It keeps me awake.*
B: *That must be really annoying. Have you ever talked to him about it?*

Neighbors **221**

Multilevel Strategy

Pre-level: After students have completed Exercise A, give them a copy of the audioscript to read as they complete Exercise B.

Teaching Tip

Time to Talk. Students sometimes have trouble getting a discussion started or keeping it going. If you see that a group is stuck or seems to have finished a group discussion prematurely, join them. Share your own experience or opinions, and then ask them questions to stimulate more discussion. For this discussion, for example, you could tell about a problem you've had with a neighbor—or invent one if necessary! If your story is interesting, it will provoke student interest in the discussion topic, and they will start asking questions. Then you can turn the attention away from yourself and onto other students in the group.

TIME to TALK

Teaching Time: 5–10 min.

- Call on two students to read the example.
- GROUPS. Have students complete the task. Walk around and help as needed.

Getting Ready to Read

Teaching Time: 5–10 min.

- **Warm-up.** Ask: *What is the word in English to describe people who sleep on the streets because they don't have a place to live?* (homeless)

- Write *the homeless* and *homelessness* on the board. Explain that when we refer to homeless people in general, we say *the homeless*. When we refer to the state or condition of being homeless, we use the word *homelessness*. Both *the homeless* and *homelessness* are nouns.

- Call on a student to read the information in the Reading Skill box aloud.

- Have students complete the task.

- Write the question on the board, and leave it up as students read the article.

Reading

Teaching Time: 15–20 min.

- Have students read the article.

- Point to the question on the board. Ask a volunteer to answer it. Correct as needed. Write the answer on the board.

Multilevel Strategy

- **Pre-level:** Give students more time to read the article.
- **At-level, Above-level:** Have students circle the logical conclusions in the text.

Reading Skill:
Understanding Questions

Writers often use questions to get the reader's attention and to highlight important ideas. Sometimes they answer the questions and sometimes they don't. Pay attention to questions. Then read carefully to see if you can find the answers.

Getting Ready to Read

Read only the first paragraph of the article. How do you think the writer will answer the question at the end of the paragraph?

_____ yes   ✓ no   _____ The writer will not answer the question.

Reading

Read the article. Then check your answer to Getting Ready to Read.

A Difficult Question

"Why does the richest country in the world have so many people living on the streets?" This is a question that visitors to the United States often ask. Americans **respond to** this question in different ways. Some Americans think that homeless people must not be able to find jobs. Others believe that they must not want to work. Others think that the homeless must all be **addicted to** alcohol. And many believe that the government must not be doing enough to help. However, there is one thing that most Americans agree on: homeless people cannot be working. After all, anyone with a job must be able to afford a place to live, right?

Some of the things that Americans believe about the homeless are true. For example, it is true that some homeless people have a problem with alcohol. It is also true that the government could help more. However, it is *not* true that all homeless people do not work. According to **advocates** for the homeless, 25 to 40% of homeless people work full-time or part-time. And 38% of the homeless population is **made up of** families with children.

So how does someone with a job and family end up living on the street? The answer to that question is **controversial.** People on both sides have strong opinions about it. However, most advocates say there are three main causes of homelessness: not enough **affordable** housing, jobs that do not pay enough, and the high cost of health care.

Unfortunately, most of the programs for the homeless help mainly with **temporary** solutions, such as housing for a short time, food, clothing, and emergency health care. These temporary solutions are important, but they do not solve the real causes of homelessness.

After You Read

A Look at the **boldface** words and expressions in the article. Guess their meaning. Then complete the sentences with the words in the box.

addicted to	afforable	made up of	temporary
advocates	controversial	~~respond to~~	unfortunately

1. You have to _____respond to_____ this e-mail immediately. They need an answer today.

2. When you are _____addicted to_____ something, you don't stop taking it, even if it is very bad for you.

3. The United States does not have just one culture. It is _____made up of_____ many different cultures.

4. The job of _____advocates_____ is to help people.

5. This solution to the problem is _____temporary_____: it will only work for a short time.

6. Health care needs to be _____affordable_____. Both poor and rich people should be able to pay for it easily.

7. It's a _____controversial_____ topic. People feel very strongly about it.

8. _____Unfortunately_____, the fact is that many homeless people in the U.S. are families with children.

B Read the article again. Then check (✓) the statements that are true.

- ❑ 1. The U.S. is a rich country, so there aren't many homeless people.
- ❑ 2. Most people understand the causes of homelessness.
- ☑ 3. Some homeless people work.
- ☑ 4. The U.S. government could do more to help the homeless.
- ❑ 5. Most homeless people are old and sick.
- ☑ 6. Many homeless people in the U.S. are families with children.
- ❑ 7. Health care does not cost a lot of money.

After You Read

A Teaching Time: 10–15 min.

- Read the example with the class.
- Have students complete the task.
- PAIRS. Have students compare their answers with a classmate. If their answers are different, tell them to decide whose answer is correct.
- Call on students to read the sentences with their answers.

B Teaching Time: 10–15 min.

- Have students complete the task. Tell them to underline the sentences in the article where they find the answers.
- Call on students to give the answers. As they give their answers, have them tell you the paragraph and the line number where the answer can be found in the article. (3. paragraph 2, line 8; 4. paragraph 2, line 4; 6. paragraph 2, line 9) Then have them read those sentences from the article aloud as the other students follow along in their books.

Multilevel Strategy

All Levels: Pair pre-level students with at-level and above-level students. Walk around the class and encourage the more advanced students to help the less advanced ones by explaining how and where they found the answers.

Getting Ready to Write

Writing

A Teaching Time: 10–15 min.

- Have students study the Writing Tip.
- Read the example with the class.
- Have students complete the task.
- Call on students to say answers. Correct as needed.

B Teaching Time: 10–15 min.

- Have students read the model paragraph. As they read, have them underline the questions and circle the answers.
- PAIRS. Have students complete the task.

Getting Ready to Write

A Read the paragraphs. For each paragraph, underline the question that gets the reader's attention. Then circle the answer to the question.

> **Writing Tip**
>
> Use questions in your writing to get your reader's attention and highlight important ideas. Your reader will then try to find the answer to your question.
> Example:
> **So how does someone with a job and family end up living on the street?**

1. Anyone with a job must be able to afford a place to live, right? Well, it is true that many people who live on the streets don't have jobs. But up to 40 percent of homeless people do work full or part-time and still can't afford a place to live.

2. Is the government doing enough to help the homeless? It does pay for some programs to help the homeless. The programs offer homeless people temporary housing, food, clothing, and free emergency health care. However, there are still far too many homeless people, so the government must not be doing enough to solve this problem.

3. Homelessness is a difficult problem to solve in the U.S. Are the homeless people the same in every U.S. city? No, they aren't. For example, in Portland, Oregon, many of the homeless are teenagers who have run away from home. In other cities, the homeless are mostly adult men or single mothers with small children.

B Read the model paragraph.

> There are thousands of homeless people in our city. What is the best way to help them? Some people choose to make free food for the homeless. Others donate clothing that they don't need anymore. The government builds apartments for the homeless to live in for a short time. All of these things are helpful. However, some homeless people have also started helping themselves. They write their own newspapers and sell them to people on the streets. These newspapers must be a good way to help. Why? Because when you buy a newspaper, you are helping homeless people help themselves.

PAIRS. Read the model again. Are these good solutions to help the homeless?

Now choose a problem in your country. Talk about ways to solve the problem. You can talk about economic problems, political problems, or your own ideas.

Prewriting: Using Questions

You are going to write a paragraph about a problem in your country. Before you write, make a list of questions to ask about the problem. Write answers to the questions. Then use the best question and answer for your paragraph.

Question 1:

Answer:

Question 2:

Answer:

Question 3:

Answer:

Writing

Now write a paragraph about a problem in your country and a possible solution. The writing tip, the model paragraph, and your notes will help you. Write in your notebook.

Prewriting

Teaching Time: 10–15 min.

- Have students complete the task. Walk around and help as needed.
- GROUPS. Each student reads his or her questions and answers to the group. Students in the group give their opinions about which questions and answers are the most interesting.

Writing

Teaching Time: 15–20 min.

Have students complete the task. Encourage them to consider the feedback of their groups as they write their paragraphs.

Multilevel Strategy

Pre-level: While the other students are writing their questions and answers, work with the pre-level students in a group. Help them come up with questions and answers about a problem in your city. Then, while other students are writing their paragraphs, use the questions and answers to construct a paragraph on the board with the group. Have students copy the final paragraph into their notebooks.

Unit 17
Health

Learning Goals

- Learn vocabulary related to health
- Learn how to use *it* + infinitive; *too* and *enough* + infinitive; and infinitives of purpose
- Listen to a conversation between a doctor and a patient and to a report about the importance of a healthy diet
- Read an article about common health myths and write a paragraph about a health myth
- Talk about health

Learner Persistence

Address the needs of older learners.

Warm-up

Teaching Time: 3–5 min.

- Have students look at each picture.
- For each picture, ask: *Why is the person at the clinic?*

Vocabulary

Teaching Time: 10–15 min.

- Have students complete the task.
- 🎧 Play Track 18 while students listen and check their answers.
- Read the words in boldface and have students repeat chorally.

Expansion Have students put the words in boldface into categories according to part of speech.

- Write three headings on the board:
  Verbs and verb phrases
  Nouns and noun phrases
  Adjectives
- Read the words and phrases aloud, and have the class tell you where to write each one.
  (Verbs and verb phrases: *gained, get in shape, has surgery, get shots*
  Nouns and noun phrases: *high cholesterol, blood pressure, vitamin C, calcium*
  Adjectives: *common, weak, strong*)

Grammar
- *It* + Infinitive
- *Too* and *Enough* + Infinitive
- Infinitives of Purpose

Vocabulary

🎧 **18** Match the sentences with the pictures. Then listen and check your answers.

<u> 2 </u> **a.** "You **gained** 15 pounds in six months. You also have **high cholesterol**. You must go on a diet and lose weight, at least 25 pounds."

<u> 1 </u> **b.** "Your **blood pressure** used to be low, but now it's a little high. That's **common** for people your age. You need to **get in shape**. Exercise more."

<u> 5 </u> **c.** "After your grandfather **has surgery**, he's going to be very **weak**. He won't be able to do things for himself, so he'll need your help."

<u> 4 </u> **d.** "Most people hate to **get shots**. They're painful."

<u> 3 </u> **e.** "You and the baby need **vitamin C**. Eat oranges or drink orange juice. You also need **calcium**. Drink milk every day and eat yogurt. You can also take calcium pills, but don't take more than 500 mg. at one time. 1,000 mg. pills are too **strong**."

226 Unit 17

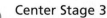

Listening

A 🔊 **TRACK 19** Listen. What is Mr. Harris's problem? Check (✓) the correct answer.

> **Look**
> normal = usual, not special

- ☐ 1. He is normal for his age.
- ☑ 2. His blood pressure is high.
- ☐ 3. He goes on too many diets.
- ☐ 4. He works two jobs.
- ☐ 5. He's very young.

B 🔊 **TRACK 20** Listen again. For each pair of sentences, check (✓) the sentence that you hear.

1. ☑ a. It's unhealthy to go on a diet.
   ☐ b. It's healthy to go on a diet.
2. ☑ a. You need to eat less and exercise more.
   ☐ b. You don't need to eat less and exercise more.
3. ☐ a. You're not old enough to make these changes.
   ☑ b. You're not too old to make these changes.
4. ☑ a. I'm too busy to exercise.
   ☐ b. I'm too lazy to exercise.
5. ☑ a. I don't have enough time to cook every day.
   ☐ b. I don't have enough time to cook today.
6. ☐ a. It's easy to do, I think.
   ☑ b. It's easier to do than you think.

C 🔊 **TRACK 21** Listen again. Answer the questions. Write complete sentences. *Wording of answers may vary.*

1. What advice does the doctor give to Mr. Harris?
   He should lose weight. He should change his diet and eat more healthy food.

2. How does Mr. Harris feel about the doctor's advice?
   He is not very happy about it.

3. Do you think that Mr. Harris will follow the doctor's advice? Explain why or why not.
   Answers will vary.

Health **227**

Option

Assign Unit 17 Supplementary Vocabulary Exercises on the Teacher's Resource Disk as homework or on the Student Persistence CD-ROM as self-access practice.

Listening

A **Teaching Time: 10–15 min.**

- **Warm-up.** Tell students that they are going to listen to a conversation between a doctor and a patient. Start a discussion about doctors. Ask: *How often do you go to the doctor? Do you always go to the same doctor? Do any of your friends or family members go to the same doctor?*
- Have students read the answer choices.
- 🎧 Play Track 19 as students listen and complete the task.
- Call on a student to say the answer. Play the conversation again if necessary.

B **Teaching Time: 10–15 min.**

- Have students read the answer choices.
- 🎧 Play Track 20 as students listen and complete the task.
- Call on students to say answers.
- 🎧 Play Track 20 again, this time pausing the recording after each answer is given. Confirm the answers students gave previously.

C **Teaching Time: 10–15 min.**

- Have students complete the task before listening again.
- 🎧 Play Track 21 as students listen and check their answers.
- Call on students to read their answers.
- 🎧 Play Track 21 again, pausing the recording as the answers to numbers 1 and 2 are given. Confirm the answers students gave previously.
- Question 3 is an opinion question. Ask students for their opinions, and have them explain their answers.

Multilevel Strategy

- **Pre-level:** Make photocopies of the audioscript. Give it to students to look at as they write the answers to Exercise C.
- **At-level, Above-level:** Have students answer the questions before they listen again.

Grammar to Communicate 1

It + Infinitive

Teaching Time: 5–10 min.

- Have students study the chart and the Look Box.
- Write on the board:

  If you want to learn a foreign language, it is important to ___.

- Call on students to complete the sentence on the board. Have them read the full sentence when they answer. Write their answers on the board. Make sure students understand that an infinitive is always *to* + a verb (not a noun).
- Say: *Here are some other adjectives that are commonly used with It + infinitive.* Write on the board:

  necessary / not necessary; unusual / common; dangerous / safe; difficult / easy; healthy / unhealthy

- Point out that *common* or *not unusual* are used as the opposite of *unusual* (not, as we might expect, the word *usual*).

A Teaching Time: 10–15 min.

- Read the example with the class.
- Have students complete the task.
- Call on students to say answers. Correct as needed.

Expansion Start a discussion about the health information in the exercise. Ask students questions as follows:

1. *Why is it important to brush your teeth after every meal? Do you brush your teeth after every meal?*
2. *Do you usually get a flu shot? How many people got a flu shot last year? Raise your hands.*
3. *Which age group often has high blood pressure? Does anyone in the class have high blood pressure? Raise your hands.*
4. *Who has had surgery? Raise your hands. Were you nervous before the surgery?*
5. *How many people go to the dentist to get a cleaning every six months?*

B Teaching Time: 10–15 min.

- Read the example with the class. Ask students to raise their hands if they know how to do CPR. Ask if anyone knows what the letters C-P-R stand

for. (cardiopulmonary resuscitation)
- Have students complete the task.
- 🎧 Play Track 22 while students listen and check their answers.
- Call on students to say answers. Correct as needed.

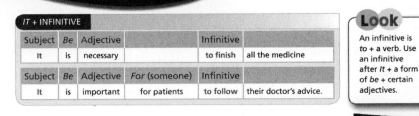

Grammar to Communicate 1

IT + INFINITIVE					
Subject	*Be*	Adjective		Infinitive	
It	is	necessary		to finish	all the medicine

Subject	*Be*	Adjective	*For* (someone)	Infinitive	
It	is	important	for patients	to follow	their doctor's advice.

Look
An infinitive is *to* + a verb. Use an infinitive after *It* + a form of *be* + certain adjectives.

A Underline the infinitives.

1. It's important to brush your teeth after every meal.
2. It's important for you to get a flu shot.
3. It's unusual for a child to have high blood pressure.
4. It's normal to be nervous before surgery.
5. It's important to go to the dentist for a cleaning every six months.
6. It can be dangerous to drive after you take this medicine.

get a cleaning

B 🎵 22 Read the conversations. Rewrite B's response with *for*. Then listen and check your answers.

1. **A:** If I get the job, do I need to take a course in CPR?
   B: Yes. It is necessary to know CPR.
   Yes, it's necessary for all employees to know CPR.
   (all employees)

2. **A:** My dad hasn't been to your office in a year. Should he make an appointment?
   B: Yes. It's important to check his cholesterol once a year.
   Yes, it's important for me to check his cholesterol once a year.
   (me)

3. **A:** Should I go on a diet?
   B: Yes, it's necessary to lose weight.
   Yes, it's necessary for you to lose weight.
   (you)

4. **A:** Should he have the surgery soon?
   B: Yes, it's important to have it as quickly as possible.
   Yes, it's important for him to have the surgery as quickly as possible.
   (him)

5. **A:** Should I keep my children home from school?
   B: Yes, it's important to stay away from other children.
   Yes, it's important for them to stay away from other children.
   (them)

CPR

228 Unit 17

Grammar Notes

1. An infinitive is *to* + verb. Use an infinitive after *It* + a form of *be* + certain adjectives (for example, *important* and *necessary*). Turn to page 300 for a more complete list of adjectives that can be followed by infinitives.

2. Add *for* + (a person) before the infinitive when you want to say *who*. If the information in the sentence is general information that is true for most or all people, do not use *for*.

3. For more information about this grammar topic, see page 292.

C Write sentences. Use a phrase from the box where necessary.

for babies	for elderly people	for teenagers

Look

Use *for* (someone) only when necessary. We usually don't use it in a general statement about people.
It is normal to eat a few times a day.
NOT It is normal ~~for people~~ to eat a few times a day.

1. It is difficult for elderly people to climb stairs.
   (difficult / climb stairs)
2. It is unhealthy to smoke.
   (unhealthy / smoke)
3. It is not healthy to eat a lot of sweets.
   (not healthy / eat a lot of sweets)
4. It is important to get enough exercise.
   (important / get enough exercise)
5. It is important for babies to see the doctor every three months.
   (important / see the doctor every three months)
6. It is common for elderly people to take several different pills every day.
   (common / take several different pills every day)
7. It is normal for elderly people to need to eat less.
   (normal / need to eat less)
8. It is good for teenagers to play sports for exercise.
   (good / play sports for exercise)
9. It is normal for teenagers to spend time with their friends.
   (normal / spend time with their friends)

TIME to TALK

PAIRS. What do you do to stay healthy? What is easy, difficult, and impossible for you to do? Explain your answers. Use the words in the box and your own ideas.

avoid junk food	gain weight	get enough sleep
eat three healthy meals a day	get a cleaning every six months	lose weight
exercise every day	get a physical once a year	

Example:
A: It's really difficult for me to exercise every day. I'm so busy.

B: I agree. In fact, I think it's impossible for most people to exercise every day.

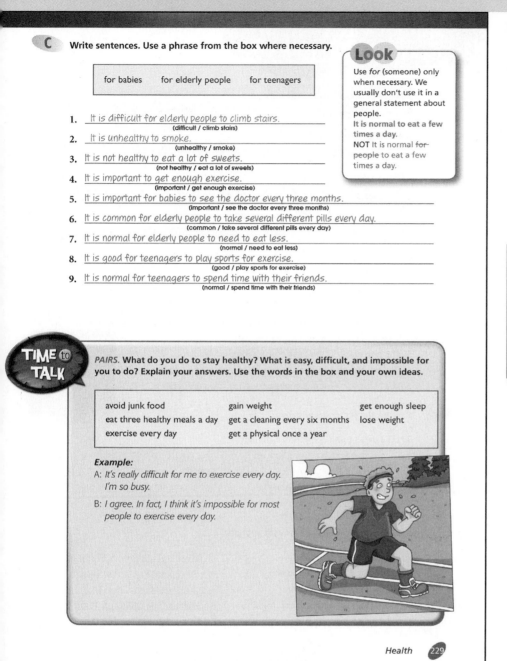

Health 229

C **Teaching Time: 10–15 min.**

- Call on a student to read the information in the Look Box aloud.
- Read the directions and the examples with the class. Make sure students understand that they should use *for* only when the sentence does not apply to all or most people.
- Have students complete the task.
- Call on students to say answers. Correct as needed. Discuss any differences in opinion.

Multilevel Strategy

- **All-levels:** Pair pre-level students with at- or above-level students for this activity. That way, if pre-level students have difficulty with the grammar, their partners can help them.

Option

Assign Unit 17 Supplementary Grammar to Communicate 1 Exercises on the Teacher's Resource Disk as homework or on the Student Persistence CD-ROM as self-access practice.

TIME to TALK

Teaching Time: 10–15 min.

- Have two students read the example.
- PAIRS. Have students complete the task.
- Call on volunteers to share their answers. Correct as needed.

Grammar to Communicate 2

Too and *Enough* + Infinitive

Teaching Time: 5–10 min.

- Copy the chart onto the board, or make a transparency of it and project it so everyone can see.
- Read the examples aloud.
- Point to the subjects *Your son* and *He* in the first and third examples in the left column, and then point to the corresponding example sentences in the right column. Say: *When the subjects are the same, don't use* for *before the infinitive.*
- Now point to the subjects *Your son* and *You* in the second and fourth examples in the left column, and then point to the corresponding example sentences in the right column. Say: *When the subjects are different, we must use* for *before the infinitive.*
- Point to *too* in the first two examples in the right column, and say: *We put* too *in front of the adjective. When we use* too *with an affirmative verb, it means that there will be a negative result. In this example, the negative result is that he won't be able to leave the hospital.*
- Point to *enough* in the next two examples in the right column, and say: *We put* enough *after the adjective. When we use* enough *with a negative verb, it also means that there will be a negative result. In this example, the negative result is that you won't be able to take him home.*

 Teaching Time: 5–10 min.

- Read the example with the class. Ask: *Why do people wear hearing aids?* (Because they can't hear well.)
- Have students complete the task.
- Call on students to say answers. Correct as needed.

 Teaching Time: 10–15 min.

- Call on a student to read the directions and the two examples (1 and 6).
- Have students complete the task.
- Call on students to say answers. Correct as needed.

Grammar to Communicate 2

TOO AND ENOUGH + INFINITIVE

Too + Adjective	*Too* + Adjective + Infinitive
Your son is too weak. [He can't leave the hospital.]	Your son is too weak to leave the hospital.
	Too + Adjective + *For* (Someone) + Infinitive
Your son is too weak. [You can't take him home.]	Your son is too weak for you to take him home.
Adjective + *Enough*	Adjective + *Enough* + Infinitive
Your son isn't strong enough. [He can't leave the hospital.]	Your son isn't strong enough to leave the hospital.
	Adjective + *Enough* + *For* (Someone) + Infinitive
Your son isn't strong enough. [You can't take him home.]	Your son isn't strong enough for you to take him home.

A Circle the correct words.

1. The hearing aid isn't **too comfortable** / **comfortable enough** for him to use.
2. It's **too painful** / **painful enough** to stand up.
3. The pharmacist is **too busy** / **busy enough** to talk.
4. She isn't **too strong** / **strong enough** to leave the hospital.
5. The baby is **too young** / **young enough** to take adult aspirin.

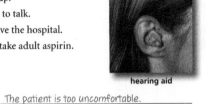

hearing aid

B Rewrite the sentences with *too*.

1. The patient isn't comfortable enough. _The patient is too uncomfortable._
2. These glasses aren't strong enough. _These glasses are too weak._
3. The nurse isn't fast enough. _The nurse is too slow._
4. The hearing aid isn't small enough. _The hearing aid is too big._
5. The hospital isn't modern enough. _The hospital is too old._

Now rewrite these sentences with *enough*.

6. The patient is too nervous. _The patient isn't relaxed enough._
7. Your blood pressure is too high. _Your blood pressure isn't low enough._
8. These pills are too big. _These pills aren't small enough._
9. The letters on the bottle are too small. _The letters on the bottles aren't big enough._
10. The man is too unhealthy. _The man is not healthy enough._

230 Unit 17

Expansion Have students make follow-up sentences with *can't*. For example, sentence 1: The patient is too uncomfortable. *He can't sleep.*

Multilevel Strategy

- **Pre-level:** Give students more time to complete Exercise B.
- **At-level:** Have students complete the Expansion activity.
- **Above-level:** Have students complete the Expansion activity, and then combine the sentences by using an infinitive, for example, sentence 1: *The patient is too uncomfortable to sleep.*

Grammar Notes

1. Use *too* before adjectives and adverbs. *Too* has a negative meaning. It means more than is good or necessary.
2. Use *enough* after adjectives and adverbs. *Enough* means the correct amount.
3. *Not enough* means less than the correct amount.
4. An infinitive often comes after *too* or *enough*. Add *for* + (a person) before the infinitive when the subject of the main verb is different from the subject of the infinitive.
5. Don't confuse *too* and *very*. *Too* causes a negative result. *Very* makes the meaning of an adjective stronger.
6. For more information on this grammar topic, see page 292.

Combine the sentences with *for*. Use *too* or *enough*.

1. I can't read the letters in the eye chart. They are too small.
   The letters in the eye chart are too small for me to read.

2. Children can't take this medicine. It's too strong.
   This medicine is too strong for children to take.

3. You can't go out and play. Your fever is too high.
   Your fever is too high for you to go out and play.

4. You can't use that Band-Aid. It's too small.
   That Band-Aid is too small for you to use.

5. I can't stay on a diet. It's too hard.
   It's too hard for me to stay on a diet.

6. My mother can't take a walk with me. It isn't warm enough.
   It isn't warm enough for my mother to take a walk with me.

eye chart

Complete the sentences. Use *too* or *very*.

1. You should see Dr. Norton. He's a _____very_____ good doctor.

2. My mother's _____very_____ old, but she is still able to live by herself.

3. You're _____too_____ thin. You must gain weight.

4. I couldn't see the dentist yesterday. She was _____too_____ busy to talk to me.

5. They can't be doctors. They're _____too_____ young.

6. I'm upset because Dr. Tran moved. Her office is _____too_____ far away now.

7. I'm _____very_____ tired, but I'll help you.

8. He's _____too_____ weak to walk home. You should call him a cab.

Look

Too has a negative meaning. *Very* makes an adjective stronger.
I'm **too tired**. I can't drive.
I'm **very tired**, but I can drive.

TIME to TALK

PAIRS. Talk about a time when you were _____ to _____.
                                                              (your idea)

| not old enough | not strong enough | too scared | too tired |
| not rested enough | not well enough | too sick | too worried |

Example:
I worked for 12 hours yesterday. When I got home, I was too tired to study.

Health 231

Watch Out!

It is common for students from some language groups to confuse *too* and *very*. It is especially common for students to ignore the negative meaning of *too*, and think that it is just a stronger form of *very*. Errors such as the following are common: *Your English is too good! How did you learn?* Listen for and correct these errors.

Option

Assign Unit 17 Supplementary Grammar to Communicate 2 Exercises on the Teacher's Resource Disk as homework or on the Student Persistence CD-ROM as self-access practice.

C **Teaching Time: 10–15 min.**

- Read the example with the class.
- Have students complete the task.
- Call on students to say answers. Correct as needed.

D **Teaching Time: 5–10 min.**

- Call on a student to read the information in the Look Box aloud.
- Explain: Too *always has a negative meaning or causes a negative result. In the first sentence,* I'm too tired, *the negative result is that you can't drive.* Very *makes the adjective stronger, but it doesn't always have a negative meaning or lead to a negative result. In the second sentence,* I'm very tired, *but there is no negative result; you can still drive.*
- Read the example with the class.
- Have students complete the task.
- Call on students to say answers. If a student gives the wrong answer, prompt him or her to self-correct by asking: *Is there a negative meaning or result? If so, what is it?* If the student is able to identify a negative meaning or result, the answer should be *too*. If there is no negative meaning or result, then the answer should be *very*.

  (1. no negative result or meaning; 2. no negative result or meaning; 3. negative meaning implied = you must do something to correct the problem; 4. negative result = I couldn't see the dentist; 5. negative meaning = They're not doctors; 6. negative result or meaning = I'm upset; 7. no negative result or meaning; 8. negative result implied = He can't walk home. You should do something to correct the problem.)

TIME to TALK

Teaching Time: 5–10 min.

- Have a student read the example.
- PAIRS. Have students complete the task.
- Call on students to tell the class something about their partner. Correct as needed.

Infinitives of Purpose

Teaching Time: 5–10 min.

- Have students study the chart and the Look Box.
- Ask: *Why are you taking this class?* If nobody in the class answers with an infinitive, write one student's answer on the board. Have the student restate it with an infinitive. For example, if the student says: *Because I want to speak English better,* write that on the board, and below it write: *I'm taking this class to ___.* Have the student complete the sentence with the infinitive *to speak English better.*
- Ask several students the same question. Write their responses on the board.

Multilevel Strategy

All levels: During a grammar presentation or practice activity, call on above-level students first to elicit the grammar that you want. Once the above-level students have modeled the correct grammar, call on one or two at-level students to reinforce the point. Call on pre-level students only after they have had a chance to hear and see the structure several times.

A   Teaching Time: 10–15 min.

- Read the example with the class.
- Have students complete the task.
- Call on students to say answers. Correct as needed.
- Then have them say full sentences, for example: *People go on diets to lose weight.*

Expansion To reinforce the meaning of the infinitive of purpose, after students have read the answers to Exercise A, have them restate the answers without an infinitive. For example, in sentence 1, first the student reads: *People go on diets to lose weight.* Then the student says: *People go on diets because* (or *when*) *they want to lose weight.*

Grammar to Communicate 3

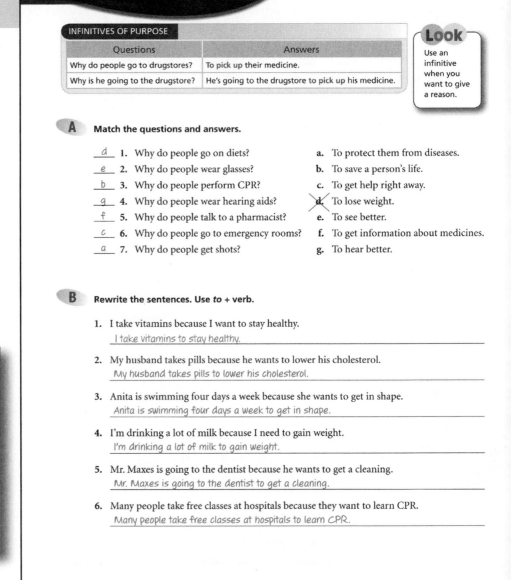

INFINITIVES OF PURPOSE

Questions	Answers
Why do people go to drugstores?	To pick up their medicine.
Why is he going to the drugstore?	He's going to the drugstore to pick up his medicine.

Look
Use an infinitive when you want to give a reason.

A   Match the questions and answers.

d 1. Why do people go on diets?
e 2. Why do people wear glasses?
b 3. Why do people perform CPR?
g 4. Why do people wear hearing aids?
f 5. Why do people talk to a pharmacist?
c 6. Why do people go to emergency rooms?
a 7. Why do people get shots?

a. To protect them from diseases.
b. To save a person's life.
c. To get help right away.
d. To lose weight.
e. To see better.
f. To get information about medicines.
g. To hear better.

B   Rewrite the sentences. Use *to* + verb.

1. I take vitamins because I want to stay healthy.
   I take vitamins to stay healthy.

2. My husband takes pills because he wants to lower his cholesterol.
   My husband takes pills to lower his cholesterol.

3. Anita is swimming four days a week because she wants to get in shape.
   Anita is swimming four days a week to get in shape.

4. I'm drinking a lot of milk because I need to gain weight.
   I'm drinking a lot of milk to gain weight.

5. Mr. Maxes is going to the dentist because he wants to get a cleaning.
   Mr. Maxes is going to the dentist to get a cleaning.

6. Many people take free classes at hospitals because they want to learn CPR.
   Many people take free classes at hospitals to learn CPR.

232   Unit 17

B   Teaching Time: 10–15 min.

- Read the example with the class.
- Have students complete the task.
- Call on students to say answers. Correct as needed.

Expansion PAIRS. Have students ask and answer questions about the things in the exercise that they do and don't do. For example:

A: *Do you take vitamins to stay healthy?*
B: *No, I don't. I don't like to take vitamins. I eat fruit and vegetables to stay healthy.*

Grammar Notes

1. We often use an infinitive (*to* + verb) to say the reason for doing something (sometimes called the infinitive of purpose). It answers the question *Why.*
2. *To* can have the same meaning as *in order to.*
3. The infinitive of purpose can come at the beginning of the sentence, before the main clause, or after the main clause. If it comes at the beginning of the sentence, put a comma between the infinitive and the subject of the sentence.
4. For more information on this grammar topic, see pages 292–293.

C PAIRS. Complete the list of Healthy Tips for Children. Use the words in the box and to. Some sentences may have more than one correct answer.

be ready to learn	have strong bones	protect your skin
~~get in shape~~	prevent colds	stop germs
have energy during the day	prevent tooth decay	

Healthy Tips for Children

- Exercise every day
  to stay in shape
- Brush your teeth
  to prevent tooth decay
- Get plenty of calcium
  to have strong bones
- Wash your hands often
  to stop germs
- Wear sunscreen
  to protect your skin
- Sleep 10 hours a night
  to have energy during the day
- Eat a good breakfast
  to be ready to learn
- Get enough vitamin C
  to prevent colds

TIME to TALK

PAIRS. Write a brochure about health for one of the groups in the box. Use the brochure in Exercise C as a model.

babies	middle-aged men	pregnant women
the elderly	middle-aged women	teenagers

Example: Middle-aged women: Take calcium to make your bones stronger.

Health 233

- Read the directions and the words in the box. Explain any unfamiliar vocabulary.
- Read the example with the class.
- PAIRS. Have students complete the task.
- Call on students to say answers. Correct as needed.

Option

Assign Unit 20 Supplementary Grammar to Communicate 3 Exercises on the Teacher's Resource Disk as homework or on the Student Persistence CD-ROM as self-access practice.

TIME to TALK

Teaching Time: 10–15 min.

- Make sure students understand that first they should agree on which group they are writing the brochure for.
- PAIRS. Have students complete the task.
- Have students exchange papers and say any information that they are not sure of or that they don't agree with. Write the sentences on the board.
- Discuss whether the information on the board is accurate or not.

Expansion Bring in markers, magazines, scissors, poster board, and tape or glue. Give each pair of students a piece of poster board and have them design a poster rather than a brochure. Have them cut out pictures from the magazines or draw their own pictures. Have students write their sentences in their notebooks so that you can correct their grammar and any inaccurate information before they write them on the poster. Mount the completed posters on the walls of the classroom. Have students walk around and read their classmates' posters.

Grammar

Teaching Time: 5–10 min.

- Read the example with the class.
- Have students complete the task.
- 🎧 Play Track 23 while students listen and check their answers.
- Call on two students to read each conversation. Correct as needed.

Dictation

Teaching Time: 5–10 min.

- 🎧 Play Track 24 while students listen and write what they hear.
- 🎧 Play Track 24 again while students check their answers.
- Ask for volunteers to write the sentences on the board.
- 🎧 Play Track 24 again and correct the sentences on the board.

Multilevel Strategy

- **Pre-level:** Give students a worksheet with some of the words from the dictation already provided.

Speaking

Teaching Time: 5–10 min.

- Read the directions and the example with the class. Tell students that they should use an infinitive of purpose in each sentence.
- PAIRS. Have students complete the task.

Expansion

- Write the example on the board. (*Doctors wear gloves and masks to protect themselves and their patients from germs.*)
- Then write this question on the board:

  What do doctors wear to protect themselves and their patients from germs?

- Read the question aloud and call on a student to answer. Tell the student to use a full sentence.

Review and Challenge

Grammar

🎧 **23** Correct the mistake in each conversation. Then listen and check your answers.

1. **A:** You're ~~very~~ *too* sick to go to work.

   B: But I have to go! I have a very important meeting.

2. **A:** Does he need surgery?

   B: No, the problem's ~~for him not~~ *not* serious enough to have surgery.

3. **A:** The doctor's too busy ~~for seeing~~ *to see* you today.

   B: But I have an appointment!

4. **A:** What do you take when you have a cold?

   B: Sweet Night. It's ~~too~~ *very* good. It helps me sleep.

5. **A:** Where are you going?

   B: I'm going downtown ~~for~~ to see the doctor. I have an appointment.

Dictation

🎧 **24** Listen. You will hear five sentences. Write them in your notebook. *See the audioscript on p. 325 for the sentences.*

Speaking

PAIRS. Look at the pictures. Why do doctors use these things? Make a sentence for each picture. Use the verbs in the box.

| give | listen to | protect | take | weigh |

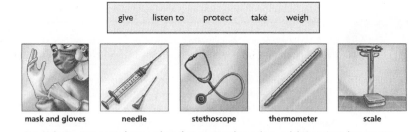

| mask and gloves | needle | stethoscope | thermometer | scale |

Example: Doctors wear gloves and masks to protect themselves and their patients from germs.

- Have students make questions from their sentences.
- Call on students to ask their questions. Their classmates should answer in full sentences. Correct as needed.

Multilevel Strategy

- **Pre-level, At-level:** Students look at the pictures as they answer their classmates' questions.
- **Above-level:** Students answer from memory.

Listening

A 🎧 **25** Listen to the interview. Check (✓) the questions that the doctor answers.

☑ 1. What are the secrets to a healthy life?

☐ 2. Which countries in the world have healthy diets?

☑ 3. Who eats more vegetables and fruit: new immigrants or people born in the United States?

☑ 4. Why is fast food unhealthy?

☑ 5. Where can people find out what is in their food?

☐ 6. How much sugar should we eat a day?

☑ 7. How much salt should we eat a day?

☑ 8. How much fat should we eat a day?

☑ 9. How much exercise do most people need to stay healthy?

☐ 10. Which fast-food restaurants serve the healthiest food?

B 🎧 **25** Listen again. Answer the questions that you checked in Exercise A.

a healthy diet and regular exercise

new immigrants

It has too much salt and too much fat.

on the Internet

fewer than 2,400 milligrams

fewer than 20 grams of saturated fat a day, and fewer than 65 grams of total fat

30 minutes a day, 5 days a week

TIME to TALK

GROUPS. Discuss the questions.

1. Compare what you eat now to what other people your age probably eat in your country. Who has the healthier diet?

2. What kinds of food have a lot of vitamin C?

3. What kinds of food have a lot of calcium?

4. What kinds of food have a lot of protein?

5. What kinds of food are bad to eat if you have heart disease?

Example: I eat a lot of meat and rice. People in my country eat more vegetables. It is unhealthy to eat too much meat, so I am going to try to change my diet.

Health **235**

Listening

A Teaching Time: 10–15 min.

- **Warm-up.** Tell students that they are going to listen to a radio interview. Tell them to look at the picture and read the answer choices. Have them guess what the topic of the interview will be. Write their guesses on the board.
- 🎧 Play Track 25 as students listen and complete the task.
- 🎧 Play Track 25 again as students check their answers to the task.
- Call on students to say answers. Correct as needed.
- Ask students what the topic of the interview is. Were any of their guesses correct? Cross out the incorrect guesses and check (✓) the correct ones.

B Teaching Time: 10–15 min.

- Have students answer as many questions as they can before listening.
- 🎧 Play Track 25 while students listen and complete the task.
- 🎧 Play Track 25 again, this time pausing the recording as each answer is given.
- Call on students to say answers. Correct as needed.

Multilevel Strategy

Pre-level: Give students a copy of the audioscript to read as they answer the questions. Then have them read along as they listen again.

Teaching Tip

Time to Talk. As students work on the unit, make a note of those who are knowledgeable about health issues. If possible, put at least one knowledgeable student in each group for this discussion.

Option

Assign Unit 17 Review and Challenge Supplementary Exercises on the Teacher's Resource Disk as homework or on the Student Persistence CD-ROM as self-access practice.

TIME to TALK

Teaching Time: 5–10 min.

- Call on a student to read the example.
- GROUPS. Have students complete the task. Walk around and help as needed.
- WRAP UP. Call on students from different groups to answer the questions.

Reading

Getting Ready to Read

Teaching Time: 10–15 min.

Warm-up. Tell students that in American magazines, short quizzes on topics such as health, relationships, and money are common. The quizzes are usually written by experts in that particular field. For example, a health quiz might be written by a medical doctor or a nutritionist. Readers take the quiz and then check their answers, which are either at the bottom of the same page, or on a different page in the back of the magazine. Often there are comments next to the answers that give additional information. Ask students if such quizzes are common in magazines in their countries.

- Have students complete the task. While students are working, draw a chart on the board, as follows:

Myth	True	False
1 Swimming		
2 Television		
3 Carrots		
4 Wet hair		
5 Chicken soup		

- Point to the word *myth* and say: *a myth is a popular belief that is false or not supported by facts.*
- Take a poll for each myth. Write the number of students who answered true and false for each myth in the chart. Leave the chart on the board as the students read the article.

Reading

Teaching Time: 15–20 min.

- Have students read the answers to the quiz.
- Point to the chart on the board. Have students say the correct answers, and explain why the statement is true or false, according to the article.

Reading

Getting Ready to Read

Check (✓) *T* (true) or *F* (false) for each statement.

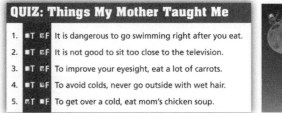

QUIZ: Things My Mother Taught Me

1. ▢T ▢F It is dangerous to go swimming right after you eat.
2. ▢T ▢F It is not good to sit too close to the television.
3. ▢T ▢F To improve your eyesight, eat a lot of carrots.
4. ▢T ▢F To avoid colds, never go outside with wet hair.
5. ▢T ▢F To get over a cold, eat mom's chicken soup.

Reading

Read the article with the answers to the quiz. Then check your answers in Getting Ready to Read.

Answers to this month's quiz

IT IS DANGEROUS TO GO SWIMMING RIGHT AFTER YOU EAT.
False. There is no proof that swimming with a full stomach is more dangerous than swimming at any other time. In fact, there is no **evidence** that anyone has ever drowned because he or she went swimming after eating.

IT IS NOT GOOD TO SIT TOO CLOSE TO THE TELEVISION.
False. It might make your eyes tired, but it doesn't **harm** them because it doesn't cause any permanent damage to your eyesight. It is not good for children to watch too much television, although the distance from the television set is not the problem. The problem is the amount of time children spend watching TV when they should be doing healthier activities such as riding their bikes or playing a sport.

TO IMPROVE YOUR EYESIGHT, EAT A LOT OF CARROTS.
False. Carrots, like all vegetables, are very good for your health, so Mom was right to tell you to eat them. However, no matter how many you eat, they will not improve your ability to see.

TO AVOID COLDS, NEVER GO OUTSIDE WITH WET HAIR.
False. We catch colds from viruses, not from the cold air. If you go outside with wet hair, you might feel cold and uncomfortable, but you won't catch a cold from it. To avoid colds, wash your hands frequently, and stay away from people who are coughing and sneezing.

TO GET OVER A COLD, EAT MOM'S CHICKEN SOUP.
True...sort of. To get over a cold, it helps to drink a lot of liquids, so chicken soup (or anything else that contains a lot of water) is good for you. And since there is strong evidence that people who feel loved recover faster from an illness, homemade soup from your Mom might be just what the doctor ordered!

Multilevel Strategy

- **Pre-level:** Give students more time to read the article.
- **At-level, Above-level:** Have students underline all of the infinitives in the article.

After You Read

A Look at the **boldface** words in the article. Find a synonym in the same paragraph. Write the synonyms next to the words below. Be careful. You might need to write more than one word.

> **Reading Skill:**
> **Recognizing Synonyms**
>
> **Synonyms** are words that have similar meanings, such as *large* and *big*. When you read, look for words or expressions with similar meanings. This will help you understand the writer's main point.

1. evidence
   proof

2. harm
   damage

3. eyesight
   ability to see

4. avoid
   stay away from

5. get over
   recover

B Read the article again. Complete the sentences.

1. Quiz answer 1: It is safe to _go swimming after you eat_.

2. Quiz answer 2: It is not harmful for children to _sit close to the television_. However, it isn't good for children to _watch too much TV_.

3. Quiz answer 3: It is healthy to _eat carrots_. However, it doesn't _improve your ability to see_.

4. Quiz answer 4: It is not dangerous to _go outside with wet hair_.
   To _prevent_ a cold, it is important to _wash your hands frequently_ and _stay away from people who are coughing and sneezing_

5. Quiz answer 5: To _get over_ a cold faster, you should _drink a lot of liquids_.

After You Read

A **Teaching Time: 10–15 min.**

- Read the information in the Reading Skill box with the class.
- Have students complete the task.
- PAIRS. Have students compare their answers with a classmate. If their answers are different, tell them to decide whose answer is correct.
- Call on students to say answers. Correct as needed

B **Teaching Time: 10–15 min.**

- Have students complete the task. Tell them to underline the sentences in the article where they find the answers.
- Call on students to say answers. As they give their answers, have them tell you the paragraph and the line number where the answer can be found in the article. Then have them read those sentences from the article aloud as the other students follow along in their books.

Expansion Start a discussion on health myths. Ask students if they had ever heard any of the health myths in the article before. If so, which ones? Who did they hear them from? Then ask them if they disagree with anything in the article. Ask them to explain.

Writing

Getting Ready to Write

A — Teaching Time: 10–15 min.

- Have students study the Writing Tip.
- Read the example with the class.
- Have students complete the task. Tell them to try to think of words that they already know first. Have some dictionaries and thesauruses available for students to refer to as needed.
- PAIRS. Have students compare their answers.
- Call on students to say answers. Correct as needed.

B — Teaching Time: 10–15 min.

- Have students read the model paragraph.
- PAIRS. Have students complete the task.

Expansion

- Have students read the model paragraph again. Tell them to look at the words in Exercise A and find synonyms in the model for the first five. Have them circle them.
- Have them compare their answers with a classmate.
- Call on students to say answers, and write them on the board:

  believe: claim (line 2)

  sleep: rest (line 5)

  important: essential (line 5)

  eat: give your body food (line 4)

  exercise: work out (line 8)

Writing

Getting Ready to Write

A Write as many synonyms for each word as you can. Use a dictionary or a thesaurus (a dictionary that gives synonyms) if you need help. *Answers will vary.*

1. believe = _____think, guess_____
2. sleep = _____
3. important = _____
4. eat = _____
5. exercise = _____
6. safe = _____
7. sick = _____
8. healthy = _____
9. fat = _____
10. thin = _____

> **Writing Tip**
>
> Use synonyms to make your writing more interesting.
>
> Example:
>
> *stay away from*
>
> To **avoid** colds, **avoid** people who are coughing and sneezing.

B Read the model paragraph.

> Many people believe that you should eat most of your food in the morning or afternoon. They claim that if you eat late at night, the food will turn to fat, and you will gain weight. This is not true. Your body does not shut down when you go to sleep. It is important to give your body food so that it keeps working while you rest. However, it is essential to avoid eating junk food. To stay thin, you should eat healthy food, like vegetables, late at night — or at any time of day! And, of course, you should exercise regularly. Experts say that you should try to work out for at least an hour, three or four times a week.

PAIRS. **Read the model again. Were you surprised by what was true and what wasn't true?**

Now, choose a health myth from your country (something people think is true but is actually false). Talk about what people believe.

Language Note

Point out that although two words are synonyms, that doesn't mean that we can use either word in all situations. Write the words *fat* and *heavy* on the board as an example. Say: *The words* fat *and* heavy *can be synonyms. However, they are only synonyms when we are talking about the weight and size of people or animals. For example, we can say that a suitcase is heavy, but we can't say that it's fat. Also, you need to be careful about whether the synonym has a positive, negative, or neutral (not positive or negative) meaning. For example,* fat *has a negative meaning, but* heavy *has a neutral meaning. As you listen to and read more English, you will get better at knowing which synonyms work in different contexts.*

Prewriting: Using a Cluster

You are going to write a paragraph about a common health myth in your country. Before you write, look at the cluster for the writing model. Then complete a new cluster to get ideas for your writing. Write any ideas you can think of about your topic.

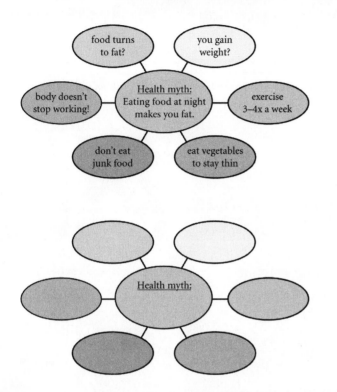

Writing

Now write a paragraph about a common health myth in your country. The writing tip, the model paragraph, and your notes will help you. Write in your notebook.

Prewriting

Teaching Time: 15–20 min.

- Have students complete the task. Walk around and help as needed.
- PAIRS. Have students exchange clusters. Tell them to ask questions about anything they don't understand.

Writing

Teaching Time: 15–20 min.

- Have students complete the task. Encourage them to consider the feedback they got from their partner as they write their paragraphs.

Multilevel Strategy

Pre-level: While the other students make their clusters and exchange them with their partners, assist the pre-level students in completing their clusters. If they don't have time to finish their paragraphs in class, assign them for homework.

Teaching Tip

If you see that a student is struggling to come up with an idea, suggest one of the myths below. However, make sure that students write about myths with which they are familiar.

Common health myths

- You will catch a cold if you sleep with your windows open or if you sleep in a room with a lot of drafts.
- If someone has the hiccups, scare them and the hiccups will go away.
- Never let a cat sleep in a baby's room. The cat will steal the baby's breath.

Unit 18
Free Time

Learning Goals

- Learn vocabulary related to likes and dislikes
- Learn how to use gerunds as subjects; gerunds as objects of prepositions; and gerunds and infinitives as objects of verbs
- Listen to a conversation about free-time activities and to a report about the most common free-time activities in the United States
- Read an article about the origins of surfing and write a paragraph about a free-time activity
- Talk about hobbies, interests, and general likes and dislikes, and the ways that people around the world spend their free time

Learner Persistence

Help students identify their next educational step.

Warm-up

Teaching Time: 3–5 min.

- Have students look at the pictures. Ask: *What are the people doing? Are they enjoying themselves?*

Vocabulary

Teaching Time: 10–15 min.

- Read the example with the class.
- Have students complete the task.
- 🎧 Play Track 26 while students listen and check their answers.
- Read the words in the box and have students repeat chorally.

Expansion PAIRS. Have students talk about the activities in the pictures. Write these questions on the board, and have students ask and answer in pairs.
Which activities do you like to do? How often do you do them? Which activities don't you like to do? Why not? Which activities have you never done?

Unit 18
Free Time

Grammar
- Gerunds as Subjects
- Gerunds as Objects of Prepositions
- Gerunds or Infinitives as Objects of Verbs

Vocabulary

CD 3 TRACK 26 Match the numbers with the words. Then listen and check your answers.

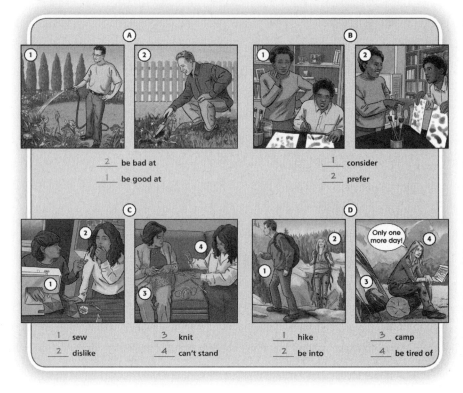

A	B
2 be bad at	1 consider
1 be good at	2 prefer

C	D
1 sew	1 hike
2 dislike	2 be into
3 knit	3 camp
4 can't stand	4 be tired of

240 Unit 18

Listening

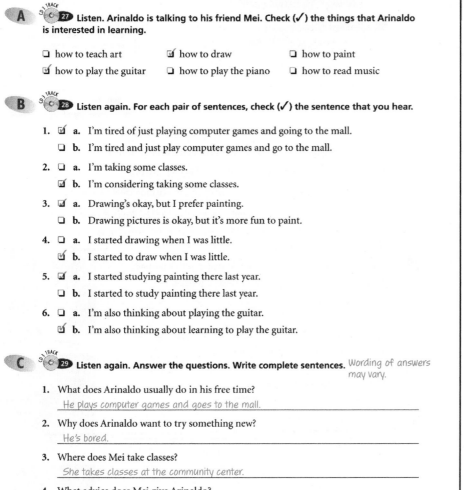

A 🎵 **27** Listen. Arinaldo is talking to his friend Mei. Check (✓) the things that Arinaldo is interested in learning.

- ☐ how to teach art
- ☑ how to draw
- ☐ how to paint
- ☑ how to play the guitar
- ☐ how to play the piano
- ☐ how to read music

B 🎵 **28** Listen again. For each pair of sentences, check (✓) the sentence that you hear.

1. ☑ **a.** I'm tired of just playing computer games and going to the mall.
   ☐ **b.** I'm tired and just play computer games and go to the mall.

2. ☐ **a.** I'm taking some classes.
   ☑ **b.** I'm considering taking some classes.

3. ☑ **a.** Drawing's okay, but I prefer painting.
   ☐ **b.** Drawing pictures is okay, but it's more fun to paint.

4. ☐ **a.** I started drawing when I was little.
   ☑ **b.** I started to draw when I was little.

5. ☑ **a.** I started studying painting there last year.
   ☐ **b.** I started to study painting there last year.

6. ☐ **a.** I'm also thinking about playing the guitar.
   ☑ **b.** I'm also thinking about learning to play the guitar.

C 🎵 **29** Listen again. Answer the questions. Write complete sentences. *Wording of answers may vary.*

1. What does Arinaldo usually do in his free time?
   He plays computer games and goes to the mall.

2. Why does Arinaldo want to try something new?
   He's bored.

3. Where does Mei take classes?
   She takes classes at the community center.

4. What advice does Mei give Arinaldo?
   She tells him to take drawing classes instead of guitar classes because the art teachers are good at the community center.

Free Time **241**

Option

Assign Unit 18 Supplementary Vocabulary Exercises on the Teacher's Resource Disk as homework or on the Student Persistence CD-ROM as self-access practice.

Listening

A Teaching Time: 10–15 min.

- **Warm-up.** Have students read the answer choices. Ask them if they know how to do any of the activities. Ask for a show of hands for each activity. For example, say: *Raise your hand if you know how to draw.* Then ask students if they would like to learn how to do any of the activities. For example, say: *Raise your hand if you would like to learn how to draw.*
- Read the directions with the class. Make sure they understand that *interested in learning* means *wants to learn.*
- 🎧 Play Track 27 as students listen and complete the task.
- Call on students to say answers. Play the conversation again if necessary, this time pausing the recording as each answer is given.

B Teaching Time: 10–15 min.

- Have students read the answer choices.
- 🎧 Play Track 28 as students listen and complete the task.
- Call on students to say answers.
- 🎧 Play Track 28 again, this time pausing the recording after each sentence. Confirm the answers students gave previously.

Expansion Have students say whether the sentences in each set have the same or different meanings.

(1: different; 2: different; 3: same; 4: same; 5: same; 6: different)

C Teaching Time: 10–15 min.

- Have students complete the task.
- 🎧 Play Track 29 as students listen and check their answers.
- Call on students to read their answers.
- 🎧 Play Track 29 again, pausing the recording as the answers are given. Confirm the answers students gave previously.

Multilevel Strategy

Pre-level: Make photocopies of the audioscript. Give it to students to look at as they write the answers to Exercise C.

Grammar to Communicate 1

Gerunds as Subjects

Teaching Time: 5–10 min.

- Have students study the chart and the Look Box.
- Write on the board:
  It is difficult to study.
  ___ is difficult.
- Ask students to complete the sentence. (*Studying is difficult.*)
- As you point to the example, say: *Subjects must always be nouns in English. But what happens if you want to use an action such as* study *as the subject of a sentence? Actions are verbs, not nouns, and a subject cannot be a verb. So we change the verb to a noun by adding* –ing.
- Write on board: *Verb* + ing = *gerund.* Say: *A gerund is the name for the noun that is formed when we add* –ing *to the verb.*
- Write the following sentence on the board under the gerund example:
  I am studying English.
- Say: *Not all words that end in* –ing, *however, are gerunds. In this example,* studying *is a verb, not a gerund. How do we know? Because it comes after the subject* I *and the auxiliary verb* am. *It is the main verb of the sentence, in the progressive form:* be + verb + –ing.
- Write the first sentence in Exercise A on the board: *My husband is hiking this weekend. Hiking is good for him.*
- Say: *There are two words that end in* –ing *in these sentences. Which one is the gerund, and which one is the verb?* (verb = is *hiking*—first sentence; gerund = *Hiking*—second sentence)

A **Teaching Time: 5–10 min.**

- Have students complete the task.
- Call on students to write the sentences with the circled gerunds on the board. Correct as needed. Point out that when the subject of the sentence is a gerund, we use the singular form of the verb.

B **Teaching Time: 10–15 min.**

- Write the example on the board:
  It takes me a long time to do crossword puzzles.

GERUNDS AS SUBJECTS

Gerund (Subject)	Verb	
Watching TV	is	fun.
Playing cards	isn't	

Look
Verbs in the progressive form end in *–ing*, but they are not gerunds.

I'm knitting a hat for my son. (verb)
Knitting is a fun hobby. (gerund)

A **Circle the gerunds.**

1. My husband is hiking this weekend. (Hiking) is good for him.
2. (Doing) crossword puzzles is fun. I've been doing a lot of them lately.
3. I've been singing with a chorus for years. (Singing) relaxes me.
4. We aren't going on vacation this year. (Going) on vacation costs a lot of money.
5. Next year, I'm going to swim more. (Swimming) helps people lose weight.
6. (Drawing) takes a lot of practice. I've been drawing for years, but I'm not very good.

B **Rewrite the sentences. Begin each sentence with a gerund.**

1. It takes me a long time to do crossword puzzles.
   <u>Doing crossword puzzles takes me a long time.</u>
2. It isn't easy to play the piano.
   <u>Playing the piano isn't easy.</u>
3. It is sometimes dangerous to ride horses.
   <u>Riding horses is sometimes dangerous.</u>
4. It is expensive to take tennis lessons.
   <u>Taking tennis lessons is expensive.</u>
5. It is fun to play chess.
   <u>Playing chess is fun.</u>
6. It takes practice to be a good chess player.
   <u>Being a good chess player takes practice.</u>
7. It is sometimes scary to hike alone.
   <u>Hiking alone is sometimes scary.</u>
8. It takes a lot of work to be in a chorus.
   <u>Being in a chorus takes a lot of work.</u>

crossword puzzle

chess

chorus

242 **Unit 18**

- Say: *Change the infinitive to a gerund,* (cross out the infinitive *to do* and write *Doing* above it) *move the gerund into the subject position* (circle *Doing crossword puzzles,* and draw an arrow to the beginning of the sentence) *cross out It* (cross out *It*). *You have a new sentence with the same meaning, but different grammar.* (Rewrite new sentence below it: *Doing crossword puzzles takes me a long time.*)
- Have students complete the task.
- Call on students to say answers. Correct as needed.

Grammar Notes

1. Gerunds are used as nouns. We form a gerund by adding *–ing* to the end of a verb.
2. Like nouns, gerunds can be the subject of a sentence.
3. Use the singular form of the verb after a gerund.
4. Use the plural form of the verb after two or more gerunds.
5. Gerunds and the present participle of verbs look the same. They both end in *–ing.*
6. Turn to page 295 for information about the spelling of gerunds.
7. For more information about this grammar topic, see page 293.

C Answer the questions. Begin each sentence with *I think*. Answers will vary.

1. Which is better for your health: swimming or running?
   I think swimming is better. OR *I think running is better.*

2. Which is more dangerous: riding a horse or hiking?
   _____

3. Which is less expensive: fishing or playing tennis?
   _____

4. Which is harder: knitting or sewing?
   _____

5. Which takes more practice: singing in a chorus or playing a musical instrument?
   _____

6. Which is more important for most boys: being a good dancer or being good at sports?
   _____

D Write sentences with the words in the boxes. Use gerunds. Answers will vary.

bake	knit	bad for you	fun
camp	play computer games	boring	good for you
draw	ride a bike	dangerous	popular
fish	ride a horse	difficult	relaxing
hike	sew	easy	scary

1. *Camping is often fun, but sometimes there are mosquitoes.*
2. _____
3. _____
4. _____
5. _____
6. _____

TIME to TALK

GROUPS. **Make a list of several activities. Describe an activity on your list to a different group. The other group tries to guess what the activity is. Take turns.**

Example:
A: *Learning this is difficult and takes practice.*   C: *Playing the piano?*
B: *Playing chess?*   A: *That's right.*
A: *No. Lessons are very expensive.*

Free Time 243

C Teaching Time: 10–15 min.

- Call on a student to read the example.
- Have students complete the task. Remind them that they're giving their opinions.
- Call on students to read their answers. Correct as needed.
- For each sentence, ask other students if they agree. Encourage students to explain their opinions.

Multilevel Strategy

- **At-level, Above-level:** When students give their opinions, have them use this pattern: *I think hiking is more dangerous than riding a horse because . . . .*

D Teaching Time: 10–15 min.

- Call on a student to read the example.
- Have students complete the task.
- PAIRS. Have students read their sentences to each other, and ask if their partner agrees with them. If their partners don't agree, they should explain why.
- Call on students to read some of their sentences. Correct as needed. Ask the rest of the class if they agree with the student's opinion. If they don't agree, have them explain why.

Option

Assign Unit 18 Supplementary Grammar to Communicate 1 Exercises on the Teacher's Resource Disk as homework or on the Student Persistence CD-ROM as self-access practice.

TIME to TALK

Teaching Time: 3–5 min.

- Read the instructions with the class. Call on two students to read the example.
- GROUPS. Have students complete the task. Give them five minutes in their groups to come up with a list of activities.
- Have the groups take turns giving hints and guessing. Make a note of any errors that they make in the use of gerunds, but don't interrupt the activity.
- After each group has had at least one turn describing and one turn guessing, write the errors that you noticed on the board. Call on students to correct them.

Gerunds as Objects of Prepositions

Teaching Time: 5–10 min.

- Have students study the chart.
- Write on the board:

  He is into sports.

  He is into swimming.

- Say: *Prepositions are words like* in, into, at, about, *and* on. *We use nouns after prepositions. For example, in the first sentence on the board,* into *is a preposition, and* sports *is a noun.* (Underline *into* and write *prep*; underline *sports* and write *noun*).

- Say: *But what happens if we want to use a verb after a preposition? The only way we can do it is if we add –ing to the verb, and make it a gerund. For example, in the second sentence, we can't use* swim *after* into, *because* swim *is a verb. So we turn the verb into a gerund—swimming.* (Underline *swimming* and write *gerund = noun*) *Whenever you use a verb after a preposition, you must use the gerund form.*

A Teaching Time: 10–15 min.

- Have students study the Look Box. Tell them that these are very common verb + preposition combinations in English. Tell them that they need to memorize the expressions and learn their meaning. Point out that in many of the expressions, the meaning of the verb + preposition is different from the meaning of the verb alone, for example, *give up* vs. *give.*
- Call on a student to read the example.
- Have students complete the task.
- Call on students to say answers. Correct as needed.

B Teaching Time: 10–15 min.

- Call on a student to read the example. Ask the student: *Are you interested in learning new things?*
- Write on the board *interested in*. Point out that *interested* is an adjective. Explain that there are many adjective + preposition combinations in English, and the only way to learn them is to memorize them.

- Have students complete the task. Remind them to use the verb *be* before the adjectives.
- Call on students to read their answers. Correct as needed.

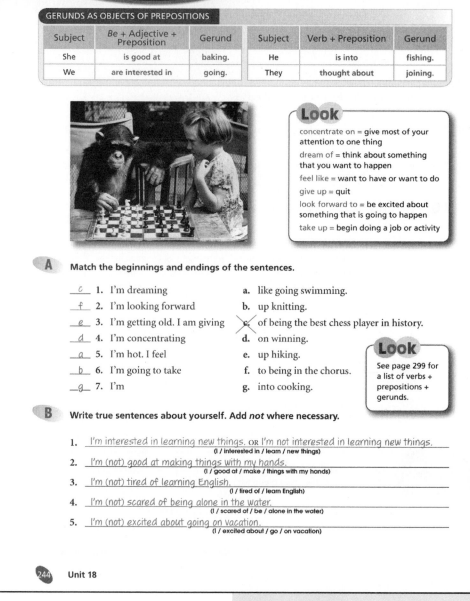

GERUNDS AS OBJECTS OF PREPOSITIONS

Subject	Be + Adjective + Preposition	Gerund	Subject	Verb + Preposition	Gerund
She	is good at	baking.	He	is into	fishing.
We	are interested in	going.	They	thought about	joining.

Look

concentrate on = give most of your attention to one thing

dream of = think about something that you want to happen

feel like = want to have or want to do

give up = quit

look forward to = be excited about something that is going to happen

take up = begin doing a job or activity

A Match the beginnings and endings of the sentences.

_c_ 1. I'm dreaming
_f_ 2. I'm looking forward
_e_ 3. I'm getting old. I am giving
_d_ 4. I'm concentrating
_a_ 5. I'm hot. I feel
_b_ 6. I'm going to take
_g_ 7. I'm

a. like going swimming.
b. up knitting.
c. of being the best chess player in history.
d. on winning.
e. up hiking.
f. to being in the chorus.
g. into cooking.

Look

See page 299 for a list of verbs + prepositions + gerunds.

B Write true sentences about yourself. Add *not* where necessary.

1. I'm interested in learning new things. OR I'm not interested in learning new things.
   (I / interested in / learn / new things)
2. I'm (not) good at making things with my hands.
   (I / good at / make / things with my hands)
3. I'm (not) tired of learning English.
   (I / tired of / learn English)
4. I'm (not) scared of being alone in the water.
   (I / scared of / be / alone in the water)
5. I'm (not) excited about going on vacation.
   (I / excited about / go / on vacation)

Grammar Notes

1. Use a gerund after a preposition. The preposition can come after a verb, an adjective, or a noun.
2. For a negative gerund, add *not* before the gerund.
3. For more information on this grammar topic, see page 293.

Watch Out!

Students are often confused by the fact that the word *to* has different grammatical functions: It is the marker for the infinitive, and it is a preposition. Errors such as the following are common: *I am looking forward to see him.* Listen for and correct these errors.

C   **Combine the sentences. Take out or change words where necessary.**

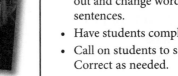

1. I want to be the star of the team. I dream of it.
   I dream of being the star of the team.

2. We might try out for the chorus. We talked about it.
   We talked about trying out for the chorus.

3. I joined a new team. I'm excited about it.
   I'm excited about joining a new team.

4. I might take up chess. I'm thinking about it.
   I'm thinking about taking up chess.

5. We're going to play next week. I'm looking forward to it.
   I'm looking forward to playing next week.

6. They finished the crossword puzzle. They concentrated on it.
   They concentrated on finishing the crossword puzzle.

7. He cooked last night. He felt like it.
   He felt like cooking last night.

TIME to TALK

GROUPS. Discuss the questions.

1. What kinds of things are difficult for you to concentrate on?

2. What do you feel like doing after class today? Are you going to do it?

3. Have you ever given anything up? If so, what have you given up? When did you give it up? Why?

4. Have you taken anything up in the past few years? What have you taken up? Are you happy that you took it up?

5. Are you looking forward to anything these days? If so, what?

6. What did you dream of doing when you were young?

Example:
A: *What kinds of things are difficult for you to concentrate on?*
B: *It is difficult for me to concentrate on studying. I have two kids, and they are very noisy.*

Free Time **245**

C   **Teaching Time: 10–15 min.**

- Call on a student to read the example. Point out that they will need to take out and change words to combine the sentences.
- Have students complete the task.
- Call on students to say answers. Correct as needed.

Watch Out!

The use of *like* as a preposition in the expression *feel like* might confuse students. Make sure they understand that the word *like* in this expression has no connection to *like* the verb, either in meaning or grammar. Before you correct student errors with *feel like*, find out what the student really means.

> **Student:** *I feel like to dance.*
> **Teacher:** *So you like to dance in general, but not right now, right?*

Option

Assign Unit 18 Supplementary Grammar to Communicate 2 Exercises on the Teacher's Resource Disk as homework or on the Student Persistence CD-ROM as self-access practice.

TIME to TALK

Teaching Time: 10–15 min.

- Read the directions and the first question with the class.
- Call on two students to read the example.
- GROUPS. Have students complete the task.
- Have one student from each group tell the class something interesting about a person in the group. Correct as needed.

Multilevel Strategy

- **Pre-level:** Have pre-level students work together for this activity. Have them ask and answer three questions. Have them write their answers in their notebooks.
- **At-level, Above-level:** Have these students ask and answer all the questions. Encourage them to ask additional questions to find out more information.

Grammar to Communicate 3

Gerunds or Infinitives as Objects of Verbs

Teaching Time: 5–10 min.

- Have students study the chart and the Look Box.
- Write on the board:

CORRECT

I enjoy reading.
          object

INCORRECT

~~I enjoy to read.~~   ~~I enjoy read.~~

CORRECT

I want to read.
          object

INCORRECT

~~I want reading.~~   ~~I want read.~~

CORRECT

I like to read. / *I like reading.*
      object   object

INCORRECT

~~I like read.~~

- As you point to the sentences on the board, say:

When we use a verb as the object of another verb, the verb in the object position must be in the gerund or infinitive form. Some verbs, such as enjoy, can only take gerunds as their object. Other verbs, such as want, can only take infinitives as their object. But some verbs, such as like, can take either an infinitive or a gerund as their object. How do you know whether a verb is followed by a gerund, an infinitive, or either? You have to memorize them.

A Teaching Time: 10–15 min.

- Read the example with the class.
- Have students complete the task. Make sure they understand that they can say *Nobody I know* + verb when they answer.
- PAIRS. Have students complete the task.
- Call on students to read their sentences. Correct as needed.

Grammar to Communicate 3

Some verbs can be followed only by a gerund, some only by an infinitive, and some by either a gerund or an infinitive.

GERUNDS OR INFINITIVES AS OBJECTS OF VERBS

Verb + Gerund		Verb + Infinitive		Verb + Gerund or Infinitive	
I considered She finished We stopped	playing.	I've decided We want They expect	to play.	I can't stand You prefer They started	playing. to play.

A Change the names to make true sentences about people you know, or write *Nobody I know*. Answers will vary.

                My mother   Nobody I know
Example: ~~My nephew Jack~~ loves reading. OR ~~My nephew Jack~~ loves reading.

1. My nephew Jack loves reading.
2. My friend Lynn loves to sing.
3. My mother enjoys knitting.
4. My father likes to fish.
5. My friend Ari likes listening to music.
6. My brother misses being on a team.
7. My friend Bob dislikes going for walks.
8. My sister is learning to play the guitar.
9. My niece hopes to become a writer.
10. My sister-in-law hates to watch TV.
11. My husband hates dancing.

PAIRS. Tell each other your sentences.

Look

See page 299 for information about verbs with gerunds and infinitives.

B Check (✓) what comes after each verb: gerund, infinitive, or either (gerund or infinitive). Look at the sentences on this page for help.

VERB +	GERUND	INFINITIVE	GERUND OR INFINITIVE
can't stand			✓
consider	✓		
decide		✓	
dislike	✓		
enjoy	✓		
expect		✓	
finish	✓		
hate			✓
hope		✓	

VERB +	GERUND	INFINITIVE	GERUND OR INFINITIVE
learn		✓	
like			✓
love			✓
miss	✓		
prefer			✓
start			✓
stop	✓		
want		✓	

Unit 18

B Teaching Time: 10–15 min.

- Read the examples with the class.
- Have students complete the task.
- Call on students to say answers. Correct as needed.

Grammar Notes

1. Use a gerund after some verbs—for example, *dislike, finish*.
2. Use an infinitive after some verbs—for example, *expect, hope*.
3. You can use a gerund or infinitive after some verbs—for example, *love, hate*. There is little difference in meaning.
4. Turn to page 299 for a list of the verbs that take gerunds or infinitives or both.
5. For more information on this grammar topic, see page 293.

T-246 Center Stage 3

C Complete the sentences. Use the infinitive or gerund. Sometimes both the gerund and the infinitive are correct.

1. I like _____being_____ with friends. I don't like _____to be_____ alone. (be)
2. I love _going / to go_ for long walks, but I dislike _____going_____ alone. (go)
3. I dislike _swimming_ in a pool. I prefer _swimming / to swim_ in the ocean. (swim)
4. I finished _____doing_____ one puzzle, so I started _doing / to do_ a new one. (do)
5. My husband always wants _____to eat_____ out, but I prefer _eating / to eat_ at home. (eat)
6. I miss _____singing_____. I want _____to sing_____ with a chorus. (sing)
7. I can't stand _____playing_____ chess, but I enjoy _____playing_____ computer games. (play)
8. I don't like _gardening / to garden_. I stopped _____gardening_____ when I sold my house. (garden)
9. I love _drawing / to draw_. I want _____to draw_____ well. (draw)
10. I considered _____taking_____ art classes, but I decided _____to take_____ sewing classes. (take)

PAIRS. Now change the verbs above to infinitives or gerunds where possible.

Example: *I like to be with friends. I don't like being alone.*

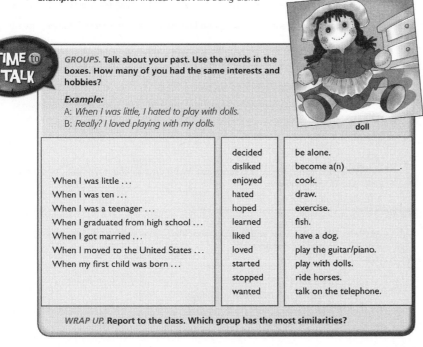

GROUPS. Talk about your past. Use the words in the boxes. How many of you had the same interests and hobbies?

Example:
A: *When I was little, I hated to play with dolls.*
B: *Really? I loved playing with my dolls.*

doll

	decided	be alone.
	disliked	become a(n) _____.
When I was little …	enjoyed	cook.
When I was ten …	hated	draw.
When I was a teenager …	hoped	exercise.
When I graduated from high school …	learned	fish.
When I got married …	liked	have a dog.
When I moved to the United States …	loved	play the guitar/piano.
When my first child was born …	started	play with dolls.
	stopped	ride horses.
	wanted	talk on the telephone.

WRAP UP. Report to the class. Which group has the most similarities?

- Read the example with the class.
- Have students complete the task.
- PAIRS. Have students complete the task.
- Call on students to say answers. If either a gerund or infinitive is possible, have them read the sentence both ways. Correct as needed.

Teaching Tip

Make your lessons as interactive as possible. When students are reading answers to an exercise, for example, stop and ask their opinion about what the sentence says, or ask if the information in it is true about them. For example, for sentences 1, 2, 3, 5, and 9 in Exercise C, ask questions such as: *Do you like being with friends? Do you like to be alone?*

Option

Assign Unit 18 Supplementary Grammar to Communicate 3 Exercises on the Teacher's Resource Disk as homework or on the Student Persistence CD-ROM as self-access practice.

TIME to TALK

Teaching Time: 10–15 min.

- Call on two students to read the example.
- GROUPS. Have students complete the task. Tell them to keep track of the number of similarities they discover in their groups.
- WRAP UP. Have one student from the group report on the number of similarities in the group. Write on the board:
  We found ___ similarities in our group.
- Now ask another student from each group to give an example of an interesting or surprising similarity in the group.

Review and Challenge

Grammar

Teaching Time: 5–10 min.

- Read the example with the class.
- Have students complete the task.
- 🎧 Play Track 30 while students listen and check their answers.
- Call on students to say answers. Correct as needed.

Multilevel Strategy

- **Pre-level:** Tell students what the mistakes are and have them rewrite the advertisement correctly.

Dictation

Teaching Time: 5–10 min.

- 🎧 Play Track 31 while students listen and write what they hear.
- 🎧 Play Track 31 again while students check their answers.
- Ask for volunteers to write the sentences on the board.
- 🎧 Play Track 31 again and correct the sentences on the board.

Multilevel Strategy

- **Pre-level:** Give students a worksheet with some of the words from the dictation already provided.

Speaking

Teaching Time: 10–15 min.

- GROUPS. Have students complete the task.
- WRAP UP. Go around the room, saying each student's name. When you say a name, have the other students tell you something about that student using a verb or expression from the box.

Review and Challenge

Grammar

💿 **30** Correct the advertisement. There are seven mistakes. The first mistake is corrected for you. Then listen and check your answers.

BAY AREA HIKING CLUB

Do you feel like ~~to do~~ *doing* something new? Are you tired of ~~be~~ *being* in the office all the time? Are you interested in ~~spend~~ *spending* time with fun people? Then ~~hike~~ *hiking* is the answer for you. Being in the fresh air and ~~see~~ *seeing* all the beautiful flowers and trees will make you feel wonderful.

You don't need to be an experienced hiker. You just have to enjoy ~~to~~ ~~go~~ *going* for long walks. If you want ~~getting~~ *to get* more information about our group, call (777) 555-3476. Great experiences are waiting for you.

Dictation

💿 **31** Listen. You will hear five sentences. Write them in your notebook. *See the audioscript on p. 326 for the sentences.*

Speaking

GROUPS. Talk about what you like (and don't like) to do in your free time. Use all the words in the box at least once.

be good at	be terrible at	can't stand	enjoy	look forward to
be into	be tired of	dislike	hate	love

WRAP UP. Now tell the class about the people in your group.

248 Unit 18

For example:

Teacher: *Svetlana?*

Student A: *Svetlana can't stand cooking.*

Continue until the class has said something about every student.

Option

Speaking. Make the WRAP UP a competition. Have each group make a statement about a student from another group using a verb or expression from the box. If their statement is correct, the group gets a point. Then it is the next team's turn. Keep going as long as students are interested, but make sure that each team has an equal number of turns.

Listening

A ⊙ **32** Listen to the report about free time in the U.S. Check (✓) the topics that the reporter discusses.

> **Look**
>
> conduct a poll = ask many people what they think about something

- ☑ how adults spend their free time
- ☑ the most popular activities
- ☐ how many hours a week people work
- ☑ changes since 1995
- ☐ how children spend their free time
- ☑ the least popular activities
- ☑ how much free time people have every week
- ☐ why people have very little free time

B ⊙ **32** Listen again. Complete the chart.

bowling

Source: Harris Interactive Poll, 2004

Favorite Free-Time Activities

Activity	2004	1995
reading	35%	28%
watching TV	21%	25%
spending time with family	20%	12%
going to the movies	10%	8%
fishing	8%	10%
using a computer	7%	2%
gardening	6%	9%
walking	6%	5%
renting movies	6%	8%
playing team sports	5%	9%
sewing	4%	7%
swimming	2%	7%
playing tennis	1%	2%
horseback riding	1%	2%
running	1%	2%
dancing	1%	1%
bowling	1%	4%

TIME to TALK

GROUPS. Discuss the questions.

1. What is the most interesting thing that you learned about free time in the U.S.? What is the most surprising thing? Which information is the same as you expected it to be?

2. How are free-time activities in your country different from those in the U.S.?

Free Time 249

Listening

A Teaching Time: 10–15 min.

- **Warm-up.** Tell students that they are going to listen to a radio report about how people in the United States spend their free time. Ask them what they think the three most popular free-time activities are in the United States. Write their guesses on the board.

- Call on a student to read the information in the Look Box and the directions.

- Have students read the answer choices.

- 🎧 Play Track 32 as students listen and complete the task.

- Call on students to say answers.

- 🎧 Play Track 32 again, this time pausing the recording as each answer is given.

- Have students look at the guesses on the board. Cross out the incorrect guesses and check (✓) the correct ones.

B Teaching Time: 10–15 min.

- Read the example with the class.

- 🎧 Play Track 32 while students listen and complete the task.

- 🎧 Play Track 32 again while students listen and check their answers.

- 🎧 Play Track 32 again, this time pausing the recording as each answer is given. Have students call out the answers.

Multilevel Strategy

- **Pre-level:** Give students a copy of the audioscript with the same information blanked out as is missing in the chart. Have them read along as they listen, and fill in the missing information on the audioscript. Then have them transfer the information from the audioscript to the chart. Have them listen again and check the answers in the chart.

- **Above-level:** Have students take notes in their notebooks rather than in the chart. Then have them fill in the chart from their notes. Play the recording one more time as they complete the chart.

Option

Assign Unit 18 Review and Challenge Supplementary Exercises on the Teacher's Resource Disk as homework or on the Student Persistence CD-ROM as self-access practice.

TIME to TALK

Teaching Time: 10–15 min.

- GROUPS. Have students complete the task. Walk around and help as needed.

Expansion Tell students to imagine that someone has conducted the same poll in their countries. Have them look at the chart in Exercise B and tell the people in their group whether they think that the percentages would be higher or lower for each activity in their countries. Have them add activities if necessary.

Getting Ready to Read

Teaching Time: 5–10 min.

- **Warm-up.** Tell students that they are going to read an article about surfing. Ask how many students have seen someone surfing. Then ask if anyone knows how to. If so, have them tell the class about surfing. If not, ask if anyone in the class has ever watched surfers, either on television or in person. Then ask if anyone would like to learn how to surf.
- Read the example with the class.
- Have students complete the task.
- Call on students to read their questions. Write them on the board.

Reading

Teaching Time: 15–20 min.

- Have students read the article.
- Have students look at the questions on the board and tell you which ones were not answered in the article. Cross those questions out. Then call on students to answer the remaining questions.

Multilevel Strategy

- **Pre-level:** Give students more time to read the article.
- **At-level, Above-level:** Have students underline the gerunds and circle the infinitives in the article. Walk around and check their work.

Getting Ready to Read

Preview the article. Read the first and last sentences of each paragraph. Then write questions that you think the article will answer. *Answers will vary.*

1. _____Who were the first surfers?_____
2. _____
3. _____

Reading

Read the article. Then check your questions in Getting Ready to Read. Can you answer them now?

SURFING

When most people hear the word *surfing,* they think of modern California teenagers in the ocean. However, surfing actually started in Hawaii **centuries** ago. No one knows exactly when Hawaiians began to surf. In 1778, James King, a British **explorer,** saw Hawaiians riding the waves. He wrote about *he'e nalu,* the Hawaiian word for surfing. King was **amazed** by the skill of the surfers. At that time, many people in England couldn't even swim.

Surfing was an important part of early Hawaiian **society.** In Hawaii, a system of laws called Kapu **ruled** everything—including surfing. For example, Hawaiian kings and queens and other members of the **royal family** had their own beaches. Other Hawaiians could never swim on those beaches. The royal family also had longer and heavier boards. The surfboard was a symbol: it showed the owner's **status** in the society.

In 1820, Christian missionaries from the U.S. arrived in Hawaii. They believed that surfing was a waste of time and tried to stop people from doing it. As a result, surfing almost **disappeared.** However, in the early 20th century, a Hawaiian teenager named Duke Paoa Kahanamoku made surfing popular again. Duke was a wonderful surfer and swimmer. He competed in the 1912 Olympics and won almost every medal in water sports. After the Olympics, Duke used his **fame** to promote both Hawaii and the **ancient** sport of surfing all over the world.

statue of Duke Kahanamoku
on Waikiki Beach

250 Unit 18

Culture Note

Explain that Hawaii did not become a state until 1959. Then write *Christian missionaries* on the board. Ask if anyone knows what a missionary is. Explain that Christian missionaries are Christians who are sent to a foreign country by their church. Their job is to teach people about Christianity and to convince the people of that country to join their religion.

After You Read

A Look at the **boldface** words in the article. Guess their meaning. Then match the words with the correct definitions.

_g_	1. centuries	**a.**	had power over a country and people
_i_	2. explorer	**b.**	very, very old
_d_	3. amazed	**c.**	did not exist anymore
_j_	4. society	**d.**	very surprised
_a_	5. ruled	**e.**	the state of being known about by a lot of people
_f_	6. royal family	**f.**	a king or queen and his or her relatives
_h_	7. status	**g.**	hundreds of years
_c_	8. disappeared	**h.**	how important a person is compared to others
_e_	9. fame	**i.**	someone who travels to a place where other people have never been before
_b_	10. ancient	**j.**	a group of people who live together and have the same laws

B Read the article again. Then check (✓) the inferences that you can make from the information in the text.

❏ **1.** Under the Kapu laws, only men were allowed to surf.

☑ **2.** The members of the Hawaiian royal family were often excellent surfers.

❏ **3.** Duke Paoa Kahanamoku was a member of the Hawaiian royal family.

❏ **4.** Duke Paoa Kahanamoku only surfed in Hawaii.

☑ **5.** Duke Paoa Kahanamoku is a hero for many Hawaiians.

> **Reading Skill: Making Inferences**
>
> An **inference** is a logical conclusion based on information. Often, writers do not say all of their ideas directly. They expect the reader to make inferences, or guesses, based on the information in the text.

Free Time 251

After You Read

A Teaching Time: 10–15 min.

- Read the example with the class.
- Have students complete the task. Tell them to circle the words in the article that helped them understand the meaning of the new words.
- Call on students to say answers. Have them read the words they circled. Correct as needed.

B Teaching Time: 10–15 min.

- Call on a student to read the information in the Reading Skill box and the instructions. Explain that an inference is much stronger than a guess. An inference is always based on specific information in the text.
- Have students complete the task. For the sentences that they check, tell them to underline the information in the article that led them to that inference.
- Call on students to say answers. Have them tell you the paragraph and the line number of the information that they based their inferences on. (2. paragraph 2, lines 5–12; 5. paragraph 3, lines 6–10 and 15–19) Then have them read those sentences from the article aloud as the other students follow along in their books. Correct as needed.

Multilevel Strategy

Pre-level: Group all pre-level students and assist them with this task.

Writing

Getting Ready to Write

A Teaching Time: 10–15 min.

- Have students study the Writing Tip.
- Read the example with the class.
- Have students complete the tasks. Encourage students to look for words that will help them figure out the order of the sentences, such as *first, final,* and *to sum up.*
- PAIRS. Have students read each other's paragraphs. Did they put the sentences in the same order?
- Call on a student to read the paragraph aloud. Correct as needed.

B Teaching Time: 10–15 min.

- Have students read the model paragraph.
- PAIRS. Have students complete the task.

Expansion PAIRS. Have students underline the gerunds and circle the infinitives in the model.

Writing

Getting Ready to Write

A Number the sentences in logical order for a paragraph.

_6_ a. Every year, sharks attack at least a few surfers.

_3_ b. And even for the best surfers, there is a high risk of broken bones and head injuries.

_2_ c. First of all, you need to be a strong swimmer and have excellent balance.

_1_ d. Surfing is a difficult and dangerous sport.

_7_ e. To sum up, before you take up surfing, you should know the difficulties and risks.

_4_ f. You also need patience, because becoming a surfer takes years.

_5_ g. Shark attacks are a final danger.

Now copy the sentences in the correct order to complete the paragraph.

Surfing is a difficult and dangerous sport. First of all, you need to be a strong swimmer and have excellent balance. And even for the best surfers, there is a high risk of broken bones and head injuries. You also need patience, because becoming a surfer takes years. Shark attacks are a final danger. Every year, sharks attack at least a few surfers. To sum up, before you take up surfing, you should know the difficulties and risks.

B Read the model paragraph.

Mountain climbing is an exciting sport. Mountain climbers have to be strong and healthy. Knowing how to use equipment such as ropes is also important. Serious climbers usually spend years training. But even for well-trained climbers, climbing the highest mountains—for example Mount Everest—is extremely dangerous. The air has very little oxygen, so breathing is difficult. And when your brain doesn't get enough oxygen, thinking clearly is impossible, and you could easily get lost. To sum up, mountain climbing is an exciting, but serious, sport.

PAIRS. **Read the model again. Do you think mountain climbing is an exciting free-time activity? Would you like to do it? Why or why not?**

Now choose another free-time activity. Talk to your partner about why it is exciting, interesting, or fun.

> **Writing Tip**
>
> When you write a paragraph, make sure that the ideas are in a logical order. Think about what the reader needs to know first, second, . . . and last. Start with the main idea, follow with supporting points, and end with a concluding sentence.

Prewriting: Using an Outline

You are going to write a paragraph about a free-time activity. Before you write, look at the outline for the model paragraph. Then complete your own outline.

Writing Model

Main idea: Mountain climbing is an exciting sport.
1. (supporting detail) must be strong, healthy
2. (supporting detail) know how to use equipment
3. (supporting detail) need years of training
4. (supporting detail) breathing difficult
5. (supporting detail) not enough oxygen = confusion; get lost
Concluding sentence = To sum up, mountain climbing is an exciting, but serious, sport.

Main idea: _____

_____

1. (supporting detail) _____
2. (supporting detail) _____
3. (supporting detail) _____
4. (supporting detail) _____
5. (supporting detail) _____

Concluding sentence = _____

_____

Writing

Now write a paragraph about a free-time activity. The writing tip, the model paragraph, and your notes will help you. Write in your notebook.

Prewriting

Teaching Time: 15–20 min.

- Have students complete the task. Tell them that it's okay if they have fewer than six pieces of support for their main idea. However, they should have at least three. Walk around and help as needed.

- PAIRS. Have students exchange outlines. Tell them to ask questions about anything they don't understand in their partner's outline.

Writing

Teaching Time: 15–20 min.

- Have students complete the task.
- Encourage them to consider the feedback they got from their partner as they write their paragraphs.

Multilevel Strategy

Pre-level: While the other students write their outlines and exchange them with their partners, assist pre-level students in completing their outlines. If they don't have time to finish their paragraphs in class, assign them for homework.

Learning Goals

- Learn vocabulary related to police, fire, and other emergency services
- Learn how to use verb + object + infinitive; verb + noun clause; replace noun clauses with *so* and *not*; and use *make* and *let*
- Listen to an interview between a crime victim and the police and to a radio call-in show about fire safety
- Read an article about fire safety and write a paragraph giving advice on how to avoid becoming the victim of a crime, fire, or accident
- Talk about crime, accident, and fire prevention

Learner Persistence

Vary your instructional strategies to keep your class interesting.

Warm-up

Teaching Time: 3–5 min.

- PAIRS. Tell students to cover the vocabulary and look at the pictures. Have them take turns describing what is happening in each picture.

Vocabulary

Teaching Time: 10–15 min.

- Have students complete the task.
- 🎧 Play Track 33 while students listen and check their answers.
- Call on students to say answers. Correct their pronunciation as needed.
- Read the words in the boxes and have students repeat chorally.

Expansion Test students' understanding of the vocabulary. Give simple definitions or descriptions, and have students call out the words. For example:

Driving too fast (speeding)

When you have an accident or are very sick, this is how you get to the hospital (ambulance)

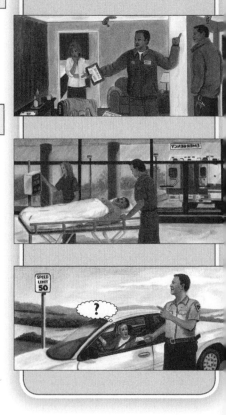

Unit 19
Emergency Services

Grammar
- Verb + Object + Infinitive
- Verb + Noun Clause and Replacing Noun Clauses
- *Make* and *Let*

Vocabulary

🎧 CD 2 TRACK 33 **Complete the sentences with the words in the box. Listen and check your answers.**

| advised | fire hazards | ordered | smoke detectors |

The apartment had a few <u>fire hazards</u>. The fire
1.
inspector <u>ordered</u> the landlord to fix the
2.
<u>smoke detectors</u> immediately. He also <u>advised</u> the
3.   4.
tenant to move the candles.

| ambulance | encouraged | paramedics | suspected |

Ali had chest pains, so he called an <u>ambulance</u>.
5.
When the <u>paramedics</u> arrived, they <u>suspected</u>
6.   7.
he was having a heart attack. They took him to the
hospital. He was okay, but the doctor <u>encouraged</u>
8.
him to lose weight.

| guess | notice | speeding | ticket |

Kay was late, so she was <u>speeding</u>. She didn't
9.
<u>notice</u> the police car. The officer gave her a
10.
<u>ticket</u>. He asked her to <u>guess</u> how fast
11.   12.
she was going.

254   Unit 19

The people who drive ambulances and take people to the hospital (paramedics)

Something that could cause a fire (fire hazard)

Listening

A 🎧 **34** **Listen. What just happened to the woman? Check (✓) the correct answer.**

❏ 1. A man stole her bag and ring when she was at a store.

❏ 2. A man stopped the woman on the street, stole her bag and ring, and drove away.

❏ 3. The woman was walking to the store when a man stole her bag and ring.

☑ 4. The woman was walking home when a man stole her bag and ring and ran away.

B 🎧 **34** **Listen again. Check (✓) the sentences that are true.**

☑ 1. The man made the woman take off her wedding ring.

☑ 2. The man let the woman go.

☑ 3. The woman believes that the man was wearing jeans.

☑ 4. The woman doesn't think that the man has a beard.

☑ 5. The operator told the woman to go to the police station.

❏ 6. The operator expects the woman to wait at the store.

☑ 7. The woman doesn't know if she will get her wedding ring back, but she hopes so.

Look

expect = think that something will happen

C 🎧 **34** **Listen again. Answer the questions. Write complete sentences.** Wording of answers may vary.

1. Where is the woman right now?

   She's at a store at the corner of 16th Avenue and Babcock St.

2. How long did the woman wait before she called 911?

   She called immediately after it happened.

3. What does the man look like?

   He was 17-years-old, white, and tall and thin.

4. Where did the man go?

   He ran down Babcock St.

5. Where is the woman going to go?

   She is going to go to the police station.

Emergency Services **255**

Teaching Tip

Some students may not be comfortable talking about painful personal experiences with crime, fire, and accidents. Others may be eager to talk about their experiences. Provide students with an opportunity to discuss their experiences if they would like to do so, but make it clear that they are not required to talk if they would prefer not to.

Option

Assign Unit 19 Supplementary Vocabulary Exercises on the Teacher's Resource Disk as homework or on the Student Persistence CD-ROM as self-access practice.

Listening

A **Teaching Time: 10–15 min.**

- **Warm-up.** Tell students that they are going to listen to someone describe a robbery. Ask if anyone has ever been robbed. Invite students to tell their experience to the class. (See Teaching Tip below.)

- Have students read the answer choices.

- 🎧 Play Track 34 as students listen and complete the task.

- Call on a student to say the answer. Play the recording again if necessary.

B **Teaching Time: 10–15 min.**

- Have students read the definition in the Look Box.

- Have students read the answer choices and check the statements that they think are true. If they are not sure, tell them to write a question mark (?).

- 🎧 Play Track 34 as students listen and complete the task.

- 🎧 Play Track 34 again, this time pausing the recording as each answer is given.

- Call on students to read the true statements.

Multilevel Strategy

Pre-level: Make photocopies of the audioscript. Give it to students and have them read along as they listen and complete Exercises B and C.

C **Teaching Time: 10–15 min.**

- Have students complete the task.

- 🎧 Play Track 34 as students listen and check their answers.

- Ask volunteers to write their answers on the board.

- 🎧 Play Track 34 again, pausing the recording as the answers are given. Correct the sentences on the board as needed.

Grammar to Communicate 1

Verb + Object + Infinitive

Teaching Time: 5–10 min.

- Have students study the chart.
- Write on the board:

  1. Tony wants to leave.

  2. Tony wants Sue to leave.

- Ask: *In the first example, who wants something?* (Tony) *Who might leave?* (Tony) *In the second example, who wants something?* (Tony) *Who might leave?* (Sue)
- As you point to the examples on the board, say: *Certain verbs, for example,* want, *can take an infinitive or an object + an infinitive. If the subject of the main verb and the infinitive are the same, then the pattern is verb + infinitive, as in example 1. If the subject of the main verb and the infinitive are different, as in example 2, then the pattern is verb + object + infinitive.*
- Write on the board: *He wants her to leave.* (NOT ~~He wants she to leave.~~) Say: *Use an object pronoun between the main verb and the infinitive. Do not use a subject pronoun before the infinitive.*
- Make two columns on the board:

verb + infinitive	verb + object + infinitive
want	want
need	need
would like	would like
expect	expect
—	advise
—	allow
	convince
—	encourage
—	order
	tell

- Say: *Certain verbs, such as* want, need, would like, *and* expect, *can follow either pattern. You can use them with or without an object before the infinitive, but of course with a difference in meaning.* Write on the board:

  I expect to study hard.

  I expect you to study hard.

- Say: *Other verbs, such as* advise, allow, convince, encourage, order, *and* tell *must have an object before*

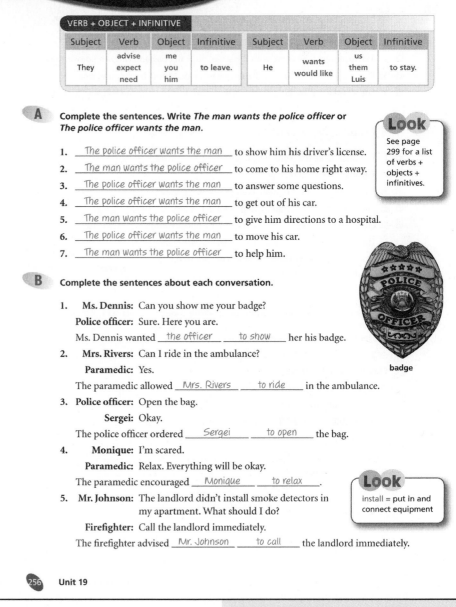

the infinitive. You cannot use these verbs without an object. Write on the board:

I advise you to study hard. (NOT ~~I advise to study hard.~~)

A Teaching Time: 10–15 min.

- Read the examples with the class.
- Have students complete the task.
- Call on students to read the sentences. Correct as needed.

B Teaching Time: 10–15 min.

- Call on a student to read the example.
- Have students complete the task.
- Call on students to say answers. Correct as needed.

Grammar Notes

1. Use an object + infinitive after some verbs—for example, *advise, order.*
2. You can use two different patterns after some verbs—for example, *need, want:* verb + infinitive *or* verb + object + infinitive.
3. Turn to page 299 for a list of the verbs that take object + infinitive.
4. For more information about this grammar topic, see page 293.

Read the situation. Then complete the sentences with your ideas.

1. Al is driving on the highway. Suddenly, he sees a police car behind him. The flashing lights are on.
   The police expect _Al to move over._

2. Roger smelled smoke and called the fire department.
   Roger wanted _the fire department to come right away._

3. The firefighter is talking to students about smoke detectors in their homes.
   The firefighter is encouraging _the students to check their smoke detectors._

4. The paramedic has asked the patient his name three times, but he hasn't answered.
   The paramedic wants _the patient to tell him his name._

5. Rita's elderly grandmother has fallen and can't move. Rita calls 911 for an ambulance.
   Rita needs _an ambulance to come._

6. Drivers can't use Beacon Street today. The police are sending drivers to Market Street.
   The police are not allowing _drivers to use Beacon St. today._

> **Look**
> A police officer **is** here.
> The police **are** there.

TIME to TALK

PAIRS. Read the situations. Then say what you think happened next. Use the verbs in the box and your own ideas.

advised	asked	didn't allow	ordered
allowed	convinced	encouraged	told

1. Tina was driving the wrong way down a one-way street. She saw a police car behind her. What happened next?

2. The police stopped Jim on the highway because he was driving fast. They thought he was acting strange. What happened next?

3. The police saw some teenagers with cans of spray paint writing on a building. What happened next?

4. It was 2:00 A.M. The fire alarm went off in a hotel. What happened next?

Example: *The police officer ordered Tina to pull over. He asked her to take out her driver's license and registration. Then he told her to wait in her car. She had a clean driving record, so he didn't give her a ticket....*

Emergency Services (257)

C Teaching Time: 10–15 min.

- Have students read the information in the Look Box. Explain that *police* is an irregular plural, like *people*. The singular form of *people* is *person*; the singular form of *police* is *police officer*.
- Call on a student to read the example.
- Have students complete the task. Tell them that more than one answer is correct for many of the sentences.
- PAIRS. Have students compare their sentences.
- Call on students to read their answers. Correct as needed.

Multilevel Strategy

- **Pre-level:** Give students more time to complete the task.
- **At-level, Above-level:** Have students complete Unit 19, Grammar to Communicate 1, Exercise B, on the Teacher's Resource Disk. Give them the answer key so that they can correct themselves.

Option

Exercise C. Since students are likely to have different answers, have them write their answers on a separate piece of paper so that you can collect and correct them.

Option

Assign Unit 19 Supplementary Grammar to Communicate 1 Exercises on the Teacher's Resource Disk as homework or on the Student Persistence CD-ROM as self-access practice.

TIME to TALK

Teaching Time: 10–15 min.

- Call on a student to read the example.
- Read the verbs in the box. Make sure the students understand what *convince* means. Explain that when you convince someone to do something, at first they don't want to do it, but then you talk to them and get them to change their mind.
- PAIRS. Have students complete the task. Walk around and help as needed.
- Have each pair tell you one of their sentences. Have the class guess which situation the sentence is about. Then write the sentence on the board and have the class correct it as necessary.

Grammar to Communicate 2

Verb + Noun Clause / Replacing Noun Clauses

Teaching Time: 5–10 min.

- Have students study the charts.
- Write on the board:

The police know   him.
        verb   object = pronoun

They know   that his name is Jim Smith.
    verb   object = noun clause with "that"
            his name is Jim Smith.
        object = noun clause without "that"

- Say: *Some verbs, such as* know, *can be followed by a noun, a pronoun, or a noun clause. A noun clause always has a subject and a verb, but in the sentence, it acts like a noun. That is why it is called a NOUN clause. Noun clauses that are objects often begin with the word* that. *However, you do not need to include* that. *It is optional.*
- Write on the board:

Did the police catch Jim Smith?
I think <u>so</u>. / I believe <u>so</u>.
I don't think <u>so</u>. / I don't believe <u>so</u>.

- Ask: *What does* so *mean here?* (that the police caught Jim Smith) Write on the board after *I don't believe so:*

= I don't think or believe that the police caught him.

- Write: *So after* believe *or* think = *a noun clause*

Affirmative: believe or think + so
Negative: not + believe or think + so

- Point to the board and say: *So can replace a noun clause after the verbs* believe *and* think. *The affirmative is* think *or* believe + so. *The negative is* not + think *or* believe + so.

A   Teaching Time: 10–15 min.

- **Warm-up.** Have students look at the picture. Ask: *What is a pickpocket?* (Someone who steals things out of people's pockets or handbags. The victim usually doesn't realize that he has been robbed until later.) Ask if anyone has ever been robbed by a pickpocket. If so, invite them to tell the class about the experience. (See Teaching Tip, page 255.)
- Call on a student to read the first two sentences. Remind them that in a noun clause, *that* is optional.

Grammar to Communicate 2

VERB + NOUN CLAUSE

Subject	Verb	Noun (Object)	Subject	Verb	Noun Clause (Object)
The police	know	his name.	The police	know	that his name is Jim Smith. his name is Jim Smith.

REPLACING NOUN CLAUSES

	Affirmative	Negative
Did the police find him?	I think so. (= I think that the police found him.)	I don't think so. (= I don't think that the police found him.)
	I believe so.	I don't believe so.
	I hope so.	I hope not.
	I guess so.	I guess not.

 A   This article has seven noun clauses. The first one is underlined. Find and underline the other six noun clauses.

Belmont Pickpocket Steals Again

This time the unlucky person was Ana Fremi. When Ms. Fremi went to pay for her groceries, she noticed <u>that her wallet wasn't in her bag</u>. The cashier saw that she was upset and guessed that the reason was the Belmont Pickpocket. The cashier immediately called the police. The police know that the pickpocket is a young man. They suspect he's from the area. They also believe that he works nearby. The manager at Belmont Market hopes the police catch the person soon.

B   Combine the sentences. Use a noun clause.

1. The fire started in an apartment on the third floor. The firefighters know this.
   The firefighters know that the fire started in an apartment on the third floor.

2. Someone was smoking in bed. The firefighters think this.
   The firefighters think that someone was smoking in bed.

3. Mr. Johnson in Apartment 3D was probably the smoker. The firefighters suspect this.
   The firefighters suspect that Mr. Johnson in Apartment 3D was probably the smoker.

4. Everybody got out of the building. The police believe this.
   The police believe that everybody got out of the building.

5. There will never be another fire. The people in the building hope this.
   The people in the building hope that there will never be another fire.

258   Unit 19

- Have students complete the task.
- Call on a student to read the paragraph and say what the noun clauses are. Correct as needed.

B   Teaching Time: 10–15 min.

- Call on a student to read the example.
- Have students complete the task.
- Call on students to say answers. Correct as needed.

Multilevel Strategy

Pre-level: Give students more time to complete Exercises A and B.

Grammar Notes

1. Use a noun clause after certain verbs—for example, *think, know, believe.* You can use *that* after the verb, but you don't have to. Both ways are correct.

2. When you answer a *yes / no* question affirmatively or negatively with *believe* or *think,* you can replace the noun clause in the question with *so.*

3. When you answer a *yes / no* question affirmatively with *hope* or *guess,* you can replace the noun clause in the question with *so.*

4. Turn to page 300 for a list of the verbs that take noun clauses.

5. For more information on this grammar topic, see page 293.

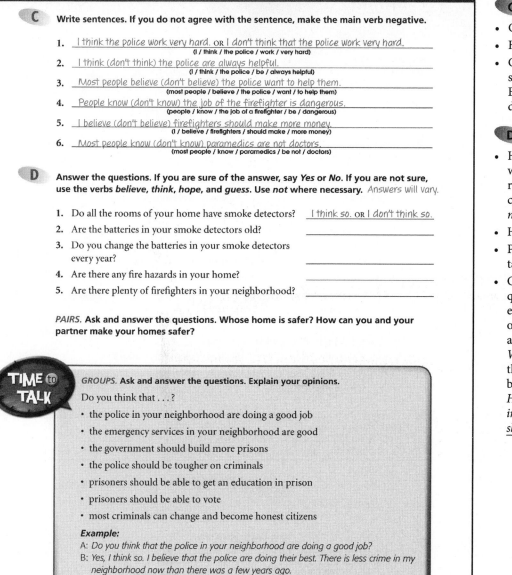

C Write sentences. If you do not agree with the sentence, make the main verb negative.

1. I think the police work very hard. OR I don't think that the police work very hard.
   (I / think / the police / work / very hard)
2. I think (don't think) the police are always helpful.
   (I / think / the police / be / always helpful)
3. Most people believe (don't believe) the police want to help them.
   (most people / believe / the police / want / to help them)
4. People know (don't know) the job of the firefighter is dangerous.
   (people / know / the job of a firefighter / be / dangerous)
5. I believe (don't believe) firefighters should make more money.
   (I / believe / firefighters / should make / more money)
6. Most people know (don't know) paramedics are not doctors.
   (most people / know / paramedics / be not / doctors)

D Answer the questions. If you are sure of the answer, say *Yes* or *No*. If you are not sure, use the verbs *believe, think, hope,* and *guess.* Use *not* where necessary. Answers will vary.

1. Do all the rooms of your home have smoke detectors?   I think so. OR I don't think so.
2. Are the batteries in your smoke detectors old?   _____
3. Do you change the batteries in your smoke detectors every year?   _____
4. Are there any fire hazards in your home?   _____
5. Are there plenty of firefighters in your neighborhood?   _____

PAIRS. Ask and answer the questions. Whose home is safer? How can you and your partner make your homes safer?

TIME to TALK

GROUPS. Ask and answer the questions. Explain your opinions.

Do you think that . . . ?

- the police in your neighborhood are doing a good job
- the emergency services in your neighborhood are good
- the government should build more prisons
- the police should be tougher on criminals
- prisoners should be able to get an education in prison
- prisoners should be able to vote
- most criminals can change and become honest citizens

Example:
A: *Do you think that the police in your neighborhood are doing a good job?*
B: *Yes, I think so. I believe that the police are doing their best. There is less crime in my neighborhood now than there was a few years ago.*
C: *I agree.*

Emergency Services 259

C **Teaching Time: 10–15 min.**

- Call on a student to read the example.
- Have students complete the task.
- Call on students to read their sentences. Correct as needed. Encourage students to express and defend their opinions.

D **Teaching Time: 10–15 min.**

- Have a student read the example. Ask what *so* replaces. Have the student read the full answer with the noun clause. (*I think that all the rooms in my home have smoke detectors.*)
- Have students complete the task.
- PAIRS. Have students complete the task.
- Call on students to answer the questions. Discuss the content of the exercise. Have students give each other advice. For example, if a student answers *I think so* to question 2, ask: *What should he do?* (He should test them.) Then broaden the discussion by asking the class questions such as: *How often do you change the batteries in your smoke detector? How often should you change them?*

Language Note

Remind students that some verbs cannot be followed by a noun clause, for example, *want.* Write on the board:

The police want Jim to call them. (NOT ~~*The police want that Jim calls them.*~~*)*

Option

Assign Unit 19 Supplementary Grammar to Communicate 2 Exercises on the Teacher's Resource Disk as homework or on the Student Persistence CD-ROM as self-access practice.

TIME to TALK

Teaching Time: 5–10 min.

- Read the directions and the questions. Make sure everyone understands the questions. Explain vocabulary as needed.
- Call on two students to read the example.
- GROUPS. Have students complete the task.
- Have students from different groups take turns answering the questions. If another group disagrees, have someone from the group explain why.

Grammar to Communicate 3

Make and *Let*

Teaching Time: 5–10 min.

- Have students study the chart and the Look Box.
- Write on the board:
  Verb + object + infinitive
  He ordered <u>me to stop</u>.
  He forced <u>me to stop</u>.

  Verb + object + base form
  He made <u>me stop</u>.

  Verb + object + infinitive
  He didn't allow <u>me to go</u>.
  He didn't permit <u>me to go</u>.

  Verb + object + base form
  He didn't let <u>me go</u>.

- As you point to the sentences on the board, say: *As you know, many verbs are followed by an object + infinitive, for example, the verbs* order *and* allow. *However, a small group of verbs are followed by an object and the base form of the verb. The two most common verbs that follow this pattern are* make *and* let.

- Explain: Make *has the same meaning as* order *or* force, *and* let *has the same meaning as* allow *or* permit. *However, the grammar is different.* Order, force, allow, *and* permit *are followed by an object + the infinitive form of the verb.* Make *and* let *are followed by an object + the base form of the verb.*

A   Teaching Time: 10–15 min.

- Read the example with the class.
- Have students complete the task. Tell them to guess if they are not sure what the procedure is in the United States.
- Call on students to say answers. Correct as needed.
- PAIRS. Have students compare what happens in their countries to what happens in the United States.
- Ask if anyone has ever been stopped for speeding. If so, invite them to tell the class about their experience. (See Teaching Tip on page 255.)

B   Teaching Time: 10–15 min.

- **Warm-up.** Write *fire drill* on the board. Explain that a fire drill is a way to practice for a real fire. People

pretend that there is a fire, and practice leaving the building. Ask students to raise their hands if they have ever participated in a fire drill. Ask how often there are fire drills at schools in their countries. Then ask how many people have done their own fire drills at home with their families. If they haven't, suggest that they do so.
- Read the example with the class.
- Have students complete the task.
- Call on students to say answers. Correct as needed.

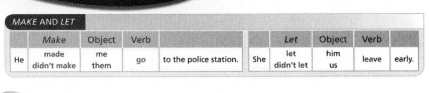

Grammar to Communicate 3

	Make	Object	Verb			**Let**	Object	Verb	
He	made didn't make	me them	go	to the police station.	She	let didn't let	him us	leave	early.

A   What happens in the U.S. when a police officer stops you for speeding? Circle the correct answers.

1. The police officer _____ him your license.
   (a.) makes you give   **b.** doesn't make you give
2. The police officer _____ in your car.
   (a.) makes you stay   **b.** doesn't make you stay
3. The police officer _____ of your car.
   a. lets you get out   **(b.)** doesn't let you get out
4. The police officer _____ for a long time.
   (a.) makes you wait   **b.** doesn't make you wait
5. The police officer _____ to the police station.
   a. makes you go   **(b.)** doesn't make you go
6. After the police officer gives you a ticket, he _____.
   (a.) lets you drive away   **b.** doesn't let you drive away

> **Look**
> make someone do something = force someone to do something
>
> let someone do something = allow someone to do something

PAIRS. Are the answers the same in your country? If not, what is different?

B   There was a fire alarm at work yesterday. Complete the sentences with *let, made, didn't let,* or *didn't make.*

1. I couldn't stay in my office because the firefighters ___made___ us leave the building.
2. They ___didn't let___ us use the elevator. We had to walk down the stairs.
3. I forgot my coat, but the firefighters ___didn't let___ me go back in the building.
4. They ___made___ us wait a long time outside. We waited for over an hour!
5. They ___didn't make___ us go far away. We waited across the street.
6. They ___didn't make___ us show any identification. They didn't need our names.
7. After they were sure there was no fire, they ___let___ us go back in the building.
8. When we went in the building, they ___let___ us use the elevator. Some people walked up the stairs, but I used the elevator. My office is on the tenth floor.

Grammar Notes

1. The verb *make* can mean *force*. When it has this meaning, it is followed by an object + the base form of the verb.
2. The verb *let* can mean *permit* or *allow*. When it has this meaning, it is followed by an object + the base form of the verb.
3. For more information on this grammar topic, see page 294.

C Look at the scenes from a TV show. Write sentences. Use the words in the box and *made*, *didn't make*, *let*, or *didn't let*. Then compare answers with a partner.

get in the police car	make one phone call	~~stop~~
leave	put his hands up	talk

1. _____They made him stop._____ 2. _____They made him put his hands up.____

3. _They made him get in the police car._ 4. _____They let him make one phone call.___

5. _____They didn't make him talk._____ 6. _____They didn't let him leave._____

TIME to TALK

PAIRS. **How can parents help their children stay out of trouble? Complete the chart with your opinions. Write two or more ideas for each column.**

To help their children stay out of trouble, parents should . . .

NOT LET THEM . . .	MAKE THEM . . .	NOT MAKE THEM . . .

WRAP UP. **Share your ideas with the class.**

Emergency Services (261)

C Teaching Time: 10–15 min.

- Read the example with the class.
- Have students complete the task.
- PAIRS. Have students compare their answers.
- Call on students to read their sentences. Correct as needed.

Multilevel Strategy

- **Pre-level:** Give students extra time to complete the exercise. Call on pre-level students to give the answers with *make* and *let* when you go over the exercise.
- **At-level, Above-level:** When students finish comparing their sentences, have them repeat the sentences, replacing *make* with *order* and *let* with *allow*. Call on above-level students to say the sentences with *order* and *allow* when you go over the exercise.

Option

Assign Unit 19 Supplementary Grammar to Communicate 3 Exercises on the Teacher's Resource Disk as homework or on the Student Persistence CD-ROM as self-access practice.

TIME to TALK

Teaching Time: 10–15 min.

- Read the directions with the class.
- Ask a volunteer to tell you one thing that parents shouldn't let their children do. Write the example on the board. Correct as needed.
- PAIRS. Have students complete the task.
- WRAP UP. Have one student from each pair tell the class one of their ideas. Have them say their ideas in complete sentences. Ask them to explain their answers. Correct as needed.

Grammar

Teaching Time: 5–10 min.

- Read the example with the class.
- Have students complete the task.
- 🎧 Play Track 35 while students listen and check their answers.
- Call on students to say answers. Correct as needed.

Dictation

Teaching Time: 5–10 min.

- 🎧 Play Track 36 while students listen and write what they hear.
- 🎧 Play Track 36 again while students check their answers.
- Ask for volunteers to write the sentences on the board.
- 🎧 Play Track 36 again and correct the sentences on the board.

Multilevel Strategy

- **Pre-level:** Give students a worksheet with some of the words from the dictation already provided.

Speaking

Teaching Time: 5–10 min.

- Call on students to read the directions and the example.
- GROUPS. Have students complete the task. While the students are talking, walk around and take notes on any mistakes that you hear.
- Write errors that you noticed on the board. Have the class correct them together.

Review and Challenge

Grammar

🔘 **35** Complete the letter with the words in the box. Then listen and check your answers. Be careful. There are two extra words.

| didn't | I | it | let | made | make | me | so | that | ~~think~~ | us | we |

To whom it may concern:

I'm writing this letter because I ___think___ you should know about my experience
1.
at your hospital last Saturday. My ten-year-old daughter had an accident on her bike,
and I noticed ___that___ she couldn't move her arm. I thought ___it___ might
2.   3.
be broken, so I drove her to the emergency room. We got there at 1:00. The nurse
saw that my daughter was in pain, but she ___didn't___ let us see a doctor right away.
4.
She told the two of ___us___ to wait in the waiting area and ___made___ me fill
5.   6.
in four different forms. We waited and waited. Finally, at 4:00 the nurse called my
daughter's name. My daughter wanted ___me___ to go with her, but the nurse didn't
7.
___let___ me go. She was very rude to me. I am writing because I would like to know
8.
your policy on this. Did the nurse have the right to ___make___ me stay in the waiting
9.
room? I don't think ___so___, but maybe there is a new policy.
10.

Dictation

🔘 **36** Listen. You will hear five sentences. Write them in your notebook. *See the audioscript on p. 327 for the sentences.*

Speaking

GROUPS. **What problems have you noticed in your neighborhood? What would you like the police or other local officials to do about the problems?**

Example:
A: *The streets are dirty. I'd like the city to clean them more often.*
B: *I agree. And the police should make people pick up their trash.*

Listening

A 🎧 **37** Listen to the radio show. What is the caller's problem? Check (✓) the correct answer.

❑ 1. He has no smoke detectors in his apartment.

❑ 2. There are no smoke detectors in his apartment building.

☑ 3. The smoke detectors in the hallway of his apartment building are not working.

❑ 4. He doesn't have a fire extinguisher in his apartment.

❑ 5. His apartment has only one exit.

❑ 6. The sprinkler system in his building isn't working.

fire extinguisher

sprinkler system

B 🎧 **37** Listen again. Answer the questions.

1. Who must make sure that the smoke detectors are working? ___the landlord___

2. What must there be in every apartment? ___a fire extinguisher___

3. What must there be in all new buildings? ___a sprinkler system___

4. How many exits must each apartment have? ___two___

TIME to TALK

GROUPS. Discuss the answers to the questions. Think of four things for each category.

What does the fire department advise people to do to prevent fires?	What do the police advise people to do to protect themselves from crime?	What do the police advise people to do to avoid car accidents?
_____	_____	_____
_____	_____	_____
_____	_____	_____
_____	_____	_____

WRAP UP. Now share your ideas with another group. Do you have any of the same ideas?

Example:
A: *The fire department advises people not to use electric heaters.*
B: *And they also advise people not to smoke in bed.*

Emergency Services 263

Listening

A **Teaching Time: 10–15 min.**

- **Warm-up.** Tell students that they are going to listen to a radio call-in show about fire safety. Have them predict the topics that will be discussed on the show. Write their predictions on the board.
- Have students read the answer choices.
- 🎧 Play Track 37 as students listen and complete the task.
- 🎧 Play Track 37 again, this time pausing the recording when the answer is given.
- Have students look at the predictions on the board. Ask which ones were discussed on the show.

B **Teaching Time: 10–15 min.**

- Have students answer as many of the questions as they can.
- 🎧 Play Track 37 while students listen and check their answers.
- 🎧 Play Track 37 again, this time pausing as each answer is given. Have students call out the answers.

Multilevel Strategy

Pre-level: Give students a copy of the audioscript. Have them read along as they listen and complete Exercise B.

Option

Assign Unit 19 Review and Challenge Supplementary Exercises on the Teacher's Resource Disk as homework or on the Student Persistence CD-ROM as self-access practice.

TIME to TALK

Teaching Time: 5–10 min.

- Read the directions and the questions for each category with the class.
- Call on two students to read the example.
- GROUPS. Have students complete the task. Walk around and help as needed.
- WRAP UP. Write the three questions on the board. Have one student from each group come up to the board and write one of the group's suggestions under each category. Correct as needed.

Reading

Getting Ready to Read

Teaching Time: 5–10 min.

- **Warm-up.** Tell students that they are going to read an article about fire safety. Ask if anyone has ever been in a fire. If so, invite them to tell the class about their experience. (See Teaching Tip on page 255.)
- Have students complete the task.
- Call on students to read their suggestions. Write them on the board.

Reading

Teaching Time: 15–20 min.

- Have students read the article.
- Have students look at the suggestions on the board and tell you which ones were mentioned in the article.

> **Multilevel Strategy**
>
> - **Pre-level:** Give students more time to read the article.
> - **At-level, Above-level:** Have students underline sentences with *make* and *let* and sentences that follow the verb + object + infinitive pattern.

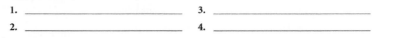

Reading

Getting Ready to Read

Make a list of four things that you can do to prevent a fire in your home. *Answers will vary.*

1. _____   3. _____
2. _____   4. _____

Reading

Read the article. Does the writer talk about any of your ideas in Getting Ready to Read?

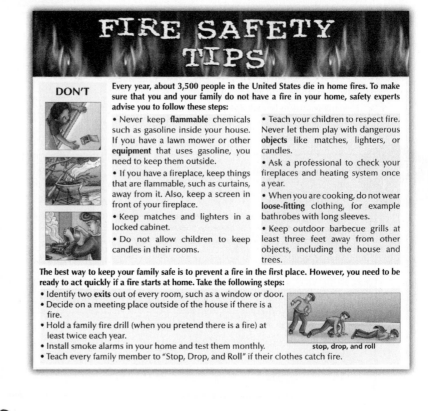

FIRE SAFETY TIPS

DON'T

Every year, about 3,500 people in the United States die in home fires. To make sure that you and your family do not have a fire in your home, safety experts advise you to follow these steps:

- Never keep **flammable** chemicals such as gasoline inside your house. If you have a lawn mower or other **equipment** that uses gasoline, you need to keep them outside.
- If you have a fireplace, keep things that are flammable, such as curtains, away from it. Also, keep a screen in front of your fireplace.
- Keep matches and lighters in a locked cabinet.
- Do not allow children to keep candles in their rooms.

- Teach your children to respect fire. Never let them play with dangerous **objects** like matches, lighters, or candles.
- Ask a professional to check your fireplaces and heating system once a year.
- When you are cooking, do not wear **loose-fitting** clothing, for example bathrobes with long sleeves.
- Keep outdoor barbecue grills at least three feet away from other objects, including the house and trees.

The best way to keep your family safe is to prevent a fire in the first place. However, you need to be ready to act quickly if a fire starts at home. Take the following steps:

- Identify two **exits** out of every room, such as a window or door.
- Decide on a meeting place outside of the house if there is a fire.
- Hold a family fire drill (when you pretend there is a fire) at least twice each year.
- Install smoke alarms in your home and test them monthly.
- Teach every family member to "Stop, Drop, and Roll" if their clothes catch fire.

stop, drop, and roll

264   Unit 19

After You Read

After You Read

A Write the examples from the article. Then write a definition of the **boldface** word. Use a dictionary for help.

1. Things that are **flammable**:
   gasoline, curtains

   Flammable means
   something that burns easily

2. One type of **equipment**:
   a lawn mower

   Equipment means
   a machine you use to do a particular job

3. **Objects**:
   matches, lighters, candles

   Objects are
   things

4. **Loose-fitting** clothing:
   bathrobes with long sleeves

   Loose-fitting means
   clothing that is very loose on the body

5. Two types of **exits**:
   a window or a door

   Exits are
   ways to get out of a building

> **Reading Skill:**
> **Understanding Examples**
>
> Writers often use examples to explain their main points. When you are reading, pay close attention to the examples. They will help you to understand the writer's main points.
>
> Never let them play with **dangerous objects like matches, lighters, or candles.**

B Read the article again. As you read, remember as many of the fire safety tips as you can. Then take notes. Do *not* look at the article when you take notes. Answers may include the following:

1. TO PREVENT A FIRE:
no flammable chemicals inside house, no flammable things near fireplaces, screen in front of fireplace, matches and lighters in locked cabinets, children must not have candles or play with matches, lighters, or candles, check fireplaces and heating system every year

2. TO PREPARE FOR A FIRE:
identify exits from every room in your house, find two exits out of house, decide on meeting place, family fire drill 2 or more times a year, install smoke detectors and check monthly, learn how to "stop, drop, and roll"

Now read the article one more time. How many of the fire safety tips did you remember?

Emergency Services 265

Teaching Tip

Exercise A. A dictionary is a powerful tool, but many students do not know how to use it effectively. Give students frequent practice in using a dictionary. For this exercise, point out that one dictionary entry often contains several meanings. Have students practice choosing the definition that fits the context.

After You Read

A Teaching Time: 10–15 min.

- Have students study the information in the Reading Skill box.
- Read the example with students.
- Have students complete the task.
- Call on students to give the answers. Correct as needed.

Multilevel Strategy

- **Pre-level:** Allow students to copy the definitions from a dictionary. Assist them in choosing the appropriate meaning for each word.
- **At-level, Above-level:** Have students write their own definitions. Call on above-level students to write their definitions on the board. Have the at-level students read the dictionary definitions aloud. Correct the definitions as needed.

B Teaching Time: 10–15 min.

- Read the example with the class.
- PAIRS. Have students complete the task in pairs.
- Write two columns on the board. Have students tell you what to write in each column.

  To prevent a fire: To prepare for a fire:
- Have students read the article again and compare the information to what is on the board.
- Have students tell you what to change or add to the notes on the board.

Multilevel Strategy

All levels: Pair pre-level with at- and above-level students for this task. The more advanced students can help the others to write what they remember.

Writing

Getting Ready to Write

A Teaching Time: 10–15 min.

- Have students study the Writing Tip.
- Read the example with the class.
- PAIRS. Have students complete the task.
- Call on students to read their answers.
- Write their examples on the board. Correct as needed.

B Teaching Time: 10–15 min.

- Have students read the model paragraph.
- PAIRS. Have students complete the task.

Expansion

- Have students find the examples in the model, and circle the word or words that the examples explain.
- Have students read the words they circled. Write them on the board:
  1. *security systems*
  2. *valuables*
  3. *belongings*
  4. *surroundings*
  5. *clothes that are difficult to move in*
- Have students look the first four up in their dictionaries, and choose the definition that fits the context.

Writing

Getting Ready to Write

Writing Tip

When you give advice, be very specific and give examples to make your advice clear and useful. Use these expressions: *for example, such as, like, including, for instance.*

Example:

Keep outdoor barbecue grills at least three feet away from other objects, **including the house and trees.**

A Complete the sentences with examples. Use your own ideas.

1. Products that contain flammable chemicals, including _____ paint and gasoline _____, can be dangerous.

2. Never store anything flammable near a heating source such as a _____ wood stove or furnace _____.

3. For your bedroom, only buy things made out of non-flammable material, for instance, non-flammable _____ blankets and pajamas _____.

4. When you are with your family in a crowded building, identify a meeting place, like _____ in front of the building _____, in case someone gets lost.

5. When you are cooking, pull your hair back to keep it away from hot surfaces, especially _____ the stove _____.

6. Keep cleaning products in a place where small children cannot find them, for example, in _____ a very high cabinet _____.

B Read the model paragraph.

> What are some things that the police advise people to do to protect themselves from crime? First of all, they encourage homeowners to <u>buy security systems, including special window locks and burglar alarms.</u> They also tell people to <u>avoid keeping valuables like jewelry in their homes.</u> They advise car owners to <u>put all of their belongings, including briefcases, backpacks, and shopping bags, in the trunk.</u> The police also tell people to <u>pay attention to their surroundings.</u> In parking garages, for example, they warn people not to park next to vehicles with dark windows. Finally, they tell people to <u>avoid wearing clothes that are difficult to move in, especially high heels or tight clothing.</u>

PAIRS. **Read the model again. According to the writer, how can people protect themselves from crime?** Wording of answers may vary.

Now talk about other ways people protect themselves from crimes or accidents.

266 **Unit 19**

Teaching Tip

Exercise A. Pairing students for vocabulary exercises allows them to pool their knowledge. Students often know different words; by working together, they can teach each other words and expand their vocabulary more rapidly.

Prewriting: Using Examples

You are going to write a paragraph about advice that experts, such as the police or paramedics, give to protect people from crimes or accidents. Before you write, organize your ideas in the chart. Write two pieces of safety advice. Then write at least two examples for each piece of advice.

If you need more information, look in the library or on the Internet. To search the Internet:

- Go to an Internet search engine such as www.google.com
- Choose topics you want to write about. For example, type in "fire prevention".
- Choose a site and click on its Web address.
- Read some of the information on the site. Write notes in the chart.

Writing Model
Topic: Robbery
Expert: Police
Safety advice # 1:
Buy security systems
Examples: special window
locks and burglar
alarms

Topic: _____ Expert: _____ Safety Advice: _____ _____	Topic: _____ Expert: _____ Safety Advice: _____ _____
Example 1:	Example 1:
Example 2:	Example 2:

Writing

Now write a paragraph about advice that experts give. The writing tip, the model paragraph, and your notes will help you. Write in your notebook.

Emergency Services 267

Prewriting

Teaching Time: 15–20 min.

- Assign the task for homework. Give students enough time to search for information in the library or on the Internet.
- PAIRS. In class, have students exchange notes and ask questions about anything that they don't understand.

Multilevel Strategy

- **Pre-level:** Have pre-level students sit together in a group. Sit with them, and help them get started on their notes.
- **At-level, Above-level:** After the pre-level students have gotten started, walk around and assist other students. If possible, pair each at-level student with an above-level writer to exchange notes.

Writing

Teaching Time: 15–20 min.

- Have students complete the task.
- Encourage them to consider the feedback they got from their partner as they write their paragraphs.

Option

Prewriting. Arrange a class library visit. If you make arrangements ahead of time, most libraries are happy to introduce groups of students to the library facilities. Often, research librarians are available to help library visitors find the best resources for the topic they are interested in. Nowadays, most libraries have computers that visitors can use for their research.

Unit 20
Taking a Trip

Learning Goals

- Learn vocabulary related to travel
- Learn how to use reported speech for statements, commands, and requests
- Listen to a conversation between two people at the airport and to a report about air travel
- Read travel anecdotes from a Web page and write a story with direct and reported speech
- Talk about travel and practice functional language used in common travel scenarios

Learner Persistence

Continually involve yourself in professional development in order to meet the ongoing challenges of learner persistence.

Warm-up

Teaching Time: 3–5 min.

- Write *plane, train,* and *bus* on the board.
- Have students call out as many words as they can think of that are related to traveling by plane, train, or bus.
- Write the words they call out under the appropriate heading(s). Many words will probably fit under more than one heading.

Vocabulary

Teaching Time: 10–15 min.

- Have students read the words in the box. Check the words on the board that appear in the box.
- Read the example with the class.
- Have students complete the task.
- 🎧 Play Track 38 while students listen and check their answers.
- Read the words in the box and have students repeat chorally.

Expansion Test students' understanding of the vocabulary. Give simple definitions or descriptions, and have students call out the words. For example:

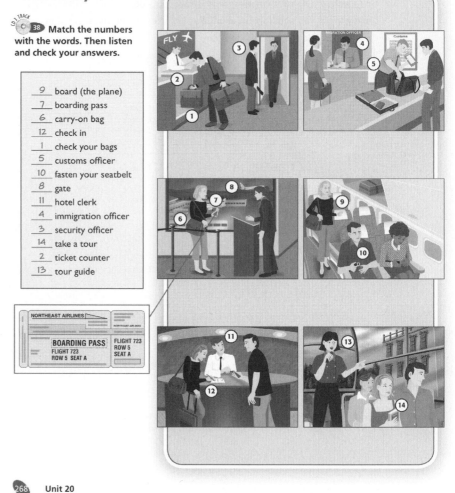

Unit 20
Taking a Trip

Grammar
- Reported Speech: Present Statements
- Reported Speech: Commands
- Reported Speech: Requests

Vocabulary

🎵 **38** Match the numbers with the words. Then listen and check your answers.

_9_	board (the plane)
_7_	boarding pass
_6_	carry-on bag
_12_	check in
_1_	check your bags
_5_	customs officer
_10_	fasten your seatbelt
_8_	gate
_11_	hotel clerk
_4_	immigration officer
_3_	security officer
_14_	take a tour
_2_	ticket counter
_13_	tour guide

268 Unit 20

Get on a train, plane, or bus. (board)

You need this to get on the plane. (boarding pass)

The flight attendants always tell you to do this as soon as you sit down. (fasten your seatbelt)

The person you pay to show you around a new place. (tour guide)

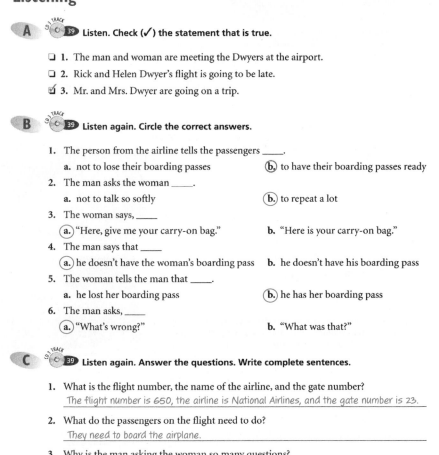

Listening

A 🎵 **39** **Listen. Check (✓) the statement that is true.**

- ❏ **1.** The man and woman are meeting the Dwyers at the airport.
- ❏ **2.** Rick and Helen Dwyer's flight is going to be late.
- ☑ **3.** Mr. and Mrs. Dwyer are going on a trip.

B 🎵 **39** **Listen again. Circle the correct answers.**

1. The person from the airline tells the passengers _____.
   - **a.** not to lose their boarding passes
   - **(b.)** to have their boarding passes ready
2. The man asks the woman _____.
   - **a.** not to talk so softly
   - **(b.)** to repeat a lot
3. The woman says, _____
   - **(a.)** "Here, give me your carry-on bag."
   - **b.** "Here is your carry-on bag."
4. The man says that _____
   - **(a.)** he doesn't have the woman's boarding pass
   - **b.** he doesn't have his boarding pass
5. The woman tells the man that _____.
   - **a.** he lost her boarding pass
   - **(b.)** he has her boarding pass
6. The man asks, _____
   - **(a.)** "What's wrong?"
   - **b.** "What was that?"

C 🎵 **39** **Listen again. Answer the questions. Write complete sentences.**

1. What is the flight number, the name of the airline, and the gate number?
   The flight number is 650, the airline is National Airlines, and the gate number is 23.

2. What do the passengers on the flight need to do?
   They need to board the airplane.

3. Why is the man asking the woman so many questions?
   He probably can't hear very well.

4. What is in the man's carry-on bag?
   Their boarding passes are in his carry-on bag.

5. Why do you think the Dwyers need to go up to the check-in counter? _Answers will vary._
   _____

Taking a Trip **269**

Listening

A **Teaching Time: 10–15 min.**

- **Warm-up.** Tell students that they are going to listen to two people at an airport. Call on students and ask: *Are you a good traveler? Do you enjoy traveling? Why or why not?*
- Have students read the answer choices.
- 🎧 Play Track 39 as students listen and complete the task.
- Call on a student to say the answer. Play the conversation again if necessary.

B **Teaching Time: 10–15 min.**

- Read the example with the class.
- Have students read the answer choices.
- 🎧 Play Track 39 as students listen and complete the task.
- 🎧 Play Track 39 again, this time pausing after each answer is given.
- Call on students to read the completed sentences. Correct as needed.

Multilevel Strategy

- **Pre-level:** Make photocopies of the audioscript, but blank out the words in the script that give the answers to Exercises B and C. Have students complete the audioscript as they listen. Then have them answer the questions to B and C.
- **At-level, Above-level:** While the pre-level students are completing Exercises B and C, put the other students in pairs and have them role-play the conversation between the Dwyers from memory. Ask volunteers to perform their role play for the class.

C **Teaching Time: 10–15 min.**

- Have students complete the task. Point out that question 5 is an opinion question.
- 🎧 Play Track 39 as students listen and check their answers.
- 🎧 Play Track 39 again, pausing as the answers are given.
- Call on students to say answers. Correct as needed.

Option

Assign Unit 20 Supplementary Vocabulary Exercises on the Teacher's Resource Disk as homework or on the Student Persistence CD-ROM as self-access practice.

Unit 20 **T-269**

Grammar to Communicate 1

Reported Speech: Present Statements

Teaching Time: 5–10 min.

- Have students study the chart and the Look Box.
- Write on the board:

  She says that she wants to travel to his country someday.

  He says, "You are welcome to visit me anytime."

- As you point to the first sentence on the board, say: *We use reported speech when we report what someone says. We don't say their exact words. We report their words with a verb like say or tell + a noun clause. We do not use any special punctuation for reported speech.*

- As you point to the second sentence on the board, say: *We use quoted speech when we write the exact words that someone says. We put a comma after the verb say or tell, and then put the words that the person said between quotation marks. Put the final punctuation, for example, the period or question mark, inside of the final quotation mark.*

- Ask a volunteer to come up to the board and change the reported speech to direct speech in the first example. Correct as needed. Remind the student to change the pronouns. Then ask another volunteer to change the quoted speech to reported speech. Correct as needed.

  She says, "I want to travel to your country someday."

  He says that she is welcome to visit him anytime.

A Teaching Time: 10–15 min.

- Explain that the statements are from the postcards. Read the example with the class.
- Have students complete the task.
- Call on students to say answers. Correct as needed.

B Teaching Time: 10–15 min.

- Read the example with the class.
- Have students complete the task.
- Call on students to write their answers on the board. Correct as needed.

 T-270   Center Stage 3

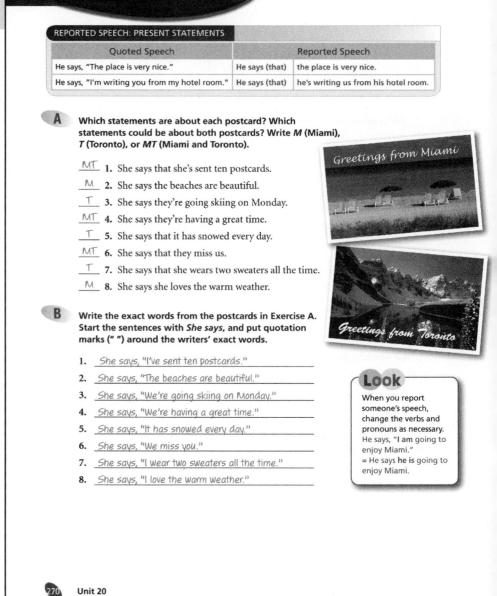

Grammar to Communicate 1

REPORTED SPEECH: PRESENT STATEMENTS		
Quoted Speech	Reported Speech	
He says, "The place is very nice."	He says (that)	the place is very nice.
He says, "I'm writing you from my hotel room."	He says (that)	he's writing us from his hotel room.

A Which statements are about each postcard? Which statements could be about both postcards? Write *M* (Miami), *T* (Toronto), or *MT* (Miami and Toronto).

<u>MT</u> 1. She says that she's sent ten postcards.

<u>M</u> 2. She says the beaches are beautiful.

<u>T</u> 3. She says they're going skiing on Monday.

<u>MT</u> 4. She says they're having a great time.

<u>T</u> 5. She says that it has snowed every day.

<u>MT</u> 6. She says that they miss us.

<u>T</u> 7. She says that she wears two sweaters all the time.

<u>M</u> 8. She says she loves the warm weather.

B Write the exact words from the postcards in Exercise A. Start the sentences with *She says*, and put quotation marks (" ") around the writers' exact words.

1. She says, "I've sent ten postcards."
2. She says, "The beaches are beautiful."
3. She says, "We're going skiing on Monday."
4. She says, "We're having a great time."
5. She says, "It has snowed every day."
6. She says, "We miss you."
7. She says, "I wear two sweaters all the time."
8. She says, "I love the warm weather."

Greetings from Miami

Greetings from Toronto

Look

When you report someone's speech, change the verbs and pronouns as necessary.
He says, "**I am** going to enjoy Miami."
= He says **he is** going to enjoy Miami.

270   Unit 20

Grammar Notes

1. Use quotation marks (" ") when you write someone's exact words. This is called *quoted speech.*

2. Use a form of *say* when you write someone's exact words. Put a comma (,) after *say* and before the quotation marks.

3. Use a form of *say* and a noun clause when you report someone's statement. Do <u>not</u> put a comma or quotation marks. This is called *reported speech.*

4. You can use *that* in reported speech, but it is not necessary.

5. For more information about this grammar topic, see page 294.

C 🔘 **40** A woman and her 86-year-old mother are taking a tour. The mother can't hear well. Complete the conversation with reported speech. Then listen and check your answers.

You're going to have lunch soon.
The restaurant is famous for its soups.
I'm not going to have lunch with you.
I need to go to the museum to buy the tickets for today's visit.
You'll have 90 minutes for lunch.
This restaurant is great. You're going to enjoy it.

Anna: "I can't understand a word that young man is saying."

Sammi: _He says that we're going to have lunch soon._
                                                                    1.

Anna: "Where? What kind of restaurant? I hope it's good."

Sammi: _He says the restaurant is famous for its soups._
                                                                    2.

Anna: "I hope he's going to sit next to me and explain everything on the menu."

Sammi: _He says he's not going to have lunch with us._
                                                                    3.

Anna: "Huh! The restaurant must not be very good. And what's that about the museum?"

Sammi: _He says he needs to go to the museum to buy the tickets for today's visit._
                                                                    4.

Anna: "Why didn't he have the tickets? He's not organized. Anyway, how long is lunch?"

Sammi: _He says we'll have 90 minutes for lunch._
                                                                    5.

Anna: "Do we need 90 minutes? Is the service slow? Oh, look, we're here. What's that about the restaurant?"

Sammi: _He says the restaurant is great. We're going to enjoy it._
                                                                    6.

Anna: "Well, we'll see about that!"

TIME to TALK

PAIRS. Student A: Look at page 305. Student B: Look at page 306.

Student A, tell Student B what the writer of Postcard 1 says. Say one sentence at a time. Student B, look at the list of places. Guess which city Student A is talking about. Then Student B tells Student A what the writer of Postcard 2 says, and Student A guesses.

Example:
A: *They say they are really enjoying themselves.*
B: *That could be anywhere. What else do they say?*

Taking a Trip 271

C **Teaching Time: 10–15 min.**

- **Warm-up.** Write *hard of hearing* on the board, and explain that we use this expression to describe people who are losing their hearing, usually because of old age. Explain that we often use reported speech when we are talking to someone who is hard of hearing.

- Have a student read the example. Make sure students understand that they should report the tour guide's words, which are in the speech bubble next to the picture.

- Have students complete the task.

- 🎧 Play Track 40 while students listen and check their answers.

- Call on two students to read the conversation. Correct as needed.

- Ask students if they know anyone like the old woman in the conversation.

Multilevel Strategy

- **Pre-level:** Give students more time to complete the task.

- **At-level, Above-level:** Have students complete Unit 20 Grammar to Communicate 1, Exercise B, on the Teacher's Resource Disk. Give them the answer key so that they can correct themselves.

Option

Assign Unit 20 Supplementary Grammar to Communicate 1 Exercises on the Teacher's Resource Disk as homework or on the Student Persistence CD-ROM as self-access practice.

TIME to TALK

Teaching Time: 10–15 min.

- Read the directions with the class.
- Call on two students to read the example.
- PAIRS. Have students complete the task. Walk around and help as needed.
- Make sure that students change the pronouns where necessary.
- Call on students to read the pairs of sentences. Write the sentence with reported speech on the board. Correct as needed.

Grammar to Communicate 2

Reported Speech: Commands

Teaching Time: 5–10 min.

- Have students study the chart.
- Say: *When you report a command (an order), use tell + object + infinitive. Do not use a noun clause.*
- Write on the board:
  The teacher said, "Open your books."
  The teacher told us to open our books.
- Say: *When you report a negative command, use tell + object + NOT + infinitive.*
- Write on the board:
  The teacher said, "Don't talk."
  The teacher told us not to talk.

A Teaching Time: 10–15 min.

- Read the example with the class.
- Have students complete the task.
- Call on students to read the sentences that they underlined. Correct as needed.
- Ask where Donna was when this happened to her.

B Teaching Time: 10–15 min.

- Call on a student to read the example.
- Have students complete the task.
- Call on students to say answers. Correct as needed.

Grammar to Communicate 2

REPORTED SPEECH: COMMANDS			
	Quoted Speech (Commands)	**Reported Speech**	
AFFIRMATIVE	He told her, "Open the bag."	He told her	to open the bag.
NEGATIVE	He told her, "Don't walk fast."		not to walk fast.

 A Read what happened to Donna. Underline the reported speech.

Today wasn't fun. <u>First, I told the man behind me in line not to push.</u> <u>He told me to stop talking on my cell phone and not to let people get in front of me.</u> Then after we sat down, the children started fighting. <u>I told them not to make too much noise,</u> but they didn't listen. <u>Then, a woman behind us told them to behave themselves,</u> so the little one started crying. Finally, he fell asleep. When the movie started, <u>I told the older boy to sit down and watch the movie.</u> But the movie wasn't for children, so he watched it for only five minutes. Then he started to run around. <u>An older man walked over to him and told him to go back to his seat.</u> Then the man came over to me and <u>told me not to let my son run around.</u> The man was very annoyed, and I was embarrassed.

annoyed

embarrassed

Where was Donna? Circle the correct answer.

a. at a restaurant   b. in a hotel room   c. on an airplane

B There are different speakers in Exercise A. Write their exact words.

1. Donna told the man, "_____Don't push._____"
2. The man told Donna, "_Stop talking on your cell phone, and don't let people get in front of you._"
3. Donna told her children, "_____Don't make too much noise._____"
4. A woman told the children, "_____Behave yourselves._____"
5. Donna told her older son, "_____Sit down and watch the movie._____"
6. An older man told her son, "_____Go back to your seat._____"
7. The man told me, "_____Don't let your son run around._____"

272 Unit 20

Grammar Notes

1. When you report an order, use *tell someone to do something.*
2. When you report a negative order, use *tell someone not to do something.*
3. Another way to report orders is to use the reporting verb *say* + a noun clause with the verb *should* or *should not.* For example:

He told	me to be quiet.
He said that	I should be quiet.
He told	me not to talk.
He said that	I should not talk.

4. For more information on this grammar topic, see page 294.

C **41** Look at what Jack said before he and Ruth left on vacation. Then complete Ruth's part of the conversation. Then listen and check your answers.

Before vacation, Jack said to Ruth:

> Take the brown suitcase, not the red one.
> Don't bring my jacket.
> Leave my credit card at home.
> Don't put my cell phone in the suitcase.
> Don't pack too many things for me.
> Buy some new clothes for yourself.

During the vacation, Jack and Ruth are talking in their hotel room.

Jack: Why did you take the brown suitcase?

Ruth: You _____ told me to take the brown suitcase. _____
1.

Jack: You forgot to bring my jacket.

Ruth: No, I didn't. You _told me not to bring your jacket._
2.

Jack: Where's my credit card?

Ruth: You _told me to leave your credit card at home._
3.

Jack: My cell phone isn't in the suitcase. Where is it?

Ruth: _You told me not to put your cell phone in your suitcase._
4.

Jack: I have only three shirts. That's not enough.

Ruth: _You told me not to pack too many things for you._
5.

Jack: And what are all these new clothes? I've never seen them before.

Ruth: _You told me to buy some new clothes for myself._
6.

Jack: I did?

TIME to TALK

PAIRS. Make a conversation. A teenager is going to travel alone. The teenager's parent is telling the teenager what to do and what not to do. Student A: You are Student B's parent. Student B: You are Student A's teenage child.

Example:
Parent: *Don't forget your tickets.*
Teenager: *Don't worry. They're in my carry-on bag.*

WRAP UP. Now act out your conversation. Your classmates will report what you said. Then listen to your classmates' conversation and report what they said.

Example:
A: *She told him not to forget his tickets . . .*

Taking a Trip 273

C Teaching Time: 10–15 min.

- Call on two students to read the example.
- Have students complete the task.
- Call on students to read their sentences. Correct as needed.
- 🎧 Play Track 41 while students listen and check their answers.

Multilevel Strategy

- **All-levels:** Pair pre-level students with at- or above-level students for this task. Ask the more advanced students to explain the answers to their partners.

Option

Assign Unit 20 Supplementary Grammar to Communicate 2 Exercises on the Teacher's Resource Disk as homework or on the Student Persistence CD-ROM as self-access practice.

TIME to TALK

Teaching Time: 10–15 min.

- Read the situation.
- Call on two students to read the example.
- PAIRS. Have students complete the task.
- WRAP UP. Have students role-play their conversation for the class. Have the class report on what they said. Correct as needed.

Grammar to Communicate 3

Reported Speech: Requests

Teaching Time: 5–10 min.

- Have students study the chart.
- Say: *When you report a request, use ask + object + infinitive. Do not use ask + a noun clause.*
- Write on the board:
  The teacher asked, "Could you please shut the door?"
  The teacher asked me to shut the door.

A Teaching Time: 10–15 min.

- Have students complete the task.
- Call on students to say answers. Correct as needed.
- Ask: *Where are the people?* (at airport security)

B Teaching Time: 10–15 min.

- Read the example with the class.
- Have students complete the task.
- Call on students to say answers. Correct as needed.
- 🎧 Play Track 42 while students listen and check their answers.

Grammar to Communicate 3

REPORTED SPEECH: REQUESTS

Quoted Speech (Requests)		Reported Requests	
She asked,	"Would you sit here, please?"	She asked me	to sit here.
	"Can you please sign your name?"		to sign my name.
	"Could you wait a few minutes?"		to wait a few minutes.

A What did the people say? Circle the exact words.

1. She asked us to check our carry-on bags.
   - **a.** "Could you please check your carry-on bags?"
   - **b.** "Are you able to check your carry-on bags?"

2. He asked me to take off my shoes.
   - **a.** "Can you take off your shoes, please?"
   - **b.** "Can you take off my shoes, please?"

3. She asked me to take everything out of my carry-on bag.
   - **a.** "Can I take everything out of your bag, please?"
   - **b.** "Would you take everything out of your bag, please?"

4. She asked me to put my arms up.
   - **a.** "Could you please put your arms up?"
   - **b.** "Are you able to put your arms up?"

B 🎧 42 Complete the conversations. Use *asked*. Then listen and check your answers.

1. **A:** Why did you close the window?
   B: The cab driver ___asked me to close___ it.

2. **A:** Why are you fastening your seat belt? The plane isn't moving.
   B: The flight attendant ___asked us to fasten___ our seat belts.

3. **A:** Why is Jack showing his passport to the immigration officer again?
   B: The immigration officer ___asked him to show___ it to her again.

4. **A:** Why do you want to wait at the gate?
   B: My husband ___asked me to wait___ at the gate.

5. **A:** Why did you give the hotel clerk our credit card?
   B: She ___asked me to give___ it to her.

274 Unit 20

Grammar Notes

1. Look at the different language for requests:
   "Can you tell me your name, please?"
   "Could you tell me your name, please?"
   "Would you tell me your name, please?"
   "Please tell me your name."

2. When you report a request, use *ask* + object + infinitive. Do not use *ask* + a noun clause.

3. For more information on this grammar topic, see page 294.

C Look at the pictures. What requests did the airport workers make? Write sentences in reported speech. Use the words in the box or your own ideas.

answer some questions	~~hand (someone something)~~	show (someone something)
empty (one's) pockets	open (something)	sit down and wait

1. The ticket agent asked the woman to hand him her bag.

2. The ticket agent asked the man to show her his identification.

3. The security officer asked the man to empty his pockets.

4. The security officer asked the woman to sit down and wait.

5. The customs officer asked the woman to open her bag.

6. The customs officer asked the man to answer some questions.

TIME to TALK

PAIRS. **Talk about an experience you had at an airport. What did the airport workers and officers ask you to do? What did they tell you to do?**

Example: When I moved to Miami, I didn't speak any English. When the customs officer asked me to show him my passport, I handed him my carry-on bag.

Taking a Trip 275

C Teaching Time: 10–15 min.

- Read the directions. Make sure students understand that they need to use the words in the box and one of the subjects: ticket agent, security officer, or customs agent. If they don't know the meaning of a word, have them look at the pictures and try to figure out the meaning.
- Read the example with the class.
- Have students complete the task.
- PAIRS. Have students compare their answers.
- Call on students to read their sentences. Correct as needed. Explain any vocabulary that students weren't able to figure out from the pictures.

Multilevel Strategy

- **Pre-level:** Give students extra time to complete the exercise. Call on the pre-level students to read their sentences.
- **At-level, Above-level:** When students finish comparing their sentences, have them rewrite them using quoted speech. For example: *The ticket agent asked, "Could you hand me your bag, please?"* or *The ticket agent said, "Hand me your bag, please."*

Option

Assign Unit 20 Supplementary Grammar to Communicate 3 Exercises on the Teacher's Resource Disk as homework or on the Student Persistence CD-ROM as self-access practice.

TIME to TALK

Teaching Time: 10–15 min.

- Call on a student to read the example.
- PAIRS. Have students complete the task.

Expansion Ask two or three volunteers to tell the class about their experience. As they talk, take notes on any errors they make, but do not interrupt the stories. When they finish, write the errors on the board and have the other students correct them.

Grammar

Teaching Time: 5–10 min.

- Read the example with the class.
- Have students complete the task.
- 🎧 Play Track 43 while students listen and check their answers.
- Call on students to say answers. Correct as needed.

Dictation

Teaching Time: 5–10 min.

- 🎧 Play Track 44 while students listen and write what they hear.
- 🎧 Play Track 44 again while students check their answers.
- Ask for volunteers to write the sentences on the board.
- 🎧 Play Track 44 again and correct the sentences on the board.

Speaking

Teaching Time: 5–10 min.

- PAIRS. Have students complete the task. Walk around and help as needed. Make a note of any errors that you hear.
- Write errors that you heard on the board. Have the class correct them together.

Grammar

🎧 **43** **Correct the mistake(s) in each conversation. Then listen and check your answers.**

1. **A:** Why did that man tell us ~~that~~ *to* go to the ticket counter?

   B: Because we need to check in.

2. **A:** Is Annie having a good time?

   B: She says ~~I am.~~ *she is.*

3. **A:** When do we need to check in?

   B: The travel agent told us to ~~we~~ check in an hour before the flight.

4. **A:** The hotel clerk told us to leave the passports in our room.

   B: No. He told us ~~to not~~ *not to* leave them in our room.

5. **A:** Would you sit in the seats near the door, please?

   B: What did she say?

   C: She asked ~~that~~ *us* to sit near the door.

Dictation

🎧 **44** **Listen. You will hear five sentences. Write them in your notebook.** *See the audioscript on p. 328 for the sentences.*

Speaking

PAIRS. **Student A:** You had a difficult day at work yesterday. Choose a situation and tell Student B what happened.

Student B: Listen and ask questions. Then switch roles.

1. You are a tour guide. A tourist on the bus was not enjoying the tour.
2. You are a ticket agent at the airport. A traveler's flight was cancelled.
3. You are an immigration officer. A traveler forgot his passport.
4. You are a customs officer. A passenger had fruit and meat in a carry-on bag.

Example:
A: *This man came through customs. His bag smelled strange, so I asked him to open it. . . .*
B: *What happened next?*

276 **Unit 20**

Listening

A 🎧 **45** **Listen to the report. Check (✓) the best title.**

❏ 1. Enjoying your vacation: It's harder than you think!

❏ 2. Flying: The best part of the trip

❏ 3. Packing for your next vacation: Control yourself!

☑ 4. Traveling: How to get there comfortably

❏ 5. Traveling alone: How to do it safely

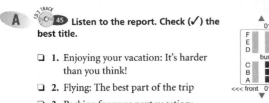

Aircraft Seating Chart

business class   economy class

<<< front 01 02 03 04   05 06 07 08 09 10

NORTHEAST AIRLINES   NORTHEAST AIRLINES

BOARDING PASS   FLIGHT 723
FLIGHT 723   ROW 5
ROW 5 SEAT A   SEAT A

B 🎧 **46** **Listen again. Complete the sentences.**

1. The reporter says that ____she has to travel____ a lot for her job.

2. Her friends always say to her, "____You are____ lucky."

3. She tells them that ____she doesn't like to____ travel, but they don't believe her.

4. People often ask ____her to tell them____ how to pack.

5. She tells them ____not to pack____ a suitcase.

6. She says, "____Pack everything in your____ carry-on bag."

7. She says, "Always ____take____ the first flight of the day."

8. She says, "Always ____ask for a seat close____ to the front of the airplane."

9. She tells travelers ____to get up and walk around____ and ____drink a lot of____ water during the flight.

TIME to TALK

GROUPS. Discuss the questions.

1. Do you like flying? Why or why not? If not, how do you like to travel?

2. When you travel, how much luggage do you usually take with you?

3. Have you ever gone on a tour? If so, where? When? Did you enjoy it?

4. Have you ever traveled alone? If so, tell your group about your experience.

WRAP UP. Now tell the class something interesting about someone in your group.

Example: *Jairo told us that he is scared of flying. When his sister got married in Arizona, his family flew there for the wedding, but he drove all the way by himself.*

Taking a Trip **277**

Option

Assign Unit 20 Review and Challenge Supplementary Exercises on the Teacher's Resource Disk as homework or on the Student Persistence CD-ROM as self-access practice.

Listening

A **Teaching Time: 10–15 min.**

- **Warm-up.** Ask students how often they fly. If they rarely travel by airplane, ask them if they can tell you how many times they've been on a plane in their lives. Is there anyone in the class who has never been on an airplane? Is there anyone in the class who is afraid of flying?

- Have students read the answer choices.

- 🎧 Play Track 45 as students listen and complete the task.

- Call on a student to say the answer. Play the recording again if necessary.

B **Teaching Time: 10–15 min.**

- Read the examples with the class.

- Have students answer as many of the questions as they can.

- 🎧 Play Track 46 while students listen and check their answers.

- 🎧 Play Track 46 again, this time pausing as each answer is given.

- Have students read the completed sentences. Correct as needed.

Multilevel Strategy

After you have gone over the answers to Exercise B, have students complete the following tasks.

- **Pre-level:** Give students a copy of the audioscript. Have them underline the sentences in the audioscript where the reporter uses reported speech, and circle the sentences where she uses quoted speech.

- **At-level, Above-level:** Have students rewrite the sentences from Exercise B in their notebooks. If the sentence is in reported speech, have them rewrite it in quoted speech and vice versa. Call on students to read their rewritten sentences. Correct as needed.

TIME to TALK

Teaching Time: 5–10 min.

- GROUPS. Have students complete the task. Walk around and help as needed.

- WRAP UP. Have one person from each group tell the class something interesting about someone in their group.

Getting Ready to Read

Teaching Time: 5–10 min.

- **Warm-up.** Tell students that they are going to read a Web page called *True Stories from Travel Agencies*. Have them read the answer choices, and guess which one is the correct answer based only on the title. Ask for a show of hands for each answer. Write the results on the board.

- Have students complete the task. Tell them they have thirty seconds to skim the article.

- Ask them to raise their hands if they changed their answer.

Reading

Teaching Time: 15–20 min.

- Have students read the article.

- Have students vote again on the correct answer to Getting Ready to Read.

Multilevel Strategy

- **Pre-level:** Give students more time to read the article.

- **At-level, Above-level:** Have students underline sentences in the Web page article that contains quoted and reported speech.

Reading

Getting Ready to Read

Skim the Web page. What is the writer is trying to do? Check (✓) the correct answer.

- ❏ teach people about the travel business
- ☑ make other travel agents laugh
- ❏ convince people not to become travel agents
- ❏ convince people to travel more

Reading

Read the Web page. Then check your answer to Getting Ready to Read.

True Stories From Travel Agencies

A client called and asked me to give her information about a trip to Hawaii. After we discussed the cost, she asked, "Would it be cheaper to fly to California and then take the train to Hawaii?"

A man called to complain about his trip to Orlando, Florida. I asked him what was wrong. He said he was expecting an ocean-view room. I tried to explain that that is not possible, since Orlando is in the middle of the state. He replied, "Don't lie to me. I looked on the map and Florida is a very thin state."

I got a call from a man who asked, "Is it possible to see England from Canada?" When I answered, he said, "But they look so close on the map!"

A woman called and asked, "Do airlines put your **physical description** on your bag?" I said, "No, why do you ask?" She answered, "Well, I was on my way to Fresno, California. I'm overweight, and they put a **tag** on my **luggage** that said 'FAT.'" I told her that the luggage tag is for the bag's **destination**, not the owner's appearance. The city **code** for Fresno is "FAT."

I just **got off** the phone with a man who asked, "How do I know which plane to get on? They announced that flight 823 was ready for boarding, but none of the planes in the parking lot have numbers on them."

A businessman called with a question about the **documents** he needed in order to fly to China. After a long discussion about passports, I told him to **apply for** a visa several months in advance. He replied, "Oh no, I don't need a visa. I've been to China many times and never had to have one of those." I checked again, and sure enough, his visit **required** a visa. When I told him this he said, "Look, I've been to China four times and every time they have accepted my American Express."

Adapted from http://www.scaruffi.com/travel/jokes.html

Culture Note

Although these stories use simple vocabulary and concepts, students might have a hard time understanding the humor. What is considered funny varies widely from one culture to another. To make these stories more accessible to your students, give with them the following information:

- A big part of American humor involves laughing at ourselves. Being able to laugh at your own mistakes or weaknesses is considered an admirable quality in American culture.

- Because Americans think that people should be able to laugh at themselves, they find it very easy to laugh at the mistakes of others.

After You Read

A Find the **boldface** words in the Web page that have similar meanings to the words below.

1. ask for — apply for
2. what someone looks like — physical description
3. needed — required
4. the place that you are going to — destination
5. a piece of paper that the airlines put on your suitcase — tag
6. a set of numbers or letters that represent something, such as the name of a place — code
7. answered — replied
8. suitcases and bags for travel — luggage
9. papers that give information, for example, about a person — documents
10. ended a telephone conversation — got off

B Read the Web page again. Write the sentences where the writer reports the statements below.

> **Reading Skill:**
> **Recognizing Reported Speech**
>
> It is important to understand when the writer is reporting someone else's words. Some common verbs that are used to report speech are *say*, *ask*, and *tell*.

1. "Apply for a visa."
   I told him to apply for a visa months in advance.

2. "Please give me information about a trip to Hawaii."
   A client called and asked me to give information about a trip to Hawaii.

3. "What's wrong?"
   I asked him what was wrong.

4. "Get on flight 823."
   They announced that flight 823 was ready for boarding.

After You Read

A Teaching Time: 10–15 min.

- Read the example with the class.
- Have students complete the task.
- Call on students to say answers. Correct as needed.

B Teaching Time: 10–15 min.

- Have students read the information in the Reading Skill box.
- Have students complete the task.
- Call on students to say answers. Correct as needed.

Expansion The humor in these stories comes from the ignorance of the travel agent's customers. Call on students to explain the mistake or misunderstanding in each story.

Answers:

Story 1: This person doesn't have any idea where Hawaii is. Either that, or she doesn't understand that trains cannot cross thousands of miles of open ocean!

Stories 2 and 3: These men do not understand what maps are, or how to read them and judge distance.

Story 4: This woman must not travel very much. She's not familiar with airport codes.

Story 5: This man must not travel very much either. First of all, the place where planes are parked is not called the parking lot. Second, flight numbers aren't written on the sides of planes.

Story 6: This man doesn't know what a travel visa is. He thinks it is a Visa credit card.

Writing

Getting Ready to Write

A   Teaching Time: 10–15 min.

- Have students study the Writing Tip.
- PAIRS. Have students complete the task.
- Call on students to write the sentences on the board. Correct as needed.

B   Teaching Time: 10–15 min.

- Have students read the model paragraph.
- PAIRS. Have students complete the task.

Writing

Getting Ready to Write

A   Read the sentences. Add commas, quotation marks, and capital letters where necessary.

1. She asked him to change the flight number.
2. I told him, "don't forget to get a visa."
3. The man said, "your seat is next to the window."
4. He told me to look for a different hotel.
5. I asked him to get a travel guide.
6. She asked me, "where did you stay in London?"
7. They told her to take a train to the airport.

B   Read the model paragraph.

> Ten years ago, I flew home for my sister's birthday. I had a big blue bag. When I got off the plane, <u>I waited and waited for my bag, but it never came.</u> All the other people on the plane got their bags and went to line up at the customs desk. <u>I started to get worried.</u> I asked an airport worker to help me find my bag, but he just said, "Look over there, in the corner." Then he walked away. I saw a bag that looked like my bag, but I opened it and it wasn't mine. <u>Then I saw a woman in the customs line. She had a bag that looked just like mine.</u> I asked her to open the bag, but she told me to go away. She was in a hurry. <u>So I grabbed the bag and opened it. My things were inside.</u> The woman looked surprised, but <u>she didn't apologize. She just said</u>, "Have a good trip."

PAIRS. Read the model again. What happened to the writer? How did the writer feel about it? Wording of answers may vary.

Now talk about something funny or interesting that happened to you or someone you know while you were traveling.

Writing Tip

Stories usually include information about what people said. You can use quoted speech or reported speech to report what people said. Pay attention to the difference in punctuation.

Examples:

Quoted speech:

She asked, **"C**an you give me information about a trip to Hawaii?**"**

Reported speech:

She asked me to give her information about a trip to Hawaii.

Prewriting: Using Quoted and Reported Speech

You are going to write a paragraph about something funny or interesting that happened to you or someone you know while you were traveling. Before you write, read the notes for the student model. Then write some of the things that the people in your story said. Use both quoted and reported speech.

**Model Story
My Missing Bag**

Quoted speech
- "Look over there, in the corner."
- "Have a good trip."

Reported speech
- I asked an airport worker to help me find my bag.
- I asked her to open the bag.
- She told me to go away.

My Story:

Quoted speech

Reported speech

Writing

Now write a paragraph about something funny or interesting that happened to you or someone you know while you were traveling. The writing tip, the model paragraph, and your notes will help you. Write in your notebook.

Taking a Trip 281

Prewriting
Teaching Time: 15–20 min.

- Have students read the notes from the model.
- Have students complete the task. If they can't remember exactly what someone said, they can use reported speech. If they can't remember an interesting travel experience, tell them to make one up.
- PAIRS. Have students practice telling their stories. Have them work with a different partner from the one they worked with in the previous activity. Tell them to ask each other questions about anything they don't understand.

Writing
Teaching Time: 15–20 min.

- Have students complete the task.
- Encourage them to consider the feedback they got from their partner as they write their stories.

Grammar Summaries

UNIT 1 Getting to Know You

Have got: Statements

1. *Have got* and *have* mean the same thing. We use *have got* more in speaking than in writing.
   > **Have** they **got** any children?
   > = **Do** they **have** any children?

2. The contracted forms (*'ve got* or *'s got*) are more common than the full forms.
   > I **have got** black hair.   He **has got** gray hair.
   > (Full forms)
   > I**'ve got** black hair.   He**'s got** gray hair.
   > (Contracted forms)

3. Use *have got* with *I*, *you*, *we*, and *they*.
   > I**'ve got** a lot of free time.
   > We**'ve got** a lot of free time.

4. Use *has got* or *'s got* with the third person singular (*he, she, it*).
   > He **has got** short hair.   She**'s got** long hair.

5. Be careful! Do not confuse the contraction for *has got* and the contraction for *is*.
   > She**'s got** a new boyfriend.
   > = She **has** got a new boyfriend.
   > She**'s** nice. = She **is** nice.

6. We use *have got* (or *has got*) only in the present.
   > He**'s got** gray hair. (present)
   > He **had** gray hair. (past)

Present Progressive: Extended Time

1. Use the present progressive to talk about activities happening right now, at the time of speaking.
   > Look! The baby**'s walking**. (= right now)

2. Use the present progressive to talk about activities happening these days: this week, this month, or this year.
   > Look at the baby! He**'s getting** big. (= these days, not right this moment)

3. Look at page 295 for information about the spelling and forms of the present progressive.

Simple Present and Present Progressive

1. Use the present progressive to talk about activities that are temporary (will probably change soon):
   > I can't talk. I**'m eating** dinner. (= now)
   >
   > It**'s getting** hot. Summer is almost here. (= these days)
   >
   > He**'s smoking**. (= cigarette in his hand at this minute)

2. Use the simple present to talk about activities that are permanent (will probably stay the same for a long time):
   > We **eat dinner** at 6 o'clock. (habit or routine)
   > It **gets** hot in the summer. (scientific fact)
   > He **smokes** (habit) but **he's not smoking** now. (now)

3. Use the simple present with stative verbs. Do not use the present progressive. (Look at page 298 for a list of stative verbs.)
   > I **like** this party a lot.
   > NOT ~~I'm liking this party a lot.~~

UNIT 2 The World We Live In

Count and Noncount Nouns: Quantifiers

1. Count nouns are singular (*1 tourist*) or plural (*3 tourists*). Noncount nouns have only one form (*tourism*) and no plural.
   > There **are** a lot of tourist**s** in my country.
   > Tourism **is** important. (NOT ~~tourisms~~)

2. Use *some* with noncount nouns and plural nouns in affirmative sentences.
   > There is **some traffic** on Pine Street.
   > There are **some cars** on Pine Street.

3. Use *any* with noncount nouns and plural nouns in negative sentences and *yes/no* questions.
   > There **aren't any** parking spaces here.
   > Is there **any** parking on your street?

4. Use *a lot of* with noncount nouns and plural nouns.
   > There is **a lot of pollution.**
   > Are there are **a lot of cars?**

5. Use *no* with noncount nouns and plural nouns. *No* + noun has the same meaning as *not any* + noun. This form is less common than *not any* + noun.
   > We **have no** oil. = We **don't have any** oil.

6. Use *a little* and *little* with noncount nouns. *A little* means *some*. *Little* means *not much*. We often use *very* with *little*.
   > We've got **a little** food. (We can give you some of ours.)
   >
   > We've got **very little** food. (We can't give you any of ours.)

7. Use *much* with noncount nouns in negative sentences and questions. Use *a lot of*, not *much*, in affirmative sentences.
   > How **much** money do you have?
   > We don't have **much** money.
   > There's **a lot of** oil in Texas.
   > (NOT ~~There's much oil.~~)

8. Use *many*, *a few*, *few*, and *several* with plural nouns. *Many* means *a lot of*. *A few* and *several* mean *some*. *Few* means *not many*. We often use *very* with *few*.
   > I have **a few** quarters. (I can give you one.)
   > I have **very few** quarters. (I can't give you any.)

Count and Noncount Nouns: *Plenty of / Enough / Too much / Too many*

1. Use *plenty of* and *enough* with noncount nouns and plural nouns.

    > There is **plenty of** tourism in Paris.
    > (= a lot; no more needed)

    > There are **plenty of** restaurants.
    > (= a lot; no more needed)

    > There is **enough** parking.
    > (= the correct amount; no more needed)

    > There isn't **enough** parking.
    > (= less than is needed)

2. Use *too much* with noncount nouns. Use *too many* with plural nouns.

    > There is **too much** noise.
    > There are **too many** people.

3. Be careful! *Too much* and *too many* have a negative meaning.

    > I hate big cities. There is **too much** noise.
    > I love big cities. There are **a lot of** things to do.
    > (NOT ~~There are too many things to do.~~)

Both / Neither / Either

1. Use *both*, *neither*, and *either* to talk about two count nouns.

    > I like **both** New York and Los Angeles. (I like the two cities.)

    > I like **neither** of them. (I don't like New York or Los Angeles.)

    > I could live in **either** city. (New York is OK; Los Angeles is OK, too.)

2. After *both* and before a plural noun, you can use *of* + qualifier or leave it out.

    > I like **both** boys.
    > I like **both of the** boys.

    With *of*, use a qualifier (*the, those, my*, etc.).
    > NOT ~~I like both of boys.~~

3. Use *neither* + singular noun for a negative meaning.
    > I like **neither** city. (I don't like New York and I don't like Los Angeles.)

4. Be careful! Do not use *neither* with a negative verb.
    > ~~I don't like neither city.~~

5. Use a singular noun after *neither* or *either*, or a plural noun after *neither* + *of* + qualifier or *either* + *of* + qualifier.
    > I like **neither** boy. (I don't like John, and I don't like Bill.)
    > I like **neither of the** boys.

Simple Past: Regular and Irregular Verbs

1. For the simple past tense of regular verbs, add *–ed* to the verb.
    > The Tigers **played** last Sunday.
    > They **play** every Sunday in the winter.

2. Look at page 296 for information about spelling rules for regular simple past verbs. Look at page 300 for information about the pronunciation of the *–ed* endings.

3. Many verbs are irregular. The simple past of these verbs do not have *–ed* at the end. Look at page 298 for information about irregular simple past verbs.
    > catch—**caught**

4. For the negative of past tense verbs, use *did not* (or *didn't*) and the base form of the verb.
    > He **did not score** two goals.
    > (He **scored** one goal.)

    > We **didn't see** Sunday's game.
    > (We **saw** Saturday's game.)

5. Be careful! The past tense of *be* is *was / wasn't* and *were / weren't*. Do not use *didn't* with the past tense of *be*.
    > I **wasn't** at home last night.
    > NOT ~~I didn't be at home last night.~~

Simple Past: Questions

1. To make a *yes/no* question, add *did* before the subject and use the base form of the verb.
    > They **had** two tickets last week.
    > **Did** they **have** two tickets last week?

2. Use *did* or *didn't* in short answers.
    > Did she play last week?
    > Yes, she **did**. OR No, she **didn't**.

3. In information questions, *did* comes after the question word (*what, where, why*, etc.)
    > **Where did** the Tigers **play**?
    > **How many** points **did** they **score**?

4. For questions with the verb *to be*, do not use *did*. Use *was* or *were*.
    > **Was** the game good?
    > Yes, it **was**. OR No, it **wasn't**.

5. When *who* or *what* is the subject of the question, do not use *did* in the question. Use the past form of the verb.

SUBJECT	VERB		
Who	**saw** the game?	We did.	
What	**happened**?	They lost.	

6. When *who* or *what* is the object of the question, use *did* and a subject word in the question.

OBJECT		SUBJECT	VERB	SUBJECT	VERB	OBJECT
Who **did**		you	see?	I		saw the Tigers.
OBJECT		SUBJECT	VERB	SUBJECT	VERB	OBJECT
What team **did you**			see?	I		saw the Tigers.

Clauses with *Because, Before, After, As soon as*

1. A clause is a group of words that has a subject and a verb. Some sentences have just one clause. That clause is the main clause.

   SUBJECT   VERB
   We   won   the game.

2. Some sentences have more than one clause. One clause is the main clause, and the other clause is the subordinate clause.

   After we scored a goal, we won the game.
   [subordinate clause]   [main clause]

3. The subordinate clause begins with a connecting word like *after, as soon as, because,* and *before.* A subordinate clause is not a complete sentence. It needs a main clause.

   After we scored a goal . . .

4. When the subordinate clause comes at the beginning of the sentence, put a comma between the subordinate clause and the main clause.

   After we won the game,   we celebrated.

   [subordinate clause]   [comma]   [main clause]

5. When the subordinate clause comes after the main clause, do not put a comma.

   We celebrated after we won the game.

   [main clause]   [subordinate clause]

UNIT 4 Accidents

Past Progressive: Statements

1. For the past progressive, use the past of the verb *to be* and verb + *–ing*.

   I **was** play**ing** with the children yesterday morning.

   Joe and Sue **were** visit**ing** Joe's parents at the time of the fire.

2. Use the past progressive to talk about activities in progress at a specific time in the past.

   The children **were sleeping** at 10 last night.
   (= They began sleeping before 10 and continued sleeping after 10.)

3. For the negative, use *was not* (or *wasn't*) or *were not* (or *weren't*) and a verb + *–ing*.

   She **wasn't** iron**ing** early this morning.
   We **weren't** work**ing** at 4 yesterday.

4. Use the simple past with stative verbs. Do not use the progressive. (Look at page 298 for a list of stative verbs.)

Past Progressive: Questions

1. To make a *yes/no* question, change the word order of the subject and the verb.

   They were eating dinner at 6:30.
   Were they eating dinner at 6:30?

2. Use *was/wasn't* or *were/weren't* in short answers.

   Was he driving at the time of the accident?
   Yes, he **was.** OR No, he **wasn't.**

   Were you going home at the time of the accident?
   Yes, we were. OR No, we **weren't.**

3. In information questions, *was* or *were* comes after the question word (*what, where,* etc.)

   What was your neighbor **doing** yesterday?
   Where were you **going** at 7 this morning?

4. When *who* or *what* is the subject of the question, there is no subject after *was.*

   SUBJECT   VERB
   Who   **was smoking?**   Mr. Jackson was.
   What   **was burning?**   Some food in the oven was burning.

5. When *who* or *what* is the object of the question, use *was* or *were* and a subject word in the question.

   OBJECT   SUBJECT   VERB
   What   **was**   he   **smoking?**   A cigarette.
   Who   **was**   he   **talking to?** The doctor.

Past Progressive and Simple Past: *When* and *While*

1. Use the past progressive and the simple past to say that one activity was in progress when another activity happened.

   While we **were watching** TV, Gus **arrived.**
   (= We began watching TV before Gus arrived.)

   When Gus **arrived,** we **were watching** TV.
   (= We began watching TV before Gus arrived.)

2. Use the simple past two times to say that one activity happened *after* another activity.

   We **watched TV** when Gus **arrived.**
   (= First, Gus arrived. Then we watched TV.)

3. Use *while* with the past progressive to say that two activities were in progress at the same time.

   While I was washing the dishes, he **was making** the beds.

4. When the subordinate clause with *when* or *while* comes at the beginning of the sentence, put a comma between the subordinate clause and the main clause.

   While they were talking,   I was working.

   [subordinate clause]   comma   [main clause]

5. When the subordinate clause comes after the main clause, do not put a comma.

   I was working while they were talking.

   [main clause]   [subordinate clause]

Used to: Statements

1. We use *used to* + verb to talk about things that happened often in the past. These things usually do not happen often or at all now.

   Women **used to wear** skirts all the time. (Now they often wear pants.)

   I **used to** work downtown. (Now I work in a different place.)

2. The negative of *used to* is *didn't use to*.

   Women **didn't use to work** outside the home.

3. Be careful! Use the simple past, NOT *used to* + verb for actions in the past that happened once or only a few times.

   I wore that dress to my brother's wedding. NOT ~~I used to wear that dress to my brother's wedding.~~

   He took care of the children three times last month. NOT ~~He used to take care of the children three times last month.~~

4. For past habits or customs, both *used to* + verb and the simple past are sometimes possible. The meaning is similar.

   Women used to stay at home. OR Women stayed at home.

   Men didn't use to do housework. OR Men didn't do housework.

Used to: Yes/No Questions

1. To make a *yes/no* question, add *did* before the subject and use *use to* + verb after the subject.

   They **used to go out** on Fridays. **Did** they **use to go out** on Saturdays?

   He **used to feed** the baby. **Did** he **use to feed** the baby?

2. Use *did* in short answers.

   Did you use to live in London? Yes, I **did**. OR No, I **didn't**.

   Did she use to be a teacher? Yes, she **did**. OR No, she **didn't**.

Used to: Information Questions

1. In information questions, *did* comes after the question word (*what, how much,* etc.) and *use to* + verb comes after the subject.

   Where did you **use to go** on weekends? We used to go to the movies.

   How much did a movie **use to** cost? A movie used to cost 25 cents.

2. When *who* or *what* is the subject of the question, do not use *did* in the question. Use *used to* + verb.

   SUBJECT   VERB
   Who   **used to live** there?
   A young couple **used to live** here.

   SUBJECT   VERB
   What   **used to happen** on dates?
   Young people **used to go** bowling on dates.

3. When *who* or *what* is the object of the question, use *did* in the question. Use *used to* + verb.

   OBJECT   SUBJECT
   What **did** you **use to do** after school?

   SUBJECT   OBJECT
   I   **used to do** my homework.

Future: *Will* for Decisions and Promises

1. Use *will* for an action that you decide to do at the time you are talking.

   A: The phone's ringing.
   B: I**'ll get** it.

2. Use *will* or *won't* when you make a promise.

   I **won't spend** all the money on clothes. I**'ll put** some of the money in the bank.

Future: *Be going to* and *Will*

1. Use *will* for an action that you decide to do at the time you are talking.

   A: The phone's ringing.
   B: I**'ll answer** it. (= decides to answer the phone at the moment it rings)

2. Use *be going to* for an action that you already have decided to do.

   A: Why are you calling Joe's Pizzeria?
   B: We**'re going to have** pizza for dinner. (= decided to have pizza for dinner before starting to call)

3. Use *be going to* when you see something now that tells you about the future.

   Look at the clouds. It**'s going to rain**. (The clouds give information about the future.)

4. Use *will* or *won't* when you make a promise.

   I**'ll be** on time. I promise.

5. Use either *will* or *be going to* to make predictions about the future. (You think something will happen, but you aren't sure.)

   I think they**'ll attend** the meeting.
   I think they're **going to** attend the meeting.

Future: Present Progressive for Future Arrangements

1. Use the present progressive for the future when the future activity was planned or arranged in advance (= before the moment of speaking).

   I**'m working** tomorrow.
   The teacher **is giving** us a test next week.

2. When we use the present progressive for the future, we usually use a time expression. Without a time expression, people understand the present progressive is for *now*.

> What **are** you **doing** on Saturday night?
> (= a question about the future)

> What **are** you **doing**?
> (= a question about now)

3. You can also use *be going to* + verb instead of the present progressive for future activities that are planned or arranged in advance. Often the meaning is the same. Do not use *will* in these situations.

> **I'm going** to the dentist today. =
> **I'm going to go** to the dentist today. (= I have an appointment.) NOT ~~I'll go to the dentist today.~~

UNIT 7 Education

Future: *If* Clauses for Possibility

1. Sentences with *if* have a subordinate clause and a main clause. The *if* clause is the subordinate clause. It gives a possible situation in the future. The main clause gives the result of the possible situation.

> If you study hard, . . .
> (= It is possible you will study hard.)
> . . . you will do well in the course.
> (= This will be the result of studying hard.)

2. The *if* clause is about the future, but do not use *will* or *be going to* in the *if* clause. Use the simple present.

> If he **doesn't graduate** in June, he'll graduate in January.
> NOT ~~If he won't graduate in June, he'll graduate in January.~~

3. Use *be going to* or *will* in the main clause of the sentence.

> If I get a scholarship, **I'll go** to college full-time.
> If I get a scholarship, **I'm going to go** to college full-time.

4. When the *if* clause comes at the beginning of the sentence, put a comma between the *if* clause and the main clause. When the *if* clause comes after the main clause, do not put a comma.

> If they fail the final exam**,** they will not pass the course.
> They will not pass the course if they fail the exam.

Future: Time Clauses

1. Future time clauses begin with a time word: *after, as soon as, before, until,* or *when.*

> I will stay in college **until I graduate**.

2. Use the simple present, <u>not</u> *will* or *be going to*, after future time words.

> Before I **take** the test next week, I'm going to study a lot.
> NOT ~~Before I will take the test next week, I'm going to study a lot.~~

3. Use *be going to* or *will* in the main part of the sentence.

> **I'm going to get** a job after I graduate.
> **I'll get** a job after I graduate.

4. When the future time clause comes at the beginning of the sentence, put a comma between the time clause and the main clause. When the time clause comes after the main clause, do not put a comma.

> As soon as he gets his diploma**,** he'll start college.
> He'll start college as soon as he gets his diploma.

Future: *May* and *Might* for Possibility

1. Use *may* and *might* + the base form of a verb to talk about future possibility. Use the base form of the verb after *may* or *might*.

> He **may go** to Colson College next year, but he's not sure.
> They **might have** a test next week.

2. Use *may not* or *might not* for negative statements. Do not contract them.

> You **might not pass** the course.
> NOT ~~You mightn't pass the course.~~

3. The forms are the same for all persons (*I, you, he, she, it, we, they*).

> I **may get** a scholarship.
> She **might apply** to college.

4. Be careful! *May* + *be* is a modal + a verb. *Maybe* is an adverb that comes at the beginning of the sentence. It means *possible*. We often use *maybe* with *will*.

> **Maybe** Gloria **will take** another English class.

UNIT 8 Getting a Job

Present Perfect: Regular Verbs
[+ *Ever* and *Never*]

1. Use the present perfect to talk about actions at an indefinite time in the past.

> **I've worked** in many restaurants. (= indefinite time: The sentence doesn't say when.)

2. To make the present perfect, use *has* or *have* and the past participle of the verb. To make the past participle of regular verbs, add *–ed* to the verb. Look at page 296 for information about the spelling rules for past participles, and page 300 for information about the pronunciation of the *–ed* endings.

> He **has talked** to the owner.
> I **have contacted** the manager.

3. Use the contracted form of the verb *have* in conversations.

> She**'s applied** for a job.
> They**'ve applied** for jobs.

4. Add *not* to *have* or *has* for negative statements. Use the contracted forms *hasn't* or *haven't* in conversations.

> He **hasn't started** his new job.
> They **haven't finished** the interview.

5. Be careful! Use the simple past, not the present perfect, to talk about actions at a *definite* time in the past.

> I **worked** at that restaurant two years ago.
> (Definite time: We know when—two years ago.)

6. *Never* and *not ever* have the same meaning.

> We**'ve never** worked.   = We haven**'t** ever worked.
>
> NOT ~~We've not never worked.~~   NOT ~~We've ever worked.~~

Present Perfect: Irregular Verbs [+ *Already* and *Yet*]

1. Many verbs have irregular past participles. The past participles of these verbs do not have *–ed* at the end. Look at page 298 for a list of irregular past participles. Some common irregular past participles are:

> be—**been**   do—**done**   have—**had**
> see—**seen**   take—**taken**   quit—**quit**

2. We often use *already* in affirmative sentences with the present perfect. Put *already* between *has* or *have* and the past participle.

> I've **already** been on an interview.
> (= Before now, but not an exact time)

3. We often use *yet* in negative sentences with the present perfect. Put *yet* at the end of a sentence.

> She hasn't heard from the manager **yet**. (But she will probably hear from the manager soon.)

4. Be careful! The contraction *'s* can mean *has* or *is*. In the present perfect, the contraction *'s* always means *has*.

> It**'s been** hard to find a good job.
> (= It **has** been hard to find a good job.)
> It**'s** hard to find a good job.
> (= It **is** hard to find a good job.)

Present Perfect: *Yes / No* Questions

1. To make a *yes/no* question, add *has* or *have* before the subject and the past participle of the verb. Use *has* or *have* in short answers.

> **Has** she ever **talked** to you about the problem?
> Yes, she **has**.
> **Have** you ever **found** a job online? No, I **haven't**.

2. When we ask someone a question with *Have you ever . . .* , we are asking about the time period from any time in the past until now. The time is indefinite.

> **Have** you **ever worked** as a waitress?
> (= indefinite time, at any time in the past)

3. We can also ask a question with *yet*. Put *yet* at the end of the question.

> Have you found a job **yet**?

Present Perfect: *For* and *Since*

1. Use *for* and *since* with the present perfect to show that something began in the past and is continuing now.

> Joe **has been** here for a month. (= Joe came here a month ago and is here now.)

2. Use *for* with a period of time.

> I've known him **for** a week / **for** a long time / **for** years.

3. Use *since* with a specific time.

> They've been married **since** 2005 / **since** last year / **since** two years ago.

Present Perfect Progressive: *For* and *Since*

1. Use the present perfect progressive to talk about actions that began in the past and are continuing now.

> I**'ve been reading** a lot lately.
> (= I started reading at some point in the past, and I am still reading now.)

2. To make the present perfect progressive, use *has* or *have* + *been* + the present participle of the verb. To make the present participle of verbs, add *–ing* to the verb.

> We **have been sitting** in class for an hour.
> The teacher **has been teaching** for an hour.

3. Use the contracted form of the verb *have* in conversations.

> She**'s** been going out with him for a month.
> They**'ve** been going out for a month.

4. Be careful! The contraction *'s* can mean *has* or *is*. In the present perfect progressive, the contraction *'s* always means *has*.

> It**'s** been raining since 11 o'clock.
> (= It **has** been raining.)
> Look! It**'s** raining. (= It **is** raining.)

5. Add *not* to *have* or *has* for negative statements. Use the contracted forms *hasn't* or *haven't* in conversations.

> It **hasn't been raining** for long.
> We **haven't been waiting** for long.

6. We often use the present perfect progressive expressions with these time expressions: *recently, lately, for* (+ period of time), *since* (+ specific time).

> Lee and Al **have been fighting** a lot **recently**.
> I**'ve been spending** a lot of time with Americans **lately**.

7. We use the present perfect progressive and *for* and *since* with <u>action</u> verbs (for example, *go*) to show that something began in the past and continues now.

> We **have been dancing** for two hours.

We use the present perfect simple with <u>non-action</u> (stative)verbs (for example, *know*) to show that something began in the past and continues now.

> I **have known** her for two years.

Be careful! Do not use the present perfect progressive with stative verbs. Look at page 298 for a list of stative verbs.

8. With some verbs (*work*, *live*, *teach*), you can use either the present perfect progressive or the present perfect simple, with no change in meaning.

> We've **been living** here since 1999.
> We **have lived** here since 1999.
> She's **been teaching** for 35 years.
> She **has taught** for 35 years.

Present Perfect Progressive: Questions

1. To make a *yes/no* question, add *has* or *have* before the subject + *been* + the present participle of the verb. Use *has* or *have* in short answers.

> **Has** he **been working** a lot lately? Yes, he **has**.
> **Have** you **been living** alone for a long time? No, I **haven't**.

2. To make information questions, use *has* or *have* after the question word (*how long*, *what*, etc.)

> How long **has** Chris been going out with Steve?
> What **have** you been doing lately?

UNIT 10 Television

Adverbs and Adjectives

1. Adverbs describe verbs. Adjectives describe nouns.

> VERB   ADVERB   ADJECTIVE   NOUN
> She speaks **well**.   She's a **good**   speaker.

2. Some verbs describe our senses. We use adjectives, not adverbs, after these verbs: *feel*, *look*, *smell*, *sound*, *taste*.

> This food **tastes good**.
> NOT ~~This food tastes well.~~

3. Adverbs also describe adjectives and other adverbs.

> ADVERB ADJECTIVE   ADVERB ADVERB
> He is **often happy**.   She is late **too often**.

Adverbs of Manner

1. Adverbs of manner answer the question *How*. Put adverbs of manner after the verb.

> (How does he run?)   He runs **quickly**.

To form an adverb of manner from most adjectives, add –*ly*.

> ADJECTIVE   ADVERB
> quick   quick**ly**

2. For adjectives with two syllables or more ending in –*y*, change the –*y* to –*i* and add –*ly*.

> ang**ri**ly   [an·gry]   happ**i**ly   [hap·py]
> | 2 | 2

3. For adjectives ending in –*ic*, add –*ally*.

> realist**ically**   [realistic]
> romant**ically**   [romantic]

4. For adjectives ending in –*le*, change the –*e* to –*y*.

> terri**bly**   [terrible]
> comforta**bly**   [comfortable]

5. Some adverbs are the same as the adjectives.

> She's a **fast** talker.   She talks **fast**.
> He's a **hard** worker.   He works **hard**.

6. The adverb of *good* is *well*.

> They're **good** singers.   They sing **well**.

7. Some adjectives do not have adverb forms. For example, adjectives that end in –*ly* (for example, *friendly*, *lovely*, *ugly*, *elderly*) do not have adverb forms.

Adverbs of Degree

1. Adverbs of degree (intensifiers) change how strong an adjective or adverb is. Put adverbs of degree in front of the adjective or adverb that they describe.

> They're **really** good dancers.
> (= stronger than *good*)
>
> They dance **very** well.
> (= stronger than *well*)

2. Do not use *very* or *extremely* with words that mean *very*. Use *pretty* or *really* with these words.

> The show's really great.   (great = very good)
> NOT ~~The show's very great.~~

3. Be careful! *Pretty* is an adjective and adverb, but the meaning is different. The adverb *pretty* goes before an adjective and makes the adjective less strong.

>   ADJECTIVE
> She's a very **pretty woman**.
> (= She's beautiful.)
>   ADJECTIVE   ADJECTIVE
> She's a **pretty**   **nice** person.
> (= She's nice, but she's not very nice.)

UNIT 11 The Animal Kingdom

Comparative and Superlative of Adjectives and Adverbs

1. Use the comparative to compare two people, places, or things.

> Elephants are **bigger than** lions.

2. You can put an auxiliary (for example, *is*, *are*, *does*, or *do*) at the end of a comparative sentence, but it is not necessary. The auxiliary depends on the main verb.

> The dog **is** bigger than the cat **is**.
> OR The dog is bigger than the cat.
>
> A cheetah **runs** faster than a lion **does**.
> OR A cheetah runs faster than a lion.

3. In formal English, use the subject pronoun (*I*, *you*, *he*, *she*, *we*, *they*) after *than*. In informal English, use the object pronoun (*me*, *you*, *him*, *her*, *us*, *them*).

> FORMAL: My brother has more pets than I.
> INFORMAL: My brother has more pets than me.

4. We sometimes put *a little*, *a lot*, or *much* before the comparative of adjectives and adverbs. *Much* and *a lot* have the same meaning.

> A rat is **a little bigger** than a mouse.
> A rat is **a lot more frightening** than a mouse.
> A rat is **much more frightening** than a mouse.

5. The opposite of *more . . . than* is *less . . . than*. Use *less . . . than* with most adjectives and adverbs that have two or three syllables. Use *not as . . . as* with adjectives and adverbs that have one syllable.

> A snake is **more** dangerous **than** a cat. =
> A cat is **less** dangerous **than** a snake.
>
> My cat is small**er than** my dog. =
> My cat is**n't as** big **as** my dog.

6. Use the superlative to compare three or more people, places, or things.

> The blue whale is **the biggest** animal in the world.

7. Look at page 297 for information about the forms of the comparative and superlative.

Comparative and Superlative of Nouns

1. Use *less* or *more* to compare two noncount nouns.

> Cats eat **less food** than dogs. =
> Dogs eat **more food** than cats.
>
> Rabbits make **much less noise** than parrots. =
> Parrots make **much more noise** than rabbits.

2. Use *fewer* or *more* to compare two count nouns.

> Dogs sleep **fewer hours** than cats. =
> Cats sleep **more hours** than dogs.

3. Use *the least* or *the most* to compare three or more noncount nouns.

> Snakes need **the least space** of all the animals in the zoo.
> Gorillas need **the most space**.

4. Use *the fewest* or *the most* to compare three or more count nouns.

> Sharks have **the most** teeth of any animal.
> The snakes had **the fewest** visitors last year.

Equatives

1. Use *as . . . as* to say two people, places, or things are the same.

> A giraffe is **as beautiful as** a bear.
> (= They are both beautiful.)
>
> A giraffe moves **as quickly as** a horse.
> (= They both move quickly.)

2. We use *not as . . . as* for the opposite of *more than*.

> The chimpanzee is **not as dangerous as** the lion.
> (= The lion is more dangerous.)

Reflexive Pronouns

1. We use reflexive pronouns when the subject and the object are the same.

> **He** is looking at **himself** in the mirror.

2. We often use reflexive pronouns after these verbs: *burn, cut, enjoy, hurt*.

> I **hurt myself** when I was cooking.

3. Do not confuse reflexive pronouns and *each other*.

> **Jim and Laura** are talking to **each other**.
> (= Jim is talking to Laura. Laura is talking to Jim.)
> NOT Jim and Laura are talking to ~~themselves.~~
> (= Jim is talking to himself and Laura is talking to herself.)

4. *By* + reflexive pronoun means *alone*.

> She lives **by herself**.   (= She lives alone.)

One / Ones

1. We use *one* or *ones* when we do not want to repeat a noun.

> I want a small glass, not a large **one**.
> (NOT ~~I want a small glass. I don't want a large glass.~~)
> I like red apples, but I don't like green **ones**.
> (NOT ~~I like red apples, but I don't like green apples.~~)

2. Use *one* for singular count nouns. Use *ones* for plural count nouns. Do not use *one* or *ones* for noncount nouns.

> I don't want a hot **sandwich**. I want a cold **one**.
> We don't want hot **sandwiches**. We want cold **ones**.
> I don't want hot tea. I want iced tea. (NOT ~~I want iced one.~~)

3. We often use *the* before *one* or *ones*.

> Which salad would you like?
> The smallest **one**, please.
>
> Which tables are ours?
> **The ones** near the window.

4. Be careful! Use *it* or *they* to refer to "*the* + a noun." Do not use *one* or *ones*.

> A: Where's **the** Italian **restaurant**?
> B: **It's** on Winter Street.

5. Use *it* or *they* to refer to a possessive adjective (*my, your, his, her*, etc.) + a noun. Do not use *one* or *ones*.

> A: Where are **our menus**?
> B: **They're** here.

Other: Singular and Plural

1. *One* is a pronoun. We use it when we do not want to repeat a singular count noun.

> They have chicken sandwiches. Do you want **one**?

2. *Another* means "an additional . . ." or "a different . . ." It can be an adjective or a pronoun.

> ADJECTIVE
>
> There are three places. One place has Chinese food. **Another place** has Italian food.
>
> PRONOUN
>
> There are three places. One place has Chinese food. **Another** has Italian food.

3. *The other* means "the last one in a group." We use *the other* before singular and plural nouns.

> There are two places. One place has Chinese food. **The other place** has Italian food.
> There are four places. One place has Chinese food. **The other places** have Italian food.

4. *The other* is an adjective or a pronoun. *The others* is a pronoun.

> ADJECTIVE
>
> This dessert is okay, but **the other** one is better. (= the other dessert)
>
> PRONOUN
>
> This dessert is okay, but **the other** is better. (= the other dessert)
>
> PRONOUN
>
> These eggs are good, but **the others** are better. (= the other eggs)

UNIT 13 Technology

Can and *Be able to*

1. Use *can* or *can't* to talk about ability. *Can* and *can't* are the same for all subjects (*I, you*, etc.).

> I **can download** music.
> I **can't download** pictures.
> She **can download** music.
> She **can't download** pictures.

2. We also use *be able to* and *not be able to* to talk about ability. The verb *be* changes for different subjects (*I am able to, He is able to, They are able to*, etc.).

> I'm **able to access** the Internet at work.
> I'm **not able to access** the Internet at home.
> He's **able to access** the Internet at work.
> He **isn't able to access** the Internet at home.

3. *Can* and *can't* are more common when we are talking about present ability. We use *be able to* with other forms—for example, the present perfect (*have/has been able to*) and modals (*might be able to*).

> People **have been able to send** e-mail messages for more than ten years.
> I **might be able to help** you, but I'm not sure.

Could and *Be able to*

1. *Could* and *couldn't* are the past forms of *can't*. Use *could* and *couldn't* to talk about general ability in the past.

> People **could talk** on the phone 30 years ago.
> People **couldn't talk** on cell phones 30 years ago.

2. Use *was/were able to* (not *could*) to talk about a specific event in the past.

> My son fixed my computer yesterday, so I **was able to use it** today.
> NOT I could use it today.

3. We also use *was/were able to* and *was not/were not able to* to talk about general ability in the past.

> I **was able to play** soccer well when I was younger.
> More people **were able to ride** horses a long time ago.

4. *Couldn't* and *wasn't/weren't able to* have the same meaning.

> I tried to fix it, but I **couldn't**.
> = I tried to fix it, but I **wasn't able to**.

5. Be careful! *Could* is also a way to ask a polite question. In this situation, it doesn't mean ability.

> **Could** I sit here?

Will be able to

1. Use *will be able to* and *won't be able to* to talk about ability in the future.

> I **will be able to download** the music next week.
> You **won't be able to access** the Internet tomorrow.

2. To make a *yes/no* question, put *will* before the subject. We use *will* or *won't* in short answers.

> **Will** they **be able to help** me?
> Yes, they **will**. OR No, they **won't**.

UNIT 14 A Kid's Life

Have to / Have got to / Must: Affirmative Statements and *Have to*: Yes / No Questions

1. Use *have to, have got to*, and *must* to talk about necessity. *Have to* and *have got to* are more common than *must* in conversation.

> You **have to** respect her.
> = You **have got to** respect her.
> = You **must** respect her.

2. Use *have to* or *have got to* with *I, you, we*, and *they*. Use *has to* or *has got to* with the third person singular (*he, she, it*).

> We **have to** be home at 8.
> = We **have got to** be home at 8.
> = We'**ve got to** be home at 8.
> He **has to** be home at 6.
> = He **has got to** be home at 6.
> = He'**s got to** be home at 6.

3. Use *have to* to ask questions about necessity. Use *do/does* or *don't/doesn't* in short answers. Do not use *have got to* or *must* in questions.

> **Do** you **have to** leave now?
> Yes, I **do**. OR No, I **don't**.
>
> **Does** the party **have to** be on Saturday?
> Yes, it **does**. OR No, it **doesn't**.

4. In information questions, *do* or *does* comes after the question word (*where, how often,* etc.).

> **Where do** you have to go?
> **How often does** he have to do chores?

5. When *who* is the subject of the question, do not use *do* or *does* in the question. Use *has to*.

> SUBJECT   VERB
> Who   **has to** do the dishes?   I do.

6. When *who* is the object of the question, use *do* or *does* and a subject word in the question.

> OBJECT   SUBJECT   VERB
> Who   **do** you   **have to** tell?   My mother.

Does not have to and *Must not*

1. *Don't / Doesn't have to* means that something is <u>not</u> necessary.

> The children **don't have to** stay in the house. They can go outside.
>
> Chris **doesn't have to** stay in her bedroom. She can play in the living room.

2. *Must not* or *mustn't* means that something is <u>not</u> permitted.

> The children **mustn't** leave the house. They have to stay in the living room.
>
> Chris **mustn't** leave her room. She **has to** stay there.

Had to: Statements and Questions

1. Use *had to* to talk about things that were necessary in the past. *Had to* is the past of *have to, have got to,* and *must.*

> I **had to** leave early yesterday.
> I **have to / have got to / must leave** early today.

2. For the negative, use *did not* (or *didn't*) + *have to* + the base form of the verb.

> We **didn't have to** go to school on Saturdays.

3. To make a *yes/no* question, add *did* before the subject and use the base form of the verb. Use *did* in short answers.

> **Did** you **have to go** to school on Fridays?
> Yes, we **did**. OR No, we **didn't**.

4. In information questions, *did* comes after the question word (*what, where, why,* etc.).

> **What time did** you **have to** leave in the morning?

5. When *who* is the subject of the question, do not use *did* in the question. Use *had to*.

> SUBJECT   VERB
> Who   **had to** take out the trash?   I did.

6. When *who* is the object of the question, use *did* and a subject word in the question.

> OBJECT   SUBJECT   VERB
> Who   **did** you   **have to** wait for?
> My sister.

Should (not) + Verb

1. Use *should* and *shouldn't* (*should not*) to give advice and express opinions. *Should, shouldn't* and *should not* are the same for all subjects (*I, you, he, she,* etc.).

> I **should** wait for her.   He **should** wait for her.
> I **shouldn't** be late.   He **shouldn't** be late.

2. Use the base form of the verb after *should* or *should not*. Use *shouldn't* for negative statements when speaking.

> She **should respect** her elders.
> You **shouldn't be** rude to people.

3. To make a *yes/no* question, put *should* before the subject and use the base form of the verb. Use *should* or *shouldn't* in short answers.

> **Should** I **give** him a present?
> Yes, you **should**. OR No, you **shouldn't**.

4. In information questions, *should* comes after the question word (*when, what,* etc.).

> **When should** I **go**?
> **What should** they **bring**?

5. *Who* can be the subject of a question with *should*.

> SUBJECT
> Who **should help**?   You should.

6. *Who* can also be the object of a question with *should*.

> OBJECT
> Who **should** I **help**?   You should help your grandparents.

Should (not) + *Be* + Present Participle

1. Use *should (not)* + *be* + present participle to give advice and opinions about something happening now.

> Why is your grandfather carrying all those bags?
> You **should be helping**.
>
> Look at that boy. He's pushing the other children. He **shouldn't be pushing**.

2. Use *should (not)* + *be* + present participle to talk about something happening now. Use *should (not)* + base form of the verb to talk about something that is true all the time.

> You **should be helping** me with the bags. (= now)
>
> You **should help** older people with their bags. (= all the time)

Should and *Have to*

1. Use *should* to say that it is a good idea for someone to do something.

> You **should be** kind to strangers. (= It's the right thing to do.)

2. Use *has to* or *have to* to say that it is necessary for someone to do something.

> Carly, you **have to be** nice to the other children. (= Carly doesn't have a choice.)

3. Use *shouldn't* to say that it is not a good idea for someone to do something.
> People **shouldn't be** rude to each other.
> (= It's not the right thing to do.)

4. Use *doesn't have to* or *don't have to* to say that it is <u>not</u> necessary for someone to do something.
> My brother's going to help tomorrow. You **don't have to help**. (= It's not necessary.)

Unit 16 Neighbors

Must + Verb

1. Use *must* when you are 95% sure that something is true, but you are not 100% sure.
> Alice and Mark **must need** the money. They both work two jobs.

2. Do not use *must* when you are 100% sure.
> That's George.
> (= I work with him and know him well.)
> That **must be** George.
> (= I've never met him, but he's with Mary and her boyfriend's name is George.)

3. Use *may* or *might* when you are less than 50% sure that something is true. You don't really know. You are just guessing.
> Carly's not in class. She **might be** sick.
> (= Maybe she is, and maybe she isn't.)

4. Remember! *Must* also means "necessary."
> You **must fix** the door today. (= It's necessary.)
> You **must be** tired.
> (= I think so, because of how you look.)

Must + Be + Present Participle

1. Use *must + be +* present participle when you are 95% sure that something is happening, but you are not 100% sure.
> Barbara **must be cooking**. It smells great in here.
> (Barbara's a good cook, and she lives here.)

2. Do not use *must + be +* present participle when you are 100% sure that something is happening.
> Barbara can't come to the phone. She's cooking.
> (You are with Barbara in the kitchen.)

3. Be careful! Do not use *must + be +* present participle to say that something is necessary.

Must not and Can't

1. Use *must not* when you are 95% sure that something is not true, but you are *not* 100% sure.
> The neighbor upstairs **must not be** home much. I never hear him.

2. We often use the contracted form *mustn't* in conversation.
> He **mustn't pay** a lot in rent. The apartment is very small.

3. Use *can't* when you think that something is impossible.
> She **can't have** four children! She's so young.

4. We also say *couldn't* when we think that something is impossible.
> She **couldn't have** four children! She's so young.

5. Use *be +* present participle with *must not, can't,* or *couldn't* when you are talking about something now.
> Louisa **must not be working** today. Her car is in the driveway.
> Norman **can't be watching** TV. He doesn't have a television.
> The children **couldn't be playing** in the yard. It's raining.

Unit 17 Health

It + Infinitive

1. An infinitive is *to* + verb. Use an infinitive after *It* + a form of *be* + certain adjectives (for example, *important* and *necessary*). Look at page 300 for a list of adjectives that can be followed by infinitives.
> It is **important to exercise** every day.

2. Add *for* + (a person) before the infinitive when you want to say "who".
> It is necessary **for me** to talk to the doctor. = I must talk to the doctor.

Too and Enough + Infinitive

1. Use *too* before an adjective. *Too* has a negative meaning. It means "more than is good."
> Your blood pressure is **too high**. You have to take medicine.

2. *Not enough* means "less than the correct amount."
> He **isn't strong enough**. He can't walk alone.

3. Use *enough* after an adjective but before a noun.
> ADJECTIVE + ENOUGH
> Your diet isn't **healthy enough**.
> ENOUGH + NOUN
> You don't eat **enough fruits and vegetables**.

4. An infinitive often comes after *too* or *enough*.
> The doctor is **too** busy **to see** you.
> You're not **strong** enough **to leave** the hospital.

5. Use these patterns with *too* and *enough* when you want to say "who".
> i) *too* + adjective + *for* + (a person) + infinitive:
> Your fever is **too high for you to go** to school. (You can't go to school.)
>
> ii) (*not*) + adjective + *enough* + *for* + (a person) + infinitive:
> The doctor's office is**n't close enough for us to walk**. (We can't walk.)

6. You can also use *too* and *enough* before an adverb.
> The doctor speaks **too quickly** for me to understand.
> The doctor does**n't** speak **clearly enough**.

7. Be careful! Don't confuse *too* and *very*. *Too* has a negative meaning; it causes a negative result. *Very* makes the meaning of an adjective stronger.
> I'm **too tired**. I can't drive.
> I'm **very tired**, but I can drive.

Infinitives of Purpose

1. We often use an infinitive (*to* + verb) to say the reason for doing something. It answers the question *Why*.

    Why does she take a pill every day?
    She takes it **to lower** her cholesterol.

2. *To* can have the same meaning as *in order to*.

    People go on diets **to lose** weight.   =
    People go on diets **in order to lose** weight.

3. You can use *for* + noun to give a reason. You cannot use *for* + verb to give a reason.

    I went to the drugstore **to get** some aspirin.
    I went to the drugstore **for aspirin**.
    NOT I went to the drugstore for get some aspirin.

Unit 18 Free Time

Gerunds as Subjects

1. Gerunds are used as nouns. We form a gerund by adding *–ing* to the end of a verb.

    (BE + ING)
    Being on a basketball team is fun.

2. Like nouns, gerunds can be the subject of a sentence.

    GERUND   NOUN
    Playing chess is fun. OR Chess is fun.

3. Use the singular form of the verb after a gerund.
    Running 10 kilometers **is** easy.

4. Use the plural form of the verb after two or more gerunds.
    Swimming and **hiking are** popular.

5. Be careful! Gerunds and the present participle of verbs look the same. They both end in *–ing*.

    VERB (present participle form)
    Tom and Jack are **taking** an art class.

    GERUND
    Taking an art class is expensive.

6. Look at page 295 for information about the spelling of gerunds.

Gerunds as Objects of Prepositions

1. Use a gerund after a preposition. The preposition can come after a verb, an adjective, or a noun.

    (verb + preposition + gerund)
    I'm thinking **about taking** a dance class.

    (adjective + preposition + gerund)
    Are you interested **in learning** how to bake?

    (noun + preposition + gerund)
    What's your reason **for being** late?

2. For a negative gerund, add *not* before the gerund.
    I enjoy **not going** to work on the weekend.

Gerunds or Infinitives as Objects of Verbs

1. Use a gerund after some verbs—for example, *dislike*, *finish*.

    I **dislike going** for walks alone.
    I'm going to **finish doing** the puzzle soon.

2. Use an infinitive after some verbs—for example, *expect*, *would like*.

    We **expect to go** to the game.
    I **would like to learn** Chinese.

3. You can use either a gerund or infinitive after some verbs—for example, *love*, *hate*. There is little difference in meaning.

    I **love swimming**.   I **love to swim**.
    Chris **hates cooking**.   Chris **hates to cook**.

4. Look at page 299 for a list of verbs that take gerunds or infinitives or both.

Unit 19 Emergency Services

Verb + Object + Infinitive

1. Use an object + infinitive after some verbs—for example, *advise*, *order*.

    OBJECT   INFINITIVE
    The police advised **him** **to get** a lawyer.

2. You can use two different patterns after some verbs—for example, *need*, *want*:

    i) verb + infinitive   I want **to go**.
    ii) verb + object + infinitive   I want **you to go**.

3. Look at page 299 for a list of verbs that take objects + infinitive.

Verb + Noun Clause and Replacing Noun Clauses

1. A noun clause is part of a sentence. It has a subject and a verb, and it is used as a noun. You can use a noun clause as the object of a verb.

    NOUN [OBJECT]
    I know the **police officer**.
    I know **that the police officer's name is Bill**.

    NOUN CLAUSE [OBJECT]

2. Use a noun clause after certain verbs—for example, *think*, *know*, *believe*. You can use *that* after the verb, but you don't have to. Both ways are correct.

    I think **that the firemen are here**.
    I think **the firemen are here**.

3. Look at page 300 for a list of verbs that take noun clauses.

4. When you answer a *yes/no* question, you can use one of these expressions in place of a noun clause.

    I **think so**.   I **believe so**.
    I **don't think so**.   I **don't believe so**.
    I **hope so**.   I **guess so**.
    I **hope not**.   I **guess not**.

    Are the firefighters coming? **I hope so**.
    (= I hope that they are coming.)

    Was the accident serious? **I hope not**.
    (= I hope that the accident wasn't serious.)

Make and Let

1. The verb *make* can mean "to force." When *make* has this meaning, use this pattern:
   make + an object (*someone*) + the base form of the verb
   > The firefighters **made everyone leave** the building.
   > NOT ~~The firefighters made everyone to leave the building.~~

2. The verb *let* can mean "to permit." When *let* has this meaning, use this pattern:
   let + an object (*someone*) + the base form of the verb
   > The firefighters **let us go** back into the building an hour later.
   > NOT ~~The firefighters let us to go back in the building an hour later.~~

UNIT 20 Taking a Trip

Reported Speech: Present Statements

1. Use a form of *say* and quotation marks (" ") when you write someone's exact words. Put a comma (,) after *say* and before the quotation marks.
   > Rick **says,** "The weather's beautiful in Santa Rita."

2. Use a form of *say* and a noun clause when you report someone's statement. Do <u>not</u> put a comma or quotation marks.
   > Rick **says that** the weather is beautiful in Santa Rita.

3. You can use *that*, but it is not necessary.
   > Rick **says** the weather is beautiful in Santa Rita.

4. When you report someone's statement, change the pronouns and verbs when necessary.
   > Susan says, **"I am** really enjoying **myself."**
   > Susan says (that) **she is** really enjoying **herself**.

Reported Speech: Commands

1. When you report an order, use *tell* [someone to do something].
   > The driver said, "Open the door."
   > The driver **told me to open** the door.

2. When you report a negative order, use *tell* [someone not to do something].
   > The flight attendant said, "Don't leave your bags on the floor."
   > The flight attendant **told us not to leave** our bags on the floor.

3. Be careful! After *tell* (or *told*), use an object + infinitive. After *say* (or *said*) use a noun clause.
   > OBJECT   INFINITIVE
   > They told **us   to come** early.
   > NOUN CLAUSE
   > She says **(that) she's coming** early.

Reported Speech: Requests

1. We use a lot of different language to make requests:
   > "Can you tell me your name, please?"
   > "Could you tell me your name, please?"
   > "Would you tell me your name, please?"
   > "Please tell me your name."

2. When you report a request, use *ask someone to do something*.
   > The woman **asked me to tell** her my name.

Charts

Spelling Rules: Present Progressive and Gerunds

1. Add *–ing* to the base form of the verb.		rain	→	rain**ing**
2. If a verb ends in *–e*, drop *–e* and add *–ing*.		smoke	→	smok**ing**
3. If a verb ends in *–ie*, change *–ie* to *–y* and add *–ing*.		die	→	d**ying**
4. If a verb is one syllable and ends in consonant + vowel + consonant (CVC), double the final consonant and add *–ing*.		stop	→	stop**ping**
5. Do not double the consonant if it is *w*, *x*, or *y*. Simply add *–ing*.		snow	→	snow**ing**
		fix	→	fix**ing**
		play	→	play**ing**
6. If the word has two or more syllables and ends in consonant + vowel + consonant (CVC), double the final consonant only if it is stressed. Then add *–ing*.		permit	→	permit**ting**
		visit	→	visit**ing**

Spelling Rules: Simple Present Third Person Singular

1. Add *–es* to words that end in *–ch*, *–s*, *–sh*, *–ss*, *–x*, or *–z*.		teach	→	teach**es**
		wash	→	wash**es**
		miss	→	miss**es**
		fix	→	fix**es**
		fizz	→	fizz**es**
2. Add *–es* to words that ends in *–o*.		do	→	do**es**
3. If the word ends in consonant + *–y*, change *–y* to *–i* and add *–es*.		cry	→	cr**ies**
4. Add *–s* to words that end in vowel + *–y*.		play	→	play**s**

Spelling Rules: Simple Past and Past Participle of Regular Verbs

1. Add –*ed* to the base form of the verb.   rain ⟶ rain**ed**

2. If a verb ends in –*e*, add –*d*.   smoke ⟶ smoke**d**

3. If a verb ends in –*ie*, add –*d*.   die ⟶ die**d**

4. If the verb is one syllable and ends in consonant + vowel + consonant (CVC), double the final consonant and add –*ed*.   stop ⟶ stop**ped**

5. Do not double the consonant if it is *w*, *x*, or *y*. Simply add –*ed*.
   - snow ⟶ snow**ed**
   - fix ⟶ fix**ed**
   - play ⟶ play**ed**

6. If the word has two or more syllables and ends in consonant + vowel + consonant (CVC), double the final consonant only if it is stressed. Then add –*ed*.
   - permit ⟶ permit**ted**
   - visit ⟶ visit**ed**

Spelling Rules: Plural Nouns

1. Add –*es* to words that end in –*ch*, –*s*, –*sh*, –*ss*, –*x*, or –*z*.
   - watch ⟶ watch**es**
   - bus ⟶ bus**es**
   - dish ⟶ dish**es**
   - pass ⟶ pass**es**
   - box ⟶ box**es**

2. Add –*es* to words that end in –*o*.   potato ⟶ potato**es**

3. If the word ends in consonant + –*y*, change –*y* to –*i* and add –*es*.   country ⟶ countr**ies**

4. Add –*s* to words that end in vowel + –*y*.   day ⟶ day**s**

Comparative Form of Adjectives

One-syllable words

1. If the word ends in a consonant, add –er.

old ⟶ old**er**

2. If the word ends in 1 vowel + 1 consonant, double the consonant and add –er.

thin ⟶ thin**ner**

3. If the word ends in –e, add –r.

nice ⟶ nice**r**

Two-syllable words

If the word ends in –y, change –y to –i and add –er.

pretty ⟶ prett**ier**

Superlative Form of Adjectives

One-syllable words

1. If the word ends in a consonant, add –est.

old ⟶ old**est**

2. If the word ends in 1 vowel + 1 consonant, double the consonant and add –est.

thin ⟶ thin**nest**

3. If the word ends in –e, add –st.

nice ⟶ nice**st**

Two-syllable words

If the word ends in –y, change –y to –i and add –est.

pretty ⟶ prett**iest**

Comparative and Superlative Forms of Adverbs

Comparative

<u>One-syllable words</u>

1. If the word ends in a consonant, add –er.

fast ⟶ fast**er**

2. If the word ends –e, add –r.

late ⟶ late**r**

<u>Two-syllable words</u>

If the word ends in –ly, add *more* before the word.

quickly ⟶ **more** quickly

Superlative

<u>One-syllable words</u>

1. If the word ends in a consonant, add –est.

fast ⟶ fast**est**

2. If the word ends –e, add –st.

late ⟶ late**st**

<u>Two-syllable words</u>

If the word ends in –ly, add *the most* before the word.

quickly ⟶ **the most** quickly

Irregular Verbs

Base form	Simple Past	Past Participle	Base form	Simple Past	Past Participle
be	was	been	make	made	made
become	became	become	meet	met	met
buy	bought	bought	pay	paid	paid
catch	caught	caught	put	put	put
come	came	come	read	read	read
cost	cost	cost	ride	rode	ridden
cry	cried	cried	ring	rang	rung
cut	cut	cut	run	ran	run
do	did	done	say	said	said
drink	drank	drunk	see	saw	seen
drive	drove	driven	sell	sold	sold
eat	ate	eaten	send	sent	sent
feel	felt	felt	shine	shone	shone
find	found	found	sit	sat	sat
fly	flew	flown	sleep	slept	slept
forget	forgot	forgotten	speak	spoke	spoken
get	got	gotten	spend	spent	spent
give	gave	given	stand	stood	stood
go	went	gone	steal	stole	stolen
have	had	had	swim	swam	swum
hear	heard	heard	take	took	taken
hit	hit	hit	teach	taught	taught
hold	held	held	think	thought	thought
hurt	hurt	hurt	try	tried	tried
know	knew	known	wake	woke	woken
leave	left	left	wear	wore	worn
lose	lost	lost	win	won	won
			write	wrote	written

Common Stative Verbs

Senses	Possession	Likes	Needs	Mental States	Measurement	Description
feel	belong	hate	need	agree	cost	be
hear	have	like	want	believe	weigh	look
see	own	love		forget		seem
smell				know		
sound				remember		
taste				think		
				understand		

Verb + Gerund

acknowledge	consider	enjoy	justify	prohibit	risk
admit	delay	escape	keep (*continue*)	quit	suggest
advise	deny	explain	mention	recall	support
appreciate	detest	feel like	mind (*object to*)	recommend	
avoid	discontinue	finish	miss	regret	
can't help	discuss	forgive	postpone	report	
celebrate	dislike	give up (*stop*)	practice	resent	
	endure	imagine	prevent	resist	

Verb + Preposition + Gerund

adapt to	approve of	be into	consist of	engage in
adjust to	argue (with	blame for	decide on	forgive (someone)
agree (with	someone)	care about	depend on	for
someone) on	about	complain (to	disapprove of	help (someone)
apologize (to	ask about	someone) about	discourage (someone)	with
someone) for	believe in	concentrate on	from	

Verb + Infinitive

agree	choose	hesitate	need	promise	want
appear	consent	hope	neglect	refuse	wish
arrange	decide	hurry	offer	request	would like
ask	deserve	intend	pay	rush	
attempt	expect	learn	plan	seem	
can't afford	fail	manage	prepare	volunteer	
can't wait	help	mean (*intend*)	pretend	wait	

Verb + Object + Infinitive

advise	encourage	hire	persuade	tell
allow	expect	invite	promise	urge
ask	forbid	need	remind	want
cause	force	order	request	warn
choose	get	pay	require	wish
convince	help	permit	teach	would like

Verbs Followed by the Gerund or the Infinitive

begin	continue	hate	love	remember	stop
can't stand	forget	like	prefer	start	try

Go + Verb + *–ing*

go bowling	go hiking	go sailing
go camping	go horseback riding	go shopping
go dancing	go hunting	go skating
go fishing	go jogging	go skiing
go golfing	go running	go swimming

Verbs Followed by a Noun Clause

believe	hear	say
feel	hope	suspect
guess	know	think

It + Adjective + Infinitive

dangerous	embarassing	good	normal
difficult	exciting	important	unhealthy
easy	frightening	necessary	unusual

Pronunciation Rules

Simple Present Third Person Singular

1. If the word ends in a vowel sound or /b/, /d/, /g/, /l/, /m/, /n/, /ŋ/, /ɹ/, /θ/, /v/ or /w/,

   it is pronounced /z/.
   gives   onions   Tom's

2. If the word ends in /f/, /h/, /k/, /p/, /t/ or /ð/,

   it is pronounced /s/.
   walks   maps   Matt's

3. If the word ends in /tʃ/, /dʒ/, /s/, /ʃ/, /z/ or /ʒ/,

   it is pronounced /ɪz/.
   sneezes   watches   Nash's

Simple Past and Past Participle of Regular Verbs

1. If the base form ends in a vowel sound or /b/, /dʒ/, /g/ /l/, /m/, /ŋ/, /ɹ/, /θ/, /v/, /w/, /z/, or /ʒ/,

   it is pronounced /d/.
   snowed   mailed

2. If the base forms ends in /tʃ/, /f/, /h/, /k/, /p/ or /s/,

   it is pronounced /t/, /ʃ/, or /ð/.
   stopped   laughed

3. If the base form ends in /d/ or /t/,

   it is pronounced /ɪd/.
   needed   wanted

Partner Activities

From Time to Talk, PAGE 53

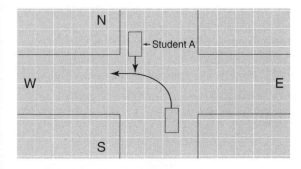

From Time to Talk, PAGE 91

Spring of your junior year

☐ Meet with a guidance counselor.

☐ Discuss several different colleges.

Fall of your senior year

☐ Study for the SAT.

☐ Decide on three colleges.

☐ Register for the December SAT.

Winter of your senior year

☐ Take the SAT in December.

☐ Start working on college applications.

☐ Start working on financial aid forms.

☐ Write college application essays.

Spring of your senior year

☐ Ask high school to send your transcript to the colleges.

☐ Submit completed application packet before the deadline.

☐ Submit completed financial aid form before the deadline.

☐ Relax and wait for an answer!

From Time to Talk, PAGE 119

Student A, read each sentence twice.

1. You haven't been listening to me.

2. We didn't speak at your wedding.

3. I haven't heard from them for months.

4. She's known him since college.

Now listen to Student B and check (✓) the sentences you hear.

5. ❑ **a.** They've been arguing for an hour.

   ❑ **b.** They argued for an hour.

6. ❑ **a.** She's been crying all day.

   ❑ **b.** She cried all day.

7. ❑ **a.** We've been getting along better.

   ❑ **b.** We're getting along better.

8. ❑ **a.** She's been talking for hours.

   ❑ **b.** She talked for hours.

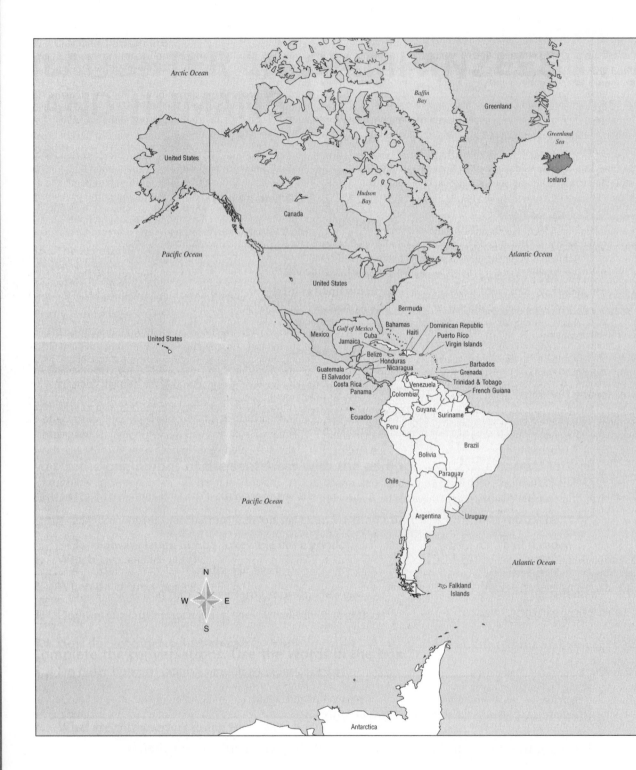

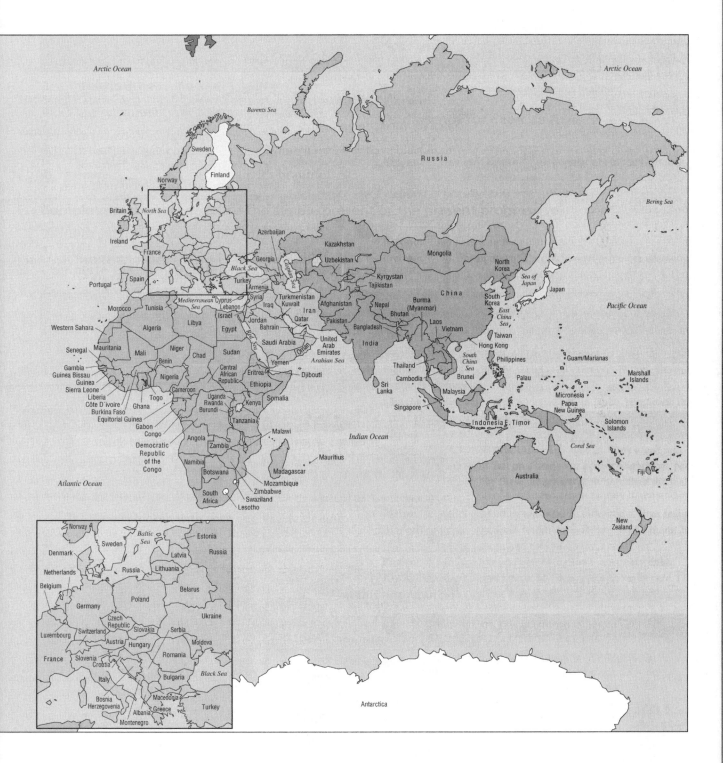

Arctic Ocean

Arctic Ocean

Barents Sea

Bering Sea

Sweden

Norway

Finland

Russia

Britain

North Sea

Ireland

France

Azerbaijan

Kazakhstan

Mongolia

North
Korea

Sea of
Japan

Japan

Pacific Ocean

Portugal

Spain

Georgia

Caspian Sea

Uzbekistan

Kyrgystan

Tajikistan

China

South
Korea

Black Sea

Turkey

Armenia

Morocco

Tunisia

Mediterranean
Sea

Cyprus
Lebanon
Syria

Iraq

Turkmenistan
Kuwait

Iran

Afghanistan

Nepal

Bhutan

Burma
(Myanmar)

East
China
Sea

Taiwan

Israel

Qatar

Pakistan

Laos

Hong Kong

Western Sahara

Algeria

Libya

Jordan

Bahrain

India

Vietnam

Egypt

Saudi Arabia

Oman

United
Arab
Emirates

Bangladesh

Guam/Marianas

Senegal

Mauritania

Mali

Niger

Chad

Sudan

Yemen

Arabian Sea

Thailand

South
China
Sea

Philippines

Marshall
Islands

Gambia
Guinea Bissau
Guinea
Sierra Leone

Benin

Eritrea

Djibouti

Sri
Lanka

Cambodia

Brunei

Palau

Micronesia

Nigeria

Central
African
Republic

Ethiopia

Malaysia

Papua
New Guinea

Liberia
Côte D´ivoire
Burkina Faso
Equitorial Guinea

Ghana

Togo

Cameroon

Uganda
Rwanda
Burundi

Kenya

Somalia

Singapore

Indonesia E. Timor

Solomon
Islands

Gabon
Congo

Tanzania

Indian Ocean

Coral Sea

Angola

Malawi

Fiji

Democratic
Republic
of the
Congo

Namibia

Zambia

Mauritius

Australia

Botswana

Madagascar

South
Africa

Mozambique
Zimbabwe
Swaziland

Atlantic Ocean

New
Zealand

Lesotho

Norway

Baltic
Sea

Estonia

Denmark

Sweden

Latvia

Russia

Netherlands

Russia

Lithuania

Belgium

Germany

Poland

Belarus

Luxembourg

Czech
Republic

Slovakia

Serbia

Ukraine

Switzerland

Austria

Moldova

France

Slovenia
Croatia

Hungary

Romania

Italy

Bulgaria

Black Sea

Bosnia
Herzegovenia

Macedonia
Greece

Antarctica

Albania

Turkey

Montenegro

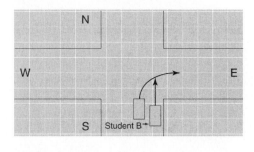

Student B, listen to Student A and check (✓) the sentences you hear.

1. ❑ **a.** You haven't been listening to me.

   ❑ **b.** You're not listening to me.

2. ❑ **a.** We haven't spoken since your wedding.

   ❑ **b.** We didn't speak at your wedding.

3. ❑ **a.** I haven't heard from them for months.

   ❑ **b.** I didn't hear from them for months.

4. ❑ **a.** She's known him since college.

   ❑ **b.** She knew him in college.

Now read these sentences for Student A. Read each sentence twice.

5. They argued for an hour.

6. She's been crying all day.

7. We've been getting along better.

8. She's been talking for hours.

Answers to Time to Talk Quiz, PAGE 147

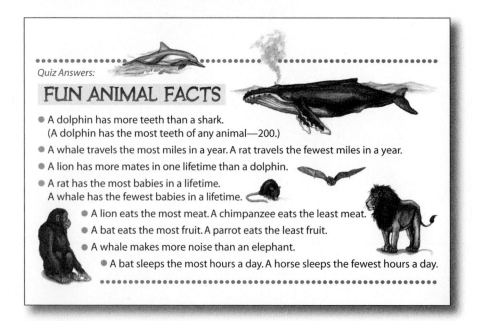

Quiz Answers:

FUN ANIMAL FACTS

- A dolphin has more teeth than a shark.
  (A dolphin has the most teeth of any animal—200.)
- A whale travels the most miles in a year. A rat travels the fewest miles in a year.
- A lion has more mates in one lifetime than a dolphin.
- A rat has the most babies in a lifetime.
  A whale has the fewest babies in a lifetime.
    - A lion eats the most meat. A chimpanzee eats the least meat.
    - A bat eats the most fruit. A parrot eats the least fruit.
    - A whale makes more noise than an elephant.
      - A bat sleeps the most hours a day. A horse sleeps the fewest hours a day.

Student A

(knock)
(apologize)

(offer to help)
(touch the dog)

(shake her hand)
(kiss her)

Student B

(cover her mouth)
(say "Excuse me")

(say "Sorry")
(say "Bless you!")

(interrupt)
(whisper to a classmate)

Postcard 1:

SYDNEY OPERA HOUSE

Dear Linda,
We're really enjoying ourselves. Our hotel is beautiful, and there are many interesting things to do. We go to the beach every day. The people are friendly, but it's hard for me to understand their English. They have a different accent and use different expressions than Americans do. It's also strange to be in a place where it's summer in January, but we love the warm temperatures. Hope you're keeping warm in Chicago.

Love, Jacquie and Paul

Ms. Linda Wong
28 West Kinzie Street
Chicago, IL 60610

Choices for Postcard 2:

❏ Cairo, Egypt

❏ New York, New York, USA

❏ São Paulo, Brazil

❏ Montreal, Canada

Postcard 2:

Times Square, New York City

Dear Mom and Dad,
I've been here for five days, and it's
been great so far. I've seen many famous
places already. All the skyscrapers are
amazing. My hotel is in a great location,
with a wonderful view of Central Park.
The only problem is the weather. It's
been cold every day, and it's snowed
twice. But that hasn't stopped me from
going out to the theater! I've seen two
Broadway shows, and have tickets for
another one tonight. I miss you!

Love, Annie

Mr. and Mrs. James Nieves
240 Hogan Street
Houston, TX 77009

Choices for Postcard 1:

❏ Hong Kong, China   ❏ Miami Beach, Florida, USA

❏ San Juan, Puerto Rico   ❏ Sydney, Australia

Answers to Exercise C, PAGE 35

2. The first World Cup took place in Uruguay.

3. People watched the World Cup on TV for the first time in 1958.

4. England won the World Cup in 1966.

5. Brazil won the 2002 World Cup.

6. 1.7 billion people saw the 2002 World Cup on TV.

Answers to Exercise D, PAGE 145

2. T 3. T 4. T 5. T 6. F 7. T 8. F

Audioscript

Unit 1: Getting to Know You

Listening, A, B, and C, page 3

Marco: Hey Betsy! How are you doing?

Betsy: Hi, Marco. I'm great. It's good to see you. What's new with you?

Marco: Oh, you know, the same old stuff. I'm taking classes at Spencer, and working nights at Clarks. Look at all these people! I can't believe that they all live in our neighborhood.

Betsy: I know. A lot of new people are moving in.

Marco: Hey, who's that?

Betsy: The woman in the kitchen? That's Felicia Banks. She lives in the Long's old house.

Marco: What's she like?

Betsy: I'm just getting to know her, but I think she's got a nice personality.

Marco: Is she going out with anyone?

Betsy: Yeah, she's got a boyfriend.

Marco: Oh well, too bad. Hey, is that Amy Parsons?

Betsy: No. Amy Parsons doesn't look like that. Amy's got long hair, and she's a lot shorter.

Marco: Oh, yeah, you're right. So who is she?

Betsy: I don't know her name, but she lives on Elm St., next to the Fosters. She works at the mall.

Marco: Has she got a boyfriend?

Betsy: No . . . but she's got a husband. Hey, what's going on with you? Are you and Jenny fighting again?

Marco: No . . . but we're not going out anymore. We're still friends, but she's going to college now, and she hasn't got time for a boyfriend. So, if you've got any single friends . . .

Grammar, page 10

Stan: Hi, Jack. How are things going?

Jack: I'm pretty busy. I'm taking five classes this semester.

Stan: Really? That's a lot. I'm just taking three. Do you like your teachers?

Jack: Yes. I get along with all of them. I really like my math teacher. He's got a good sense of humor, and he explains things really well.

Stan: I like my teachers, too. So, where are you going now?

Jack: I'm going home. Peggy's waiting for me in the car.

Stan: Oh, are you two going out these days?

Jack: No, we're just friends. She's got a boyfriend.

Dictation, page 10

1. My daughters have got wavy hair.
2. My husband's got a beard and a mustache.
3. She hasn't got a good sense of humor.
4. Who are you going out with these days?
5. These days my sister and I are getting along better.

Listening, A and B, page 11

Reporter: This is Evangeline Lopez with *Spotlight on the City*. People in the city often complain that nobody knows their neighbors anymore. We decided to find out if that's true. We are downtown, standing in front of an apartment building. Excuse me, I'm with *Spotlight on the City*. Do you live in this building?

Woman 1: Here? No. I'm just visiting a friend.

Reporter: Thank you. Excuse me, sir? Have you got time for a few questions? I'm with *Spotlight on the City*, and we're talking to people today about their neighbors.

Man: Their neighbors?

Reporter: Yes. Do you know your neighbors' names?

Man: Hmmm . . . Let me think . . . well, I know the name of my neighbor's dog—it's Lucy—but I don't know *his* name. And the woman next door to me. . . . she's got a cat . . . I think her name is Mrs. Carson . . . or is it Carter? I'm not sure. I guess that's it.

Reporter: And how long have you lived here?

Man: Ten years.

Reporter: Thank you very much.

Man: No problem.

Reporter: Excuse me, ma'am?

Woman 2: Yes?

Reporter: I'm with *Spotlight on the City*. Can I ask you a few questions?

Woman 2: Yes, of course, dear.

Reporter: Do you live in this building?

Woman 2: Yes.

Reporter: And do you know your neighbors?

Woman 2: Of course. I know all of them . . .

Reporter:	Really? All of them? How many are there?
Woman 2:	Well, there's Mr. Rupert on the first floor— He's got a bad heart. And there's poor Jenny in 3A. She's working so much these days. She's making herself sick . . . and then there's Molly in 3B. She's looking for a job. Maybe you've got something for her at the radio station?

Unit 2: The World We Live In

Listening, A, B, and C, page 17

Rita:	I'm sick of living in the city. There are very few good schools, too much crime, and very little open space. I want to move somewhere safe where there's plenty of space for my kids to run around.
Ben:	Let me guess—you're thinking about moving to the suburbs, right?
Rita:	Yeah, why?
Ben:	Don't do it! My wife and I moved out of the city two years ago, and neither of us is happy with the decision.
Rita:	Why do you say that?
Ben:	Well, you're right about the open space— there's plenty. But I don't have any time to enjoy it. I have no time with my kids.
Rita:	Why is that?
Ben:	There are a lot of reasons. First of all, a lot of people are moving out of the city. There aren't enough houses and apartments for them all in the suburbs, so the prices are really high. I have to work extra hours to pay for our new house, and we still don't have enough money to pay our bills. And the traffic is terrible. I spend several hours a day in my car. I'm spending too much on gas, but what can I do?
Rita:	Why don't you take public transportation?
Ben:	Because there are no trains before 7:00 A.M., and only a few after 5:00. There's one at 5:30 and one at 6:30, but as you know, I work until 7.
Rita:	That's a real problem. So where do you park? There's very little parking out back, and the public lots are expensive, aren't they?
Ben:	Well, there aren't a lot of parking spaces here, but there are a few. That's why I get here so early every day.
Rita:	Hmmm . . . I'll think about what you said.
Ben:	Well, if you *do* decide to move to the suburbs, let me know. Maybe we can sell you our house . . . and move into your apartment.

Grammar, page 24

I'm writing from my new home. The neighborhood is safe, and it's quiet most of the time. There's a little noise in the morning, but I get up early anyway. The rent is very cheap, but there is very little public transportation. Just one bus stops on my street. That's not great, but I'm lucky because there are plenty of inexpensive stores and restaurants.

My apartment's fine, but there are a few problems. First of all, the rooms are small, so there isn't a lot of space. Second, there isn't enough light. There isn't much sunshine around here, and my bedroom has no windows, zero! There are two windows in the living room, but both of them are very small. I miss the sunshine back home!

Dictation, page 24

1. We haven't got too much crime.
2. There isn't enough public transportation.
3. There's plenty of sunshine all the time.
4. We've got too many tourists.
5. We have a little traffic and a little crime, but neither problem is very serious.

Listening, A and B, page 25

Good evening. This is Jeff Woodman for *Spotlight on Our World*. Tonight's Spotlight Report is on the island nation of Cape Verde. The Republic of Cape Verde is located in the North Atlantic Ocean. It is about 500 kilometers from the West African coast. There were no people on the islands when they were discovered by the Portuguese in 1460. Today, the islands are home to approximately 400,000 people. Like many other island people, Cape Verdeans eat a lot of fish. However, they sell very little to other countries. It is difficult and expensive to keep the fish fresh. Other than fish, there are very few natural resources in Cape Verde.

Cape Verde is warm and dry all year, with plenty of sunshine. Most Cape Verdeans do not live in the big cities. About 70% live on farms or in small towns. They grow bananas, corn, beans, sweet potatoes, sugarcane, coffee, and peanuts. However, there are very few large farms because there isn't enough water. Most years, there is very little rain. In fact, in the 20th century there was no rain at all for several years. As a result, Cape Verdeans cannot grow enough food to feed their population, so they have to buy food from other countries. They import about 80% of their food.

Cape Verdeans are proud of their culture. Cape Verdean art and music is well known all over the world. Tourism is very important to Cape Verde. There are many beautiful beaches and several great hotels on the islands. Every year, more tourists choose Cape Verde for their vacations. Most of the tourists are from Western Europe, but Cape Verdeans hope there will soon be more tourists from other parts of the world too.

For *Spotlight on Our World*, this is Jeff Woodman. Tune in again tomorrow night, when we visit the beautiful Mexican island of Cozumel.

Unit 3: Sports

Listening, A, B, and C, page 31

Mina: Hi, honey. What time are you picking me up tonight?

Tony: Tonight? I can't go out tonight. I have tickets for the soccer match.

Mina: But you went to a match last night!

Tony: Yeah. And it was great. As soon as we sat down, our team scored a goal. Didn't you watch it on TV? It was . . .

Mina: No, Tony, I didn't. Tony, didn't you promise me something?

Tony: Did I? What did I promise?

Mina: A movie . . . do you remember anything about a movie?

Tony: Oh . . . yeah . . . I remember now . . . You wanted to see a movie because your sister liked it.

Mina: And who did I want to see it with?

Tony: Me? Did you want to see it with me?

Mina: Yes, I did.

Tony: But I didn't know that it was tonight.

Mina: Yes, you did. Before I got the tickets, I called you and asked. You said tonight was fine.

Tony: Uh oh . . . Now I remember. After I talked to you, Barney stopped by and invited me to go to tonight's game with him. I'm sorry, honey. I was so excited that I completely forgot about our date.

Mina: Well, just call Barney and tell him you can't go.

Tony: But, Mina, I'll take you to the movies another night.

Mina: Forget it, Tony. It's either me or soccer . . .

Tony: [silence—thinking]

Mina: Goodbye, Tony.

Grammar, page 38

Inez: I called you last night, but you weren't home.

Anton: I went to the Stars game.

Inez: How did the Stars do? Did they win?

Anton: No, they lost 3 to 1.

Inez: What happened?

Anton: Bond left the game because he got hurt. After he left, they didn't score again.

Dictation, page 38

1. They beat the other team by ten points.
2. Did the game take place at night?
3. How many times did your team lose to them?
4. The fans cheered after the team scored a goal.
5. Because he missed the shot, the player got angry.

Listening, A and B, page 39

Reporter: Good morning. This is June Vero, with *Spotlight on Sports*. Today we are talking about the first team sport with Dr. Ramon Perez, an expert in ancient Mesoamerican civilizations. Dr. Perez, welcome!

Dr. Perez: Thank you, June.

Reporter: So, Dr. Perez, where and when did the first team sport appear?

Dr. Perez: We now believe that the native people of Central America invented the first team sport about 3,500 years ago.

Reporter: What kind of game was it?

Dr. Perez: Well, there were several different versions of the game. We don't know all of the details, but we do know that in most places, the two teams played on a court in the shape of a capital I. They played with a large, heavy rubber ball.

Reporter: And what did they do with the ball?

Dr. Perez: We think that the players tried to pass the ball through a ring high on the wall of the court. They couldn't touch the ball with their hands, and the ball could never touch the ground.

Reporter: So how did they pass the ball?

Dr. Perez: We think they used their hips and elbows.

Reporter: How did the game end?

Dr. Perez: The game ended as soon as one team put the ball through the ring, or as soon as the ball touched the ground.

Reporter: So as soon as one team scored, the game was over?

Dr. Perez: Well, in fact, in most games there was no score. The ball usually touched the ground before any of the players put it in the ring.

Reporter:	But then who was the winner?
Dr. Perez:	The team that touched the ball right before it hit the ground lost the game. The other team won.
Reporter:	What happened after the game?
Dr. Perez:	There was a big celebration for the winning team.
Reporter:	And what happened to the losers?
Dr. Perez:	That was different in different places and at different times in history. In the earliest days of the game, the captain of the losing team was killed.
Reporter:	Well thank you, Dr. Perez, for being here.

Unit 4: Accidents

Listening, A, B, and C, page 45

Emily:	Manny, what happened to you? You look terrible!
Manny:	I had the worst weekend of my life.
Emily:	Why? What happened?
Manny:	Well, I was working with my father-in-law. We were painting his house. I was climbing up a ladder to paint the top of the house, and my father-in-law was standing below me. Suddenly, I heard a loud BANG. I was so surprised that I dropped my paintbrush ... When I looked down, my father-in-law was standing there with paint all over him.
Emily:	Oh, no!
Manny:	Then my wife and mother-in-law ran out of the house. They were screaming.
Emily:	What was going on?
Manny:	I didn't have any idea at first. While I was climbing down the ladder, I heard another bang. And then I smelled smoke.
Emily:	Where was it coming from? Was it coming from inside the house?
Manny:	No, it wasn't. It was coming from the house next door.
Emily:	Oh no! Was anyone in the house?
Manny:	No, thank goodness. They were away for the weekend, visiting their daughter.
Emily:	Well, that's one good thing. Did the house burn down?
Manny:	Yes, it did. It was awful.
Emily:	How did the fire start?
Manny:	They don't know yet.

Emily:	Did anything happen to your father-in-law's house?
Manny:	No, we were very lucky.

Dictation, page 52

1. I was daydreaming when the teacher called my name.
2. What were you doing when you fell off the ladder?
3. Was he paying attention when the accident happened?
4. Last night at nine I was ironing.
5. She was talking on the phone while she was standing on the ladder.

Listening, A and B, page 53

Insurance Agent:	Capital Insurance. May I help you?
Maddy:	Hello? This is Maddy White. I have an insurance policy with you.
Insurance Agent:	Yes, of course, Mrs. White. Are you OK? You sound a little upset.
Maddy:	I am. I just had an accident.
Insurance Agent:	Oh, that's terrible. Are you okay?
Maddy:	Yes. I was wearing my seatbelt, thank goodness.
Insurance Agent:	Was anyone else injured?
Maddy:	Yes, the driver of the car that hit my car wasn't wearing her seatbelt, and she hit her head. She was bleeding a lot. They took her to the hospital.
Insurance Agent:	I'm sorry, Mrs. White. I know you're upset, but I have a few more questions.
Maddy:	OK, go ahead.
Insurance Agent:	When and where did the accident happen?
Maddy:	I was driving down Seventh Ave. when—
Insurance Agent:	Were you driving east or west on Seventh?
Maddy:	I was driving east.
Insurance Agent:	And when was this?
Maddy:	About two hours ago.
Insurance Agent:	OK, go ahead.
Maddy:	As I was saying, I was driving down Seventh Ave. There was a red light ahead at the intersection with Grove St. I was slowing down to stop when I saw a car behind me. It was coming very fast— maybe 30 miles an hour. The driver wasn't paying attention, so she didn't see the red light. She was talking on her cell phone while she was driving! Then she hit me, and my car hit a van in front of me.

Insurance Agent:	Was anyone in the van injured?
Maddy:	No, thank goodness. They were wearing their seatbelts.
Insurance Agent:	And how fast do you think you were going when she hit you?
Maddy:	I told you, my car wasn't moving! I was at a stop sign.
Insurance Agent:	Please calm down, Mrs. White. These are just routine questions. Did the police come to the scene?
Maddy:	Yes, they did. They gave me a copy of the accident report.
Insurance Agent:	Great. That will make things a lot easier. OK, so here's what you need to do . . .

Unit 5: Then and Now

Listening, A, B, and C, page 59

Tina:	Grandma, what were things like when you were young?
Grandma:	What do you mean?
Tina:	I mean, well, between boys and girls. Did you use to go on dates?
Grandma:	Yes, of course we did.
Tina:	Well, what did you use to do?
Grandma:	Well, we used to go bowling, or go out for an ice cream, or go to a movie.
Tina:	Who used to pay?
Grandma:	The boy did. It wasn't like today. In those days, the girl never paid.
Tina:	Did the guy pick you up, or did you meet him somewhere?
Grandma:	Oh, when I was your age, the boy used to pick the girl up at her house and meet her parents. We didn't use to meet at the mall, like kids do today. In fact, there didn't use to be any malls!
Tina:	No malls? You're kidding!
Grandma:	No, I'm serious. All of the stores used to be downtown, on Main Street.
Tina:	Wow. Did you go on dates every Saturday night?
Grandma:	No, I didn't. I wasn't that popular. I used to study a lot.
Tina:	So how did you meet grandpa?
Grandma:	At a dance.
Tina:	Was he your first boyfriend?
Grandma:	I think that's quite enough questions for tonight.

Grammar, page 66

Rob:	Do you always take your son to school?
Dan:	Always.
Rob:	Did your father use to take you to school?
Dan:	No, never.
Rob:	Did your father use to help around the house?
Dan:	My father didn't use to do a thing. He used to come home, have dinner, and watch TV.
Rob:	Who used to take care of the house?
Dan:	My mother, of course.
Rob:	Did you use to help her?
Dan:	No, I didn't. My brothers and sisters and I used to be the same as my father.

Dictation, page 66

1. Men never used to change children's diapers.
2. People didn't use to throw old things away.
3. Women used to make their own clothes, but men didn't.
4. Did men use to wear casual clothes to work?
5. How often did women use to get dressed up?

Listening, A and B, page 67

Reporter:	This is Ellie McDermott for *Spotlight on Women*. On today's program, we are taking a trip back in time with Alice and Lynn Thomas. They are twins. They are 102 years old today, and they are here to talk to us about the changes in women's lives in the past century. First of all, happy birthday!
Alice and Lynn:	Thank you.
Reporter:	So, what can you tell us about life when you were young? How were things different for women then?
Lynn:	Oh, my goodness. Well, life was very difficult for the girls and women of our generation.
Alice:	What do you mean?
Lynn:	Take housework, for example. In those days men didn't use to do any housework at all. And remember, there didn't use to be any washing machines, dishwashers, hot water, vacuum cleaners, electric stoves, or refrigerators.
Alice:	Lynn, do you remember laundry day?
Lynn:	Of course I do!
Reporter:	Why? What happened on laundry day?
Alice:	Every Monday, we had to wash the family's clothes, sheets, and towels—everything by hand.

Lynn:	Oh, we used to hate Mondays, didn't we, Alice?
Alice:	Yes, we certainly did! We used to get up at 4:00 A.M., and we didn't finish until 8:00 or 9:00 at night.
Lynn:	And do you remember how our hands used to hurt?
Alice:	How could I forget??!!! Sometimes they even bled.
Reporter:	Your hands used to bleed?
Lynn:	Oh, yes.
Reporter:	That sounds terrible. Was the rest of the week any easier?
Alice:	Not really. Now, don't get the wrong idea. The men used to work really hard too, but at least they got Sundays off. Not the women! Even on Sundays we had to eat, and there didn't use to be any fast food. My mother used to spend hours preparing the Sunday meal. And of course my sister and I had to help her.
Reporter:	Well, I guess I feel pretty lucky! *Spotlight on Women* will be back after a short break, with more from our guests, Lynn and Alice Thomas, who are 102 years old today . . .

Unit 6: Busy Lives

Listening, A, B, and C, page 73

Mom:	Hurry up! You're going to miss the bus!
Billy:	I'm not taking the bus today. Luz is picking me up.
Mom:	What time is she coming? It's really late.
Billy:	Relax, Mom. We'll get to school on time. I promise.
Billy:	I'll get it. It's probably Luz . . . Hello? Yeah, hi Luz. . . . Uh oh . . . okay, I'll ask. Mom?
Mom:	Yes, Billy?
Billy:	Can you drive Luz and me to school?
Mom:	What? But Luz is picking you up!
Billy:	Her mother needs the car today.
Mom:	Well, too bad. I'm already late for work. Come on. I'll drop you off at the bus stop.
Billy:	That's okay. I'll call Tad. He'll give us a ride.
Mom:	Forget it! It's already 7:30. Now say goodbye to Luz and get in the car.
Billy:	Luz? My mother can't give us a ride. I'm going to take the bus. I'll see you at school.

Mom:	What time are you going to be home tonight?
Billy:	Pretty late. I'm trying out for the soccer team after school.
Mom:	Oh, that's right. Good luck.
Billy:	Thanks . . . What are we having for dinner?
Mom:	I don't know. I need to run some errands after work. I'm not going to have time to cook, and your father's not going to be home. It's just going to be you and me.
Billy:	I'll cook. I'll make pizza.
Mom:	Really? That's great, honey.

Grammar to Communicate 1, B, page 74

1. **A:** What's fresh today?
   B: Everything's fresh. These muffins are hot out of the oven.
   A: Mmmm. I'll take six.
2. **A:** Mr. Roberts, Charlie Parker is on the line.
   B: Tell him I'm busy. I'll call him back later.
   A: But he said it was important.
3. **A:** Hello? Jimmy, it's Mom. I'm working late again tonight.
   B: But what about the movie? You promised.
   A: I'm sorry. Dad isn't busy. Maybe he'll take you.
4. **A:** Are you dropping off or picking up?
   B: Dropping off. Wow, you're busy. I'll run some errands and come back at noon.
   A: OK. I'll have your prescription ready for you then.
5. **A:** A table for two, please.
   B: And your name, please?
   A: Oh, is there a wait? We're in a hurry. We'll get something to go.

Grammar, page 80

1. **A:** Bye, darling. Have a good day.
   B: Bye-bye. I'll call you later.
2. **A:** Oh, no! I haven't got my wallet with me!
   B: That's OK. I'll pay. You can pay next time.
3. **A:** Is Linda pregnant?
   B: Yes, she's going to have a baby in three months.
4. **A:** So, what did you decide? Are you going to New York this weekend?
   B: No, we haven't got the money.
5. **A:** Don't forget about tonight.
   B: Don't worry. We won't be late.
6. **A:** Which days are you going to work this week?
   B: Monday to Saturday. I'm off on Sunday.

Dictation, page 80

1. I'll give you a ride.
2. I'm sorry, but I won't have time to pick you up.
3. When is she going to try out for the team?
4. Are you babysitting on Friday night?
5. My husband and I are attending an important meeting tonight.

Listening, A and B, page 81

CONVERSATION 1

Woman: Oh, that's too bad. So . . . what are you going to do?

Man: I'm not sure. The job market is really bad here. Maybe I'll move.

CONVERSATION 2

Female Passenger: Look at all this traffic! We're going to be late.

Cab Driver: Sorry, lady, but it's rush hour.

Male Passenger: Just drop us off at the next corner. We'll walk the rest of the way.

CONVERSATION 3

Mona: Hello?

Barry: Hi, it's me.

Mona: Oh, hi, Barry. What's up?

Barry: I was just wondering . . . Are you and Dad going to Billy Rose's wedding next month?

Mona: Billy Rose is getting married?

Barry: Yes. Didn't you get an invitation?

Mona: No, I didn't.

Barry: Oh, that's strange.

CONVERSATION 4

Man 1: So, who's going to pick up the cake?

Man 2: I'm off tomorrow. I'll do it.

Man 1: Thanks. And who's going to buy the card?

Woman 1: We're not going to buy a card. Jose and I are going to make one.

Man 1: Oh, that's a great idea. Now remember—don't say a word to the teacher. It's a surprise.

Woman 2: Don't worry, we won't say anything.

CONVERSATION 5

Man: Do you want it for here or to go?

Woman: I'll take it to go.

Man: Do you need plates and forks?

Woman: No, thanks. We're going to eat at home.

Man: OK then. That'll be $15.75.

Woman: Here you go. I'm going to run some errands. When will it be ready?

Man: In about 15 minutes.

Woman: OK. I'll be back.

Unit 7: Education

Listening, A, B, and C, page 87

Mrs. Parker: Hello, Mrs. Martin?

Mrs. Martin: Yes?

Mrs. Parker: This is Helen Parker, your son Tommy's teacher.

Mrs. Martin: Oh, yes. Mrs. Parker. How are you?

Mrs. Parker: I'm fine. Is this a bad time?

Mrs. Martin: No, of course not. What can I do for you?

Mrs. Parker: Well, I'm worried about Tommy. He's not doing his work. If something doesn't change, he won't finish the year with the rest of his class.

Mrs. Martin: What do you mean?

Mrs. Parker: He might not be ready for high school next year. And he will definitely need to attend summer school.

Mrs. Martin: Why didn't you call me before?

Mrs. Parker: I did call you Mrs. Martin. And I sent you several e-mails. The principal also tried to contact you.

Mrs. Martin: You're right. You did . . . but I've been so busy . . . Anyway . . . as soon as I get home tonight, I'll take care of this. Tommy's not going to leave the house until he improves his grades. After I talk to him, he'll do his work.

Mrs. Parker: Mrs. Martin, can I make a suggestion?

Mrs. Martin: Yes?

Mrs. Parker: Well, Tommy's a smart boy . . .

Mrs. Martin: I know! He's just lazy. If he tries harder, he'll be fine.

Mrs. Parker: That's not what I was going to say. Tommy's very smart, but I think he might have a learning problem.

Mrs. Martin: A learning problem? What do you mean?

Mrs. Parker: We won't know exactly until we test him.

Mrs. Martin: Test him? What kind of test?

Secretary: Mrs. Martin? Mr. Bradley is waiting for you in the conference room.

Mrs. Martin: I'm sorry, but I have a meeting right now. I'll call you when we finish—in about an hour?

Mrs. Parker: That will be fine. My number is . . .

1. I might major in English.
2. If you cheat on the test, you'll fail.
3. I may not take the final exam.
4. I won't go to college until I get a scholarship.
5. As soon as I get my degree, I'm going to look for a job.

Listening, A and B, page 95

Reporter: Good evening. This is Lisette Bouvier for *Spotlight on Education*. Tonight I am talking with this year's candidates for mayor, Tim Lee and Maureen West, about their views on education. Welcome to the show.

Lee: Thanks. Glad to be here.

West: Thank you for inviting us.

Reporter: As you both know, the public schools in our city are not doing very well. In fact, student test scores in our city are among the lowest in the country. Ms. West, if you become mayor, what will you do about this serious problem?

West: As soon as I become mayor, I am going to meet with the principals of all of the public schools in the city. I will listen carefully to their ideas, but before I do anything, I am also going to visit every school in the city. I want to talk to the teachers and the students directly. We won't be able to find a solution until we talk to all of the people involved.

Reporter: And you, Mr. Lee?

Lee: Ms. West's plan sounds good, but it will take too much time. This is an emergency. If we don't act quickly, hundreds of students will lose another year. And they might not get another chance to get a good education.

Reporter: So what's your plan, Mr. Lee?

Lee: As you know, Lisette, early in my career I was a teacher. I know how important good teachers are. But right now, there aren't enough good teachers in our schools, because we don't pay them enough. When I become mayor, I will work quickly to increase teachers' salaries. If we pay the teachers in public schools more, we will be able to hire the best.

Reporter: Well, let's see what the people who live in the city think of your plans. Our first caller is a teacher at Brookside Elementary School.

Unit 8: Getting a Job

Listening, A, B, and C, page 101

Ignacio: Hey, Natalia. How's the job search going? Have you found anything?

Natalia: No, not yet. I've applied at a few places at the mall, but no one has called me back. Have you heard about any jobs?

Ignacio: In fact, I have. Have you been to Danny's?

Natalia: No, I haven't. Why?

Ignacio: I think they're looking for a cashier.

Natalia: But I haven't ever worked as a cashier.

Ignacio: Don't worry about it. They'll train you.

Natalia: How do you know that?

Ignacio: Because several of my friends have worked there. Have you ever handled money?

Natalia: Just when I sold vegetables at a farm last summer. But I've never used a cash register.

Ignacio: Oh, it's easy.

Natalia: Really? Have you ever used one?

Ignacio: Uh, no, I haven't. But a lot of my friends have. Just go in and apply.

Natalia: Hmmm . . . maybe I will. Thanks for the information. So, how about Tracy? Has she started her new job?

Ignacio: Yes, she has.

Natalia: And how does she like it?

Ignacio: She loves it.

Natalia: Has she gotten her first paycheck yet?

Ignacio: No, she hasn't, but I think she's already spent more than she's made!

Natalia: What do you mean?

Ignacio: Well, she's borrowed at least a hundred dollars from me, and another hundred from her Mom. If she's not careful, she's going to need another part-time job.

Grammar, page 108

Raj: Hi, Liz. How are you and the family? Has Annie found a job?

Liz: No, she hasn't. It's never been easy for her to find a job.

Raj: Has she ever searched for a job online? I've found lots of jobs that way.

Liz: I'm not sure. But she's gone to several employment agencies. How about your new job? Have you started yet?

Raj: Yes, I have. It's a little hard because I have to work the night shift.

Liz: Oh, that is hard. I guess I'm lucky. I've always had the day shift.

Dictation, page 108

1. Have you ever owned a business?
2. I've never hired people.
3. She hasn't quit yet.
4. They've already contacted me.
5. Has the manager fired her yet?

Listening, A and B, page 109

Interviewer: Please, Ms. Yu, have a seat. So, did you have any trouble finding us today?

Ms. Yu: No, not at all. Your directions were perfect.

Interviewer: Good. So, you're interested in our management training program.

Ms. Yu: Yes.

Interviewer: Have you ever worked as a manager?

Ms. Yu: No, I haven't. But I've owned my own business for five years.

Interviewer: Yes, I see that on your application. It's a house-cleaning service, right?

Ms. Yu: Yes, that's right.

Interviewer: I see. And how many workers do you have?

Ms. Yu: Oh, I've always worked alone.

Interviewer: I see. So you've never hired or trained anyone.

Ms. Yu: No, I haven't.

Interviewer: And has your business been successful?

Ms. Yu: Well, I haven't gotten rich, but I'm a single parent and I've made enough to put food on the table and a roof over our heads.

Interviewer: It sounds like you've done very well. If you get into our program, what will happen to your business?

Ms. Yu: My oldest son will take over when he graduates from high school next month.

Interviewer: I see. Have you ever worked for a large company? It's very different from working for yourself. You'll have a lot less freedom. Have you thought about that?

Ms. Yu: Yes, I have thought about it a lot. In fact, I've always wanted to work for a large company.

Interviewer: Why?

Ms. Yu: Well, I've learned a lot in the five years that I've had my own business. One of the things that I've learned is that I don't really like to work alone. I'm a people-person. And I don't want to clean houses my whole life. I'm looking for a job with a future.

Interviewer: You haven't ever been a manager. How do you know that you will be good at it?

Ms. Yu: You're right, I haven't managed people. But I have managed a business. And I've had a lot of experience with different kinds of people. My life hasn't been easy, but when I decide to do something, I give it 100%.

Interviewer: Well, Ms. Yu, I must say that I like your positive attitude ...

Unit 9: Relationships

Listening, A, B, and C, page 115

Rachel: Hello, Lauren? It's Rachel.

Lauren: Rachel! I've been meaning to call you for days.

Rachel: Well, here I am.

Lauren: So, how have the newlyweds been doing? Have you and John had your first fight yet?

Rachel: Stop it! No, we haven't. We've been getting along great. We've been busy with the new house, and I've been making friends in the neighborhood. And I've been learning how to cook.

Lauren: You've been cooking? Poor John!

Rachel: Come on, Lauren. I'm not that bad, and Mom's been helping me.

Lauren: And have you been running much?

Rachel: No, I haven't. The weather's been awful. It's been raining for weeks.

Lauren: Really? It's been beautiful out here. We've been wearing summer clothes since the beginning of June.

Rachel: That's early. And how are my favorite nephews?

Lauren: They've been out of school for two weeks, and I'm ready to send them back. They've been fighting constantly!

Rachel: You know, I've been thinking ... Why don't you send them out to visit us? John would really love to get to know them better.

Lauren: Really? But you've only been married since February. You and John haven't had enough time alone together.

Rachel: We have the rest of our lives together, but my nephews won't be young forever.

Lauren: I don't know, Rachel. I'm not sure it's a good idea. Has John ever been around young kids?

Rachel:	No, but it will be good practice for him.	**Walter:**	And do you have any children?
Lauren:	Practice? For what? Rachel, are you trying to tell me something? Are you . . . ?	**Mary:**	No, not yet, but we've been thinking about starting a family soon.
Rachel:	Yup! Your little sister is going to be a mom!	**Walter:**	Okay, so back to your money problems. You said that you've known each other for a long time. Are these arguments something new, or has money always been a problem?

Grammar, page 122

Kate:	John, how long have we been going out?
John:	Let's see. It's December. I moved back here in June. So we've been going out for six months.
Kate:	And how long have we known each other?
John:	For a year.
Kate:	And have we had any conversations since last year?
John:	Sure. Every day. We're having a conversation right now.
Kate:	No. I mean a real conversation, a conversation about our relationship.
John:	About our relationship?
Kate:	Yeah. This is probably a surprise to you, but I haven't been happy for about a month.
John:	Really? Why not?
Kate:	You've been working a lot and you have not been paying attention to me.
John:	Oh, come on, Katie. You know I love you.

Dictation, page 122

1. How long have you been on your honeymoon?
2. They've been arguing a lot lately.
3. She's hasn't made any new friends since childhood.
4. They haven't had a fight since the birth of their daughter.
5. The newlyweds have been looking for an apartment for months.

Listening, A and B, page 123

Walter:	Good evening. This is Walter Sussman with *Heart to Heart*. Tonight we are taking calls from couples with relationship problems. Our first caller is Mary.
Mary:	Hello?
Walter:	Yes, Mary, you're on the air. Go ahead.
Mary	I'm a little nervous. I've never called your show before.
Walter:	Well, welcome. So, tell us what's going on.
Mary:	Well, my husband and I love each other a lot, but recently, we've been arguing a lot.
Walter:	What have you been arguing about?
Mary:	Everything . . . well, mostly money, I guess.
Walter:	How long have you been married?
Mary:	Just one year—we're newlyweds—but we've known each other since we were kids.

Walter:	And do you have any children?
Mary:	No, not yet, but we've been thinking about starting a family soon.
Walter:	Okay, so back to your money problems. You said that you've known each other for a long time. Are these arguments something new, or has money always been a problem?
Mary:	Hmmm . . . well, we've never had much money, but we didn't use to fight about it.
Walter:	Have there been any changes in your situation recently?
Mary:	No, not really . . . except that since our marriage, we've been trying to save enough money to buy a house.
Walter:	You said "we've." Are you sure that your husband wants a house and children?
Mary:	Of course I'm sure! That's why we got married.
Walter:	Okay, so you've been trying to save. Has your husband been helping you?
Mary:	No, not at all. He's a very hard worker, but I've found out that he's also a big spender. He loves music. He buys a lot of CDs. And he goes to a lot of concerts.
Walter:	Do you both work?
Mary:	Yes, we both work full-time. Now don't get me wrong. My husband's a very hard worker. He's been working since he was 15 years old.
Walter:	Has he saved anything?
Mary:	No, he hasn't. I didn't know that before our marriage. I thought he had at least some savings.
Walter:	Well, Mary, I'm glad that you called tonight. It sounds like you really need some help . . .

Unit 10: Television

Listening, A, B, and C, page 129

Lisa:	Oh Brad, this is really romantic. The food looks delicious, and the flowers are wonderful. And look at the sky. It's really beautiful tonight. Everything is just perfect.
Brad:	And you look beautiful. Mmm . . . and you smell pretty terrific, too.
Lisa:	Oh Brad . . . What was that?
Brad:	What? Come here . . .
Lisa:	No, I'm serious. I heard a strange noise. Listen . . . There it is again!

Brad:	Relax, Lisa. It's very safe out here. Now, where were we?
Lisa:	No, Brad, I'm really serious. Be quiet and listen carefully. Don't you hear that? It's pretty loud now. Look, over there, in the water! It's swimming really quickly! And it's pretty big. Oh no! It's coming directly this way!
Brad:	What the heck? Run, Lisa, run! We need to get out of here fast!
Narrator:	And now, scenes from next week's dramatic season finale of "The Secret."
Brad:	Lisa, Lisa, where are you? Answer me, please.

Grammar to Communicate 2, A, page 132

1. Umm . . . I think . . . umm . . . I think the . . . um . . . answer . . . the answer is . . . umm . . . umm . . . it's B . . . the answer is B.
2. Oh darling, I love you. You are so beautiful, so perfect. Come to me.
3. I already told you. I don't know the guy.
4. Leave now. Never come back.
5. Look at those people over there. Do you see them?

Dictation, page 136

1. Stars always dress fashionably.
2. The actor looks really nervous.
3. That talk show isn't very interesting.
4. That newscaster doesn't speak clearly.
5. They did pretty well on the game show.

Listening, A and B, page 137

SCENE 1

Detective:	You look worried. What's wrong?
Suspect:	Nothing. I feel perfectly fine.
Detective:	You don't look fine to me.
Suspect:	Well, I am. Can I call my lawyer now?
Detective:	I told you, you can call in a minute.

SCENE 2

Man:	Let's get out of here. I need to talk to you . . . privately.
Woman:	Right now?
Man:	I can't wait even one more minute. It's extremely important.
Woman:	Well, if it's that important . . .
Man:	It is. Come quickly . . .

SCENE 3

| **Woman:** | This recipe is delicious, and you can prepare it quickly and easily—in about 30 minutes. |

| **Man:** | But remember . . . I'm the world's worst cook . . . |
| **Woman:** | That is ridiculous. Anyone can learn to cook well. Just watch carefully and learn. |

SCENE 4

Man:	The rivers here are already dangerously high, and it continues to rain heavily.
Woman:	Did all of the people in the surrounding neighborhoods get out safely yesterday?
Man:	We are not sure right now. It is extremely difficult to get any information. There is no electricity, and there is almost no telephone service.

SCENE 5

Woman:	Look up there, in the top of that tree. Do you see it?
Man:	Where? I can't see anything.
Woman:	It's right up there. You have to look very carefully. It moves really fast.
Man:	Oh, there it is! It's fantastic.
Woman:	This is really amazing. It is extremely unusual to find this kind of bird so easily in this area.

Unit 11: The Animal Kingdom

Listening, A, B, and C, page 143

Ahmed:	Hi, May. What are you doing?
May:	Hey, Ahmed. I'm reading a report about pets. It says that the most popular pet in the United States today is the cat.
Ahmed:	Really? I was sure that dogs were more popular than cats.
May:	This says that a lot more people own cats than dogs.
Ahmed:	Not in my neighborhood. There are as many dogs as children. Things are really different in Morocco. Pets aren't as popular as they are in the United States. And very few people have dogs. In fact, dogs are the least popular pets.
May:	Why is that? Don't you believe that the dog is man's best friend?
Ahmed:	No, many people think that dogs are dirty.

(continued on next page)

May:	That's interesting. In China people like dogs, but our houses and apartments are a lot smaller than in the U.S. We don't have as much space as Americans do, so big dogs are less popular than cats and small dogs. So, what is the most common pet in Morocco?
Ahmed:	I'm not sure, but in my family, we have falcons.
May:	Falcons? What's a falcon?
Ahmed:	It's a bird. In Morocco we keep falcons as pets, and we teach them how to hunt. Hunting with falcons is called falconry. I'm surprised you don't know about falconry. It's one of the oldest sports in Asia.
May:	Really? I had no idea.
Ahmed:	Falcons are the best hunters of all the birds, and they are the easiest to train. They also fly the fastest.
May:	That's really interesting.

Grammar, page 150

I have two parrots, Gertie and Peter. Gertie is older. She's 25 years old. Peter's only 10. He is gray. Gertie is more colorful than Peter. She's green, blue, and yellow. Both parrots talk a lot. Gertie is as talkative as Peter. Gertie knows fewer words than Peter, but Peter doesn't know as many big words as Gertie does. And they both say the funniest things. Parrots are always messy, but Gertie isn't as messy as Peter. He always makes a big mess. I love both my parrots. They cause the fewest problems of any pet, and they are the most fun.

Dictation, page 150

1. Little dogs aren't as frightening as big dogs are.
2. Do lions move as quickly as giraffes?
3. Parrots live a lot longer than other birds.
4. Elephants have the biggest ears.
5. Lions eat the most meat.

Listening, A and B, page 151

Reporter:	I'm Liz Baker with *Spotlight on Science*. Today, Dr. Richard Downey of the San Diego Zoo is with us, answering your questions about the animal kingdom. Welcome, Dr. Downey.
Downey:	Thanks, Liz. I'm happy to be here.
Reporter:	There are a lot of kids out there with questions for you, so let's get started. Our first caller is Jeremy. Go ahead, Jeremy.
Jeremy:	Ummm . . . yes . . . Is it true that pigs are the dirtiest animals?
Downey:	Well, it isn't really possible to say that one animal is dirtier than another. But I can say that the pig is definitely not the dirtiest. People think that pigs are dirty because they like to roll in mud. In fact, they do that because they don't sweat. It's the easiest way for them to stay cool. They are also very smart animals—almost as smart as the chimpanzee.
Reporter:	So which animal is the smartest? Is it the chimpanzee?
Downey:	Chimps are certainly very smart, but it's difficult to say which animal is the most intelligent. However, many people are surprised when they hear that whales, elephants, and pigs are some of the most intelligent animals.
Reporter:	OK, Jeremy, thanks for calling. Let's go to Alison. Alison?
Alison:	Hello?
Reporter:	Yes, Alison. What's your question?
Alison:	Yes . . . My brother says that cats sleep more than dogs, but I think he's wrong. Am I right, or is he?
Downey:	I'm sorry, but I'm afraid your brother is right. Cats sleep about 12 hours a day—about an hour and a half more than dogs do. The animal that sleeps the most is the brown bat. Brown bats sleep 20 hours a day. Giraffes sleep the fewest number of hours—only about 2 hours a day.
Reporter:	OK, Alison?
Alison:	Yes, thank you.
Reporter:	We've got time for just one more call. This is Josh. Do you have a question for Dr. Downey, Josh?
Josh:	Uh, yeah. Which animal is the most dangerous?
Downey:	That's easy—the mosquito.
Josh:	The mosquito? No way!!!
Downey:	It's true. Mosquitoes carry a serious disease called malaria. More than 300 million people get sick with malaria every year, and one to three million of them die.
Reporter:	And that's all we've got time for. Thank you for being on the show today, Dr. Downey.
Downey:	Oh, you're quite welcome.

Unit 12: Let's Eat!

Listening, A, B, and C, page 157

Man: Can we seat ourselves?

Waiter: No, please wait. The hostess will seat you.

Hostess: Two for lunch?

Woman: Yes, please.

Hostess: Right this way. Here you go.

Man: Could we have another table? This one is very noisy.

Hostess: Of course. Which one would you like?

Man: How about that one, over there?

Hostess: The one in the corner? It's reserved.

Man: How about the ones over there? Are they reserved too?

Hostess: By the window? One of them is, but the others are free. Enjoy your meal.

Woman: Thank you.

Waiter: Good afternoon.

Woman: Good afternoon.

Man: We're ready to order.

Waiter: What would you like?

Man: I'll have the lunch special.

Waiter: Which one?

Man: The one on the menu!

Waiter: There are several specials on the menu.

Man: The one that comes with a salad.

Waiter: They all come with salads.

Woman: He'll have the number three, please.

Man: I can order for myself. I'll have the number three. And make sure the soup is warm. The last time it was cold.

Waiter: Of course. And for you, ma'am?

Woman: I'll take the number three, too. Thank you.

Waiter: The salad bar is over there. You can serve yourselves whenever you're ready.

Man: I need another fork. This one is dirty.

Waiter: Oh, I'm sorry. I'll get you another one.

Man: And another glass. This one has a hair in it.

Waiter: Of course.

Woman: Could you behave yourself?

Man: What?

Woman: Why are you always so rude?

Man: Me, rude?

Woman: Oh, forget it. Next time, I'm sitting by myself.

Grammar, page 164

Amy: Come in. Make yourself at home. Here, give me your jacket.

Jan: Sorry I'm late. I missed the bus and waited an hour for the next one.

Amy: Don't worry. Two couples, the ones from Chester, still aren't here.

Jan: Yeah, Chester is far away. Bill, is that you? How are you?

Bill: Oh, Jan, nice to see you. I'm great.

Amy: How do you two know each other? Did you meet at another party?

Jan: Yeah. We met at Lin's. It was great. We really enjoyed ourselves.

Amy: So Jan, do you know the other people here?

Jan: Well, I know your boyfriend, of course, but I don't think I know the others.

Dictation, page 164

1. Please give me the other menu. This one is the lunch menu.
2. The main dish with chicken isn't expensive, but the others are.
3. The ice cream is two dollars, but the other desserts are more expensive.
4. Please serve yourselves at the salad bar.
5. We'd like two hot appetizers and two cold ones.

Listening, page 165

Reporter: These days, there are fast-food restaurants everywhere, in almost every country of the world. But it was not always that way. Today, Bryant Jones reports on the birth of the fast-food industry.

Jones: In the 1940s, as large numbers of Americans began to buy cars, drive-in restaurants became popular. At a drive-in restaurant, customers ordered their food, ate it, and paid for it without leaving their cars. Waiters, called car hops, took orders and served customers in their cars. In all other ways, however, drive-in restaurants were typical restaurants. There were different kinds of food on the menu, and all of it was made-to-order. For example, at a table with two customers, one person might order a rare hamburger with onions, while the other might order a well-done one with tomatoes. One customer's hamburger was cooked differently from the other's.

In the 1940s, two brothers, Richard and Maurice McDonald, owned a drive-in restaurant in California. Like the other drive-in restaurants in the area, theirs had a large menu. However, most of the money that they made came from just three items: hamburgers, French fries, and milkshakes. The McDonald brothers decided to try something new. They limited the menu to those three items, and they developed the "Speedy Service System." The Speedy Service System used an assembly line like the one in the automobile industry. Nothing was made-to-order. One hamburger was exactly the same as all the other hamburgers, just as one Model-T Ford was exactly the same as all the others.

Another feature of the Speedy Service System was that there were no waiters. Customers served themselves. They walked up to a window, ordered, and paid. Within minutes, their order came off the "assembly line." They then chose a table and seated themselves. They even cleaned up after themselves. Cleaning up was easy because there were no dishes, just paper cups and bags. Customers just threw everything away.

Today, fast-food restaurants still follow the McDonald brothers' Speedy Service System—the system that put the "fast" in fast food.

Unit 13: Technology

Listening, A, B, and C, page 171

Rashida: I hope that you can help me. My computer isn't working.

Technician: What's the problem?

Rashida: I don't know. That's your job!

Technician: Ma'am, please calm down. I'm trying to help you.

Rashida: I'm sorry. I know it's not your fault, but I really need my computer.

Technician: First of all, are you able to turn it on?

Rashida: Yes, but that's all I can do. Two weeks ago I had the same problem, but my husband was able to fix it. I still couldn't access my e-mail, but at least I was able to use it for other things. But then this morning when I turned it on, I couldn't do anything.

Technician: What do you mean, you couldn't do anything?

Rashida: I mean exactly that. I wasn't able to do anything. What do you think? Will you be able to repair it?

Technician: I don't know, but we'll do our best.

Rashida: Can you look at it right now?

Technician: Right now? No, I'm sorry, but I can't.

Rashida: Well, when will you be able to repair it? I really need my computer. I can't work without it! Will you be able to look at it later today?

Technician: Lady, I'm not even sure we'll be able to fix it at all. But we won't be able to do it by tomorrow. It's going to take at least a week.

Rashida: A week! Why so long?

Technician: Because the only person that can fix that kind of computer is on vacation.

Rashida: Oh, forget it. I'll take it someplace else.

Grammar, page 178

Hi, I have good news and bad news. First, the bad news. I haven't been able to fix the TV yet. When I turn it on, I can see a picture; but I can't hear a thing. That's strange because yesterday I could hear things, but I wasn't able to see anything. I'm going to look at the TV again tomorrow. Maybe I can fix it then.

Now, the good news. I was able to fix the radio yesterday. At first, I wasn't able to find the problem, but actually there wasn't really a problem. It only needed new batteries. Sam

Dictation, page 178

1. I'm usually able to access the Web from my home.
2. I couldn't install the software yesterday.
3. Can you record my TV program for me?
4. In the future, people will be able to get married online.
5. We were able to repair the DVD player yesterday.

Listening, A and B, page 179

Judd: With *Spotlight on Technology*, this is Judd Newman. With us today is our science and technology reporter, Jasmine Thomas, who is just back from this year's international auto show. So, tell us, Jasmine, what will our cars be able to do next?

Jasmine: Well, Judd, several car companies have come out with concept cars that can interact with the driver, and are able to prevent accidents.

Judd: What do you mean, interact with the driver? Do you mean talk to the driver?

Jasmine: No, not exactly. It's more like listening to or "feeling" the driver. Here's how it works. You're driving and you begin to feel sleepy. Your hand relaxes on the steering wheel, and your car starts to go off the road. The car knows what is happening, and wakes you up by setting off an alarm, moving the seat, or spraying water in your face.

Judd: How can a car know that you're falling asleep?

Jasmine: When we are falling asleep, our heart starts beating more slowly, and our muscles relax. A computer in the car is able to "feel" these

Judd: physical changes through sensors on the driver's seat and the steering wheel.

Judd: That's pretty amazing.

Jasmine: Yes, it is. And that's not all. These cars can communicate with other cars that have the same technology. Let's say you're on the east side of Los Angeles and you want to go somewhere on the west side. Your car will be able to communicate with another car on the west side, and find out the driving conditions there; for example, accidents or traffic jams. Your car can then show you the fastest and safest route to your destination.

Judd: So, where can I buy one of these cars?

Jasmine: You can't. That's why they're called concept cars. There are only a couple of them. You won't be able to buy one for at least two years. And even then most people won't be able to afford them. But I predict that within 5 years, the prices will come down. Then the average person will be able to own one.

Judd: Very interesting. Thanks, Jasmine . . .

Unit 14: A Kid's Life

Listening, A, B, and C, page 185

Mom: So, Nick, remember. You don't have to come home right after school, but you've got to call me on my cell phone and tell me where you are. And you mustn't miss the 5:00 bus. Dad's got to work late, so you have to make dinner.

Nick: Again? I had to make dinner last week, too. It's Suzy's turn.

Mom: Suzy has to babysit for the Martin boys. She won't be home until 5:30, so she won't have time to cook. We've got to eat by 6:00 at the latest because she has to get to basketball practice.

Nick: Does she have to babysit for the Martins every afternoon? Last month she didn't have to do any chores because she was always at the Martins. I have to do everything around here, and I don't get any money for it, but the Martins pay her for babysitting. It's not fair.

Mom: I'm sorry, Nick, but I haven't got time to argue with you right now. I've got to get to work.

Nick: Why did you have to go back to work, anyway? Things were so much better when you stayed at home. Then I didn't have to cook or clean.

Mom: Oh, Nick, you know that I have to work. We have to pay the bills. Besides, I like working. And you don't have to do everything in the house. That's just not true. Everyone in the family has to do chores.

Nick: Yeah, everybody except little Miss Suzy.

Mom: OK, Nick, that's enough. You've got to get to school, and I've got to get to work. We'll talk about this later.

Grammar, page 192

Lee: Why do you have to go so early? Let me guess . . . You have to pick up your sister.

Dan: That's right.

Lee: You had to pick her up yesterday, too. Why do you always have to pick her up?

Dan: I don't always have to pick her up. I didn't have to do it last week. It was Stan's turn.

Lee: So why can't Stan do it today?

Dan: Because he's got to work.

Lee: So, where does she have to go this time? Soccer practice? Piano lessons?

Dan: She's got to go to the dentist. I'm sorry, but I really have to go. She mustn't be late for her appointment.

Lee: And I've got to get a new boyfriend—one with no little sister!

Dictation, page 192

1. You've got to be strict with your children.
2. We had to obey our parents.
3. My son and daughter don't have to do chores every day.
4. The children mustn't cross the street.
5. Do you have to take out the trash every day?

Listening, A and B, page 193

Reporter: This is Doris Hamilton for *Culture Watch*. Today, we are going to compare the lives of children in the U.S. and Japan. Mrs. Eileen Aoaki is here with us. She is a professor of early childhood education, and has lived in both the United States and Japan. Welcome, Mrs. Aoaki.

Mrs. Aoaki: Thank you, Doris.

Reporter: So, what are the biggest differences that you've found?

Mrs. Aoaki: Well, the differences start as soon as the baby is born. In the United States, as you know, most parents believe that children have to learn to sleep alone from a very early age.

If there's enough space in the house, infants in the U.S. usually have their own rooms. That usually doesn't happen in Japan. In Japan, children sometimes sleep in their parents' room for years, often because space is limited. Also, many American doctors tell parents that they mustn't pick up their babies every time they cry, because babies have to learn how to comfort themselves. In Japan, many mothers believe that they must pick up a crying child immediately. If they don't, they are not good mothers.

Reporter: Those are big differences.

Mrs. Aoaki: Yes, they are. And the differences get bigger when children begin school. For example, in Japan, children learn that they must obey their teachers.

Reporter: Wait a minute! Children in the U.S. have to obey their teachers too!

Mrs. Aoaki: Yes, of course, let me explain. Japanese children are taught that they must not question their teachers. This is changing a little, but is still a pretty common way of thinking in Japan. In contrast, American children learn that they have to ask questions in class. And many American parents teach their children that they must speak up if the teacher does or says something wrong.

Reporter: Now I see.

Mrs. Aoaki: Another difference is in the amount of time that children spend studying. In the past, children had to go to school 6 days a week. Today, Japanese children don't have to go to school on Saturday. However, most Japanese parents pay for their children to take classes on Saturdays. That's because kids have to pass very difficult exams to get into a good high school. They've got to start preparing at a young age.

Reporter: Interesting. We have to take a break now, but don't go away. We'll be right back . . .

Unit 15: Manners

Listening, A, B, and C, page 199

Mom: Allen, what have I told you about table manners?

Allen: What? What am I doing wrong now?

Mom: You shouldn't be asking me that. You should know.

Allen: Oh come on, just tell me.

Mom: Well, first of all, you shouldn't be eating with your fingers.

Allen: But I'm eating French fries!

Mom: So what? You should be using a fork.

Allen: Why do I have to use a fork? None of my friends has to eat French fries with a fork!

Mom: As I've told you many times, I don't care about your friends' table manners. I don't have to live with them. You don't have to like my rules, but you have to obey them. And one more thing—you shouldn't be talking with your mouth full. It's disgusting. Allen . . .

Allen: What now?

Mom: Should your elbows be on the table?

Allen: OK, OK, I'm sorry. I forgot. [phone rings]

Mom: Sit back down.

Allen: But, Mom, it's probably Blanca. I have to talk to her. It's important.

Mom: I don't care. She shouldn't be calling at dinner time. She should know better.

Grammar, page 206

Lori: Listen to that woman with the cell phone. She shouldn't be talking on her cell phone here. You should tell her.

Kirk: What should I say?

Lori: You should say, "Stop talking on your cell phone."

Kirk: That's not very polite. I don't think I should be rude because she's rude.

Lori: Sometimes you have to be rude to people. They don't listen if you're polite.

Kirk: I don't agree. Watch. Excuse me?

Stranger: What?

Kirk: I'm sorry, but you really shouldn't be using your cell phone here.

Stranger: And you shouldn't interrupt other people's conversations.

Dictation, page 206

1. You shouldn't talk with your mouth full.
2. You don't have to hold the door open but you should.
3. He should be carrying his grandmother's bag.
4. You should knock on my door before you come in.
5. I have to do a favor for my mother.

Listening, A and B, page 207

Reporter: This is Joanna Bergman for *Culture Watch*. This week's topic is table manners. As anyone who has traveled to another country knows, table manners are quite different in different countries. You don't have to know everything, but you should find out the most important rules before you visit a country. Here are some things you will probably want to find out.

First, seating. Where should guests sit at the table? Should you wait for others to sit down, or should you just sit down in the nearest chair? Do men and women eat together, or do they have to sit in separate rooms?

The second set of rules involves how you eat. Which utensils should you use? How should you use them? How shouldn't you use them? In countries where people eat with their hands, can you use both hands, or should you use only one hand? Which hand?

The third set of rules involves body language at the table. How should you sit? For example, should you put your hands on the table, or in your lap? Is it okay to put your elbows on the table? If you have to sit on the floor to eat, what should you do with your legs?

Next, what about conversation at the table? Should you talk while you are eating, or wait until you finish? Which topics should you discuss? Which topics shouldn't you discuss?

And what about food? Do you have to eat everything on your plate? What should you do if you don't like something? If you want more food, can you ask for it, or do you have to wait for the host or hostess to offer it?

Tomorrow, we will be interviewing people from all over the world to learn the answers to these questions and more. Until then, this is Joanna Bergman for *Culture Watch*.

Unit 16: Neighbors

Listening, A, B, and C, page 213

Ann: Hi, Bob. How was your flight?

Bob: Long. I left Detroit at 7:00 A.M.

Ann: You must be tired. So, how are the grandchildren?

Bob: It was great to see them, but I'm glad to be home. So, what's been going on around here?

Ann: I just saw Emily Rose on the elevator. She was wearing a new suit. She must be doing well at work.

Bob: Are you kidding? She lost her job last week.

Ann: Really? She must not be very happy about that.

Bob: No, I'm sure she isn't. And speaking of unhappy, how's Roberta doing?

Ann: She and Andy must be getting along. I haven't heard them fighting lately.

Bob: But they can't be getting along. Haven't you heard? He moved out. They're getting a divorce.

Ann: Really? So that's why it's so quiet over there. He must be at his mother's.

Bob: Actually, he's staying with his brother. What about the Russels?

Ann: Mr. and Mrs. Russel are on vacation, but I saw little Sarah Russel on her way to school this morning. She must be staying with Mrs. O'Hara.

Bob: She can't be staying with Mrs. O'Hara. Mrs. O'Hara is visiting her son.

Ann: Well then who's taking care of her? She's only 10 years old. She can't be alone!

Bob: Her grandmother must be staying with her. I saw her car when I came in.

Ann: You're amazing. You've been away for a month, and you know more about what's going on around here than I do!

Grammar, page 220

1. **A:** It must be difficult to find a good apartment around here.
   B: You're right. It is. I've been looking for a place for three months.
2. **A:** Laura's walking to the bus stop. That's strange.
   B: Her husband must be using her car today.
3. **A:** Mrs. Olsen must be feeling lonely since her husband's death.
   B: I know. We should visit her next weekend.
4. **A:** Look, there's Tommy. He must be going to school.
   B: But it's Saturday. He can't be going to school.
5. **A:** Hello? Could I please speak to Donna?
   B: Donna? There's no Donna here. You must have the wrong number.

1. My wife isn't answering the phone. She must be chatting with a neighbor.
2. The flowers in that yard are beautiful. The owners must be good gardeners.
3. The kids can't be next door. Our neighbors are on vacation.
4. My dog can't be barking in the yard. He's in the house.
5. The Smiths must not be at home. Their car isn't in their driveway.

Listening, A and B, page 221

Vicki: Good evening, this is Vicki Hernandez for *Your Turn*. Tonight's topic is getting along with your neighbors. Our first caller is Randy. So, Randy, how are things in your neighborhood?

Randy: Not great, I'm afraid. A family moved in next-door a few months ago. The houses in our neighborhood are very close together, and their kitchen window is across from ours. Every time they see me through the window, they wave. At first, I thought it was sweet. But lately it's really started to bother me. I feel like they're watching me all the time.

Vicki: That must be uncomfortable.

Randy: Yeah, especially after someone told me that they are police officers.

Vicki: Is there some reason that the police should be interested in you?

Randy: No, of course not.

Vicki: So you can't be worried about that. They probably just want to be friendly with you. They must not know how you feel. Do you have curtains?

Randy: Uh, no . . .

Vicki: Well, Randy, it's time to get some! Good luck . . . Well, that was easy! Let's take another call. Hello, Sue?

Sue: Yes. Hello. My problem is not my neighbors; it's my husband. He doesn't get along with our neighbors. Take last night, for example. The doorbell rang at dinnertime. My husband thought that it must be someone asking for money. He answered the door, and shouted "Why are you bothering people at dinner time!" and slammed the door. Just then I looked out the window, and saw my next-door neighbor walking away from our house. I opened the door, and found a box of cookies. It was a birthday gift for me!

Vicki: Oh dear. Your husband must not like your neighbor very much.

Sue: He didn't know it was her. It was dark, and he wasn't wearing his glasses . . .

Vicki: Did he apologize?

Sam: Yes, but I don't think she believed him. She hasn't been very friendly to me since then.

Vicki: Really? Your neighbor mustn't have a very good sense of humor. It's a pretty funny story.

Unit 17: Health

Listening, A, B, and C, page 227

Doctor: Mr. Harris, it isn't normal for someone of your age to have high blood pressure. You must lose weight.

Mr. Harris: But, doctor, diets have never worked for me. Maybe it's impossible for me to lose weight.

Doctor: I'm not talking about a diet. In fact, it's unhealthy to go on a diet.

Mr. Harris: If I don't go on a diet, how will I lose weight?

Doctor: It's simple. You need to eat less and exercise more.

Mr. Harris: Isn't that a diet?

Doctor: Usually when people talk about a diet, they're talking about doing something for a few weeks to lose weight. But you need to change your eating and exercise habits—not just for a few weeks, but for the rest of your life.

Mr. Harris: So I have to be on a diet for the rest of my life?

Doctor: No, you need to eat healthy food and exercise regularly. And you're not too old to make these changes.

Mr. Harris: But I'm too busy to exercise. I work two jobs.

Doctor: It isn't necessary to go to the gym and spend hours a day exercising. Just small changes will make a big difference.

Mr. Harris: Like what?

Doctor: Even just a few minutes of fast walking a day will help. Most people can find enough time to take a 15-minute walk.

Mr. Harris: But what about the healthy food part? I don't have enough time to cook every day.

Doctor: You can make a healthy, delicious meal in less than 15 minutes.

Mr. Harris: Really?

Doctor: Yes. It's easier to do than you think.

Grammar, page 234

1. **A:** You're too sick to go to work.
   B: But I have to go! I have a very important meeting.
2. **A:** Does he need surgery?
   B: No, the problem is not serious enough for him to have surgery.
3. **A:** The doctor's too busy to see you today.
   B: But I have an appointment!
4. **A:** What do you take when you have a cold?
   B: Sweet Night. It's very good. It helps me sleep.
5. **A:** Where are you going?
   B: I'm going downtown to see the doctor. I have an appointment.

Dictation, page 234

1. It's important for him to gain weight.
2. You should exercise more to get in shape.
3. She's not strong enough to leave the hospital yet.
4. Your blood pressure is too high for someone your age.
5. He's too weak to have surgery.

Listening, A and B, page 235

Talk Show Host: Please join me in welcoming Dr. Paul Wade. Dr. Wade, what can we do to stay healthy?

Dr. Wade: There are two secrets to a healthy life: a healthy diet and regular exercise. Did you know that new immigrants often have a healthier diet than Americans born in the U.S.?

Talk Show Host: Really?

Dr. Wade: Yes. American-born women eat fewer fruits and vegetables than new immigrants: two and a half fewer servings every day. After a few years in the United States, however, most immigrants have the same diet as people born in the U.S. And that's not a good thing.

Talk Show Host: But the United States is a rich country. Why is the American diet so unhealthy?

Dr. Wade: In the United States it's often cheaper to buy fast food than fresh fruits and vegetables. And people don't have time to cook. So it's faster to pick up dinner from a fast-food restaurant or to buy a frozen meal from the supermarket. The problem is, fast food is unhealthy. It has too much salt and too much fat.

Talk Show Host: How can we find out how much salt and fat is in our food?

Dr. Wade: Learn to read food labels. The chemical name for salt is sodium. Most adults should eat fewer than 2,400 milligrams of sodium a day. There are two kinds of fat—saturated and unsaturated. You shouldn't eat more than 20 grams of saturated fat a day, and not more than 65 grams of total fat.

Talk Show Host: How do we know what's in the food at fast-food restaurants?

Dr. Wade: It's easy to find that information on the Web. But let me save you time. Most of the food at fast-food restaurants is bad for you. The average cheeseburger at a fast-food restaurant has about 10 grams of saturated fat, and over 1,000 milligrams of salt.

Talk Show Host: That is a lot. Now let's talk about exercise.

Dr. Wade: Most people need about 30 minutes of exercise a day, five days a week. People think that they don't have time to exercise. But on average, Americans watch 2 to 3 hours of TV a day. . . . So they have free time. They just don't use it to exercise.

Talk Show Host: It's time for a short break, but don't go away.

Unit 18: Free Time

Listening, A, B, and C, page 241

Arinaldo: I'm bored. I'm tired of just playing computer games and going to the mall.

Mei: Well, what else are you interested in?

Arinaldo: Lots of things. I'm considering taking some classes.

Mei: In what?

Arinaldo: Well, drawing, for example. I'm good at drawing, but I've never taken any classes.

Mei: You like drawing? I didn't know that. Drawing's okay, but I prefer painting.

Arinaldo: I started to draw when I was little. Anyway, I'm thinking about taking a class at the community center.

Mei:	I started studying painting there last year. It's great. I love going . . . And it's not very expensive.
Arinaldo:	Yeah, that's what I've heard. I'm also thinking about learning to play the guitar. I've taken piano lessons, so I can read music, but I've never really liked to listen to piano music. I prefer to listen to the guitar.
Mei:	Playing is very different from listening, though. It's pretty difficult to play the guitar.
Arinaldo:	Harder than playing the piano?
Mei:	Maybe not. So, do you want to take both guitar and drawing classes?
Arinaldo:	Oh no, I don't want to do both. I'm trying to decide between them. What do you think?
Mei:	Hmmm . . . well, if you've decided to take classes at the community center, then you should take drawing.
Arinaldo:	Why?
Mei:	Because I know they have great art teachers, but I haven't heard good things about the music teachers.
Arnaldo:	That's good to know. Thanks!
Mei:	No problem.

Grammar, page 248

Do you feel like doing something new? Are you tired of being in the office all the time? Are you interested in spending time with fun people? Then hiking is the answer for you. Being in the fresh air and seeing all the beautiful flowers and trees will make you feel wonderful. You don't need to be an experienced hiker. You just have to enjoy going for long walks. If you want to get more information about our group, call (777) 555-3476. Great experiences are waiting for you.

Dictation, page 248

1. I can't stand knitting because I'm not good with my hands.
2. I'm good at drawing, but I don't like painting.
3. I'm considering taking up chess.
4. I'm tired of being alone all the time.
5. When I got sick, I gave up singing in the chorus.

Listening, A and B, page 249

Reporter: Good morning. This is Martha Hong reporting. Today we are looking at the ways that adults in the United States spend their free time. The information in this report comes from a poll of 1,014 adults conducted by Harris Interactive in the year 2004.

According to the poll, reading, watching TV, and spending time with family were the three most popular free-time activities in the U.S. in 2004—35% of adults in the poll said reading, 21% said watching TV, and 20% said spending time with family. Next on the list were going to the movies—10%; fishing—8%; and using a computer—7%. Gardening, walking, and renting movies were all equally popular, at 6%.

And what were the least popular activities? Playing tennis, horseback riding, running, dancing, and bowling were at the bottom of the list, with only 1% each.

Since the poll was first conducted in 1995, the biggest increases in popularity have been in spending time with family—from 12% in 1995 to 20% in 2004; reading—from 28% to 35%; and using computers, from 2% to 7%. The biggest decreases in popularity from 1995 to 2004 were in swimming (from 7% to 2%), TV watching (from 25% to 21%), and playing team sports (from 9% to 5%).

And how about the amount of free time people have per week? That has not changed at all since 1995—19 hours a week. But if you go back to 1973, you'll see a big difference. On average, adults in the U.S. had 26 hours a week of free time in 1973. For *Spotlight on Culture*, I'm Martha Hong.

Unit 19: Emergency Services

Listening, A, B, and C, page 255

Operator:	911. What's your emergency?
Woman:	A man just stole my bag! I was walking home . . . He told me to give him my money and jewelry. He made me give him my wedding ring!
Operator:	Are you safe now? Did he hurt you?
Woman:	No, he didn't. He let me go when I gave him my bag and my ring.
Operator:	Where are you now?
Woman:	In a store on the corner of 16th Avenue and Babcock St.
Operator:	How long ago did this happen?
Woman:	Just a minute ago.
Operator:	Can you describe him?
Woman:	I think so. He was about 17-years-old, white. He was tall and thin. I believe he was wearing a black sweatshirt and jeans.
Operator:	Did you notice anything else? Did he have a mustache or a beard?
Woman:	I don't think so.

Operator:	Did you see where he went?
Woman:	Yes, he ran down Babcock St.
Operator:	OK, ma'am. I've contacted the police.
Woman:	Please, make them come right away. You can't let him get away with my wedding ring!
Operator:	I can only report the emergency, ma'am. Now, can I have your name, address, and telephone number?
Woman:	Marianne Jackson, 230 Westfield Terrace, 555-660-2050. Will the police expect me to wait here?
Operator:	No, ma'am. You need to go to the police station and fill out a report.
Woman:	But shouldn't I wait here for the police?
Operator:	No, you should go to the police station.
Woman:	OK, thank you. You've been very kind.
Operator:	You're welcome. I hope you get your wedding ring back.
Woman:	Thank you. I hope so, too.

Grammar, page 262

To whom it may concern,

I'm writing this letter because I think you should know about my experience at your hospital last Saturday. My ten-year-old daughter had an accident on her bike, and I noticed that she couldn't move her arm. I thought it might be broken, so I drove her to the emergency room. We got there at 1:00. The nurse saw that my daughter was in pain, but she didn't let us see a doctor right away. She told the two of us to wait in the waiting area and made me fill in four different forms. We waited and waited. Finally, at 4:00 the nurse called my daughter's name. My daughter wanted me to go with her, but the nurse didn't let me go. She was very rude to me. I am writing because I would like to know your policy on this. Did the nurse have the right to make me stay in the waiting room? I don't think so, but maybe there is a new policy.

Dictation, page 262

1. I hope that you don't get another speeding ticket.
2. The firefighter advised us to look for fire hazards in our home.
3. The woman wants an ambulance to come right away.
4. The paramedic didn't let me go in the ambulance with my friend.
5. I made the police officer show me his badge when he stopped me.

Listening, A and B, page 263

Reporter:	It's Fire Prevention Week. I'm Cynthia Steiner and Captain Will Farrell is with us to talk about fire safety. Thank you for coming in, Captain Farrell.
Captain:	Thank you for inviting me.
Reporter:	I know that there are several listeners waiting to talk to you, so let's get started.
Caller 1:	Hello? Captain Farrell?
Captain:	Yes?
Caller 1:	I live in a large apartment building, but I have noticed that the smoke detectors in the hallways are not working.
Captain:	How do you know that they aren't working?
Caller 1:	The other night my wife was cooking, and she burned our dinner. There was a lot of smoke. The smoke detectors in our apartment went off, but the ones in the hallway didn't. I suspected that they weren't working, so I checked them.
Captain:	Well, I hope that you called the landlord right away.
Caller 1:	Yes, I did, but he hasn't called me back yet.
Captain:	Well, I advise you to call him again, and tell him to fix the problem immediately or you will call the fire department. If he doesn't call you after that, I want you to call your local fire station, and ask them to call him, OK? I'm pretty sure he will listen to them.
Caller 1:	OK. Thank you very much.
Captain:	You're very welcome. You know, Cynthia, not enough tenants know that they have rights. They can make their landlords fix fire hazards like the one that the caller described.
Reporter:	What other things should tenants know?
Captain:	By law, there must be a fire extinguisher in every apartment. And in all new buildings, there must be a sprinkler system.
Reporter:	I understand that every apartment must also have two exits. Is that correct?
Captain:	Yes, absolutely. That's very important.
Reporter:	So, if any of our listeners have problems with their landlords, what do you advise them to do?
Captain:	First they need to talk to their landlords, and ask them to fix the problem. Then, if they don't, they need to call their local fire department.

Reporter: Thank you, Captain. In a minute we'll be back to take more of your calls.

Unit 20: Taking a Trip

Listening, A, B, and C, page 269

Announcer: National Airlines flight #650 is now boarding at gate 23. Passengers, please have your boarding passes and identification ready.

Man: What's that? What's he saying?

Woman: Our flight must be leaving. He told us to take out our boarding passes and identification. Here, give me your carry-on bag.

Man: What?

Woman: I asked you to give me your carry-on bag.

Man: Why do you need my carry-on bag?

Woman: I need to find our boarding passes.

Man: You need to find what?

Woman: Our boarding passes . . . I said that I need to find our boarding passes.

Man: Your boarding pass? I don't have your boarding pass. I only have mine.

Woman: What did you say?

Man: I said that I have my boarding pass, but I don't have yours.

Woman: You're kidding.

Man: What?

Woman: Oh, never mind. Just give me your carry-on bag.

Man: What?

Woman: I told you to give me your carry-on bag.

Man: But I told you that I don't have your boarding pass.

Woman: Yes, you do. It's right here. See?

Announcer: Would passengers Rick and Helen Dwyer please check in at the ticket counter?

Woman: That's us! He just asked us to check in.

Man: What? What's wrong? We already checked in.

Woman: I don't know. We'd better go up and see.

Grammar, page 276

1. **A:** Why did that man tell us to go to the ticket counter?
   B: Because we need to check in.
2. **A:** Is Annie having a good time?
   B: She says she is.
3. **A:** When do we need to check in?
   B: The travel agent told us to check in an hour before the flight.
4. **A:** The hotel clerk told us to leave the passports in our room.

B: No. He told us not to leave them in our room.

5. **A:** Would you sit in the seats near the door, please?
   B: What did she say?
   C: She asked us to sit near the door.

Dictation, page 276

1. The woman says that your carry-on bag is too big.
2. My wife says she doesn't want to take a tour.
3. The hotel clerk told us not to leave the key in the room.
4. The immigration officer asked me to wait in a small room.
5. I told you to ask the tour guide.

Listening, A and B, page 277

This is Karen Saunders with *Spotlight on Travel*. As you know, I have to travel a lot for my job. My friends always tell me that I'm lucky. They don't believe me when I tell them that I don't like to travel. But it's true. I love visiting new places, but I don't really enjoy getting there. I especially dislike flying. However, over the years, I have found some ways to make my trips a little easier.

First, let's talk about what I do before I get to the airport. People often ask me to tell them how to pack. My advice? Don't pack a suitcase. Yes, you heard me . . . I said, "Never pack a suitcase." When I travel, I pack everything in my carry-on bag. That way, I don't have to check any bags. At the end of the flight, I can just leave the airport. I don't have to wait, and I don't have to worry about losing my suitcase.

My next piece of advice? Always take the first flight of the day. It usually leaves on time. And when you make your reservation, ask the ticket agent to give you your seat assignment. That way you will be able to choose your seat. If you wait until you get to the airport, you won't have a choice. Always ask for a seat close to the front of the airplane. That way, you can get off the plane more quickly.

Now let's talk about the flight. Make sure that you get up and walk around, especially on a long flight. It's good for you. It's also good to drink a lot of water, because the air on an airplane is very dry. You will look and feel much better at the end of the flight.

Finally, I definitely agree with the saying, "When in Rome, do as the Romans do." If you are traveling into a new time zone, don't forget to change your watch on the airplane. And don't think about what time it is back home. Even if you are very tired, wait until it is nighttime to go to bed. Likewise, go to bed at a normal hour, even if it feels very early to you.

For *Spotlight on Travel*, I'm Karen Saunders. Have a great trip!

Index

Writing

LIFESKILLS

Business and Employment

Name: _____   **Date:** _____

A 🔘 **2** **Listen. Then complete each sentence. Circle the letter of the correct answer.**

1. Gary and Susan are _____.

    a. looking for a job   b. working at new jobs

2. Susan is _____ at work right now.

    a. having a party   b. meeting new people

3. Susan's boss has got _____.

    a. curly brown hair   b. straight blonde hair

4. _____ is moving up in the company fast.

    a. Susan   b. Susan's boss

5. The accountant has got _____.

    a. a bad temper   b. a good sense of humor

6. Gary _____ going out with his girlfriend.

    a. is   b. isn't

7. Susan is _____ Anya.

    a. getting to know   b. getting along with

8. Anya's got _____.

    a. a boyfriend   b. a husband

B **Match the beginnings of the sentences with the endings. Write the correct letters.**

_____ **1.** Mei-Ling's hair isn't curly or wavy. It's   a. beard.

_____ **2.** The young man had no hair on his chin. He didn't have a   b. mustache.

_____ **3.** I always laugh at Ed's jokes. He has a good   c. bad temper.

_____ **4.** Rick is very unfriendly. He has a   d. straight.

_____ **5.** Look at that hair above Tim's mouth! He's got a   e. nice personality.

_____ **6.** We all like Tom. He has a   f. sense of humor.

C **Complete the conversations. Use the words in the box.**

gets along with	is getting to know	is going out with

1. **A:** Did you hear? Pedro _____ Jen.

     B: I know! They're in love!

2. **A:** Does Sylvie like children?

     B: Yes. She really _____ them.

3. **A:** Does your daughter like her new roommate?

     B: She's not sure yet. She _____ her.

Name: _____   Date: _____

D **Complete the sentences. Use the words in the box.**

has got	have got	hasn't got	haven't got

1. That store _____ the new computer game. Let's buy it!

2. He _____ a new girlfriend. He's still going out with Elena.

3. Mr. and Mrs. Green _____ white hair. They have black hair.

4. Lynette _____ wavy hair. It's beautiful.

E **Complete each sentence. Use the simple present or the present progressive.**

1. We _____ a lot of fast food these days.
       (eat)

2. I love my parents. I _____ time with them every weekend.
                            (spend)

3. Jack is so friendly! He _____ well with everyone.
                             (get along)

4. Mr. Davis _____ a lot of overtime this month.
                  (work)

5. Penny and I _____ a Spanish class together this semester.
                     (take)

6. She _____ in the Brentwood area. She has a big house.
            (live)

Name: _____ Date: _____

F   Read the paragraph. Then complete each sentence. Circle the correct answer.

MEETING A MATE ... IN CYBERSPACE!

Usually, people meet their mates—their girlfriends, boyfriends, husbands, or wives—through friends or at work. But some single people are not finding mates in these places. More and more of these lonely people are trying Internet dating.

How does Internet dating work? There are special websites for Internet daters. These websites ask daters to complete a profile. In the profile, people usually answer questions about their personality. For example, they say that they are easy-going, serious, or shy. Then they give information about their favorite activities, such as bicycling, or swimming. Also, they usually send in a recent photo.

This is because most Internet daters don't like profiles without photos. They want to see what the person looks like.

The next part of the profile asks for information about the person's ideal mate. What appearance and personality is he or she looking for in a mate? Many people ask for a certain hair color or height, such as "tall, dark, and handsome." But this is probably a mistake. Personality and shared interests are more important than appearance in a good relationship.

When a profile is ready, other people can read it and e-mail the person. Sometimes, the website automatically matches two people that will probably get along well. Then it sends each person the other person's profile. After that, the two people get to know each other through e-mail. Of course, a real relationship usually doesn't start until the matches meet each other in person. Computers can do a lot, but they don't understand true love!

1.   Usually, people meet their mates **on the Internet / through friends or at work**.

2.   In the profile, users describe **their personality / the dating website**.

3.   An easy-going person **gets along / doesn't get along** with other people.

4.   More people will write to a person if he or she sends in a **profile / recent photo**.

5.   Internet daters **describe / don't describe** their ideal mate in the profile.

6.   In a good relationship, a person's appearance **is / isn't** more important than personality.

7.   Websites **can sometimes / can't** automatically match people.

8.   Internet daters usually **e-mail, then meet / meet, then e-mail** each other before they start a relationship.

Name: _____   Date: _____

A   🔘 **3**   **Listen. For each sentence, write *T* for *True* or *F* for *False*.**

1. Mei-Ling doesn't have enough space for her kids.   _____

2. Frank and his wife are happy in the city.   _____

3. There are no museums in Frank's city.   _____

4. Frank doesn't have much extra space in his apartment.   _____

5. Frank doesn't save any money on public transportation.   _____

6. Frank doesn't spend much time looking for parking.   _____

7. Frank has a little extra money for a parking space.   _____

8. Mei-Ling and her husband can't decide where to live.   _____

B   **Read the sentences. What do they describe? Check (✓) *city*, *suburbs*, or *country*.**

	City	Suburbs	Country
1. There are a lot of skyscrapers.			
2. There is no pollution.			
3. There are a lot of fields.			
4. There is plenty of public transportation.			
5. There are lots of cars and parking spaces.			
6. There is no traffic.			
7. There are factories.			
8. There are a lot of tourists at museums.			

Name: _____   Date: _____

C   Complete each sentence. Circle the letter of the correct answer.

1. New York and Tokyo are big cities. _____ cities are expensive.
   a. Neither   c. Both
   b. Either   d. Two

2. Many people can't buy a house. They don't have enough money. Houses cost _____.
   a. too much money   c. enough money
   b. much money   d. some

3. I live in a very small village. There are twenty-five families. There are _____ people there.
   a. little   c. several
   b. very few   d. a lot of

4. Parking is no problem. There are _____ parking spaces.
   a. few   c. any
   b. too many   d. plenty of

5. My wife doesn't want to move to Chicago or Los Angeles. She doesn't like _____ city.
   a. neither   c. both
   b. either   d. any

6. We don't like the city. There are _____ people there.
   a. too much   c. much
   b. too many   d. plenty of

7. My room is small! I have just _____ space for my bed and my desk!
   a. plenty of   c. enough
   b. some   d. few

8. Our city isn't very big. There are only _____ skyscrapers here.
   a. a little   c. some
   b. a few   d. many

9. I'm going to look at _____ apartments this afternoon.
   a. several   c. a little
   b. any   d. few

10. I like the Chinese and the Thai restaurants. _____ restaurant is fine with me.
    a. Both   c. Neither
    b. Either   d. Any

Name: _____   Date: _____

D   Read the article. Then answer each question. Circle the letter of the correct answer.

A FAST-GROWING CITY

Orlando is a popular vacation destination. People enjoy the nice weather and fun activities at theme parks such as Disney World. But many people also live and work in Orlando. Space scientists and engineers come to Orlando to find work at the nearby Kennedy Space Center. The University of Central Florida is attracting plenty of teachers and researchers from around the world. The university is building a new medical school. In the next ten years, more professional people will arrive. These people will want good restaurants, entertainment, and stores.

The future looks bright for this city, but it has some problems too. Housing prices in Orlando are rising. Many families live in apartments because they can't save enough money to buy a house. Also, Orlando doesn't have enough public transportation. There are many traffic jams because there are too many cars on the road. In fact, there aren't enough roads! Companies are building both houses and stores. Soon there will be very little open space in Orlando.

Many of these problems are probably going to get worse as more people move to the city. City planners are expecting 650,000 new homes in the next 25 years. They need to fix Orlando's problems soon. They don't want to diminish the quality of life for the city's residents.

1. What do tourists come to Orlando to see?

   a. theme parks   b. medical schools

2. Where do engineers work in Orlando?

   a. in the space industry   b. at the performing arts center

3. What is attracting teachers to Orlando?

   a. university jobs   b. high housing costs

4. Why isn't Orlando completely successful?

   a. The city is not growing enough.   b. The city still has problems to fix.

5. What is happening to homes in Orlando?

   a. They are becoming more expensive.   b. They are getting bigger.

6. Why does Orlando have big traffic jams?

   a. There are plenty of roads.   b. There aren't enough roads.

7. What are companies building in Orlando?

   a. houses and stores   b. open space

8. What will happen if the city planners don't fix Orlando's problems?

   a. The quality of life will go down.   b. The quality of life will go up.

Name: _____   **Date:** _____

A   **Listen. Then complete each sentence. Circle the correct answer.**

1. Cindy **is / is not** driving to a soccer game.

2. Alfredo **watched / didn't watch** his brother's soccer game last week.

3. Cindy **told / didn't tell** Alfredo about the dinner before she made the reservation.

4. Cindy **did / didn't** get a new job.

5. Alfredo **forgot / didn't forget** about the anniversary.

6. Cindy **decides / doesn't decide** to go to the soccer game.

B **Listen to the sentences. Circle the letter of each sentence you hear.**

1. a. The player scores a run.

    b. The player scored a run.

2. a. The player kicks the ball.

    b. The player kicked the ball.

3. a. They don't cheer.

    b. They didn't cheer.

4. a. Does their team play today?

    b. Did their team play today?

C **Complete the sentences. Use the words in the box.**

beat	cheer	court	is tied	loses to	miss	passes	runs

1. We always _____ when our team scores.

2. Each team has two points. The score _____.

3. The basketball players ran across the _____.

4. The baseball player scored two _____.

5. The Panthers scored five more runs to _____ the Wildcats 7 to 2.

6. Our team always _____ the Lions. It makes me so mad!

7. When I have to work on Saturday, I _____ the game.

8. When Connors _____ the ball to Rodgers, Rodgers usually scores.

Name: _____   Date: _____

D Complete each sentence. Circle the letter of the correct answer.

1. _____ tickets for the Bears game?

   a. Did Jack get   b. Jack got

2. _____ the Royals.

   a. Did the Bears play   b. The Bears didn't play

3. _____ to the game with Jack?

   a. Who went   b. Who did

4. Brown _____ the ball and scored the point.

   a. shoot   b. shot

5. _____ the Orlando Magic?

   a. The Miami Heat played   b. Did the Miami Heat play

6. How many points _____?

   a. did the Bears score   b. the Bears scored

7. When _____ the stadium?

   a. did Jack and Henry leave   b. Jack and Henry left

E Complete the sentences. Use *because*, *before*, *after*, or *as soon as*.

1. _____ Tiger Woods is a great player, he wins a lot of golf matches.

2. Michael Jordan was a basketball star. Then he became a baseball player. Jordan became a baseball player _____ he was a basketball star.

3. The fans started cheering when the Bears scored a point. _____ the Bears scored their first point, the fans didn't cheer.

Name: _____   Date: _____

F   Read the article. Then put the statements in order from 1 to 8. Write the numbers.

LANCE ARMSTRONG'S STORY

In July of 2005, Lance Armstrong won the Tour de France for the seventh time. Armstrong's performance was amazing. Some say it was a miracle. Very few athletes get cancer *before* they win the top race in their sport—seven times!

Lance Armstrong competed in sports when he was in high school. Lance was good at running, swimming, and cycling, and his favorite sport was the triathlon. At 16, he became a professional athlete. He started to train seriously as a bike racer when he was 18. Before he turned 22, he won ten racing titles. By 1996, Lance was one of the best bike racers in the world.

Then he got bad news. He had testicular cancer. It moved to his lungs and his brain. For a while, he was very sick. After treatments for cancer in the hospital, including chemotherapy, Lance began to train again. It took three years, but Armstrong got in shape. In 1999, he won the Tour de France for the first time, just before his son was born. Then Armstrong won the Tour de France six more times. After his final win, he retired from racing.

These days, Armstrong raises money for people with cancer. He is also the author of two books about his experiences with cancer and bike racing.

_____ **a.**   Armstrong became a professional athlete.

_____ **b.**   Armstrong wrote books about his experience as a cancer survivor.

_____ **c.**   Armstrong found out he had cancer.

_____ **d.**   Armstrong retired from bicycle racing.

_____ **e.**   Armstrong won his first ten racing titles.

_____ **f.**   Armstrong trained for three years to get back in shape.

_____ **g.**   Armstrong did triathlons.

_____ **h.**   Armstrong won the Tour de France for the first time.

Name: _____   Date: _____

A 🔘 **6** **Listen. Then complete each sentence. Circle the letter of the correct answer.**

1. Paul and his father were climbing the _____.

   a. stairs   b. ladder

2. Paul _____ a ladder.

   a. was dropping   b. was carrying

3. When Paul heard a cry, he _____ the ladder.

   a. picked up   b. dropped

4. Paul's father _____ down the stairs.

   a. fell   b. walked

5. Paul probably _____ while he was going up the stairs.

   a. slipped   b. stepped on the cat

6. The cat _____ under the chair.

   a. was crying   b. was sleeping

7. Paul's father _____ his back.

   a. hurt   b. didn't hurt

8. Paul and his wife painted the house while his father _____.

   a. was resting   b. was working

B **Complete each sentence. Circle the correct answer.**

1. Ed **climbed / fell off** a ladder. It was a terrible accident!

2. The children **fell down / went down** the stairs slowly and carefully.

3. Miri **chopped / cut** her finger by accident.

4. Ted **burned / ironed** his shirt. It looked beautiful.

5. Nancy **dropped / slipped** on the ice in the street.

6. Nick wasn't paying attention to the traffic. He was **daydreaming / slipping**.

7. Mrs. Williams **was breaking / was chopping** an onion when the guests arrived.

8. Pete used a ladder to **climb / go down** to the top of the house.

9. There was a fire next door. The house **burned / broke** down.

10. Bea dropped a glass and it **broke / slipped**.

Name: _____   Date: _____

C   Complete each sentence. Use the past progressive.

At the time of the accident . . .

1. The children _____ magazines.
    (read)
2. My brother _____ the house.
    (not / paint)
3. Jennifer _____ at her friend's house.
    (not / sleep)
4. Mr. and Mrs. Garcia _____ a vacation in Mexico.
    (take)
5. Where _____ you _____?
    (work)
6. _____ they _____ TV?
    (watch)

D   Complete each sentence. Use the past progressive or the simple past.

1. While I _____, I was daydreaming.
    (drive)
2. I was taking a shower when the phone _____.
    (ring)
3. Hannah burned her hand when she _____ the hot plate.
    (touch)
4. He was playing the piano while she _____ the violin.
    (play)

Name: _____   Date: _____

E   Read the article. Then answer the questions.

LIGHTNING STRIKE SURVIVORS

Lightning strikes are very dangerous. Survivors of lightning strikes are very lucky to be alive. Here are two incredible stories about lightning strike survivors.

Actor Jim Caviezel was playing the role of Jesus in Mel Gibson's *The Passion of the Christ* when lightning struck him—twice! The first time, he was holding an umbrella while he was filming in Italy. Caviezel was not hurt, but smoke came out of his ears. A few months later, he was holding an umbrella again when lightning struck him. Once again, he was not hurt.

Two other lightning strike survivors are Lorianna and her boyfriend Ed. They were riding their horses one day when the weather turned bad. They went into a barn with a metal roof to escape the storm. When the lightning hit, Ed was leaning against the wall, and Lorianna was holding onto him. Ed's horse Jamie was standing next to them. Lorianna and Ed heard a loud bang. The lightning shot through them and Lorianna fell to the ground. Ed was not able to move. His arm was paralyzed. Then an incredible thing happened. Jamie touched Ed's arm with her nose and he was able to move his arm. But then Jamie fell to the ground. Ed helped Lorianna stand up, and then they both helped Jamie stand up. All three survived. Ed and Lorianna almost died, but Jamie saved them with a touch of her nose.

1. Where was Caviezel when he was struck by lightning?

   _____

2. What was Caviezel holding when he was hit?

   _____

3. What were Lorianna and Ed doing when the weather turned bad?

   _____

4. Why did Lorianna and Ed go into the barn?

   _____

5. When the lightning hit, what was Ed doing?

   _____

6. Where was Ed's horse standing when the lightning hit?

   _____

7. What did Jamie do while the lightning was shooting through Ed?

   _____

8. After Jamie fell to the ground, what did Ed and Lorianna do?

   _____

Name: _____ **Date:** _____

A 🔘 **7** **Listen. For each sentence, write *T* for *True* or *F* for *False*.**

1. Grandpa used to meet girls at dances. _____

2. Sam's grandma didn't use to dance well. _____

3. Grandpa used to like fast dances. _____

4. Young women used to ask the men to dance when Grandpa was young. _____

5. Grandpa used to wear casual clothes to the dances. _____

6. Grandpa used to wear a flower on his jacket. _____

7. Young men used to pay for everything when Grandpa was young. _____

8. Sam is still going out with his girlfriend Ashley. _____

B **Match the sentences. Write the correct letters.**

_____ 1. That dog smells terrible!

_____ 2. The kids are hungry.

_____ 3. The baby's wet.

_____ 4. It's cold today.

_____ 5. The refrigerator isn't working.

_____ 6. This milk smells bad!

_____ 7. It's a very fancy party.

_____ 8. Mrs. DeLucca is at the hospital.

_____ 9. I'm a fashion designer.

_____ 10. Come to my pool party.

a. I make my own clothes.

b. She's giving birth to a little boy!

c. Please wear casual clothes.

d. Please dress the kids in warm clothes.

e. Let's feed them some spaghetti.

f. Please give it a bath today!

g. Please change her diaper.

h. I'm going to call someone to repair it.

i. Please throw it away.

j. We should get dressed up.

Name: _____   Date: _____

C   Complete the conversations. Use the correct form of *used to*.

1. **A:** When I was a child, I _____ play with dolls.

   B: I never did that.

2. **A:** Did you enjoy dancing when you were young?

   B: No. I _____ dance when I was young.

3. **A:** _____ girls _____ ask boys to go on a date?

   B: No. Boys asked girls.

4. **A:** When _____ Ken _____ date Maddie?

   B: When they were in college.

5. **A:** I _____ make my own clothes. I don't make clothes anymore.

   B: Oh, really? Do you buy them in stores now?

6. **A:** Teresa goes to the gym every day.

   B: Wow! I'm surprised! She _____ exercise at all!

7. **A:** How often _____ you _____ go the dances, Grandpa?

   B: Every Saturday.

8. **A:** Women _____ work after they got married. Now most married women work outside the home.

   B: I know. But some women stop working when they have children.

9. **A:** People _____ write letters. Now they send e-mails.

   B: Yes. I miss letters!

10. **A:** _____ Mrs. Williams _____ work at the post office?

   B: No, she didn't.

Name: _____   Date: _____

D   Read the article. Then match the paragraphs with the topics. Write the correct letters.

The History of the Bicycle

1 The first bicycles appeared in 1817, but they didn't look like the bicycles we ride today. What did bicycles use to look like? The first bicycle was called a hobby horse. It had two wheels, but it didn't have pedals. Riders used to sit on the seat and push their feet against the ground. The hobby horse was very slow. It wasn't very comfortable or practical.

2 In 1865, inventors added pedals to the bicycle. They put the pedals on the front wheel. Riders used to sit above the front wheel. It wasn't easy to balance on this bicycle, called a velocipede. Riders used to fall off and get hurt a lot. The velocipede was also uncomfortable and heavy because it had metal wheels.

3 Bicycles improved in the 1880s. Inventors used rubber for the wheels. The front wheel was very big and the back wheel was very small. Riders used to sit above the big front wheel. They sat very far from the ground on these "high wheel" bikes. Riders used to fall off when they hit a stone in the road. Women didn't use to ride high wheel bicycles because they wore big skirts. They used to ride high wheel tricycles. These tricycles had a seat between two high wheels. They had a small wheel in front.

4 In the 1890s, bicycles changed forever. Inventors made the wheels the same size. They put the pedals on a chain with gears. They also put air in the rubber tires. Bicycles were lighter, faster, and more comfortable. They were also very popular with women. Some women stopped wearing big skirts because they wanted to ride bicycles!

_____ **1.** Paragraph 1   a. the velocipede

_____ **2.** Paragraph 2   b. the modern bicycle

_____ **3.** Paragraph 3   c. the hobby horse

_____ **4.** Paragraph 4   d. the high wheel bicycle

E   Read the article again. Then complete each sentence. Circle the correct answer.

1. Bicycles didn't use to have **pedals / seats**, but they always do now.

2. Riders used to sit **between the wheels / above the front wheel** of the velocipede.

3. Bicycles used to be heavy because they **had metal wheels / were dangerous**.

4. Riders used to **balance on / fall off** bicycles and get hurt.

5. Women used to ride tricycles because **they wore long skirts / bicycles were too heavy**.

6. **High wheel / Modern** bicycles were very popular with women.

Name: _____   **Date:** _____

A   **8**   **Listen. Answer each question. Circle the letter of the correct answer.**

1. What is Linda going to do in the morning?

   a.   She's staying home.   b.   She's meeting an accountant.

2. What is Rick doing in the afternoon?

   a.   He's picking up his mother.   b.   He's running errands.

3. Is Linda going to call Amy?

   a.   No. Amy is on vacation.   b.   No. She's going to call the accountant.

4. How will Linda get to work?

   a.   She'll take the train.   b.   Rick will drop her off.

5. Where is Linda going to have breakfast?

   a.   She's going to eat at home.   b.   She's going to eat at the meeting.

6. What time is Linda coming home?

   a.   7:00   b.   7:30

7. Is Linda going to cook tonight?

   a.   Yes, she is.   b.   No, she isn't.

8. How many people are going to go to dinner tonight?

   a.   two   b.   three

B   **Match the questions with the answers. Write the correct letters.**

_____ **1.** Can they come to the movies with us tonight?	a.	Yes! I love to babysit.
_____ **2.** Do you have your car today?	b.	No, but I'll get some coffee to go.
_____ **3.** Is that my cell phone ringing?	c.	Yes. I'm going to pick it up now.
_____ **4.** Did you get a part in the play?	d.	Yes, I can answer it for you.
_____ **5.** Can you take care of my kids?	e.	Yes. I can give you a ride.
_____ **6.** Do you have time for breakfast?	f.	Yes, I need to drop off some film.
_____ **7.** Is Mike having trouble with his homework?	g.	No. I didn't try out for it.
_____ **8.** Did you miss an important meeting today?	h.	Yes. I'll help him do it later.
_____ **9.** Are you going to the camera store?	i.	Yes. I wasn't able to attend.
_____ **10.** Did you order the pizza?	j.	Yes, they're free.

Name: _____   **Date:** _____

C   Complete each conversation. Use *will* or *be going to*.

1.   **A:**   I _____ ask Jessica to marry me.

     B: Well, finally! After five years of dating!

2.   **A:**   What does Mom want for her birthday?

     B: I _____ get her a digital camera. I bought one yesterday.

3.   **A:**   Your room is a mess!

     B: Oops! I'm sorry, Mom. I _____ clean it.

4.   **A:**   Susie's sick. She has a fever.

     B: Oh, no! I _____ take her to the doctor right away.

5.   **A:**   Is Ed in town this week?

     B: Yes. I _____ meet him for lunch on Tuesday.

D   Complete each conversation. Use *will* or the present progressive.

1.   **A:**   The house is on fire!

     B: Oh, my gosh! I _____ the fire department!
                                  (call)

2.   **A:**   I _____ my job.
                      (quit)

     B: Did you discuss this with your wife?

     A: Oh, yes. She thinks it's the right thing to do too.

3.   **A:**   What _____ we _____ for dinner?
                                              (have)

     B: Spaghetti.

4.   **A:**   Please stay another night. We enjoy your visits.

     B: All right, I _____.
                               (stay)

5.   **A:**   I _____ to Alaska this weekend!
                      (fly)

     B: You are?

     A: Yes, I bought my ticket today.

Name: _____   Date: _____

E   Read the article. Then read the sentences. For each sentence, write *T* for *True* or *F* for *False*.

RENT-A-HUSBAND

It's 7:00 A.M. and George is checking his work schedule. First, he's fixing a window at Mrs. Garcia's house. Then he's repairing a door at Mrs. Brown's house. In the afternoon, he's going to paint a bathroom for Mr. Parson.

George is a typical husband—a typical "Rent-a-Husband." He does home repair projects. The projects take from two hours to two days. Most real husbands don't have time to do little jobs around the house. George will work on those little jobs . . . and he'll finish them, too!

In 1996, Kaile Warren noticed that many homeowners needed small home repairs. These people were not able to find good repairmen. The repairmen came late, and their work wasn't good. They charged too much. The homeowners weren't happy. They wanted better service. So Kaile started the Rent-a-Husband business. With Rent-a-Husband, a homeowner pays only for the hours a man works. The fee is reasonable. If a repairman is late, he'll call and tell the homeowner. And Rent-a-Husband guarantees its work. Repairmen will do a job again if the homeowner is not happy.

The Rent-a-Husband company is very successful. Kaile Warren made $500,000 in 1998. Then he sold his idea to other people, like George. They began their own Rent-a-Husband companies. You can probably find a Rent-a-Husband company near you.

1. George is going to fix Mrs. Brown's window.   _____

2. Rent-a-Husband is a home repair business.   _____

3. Homeowners want good repairmen, but some repairmen don't come on time.   _____

4. George began the Rent-a-Husband business in 1996.   _____

5. Rent-a-Husband charges a lot of money for their work.   _____

6. If a Rent-a-Husband repairman is late, he won't call the homeowner.   _____

7. Rent-a-Husband guarantees the quality of their work.   _____

8. Rent-a-Husband is a very successful business.   _____

9. Other people bought Kaile Warren's idea and began Rent-a-Husband businesses.   _____

Name: _____   Date: _____

A   **9**   **Listen. For each sentence, write *T* for *True* or *F* for *False*.**

1. Mr. Artaud is Claude's teacher.   _____

2. Mrs. Jones isn't worried about Claude.   _____

3. Claude is helping the other children learn their lessons.   _____

4. Claude's father is going to talk to him about shouting out answers.   _____

5. Claude is bored in class.   _____

6. Claude might need an easier class.   _____

7. If his lessons are more difficult, Claude won't be bored.   _____

8. If Claude improves at school, he will get music lessons.   _____

B   **Complete the conversation. Use the words in the box.**

apply for	courses	grades	scholarship
cheat	fail	pass	transfer

Ed: Nancy is going to nursing school next year.

Chris: Really?

Ed: Yes. But she needs money to go to school. She's going to _____ a
1.

_____. If she gets it, she'll be able to go to school full-time.
2.

Chris: Full-time? How much will she have to study?

Ed: Well, students usually take five _____ every semester. And nursing
3.

students have to get good _____—a B or better. If they don't do well,
4.

or if they _____ a class, the school gives them a warning. And if they
5.

_____ during a final exam, they have to leave the school.
6.

Chris: That sounds hard. Is Nancy scared?

Ed: No! She's sure she will _____ her classes. She's a great student. In fact, she plans
7.

to _____ to a four-year college in two or three years. She wants to go to medical
8.

school after that.

Name: _____   **Date:** _____

C   Complete each sentence. Circle the letter of the correct answer.

1. If you don't study, you _____ the exam.
   - a. will pass
   - b. pass
   - c. won't pass
   - d. don't pass

2. Angela _____ be an engineer. She decided that last year.
   - a. is going to
   - b. might
   - c. may not
   - d. might not

3. Victor will buy the house if his wife _____ it.
   - a. will like
   - b. likes
   - c. liking
   - d. doesn't like

4. We won't celebrate until we _____ all our classes.
   - a. will pass
   - b. pass
   - c. passing
   - d. won't pass

5. Alice and Roberto _____ doctors when they graduate.
   - a. will become
   - b. become
   - c. becoming
   - d. don't become

6. Frank might look for another job, or he _____ back to school.
   - a. is going back
   - b. might not go
   - c. goes
   - d. may go

7. If Ted _____ good grades, he'll get a scholarship.
   - a. will get
   - b. gets
   - c. get
   - d. doesn't get

8. As soon as Hana _____ a new job, she'll buy a car.
   - a. will get
   - b. gets
   - c. getting
   - d. get

9. When my son _____ from his year in Costa Rica, he'll be fluent in Spanish.
   - a. will return
   - b. returns
   - c. returning
   - d. might return

10. Maria and Matt are in love. Maybe they _____ married after college.
    - a. might get
    - b. may get
    - c. will get
    - d. are

Name: _____ Date: _____

D Read the article. Then complete each sentence. Circle the letter of the correct answer.

THE LANGUAGES OF THE FUTURE

What language will the world speak in the future? If you think most people in the world will speak English, you are probably wrong. In 2000, the native language of most people was Chinese, and English was second. By 2050, experts believe that many more people will speak Chinese, Hindu-Urdu, Arabic, and Spanish. If Americans want to be successful on the **global** job market, they will need to speak a foreign language.

How can parents help their children learn another language? Well, if learning is fun, children will do it. Young children will learn if parents and teachers sing songs and play games with them. Tapes and videos may help children learn too. But kids will learn best when they talk to people and **engage in** ordinary activities with them. If parents hire a foreign babysitter, for example, their children will learn a second language much faster.

Teenagers and adults may not want to play games or sing silly songs. Instead, they might play language games on the computer. But like young children, teenagers and adults learn best with other people. That's why many colleges have special immersion language programs. The students speak only the foreign language at their dormitory or house. Over a million and a half American students are studying a foreign language in college, and the numbers are increasing. That's a good sign for the future.

1. The percentage of English speakers in the world is probably going to _____.

   a. go up   b. go down

2. In the first paragraph, **global** means _____.

   a. international   b. local

3. Parents can help their children learn another language if they make learning _____.

   a. fun   b. ordinary

4. In the second paragraph, **engage in** means _____.

   a. do   b. watch

5. The best way for young children to learn a language is to _____.

   a. watch videos   b. talk to people

6. Language games on the computer may seem _____ to teenagers and adults.

   a. fun   b. silly

7. An immersion program asks students to _____.

   a. major in a foreign language   b. speak a foreign language where they live

8. The number of students studying foreign languages in college is _____.

   a. rising   b. falling

Name: _____   Date: _____

A 🔘 **10**   Listen. Then answer the questions. Check (✓) *Kentaro*, *Emmy*, or *David*.

	Kentaro	Emmy	David
1. Who has applied for some jobs, but isn't working now?			
2. Who has gotten a job at the Hollywood Café?			
3. Who has never worked as a waiter or waitress?			
4. Who has sung "Happy Birthday" many times?			
5. Who has used a cash register?			
6. Who has served food and handled money?			
7. Who has started a job at the pool?			
8. Who has gotten a paycheck?			
9. Who has saved some money?			

B   Match the beginnings of the sentences with the endings. Write the correct letters.

_____ **1.** Jack sleeps during the day because

_____ **2.** Inez missed work and didn't call, so

_____ **3.** The new workers attended classes because

_____ **4.** Gary started looking for a new job because

_____ **5.** Mrs. Santos takes care of her son at night, so

_____ **6.** Bill handles a lot of money, so

_____ **7.** Ms. Lee is smart and organized, so

_____ **8.** Mrs. Diaz needed a job, so

_____ **9.** Suzanne applied at a store yesterday and

_____ **10.** The company needed people to work more, so

a.   Mr. Park hired her as his assistant.

b.   he quit his old job.

c.   the boss fired her.

d.   he uses a cash register.

e.   she contacted employers.

f.   the company had to train them.

g.   he works the night shift.

h.   she heard from the owner today.

i.   she only works the day shift.

j.   George had to work overtime.

Name: _____   Date: _____

C   Read the chart. Then complete the sentences. Use *has*, *have*, *hasn't*, or *haven't* and the past participle.

Past Experience	Karen	Mikhail	Sandra	Mei-Ling
handled money	yes	no	yes	yes
drove a truck	no	yes	no	no
worked with children	no	no	yes	no
took computer classes	yes	yes	no	yes
managed people	no	no	yes	yes

1. Mikhail might work as a truck driver because he _____ a truck.

2. Sandra might work as a day-care worker because she _____ with children.

3. Mikhail might not work as a manager because he _____ people.

4. Sandra, Karen, and Mei-Ling might work as cashiers because they _____ money.

5. Karen, Mikhail, and Mei-Ling might work in an office because they _____ computer classes.

6. Sandra doesn't know how to use a computer because she _____ any computer classes.

D   Complete the conversations. Use *has*, *have* and the past participle.

1. **A:** _____ you ever _____ a job?
   (quit)

   B: Yes, I have.

2. **A:** _____ Mei-Ling ever _____ in Japan?
   (be)

   B: Yes, she has.

3. **A:** _____ Mr. and Mrs. Santini ever _____ a store?
   (own)

   B: No, they haven't.

4. **B:** _____ Lillian _____ for a job yet?
   (apply)

   B: No, she hasn't.

Name: _____   Date: _____

E   Read the article. Then read the sentences. For each sentence, write _T_ for _True_ or _F_ for _False_.

RESTAURANT CRITICS

Sarah has eaten at the new Korean restaurant four times in the last few weeks. She has ordered six different dishes. But she hasn't enjoyed the food. So why has Sarah come back to the restaurant so many times? Because she is a restaurant critic.

Restaurant critics eat at restaurants. Then they write about their experiences in reviews. People read these reviews to find out if a restaurant is good or bad. Some critics are famous, but no one knows what they look like. This is important. When restaurant owners and staff recognize critics, they are nicer to them than they are to regular customers. So critics try to look and act like regular customers. That way, they can write about the experience that a regular customer will have at the restaurant.

Many food lovers want to become restaurant critics. They think that restaurant critics eat great food with their friends and then write an article about it. But restaurant critics work hard. For example, Sarah has done a lot more than eat during her visits to the Korean restaurant. She has taken secret notes on the service in the restaurant. She has read the entire menu and wine list. She has even checked the bathrooms. And she has gone back to the restaurant several times because she wanted to make sure that nothing changed before she wrote her review.

To become a restaurant critic, you need to know a lot about food and restaurants. You need to know how to write well. And you also need to be able to eat a lot of rich, and sometimes bad, food every day of the week! This is not good for your body. In fact, most people can't work as restaurant critics for more than five years!

1. Sarah has eaten at the Korean restaurant four times because she likes the food.   _____

2. Restaurant critics want people to know what they look like.   _____

3. Lots of people want to be restaurant critics.   _____

4. Food lovers think restaurant critics work hard.   _____

5. The waiters at the Korean restaurant have seen Sarah's notes on their service.   _____

6. Restaurant critics usually don't know how to write well.   _____

7. Most restaurant critics are healthy and have good bodies.   _____

8. Restaurant critics usually work for five years before they change jobs.   _____

Name: _____   Date: _____

A 🎵 **11 Listen. For each sentence, write *T* for *True* or *F* for *False*.**

1. John and Suzanne are newlyweds.   _____

2. John and Suzanne have been staying in their room all the time.   _____

3. John likes photography.   _____

4. John and Suzanne have been working in a Hawaiian restaurant.   _____

5. Suzanne hasn't gone shopping very much.   _____

6. Gina and David have been to Hawaii.   _____

7. David and Gina haven't been getting along.   _____

8. Gina hasn't been home for dinner for two months.   _____

9. David and Gina have been skiing.   _____

10. Gina has been relaxing every weekend.   _____

B **Complete the sentences. Use the words in the box.**

argued	broke up	honeymoon	newlyweds	widow
birth	fight	marriage	remarried	widower

1. Bob and Sue's _____ was short. They divorced after two months.

2. My son and his new wife will go on their _____ in Paris.

3. Henri had a _____ with his brother. They aren't speaking to each other.

4. Mr. DeSantos died. Mrs. DeSantos is a _____.

5. Maria and her boyfriend didn't get married. They're not together. They _____.

6. Cristina got divorced. Four years later, she got _____ to another man.

7. Tom and Fred were business partners. They disagreed about money. They also _____ about how to manage the company.

8. Jane and Bob just got married. They are _____.

9. When Oscar's mother died, his father became a _____.

10. Florence and her husband have two children. They are expecting the _____ of their third child in April.

Name: _____   Date: _____

C   Complete each sentence. Circle the letter of the correct answer.

1. Juan has been looking for a job _____ three months.
   a. for   c. in
   b. since   d. during

2. My nephews _____ talking on the phone all night.
   a. have   c. has
   b. have been   d. has been

3. Have they _____ to Hawaii since their honeymoon?
   a. going   c. go
   b. gone   d. went

4. Jim isn't married now. He _____ a divorce.
   a. have gotten   c. has gotten
   b. haven't gotten   d. hasn't got

5. Gilbert arrived in Chicago many years ago. He has been living here _____ 2001.
   a. for   c. in
   b. since   d. during

6. Ron and Peichi _____ for over ten years!
   a. has been going out   c. have been going out
   b. hasn't gone out   d. has gone out

D   Complete each conversation. Use *has*, *have*, *hasn't*, or *haven't*.

1. **A:** Have the children been playing computer games?

   B: Yes, they _____.

2. **A:** Have you broken up with Alfredo?

   B: No, I _____.

3. **A:** How long _____ you been working at the library?

   B: For two months.

4. **A:** _____ your husband been spending more time with the kids lately?

   B: Yes, he has.

Name: _____   Date: _____

E   Read the article. Then complete the sentences. Use the words in the box.

BIGGER FAMILIES

The population of Europe has been going down since 1970. Now families are too small in some parts of the European Union. In northern European countries like Sweden, Germany, Britain, Ireland, and the Netherlands, families haven't been having enough children.

The average Northern European woman used to have 2.4 children. But over the years, Northern European women have been going to college and working outside the home more and more. They've also been getting married when they were older and having fewer children. Now the average family has 1.5 children. The number of old people is going up, but the number of young people is going down. Young workers pay for pensions and medical costs for old people. European families need to have more children so there will be enough young workers in the future.

For these reasons, the governments of many European countries have been making it easier for families to have more children. In Sweden, for example, the government has changed its maternity leave policies. It has given parents time off from work, with pay, to have a child. If a mother gives birth to her first baby, she can stay home for over a year and still get 80 percent of her paycheck. Her husband can stay home one day a week and get 80 percent of his pay too. If they have more children, the government will give them more money.

Policies like these have raised the average number of children per family. But the number still isn't high enough. Families need to have 2.1 children to keep the population at the same level. If they want to stay out of economic trouble in the future, European governments will have to think of other ways to make their populations grow.

1970	fewer	jobs	pensions and medical costs
2.1	going up	paycheck	time off

1. Europe's population has been going down since _____.

2. Many European women are now well educated and have good _____.

3. Many European women didn't get married when they were young, and they've had _____ children.

4. The elderly population in Europe is _____.

5. The European Union needs more young workers to pay for _____ for the older population.

6. The Swedish government gives parents _____ when they have a baby.

7. If a Swedish woman has had a baby, she can stay home and get most of her _____.

8. A family needs to have an average of _____ children to keep the population at the same level.

Name: _____   Date: _____

A   **12**   **Listen. Answer each question. Check (✓) *Vanessa* or *Matthew*.**

	Vanessa	Matthew
1. Who is a bad cook?		
2. Who is angry?		
3. Who is dressed beautifully?		
4. Who wanted a romantic dinner in a restaurant?		
5. Who planned the picnic carefully?		
6. Who is nervous?		
7. Who heard a strange noise?		
8. Who is really scared?		
9. Who is running fast?		
10. Who is a rich person?		

B   **Complete each sentence. Circle the correct answer.**

1. Selma is a model. She is extremely **attractive** / **clear**.

2. Kate wasn't nervous about the interview. In fact, she was very **strange** / **calm**.

3. John and Mary didn't tell anyone about their **secret** / **nervous** marriage.

4. The cell phone connection wasn't **awful** / **clear**. It was difficult to hear.

5. Carlos surprised Angie with flowers and candy because he is a **fashionable** / **romantic** guy.

6. Tom Hanks is a very **successful** / **secret** movie actor.

7. Something is wrong with the car. It is making a **strange** / **terrific** noise.

8. I love going to Mom's house for dinner. She's a **romantic** / **terrific** cook.

9. I think you put too much salt in this food. It tastes **attractive** / **awful**.

10. Marco buys his clothes at the best shops. He is very **nervous** / **fashionable**.

Name: _____   Date: _____

C   Complete each conversation. Circle the letter of the correct answer.

1.   A: Was I going too fast, Officer?

    B: Yes, you have to drive _____ when you pass the school.

      a.   slow   b.   slowly

2.   A: Ben is the best worker in the company. I want to give him a raise.

    B: I agree. He works _____.

      a.   hard   b.   hardly

3.   A: How was the talk show last night?

    B: It was _____ boring, but some parts were OK. I liked the interview with Angelina Jolie.

      a.   extremely   b.   pretty

4.   A: Does David speak Spanish?

    B: Yes, he speaks it _____.

      a.   perfect   b.   perfectly

5.   A: I watched a nature show about hikers on Mount Everest last night. They almost died!

    B: I know. That mountain is a _____ place!

      a.   dangerous   b.   dangerously

6.   A: Is Sheila going to take part in the singing contest?

    B: Yes, and she might win. She sings _____.

      a.   good   b.   well

7.   A: Are you going to ask Betsy to marry you tomorrow?

    B: Yes! But I'm _____ nervous! She'll probably say no. And then I'll feel terrible!

      a.   pretty   b.   very

8.   A: Elena doesn't talk much.

    B: No, she's a _____ person.

      a.   quiet   b.   quietly

9.   A: I can't hear the newscaster.

    B: I can't either. He's speaking very _____. Turn up the volume on the TV!

      a.   soft   b.   softly

10.   A: These roses are for you.

    B: Thank you! Mmmm, they smell _____.

      a.   wonderful   b.   wonderfully

Name: _____   Date: _____

D   Read the article. Then complete each sentence. Circle the letter of the correct answer.

REALITY TV

Reality TV shows have become very popular in the last few years. In most reality shows, ordinary people compete with each other. But there are some important differences in the ways they compete on the different shows.

One type of reality show puts ordinary people in stressful, dangerous situations. The people have to learn to get along with each other. If they don't, they might not survive. One extremely popular example of this type of show is *Survivor. Survivor* puts its contestants on a faraway island. The people have to build a place to live and find food to eat. They also compete in games to win food or items they need. Sometimes people behave badly. Some of them tell lies to win. Audiences enjoy the dramatic social situations and the exciting games.

In contrast, other reality shows are talent competitions. Contestants sing or dance in front of judges. The contestants have to look and sound terrific. If they don't, the judges are very nasty. For example, the judges on *American Idol* sometimes say things like: "You have no talent." "You are too fat." "You should buy new clothes." Some competitors get very upset. The competition is really difficult, but successful competitors become stars overnight.

Finally, some reality shows are about helping others. For example, *Extreme Home Makeover* builds homes for families. The builders design the homes carefully. Then they decorate the homes beautifully. When the family sees their new house, they are extremely happy and thankful. Many people think these types of reality TV shows are the best. They are exciting and entertaining, and they affect their audiences positively. What's better than helping people solve real problems?

1. People usually _____ in reality TV shows.
   a. compete with each other   b. win

2. On shows like *Survivor*, competitors have to learn to get along in _____ situations.
   a. ordinary   b. stressful

3. Contestants are not always _____ on *Survivor*.
   a. honest   b. competitive

4. The *American Idol* judges are sometimes _____.
   a. nasty   b. dishonest

5. Contestants on *American Idol* often get _____.
   a. physically hurt   b. upset

6. Successful *American Idol* contestants often _____.
   a. lose weight   b. become stars

7. People feel extremely thankful when _____.
   a. designers build a new house for them   b. they help others

8. Many people think that the best reality TV shows _____.
   a. give the winners a lot of money   b. affect their audiences positively

Name:_____   Date:_____

A **13** **Listen. For each pet, check (✓)** *Popular in Japan*, *Popular in Italy*, or *Popular in the U.S.*

	Popular in Japan	**Popular in Italy**	**Popular in the U.S.**
1. cats			
2. dogs			
3. fish			
4. birds			
5. virtual pets			

B **13** **Listen again. Then complete each sentence. Circle the correct answer.**

1. Apartments in Japan are **a lot smaller than / the same size as** apartments in the U.S.

2. Pietro has a **dog / parrot**.

3. People in Japan like Tamagotchi **less / more** than real pets.

4. Tamagotchi grow **larger than real pets / on a computer screen**.

5. Pietro thinks Tamagotchi are **easier / harder** to take care of than real pets.

C **Look at the pictures. Complete each sentence with the name of the animal.**

1. _____
    are good swimmers.

2. _____
    are the largest animals
    in the sea.

3. _____
    have big ears.

4. _____
    fly all night.

5. _____
    are excellent hunters.

6. _____
    live in the desert.

7. _____
    can be dangerous.

8. _____
    live in the Arctic.

Name: _____   Date: _____

D   Complete each sentence. Circle the letter of the correct answer.

1. A snake is _____ a penguin.

   a.   not as cute as   c.   less cute

   b.   the least cute

2. A cheetah runs _____ than any other animal.

   a.   fast   c.   fastest

   b.   faster

3. A pig is _____ than a dog.

   a.   the cleanest   c.   as clean as

   b.   cleaner

4. An elephant is _____ a whale.

   a.   not as big as   c.   the biggest

   b.   bigger

5. Parrots are the _____ birds.

   a.   most beautiful   c.   beautifully

   b.   more beautiful than

6. Dogs are _____ than rats.

   a.   the nicest   c.   nicer

   b.   nice

7. Cheetahs are _____ hunters of all the big cats.

   a.   the best   c.   better than

   b.   better

8. Bears have _____ mice.

   a.   as much fur   c.   more fur than

   b.   the most fur

9. A rabbit doesn't eat _____ a lion.

   a.   more   c.   more than

   b.   the most

10. The _____ animal at this zoo is the elephant.

   a.   oldest   c.   as old as

   b.   older than

Name: _____   Date: _____

E   Read the article. Then answer the questions.

LAUGHTER IN CHIMPANZEES AND HUMANS

Many people think that humans are the only animal species that laugh. In fact, chimpanzees laugh too. What are some of the similarities and differences between chimp and human laughter?

Both chimp and human laughter are social activities. Chimps laugh when they wrestle, play, or tickle. And studies have found that humans laugh more when they are around others. However, chimp laughter sounds different from human laughter. A chimp laugh is quieter than a human laugh. It sounds like heavy breathing, or panting. The biggest difference between chimp laughter and human laugher, however, is that older chimps tickle and laugh as much as younger chimps do. But older people laugh less and play less than children do.

Scientists who study chimp laughter wonder why this is. Do monkeys have a better sense of humor than humans? Maybe so, or maybe humans don't appreciate laughter enough. Scientists notice that laughter makes both chimps and humans happier and healthier. Scientists are not sure how laughter does this, but they know that laughter strengthens social bonds. When chimpanzees tickle one another, they are acting like parents do when they touch their babies. The tickling and laughter help maintain good relationships within a family and a community. Studies have shown that social support is good for humans too. Social support might help some humans fight illness better than others. So scientists suggest that people should act like monkeys, and laugh more!

1. Which two species laugh? _____

2. When do chimps laugh? _____

3. Do humans laugh more when they are alone or together? _____

4. How does chimp laughter sound? _____

5. Do older humans laugh as much as older chimps? _____

6. According to the reading, why is laughter important? _____

7. What are chimpanzees doing when they tickle? _____

8. What might make some humans healthier? _____

UNIT 12   TEST

Name: _____   Date: _____

A   🎵 14   Listen. For each sentence, write *T* for *True* or *F* for *False*.

1. The service at this restaurant is slow. _____

2. The couple's waiter has a mustache. _____

3. The main dishes come with salad. _____

4. The woman wants the rosemary chicken. _____

5. The man orders the spaghetti. _____

6. The waiter will serve the salad. _____

7. The man needs another fork. _____

8. The man is impatient. _____

9. Their kids are probably very patient. _____

B   Complete the conversations. Use the words in the box.

appetizers	help myself	order	specials	treat
enjoys himself	napkin	salad bar	stuff myself	

1. **A:** Do you want to go to Pizza Land for dinner?

   B: No I don't. I always _____ at that place. I don't want to get fat.

2. **A:** Juan's birthday is on Saturday. Do you want to _____ him to lunch?

   B: Yes. That's a great idea.

3. **A:** Excuse me, Miss. What are the _____?

   B: Fried chicken with corn and vegetable soup.

4. **A:** Oops! I dropped my _____.

   B: Well, ask the waitress for another one.

5. **A:** Chung always _____ at this restaurant.

   B: Yes, he does.

6. **A:** I like restaurants where I can _____.

   B: I don't. I like to be served by a waiter.

7. **A:** What did you _____ for dessert?

   B: Um . . . I don't know. I can't remember.

8. **A:** Look, the _____ is over there.

   B: It's really big! Maybe I won't get a main dish.

9. **A:** Do you want some shrimp _____ before the meal?

   B: Yes. That sounds great.

Unit 12 Test   T-367

Name: _____   Date: _____

C   **Complete the story. Use the words in the box. Use capital letters as needed.**

another	myself	ones	the others	ourselves
each other	one	other	other ones	themselves

My favorite restaurant is a Greek restaurant called Zorba's. There are three

_____ Greek restaurants on the same street, but Zorba's is the
        1.

best _____. The _____ are not as good,
        2.   3.

and they aren't as clean either. There isn't a hostess at Zorba's, so customers seat

_____. We always seat _____ by the window.
        4.   5.

That way we can see the park across the street. It's a small place, and a lot of the customers

know _____.
        6.

All of the main dishes are good, but most people like the _____
                                                                7.

with lamb. One time I ordered the spinach pie, and it was delicious.

_____ time I ordered the custard for dessert. It was good, but I
        8.

won't get it again because I don't want to make

_____ fat.
        9.

Three of the waiters at Zorba's are Greek, but

_____ aren't. All of them
        10.

are very nice, though. They always remember

me. They say I'm their best customer!

Name: _____   Date: _____

D Read the article. Then complete each sentence. Circle the letter of the correct answer.

𝓕ARMER'S MARKETS: 𝓗EALTHIER LIVING

Farmer's markets are a traditional way to sell goods. At farmer's markets, farmers sell fruits, vegetables, meats, and other products. The farmers usually set up the markets in town squares. Along with food products, shoppers will often find jellies, sauces, freshly baked goods, handcrafted jewelry, and plants. Some people come to shop. Others come for the atmosphere—farmer's markets often have live music or entertainment.

A weekly market is part of normal life in villages around the world, but farmer's markets have recently become more popular in the United States and Canada. New markets are appearing, and the older ones are seeing new growth. This may be because people are taking better care of themselves. They want healthier and fresher foods.

Many people say farmer's markets encourage healthier living. Others point out that farmer's markets are better for the environment than supermarkets, too. Farmers drive straight to the market. They don't use as much gas as truck drivers who drive food to the supermarket do. Food in supermarkets is in plastic bags and boxes. But farmers don't use a lot of plastic to keep their food products fresh. So, farmer's markets reduce pollution. To sum up, the farmer's market is a healthy tradition. Many people want it to continue.

1. The traditional way to sell goods is _____.
   a. in a supermarket   b. in a town square

2. According to the article, you will probably find _____ at a farmer's market.
   a. bread   b. soda

3. Some people like farmer's markets for the _____.
   a. cheap food   b. live music

4. Generally, farmer's markets happen _____.
   a. once a week   b. once a month

5. In the United States and Canada, _____ farmer's markets.
   a. there are no   b. people are becoming more interested in

6. Older farmer's markets _____.
   a. are closing   b. are growing

7. Today, many people are _____.
   a. buying healthier food   b. buying less food

8. Farmer's markets are good for the environment because farmers _____.
   a. don't use much plastic   b. use a lot of gas

Name: _____   Date: _____

A 🔘 15 **Listen. Then complete each sentence. Circle the correct answer.**

1. The woman **can / can't** turn on her computer.

2. The man **will be able to / won't be able to** repair the computer this week.

3. The woman **is able to / isn't able to** wait that long.

4. The woman **can / can't** rent a computer.

5. The woman's nephew **could / couldn't** use the camcorder.

6. The man **could / couldn't** fix camcorders years ago.

7. The man **can / can't** fix camcorders now.

8. The woman **can / can't** come to the store this afternoon.

B **Look at each picture. Then check (✓) the sentence that tells what is happening in the picture.**

1.    _____ The woman is recording.

     _____ The woman is downloading.

2.    _____ The battery is charging.

     _____ The software is charging.

3.    _____ The man is operating the Web.

     _____ The man is operating the remote control.

C **Complete the paragraph. Use the words in the box.**

battery	burn CDs	camcorder	install	online	software

My mom got a _____ for her birthday, but she wasn't able to operate it. First,
                                1.

when she tried to charge the _____, she couldn't find it. Then, she couldn't
                                            2.

_____ the _____ on her computer. She tried all night.
            3.   4.

I looked _____ the next day for help. I read that that kind of software won't
                    5.

work on her computer. My mom is going to take her gift back. Anyway, she doesn't need it. I can take

pictures of my son and _____ for her!
                                    6.

Name: _____   **Date:** _____

D   Find the mistake in each sentence. Circle the letter and correct the mistake.

1. Before <u>there</u> were <u>computers</u>, people <u>can</u> use typewriters.   **Correct:** _____
           A   B   C

2. I <u>was be</u> able to <u>charge</u> the battery.   **Correct:** _____
      A   B   C

3. Will <u>the computer</u> <u>can</u> run <u>faster</u> with the new software?   **Correct:** _____
         A   B   C

4. <u>What</u> will I <u>able to</u> <u>do</u> with this CD?   **Correct:** _____
      A   B C

5. <u>Is</u> you <u>able to</u> <u>download</u> software?   **Correct:** _____
     A   B   C

6. Alan <u>could</u> <u>e-mail</u> his boss when he's <u>traveling</u>.   **Correct:** _____
          A   B   C

7. I <u>can</u> ski when I was <u>younger</u>, but now I <u>can't</u>.   **Correct:** _____
      A   B   C

8. In the future, we <u>could</u> <u>to</u> <u>download</u> movies onto our phones.   **Correct:** _____
                   A B C

9. Two hundred years <u>ago</u>, people were <u>not</u> <u>able</u> travel by plane.   **Correct:** _____
                 A   B C

10. How long <u>has</u> Ivan <u>be</u> able to <u>use</u> a computer?   **Correct:** _____
           A   B   C

Name: _____   Date: _____

E   Read the article. Then read the sentences. For each sentence, write _T_ for _True_ or _F_ for _False_.

Micromachines: MEMS

In the late 1960s, computer scientists made an important discovery. They realized they could work with very small parts to create tiny machines. These micromachines, or MEMS (Micro Electro Mechanical Systems), work with microchips. The micromachines get information when they interact with the outside world. Then they give this information to the microchips. This means that the microchips are the "brains" of computer systems, while the micromachines are the eyes, ears, hands, and feet.

MEMS can do some amazing things. For example, they save many lives each year. Scientists have put MEMS in airbags in cars and planes. These airbags fill with air to protect the passengers when an accident happens. When a car hits another car, for example, the MEMS inside an airbag are able to feel the impact before people can. They make the airbag fill with air very quickly so that the people in the car are not hurt.

In the future, scientists predict MEMS will be able to do many more things. For instance, MEMS in the soles of running shoes will be able to increase the beat of music on an mp3 player. They will be able to make the music play faster as the person runs faster. MEMS will also be able to test the freshness of food. At the checkout line at the grocery store, a tiny MEM tongue will be able to taste your juice to see if it's fresh. But most exciting, scientists say, is the way MEMS will be able to assist with healthcare. They will be able to swim through blood vessels in human bodies to find and destroy harmful viruses.

1. The main topic of the article is microchips.   _____

2. Scientists discovered MEMS 20 years ago.   _____

3. MEMs are very small machines.   _____

4. Microchips give information to MEMS.   _____

5. MEMS in airbags are able to save lives.   _____

6. MEMS can now help people listen to music from their shoes.   _____

7. In the future, MEMS will be able to taste juice.   _____

8. MEMS will be able to help people by destroying human bodies.   _____

Name: _____   Date: _____

A 🔘 16-19 ▶ **Listen to each conversation. Then complete each sentence. Circle the correct answer.**

Conversation 1:   1.   **Sara / Dad** has to take out the trash tonight.

                      2.   **Sara / Dad** has to do the dishes.

Conversation 2:   3.   **Wendy / Jin** has to be home by ten o'clock on Saturdays.

                      4.   **Wendy / Jin** has to be home by 9:30.

                      5.   If **Wendy / Jin** isn't home on time, she has to do chores.

Conversation 3:   6.   **Max / Max's mom** has to apologize.

                      7.   **Bobby / Max** wants a new Game Boy.

Conversation 4:   8.   **Kano / Eva** rode a bike in the dark.

                      9.   **Kano / Mom** can drive Eva home next time.

B   **Complete each conversation. Use the words in the box.**

apologize	bothers	do chores	obey	take out the trash
behave	crosses	holds	strict	

1. **A:** My children _____ themselves very well at restaurants.
    B: Mine don't! They throw food and bang on the table.

2. **A:** It _____ me when you play with your food!
    B: Sorry, Mom.

3. **A:** Lizbeth had to _____ to her teacher.
    B: Was she late for class again?

4. **A:** Do your children have to _____ on the weekends?
    B: Yes! They have to do them on both Saturday and Sunday.

5. **A:** Susan's parents aren't very _____.
    B: I know. She doesn't have to do chores, and she can stay out late.

6. **A:** Thad _____ his little brother's hand when they walk to school.
    B: He's a very considerate older brother.

7. **A:** If you don't _____ the rules of the house, you can't go to the dance.
    B: But, Mom! That's not fair.

8. **A:** I forgot to _____ last night!
    B: Did the garbage collectors already come? Maybe you can do it now.

9. **A:** Jude _____ the street by himself now.
    B: Wow! He's getting big.

Unit 14 Test   T-373

Name: _____   Date: _____

C   Complete the sentences. Use the words in the box. Use capital letters as needed.

did	does	got to	have to	mustn't
do	don't have to	has to	have to do	what

1. _____ did he have to do after he finished his homework yesterday?

2. Do I _____ wash the dishes right now? I want to play this video game.

3. I think Mikey forgot to feed the cat. We've _____ feed her now. She looks really hungry.

4. Ellie _____ stay out late tonight. She has a test tomorrow morning.

5. _____ we have to eat Grandma's meatloaf? We can't stand it.

6. They _____ go to swim practice today. It was canceled.

7. What does he _____ after school today?

8. _____ you have to walk home from school when you were a kid?

9. Meredith _____ apologize to her mother. She forgot to take out the trash last night.

10. _____ Suzy have to study this weekend? I want her to go to the movies with us.

Name: _____   **Date:** _____

D   Read the letter. Then answer the questions.

Dear Parents:

Tomorrow night, a special council is going to discuss several important issues:

Cafeteria Food. As you know, many parents are worried about the poor quality of food at the cafeteria. We must tell the council that we do not want pizzas and cheeseburgers on the menu. We also have to remind them to get rid of all the soda machines. The machines that sell only water and juice are OK, of course.

Homework. When we were children, we didn't have to do three or four hours of homework every night. We could play sports and socialize with one another. Today, our children are under too much pressure. Often, they have to do so much homework, they don't have time for other activities. Children need homework, but not too much. How many times do we have to tell our administrators this?!

Fundraising. The art and theater departments still need money. We must help the school raise money for these very important activities. Last year, the school play had to be canceled because there wasn't enough money. This mustn't happen again.

Before we can ask for changes, we must have support from parents like you! So, I hope to see you all at the meeting tomorrow!

Tina Hamilton

Tina Hamilton
Parent Representative, Bobcat High School

1. What is wrong with the food at the cafeteria? _____

2. Does the school have to get rid of all the machines that sell drinks? _____

3. Does Ms. Hamilton think children need homework? _____

4. If children had less homework, what could they do? _____

5. Have parents asked for less homework? _____

6. Which two departments have little money? _____

7. What happened to the school play last year? _____

8. What must Ms. Hamilton have before she can ask for changes? _____

Name: _____   Date: _____

A 🔘 **20** **Listen to the conversation. Then answer the questions. Use short answers.**

1. Should David bring flowers? _____
2. Should David talk with his mouth full? _____
3. Should David put his elbows on the table? _____
4. Should David whisper to Jada at the dinner table? _____
5. Should David and Jada be leaving now? _____
6. Should David and Jada be late for dinner? _____

B 🔘 **20** **Listen again. Circle the letter of each sentence you hear.**

1. a. My parents have bad manners.
   b. My parents hate bad manners.

2. a. What should I do?
   b. What shouldn't I do?

3. a. Don't serve yourself with their fork.
   b. Don't serve yourself with your fork.

4. a. It won't make my parents angry.
   b. It will make my parents angry.

C **Complete the sentences. Use the words in the box.**

cover your mouth	put your elbows
interrupts	talks about me behind my back
knock on the door	talks with her mouth full
lick	whisper

1. You're sick, so you should _____ when you cough.

2. Kelly _____. It makes me really upset. I thought we were friends.

3. My sister _____. It's disgusting!

4. Don't _____! I can't hear you.

5. Remember, _____ before you enter my room. I don't like surprises.

6. Sometimes I forget my manners and _____ my fingers at the dinner table.

7. Sally _____ people all the time. She can't be quiet for more than two seconds.

8. Everybody knows you shouldn't _____ on the table.

Name: _____   Date: _____

D Find the mistake in each sentence. Circle the letter and correct the mistake.

1. **A:** Those kids <u>shouldn't</u> be <u>run</u> around the pool.   Correct: _____
                  A   B

    B: You're right. We <u>should</u> tell them.
                         C

2. **A:** <u>Where's</u> the waiter? He <u>be should</u> taking our order.   Correct: _____
             A   B

    B: There he is. He's <u>coming</u>.
                          C

3. **A:** <u>Should</u> <u>bring</u> Justin a present to the party?   Correct: _____
             A   B

    B: Yes. The other children should <u>bring</u> presents too.
                                  C

4. **A:** That boy <u>is</u> hitting that dog. What <u>we should</u> do?   Correct: _____
                    A   B

    B: We <u>should</u> stop him.
                 C

5. **A:** <u>Should</u> we bring flowers to Jeff's dinner?   Correct: _____
             A

    B: No. We <u>don't</u> <u>has</u> to bring flowers.
                   B   C

6. **A:** Children should <u>be</u> always <u>speak</u> politely to adults.   Correct: _____
                      A   B

    B: Yes. And adults <u>should</u> speak politely to children.
                         C

7. **A:** <u>Should</u> I <u>be</u> helping that guest with her bag?   Correct: _____
             A   B

    B: No. Robert is helping her. You don't <u>should</u> to help.
                                C

8. **A:** <u>When</u> <u>should</u> <u>pick up</u> we the kids?   Correct: _____
             A   B   C

    B: At 3:30. We shouldn't be late.

9. **A:** Seth, <u>don't</u> interrupt me! You <u>should</u> do that.   Correct: _____
                A   B

    B: Sorry, Mom. I won't <u>do</u> it again.
                           C

Name: _____   Date: _____

E   **Read the advice column. Then complete each sentence. Circle the correct answer.**

Dating Etiquette

In the past, people tried to behave very politely when they went out on dates. Many people today think they don't have to obey old-fashioned rules of dating etiquette anymore. But they could be wrong. Often, your date will like you more if you are polite. You don't have to be stiff and formal, but there are some simple rules you should follow the next time you go out on a date.

Before, men always used to pick up women at their homes for dates. They don't have to do that anymore. These days, couples will often meet each other at a restaurant or other location. But whether you pick up your date or meet him or her somewhere, you should be on time. If you are late, your date will think that you don't care that he or she had to wait for you. If you do arrive late, you should always apologize.

During the date, it is traditional etiquette for a man to hold doors open for a woman and to pay for her on the date. Many people still think that a man should do these things. But some

women don't want men to hold doors open or pay for them. If you are a man and you want to be polite, you should probably at least offer to do these things for your date. And women, you should politely refuse the man's offers if you don't want to accept them. Both men and women should also have good dining manners. Don't eat with your mouth open, and don't lick your fingers.

And don't interrupt. When your date is talking, you should be listening.

Finally, there is one thing you *must* do: be yourself! Don't try to act like somebody else. Your date wants to get to know who you are. So, above all, you should relax and remember to have a good time.

1.   Many people today think they **have to / don't have to** obey rules of etiquette when they date.

2.   People should **be stiff and formal / follow some simple rules** when they date.

3.   Men **have to / don't have to** pick up women at their homes for dates.

4.   People **should / don't have to** be on time for dates.

5.   **All / Some** women want men to open doors for them on dates.

6.   To be polite, men **should offer to / must** pay for women on dates.

7.   When your date is talking, you **should / should not** be interrupting.

8.   The most important thing is to **act like somebody else / be yourself** on a date.

Name: _____   Date: _____

A **21** **Listen. For each sentence, write *T* for *True* or *F* for *False*.**

1. Mark lives in Brazil. _____

2. Mark isn't tired. _____

3. The Everetts probably moved out. _____

4. There is a lot of junk in the Everetts' yard. _____

5. The Jordans are on vacation. _____

6. The Jordans' car is in their driveway. _____

7. Zelda doesn't have many vegetables in her garden. _____

8. The Prossers are probably visiting family in California. _____

9. Zelda knows a lot about the neighborhood. _____

B **Complete the conversation. Use the words in the box.**

bark	driveway	gardeners	musician	slam their door
chat	garden	junk	shout	yard

Rebecca: Have you noticed that the Stewarts' dogs _____ all night?
                                                                          1.

Xavier: Yes, it drives me crazy. Their kids also _____ at each other all day.
                                                                          2.

Rebecca: And they _____. One of these days, it's going to fall off.
                          3.

Xavier: I wonder why they have so much _____ in their _____.
                                                            4.   5.

There's an old car and a washing machine.

Rebecca: They must be messy. They are nice people, though. Anyway, have you seen their

_____?
          6.

Xavier: Yes! Their roses are beautiful. They must be very good _____. Do you like plants?
                                                                                      7.

Rebecca: I do. But I don't work in the yard much. In my free time, I play the cello instead. I'm a

_____.
          8.

Xavier: I didn't know that! We'll have to _____ more about that later—I see Sara waving
                                                            9.

to me from her car in the _____.
                                          10.

Rebecca: OK, see you later, Xavier.

Name: _____   Date: _____

C Look at the picture. Then complete the sentences. Use the words in the box and *must be* or *must not be*.

chatting	clean	a gardener	a musician	shouting

1. They _____.

2. She _____.

3. He _____.

4. He _____.

5. The man _____.

D Match the sentences. Write the correct letters.

_____ **1.** We've been out in the snow all day.   a. She must have a lot of time.

_____ **2.** She is sick today.   b. Someone must be cooking.

_____ **3.** She's moving out of his house.   c. They must not be getting along.

_____ **4.** She makes her own clothes.   d. You must be cold.

_____ **5.** The house smells wonderful.   e. She can't be! She was fine an hour ago.

Name: _____   Date: _____

E   Read the article. Then answer the questions.

Runaways: A Serious Problem

Runaways are a serious problem in the United States. So why do so many American children and teenagers run away from home? Many people think that runaways must be bad kids. They think these kids must be leaving home because they want to drink alcohol and take drugs or because they don't want to obey their parents. They don't realize that runaways often come from violent or abusive homes.

Many runaways think that life on the streets can't be worse than the violence and abuse they experience at home. Unfortunately, living on the streets is often very difficult and dangerous, especially for young people. Teens often have to sell drugs or steal to survive.

In most states, it is illegal for children or teens to run away. As a result, many health officials return kids to violent homes. Why does a law that was meant to protect kids often hurt them? Many people believe there must be a better way to help runaways.

Advocates say the government should have "safe places" where kids can go when their homes are unsafe. Since many states already have "safe houses" for abused women, they must be able to offer the same to runaways. Also, the government should teach violent or abusive parents to treat their children better. If parents are nicer to their kids, fewer children will decide to run away in the first place. The problem is not an easy one to solve, but good services, counseling, and parenting classes can help.

1. What are runaways?

_____

2. What do many people assume about runaways?

_____

3. According to the article, why do kids run away?

_____

4. Do runaways think that life on the street is worse than life at home?

_____

5. What do many runaways have to do to survive on the streets?

_____

6. Why are runaways often sent back to violent homes?

_____

7. What do advocates think the government should have for runaways?

_____

8. What should the government do to stop kids from running away?

_____

Name: _____   Date: _____

A 🔘 *CD1 TRACK* **22** **Listen. Then check (✓) the things Dr. Chen tells Michael to do. Cross (✗) the things that he doesn't tell him to do.**

According to Dr. Chen, Michael needs to . . .

☐ **1.** gain weight.   ☐ **4.** get shots.

☐ **2.** lower his cholesterol.   ☐ **5.** get a cat.

☐ **3.** have surgery.   ☐ **6.** eat less red meat.

B 🔘 *CD1 TRACK* **22** **Listen again. Then complete the sentences.**

1. It's difficult for me to _____.

2. Well, it's important for you to _____.

3. Some people are too busy to _____.

4. It is fun to _____.

C **Complete each sentence. Circle the letter of the correct answer.**

1. You _____ 20 pounds! You need to eat less.

a. gained   b. lost

2. You have _____. You must go on a diet and lose weight.

a. low blood pressure   b. high cholesterol

3. I hate to get _____. They're painful!

a. shots   b. in shape

4. It's important to eat oranges or drink orange juice for _____.

a. calcium   b. vitamin C

5. You can take pills to get _____.

a. calcium   b. high cholesterol

6. Is it necessary to have the _____ soon?

a. diet   b. surgery

7. I must make an appointment to check my _____.

a. shape   b. blood pressure

8. I want to get _____ so I can fit into my favorite jeans.

a. in shape   b. shots

9. That diet made me feel too _____. I want to try another one.

a. weak   b. healthy

10. It's _____ to be nervous at the dentist's office.

a. high blood pressure   b. common

Name: _____   Date: _____

D Find the mistake in each sentence. Circle the letter and correct the mistake.

1. I'm <u>taking</u> my wife <u>to the</u> hospital <u>have</u> surgery.   Correct: _____
        A   B   C

2. Sir, you are <u>enough</u> <u>heavy</u> for us <u>to</u> carry.   Correct: _____
                  A   B   C

3. <u>Why</u> do children go <u>too</u> bed <u>so</u> early?   Correct: _____
     A   B   C

4. <u>Is</u> my son <u>too</u> young <u>go</u> on a diet?   Correct: _____
     A   B   C

5. I am <u>too</u> sick <u>enough</u> to <u>go</u> back to work.   Correct: _____
          A   B   C

6. I <u>eat</u> <u>enough</u> much junk food to <u>lose</u> weight.   Correct: _____
       A   B   C

7. You must <u>to</u> go <u>to</u> the doctor soon. You're <u>very</u> sick.   Correct: _____
             A   B   C

8. <u>It</u> unhealthy <u>for</u> people <u>to have</u> high cholesterol.   Correct: _____
     A   B   C

9. <u>It is</u> important for <u>she</u> to follow <u>the doctor's</u> advice.   Correct: _____
      A   B   C

10. I need <u>to take</u> vitamin C <u>for</u> stay <u>healthy</u>.   Correct: _____
           A   B   C

Name: _____   Date: _____

E   Read the sentences. For each sentence, check (✓) T for *True* or F for *False*.

Quiz: The Truth About Some Advice

1. ☐ T   ☐ F   It's not good to listen to loud music.
2. ☐ T   ☐ F   To make yourself smarter, eat fish.
3. ☐ T   ☐ F   It is dangerous to travel on Friday the 13th.
4. ☐ T   ☐ F   To improve your skin, eat less chocolate.

F   Read the article. Then find and correct the mistake in each sentence.

Answers to this week's health quiz

IT'S NOT GOOD TO LISTEN TO LOUD MUSIC.

True. Loud noises make the eardrum shake and can damage tiny hairs in the ear. It's important to remember: When you wear headphones, if those around you can hear the music, it's too loud!

TO MAKE YOURSELF SMARTER, EAT FISH.

True. Fish contains "good fats" called omega-3's. These fats help the brain. Omega-3's are also good for hair, skin, and nails. It is a good idea to eat fish as part of a healthy diet. If you don't like fish, you can take a pill to get your omega-3's.

IT IS DANGEROUS TO TRAVEL ON FRIDAY THE 13TH.

False. Most people now realize this isn't true, but some people still worry on Friday the 13th. They won't travel on that day, or have important events like weddings.

TO IMPROVE YOUR SKIN, EAT LESS CHOCOLATE.

True . . . and false. Some people are more sensitive to chocolate than others. One person may get bad skin from chocolate, while another person won't have a problem. It is common for people to have different problems with different foods. For example, some people are very allergic to peanuts and strawberries.

1. Loud noises cannot damage the tiny hairs in your ear.

2. If other people can hear the music from your headphones, it is too quiet.

3. Fish isn't good for the skin and the brain.

4. You can't get omega-3's from pills.

5. Most people still worry on Friday the 13th.

6. Some people don't like to travel on Friday the 15th.

7. All people get bad skin from chocolate.

8. Peanuts are safe for everybody to eat.

Name: _____   Date: _____

A 🔘 **23 Listen. Then complete each sentence. Circle the correct answer.**

1. Abby is interested in **sewing** / **hiking**.

2. Isabel thinks **gardening** / **knitting** is hard.

3. Abby can't stand **staying in a hotel** / **feeling cold**.

4. Isabel is good at **knitting** / **hiking**.

5. Isabel hiked **seven** / **eleven** miles.

6. Abby loves **cooking** / **camping**.

7. Isabel isn't very good at **cooking** / **camping**.

8. Abby is considering taking a class in **Chinese cooking** / **Japanese cooking**.

B Match the pictures with the statements. Write the correct letters.

1. _____   2. _____   3. _____   4. _____

 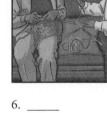  

5. _____   6. _____   7. _____   8. _____

a. "I'm into hiking."

b. "I prefer the painting on the left."

c. "I'm really bad at gardening."

d. "I can't stand knitting."

e. "I'm good at gardening."

f. "I'm tired of camping."

g. "Hmm . . . I'm considering your paintings."

h. "I dislike sewing."

Name: _____ Date: _____

C Complete the paragraph. Use the words in parentheses. Some items may have more than one answer.

My kids are interested in many different things. Fortunately, they all

_____ TV is boring. They are always doing different activities
    1. (think / watch)

on the weekends. My son Simon _____. He drives up to the
                                    2. (enjoy / hike)

mountains and sometimes he camps. In my opinion, _____ too
                                                        3. (camp / be)

much work. Also, I _____ on the ground—I have a bad back! I
                        4. (dislike / sleep)

_____. I knit scarves and sweaters. My daughter, Charlotte,
    5. (prefer / knit)

_____ too. We do it together in the evenings. Charlotte
    6. (like / knit)

_____ as well. She usually sings with a choir on Friday nights. My
    7. (be into / sing)

son Peter _____ soccer. He is getting really good! He
            8. (love / play)

_____ all the time! He _____ a professional
    9. (want / play)   10. (hope / become)

player someday.

Name: _____   Date: _____

D   Read the article. Then put the statements in order from 1 to 6.

Bowling

People have bowled for more than 5,200 years. Ancient Egyptians played a game similar to bowling. In Germany, around 200 B.C., people liked to bowl at festivals. They threw stones at nine sticks. In 1366, the English king Edward III decided that his troops were bowling too often. He ordered them to stop. In the early 1500s, the Dutch introduced a kind of bowling to America. They bowled in an area of Manhattan called "Bowling Green." Today, this area is one of the biggest financial centers in the world.

There were no bowling rules in the United States until the 19th century. The weight and size of balls, pins, and lanes were different in every state. But on September 9, 1895, the American Bowling Congress created general rules. After that, men began to play in national contests. In the beginning,

bowling

only men could bowl. Women couldn't bowl in contests until 1917.

At the beginning of the 20th century, bowling technology improved greatly. People used to make bowling balls out of wood, but in 1914 the Brunswick Corporation introduced the "Mineralite Ball." This ball was made of rubber, and it was a big success. But the biggest change in bowling came with the automatic pinsetter in 1936. This machine picked up the pins that the bowling balls knocked down, and bowling alleys didn't need "pin boys" anymore.

In 1961, ABC showed the Pro Bowlers Tour on TV. Millions of Americans watched and became interested in bowling. Today over 100 million people enjoy bowling in more than 90 different countries. And this number just seems to be growing and growing.

_____ **a.** Women began to bowl in national contests.

_____ **b.** Brunswick Corporation introduced the "Mineralite Ball."

_____ **c.** At German festivals, people threw stones at nine sticks.

_____ **d.** Ancient Egyptians played a game similar to bowling.

_____ **e.** Millions of Americans became interested in bowling.

_____ **f.** The Dutch introduced bowling to America.

E   Read the article again. Check (✓) the inferences that you can make from the information in the text. Cross (✗) the inferences that you cannot make.

☐ **1.** King Edward III loved bowling.

☐ **2.** The "Mineralite Ball" was easier to use than the wooden ball.

☐ **3.** Before 1936, "pin boys" used to pick up all the pins.

☐ **4.** Bowling is less popular now than it used to be.

Name: _____   Date: _____

A **24** **Listen. Read the sentences. For each sentence, write T for True or F for False.**

1. There are no flames in the building.   _____

2. The man is calling from inside the building.   _____

3. The smoke detectors weren't working.   _____

4. The fire started eleven minutes ago.   _____

5. The man told most of his neighbors about the fire.   _____

6. The man doesn't know how many people are still in the building.   _____

7. The operator tells the man to try to go in the building.   _____

8. The operator encourages the man to get some coffee.   _____

9. The fire trucks won't arrive for a long time.   _____

B **Complete the conversations. Use the words in the boxes.**

advised	fire hazards	ordered	smoke detector

Jane: I asked a fire inspector to look at my apartment yesterday. He found a few problems. He discovered that my

_____ was broken.
             1.

Paul: That's dangerous.

Jane: I know, but he _____ the landlord to fix it, so she has to do it. The fire inspector also
                                    2.

_____ me to move my candles.
          3.

Paul: Good. Those are _____.
                                          4.

guess	notice	speeding	ticket

Jesse: I got a _____ on Sunday because I was _____.
                            5.   **6.**

Cavon: What happened?

Jesse: I was late to work and driving too fast. I didn't _____ the police car. He asked me to
                                                                          7.

_____ how fast I was going. I didn't know. It was 90 miles an hour!
          8.

Name: _____   **Date:** _____

C   Complete the conversations. Use the words in the box.

don't think	he's	makes	to stop	you
guess	let	me	to move	your

1. **A:** I expected you _____ the thief after he stole my bag.

   B: I'm sorry. He was too fast.

2. **A:** Did Jannie go to the hospital?

   B: I _____ not. I saw her in class yesterday.

3. **A:** What happens in the U.S. when a police officer stops you for speeding?

   B: He _____ you give him your license.

4. **A:** Suzy wants _____ to call the paramedics right away. Grandpa is ill.

   B: We don't need to call the paramedics! Grandpa just has a stomachache!

5. **A:** Did the fire alarm go off?

   B: I _____ so. I didn't hear it.

6. **A:** Did the police find the pickpocket?

   B: No, but they suspect that _____ from the area.

7. **A:** When did you go back in the building?

   B: The firefighters _____ us go back in after they were sure there was no fire.

8. **A:** Did the doctor give you advice?

   B: Yes, she wants _____ to rest for another week.

9. **A:** What did the police officer want?

   B: He wanted me _____ my car.

10. **A:** I hope _____ apartment has good smoke detectors.

    B: Don't worry. It does.

Name: _____   Date: _____

D   Read the article. Then complete each sentence. Circle the correct answer.

Flooding Safety Tips

Safety experts advise you to follow these steps before, during, and after a flood:

Before a Flood:

- Start preparing for a flood before it happens. Don't wait until the flood is already at your doorstep. You won't have time to do much then! Floods happen fast, so don't let them catch you unprepared.

- Clear leaves and garbage out of the ditches and gutters near your house so that water can flow through them, and away from your house.

- Move your car to higher ground. Only two feet of water can wash a car away.

When You Hear That a Flood Is Coming:

- Move your valuable possessions to high places in your home. Remove kitchen chemicals from under your sink.

- Turn off your electricity.

During a Flood:

- Officials might advise you to leave your house. Follow their advice, and do so quickly. Your life is more important than your possessions.

- Don't drive through flood water. You can't see dangerous things in the water, and you probably won't be able to see the road.

- Don't walk in flood water that is above your knees. The water may knock you down!

After the flood:

- Flood water may be very dirty. Clean and disinfect everything in your house. Watch for broken glass or nails in the water, and wear gloves.

- If you think that any electrical equipment may be damaged, don't use it!

1. You need to start preparing for a flood **before / when** it happens.

2. You should move your car **to a ditch or gutter / to higher ground**.

3. When you hear a flood is coming, **throw out / move** your valuable possessions.

4. Your electricity should be **on / off** during a flood.

5. If officials advise you to leave your house, you should **leave / stay**.

6. If you have to leave your house, you **should / shouldn't** drive through the water.

7. Walking in water above your knees is a **good / bad** way to escape from a flood.

8. Flood water can be very **clean / dirty**.

9. Using damaged electrical equipment is **safe / dangerous**.

Name: _____   Date: _____

A 🔘 25 **Listen. Then find and correct the mistake in each sentence.**

1. National Airlines flight number 320 is now boarding at gate 14.

2. José asks Angie where she wants to go.

3. Angie asks José why the plane is boarding late.

4. The announcer told the passengers to take out their carry-on bags.

5. Angie thinks she left the magazine in the bathroom.

6. José says he found the boarding passes in the bathroom.

7. José tells Angie to hurry because they are not boarding the plane.

8. José tells Angie not to forget her identification.

B **Match the words with the definitions. Write the correct letters.**

_____ **1.** customs officer

_____ **2.** carry-on bag

_____ **3.** hotel clerk

_____ **4.** immigration officer

_____ **5.** ticket counter

_____ **6.** gate

_____ **7.** fasten your seatbelt

_____ **8.** board

_____ **9.** tour guide

_____ **10.** check in

a. get on

b. where you buy a ticket

c. something you bring on the plane

d. someone who checks people into a hotel

e. give your bags and ticket to an airport worker

f. someone who checks goods coming into the country

g. someone who leads a group on a tour

h. where people get on the plane

i. what you do on the plane when it is going to leave

j. someone who checks people coming into the country

Name: _____ Date: _____

C Change each sentence to reported speech.

1. Tom says, "We're going hiking on Tuesday."

_____

2. She says, "The place isn't very nice."

_____

3. He says, "I'm having a great time."

_____

4. He told her, "Stop talking on your cell phone."

_____

5. The captain told us, "Go back to your seats."

_____

D Change each sentence to quoted speech.

1. Meredith says it was sunny every day on her vacation.

_____

2. She says she's sent the package.

_____

3. He told his children not to push.

_____

4. They told us to leave our sweaters at home.

_____

5. The flight attendant asked me to check my carry-on bag.

_____

Name: _____   Date: _____

E   Read the Web page. Then read the sentences. For each sentence, write *T* for *True* or *F* for *False*.

Travel Horror Stories

Teya and Tom: Driving the Italian Way

Teya and I were on vacation in Italy. We were driving through the countryside when we saw a nice town. I thought I saw a parking lot with many empty spaces. As I drove into the "lot," Teya said, "Tom, stop! You're driving in the town square." I told her to calm down. But then I realized she was right. I was driving in circles in the traffic-free town square. The people in the square had to run to the sidewalks. They started yelling at us. Teya told them we were sorry as we drove away. But unfortunately, nobody spoke any English. They just yelled louder. Teya said she was so embarrassed. She wanted to go back the next day and apologize. I told her that if we wanted to leave Italy alive, we'd better not!

Brad: Naked in Key West

I went to Key West for vacation. I was on a beach and nobody else was around. I decided to take my clothes off and go for a swim. I left my clothes, my boots, my watch, and my wallet on the beach. The water was blue and clear. It was a perfect day. I swam for an hour. When I came back to the beach, a man was picking up my things. I told the man to stop. When he didn't stop, I chased him. We soon came to a crowded part of the beach. People started yelling at me to put my clothes on. I pointed at the man. "Thief! Thief!" I yelled, "He stole my clothes!" Finally, a big guy grabbed the thief and held him. I was happy to have my valuables back, but I was even happier to have my clothes back!

1. Teya and Tom decided to stop in a town for a swim.   _____
2. Teya and Tom found a parking lot with many empty spaces.   _____
3. Teya told Tom to calm down.   _____
4. The people in the square had to run from Teya and Tom's car.   _____
5. Teya yelled, "We're sorry!" as they drove away.   _____
6. Brad was swimming in the hotel pool.   _____
7. Someone stole Brad's car.   _____
8. Brad yelled "Stop!"   _____
9. Brad ran after the thief.   _____
10. The thief told Brad to put his clothes on.   _____

Unit Test Answer Key and Audioscript

Unit 1

A

1. b   3. a   5. b   7. a
2. b   4. b   6. b   8. a

B

1. d   3. f   5. b
2. a   4. c   6. e

C

1. is / 's going out with   3. is / 's getting to know
2. gets along with

D

1. has got   3. haven't got
2. hasn't got   4. has got

E

1. are eating   3. gets along   5. are taking
2. spend   4. is working   6. lives

F

1. through friends or at work   5. describe
2. their personality   6. isn't
3. gets along   7. can sometimes
4. recent photo   8. e-mail, then meet

Audioscript for Exercise A:

Gary: Hi, Susan. Great party!

Susan: I'm glad you came, Gary. What are you doing these days?

Gary: I'm starting a new job on Monday. And I go to school at night.

Susan: Oh, really? I have a new job too!

Gary: Oh, yeah? So, who are all these new people?

Susan: I'm meeting a lot of new people at work. I invited them to the party.

Gary: Who's the woman with the curly brown hair?

Susan: That's my boss. She's moving up in the company fast. She'll be vice president soon.

Gary: And the man with the beard? He's laughing about something.

Susan: That's the accountant. He's got a great sense of humor. He gets along with everyone.

Gary: And who's that woman, the blonde with the straight hair on the sofa?

Susan: The woman in the living room? That's Anya Olson.

Gary: What's she like?

Susan: I'm just getting to know her, but I think she's got a nice personality.

Gary: Is she going out with anyone?

Susan: Oh, yes. She's got a boyfriend.

Gary: Oh, too bad. So who is that beautiful woman over there?

Susan: Hey, what's going on? Are you looking for a girlfriend? What about Paula?

Gary: Well, we're not going out anymore. So, if you've got any single friends, let me know!

Unit 2

A

1. F   3. F   5. F   7. T
2. T   4. T   6. F   8. T

B

1. city   4. city   7. suburbs
2. country   5. suburbs   8. city
3. country   6. country

C

1. c   3. b   5. b   7. c   9. a
2. a   4. d   6. b   8. b   10. b

D

1. a   3. a   5. a   7. a
2. a   4. b   6. b   8. a

Audioscript for Exercise A:

Mei-Ling: I love living in the country. There are some good schools, not much crime, and a lot of open space. I feel safe and there's plenty of space for my kids to run around. But . . .

Frank: Let me guess—you miss the city, right?

Mei-Ling: Yeah, I miss it a lot. The country is very quiet.

Frank: I know! My wife and I moved to the city last year, and both of us are happy with the decision.

Mei-Ling: Why do you say that?

Frank: Well, there are plenty of museums and events. My kids love all the things to do.

Mei-Ling: But the city is very expensive.

Frank: True. There aren't enough cheap places to live. And most apartments are small. We have very little room for extra furniture. We have a few nice pieces of furniture, but that's all.

Mei-Ling: Isn't public transportation expensive too?

Frank: I save some money when I buy a subway pass. And I walk to many places. I get plenty of exercise without going to the gym.

Mei-Ling: So where do you park?

Frank: There's very little parking. It takes a long time to find parking. I'm spending too much time in my car. Well, I have a little extra money, so I'll rent a parking space at a garage.

Mei-Ling: Hmmm . . . I don't know if my husband and I are ready to move. Neither of us can decide.

Frank: Well, if you *don't* move here, please come for a visit, and we'll visit you in the country.

Unit 3

A

1. is not
2. watched
3. told
4. didn't
5. forgot
6. decides

B

1. b
2. a
3. b
4. b

C

1. cheer
2. is tied
3. court
4. runs
5. beat
6. loses to
7. miss
8. passes

D

1. a
2. b
3. a
4. b
5. b
6. a
7. a

E

1. Because
2. after
3. Before

F

a. 2
b. 8
c. 4
d. 7
e. 3
f. 5
g. 1
h. 6

Audioscript for Exercise A:

Alfredo: Hello?

Cindy: Hi, Alfredo. I'm waiting for you. Where are you?

Alfredo: I'm driving to my brother's soccer game.

Cindy: But you watched his game last Saturday!

Alfredo: Yeah. And they won! I'm going to the championship game tonight because they won last week. Didn't I tell you the good news?

Cindy: No, Alfredo, you didn't. You forgot to tell me. And I think there's something else you forgot.

Alfredo: What? Did I forget something important?

Cindy: Not important to you. But I am sitting at the Four Flowers restaurant right now . . . alone.

Alfredo: Oh . . . yeah . . . I remember now . . . You wanted to have a nice dinner.

Cindy: And why did I want to have a nice dinner?

Alfredo: Did you get a new job?

Cindy: No, I didn't. Don't you remember? Before I made the reservation, I told you to save tonight for us.

Alfredo: Us? Oh . . . us. Our anniversary. Oh honey, I'm sorry. When Larry asked me to see the game, I didn't want to say no.

Cindy: Well, just call Larry and tell him the Four Flowers can't wait.

Alfredo: But Cindy, can't we go to dinner tomorrow?

Cindy: Oh, Alfredo. You're not romantic at all.

Alfredo: But I married you because you're a good sport.

Cindy: OK, where's the game? I'll join you.

Audioscript for Exercise B:

1. The player scored a run.
2. The player kicks the ball.
3. They didn't cheer.
4. Did their team play today?

Unit 4

A

1. a
2. b
3. b
4. a
5. b
6. a
7. a
8. a

B

1. fell off
2. went down
3. cut
4. ironed
5. slipped
6. daydreaming
7. was chopping
8. climb
9. burned
10. broke

C

1. were reading
2. was not painting OR wasn't painting
3. was not sleeping OR wasn't sleeping
4. were taking
5. were, working
6. Were, watching

D

1. was driving
2. rang
3. touched
4. was playing

E

Answers will vary. Possible answers:

1. He was in Italy.
2. He was holding an umbrella.
3. They were riding their horses.
4. They wanted to escape the storm.
5. Ed was leaning against the wall.
6. The horse was standing next to Ed and Lorianna.
7. Jamie touched Ed with her nose.
8. They helped her stand up.

Audioscript for Exercise A:

Exercise A:

Olga: What's the matter, Paul? You look tired!

Paul: There was a little accident at my house.

Olga: I'm sorry to hear that. What happened?

Paul: Well, my father and I were painting his house. I was carrying the ladder upstairs and my father was following me. Suddenly, I heard a strange noise. I was so surprised that I dropped the ladder . . . and the ladder and my father fell a few steps. When I looked down, my father was sitting at the bottom of the stairs with the ladder on top of him.

Olga: Oh, no!

Paul: Then my wife and my mother ran out of the kitchen. They were yelling, "What's going on?"

Olga: What *was* going on?

Paul: I wasn't sure. While I was helping my father up, I heard the noise again.

Olga: Where was it coming from?

Paul: It was coming from under a chair. I looked under the chair and our cat Cleo was sitting there, crying. I think she was sitting on the stairs when I was going up and I stepped on her tail.

Olga: Was your father OK?

Paul: Yes, thank goodness. He didn't break anything, but his back was hurting a bit this morning.

Olga: Did you finish painting the house?

Paul: Yeah . . . My wife and I painted the bathroom while my father was resting in his bedroom.

Olga: And the cat?

Paul: Cleo! Ten minutes later she was purring again.

Unit 5

A

1. T	3. F	5. F	7. T
2. F	4. F	6. T	8. F

B

1. f	3. g	5. h	7. j	9. a
2. e	4. d	6. i	8. b	10. c

C

1. used to	5. used to	9. used to
2. didn't use to	6. didn't use to	10. Did, use to
3. Did, use to	7. did, use to	
4. did, use to	8. didn't use to	

D

1. c	2. a	3. d	4. b

E

1. pedals
2. above the front wheel
3. had metal wheels
4. fall off
5. they wore long skirts
6. Modern

Audioscript for Exercise A:

Exercise A:

Sam: Grandpa, how did you meet girls when you were young?

Grandpa: I used to go to dances on Saturday nights. That was very popular. Your grandma used to be a great dancer, you know.

Sam: What kind of dances did you use to do?

Grandpa: Oh, we used to like slow dances. When you're dancing slow, you can talk to the girl. Not now. I don't think young people talk when they dance. The music's too loud.

Sam: Who used to ask for a dance?

Grandpa: The man always did. It wasn't like today. In those days, the lady never asked the man for a dance.

Sam: Did you dress up for the dances?

Grandpa: We sure did. I used to put on my best suit. And I used to wear a flower on my jacket. If I had a date, I used to buy her flowers too.

Sam: Who used to pay for the date?

Grandpa: Oh, the man paid for everything. He used to pay for the dance, the drinks, the streetcar. . . .

Sam: Streetcar!? You're kidding!

Grandpa: No, I'm serious. Say, where's your girlfriend Ashley? Did you break up with her?

Sam: No, but I think she broke up with me! She used to call me a lot, but now she doesn't call me anymore.

Grandpa: Well, call her up . . . and take her slow dancing!

Unit 6

A

1. b	3. a	5. b	7. b
2. a	4. b	6. a	8. b

B

1. j	3. d	5. a	7. h	9. f
2. e	4. g	6. b	8. i	10. c

C

1. am going to OR 'm going to	4. will OR 'll
2. am going to OR 'm going to	5. am going to OR 'm going to
3. will OR 'll	

D

1. will OR 'll	4. will stay OR 'll stay
2. am quitting OR 'm quitting	5. am flying OR 'm flying
3. are, having	

E

1. F	3. T	5. F	7. T	9. T
2. T	4. F	6. F	8. T	

Exercise A:

Rick: Linda . . . Linda, honey. Wake up! You're going to be late for work again!

Linda: I'm not going to work today. I'm staying home.

Rick: No, you're not. You're meeting with the new accountant this morning. She's coming at 8:30.

Linda: OK, OK, I'll get up. Just five more minutes. I'll get to work on time. I promise.

Rick: I'll start making breakfast.

Rick: Linda, wake up! It's 7:30.

Linda: What?! 7:30? Oh no, Rick, I'm going to be late. Can you give me the car today?

Rick: I can't. I'm picking my mother up at the airport in the afternoon!

Linda: Oh, that's right.

Rick: Call Amy. She'll give you a ride.

Linda: Amy's on vacation this week.

Rick: All right. I'll drop you off at work, but you'll have to hurry up or *I'm* going to be late too! Do you want some coffee?

Linda: No, I'm going to have breakfast with the accountant.

Rick: What time are you going to be home tonight?

Linda: Around 7:00.

Rick: Don't be late. We're having dinner at the French Café.

Linda: We are? Is it going to be you and me? How nice!

Rick: You, me, and my mother . . . Don't forget my mother's coming.

Unit 7

A

1. F	3. F	5. T	7. T
2. F	4. T	6. F	8. F

B

1. apply to
2. scholarship
3. courses
4. grades
5. fail
6. cheat
7. pass
8. transfer

C

1. c	3. b	5. a	7. b	9. b
2. a	4. b	6. d	8. b	10. c

D

1. b	3. a	5. b	7. b
2. a	4. a	6. a	8. a

Exercise A:

Mrs. Jones: Hello, Mr. Artaud. I'm Bernadette Jones, your son Claude's teacher.

Mr. Artaud: Nice to meet you, Mrs. Jones.

Mrs. Jones: Nice to meet you too. I need to speak to you about Claude.

Mr. Artaud: Of course. What is it?

Mrs. Jones: Well, I'm worried about him.

Mr. Artaud: Worried? What's wrong?

Mrs. Jones: Well, he's causing problems in the classroom.

Mr. Artaud: What do you mean?

Mrs. Jones: He talks all the time. Before the other children can answer a question, Claude will shout out the answer. If he doesn't learn to be quiet, the other children aren't going to learn their lessons.

Mr. Artaud: I'm sorry about that, Mrs. Jones. As soon as I get home, I'll talk to him about that.

Mrs. Jones: And another thing . . . Claude isn't getting good grades. He's very smart, but he's bored in class.

Mr. Artaud: You may be right. He's not interested in his schoolwork at all. Most of the time he draws pictures.

Mrs. Jones: Claude might need a harder class. If his lessons are more difficult, he won't be bored.

Mr. Artaud: Yes. I think he might do better with harder courses.

Mrs. Jones: And about the pictures . . . Claude *is* a wonderful artist. If he takes an art class, I think he'll really enjoy it.

Mr. Artaud: If he improves in school, I'll put him in an art class.

Unit 8

A

1. Emmy	4. Emmy	7. David
2. Kentaro	5. Emmy	8. David
3. Kentaro	6. Emmy	9. David

B

1. g	3. f	5. i	7. a	9. h
2. c	4. b	6. d	8. e	10. j

C

1. has driven
2. has worked
3. hasn't managed OR has not managed
4. have handled
5. have taken
6. hasn't taken OR has not taken

D

1. Have, quit	3. Have, owned
2. Has, been	4. Has, applied

E

1. F	3. T	5. F	7. F
2. F	4. F	6. F	8. T

Audioscript for Exercise A:

Exercise A:

Kentaro: Hey, Emmy. Have you found a job yet?

Emmy: No, Kentaro, not yet. I've applied at a supermarket, but no one has called me back. Have you applied for any jobs?

Kentaro: Yes, I have. And I have a job as a waiter!

Emmy: Where?

Kentaro: Have you heard of the Hollywood Café?

Emmy: Sure . . . but you haven't ever worked as a waiter or worked a cash register!

Kentaro: I'm not worried about it. They'll train me.

Emmy: Hey, maybe I can apply there too.

Kentaro: Have you ever sung in front of people?

Emmy: Well, yeah . . . Why?

Kentaro: All the waiters and waitresses have to sing "Happy Birthday" to the customers.

Emmy: Oh, I can do that. I've sung "Happy Birthday" a million times.

Kentaro: And have you ever handled money or served food?

Emmy: Yes, I have. And I've used a cash register too.

Kentaro: So, has your brother David gotten a job?

Emmy: Yes, he has. He's working at the pool.

Kentaro: Has he gotten his first paycheck yet?

Emmy: Yes, and he's put the money in the bank! He's saving for a car.

Unit 9

A

1. T	3. T	5. F	7. T	9. F
2. F	4. F	6. F	8. T	10. F

B

1. marriage
2. honeymoon
3. fight
4. widow
5. broke up
6. remarried
7. argued
8. newlyweds
9. widower
10. birth

C

1. a	3. b	5. b
2. b	4. c	6. c

D

1. have
2. haven't
3. have
4. Has

E

1. 1970
2. jobs
3. fewer
4. going up
5. pensions and medical costs
6. time off
7. paycheck
8. 2.1

Audioscript for Exercise A:

Exercise A:

David: Hello?

John: Hi, David? It's John.

David: John! I've been thinking about you all week. How's the honeymoon?

John: Oh, Suzanne and I have been having a great time.

David: Of course, it's Hawaii! Have you gone to the beach?

John: Oh, sure. We've been swimming at the beach. I've been taking pictures, and we've been learning how to cook Hawaiian food.

David: *You've* been cooking? I can't believe it. And have you been shopping too?

John: No, I haven't, but Suzanne has. She's bought a lot of summer clothes.

David: *Summer* clothes! It's been snowing all week here at home.

John: The weather here is great. Have you and Gina ever taken a vacation in Hawaii?

David: No, we haven't. Look, John, about Gina . . . we haven't been getting along too well. She's been working at a new job and I never see her anymore. I've eaten dinner alone for two months!

John: Why don't you take a weekend vacation together? I've got a house in the mountains. You can stay there and ski.

David: That sounds terrific, but I don't know if Gina will like it. She's been working weekends too. She hasn't taken any time off in weeks.

John: It sounds like she needs to relax! Maybe Suzanne can talk to her.

David: That might help. I don't want us to break up over this job.

Unit 10

A

1. Matthew
2. Vanessa
3. Vanessa
4. Vanessa
5. Matthew
6. Matthew
7. Vanessa
8. Vanessa
9. Vanessa
10. Matthew

B

1. attractive
2. calm
3. secret
4. clear
5. romantic
6. successful
7. strange
8. terrific
9. awful
10. fashionable

C

1. b	3. b	5. a	7. b	9. b
2. a	4. b	6. b	8. a	10. a

D

1. a	3. a	5. b	7. a
2. b	4. a	6. b	8. b

Audioscript for Exercise A:

Exercise A

Matthew: Vanessa, honey, I hope you like this picnic. I made all this food for you.

Vanessa: *You* made the food? Oh Matthew, you're an awful cook! The food tastes like paper. And the weather is really awful this evening. Ugh! Mosquitoes!

Matthew: But you, Vanessa . . . You're so attractive. Mmm . . . and you dressed so beautifully for this picnic, too.

Vanessa: Yeah, because I thought we had reservations for a romantic dinner . . . in a place with chairs.

Matthew: Nature is beautiful, Vanessa. It's the perfect place to tell you. . . .

Vanessa: What? That you're too cheap to buy me dinner?

Matthew: No, honey. I planned this carefully. Look, I love you very, very. . . .

Vanessa: What, Matthew? You look nervous.

Matthew: I am a little nervous . . . because I want to ask you. . . .

Vanessa: What was that?! I heard a strange noise. Listen. . . .

Matthew: Stay calm, Vanessa. It's very safe out here. Now, where was I? Um, I really love you. . . .

Vanessa: Matthew!! Something is moving slowly behind that tree. Oh, no! It's coming directly this way! Eek!

Matthew: Wait, Vanessa, wait! Please, don't run so fast! I need to tell you . . . I want to marry you . . . and I just won a million dollars . . . Wait!

Narrator: And now, scenes from next week's dramatic season finale of "Secret Hearts."

Matthew: Vanessa, Vanessa, I love you. Answer me. Please say "yes."

Unit 11

A
1. Popular in Japan, Italy, the U.S.
2. Popular in Japan, the U.S.
3. Popular in Japan
4. Popular in Japan, Italy
5. Popular in Japan

B
1. a lot smaller than
2. parrot
3. more
4. on a computer screen
5. easier

C
1. Dolphins
2. Whales
3. Rats
4. Chimpanzees
5. Elephants
6. Bats
7. Lions
8. Camels
9. Bears
10. Penguins

D
1. a
2. b
3. b
4. a
5. a
6. c
7. a
8. c
9. c
10. a

E

Answers will vary. Possible answers:
1. Chimpanzees and humans.
2. Chimps laugh when they wrestle, play, or tickle.
3. Humans laugh more when they are together.
4. Chimp laughter is quieter than human laughter. It sounds like breathing or panting.
5. No, they don't.
6. Laughter is important because it makes humans and chimps happier, healthier, and strengthens social bonds.
7. They are acting like parents do when they touch their babies.
8. Laughing might make some humans healthier.

Audioscript for Exercise A:

Exercise A:

Kiyomi: I've heard that the most popular pet in the United States today is the cat.

Pietro: Oh really? Cats are popular in Italy, too. There are as many cats as children—maybe more! They live all over the streets.

Kiyomi: Do people in Italy like dogs?

Pietro: No, not so much. They like cats much more than dogs. What kinds of pets are popular in Japan?

Kiyomi: Dogs and cats are the most popular. But our apartments are a lot smaller than apartments in the U.S., so people often have fish or birds.

Pietro: Birds are popular in Italy, too. I have a parrot.

Kiyomi: Parrots live longer than most animals, right?

Pietro: That's right. My parrot is 20 years old. Do you have a pet, Kiyomi?

Kiyomi: Well, yes, but it's a virtual pet. In Japan, people are really into virtual pets.

Pietro: Virtual pets?!

Kiyomi: Yes, virtual pets, called Tamagotchi. They aren't real. They grow really fast on a computer screen. Right now, people in Japan like these imaginary pets more than the real thing.

Pietro: Well, I guess they are easier to take care of than real pets.

Kiyomi: Actually, you still feed them and take care of them. But they're cleaner and they make less noise!

Pietro: I think I like real pets better than imaginary ones.

Kiyomi: I don't know, Pietro. My Tamagotchi is really cute. I think it's as cute as a real pet!

Unit 12

A
1. T
2. T
3. T
4. F
5. T
6. F
7. F
8. T
9. F

B
1. stuff myself
2. treat
3. specials
4. napkin
5. enjoys himself
6. help myself
7. order
8. salad bar
9. appetizers

C

1. other
2. one
3. other ones
4. themselves
5. ourselves
6. each other
7. ones
8. Another
9. myself
10. the others

D

1. b
2. a
3. b
4. a
5. b
6. b
7. a
8. a

D

1. C: could
2. A: was
3. B: be able to
4. B: be able to
5. A: Are
6. A: can
7. A: could
8. A: will be able
9. C: able to
10. B: been

E

1. F
2. F
3. T
4. F
5. T
6. F
7. T
8. F

Audioscript for Exercise A:

Exercise A:

Gordon: This restaurant is dirty and the service is slow! All the other tables have been served already!

Mary: Oh, honey, it's not that bad. . . .

Gordon: Yes, it is. . . . Hey! Waiter! Waiter! We're ready to order now!

Mary: That's not our waiter. Ours is the one with the mustache.

Waiter 1: I'll tell your waiter you're ready to order, sir.

Waiter 2: What would you like, ma'am?

Mary: Umm. . . .

Gordon: Mary! You don't know what you want yet?

Mary: Sorry, I don't . . . Would you tell me about your specials?

Waiter 2: Well, today our specials are spaghetti with meatballs, rosemary chicken, and fried chicken.

Mary: Do the chicken ones come with salad?

Waiter 2: All of our main dishes come with salad.

Gordon: She'll have the rosemary chicken.

Mary: Honey, I can order for myself! I'll have the other chicken special—the fried chicken.

Waiter 2: Of course. And for you, sir?

Gordon: I'll have the spaghetti. And make it quick!

Waiter 2: Yes, sir. The salad bar is over there. You can serve yourselves whenever you're ready.

Gordon: Wait! I need another napkin. This one fell on the floor.

Waiter 2: Sure. I'll be right back.

Mary: Why are you always so impatient at restaurants? Can't you behave yourself?

Gordon: Me, impatient?

Mary: Yes. You're worse than the kids sometimes.

Unit 13

A

1. can
2. won't be able to
3. isn't able to
4. can
5. couldn't
6. could
7. can't
8. can

B

1. The woman is recording.
2. The battery is charging.
3. The man is operating the remote control.

C

1. camcorder
2. battery
3. install
4. software
5. online
6. burn CDs

Audioscript for Exercise A:

Exercise A:

Mack: Pro Computer Services.

Patty: Hello, can you help me? My computer isn't working.

Mack: Sure. I can try. What's the problem, ma'am?

Patty: I can turn it on, but then after a few minutes, the screen goes black.

Mack: That's not good. Have you downloaded anything onto your computer recently?

Patty: Yes. I downloaded some music from the Web a few weeks ago. I wanted to burn a CD for a friend.

Mack: You probably downloaded a bad file.

Patty: Well, will you be able to fix it?

Mack: I don't know. I need to take a look at it, but I'm very busy this week. I won't be able to start until next week.

Patty: I can't wait that long! I need to access my e-mail.

Mack: Well, you can rent a laptop from us while we repair your computer.

Patty: I can? That's great. I'll do that, then. . . . Oh, I have one more question: Are you able to fix camcorders? My little nephew couldn't get our camcorder to work, so he threw it against the wall.

Mack: Well, I could fix those things years ago, but now I can't. The technology has changed too fast for me.

Patty: So, you can't help me with the camcorder?

Mack: Sorry, I can't. But you can pick up the rental computer at our store this afternoon.

Patty: Great! I'll see you then.

Unit 14

A

1. Sara
2. Sara
3. Wendy
4. Jin
5. Jin
6. Max
7. Max
8. Eva
9. Mom

B

1. behave
2. bothers
3. apologize
4. do chores
5. strict
6. holds
7. obey
8. take out the trash
9. crosses

C

1. What
2. have to
3. got to
4. mustn't
5. Do
6. don't have to
7. have to do
8. Did
9. has to
10. Does

D

Answers will vary. Possible answers:
1. The food at the cafeteria is unhealthy.
2. No. The school doesn't have to get rid of the machines that sell only water and juice.
3. Yes, but she thinks they need less homework.
4. They could do other activities like sports, and they could socialize more.
5. Yes, they have.
6. The art and theater departments have little money.
7. It was canceled.
8. She must have support from parents.

Audioscript for Exercise A:

Exercise A:

Conversation 1

Dad: Sara, have you taken out the trash yet?
Sara: No, Dad, not yet. I've got to do the dishes first.
Dad: OK. But you have to do it tonight. The garbage collectors come at 5:00 A.M. tomorrow morning.
Sara: Don't worry, Dad. I'll do it.

Conversation 2

Wendy: Jin, my mother is too strict. She says I have to be home by ten o'clock on Saturdays.
Jin: Well, my mom is stricter than yours, Wendy. If I'm not home by 9:30, she punishes me—I have to do all the chores all week.
Wendy: Wow, that is strict. So what do your brothers have to do when you're doing the chores?
Jin: Nothing! They just watch TV.

Conversation 3

Max: Mom, I've got to apologize to the Colemans. They said Bobby had to go to bed early. But he stayed up until 10.
Mom: Max, you know kids often don't obey baby-sitters. I'm sure the Colemans understand that.
Max: I hope they do. I have to baby-sit for Bobby again. I need the money for a new Game Boy.

Conversation 4

Mom: You mustn't ride your bike after dark again, Eva. It's dangerous.
Eva: But I had to pick up some things for class tomorrow from Kano's house.
Mom: Next time, tell me, and I can drive you.
Eva: OK, Mom. I'm sorry.

Unit 15

A
1. Yes, he should.
2. No, he shouldn't.
3. No, he shouldn't.
4. No, he shouldn't.
5. Yes, they should.
6. No, they shouldn't.

B
1. b
2. a
3. b
4. b

C
1. cover your mouth
2. talks about me behind my back
3. talks with her mouth full
4. whisper
5. knock on the door
6. lick
7. interrupts
8. put your elbows

D
1. B: running
2. B: should be
3. B: Justin bring
4. B: should we
5. C: have
6. A: (delete)
7. C: have
8. C: we pick up
9. B: shouldn't

E
1. don't have to
2. follow some simple rules
3. don't have to
4. should
5. Some
6. should offer to
7. should not
8. be yourself

Audioscript for Exercise A:

Exercise A:

Jada: David, you're meeting my parents for the first time tonight, and there's something I should tell you.
David: What is it, Jada?
Jada: My parents hate bad manners.
David: I don't have bad manners!
Jada: Well. . . .
David: OK. OK. What should I do?
Jada: First, you should bring my mother flowers.
David: I can do that.
Jada: Good. Then, when we have dinner, don't talk with your mouth full. Don't lick your fingers. Don't put your elbows on the table. Don't serve yourself with your fork. . . .
David: But I don't. . . .
Jada: Don't interrupt. I'm not finished. One more thing: you shouldn't whisper to me at the dinner table. It will make my parents angry.
David: OK, OK. Got it. So, when should we leave? Didn't they tell us to come around 6?
Jada: Oh, no! It's already 5:45! We should be leaving right now. And we have to pick up flowers first. Oh, David, we might be late! Should we call?
David: Wait a minute. You want *my* advice now? Well, Miss Manners. Here's some advice: You shouldn't be late to dinner at your parents' house!

Unit 16

A
1. F
2. F
3. T
4. F
5. F
6. T
7. F
8. T
9. T

B
1. bark
2. shout
3. slam their door
4. junk
5. yard
6. garden
7. gardeners
8. musician
9. chat
10. driveway

C
1. must be chatting
2. must be a gardener
3. must be shouting
4. must be a musician
5. must not be clean

D

1. d	2. e	3. c	4. a	5. b

E

Exact wording of answers may vary.

1. Runaways are children or teenagers who leave their homes.
2. They assume runaways must be bad kids / must drink or take drugs / must not want to obey their parents.
3. They run away because they live in violent or abusive homes.
4. No, they think it's better than life at home.
5. They have to sell drugs or steal.
6. Because it is illegal for children or teens to run away.
7. They think they should have "safe places" where abused teenagers or children can go.
8. The government should teach violent or abusive parents to treat their children better.
9. Good services, counseling, and parenting classes can help to solve the problem.

Audioscript for Exercise A:

Exercise A:

Zelda: How was your trip to Brazil, Mark?

Mark: Well, Zelda, it was great, but the flight from Rio was too long and it was delayed.

Zelda: You must be tired.

Mark: Yes, I am. So, what's been going on around here?

Zelda: Well, I think the Everetts moved out. All the junk in their yard is gone, and for a whole week it's been quiet over there. Can you believe it?

Mark: No, I really can't. They were always so noisy. What about the Jordans? Have you seen them around?

Zelda: No, I haven't.

Mark: Hmm . . . They must be on vacation.

Zelda: They can't be. Their car is still in the driveway, and I hear music from their house sometimes. Maybe I should go over there and see if they're OK.

Mark: Yeah, you could bring them some vegetables from your garden. You must have a lot of them this year. Your garden looks great.

Zelda: Thanks! I'll bring you some too.

Mark: That would be nice. I brought you something from Rio. I also brought something for the Prosser kids.

Zelda: How nice! But where are the Prossers? I haven't seen them in a long time.

Mark: Oh, they must be visiting their family in California.

Zelda: I didn't know they had family in California.

Mark: Zelda, you may know a lot about this neighborhood, but you don't know everything!

Unit 17

A

Check: 2, 6

Cross: 1, 3, 4, 5

B

1. lose weight
2. get in shape
3. care for a dog
4. walk a dog

C

1. a	3. a	5. a	7. b	9. a
2. b	4. b	6. b	8. a	10. b

D

1. C: to have
2. A: too
3. B: to
4. C: to go
5. B: (delete)
6. B: too
7. A: (delete)
8. A: It's OR It is
9. B: her
10. B: to

E

Answers will vary.

F

1. ~~cannot~~, can
2. ~~quiet~~, loud
3. ~~isn't~~, is
4. ~~can't~~, can
5. ~~Most~~, Some
6. ~~15th~~, 13th
7. ~~All~~, Some
8. ~~safe~~, not safe

Audioscript for Exercise A:

Exercise A:

Dr. Chen: Well, Michael, you've gained quite a bit of weight lately. Your blood pressure is pretty high and you also have high cholesterol. I think you need to make some changes in your lifestyle.

Michael: I know I'm a little heavy, Doctor, but it's difficult for me to lose weight. . . .

Dr. Chen: Well, it's important for you to get in shape. Do you walk during the day?

Michael: No. I drive everywhere.

Dr. Chen: You should try to walk or ride your bike more. You need to exercise more, not just eat less, if you want to lose weight. Do you have a dog?

Michael: No, just a cat.

Dr. Chen: Well, it might be a good idea for you to get one. Dogs need walks, and they often help their owners to get exercise. Most people can find enough time to take a half-hour walk with their dog every day. And dogs are good companions, too. They help people to stay happy as they get older. But it's important to think about it for a while before you get one. Some people are too busy to care for a dog.

Michael: Hmmm . . . I'll think about it. It *is* fun to walk a dog.

Dr. Chen: As for your diet, try to eat less red meat and more fruits and vegetables. And make sure you get enough vitamin C. Flu season is coming.

Michael: OK. Thanks, Dr. Chen.

Dr. Chen: You're welcome.

Unit 18

A

1. sewing
2. knitting
3. feeling cold
4. hiking
5. seven
6. cooking
7. cooking
8. Japanese cooking

B

1. c	3. a	5. h	7. g
2. e	4. f	6. d	8. b

C

1. think watching
2. enjoys hiking
3. camping is
4. dislike sleeping
5. prefer knitting / to knit
6. likes knitting / to knit
7. is into singing
8. loves playing / to play
9. wants to play
10. hopes to become / is hoping to become

D

1. d	3. f	5. b
2. c	4. a	6. e

E

1. ✗	2. ✓	3. ✓	4. ✗

Audioscript for Exercise A:

Exercise A:

Isabel: Abby, what are you interested in?

Abby: Well, Isabel, lots of things. Gardening, sewing . . . oh, and knitting, too. I'm knitting a hat and gloves for my nephew.

Isabel: You like knitting? Knitting is too hard for me. I prefer hiking.

Abby: Oh, really? Where do you go hiking?

Isabel: I go to Joshua Tree a lot. I also like camping.

Abby: I can't stand camping. I prefer staying in a hotel. I don't like sleeping on the ground. And I hate feeling cold.

Isabel: You have to have good equipment. If you have bad equipment, camping is not fun.

Abby: Are you good at hiking?

Isabel: I guess so. One day I hiked seven miles.

Abby: Seven miles. That's a lot!

Isabel: Yeah, I was pretty tired by the end of the day. So, what else do you like to do?

Abby: Well, I love cooking.

Isabel: I like cooking, too, but I'm not very good at it. What do you like to cook?

Abby: I like to cook almost anything. Right now I'm learning to make Chinese food.

Isabel: That's interesting. Are you taking a class?

Abby: Not yet, but I'm considering taking a class in Japanese cooking.

Isabel: All this talk about cooking is making me hungry. Are you hungry, too?

Abby: Yes! Come over now, and I'll cook dinner for you.

Unit 19

A

1. F	3. T	5. T	7. F	9. F
2. F	4. F	6. T	8. T	

B

1. smoke detector	4. fire hazards	7. notice
2. ordered	5. ticket	8. guess
3. advised	6. speeding	

C

1. to stop	5. don't think	9. to move
2. guess	6. he's	10. your OR that your
3. makes	7. let	
4. you	8. me	

D

1. before	4. off	7. bad
2. to higher ground	5. leave	8. dirty
3. move	6. shouldn't	9. dangerous

Audioscript for Exercise A:

Exercise A:

Operator: 9-1-1. What's your emergency?

Barry: There's a fire in my apartment building! The smoke is pouring out of the windows, and I can see the flames!

Operator: Are you inside the building?

Barry: No, I got out. I'm standing across the street.

Operator: Did you hear any fire alarms?

Barry: No. It seems the smoke detectors weren't working. I saw smoke come in under my bedroom door. So I opened the window and went down the fire escape.

Operator: Where are you now, exactly?

Barry: In a store on the corner of Eleventh and Broadway.

Operator: How long ago did the fire start?

Barry: Maybe five or ten minutes ago.

Operator: Are there other people in the building?

Barry: I called most of my neighbors, and I advised them to leave, but I think there are still some people inside. Should I go get them . . . ?

Operator: No! I need you to stay where you are. Do not try to go in the building. That's a job for the firefighters. They'll be there soon.

Barry: How soon?! The smoke is getting very heavy.

Operator: There's a fire station around the corner. I encourage you to stay calm, get some coffee, and wait for them to come. They'll expect you to make a report.

Barry: OK. I think I hear the siren now. . . .

Unit 20

A

1. ~~14~~, 15
2. ~~wants to go~~, has been
3. ~~late~~, early
4. ~~carry on bags~~, boarding passes and identification
5. ~~magazine~~, boarding passes
6. ~~in the bathroom~~, under the seat
7. ~~not boarding~~, boarding
8. ~~identification~~, magazine

B

1. f	3. d	5. b	7. i	9. g
2. c	4. j	6. h	8. a	10. e

C

1. Tom says (that) we're going hiking on Tuesday.
2. She says (that) the place isn't very nice.
3. He says (that) he's having a great time.
4. He told her to stop talking on her cell phone.
5. The captain told us to go back to our seats.

D

1. Meredith says, "It was sunny every day on my vacation."
2. She says, "I've sent the package."
3. He told his children, "Don't push."
4. They told us, "Leave your sweaters at home."
5. The flight attendant asked me, "Can / Could / Would you check your carry-on bag?"

E

1. F	3. F	5. T	7. F	9. T
2. F	4. T	6. F	8. T	10. F

Audioscript for Exercise A:

Exercise A:

Airport Announcer: National Airlines flight number 320 is now boarding at gate 15. Passengers, please have your boarding passes and identification ready.

José: Angie, where have you been?

Angie: I went to the bathroom and then I bought a magazine.

José: Well, he just told us the plane is boarding.

Angie: Oh, it's early. Why is it boarding early?

José: I don't know. Please get ready. He told us to take out our boarding passes and identification.

Angie: OK. . . . José! Where are our boarding passes?

José: What?

Angie: I *said* where are our boarding passes?

José: I don't know.

Angie: Maybe I left them in the bathroom. I'll go check.

José: Wait . . . did you leave them at the check-in counter?

Angie: No, that's impossible. The attendant at the check-in counter said, "Have a nice flight," and handed them to me.

José: That's right. I remember now. OK, go check the bathrooms.

José: Wait, Angie, I found them!

Angie: What?

José: I said I found the boarding passes!

Angie: Phew! Where were they?

José: They were under the seat. They probably slipped out of your carry-on bag. Hurry! They're boarding the plane. Oh, and don't forget your magazine!

Notes

Notes

Notes

Notes

Notes

Notes

Notes

Notes

Notes

Notes

Notes

Notes

Notes

Do I need to design additional materials or develop my own lessons?

No. *Center Stage* is designed to maximize your efficiency inside and outside the classroom. Any additional materials needed to maximize multilevel classroom instruction are included in the *Center Stage* components, such as the grammar worksheets found on the Teacher's Resource Disk.

Can I use *Center Stage 2* to teach a multilevel class?

Yes. Each unit of the Teacher's Edition includes multilevel instruction strategies for many of the Student Book activities. These strategies will help you administer the activities to students based on their proficiency level, whether they be pre-level, at-level, or above-level. This way, all students can do something that is meaningful and level-appropriate, while meeting the goal(s) and objective(s) of the lesson.

Is it true that each lesson will meet the needs of the different levels of students in my class?

Yes. The only difference is the task expectations for each level. The multilevel strategies contain tasks that will comfortably fit the abilities of students at any given level. Pre-level students get the extra support and reinforcement they need, and above-level students are challenged to go a bit beyond the original task.

Will my at-level students get lost in the shuffle?

No. While the strategies target mostly pre-level and above-level students, they also offer additional instructions for at-level students. At-level students are often encouraged to join either the pre-level groups as assistants or the above-level groups as partners. Both experiences provide valuable learning opportunities for the at-level students. When they work with the pre-level students, they enhance their own learning by assisting others. While working with above-level students, they are challenged to excel, which will increase their motivation and persistence.

Won't multilevel strategies introduce confusion and disorder into the classroom?

On the contrary, the multilevel strategies are designed to enhance the productivity of your classroom. The strategies target different abilities, which will help you reach more of your students on a daily basis. Furthermore, students learn some transferable skills in the process, such as working on a team and problem-solving strategies.

Will students feel left out if I spend too much time with one group?

No, because we have incorporated a lot of variety with the multilevel strategies so that your time will be balanced among all your students. We should emphasize that the level designations into pre-level, at-level, and above-level do not strictly apply to particular student at all times. In other words, the student who is pre-level for one activity may actually be above-level for another. Therefore, groups are not static; they are always evolving as current students improve their abilities and new students enter your class. In addition, to avoid feelings of resentment among students, you can offer variations of the same task to all your students and have them choose which one they want to do. Students will welcome tasks that are appropriate for their abilities and feel a sense of validation and accomplishment once the tasks are completed.

Will I be able to manage the different groups without feeling overwhelmed?

The strategies are designed so that students can often work independently, with a partner or in a small group. This way, students become responsible for themselves and to one another. In many cases, your role will be to facilitate the different groups, monitor their progress, and be available if needed while students complete their tasks.